D0849514

PHILOMATHES

STUDIES AND ESSAYS
IN THE HUMANITIES IN MEMORY OF

PHILIP MERLAN

PHILOMATHES

STUDIES AND ESSAYS
IN THE HUMANITIES IN MEMORY OF

PHILIP MERLAN

Edited by

ROBERT B. PALMER and ROBERT HAMERTON-KELLY

MARTINUS NIJHOFF / THE HAGUE / 1971

PRINTED IN THE NETHERLANDS

TABLE OF CONTENTS

PREFACE I

I. PHILOSOPHIA ANTIQUA

PLATON UND KRATYLOS: EIN HINWEIS 3
Wolfgang Schadewaldt
ΘΕΙΑ ΣΩΜΑΤΑ. 12
Hans Herter
PHILO VON ALEXANDRIA UND DER HELLENISIERTE TIMAE-
US 25
Willy Theiler
DIE STELLUNG PLUTARCHS IM PLATONISMUS SEINER ZEIT . 36
Heinrich Dörrie
ÄHNLICHKEIT UND SEINSANALOGIE VOM PLATONISCHEN PAR-
MENIDES BIS PROKLOS 57
Johannes Hirschberger
SUR LA COMPOSITION ONTOLOGIQUE DES SUBSTANCES SEN-
SIBLES CHEZ ARISTOTE (*MÉTAPHYSIQUE Z 7–9*) 75
Suzanne Mansion
EXPLICATION D'UN TEXTE D'ARISTOTE: *DE PARTIBUS ANI-
MALIUM* I. I. 641a14–b10 88
Joseph Moreau
ARISTOTELES, *DE INTERPRETATIONE* 3. 16b19–25 95
Hans Wagner
ON THE CHARACTER OF ARISTOTLE'S ETHICS 116
C. J. De Vogel
ARISTOTLE'S DEFINITION OF SOUL 125
Joseph Owens

PER L'INTERPRETAZIONE DI ARISTOTELE, *DE AN.* 404b18
SGG 146
  Margherita Isnardi Parente
PLATO'S FIRST MOVER IN THE EIGHT BOOK OF ARISTOTLE'S
PHYSICS 171
  Friedrich Solmsen
SOME FEATURES OF THE TEXTUAL HISTORY OF MARCUS
AURELIUS' *MEDITATIONS* 183
  D. A. Rees
LES CRITIQUES DE PLOTIN CONTRE L'ENTÉLÉCHISME D'ARI-
STOTE: ESSAI D'INTERPRÉTATION DE L'*ENN.* 4. 7. 8[5] . . . 194
  G. Verbeke
ON CONSOLATION AND ON CONSOLATIONS. 223
  P. M. Schuhl
ABAMON, PSEUDONYME DE JAMBLIQUE 227
  H. D. Saffrey
DISPLACEMENT IN HIPPOLYTUS' *ELENCHOS* 240
  Miroslav Marcovich
PHILON D'ALEXANDRIE ET LE PRÉCEPTE DELPHIQUE . . . 245
  Pierre Courcelle
L. CAELIUS FIRMIANUS LACTANTIUS ÜBER DIE GESCHICHTE
DES WAHREN GOTTESGLAUBENS 251
  Fritz Wehrli
PTOLEMY'S *VITA ARISTOTELIS* REDISCOVERED. 264
  Ingemar Düring
DE NOVO PINDARI FRAGMENTO ARABICO. 270
  Marianus Plezia
LA RÉFUTATION DE LA MÉTENSOMATOSE D'APRÈS LE THÉOLO-
GIEN KARAÏTE YŪSUF AL-BAṢĪR. 281
  Georges Vajda

II. PHILOSOPHIA MODERNA

DREIERLEI PHILOSOPHIEGESCHICHTE 293
  Victor Kraft
SOCRATES IN HAMANN'S *SOCRATIC MEMORABILIA* AND
NIETZSCHE'S *BIRTH OF TRAGEDY*: A COMPARISON 306
  James C. O'Flaherty

J. G. HAMANN AND THE PRINCESS GALLITZIN: AN ECUMENI-
CAL ENCOUNTER. 330
　　Ronald Gregor Smith †
THE LOST PORTRAIT OF EDMUND HUSSERL BY FRANZ AND IDA
BRENTANO 341
　　Herbert Spiegelberg
EPICUREANISM AND SCEPTICISM IN THE EARLY 17TH CEN-
TURY. 346
　　Richard H. Popkin
PETRAŻYCKI'S CONCEPT OF ADEQUATE THEOREM IN THE LIGHT
OF EARLIER RELATED DOCTRINES. 358
　　Tadeusz Kotarbiński
VALUE AND EXISTENCE 371
　　Marvin Farber
PHENOMENOLOGY, TYPIFICATION, AND THE WORLD AS TA-
KEN FOR GRANTED. 383
　　Maurice Natanson
AUSGANGSPROBLEME ZUR BETRACHTUNG DER KAUSALEN
STRUKTUR DER WELT. 398
　　Roman Ingarden
PHILOSOPHY AS CRITICISM AND PERSPECTIVE. 412
　　Neal W. Klausner
WAS HEISST AUTORITÄT. 433
　　Helmut Kuhn

III. LITTERAE

ECLOGA EPICUREA 447
　　Thomas G. Rosenmeyer
MENANDRO E IL PERIPATO 461
　　Marcello Gigante
GOETHES "HOMMAGE À MOZART" – BEMERKUNGEN ZU "DER
ZAUBERFLÖTE ZWEITER THEIL" 485
　　Arthur Henkel
GORGIAS BEI GOETHE. 503
　　Albin Lesky
ANTIKE MOTIVE IM EPICEDION DES EOBANUS HESSUS AUF
DEN TOD DÜRERS. 508
　　Wolfgang Schmid

IV. HISTORICA

THE MEDIEVAL CANON LAW OF CONTRACTS, RENAISSANCE "SPIRIT OF CAPITALISM," AND THE REFORMATION "CONSCIENCE": A VOTE FOR MAX WEBER 525
Benjamin Nelson

TO

PHILIP MERLAN

PIETATIS CAUSA

What began as a *Festschrift* has now become a memorial: Philip Merlan died on December 23, 1968 as this book entered its final stages of preparation.

It was typical of him that he was busy with his research right up to the end. For in whatever he did Philip Merlan was a philologist, a lover of learning, and a philospher, a lover of wisdom.

Philologists lavish their love on texts. And so it was with him. He lavished his love on texts, philosophical texts, and it made no difference to him whether they were ancient or modern provided they dealt with the realities of the world of the mind.

But that is only half of the matter. As one of his distinguished colleagues recently wrote, "What I respect in Philip Merlan is that he is not only unusually versed in the history of philosophy but he *knows why* one concerns oneself with the thoughts of the past, and he *knows what such a concern can bring to the whole process of thought itself.* He has, in short, combined *eruditio* with *sapientia.*"

As his colleagues of some years standing at Scripps College, we can testify to the truth of this statement; but we must also stress an element of his career which may not be as well known to the learned colleagues with whom he corresponded over the years. He had the gift of "speaking words of great subtlety and tonal complexity to subtle souls, and he could also speak natural words to natural souls" (ποικίλῃ μὲν ποικίλους ψυχῇ καὶ παναρμονίους διδοὺς λόγους, ἁπλοῦς δε ἁπλῇ [*Phdr.* 277c]). What appears here illustrates the first quality; the deep love and affection he received from hundreds of his students at Scripps College bear witness to the second. He always cared deeply about what he taught in the humanities; but he never failed to recognize that what he taught was meaningless until it came alive in the natural minds of the young.

Plato in his *Phaedo* has Socrates say, "there are many narthex bearers, but only a few Bacchoi" (ναρθηκοφόροι μὲν πολλοί, Βάκχοι δέ τε παῦροι [*Phd.* 69c]) "and these inspired ones are those who have become true philosophers" (οἱ πεφιλοσοφηκότες ὀρθῶς). Scripps College dedicates this volume to one of the παῦροι.

As editors we would like to thank not only the many distinguished scholars who have responded so graciously to our requests but also the administrators and faculty of Scripps College who have helped us make this tribute a reality. Special thanks must go to President Mark Curtis of Scripps College who gave us both his moral and financial support, and to Rosemary Hamerton-Kelly and Professors Edith Potter and Nalsy Ewing who answered our linguistic inquiries. Nor can we forget the assistance of Professor Stephen Glass, and the dedicated labor of Parker Palmer, our typist, who remained undaunted by manuscripts which came to him in a variety of languages and a welter of scripts.

Finally we owe a special debt of gratitude to the firm of Martinus Nijhoff and its director, Dr. H. J. H. Hartgerink, who expressed an immediate willingness to publish the *Merlan Memorial Volume* and has performed his task with dispatch and imagination.

To all of us the words of our dedication, *pietatis causa*, have never meant so much as now.

Robert B. Palmer
Robert Hamerton-Kelly

Scripps College
Claremont, California
1969

BIBLIOGRAPHY OF THE PUBLICATIONS OF
PHILIP MERLAN, 1929–1970*

1929 "Zu § 51 Grundbuchsgesetz," *Juristische Blätter* (Wien) 58 (1929), 278 f. "Hat das Fruchtgenußrecht wiederkehrende Leistungen im Sinne des § 34 GBG zum Gegenstand?", *Gerichtszeitung* (Wien) 80 (1929), 299 f.

1932 "Das neue Arbeitsvertragsrecht Polens," *Zeitschrift für soziales Recht* 4 (1932), 112–115.

1933 "Das neue Arbeitsvertragsrecht Polens," *Zeitschrift für soziales Recht* 5 (1933), 133–136.
"Zwei Fragen der Epikureischen Theologie," *Hermes* 68 (1933), 196–217.

1934 "Beiträge zur Geschichte des antiken Platonismus," *Philologus* 89 (1934) 35–53; 197–214.
W. Capelle (tr.), Marc Aurel, Selbstbetrachtungen, *Gnomon* 10 (1934), 219 f. (Rezension).
J. Baudry, Atticos, *ibid.*, 263–273, 336 (Rezension).
A. Krokiewicz, Nauka Epikura, *ibid.*, 603–609 (Rezension).

1935 "Ein Simplikios-Zitat bei Pseudo-Alexandros und ein Plotinos-Zitat bei Simplikios," *Rheinisches Museum* 84 (1935), 154–160.

1936 "Überflüssige Textänderungen," *Philologische Wochenschrift* 56 (1936), 909–912.
W. S. Hinman, Literary quotation and allusion in the Rhetoric, Poetics and Nicomachean Ethics of Aristotle, *ibid.*, 56 (1936), 259–261 (Rezension).

* Reprinted with additions and corrections with the kind permission of the editorial staff of the *Zeitschrift für philosophische Forschung*, Munich. For the original impression, see *Zeitschrift für philosophische Forschung* 22 (1968), pp. 139–145.

W. Theiler, Porphyrios und Augustin, *Gnomon* 12 (1936), 527–543 (Rezension).

H. Guitton, Le temps et l'éternité chez Plotin et Saint-Augustin, *ibid.* (Rezension).

P. Henry, Plotin et l'Occident, *ibid.* (Rezension).

J. Barion, Plotin und Augustinus, *ibid.* (Rezension).

1937 P. Gohlke, Die Entstehung der Aristotelischen Logik, *Philologische Wochenschrift* 57 (1937), 1233–1249 (Rezension).

W. Schmid, Epikurs Kritik der platonischen Elementenlehre, *Deutsche Literaturzeitung* 1937, 1284 f. (Rezension).

1938 R. Walzer, Aristotelis Dialogorum fragmenta, *Philologische Wochenschrift* 58 (1938), 65–69 (Rezension).

F. Dirlmeier, Die Oikeiosis-Lehre Theophrasts, *ibid.*, 177–182 (Rezension).

1939 PLATONS FORM DER PHILOSOPHISCHEN MITTEILUNG, Lwów.

A. Becker-Freyseng, Die Vorgeschichte des philosophischen Terminus "contingens," *Gnomon* 15 (1939), 389 f. (Rezension).

1941 E. Bignone, L'Aristotele perduto e la formazione filosofica di Epicuro, *Gnomon* 17 (1941), 32–41 (Rezension).

1942 "A Certain Aspect of Bergson's Philosophy," *Philosophy and Phenomenological Research* 2 (1942), 529–545.

Essays on Maimonides, *Personalist* 23 (1942), 427 f. (Rezension).

1943 "Plotinus Enn. 2.2," *Transactions of the American Philological Association* 74 (1943), 179 –191.

"Towards the Understanding of Kierkegaard," *Journal of Religion* 23 (1943), 77–90.

Gitler, Social Thought Among the Greeks, *Personalist* 24 (1943), 332 f. (Rezension).

F. Solmsen, Plato's Theology, *Personalist* 24 (1943), 316 f. (Rezension).

1944 "An Idea of Freud's in Plato," *Personalist* 25 (1944), 54–63.

1945 "Brentano and Freud," *Journal of the History of Ideas* 6 (1945) 375–377.

1946 "Aristotle's Unmoved Movers," *Traditio* 4 (1946), 1–30.

"The Successor of Speusippus," *Transactions of the American Philological Association* 71 (1946) 103–111.

1947 "Time Consciousness in Husserl and Heidegger," *Philosophy and Phenomenological Research* 8 (1947), 23–59.

"Form and Content in Plato's Philosophy," *Journal of the History of Ideas* 8 (1947), 406–430.

1948 "Modern Philosophy on Man," *Scripps College Bulletin, Alumnae News Letter* 23, 4 (1948).

"Parva Hamanniana I. Hamann as a Spokesman of the Middle Class," *Journal of the History of Ideas* (1948), 330–334.

1949 "Epicureanism and Horace," *Journal of the History of Ideas* 10 (1949), 45–51.

"Brentano and Freud," *Journal of the History of Ideas* 10 (1949), 451.

"Parva Hamanniana II. Hamann and Schmohl," *Journal of the History of Ideas* 10 (1949), 567–574.

[Letter on Herder], *Journal of Aesthetics* 8 (1949), 129 f.

T. W. Organ, An Index to Aristotle in English Translation, *Classical Weekly* 43 (1949), 61 f. (Rezension).

1950 "Parva Hamanniana III. Hamann and Galiani," *Journal of the History of Ideas* 11 (1950), 486–489.

"Lucretius – Primitivist or Progressivist?", *Journal of the History of Ideas* 11 (1950), 364–368.

"Antiphon the Sophist or Alexander the Great?", *Classical Philology* 45 (1950), 161–166.

K. Janaček, Prolegomena to Sextus Empiricus, *Classical Philology* 45 (1950), 205 (Rezension).

1951 "From Hume to Hamann," *Personalist* 32 (1951), 11–18.

"Hermetische Pyramide und Sextus," *Museum Helveticum* 8 (1951), 100–105.

K. McLean, Agrarian Age, *Journal of the History of Ideas* 12 (1951), 311 (Rezension).

C. J. de Vogel, Greek Philosophy, *Journal of the History of Ideas* 12 (1951), 158 (Rezension).

1952 "Unearthing Aristotle," *Claremont Quarterly* 1 (1951/2), 3–8.

L. Schönberger – M. Steck, Proclus Diadochus Kommentar zum 1. Buch von Euklids Elementen, *Journal of the History of Ideas* 13 (1952), 119 f. (Rezension).

Plotino, Enneadi, ed. V. Cilento, vol. III, Part 2 (B. Mariën), *The Philosophical Review* 61 (1952), 415–418 (Rezension).

1953 FROM PLATONISM TO NEOPLATONISM, Nijhoff, The Hague.
"Ambiguity in Heraclitus," *Proceedings of the XIth International Congress of Philosophy*, vol. XII, 55–60.
"Abstraction and Metaphysics in St. Thomas' Summa," *Journal of the History of Ideas* 14 (1953), 284–291.
Foreword to H. Gomperz, *Philosophical Studies*, 7–11.
"Plotinus and Magic," *Isis* 44 (1953), 341–348.
R. Bury, Sextus Empiricus, vol. IV, *Classical Philology* 48 (1953), 39 (Rezension).
P. Henry – R. H. Schwyzer (ed.) Plotini Opera I, *Philosophical Review* 62 (1953), 622 (Rezension).

1954 [joint author] Symposium – Are Religious Dogmas Cognitive and Meaningful? *Journal of Philosophy* 51 (1954), 156 f.
[anonymous] "Humanities at Scripps," *Times*, Educational Supplement, Febr. 5, 1954, 115.
954–965.
"Isocrates, Aristotle, Alexander the Great," *Historia* III (1954), 60–81.
"Hamann et les 'Dialogues' de Hume," *Revue de Métaphysique et de Morale* 59 (1954), 285–289.
O'Flaherty, Unity and Language, *Monatshefte* 46 (1954), 59 f. (Rezension).
C. J. Keyser, The Rational and the Superrational, *Personalist* 35 (1954), 410 (Rezension).

1955 "Le 'grand inquisiteur' réinterprété," *Revue de Métaphysique et de Morale* 60 (1955), 153–160.
"The Courage to be Perplexed," *Scripps College Bulletin* 1955.
"Johann Georg Hamann," *Claremont Quarterly* 3 (1955), 33–42.
"Celsus," *Reallexikon für Antike und Christentum* II (1955),
"Aristotle, Averroës und die beiden Eckharts," *Autour d'Aristote* (1955), 543–566.
Rezensionen:
H. Reiner, Pflicht und Neigung, *Personalist* 36 (1955), 98 f.

R. Schottländer, Der philosophische Heilsbegriff, *ibid.*, 98 f.

R. S. Hartmann [tr.] Hegel, Reason in History, *ibid.*, 321.

H. Wagner, Existenz, Analogie, Dialektik, *ibid.* 217.

V. Verra, Hamann e l'incontro di tempo, *Hamann News-Letter* 1 (1954), 2f.

P. Brachin, Le cercle de Münster, *ibid.* 1 (1954), 5.

W. K. C. Guthrie, Greek Philosophy, *Journal of Philosophy* 52 (1955), 349–358.

B. Snell, The Discovery of the Mind, *ibid.*

R. Robinson, Plato's Earlier Dialectic, *ibid.*

J. Wild, Plato's Modern Enemies and the Theory of Natural Law, *ibid.*

R. Klibansky & C. Labowsky, Procli Commentarium in Parmenidem, *The Philosophical Review* 64 (1955), 146 f.

N. W. De Witt, Epicurus and His Philosophy, *ibid.*, 140–143.

1956   "Schopenhauer," *Encyclopedia of Morals* (1956).
"Minor Socratics," *ibid.*
Hamann, Briefe v. I, *Monatshefte* 48 (1956), 339 f. (Rezension).
G. Ryle, Dilemmas, *Personalist* 37 (1956), 70 (Rezension).
W. D. Oliver, Theory of Order, *ibid.*, 69 (Rezension).
V. de Magalhaes-Vilhena, Le Problème de Socrate, *Philosophische Rundschau* 4 (1956), 212–216 (Rezension).
V. de Magalhaes-Vilhena, Socrate et la Legende platonicienne, *ibid.* (Rezension).

1957   A. J. Ayer, Philosophical Essays, *Personalist* 38 (1957), 83 f. (Rezension).
R. M. Yost, Jr., Leibniz and Philosophical Analysis, *ibid.*, 82 (Rezension).
"Metaphysik: Name und Gegenstand," *Journal of Hellenic Studies* 77 (1957), 87–92.

1958   "Nietzsche Today," *Claremont Quarterly* 5 (1958), 39–50.
Artikel: Academy, Albinus, Arcesilaus, Carneades, Cleitomachus, Diogenes Laërtius, Heracleides, Lacydes, Philo, Plato (part), Speusippus, Xenocrates in: *Encyclopaedia Britannica*, copyright 1958/60.

H. Jonas, Gnosis und antiker Geist, vol. II, *Journal of Philosophy* 55 (1958), 743–748 (Rezension).

1959   "Metaphysics and Science," *Journal of Philosophy* 56 (1959), 612–618.

"Le problème de l'irrationalisme dans les 'Deux Sources' de Bergson," *Revue philosophique* 149 (1959), 305–319.

"Ὄν ᾗ ὄν und πρώτη οὐσία: Postskript zu einer Besprechung," *Philosophische Rundschau* 7 (1959), 148–153.

"Zur Biographie des Speusippos," *Philologus* 103 (1959), 198–214.

"Idéalisme, réalisme, phénoménologie," *Husserl* (Cahiers de Royaumont. Philosophie, No. III), Paris, 1959, pp. 382–410 (Les Editions de Minuit).

1960   STUDIES IN EPICURUS AND ARISTOTLE, Harrassowitz, Wiesbaden.

FROM PLATONISM TO NEOPLATONISM, 2nd ed., rev., Nijhoff, The Hague.

"Averroës über die Unsterblichkeit des Menschengeschlechtes," *L'Homme et son destin, Actes de premier congrès international de philosophie mediévale*, Louvain-Paris, 1960, 305–311.

"Neoplatonism," *The Concise Encyclopedia of Western Philosophy and Philosophers*, New York, 1960.

"Existentialism – A Third Way," *Proceedings and Addresses of the American Philosophical Association* 33 (1960), pp. 43–68.

Hegel: "Cur Deus homo?", *Sitzungsberichte des XII. Internationalen Philosophiekongresses*, vol. XII, pp. 319–326.

Rezensionen:

B. Kasm, L'idée de preuve en métaphysique, *Personalist* 41 (1960), 426 f.

A. Mercier, Thought and Being, *ibid.*, 522 f.

G. Vallin, La perspective métaphysique, *ibid.*, 554 f.

B. Lavergne, Individualisme contre autoritatisme, *ibid.*, 556 f.

J. Hessen, Das Kausalprinzip, *ibid.*, 557.

Rezensionen:

1961   G. Pflug, Henri Bergson, *Personalist* 42 (1961), 97.

J. H. Randall, Jr., Aristotle, *Philosophy and Phenomenological Research* 22 (1961), 119–121.

E. Paratore, L'Epicureismo e la sua diffusione nel mondo latino, *Gnomon* 33 (1961), 524 f.

1962 "Drei Anmerkungen zu Numenius," *Philologus* 106 (1962), 137–145.
Rezensionen:
Les sources de Plotin, *Gnomon* 34 (1962), 204–207.
C. H. Kahn, Anaximander, *Journal of Philosophy* 59 (1962), 246–248.
L. Malverne, Signification de l'homme, *Personalist* 43 (1962), 305.
J. Jalabert, Le dieu de Leibniz, *ibid.*, 305 f.
R. Muchielli, Le Mythe de la citée ideale, *ibid.*, 143.
F. Solmsen, Aristotle's System of the Physical World, *American Journal of Philology* 83 (1962), 202–204.

1963 MONOPSYCHISM, MYSTICISM, METACONSCIOUSNESS, Nijhoff, The Hague.
"Zum Schluß von Vergil's Vierter Ekloge," *Museum Helveticum* 20 (1963), 21.
"Religion and Philosophy from Plato's *Phaedo* to the Chaldaean Oracles," *Journal of the History of Philosophy* 1 (1963), 163–176.
"Das Problem der Erasten," *Horizons of a Philosopher, Essays in Honor of D. Baumgardt*, Leiden, 1963, pp. 297–314.
"Diogenes Laërtius," *Collier's Encyclopedia*, 1963.
Rezensionen:
H. Thesleff, An Introduction to the Pythagorean Writings of the Hellenistic Period, *Mind* 72 (1963), 303 f.
M. Schramm, Die Bedeutung der Bewegungslehre des Aristoteles für seine beiden Lösungen der zenonischen Paradoxie, *Isis* 54 (1963), 299 f.
J. Pieper, Begeisterung und göttlicher Wahnsinn, *Journal of the History of Philosophy* 1 (1963), 95–99.
W. F. Otto, Das Wort der Antike: Mythos und Welt, *Gymnasium* 70 (1963), 424–429.
H. A. Salmony, J. G. Hamanns metakritische Philosophie, *Hamann News-Letter* 3 (1963), 15–18.
Plato, Sämtliche Werke, *Journal of the History of Philosophy* 1 (1963), 238 f.

1964   "Religion and Philosophy from Plato's Phaedo to the
       Chaldaean Oracles" (concluded), *Journal of the History of
       Philosophy* 2 (1964), 15–21.
       "Death, Dying, Immortality," *Pacific Philosophy Forum* 3
       (1964), 3–45.
       "Aristotle, *Met.* A 6, 987 b 20–25 and Plotinus, *Enn.*
       V 4, 2, 8–9," *Phronesis* 9 (1964), 45–47.
       "Sterben, Sterblichkeit, Unsterblichkeit," *Epimeleia (Fest-
       schrift Kuhn)*, Munich, 1964, pp. 223–236.
       "Natural Law – Relevant or Irrelevant?", *Proceedings of
       the XIIIth International Congress of Philosophy, Mexico
       City, 1963*, 103–117.
       Contrib. to: S. and B. Rome (ed.), *Philosophical Inter-
       rogations* (1964).
1965   "Monismus und Dualismus bei einigen Platonikern,"
       Parusia (Festgabe für J. Hirschberger), Frankfurt, 1965,
       pp. 143–154.
       "Zur Zahlenlehre im Platonismus (Neuplatonismus) and
       in *Sefer Yezira*," *Journal of the History of Philosophy* 3
       (1965), 167–181.
       Artikel: Abammon, Aidesios, Albinus, Alexander of
       Lykopolis, Amelios, Ammonios Hermeiu, Ammonios
       Sakkas, Asklepios, Attikos, Boëthius, Calcidius, Calvisius
       Taurus, Celsus, Damaskios, Derkylides, Eudoros, Gaios,
       Herakleides v. Pontos, Hermeias, Hermodoros, Hierokles,
       Hypatia, Iamblichos, Johannes Lydos, Krantor, Krates,
       Marius Victorinus, Maximus v. Tyros, Neoplatoniker,
       Origines d. Heide, Philippos v. Opus, Plotin, Plutarch v.
       Athen, Plutarch v. Chaeronea (part), Polemon, Porphyrios,
       Proklos, Sallustius Serenus, Simplikios, Sopatros, Speu-
       sippos, Syrianos, Theodoros, Vettius Agorius Praetex-
       tatus, Xenocrates in: *Lexikon der Alten Welt*, Zürich,
       1965.
       Rezensionen:
       J. M. Rist, Eros und Psyche, *Dialogue* 3 (1965), 438–440.
       H. S. Long, Diogenes Laërtios, *Journal of the History of
       Philosophy* 3 (1965), 119–121.
       F. Muthmann, Untersuchungen zur "Einkleidung" einiger
       Platonischer Dialoge, *Gymnasium* 72 (1965), 256 f.

K. Gaiser, Platons ungeschriebene Lehre, *ibid.*, und
W. Bröcker, Platos Gespräche, *ibid.*, 543–547.

1966 "Neues Licht auf Parmenides," *Archiv für Geschichte der Philosophie* 48 (1966), 267–276.

Tὸ τί ἦν εἶναι, *Classical Philology* 61 (1966), 188.

"Two Theological Problems in Aristotle's Met. Lambda 6–9 and De caelo 9," *Apeiron* 1 (1966), 3–13.

"A Precursor of Tocqueville," *Pacific Historical Review* 35 (1966), 467 f.

"Zum Problem der drei Lebensarten," *Philosophisches Jahrbuch* 74/1 (1966), 217–219.

Rezensionen:

W. A. Luijpen, Phenomenology and Atheism; *idem*, Phenomenology and Metaphysics, *Philosophy and Phenomenological Research* 26 (1966), 589–591.

G. Reale, Teofrasto a la sua aporetica metafisica, *The Philosophical Quarterly* 16 (1966), 363.

1967 Artikel: Academy, Albinus, Arcesilaus, Carneades, Cleitomachus, Diogenes Laërtius, Heracleides, Philo, Plato (part), Speusippus, Xenocrates in: *Encyclopaedia Britannica*, copyright 1967.

Alexandrian School, Athenian School, Emanationism, Neoplatonism, Plotinus in: *The Encyclopedia of Philosophy*.

"Greek Philosophy from Plato to Plotinus," in: *The Cambridge History of Later Greek and Early Medieval Philosophy*, Cambridge, 1967, 14–132.

"ΤΟ ᾿ΑΠΟΡΗΣΑΙ ᾿ΑΡΧΑΙΚΩΣ (Arist. Met. N2, 1089a1)," *Philologus* 111 (1967), 119–121.

"Aristoteles' und Epikurs müssige Götter," *Zeitschrift für philosophische Forschung* 21 (1967), 485–498.

"Kant, Hamann-Jacobi and Schelling on Hume," *Rivista Critica di Storia della Filosofia* 22 (1967), 481–494.

Rezensionen:

W. Theiler, Forschungen zum Neuplatonismus, *The Classical Journal* 62 (1967), 371.

O. Wichmann, Platon, *Gymnasium* 74 (1967), 364–367.

H. Thesleff, The Pythagorean Texts of the Hellenistic Period, *ibid.*, 460.

H. Kremer, Die neuplatonische Seinsphilosophie und ihre

Wirkung auf Thomas von Aquin, *Zeitschrift für Religions-
und Geistesgeschichte* 19 (1967), 370.
H. Jonas, The Phenomenon of Life, *Philosophy and Phenomenological Research* 28 (1967), 277 f.
E. Straus, The Primary World of the Senses, *ibid.*, 285.

1968 FROM PLATONISM TO NEOPLATONISM, 3rd ed., Nijhoff,
The Hague.
"Zwei Bemerkungen zum Aristotelischen Plato," *Rhein-
isches Museum* 111 (1968), 1–15.
"Ammonius Hermiae, Zacharias Scholasticus and Boe-
thius," *Greek, Roman and Byzantine Studies* 9 (1968),
193–203.
"On the Terms 'Metaphysics' and 'Being-qua-Being',"
The Monist 52 (1968), 174–194.
Rezensionen:
W. Beierwaltes, Proklos, *Philosophische Rundschau* 15
(1968), 94–97.
H. J. Krämer, Der Ursprung der Geistmetaphysik, *ibid.*,
97–110.
A. Hübscher (ed.), XXXVIII. Schopenhauer-Jahrbuch
für das Jahr 1967, *Journal of the History of Philosophy* 6
(1968), 95.
C. Brosset, Schopenhauer ..., *ibid.*

1969 Artikel:
"War Platons Vorlesung *Das Gute* einmalig?," *Hermes* 96
(1969), 705–709.
"Metaphysik: Name und Gegenstand," Wiederabdruck in:
Metaphysik und Theologie des Aristoteles, Darmstadt, 1969
(Wege der Forschung 206), pp. 251–266.
"Bemerkungen zum 'neuen' Plato," *Archiv für Geschichte
der Philosophie* 51 (1969), pp. 111–126.
"Zwei Untersuchungen zu Alexander Aphrodisias mit
einem Anhang zur sogenannten Diktiertheorie," *Philolo-
gus* 113 (1969), 85–92.
Rezensionen:
H. R. Schlette, Epiphanie als Geschichte, *Philosophische
Rundschau* 16 (1969), 152–161.
H. R. Schlette, Das Eine und das Andere, *ibid.*

S. S. Jensen, Dualism and Demonology, *Gnomon* 41 (1969), 501–503.

J. O'Flaherty, Hamann's Socratic Memorabilia, *Journal of the History of Philosophy* 7 (1969), 327–355.

W. M. Alexander, Johann Georg Hamann, *ibid*.

L. Edelstein, The Idea of Progress in Classical Antiquity, *Journal of the History of Philosophy* 7 (1969), 323–325.

F. M. Bernard, Herder's Social and Political Thought, *History and Theory* 8 (1969), 395–404.

1970 MONOPSYCHISM, MYSTICISM, METACONSCIOUSNESS, 2nd edition, Nijhoff, The Hague.

Artikel:

"The Discontinuous Universe of Epicurus," *Proceedings of the 1968 G. Budé Congress*, Paris, 1970, pp. 57–63. Alexander Aphrodisias, Ammonius Hermiae, Bryson in: *Dictionary of Scientific Biography*, New York, 1970.

Im Druck:

"Alienation in Marx' Political Economy and Philosophy," *Memorial Volume for A. Schütz*.

"Ist die These-Antithese-Synthese Formel unhegelisch?", Abstract in: *Proceedings of the XIV International Congress of Philosophy*.

"Nochmals: war Aristoteles je Anhänger der Ideenlehre? Jaegers letzte Worte," *Archiv für Geschichte der Philosophie*.

"Hintikka and a Strange Aristotelian Doctrine,"*Phronesis*, Vol. XV.

"Eschatology, Sacred and Profane," *Journal of the History of Philosophy*.

"Greek Philosophy from Plato to Plotinus" in: *The Cambridge History of Later Greek and Early Medieval Philosophy*, 2nd edition, Cambridge, 1970, 14–132.

Rezensionen:

J. Düring, Aristoteles, *Journal of the History of Philosophy*.

I. PHILOSOPHIA ANTIQUA

PLATON UND KRATYLOS

EIN HINWEIS

WOLFGANG SCHADEWALDT

I

Im sechsten Kapitel des ersten Buches der Metaphysik (987a29 ff.) gibt Aristoteles[1] einen knappen, aber höchst bedeutsamen Überblick über die Entwicklung der Philosophie Platons in drei Stufen. Jede von diesen Stufen ist charakterisiert durch die Einwirkung eines bedeutenden Denkers oder einer Denkrichtung oder einer 'Schule' auf Platons eigenes Denken, und wir hätten danach im Denken Platons eine Heraklitische, eine Sokratische und eine Pythagoreische Stufe zu unterscheiden.

Die Lehre des Heraklit, sagt Aristoteles, sei dem jungen Platon durch Kratylos vermittelt worden, und die Überzeugung, dass alle Sinnendinge ständig im Fluss seien und dass es mithin ein sicheres Wissen von ihnen nicht geben könne, habe Platon auch späterhin als Grundlage angenommen. Von der Frage des Sokrates nach den sittlichen Dingen und seinen Abgrenzungen in diesem Bereich sei Platon darauf gekommen, dass dieses Fragen sich auf den Bereich anderer Dinge als der Sinnendinge bezöge, und er habe diese Wesenheiten Ideen benannt, nach deren Massgabe denn auch die Sinnendinge angesprochen und benannt würden. Auf der dritten Stufe habe Platon unter Einwirkung der Pythagoreer die Zahlen in sein Denken einbezogen,

---

[1] Auf die Probleme, die die Platondarstellung des Aristoteles in *Metaphysik* A6 stellt, kann ich hier nicht näher eingehen. Ich verweise auf H. Cherniss, *Aristotle's Criticism of Plato and the Academy*, I (Baltimore, 1944; Neuauflage, New York, 1962), pp. 177 ff., sowie H. J. Krämer, *Arete bei Platon und Aristoteles* (Heidelberg, 1959; Neuauflage, Amsterdam, 1967), pp. 530 f. Zu einer schwierigen Stelle des Textes neuerdings P. Merlan, "Aristotle," *Met.* A6, 987b20–25 and Plotinus, *Enn.* V.4 2. 8–9," *Phronesis* 9 (1964), pp. 45–47.

dies aber so weitergebildet, dass für ihn einerseits die Zahlen einen Zwischenbereich zwischen Ideen und Sinnendingen darstellten und andererseits die Seinsweise der Ideen selbst durch das Zahlenmässige begründet würde, indem das Sein der Ideen auf die beiden Grundprinzipien des Einen und der unbestimmten Zweiheit zurückginge.

Da Platon in seinen Dialogen immer wieder die Gestalt des Sokrates heraufruft, ist die zweite der von Aristoteles genannten Stufen, die Sokratische, für die moderne Platonforschung die lebendigste, vielfältigste und bedeutsamste geworden: Platon als Ethiker, Staatsethiker, Begründer der Ideenlehre, dihäretischer Methodiker und schliesslich wohl auch Kosmologe. Was die Pythagoreische Stufe angeht, mit ihren Konsequenzen für eine esoterische Prinzipienlehre Platons, nach der die beiden Prinzipien des Einen und der unbestimmten Zweiheit sowohl die Struktur der Ideen wie auch überhaupt der gesamten Wirklichkeit bis hinab zur Ethik bestimmen, so ist die Bedeutung dieses Aspekts seit einigen Jahren stark betont worden, nicht ohne einen internationalen Meinungsstreit heraufzurufen, über den noch nicht entschieden ist.[2] Was endlich die von Aristoteles behauptete Frühstufe im Denken Platons angeht,[3] wonach Platon im Umgang mit dem Herakliteer Kratylos sich in seiner Jugend *vor* der Begegnung mit Sokrates von der Richtigkeit der Flusslehre des Heraklit überzeugt habe, so ist soviel ohne weiteres klar, dass allerdings diese Flusslehre des Heraklit für Platon immer gültig geblieben ist. In seinem späteren dualistischen Weltsystem ist die Sinnenwelt ständig im Fluss, in der Veränderung, im Werden, und erlaubt bestimmte Aussagen nur soweit, wie die fliessenden Sinnendinge durch eine "Teilhabe" mit den seienden Wesenheiten der Ideen verbunden sind. Dieser Ansatz eines eigenen Bereichs der Ideen ist dem Platon aber erst auf Grund seiner Begegnung mit Sokrates und dessen Fragen nach dem "was ist" (*ti estin*) zugewachsen. Und so legt sich uns die Untersuchung nahe, ob es nicht vielleicht möglich wäre, die

---

[2] Eine wichtige Beobachtung zur Entstehung des Platonischen Prinzipiendualismus bringt neuerdings P. Merlan, "ΤΟ 'ΑΠΟΡΗΣΑΙ 'ΑΡΧΑΙΚΩΣ (Arist. *Met.* N2, 1089a1)," *Philol.* 111 (1967), pp. 119–121.

[3] Vgl. hierzu Sir David Ross, *Plato's Theory of Ideas* (Oxford, 1953), pp. 154 ff.

durch Aristoteles bezeugte früheste vorsokratische Herakliteische Jugendepoche des Denkens Platons, die durch den Umgang
mit Kratylos bezeichnet war, noch etwas näher zu charakterisieren. Die Frage verweist uns auf Platons Dialog *Kratylos.*

II

Unter den verschiedenen Problemen, die der *Kratylos* Platons
uns aufgibt,[4] ist eines der seltsamsten wohl dieses: Kratylos
tritt im Dialog am Anfang (383a–384a) und wieder am Schluss
(427e–440e) als überzeugter Anhänger der Flusslehre des Heraklit
und entschiedener Verfechter der unbedingten "Richtigkeit der
Namen (von Natur)" auf. Tatsächlich bringt der Dialog in
seinem Mittelteil (391a–427d) – dem Umfang nach weit mehr als
die Hälfte des Ganzen – die reiche Etymologien-Sammlung, die den
Dialog berühmt gemacht hat. Mit Homers Namengebung begin-
nend und von der Deutung der Götternamen über die Elemente
zu den geistig-ethischen Begriffen und schliesslich den Lauten als
den Elementen der Wörter forstschreitend, beruhen diese Etymologien auf der von Kratylos vertretenen Lehre von der "Richtigkeit der Namen," und sie fussen weitgehend, vor allem gegen
Schluss, auf der Flusslehre des Heraklit. Und doch ist es nicht
Kratylos, der die Etymologien vorträgt, sondern Sokrates.
Kratylos sagt kein Wort, während Sokrates diese Dinge im Gespräch mit Hermogenes entwickelt, und bekundet am Schluss nur
seine Zustimmung (427d–428e). Die Art, wie Kratylos zustimmt,
ist interessant genug und dürfte auch für die vielbehandelte Frage
nach der tatsächlichen Herkunft der von Sokrates vorgetragenen
Etymologien einen Hinweis geben. *Hermogenes* (nachdem Sokrates
seinen Vortrag über die Etymologien abgeschlossen hat): Kraty-

---

4 Zum *Kratylos* sei hier nur verwiesen auf P. Friedländer, *Platon*, II
(Berlin, 1957), pp. 181 ff., sowie W. Bröcker, *Platons Gespräche* (Frank-
furt/Main, 1964), pp. 331 ff. Ferner die durch G. S. Kirk mit seinem
vorzüglichen Aufsatz: "The Problem of Cratylus," *AJPh* 72 (1951),
pp. 225–253 eingeleitete Diskussion, zu der ich im einzelnen hier nicht
Stellung nehme; D. J. Allan, "The Problem of Cratylus," *AJPh* 75
(1954), pp. 271–287; H. Cherniss, "Aristotle, *Metaphysics* 987a32–b7,"
AJPh 76 (1955), pp. 184–186; Sir David Ross, "The Date of Plato's
Cratylus," *Revue Internationale de Philosophie* 9 (1955), pp. 187–196. Und
ferner K.-H. Ilting, "Aristoteles über Platons philosophische Entwicklung," *Zeitschrift für philosophische Forschung* 19 (1965), pp. 377–392.

los solle nun dem Sokrates gegenüber erklären, ob das, was
Sokrates über die Namen ausgeführt habe, seinen Beifall finde,
oder ob er auf irgendeinem anderen Wege Besseres darüber zu
sagen habe. – *Kratylos* (ausweichend): Ob er sich vorstelle, dass
es so leicht sei, über eine so bedeutende Sache in Eile etwas zu
lernen oder zu lehren! – *Hermogenes*: Auch wenn er nur Weniges
zur Förderung beitragen könne, solle er es tun. – *Sokrates* (ein-
fallend): Auch er selber wolle nicht unbedingt auf dem bestehen,
was er im Gespräch mit Hermogenes entwickelt habe. Darum
solle Kratylos nur getrost sagen, wenn er etwas Besseres wisse.
Ihn, Sokrates, würde es nicht verwundern. Kratylos habe sich
doch mit solchen Dingen beschäftigt und sie auch von anderen
gelernt. Habe er Besseres zu sagen, so sei er, Sokrates, bereit,
sich bei ihm als Schüler einzuschreiben. – Und *Kratylos*: Ja,
er habe sich damit beschäftigt und würde ihn womöglich als
Schüler annehmen. Er befürchte nur, es verhalte sich gerade umgekehrt. Er könne nur mit dem Achilleus bei Homer sagen:
"in allem habe Sokrates ihm aus dem Herzen gesprochen," ob
ihn nun Euthyphron inspiriert habe oder auch *eine andere Muse,
die unbewusst schon lange in ihm lebe.* Und Sokrates, wie schon
früher im Verlauf des Gesprächs ein paarmal (396e, 401e): Er
staune selber längst über die eigene Weisheit und misstraue ihr.
– Worauf die Wendung zur Destruktion des vorher vorgetragenen
Etymologienteiles und zur Widerlegung des Kratylos einsetzt.

III

Was wir für die Herkunft der Etymologien aus dieser abschliessenden Erörterung entnehmen können ist ungefähr folgendes:

1. Sokrates trägt die Etymologien vor, doch er weiss selbst
nicht, woher er diese Weisheit hat, wie dieser "Schwarm" ihn
anflog – eine sehr berechtigte Ungewissheit, denn Sokrates war
bestimmt nicht der Autor dieser Etymologien.

2. Ein gewisser Einfluss, eine Art Inspiration durch den
Priester Euthyphron mit seinen Götter-Etymologien wird mehr-
fach angedeutet und mag tatsächlich bestanden haben. Aber von
Euthyphron können sie nicht stammen.

3. Sie stammen aber auch gewiss nicht von Kratylos, der

sie nicht vorträgt und ihnen nur zustimmen kann, mit der Bemerkung, er habe sich zwar auch damit beschäftigt, könnte in
diesen Dingen aber nicht Sokrates' Lehrer sein, sondern es verhalte sich eher umgekehrt.

Das heisst, die vorgetragene Etymologienlehre mag im Kon-
takt mit Kratylos entstanden sein, geht aber weit über das, was
Kratylos auf diesem Feld versucht haben mag, hinaus. Doch
ist es bei rechter Würdigung der charakteristisch Platonisch
ironisch-verhüllenden und in der Verhüllung doch andeutenden
Diktion andererseits gewiss nicht nötig, sich in der Ferne umzu-
tun und etwa bei dem Platonschüler Herakleides Pontikos die
Quelle der Etymologien des Dialogs zu suchen, wie, wenig über-
zeugend, Max Warburg dies in seinem Buch getan hat.

IV

Nach allem wage ich, gestützt auf die Notiz des Aristoteles
wie die Hindeutungen Platons, die Hypothese: der grosse Etymologienteil stammt von Platon selbst, ist aber nicht erst *ad
hoc* für diesen Dialog erdacht und geschrieben, sondern reicht
in seinem Hauptbestand in Platons jugendlichen Umgang mit
Kratylos zurück, in die vorsokratische, Herakliteische Frühstufe
seines Denkens. Die Herakliteische Flusslehre ist in einem Haupt-
teil der Etymologien vorausgesetzt. Etymologien auf der anderen
Seite als Versuche, aus dem richtig gedeuteten Namen auf das
Wesen der Sache zu schliessen, kommen in tiefsinnigster Form
schon bei Heraklit selber vor (*Frg.* B 48; B 2 und B 114 Diels,
Vorsokr.[9]), und das wurde wohl von Herakliteern fortgesetzt.
Das Entscheidende aber: auch der junge Platon, der sich im
Umgang mit Kratylos von der Richtigkeit der Flusslehre über-
zeugen musste, hat sich gewiss schon in dieser Zeit mit der blossen
Annahme dieser Lehre, dass alle Sinnendinge im Fluss seien und
dass es mithin ein sicheres Wissen von ihnen nicht geben könne,
nicht zufrieden gegeben, sondern im Bereich des allgemeinen
Flusses der Dinge nach etwas Festem, Bleibendem gesucht, etwas
das eine Verständigung ermöglichte und eine Art Wissen und
Gewissheit begründen könnte. Hier aber boten sich ihm die
Namen dar. Das ausgesprochene Wort "Baum" wird von dem
anderen auch als Hinweis auf "den" Baum vernommen. Und

ist nun in dem Etymologienteil eine grosse Anzahl der wichtigsten Begriffe des Denkens, Fühlens und der Erkenntnis so gebildet, dass sie als Seelbewegungen sich zugleich als Abbilder des bewegten Flusses der Dinge und Erscheinungen offenbaren, so ist auf diesem "etymologischen" Wege und unter Voraussetzung der Flusslehre eine erste Ontologie begründet. Dass viele der Namen, recht gedeutet, auf der allgemeinen Tatsache fussen, dass die Dinge in Bewegung, im Fluss, im ständigen Werden sind, sagt Platon selbst (411c8–10), wo er auch auf die vorhergehende ausdrückliche Erwähnung des Heraklit (402ab) zurückweist. Aus diesem Gegründetsein im Fluss aller Dinge haben die Namen also ihre Wahrheit (*etymon*); in ihnen ist der Fluss der Dinge gleichsam geronnen und eingefroren zu etwas Festem, das Wissen und Verständnis ermöglicht. Dies mag der frühplatonische Ansatz in der vorsokratischen Herakliteischen Epoche seines Denkens gewesen sein. Zur weiteren Begründung seien zwei Dinge angeführt.

V

Einmal: die in dem grossen Mittelteil des Dialogs von Sokrates vorgetragenen Etymologien beginnen bei den höchsten, würdigsten Substanzen (den Namen der Götter) und gehen über die Elemente alles Seienden dann durch die ganze Welt bis zu den geistigen und ethischen Begriffen; den Abschluss bildet wieder "das Grösste und Schönste" nämlich die Deutung von *aletheia*, *pseudos*, *onoma* und *on*. Das heisst, kein zufälliges oder beliebiges Etymologisieren stellt sich in ihnen dar, sondern eine umfassende Ontologie. Es wäre eine reizvolle Aufgabe, dieser Ontologie anhand der Etymologien im einzelnen nachzugehen. Ich muss hier darauf verzichten.

Und sodann: ebenso wie die Herakliteische Flusslehre für die Platonische Ontologie ein für allemal gültig geblieben ist, indem sie in dem Platonischen Welt-Dualismus die untere Sphäre der Sinnendinge charakterisiert, so ist auch das *onoma* als eine erste, unterste Stufe des Wissens und der Vergewisserung für Platon immer gültig geblieben. Klaus Oehler hat in seinem Buch *Die Lehre vom noetischen und dianoetischen Denken bei Platon und*

Aristoteles [5] die "zentrale" hermeneutische Bedeutung des *onoma* bei Platon lichtvoll dargestellt. Wir erinnern darüber hinaus nur an die fünf Erkenntnis- und Seinsstufen im Platons siebentem Brief (342ab), wo die unterste dieser Erkenntnisstufen vor Definition, sinnlicher Darstellung und Sachverständnis immer noch das Wort, der Name ist. Nur ist das Wort, der Name, mag er noch so sehr auf der Natur der Sache aufruhen, in der Konvention auswechelbar (ich kann für "rund" "gerade" und für "gerade" "rund" sagen) und nimmt daher in der Stufenleiter der Erkenntnisweisen in Platons nachsokratisch voll entwickeltem Denken nur den untersten Platz ein, ohne jedoch diesen einzubüssen.

VI

Die im Vorstehenden gegebenen Ausführungen beruhen auf einer Kombination der Notiz des Aristoteles über die früheste Stufe des Platonischen Philosophierens mit Platons Dialog *Kratylos*. Es sei zum Schluss erlaubt, die sich aus dieser Kombination ergebenden Vorstellungen in kurzen Behauptungen zusammenzufassen.

1. Es gibt eine Früh- und Jugendstufe des Platonischen Denkens, in der Platon unter dem Einfluss des Kratylos Herakliteer war und die Flusslehre des Heraklit für sein eigenes Denken zugrunde legte. Bei seinem schon damals lebendigen Bestreben, zu etwas Festem, Gewissem zu gelangen, geriet er auf die schon bei Heraklit vorgebildeten Etymologien und meinte, in den Namen, vor allem sofern sie etymologisch in der Vorstellung des Flusses aller Dinge begründet seien, etwas Festes, Bleibendes, Wissen und Verständnis Vermittelndes zu finden. Was später nach Weiterentwicklung der Sokratischen Begriffsbestimmungen bei Platon die transzendenten Ideen leisten, bewirkten zu ihrem Teil auf dieser frühen Stufe die auf ihre wortimmanente Wahrheit (das *etymon*) hin gedeuteten Namen.

2. Im Dialog *Kratylos* ist Platon weit über diese Jugendstufe hinausgewachsen und für die Richtigkeit der Namengebung zu

---

[5] *Zetemata* 29 (München, 1962), pp. 56 ff.; ich verweise für den *Kratylos* im besonderen auf die wichtige Anmerkung bei Oehler, pp. 67 f.

der vorher im Gespräch mit Hermogenes entwickelten Auffassung gelangt, dass der Namengeber die Namen nach Anweisung des Dialektikers zu geben habe, der jedem Namen gleichsam seinen Stellenwert von der zugehörigen Idee aus anweist (*Crat.* 389–390). Das einstige Etymologisieren auf Grund der Herakliteischen Flusslehre rückt nun in eine überlegene Distanz, und dies gibt der Behandlung den ironischen Charakter, den man gelegentlich fälschlich als blossen Scherz gedeutet hat. Der Rückgriff auf das Problem der Richtigkeit der Namen gewann für Platon aber neue sachliche Bedeutung, als er sich nach dem *Staat* den denk-methodischen Dialogen zuwandte. Der *Kratylos* hat in dieser Hinsicht in Platons Dialogschriftstellerei seinen sinngemässen Ort als Vorstufe zu *Theaetet, Sophistes* und *Politikos*, ent-sprechend dem unteren Rang, der dem *onoma* unter den Denk-mitteln der Platonischen Dialektik zukommt. Wir werden also auch auf unserm Wege dazu gedrängt, denen beizupflichten, die den *Kratylos* unmittelbar vor den *Theaetet* datieren, und keines-wegs in ihm einen Frühdialog Platons zu sehen.

3. Fragen wir im ganzen schliesslich nach dem Weg Platons zur Philosophie, so werden wir nach unsern Vermutungen über jene Herakliteische Frühform des Platonischen Denkens nicht mehr der Meinung beipflichten, dass Platon im Grunde als Politiker begonnen habe und dann Philosoph geworden sei ("Philosophie die Fortsetzung der Politik mit anderen Mitteln"), dass er im Grunde Erzieher und Bildungspolitiker gewesen sei, dass er zunächst als Freund und Gefährte des Sokrates Moralist und Ethiker war und sich erst später zum Ontologen, Kosmo-logen "entwickelt" hätte. Das Philosophieren ist ein Grundan-liegen des menschlichen Geistes, wie die Poesie, die bildende Kunst, die Religion. Und niemand entwickelt sich zum Philo-sophen, der es, in welcher verhüllten Form auch immer, nicht schon ist. Auch Platon war von Anfang an im Grunde nichts ande-res als – Philosoph, d.h. der von der Frage nach Gewissheit, Seiendheit Umgetriebene, der, wie es Jahrhunderte später Cartesius neu erfahren hat, zwar sieht, dass alles, was ihm begegnet, ungewiss ist, aber "den Triebsand unter den Füssen" nicht dulden kann.

Mit alledem wollte ich dem verehrten Mann, dem dieses Buch gewidmet ist, gewiss nicht mehr als einen Hinweis geben. Er hätte aus seiner tiefbegründeten Kenntnis der Dinge, die ich hier berührt habe, am besten beurteilt, was wohl mit diesem Hinweis anzufangen sein mag oder auch nicht.

Tübingen

ΘΕΙΑ ΣΩΜΑΤΑ

HANS HERTER

Dem hervorragenden Kenner Platons und des Platonismus möchte ich zu seinem Ehrentage eine Stelle aus dem Proömium des Dialogs *Kritias* unterbreiten, die, soweit ich sehe, noch nicht die wünschenswerte Beachtung gefunden hat. Nachdem der Vortrag des Timaios in einem Gebet an den Gott des Universums ausgeklungen ist, hat Kritias seinen Beitrag zu dem geistigen Gastmahl mit der Erzählung von Urathen und Atlantis zu leisten. Er will nun begründen, dass seine Aufgabe nicht einfacher, sondern im Gegenteil schwieriger sei als diejenige seines Vorgängers, und stellt daher die Behauptung auf, es sei leichter über die Götter zu Menschen als über Sterbliche zu uns ausreichend zu reden: περὶ θεῶν γάρ, ὦ Τίμαιε, λέγοντά τι πρὸς ἀνθρώπους δοκεῖν ἱκανῶς λέγειν ῥᾷον ἢ περὶ θνητῶν πρὸς ἡμᾶς. (Pl. *Criti.* 107a–b). Eine Missdeutung dieses πρὸς ἡμᾶς hat R. Schaerer in die Irre geführt:[1] es bezieht sich nicht auf den kleinen Kreis der Gesprächsteilnehmer, sondern, wie man bisher auch immer verstanden hat, auf "uns Menschen" im allgemeinen, ist also samt περὶ θνητῶν bloss zur Variation für περὶ ἀνθρώπων πρὸς ἀνθρώπους gesetzt. Wer Belege sucht, findet einen im selben Dialog (109b) und viele weitere im *Timaios* (30d; 40c; 71d; 76e; 77a, c; 80a, e; 81a; 90a, c, d) und wieder andere in der mittleren Periode bis in späteste Zeit (*Phd.* 62b, d; *Symp.* 206c; *Alc.* 2. 149e; *Politicus* 270c; *Leg.* 672d); gelegentlich ist οἱ ἄνθρωποι sogar ausdrücklich hinzugefügt.[2] In unserem Satze liegt der Ton

---

[1] R. Schaerer, "A propos du *Timée* et du *Critias*," *Rev. Ét. Grec.* 43 (1930), pp. 26 ff. Er kommt zu der Annahme eines Gegensatzes zwischen dem Auditorium der Philosophen und einem solchen von Laien. Unerheblich R. Mugnier, *Le sens du mot θεῖος chez Platon* (Paris, 1930), pp. 88 f.

[2] Natürlich bezeichnen sich so die Menschen auch im Gegensatz zu

mehr auf περὶ θεῶν und περὶ θνητῶν als auf πρὸς ἀνθρώπους und πρὸς ἡμᾶς, denn dass die Sache umgekehrt liegen würde, wenn man zu Göttern redete, wäre eine nicht ausdenkbare Eventualität, deren sich der Sprecher gar nicht bewusst wird. Warum ist nun aber das eine leichter als das andere? Wegen der Unbekanntschaft der Hörer mit dem Gegenstande; "wie es uns aber mit den Göttern geht, das wissen wir ja." Man sieht, hier liegen die beiden *Propositiones* eines Syllogismus vor, dessen *Conclusio* vorausgenommen war.

Nunmehr ist es aber an dem, die überraschende These näher zu erläutern. Kritias stellt also fest, dass alles, was wir sagen, Nachahmung und Abbildung (μίμησις καὶ ἀπεικασία) ist; die Kombination der beiden Ausdrücke findet sich in ähnlichem Zusammenhange (*Leg.* 668bc) wieder. Es taucht damit die bekannte Wesensbestimmung der Kunst, ja der Sprache auf; in ihrer Konsequenz liegt natürlicherweise die spezielle These, die Kritias nunmehr an der Malerei exemplifiziert, wie diese ja auch im 10. Buche der *Politeia* die Sachlage besonders anschaulich macht. An unserer Stelle war die Wendung schon insofern vorbereitet, als μίμησις durch das Substantiv ἀπεικασία ergänzt war, das Platon von seinem Lieblingswort ἀπεικάζειν vielleicht selber gebildet hat. Fassen wir einmal, sagt Kritias, die malerische Darstellung göttlicher und menschlicher Körper nach Leichtigkeit und Schwierigkeit einer den Betrachter zufriedenstellenden Nachahmung ins Auge: so ist im Hinblick auf das *Demonstrandum* formuliert, dass es nämlich leicht ist, die göttlichen, und schwer, die menschlichen Körper zur Zufriedenheit abzubilden.[3] In dieser Reihenfolge betrachtet der Sprecher also die beiden Kategorien: was die göttlichen Körper anlangt, für die er die Gestirne und andere Naturobjekte nennt, werden wir, so meint er, sehen, dass wir uns mit einer auch nur geringen Ähnlichkeit der

den andern Lebewesen (*Soph.* 222c; *Politicus* 2266b, c) oder die Männer im Unterschied von den Frauen (*Tim.* 91a, *Leg.* 781a [?], vgl. b) oder die Griechen gegenüber den Barbaren (Ps. -Plat.*Minos* 315c). Dass gelegentlich Interpretationsschwierigkeiten auftreten, ist nicht zu verwundern, s. z.B. J. S. Morrison, "Socrates and Antiphon," *CR* 69 (1955), pp. 8 ff.

[3] Cornarius wollte οὐράνια aus 107d einschleppen und anstelle von ἀνθρώπινα setzen (so Stallbaum im Text); im Gegensatz zu andern Konjekturen des trefflichen Mannes sollte diese verschwinden, da sie den Sinn ruiniert.

Nachbildung begnügen und in Ermangelung eines genauen Wissens über diese Körper das Gemalte nicht prüfen und beanstanden, sondern uns mit einer undeutlichen und täuschenden "Schattenmalerei" (σκιαγραφία) genug sein lassen.[4] Umgekehrt ist es mit "unsern" Körpern, wie Kritias sich ausdrückt: wer noch zweifeln sollte, was vorher mit πρὸς ἡμᾶς gemeint war, wird jetzt jeden Bedenkens überhoben sein. Versucht also jemand die menschlichen Körper wiederzugeben, so sind wir strenge Kritiker und lassen uns infolge unserer Vertrautheit mit ihnen keinen Mangel an Ähnlichkeit gefallen. Nachdem damit der Fall der Malerei ins reine gebracht ist, muss nunmehr die Nutzanwendung auf die Redekunst[5] folgen, und wieder tritt der alte Gegensatz auf: Himmlisches und Göttliches akzeptieren wir, wenn es nur ein wenig adäquat (εἰκότα) dargestellt ist, während wir das Sterbliche und Menschliche genau prüfen. Daraufhin kommt Kritias endlich auf sein Anliegen zurück; er kann Verzeihung beanspruchen, wenn er das Gehörige nicht gänzlich wiederzugeben vermag, und ein letztes Mal prägt er dem Hörer ein: "denn man muss sich das Menschliche nicht als leicht, vielmehr als schwer erwartungsgemäss[6] abzubilden vorstellen." Zum guten Schluss wiederholt er als Fazit, dass er nicht weniger, sondern mehr Nachsicht als Timaios verdiene.

Platon hat alles getan, um den Gedankengang völlig klar und deutlich zu machen, und tatsächlich ist der Zusammenhang im ganzen meist richtig verstanden worden. Die einlässliche Argumentation ist auch psychologisch wohlbegründet, da sie die Beflissenheit fühlbar werden lässt, mit der der Sprecher zu erreichen bemüht ist, dass seine Leistung nur ja nicht gegen diejenige des Vorredners abfalle. Dieser hatte eine ähnliche *captatio benevolentiae* (*Tim.* 29b–d) angebracht, und Kritias versäumt nicht, gleich, als er ihn ablöst, an sie zu erinnern, aber es

---

[4] Das Subjekt von χρώμεθα sind wieder die Menschen, die die Bilder betrachten, nicht die Maler. Zu ἀκριβής s. H. Herter, "Die Treffkunst des Arztes in hippokratischer und platonischer Sicht," *AGM* 47 (1963), pp. 247 ff.

[5] Nicht speziell die Dichtkunst (so O. Apelt, *Platons Dialoge Timaios und Kritias übersetzt und erläutert*[2] (Leipzig, 1922), p. 212, Anm. 6.

[6] Schaerer (ebenso Canart, p. 298, s. u. Anm. 19) missversteht πρὸς δόξαν ("des choses mortelles, qui relèvent de l'opinion") und bringt so die Ideen als Gegensatz ins Spiel; in Wirklichkeit gehört der Ausdruck zu ἀπεικάζειν und dies zu χαλεπὰ ὄντα.

soll in seiner ganzen Expektoration wohl keine persönliche Spitze liegen,[7] denn er erkennt von vorneherein nicht nur die Trefflichkeit des Vortrags des andern an, sondern bezeichnet zur Entschuldigung seine Einlassung als ein recht ehrgeiziges und etwas plumpes Verlangen. Immerhin schlägt er Timaios mit dessen eigener Waffe, denn dieser hatte geltend gemacht, dass sein Thema bloss einen εἰκὼς μῦθος zulasse, und das nicht nur wegen des instabilen Charakters des dem Bleibenden lediglich nachgebildeten Universums, sondern auch wegen der Begrenztheit der menschlichen Fassungskraft; das wendet Kritias nun unter Benutzung des entscheidenden Terminus so,[8] dass er erklärt, wir Menschen seien mit dem Himmlischen und Göttlichen zufrieden, auch wenn es in noch so geringem Masse in der Darstellung als εἰκότα erscheine: es vollständig angemessen und damit wahrscheinlich zu machen, bleibt also von vorneherein ausgeschlossen, während das Menschenthema sehr wohl einen solchen Anspruch an den Vortragenden stellt. Trotzdem möchte ich hier von Ironie [9] oder Humor [10] nur in den Grenzen sprechen, die die attische Urbanität und der künstlerische Geschmack Platon verstatten.

So sehr sich der Sprecher in seinem Paradoxon gefällt, dürfen wir das, was er sagt, doch nicht etwa als blosse Spielerei abtun, die mit Platons eigenen Anschauungen nichts zu tun hätte. Es war auch abwegig, dass Stallbaum die Religionstheorie des Tyrannen Kritias heranzog,[11] selbst wenn dieser es sein sollte, dem Platon die Atlantisgeschichte in den Mund gelegt hätte.[12]

[7] So P. Grenet, *Les origines de l'analogie philosophique dans les dialogues de Platon* (Rouen, 1948), p. 60, Anm. 165.

[8] Schaerers Vergleich der beiden Stellen läuft in einer verkehrten Richtung, vgl. Anm. 1 oben. Ähnlich A.-J. Festugière, *L'idéal religieux* (Paris, 1932), p. 34, Anm. 5.

[9] So O. Reverdin, *La religion de la cité platonicienne* (Paris, 1945), p. 53, und Grenet, *op. cit.*

[10] So J. Duchemin, "Platon et l'héritage de la poésie," *Rev. Ét. Grec.* 68 (1955), p. 21.

[11] Mit ihm H. Müller in seiner Platonübersetzung, Bd. VI (Leipzig, 1854), p. 347, Anm. 3; vgl. K. Steinhart, *ibid.*, p. 340, Anm. 3; Apelt, p. 212, Anm. 5 u. a.

[12] Ich bleibe bei J. Burnets Identifikation des Sprechers mit dem im Stammbaum ergänzten Grossvater des Tyrannen (H. Herter, "Platons Atlantis," *Bonner Jahrb.* 133 (1928), p. 28, Anm. 1). Dagegen besonders Th. G. Rosenmeyer, "The Family of Critias," *AJPh* 70 (1949), pp. 404 ff. An sich war es natürlich zu erwarten, dass unser Kritias identisch sei mit

Die Distanz, die das Plädoyer gegenüber den Göttern einhält, hat nichts mit der Skepsis der Sophistik zu tun, denn sie entspringt gerade einem festen Glauben und entspricht mehr Xenophanes *frg.* 34 als Protagoras *frg.* 4; nur ist sie, wie es wohl auch schon bei dem Eleaten der Fall war, mit der Scheu verbunden, Urteile abzugeben über etwas, was nicht beurteilt werden kann, einer Haltung, die sich auch bei Alkmaion *frg.* 1, Hippokrates π. ἀρχ. ἰητρ. 1, p. 36, 15 ff. H., Herodot 2. 23 u. a. geltend macht. Dass die Götter von den Menschen unzulänglich erkannt und völlig unverbindlich dargestellt werden, sagt Platon vor allem *Phdr.* 246c–d: πλάττομεν οὔτε ἰδόντες οὔτε ἱκανῶς νοήσαντες θεόν, ἀθάνατόν τι ζῷον, ἔχον μὲν ψυχήν, ἔχον δὲ σῶμα, τὸν ἀεὶ δὲ χρόνον ταῦτα συμπεφυκότα.[13] (vgl. *Leg.* 904a); nicht einmal ihre wahren Namen, mit denen sie sich selber nennen, sind uns nach *Cra.* 400d–401a bekannt.

Sehen wir uns nun aber einmal die Naturobjekte an, die Kritias für so schwer erkennbar hält. Mit ihrer Aufzählung werden die θεῖα σώματα spezifiziert, die vorher als die eine Gruppe von Gegenständen der Malerei im Gegensatz zu den ἀνθρώπινα σώματα eingeführt worden waren. Im Bereiche der bildenden Kunst konnte es sich nur um diese "Körper" handeln; nachher, als die Erörterung wieder auf die λεγόμενα zurückkommt, sind allgemein τὰ οὐράνια καὶ θεῖα und τὰ θνητὰ καὶ ἀνθρώπινα einander gegenübergestellt:[14] οὐράνια hält aber immerhin im

dem Gesprächsteilnehmer im *Charmides* und *Protagoras*, und es käme auch mir auf einen Anachronismus mehr oder weniger bei Platon nicht an; aber der Erzähler der Atlantisgeschichte steht wirklich nicht mehr in mittleren Jahren, wie Rosenmeyer glaubt, sondern ist besonders *Tim.* 26bc mit einem glänzend beobachteten typischen Zug als alter Mann gekennzeichnet: entscheidend ist das, wie ich nirgends scharf genug betont finde, insofern, als dieser greisenhafte Gedächtniszustand absolut nicht mit dem Erinnerungsbild harmoniert, das Platon von seinem Oheim aus der Zeit seiner Tyrannis und seines Todes im Kampfe gehabt haben muss. Lit. s. H. Cherniss, "Plato, 1950–1957," *Lustrum* 4 (1959), Nr. 374.

[13] Dass es solche aus Leib und Seele für immer zusammengesetzte Wesen gibt, hat Platon auch schon in diesem Dialog nicht offen gelassen, wie R. Hackforth in seiner Übersetzung (Cambridge, 1952), p. 70, Anm. 1 meint (nicht treffend auch W. H. Thompson, *The Phaedrus of Plato* [London, 1868] z. d. St.), und erst recht nicht bestritten: mit ἀθάνατόν τι ζῷον beginnt die positive Bestimmung der Gottheit.

[14] Grenet, pp. 60 f. (vgl. M. Untersteiner, *Platone, Repubblica libro X* [Napoli, 1966], p. 81) findet eine Analogie zwischen dem Theologen, der

Anschluss an den vorher mitgenannten οὐρανός neben θεῖα noch
das äussere Erscheinungsbild fest, und so kommt es, dass auch
die andere Kategorie, sie aber ohne Not und nur der Gleich-
mässigkeit wegen, doppelt bezeichnet wird. Es ist jedoch in der
Einzelaufzählung noch mehr genannt: Erde, Berge, Flüsse, Wald
neben dem gesamten Himmel und allem, was in seinem Umkreis
steht und geht (Fixsternen und Planeten).[15] Die Gestirne unter
den θεῖα σώματα genannt zu finden, wird sich niemand wundern,
wenn er an *Tim.* 40ab neben vielen andern Stellen denkt; man
darf auch gleich Ge hinzufügen, die im Anschluss daran (40c) als
die erste und älteste der Gottheiten innerhalb des Himmels bezeichnet wird, und zieht man schliesslich *Epin.* 977ab bei, so gewinnt man noch Uranos und sogar Olympos und überhaupt den
ganzen Kosmos, der bekanntlich auch seinen eigenen göttlichen
Status hat.[16] Wenn man Platons Astralreligion ernst nimmt
– und wie sollte man nicht? – so kann man füglich auch den
Anspruch der Ge trotz A. E. Taylor[17] nicht abweisen und
desgleichen den übrigen an unserer Kritiasstelle genannten
Potenzen ihre Göttlichkeit nicht bestreiten, zumal da ja der
Wortlaut im *Timaios* 40c impliziert, dass es neben Ge noch
andere Gottheiten innerhalb des Himmels (ἐντὸς οὐρανοῦ)[18] gibt.
P. Canart hat sich in dem von ihm fortgesetzten Werke von
J. Van Camp[19] über der etymologischen, symbolischen, philo-
sophischen Tragweite des Wortes θεῖος in unserm Passus den
Kopf zerbrochen und ein Gleiten der Bedeutung von dem einen

etwas über die Götter sagt, und dem Maler, der eine Landschaft wiedergibt, aber es ist festzuhalten, dass das göttliche Objekt nicht mit der
Landschaft verglichen wird, sondern die Landschaft selber ist.

[15] F. Susemihl in seiner Übersetzung (Stuttgart, 1857), p. 917, Anm. 3
verstand unter den Göttern 107b4 irrtümlich ausschliesslich die Gestirngötter.

[16] *Tim.* 28b, 34b, 68e, 92c; *Criti.* 106a; *Leg.* 821a. Zu *Epin.* 977a
zuletzt H. Lier, *Untersuchungen zur Epinomis* (Diss. Marburg, 1966),
pp. 38 f.

[17] In seinem Timaioskommentar (Oxford, 1928), pp. 240 f.

[18] Anders τῶν ἐν οὐρανῷ θεῶν *Resp.* 508a. Vgl 592b (H. Herter,
"Platons Staatsideal in zweierlei Gestalt," *Der Mensch und die Künste*,
Festschr. H. Lützeler [Düsseldorf, 1962], p. 180 mit Anm. 10).

[19] J. Van Camp, P. Canart, *Le sens du mot θεῖος chez Platon* (Louvain,
1956), pp. 295 ff. Zur allgemeinen Kritik dieser Arbeit, s. H. Herter,
"Allverwandtschaft bei Platon," *Religion und Religionen, Festschr. G.
Mensching* (Bonn, 1967), p. 73, Anm. 30.

zum andern Vorkommen zu entdecken gesucht, aber das scheint
mir verlorene Liebesmüh zu sein: wenn θεῖα und ἀνθρώπινα so
wie hier in Opposition gestellt sind, müssen sie im Vollsinn verstanden werden, und Gott und Mensch stehen in ihrem unabding-
baren und unausweichlichen Gegensatz zueinander wie eh und je
bei Platon. Dic Aufzählung kann aber auch nicht im Sinne der
Volksanschauung genommen werden, da die Naturobjekte alle
nicht als Personen und schon gar nicht als die im Kult verehrten
erscheinen. Auch die Berge, Wälder und Flüsse werden nur als
θεῖα σώματα betrachtet und stehen damit in einer Linie mit
den im allgemeinen gar nicht verehrten Gestirnen: Platon kann
seinen Kritias nicht im selben Atem eine philosophisch anerkannte und eine andere nicht anerkannte populäre Götterkate-
gorie unterschiedslos haben nebeneinanderstellen lassen.

Wiederholen wir es also: diese Naturpotenzen sind samt und
sonders Götter, die hier nur mit ihren Leibern berücksichtigt
sind, aber auch ihre Seelen haben müssen. Die *Epin.* 983e–984a
verhandelte Frage, ob die Himmelskörper selber Gottheiten seien
oder nur deren ἀγάλματα, stellt sich in unserem Zusammenhange
nicht. Es darf nicht stören, dass in *Politeia* 596c und *Soph.*
234a[20] neben diesen und andern Objekten der Bildkunst auch
die θεοί noch besonders aufgeführt werden, denn dort geht es
nicht wie hier um den Gegensatz des Göttlichen und des Menschlichen, sondern es sollen lediglich besonders grosse Wagnisse ohne
scharfe Distinktion gekennzeichnet werden. Erhellend für das
Verständnis unseres Passus wirkt hingegen eine etwas frühere
Stelle im *Soph.* 232b–c, wo es von den Sophisten heisst, dass sie
ἀντιλογικοί seien und andere dazu machten, und zwar in allen
möglichen Dingen, zuvörderst in den göttlichen: περὶ τῶν θείων, sowohl ὅσ' ἀφανῆ τοῖς πολλοῖς wie auch ὅσα φανερὰ γῆς τε καὶ οὐρανοῦ
καὶ τῶν περὶ τὰ τοιαῦτα. Es werden also im Blick auf 234a
offenbare θεῖα, Erde und Himmel und was damit zusammenhängt, von solchen θεῖα geschieden, die der Menge unsichtbar
sind, kurz gesagt, die leiblichen Erscheinungen von den dahinter-
stehenden Wesenheiten; wenn gesagt wird, dass diese den
"Vielen" verborgen bleiben, so soll das nicht implizieren, dass
andere, wenige sie durchschauen, sondern nur soviel, dass diese

[20] Vgl. P.- M. Schuhl, *Platon et l'art de son temps* (Paris, 1952), pp.
11 f., Anm. 3.

andern sich der seelischen Natur der Götter bewusst sind. Da
Platon die Sophisten angreift, die leichterhand von allem etwas
verstehen wollen, charakterisiert er die Dinge offenbar so, wie
er selber sie sieht, und nicht im Sinne der Gegner.[21] Natürlich
ist auch wieder nicht daran zu denken, dass er von den göttlichen
Potenzen in der Sicht der Volksreligion spräche, denn wie an der
Kritiasstelle bezieht er sich ja gar nicht auf die persönlichen
Götter des offiziellen Kultes.

Man könnte den Passus, dem unsere Erörterung vor allem
gilt, auch noch nach andern Seiten betrachten, etwa auf das
Motiv der *Mimesis* hin, die wie gewöhnlich nur die Ähnlichkeit
mit dem Objekt erstrebt, ohne es zu idealisieren, aber doch nicht
abgewertet wird, oder als Illustration zu der zeitgenössischen
Malerei, die in ihrer altgewohnten Konzentration auf die ζῷα[22]
befangen die Landschaft nur als Beiwerk darbot und trotz aller
Skiagraphie die ungern bestiegenen Berge und auch die immerhin
eher erreichbaren Flüsse und Wälder nicht wiederzugeben im-
stande war. Wir müssen uns versagen, das alles zu beleuchten,
und dürfen uns auch nicht tiefer auf die religiösen Anschauungen
Platons einlassen oder sie gar in ihr geistiges Ambiente stellen,
sondern müssen uns mit den beiden besprochenen Zeugnissen
begnügen, die uns zwingen, seine Götterwelt etwas reicher zu
denken, als oftmals geschieht. Aber wir können uns nicht davon
dispensieren, eine bekannte Stelle näher in Augenschein zu
nehmen, die eben schon kurz erwähnt war. Kritias knüpft an die
Ausführungen des Timaios an, ja, ich möchte fast sagen, seine
Erörterung der θεῖα σώματα bringt eine Art Ergänzung zu dem
vorangegangenen Vortrag; vielleicht trägt dieser Umstand zur
Erklärung bei, weshalb der Abschnitt so sehr ausgesponnen ist,
dass er A. Rivaud[23] "un peu long et étranger au sujet" vorkam.
Hier haben wir eben den spekulativen Hintergrund für die
Volksgötter, die Timaios (40d ff.) zusammen mit den Gestirn-

---

[21] Anders Canart, pp. 196 ff., der aber richtig θείων auch zum zweiten
der beiden ὅσα-Glieder zieht. Cornfords (*Plato's Theory of Knowledge*
[London, 1935], pp. 190 f., Anm. 3) Eventualbeziehung des ersten
Gliedes auf die Ideen wäre nur annehmbar, wenn man zu dem zweiten
nicht θείων ergänzte.

[22] Deshalb heisst der Maler ja ζωγράφος (Untersteiner, *op. cit.*, p. 67).

[23] In seiner Budé-Ausgabe des Timaios und Kritias (Paris, 1925), p.
255, Anm. 1.

göttern als Geschöpfe und Gehilfen des Demiurgos eingeführt
hatte. Der belesene Platoniker Paul Shorey hat die Kritiasstelle
als Parallele zu der andern angemerkt;[24] ebenso hat sie schon
Friedrich Weber zitiert[25] und in seinem Gefolge Rivaud (p.
156, n. 1), ohne freilich (p. 37) zwischen seinen Eventualdeutungen
einen festen Standpunkt zu finden. Nach der Erschaffung der
Gestirngötter kommt der platonische Timaios auf den Ursprung
der Volksgötter zu sprechen, und zwar nicht ganz unvermittelt,
da er Ge schon vorher als erste und älteste unter den Gottheiten
innerhalb des Himmels erwähnt hatte. Er erklärt freilich, dass
die Entstehung der "andern" δαίμονες darzustellen und zu erkennen, über das Menschenmögliche hinausgehe; man müsse
vielmehr denen vertrauen, die vordem darüber gesprochen hätten, da sie versicherten, Abkömmlinge von Göttern zu sein,
und so über ihre Vorfahren genau Bescheid wissen müssten.
Zwar legten sie keine Wahrscheinlichkeitsgründe und zwingende
Beweise vor, aber da es nach ihrer Angabe Familiäres sei, was sie
vorbrächten, müsse man ihnen glauben und damit dem *Nomos*
folgen. Timaios schliesst sich also an die Genealogie an, die von
Ge und Uranos über Okeanos und Tethys zu Phorkys, Kronos
und Rhea samt ihrer Generation und weiterhin zu Zeus, Hera
und allen ihren Geschwistern und schliesslich zu deren Ab-
kömmlingen führt. Nachdem somit, fährt der Redner in seiner
Erzählung fort, alle Götter entstanden waren, sowohl die sichtbar
wandelnden wie die nach Belieben erscheinenden, richtete der
Demiurgos seine grosse Rede an sie, mit der er sie zur Erschaffung
der weiteren Lebewesen aufforderte. Die zeitliche Reihenfolge
der Schöpfungen ist auch in der *Epinomis* (984d) gültig geblieben; der vielberufene Passus des *Timaios* steht damit nicht
allein.

Man hat freilich längst, wenn auch nicht ganz unwider-
sprochen,[26] Ironie[27] in ihm gespürt, ja, "tiefe, fast zum Hohn

[24] P. Shorey, *What Plato Said* (Chicago, 1933, rpr. 1965), p. 335.
Weiterhin auch Reverdin, p. 53.
[25] F. Weber, *Platonische Notizen über Orpheus* (Diss., Erlangen, 1899),
p. 13.
[26] F. Solmsen, *Plato's Theology* (Ithaca, New York, 1942), pp. 117 f.
Vgl. Ed. Zeller, *Philosophie der Griechen* II 1 [5] (Leipzig, 1922), p. 932,
Anm. 4.
[27] Th. H. Martin, *Études sur le Timée de Platon* (Paris, 1841), Vol. II,

fortgehende Ironie"[28] oder auch Sarkasmus[29] oder wenigstens
"überlegenen Humor,"[30] und Weber hat es sich angelegen sein
lassen, einen solchen Eindruck zu fundieren, aber selbst seine
Ausführungen leiden an einer gewissen Unklarheit, die auch
manchen andern Äusserungen über die Stelle anhaftet. Es gilt
nämlich genau zu bestimmen, wer in dieser Weise aufs Korn genommen sein soll, und so hat F. M. Cornford[31] mit der nötigen
Deutlichkeit festgestellt, dass Platon sich nicht atheistisch,
sondern agnostizistisch zeigt:[32] offenbar legt er sich mit den
Genealogen an und nur mit diesen; es geht zu weit, wenn man
auch die Götter diskreditiert[33] oder auch nur mit Indifferenz
behandelt findet.[34] Man darf das Kind nicht mit dem Bade aus-
schütten: nicht die Unsterblichen selber, sondern bloss ihre vorgeblichen Abkömmlinge sind es, gegen die Platon seine Vorbe-
halte hat. Orpheus ist es im besonderen, wenn nicht gar allein,
auf den er zielt, Orpheus, der einzige Göttersohn unter den in
Betracht kommenden Persönlichkeiten, und seiner Sekte schreibt
man denn heute mit Proklos[35] fast allgemein den angeführten
Stammbaum zu.[36] Stolz auf eine lange Ahnenreihe schätzt

p. 146. P. Frutiger, Les mythes de Platon (Paris, 1930), p. 244. Steinhart,
op. cit., pp. 71, 75 f., 110 f. Vgl. P. Shorey, "Recent Interpretations of the
Timaeus," CPhil 23 (1928), p. 355.
[28] Ed. Zeller, op. cit., p. 932, Anm. 4.
[29] Taylor, op. cit., pp. 245 ff.
[30] Weber, op. cit., pp. 9 ff., der aber auch von Ironie spricht; ähnlich
O. Apelt, Platonische Aufsätze (Leipzig, Berlin, 1912), pp. 81 f., vgl.
Übersetzung, p. 163, Anm. 90, 92. "Humorvolle Ironie," E. Pfleiderer,
Sokrates und Plato (Tübingen, 1896), p. 643.
[31] F. M. Cornford, Plato's Cosmology (London, 1937), pp. 138 f.
[32] So auch Rivaud, op. cit.; Shorey, What Plato Said, p. 615; Th. B.
De Graff, "Timaeus 41A," CW 35 (1941–1942), p. 244; Reverdin, pp.
52 ff.; Ad. Levi, "I miti platonici," RSF 1 (1946), p. 200; Solmsen, op.
cit.; W. K. C. Guthrie, Orpheus and Greek Religion (London, 1952), p. 240.
[33] Taylor, op. cit., pp. 245 ff. hat das ganz konsequent durchgeführt.
So aber auch schon Steinhart, op. cit.; Susemihl, Übersetzung, p. 748,
Anm. 113; Susemihl, Die genetische Entwickelung der platonischen Philosophie II 2 (Leipzig, 1860), pp. 387 f.; Pfleiderer, op. cit. Vgl. Martin I,
p. 32 (dazu II, pp. 134 ff.): "Entre la lune et la terre sont placées les
divinités de la mythologie grecque, auxquelles on peut douter que Platon
ait cru bien fermement." "More or less sceptical acquiescence" (p. 129)
findet P. E. More, The Religion of Plato (Princeton, 1921), pp. 128 ff.
[34] R. D. Archer-Hind in seinem Kommentar (London, 1888), pp. 136 f.
[35] Orph. frg. 114 Kern.
[36] Orph. frg. 16 Kern, vgl. Zeller 1[6]/[7] (Leipzig, 1923), pp. 123 f., Anm.
2; K. Ziegler, RE XVIII 2, col. 1358, s.v. "Orphische Dichtung," u.v..a

Platon nicht,[37] am wenigsten wenn sie wie so oft auf Götter hinaus-
läuft.[38] Das besondere Wissen, das sich auf eine so anspruchs-
volle Abkunft gründet, gesteht er dem Orpheus und seinesgleichen
im Grunde seines Herzens nicht zu; selbst wenn das moderne Gefühl sich über den Ton seiner Auslassung täuschen sollte, ist
doch jedenfalls soviel klar, dass er die Verantwortung für die
menschenartige Entstehung der Götter von sich schiebt. Getroffen ist damit aber eben nur diese Weise ihrer Herkunft an
sich; wenn bereits Martin (I, p. 32) mit den Worten "il se moque,
sinon de leur existence, du moins de leur filiation prétendue" den
springenden Punkt richtig traf, so hätte er sich getrost energischer
ausdrücken können. In der *Politeia* 365e hören wir, dass die
Kenntnis der Menschen von den Göttern nur von den Bräuchen
(νόμοι?) und den genealogisierenden Dichtern herrühre: das
wird dort im Sinne der skeptischen Jugend gesagt, aber auch für
Platon selber ist die Berufung auf die alten Autoritäten eine
schwache Stütze (*Leg.* 886cd), und er zählt sicher zu den Weisen,
denen die Legenden der Vorzeit nicht gefallen (*Epin.* 988c); es
bleibt dabei, dass die sterbliche Natur in Sachen der Volksreligion kein Wissen haben kann (*Epin.* 985d). Timaios gesteht
den Genealogen nicht zu, dass sie auch nur εἰκότα beizubringen
haben, wenn man sich auch getreu dem *Nomos* dabei beruhigen
soll, genau so wie das Publikum nach Kritias' Worten mit den
Darlegungen über die θεῖα zufrieden ist, mögen sie καὶ μικρῶς
εἰκότα zu Tage fördern. Wenn die beiden Kategorien der er-
schaffenen Götter so unterschieden werden, dass die einen sicht-
barlich umherwandeln und die andern nur "soweit sie wollen"
sich zeigen, so scheint mir der Zusatz καθ᾽ ὅσον ἂν ἐθέλωσιν auf
gewisse Homerstellen zu deuten, unter denen besonders *Od.* 10.

Anders Apelt, *Übersetzung*, p. 163, Anm. 91; I. M. Linforth, *The Arts of
Orpheus* (Berkeley, Los Angeles, 1941), pp. 108 f; W. Staudacher, *Die
Trennung von Himmel und Erde* (Diss., Tübingen, 1942), pp. 79 f., 92 ff.
(dagegen M. P. Nilsson, *Erasmus* 1 (1947), p. 595; Nilsson, *Gesch. d.
griech. Religion*[2] I (München, 1955), p. 685). Zur Nachwirkung P. Boyancé,
"Xénocrate et les Orphiques," *Rev. Ét. Anc.* 50 (1948), pp. 224 ff.; "Le
Dieu Cosmique," *Rev. Ét. Grec.* 64 (1951), p. 310; "Théologie Cosmique
et Théologie Chrétienne," *ibid.* 77 (1964), p. 564. Lit. s. Cherniss, *Lustrum*,
op. cit., pp. 46 f.
    [37] *Tht.* 174e–175b. Vgl. H. G. Ingenkamp, *Untersuchungen zu den
pseudoplatonischen Definitionen* (Wiesbaden, 1967), p. 58.
    [38] *Resp.* 364e; vgl. *Alc.* 1. 120e–121c.

573 f. nahesteht: "Wer hätte einen Gott, der es nicht wollte
(οὐκ ἐθέλοντα), mit Augen gesehen!"[39] Findet man auch in
dieser Anspielung Ironie, so geht sie auf den Volksglauben,
der diesmal ja auch mit seinen persönlichen Kultgöttern reprä-
sentiert ist;[40] die Epiphanie dieser Götter kann nur in der
Phdr. 246c bezeichneten naiven Weise anthropomorph erlebt
werden, und das auch nur in vorübergehenden Erscheinungen,
gegen die Platon schon *Politeia* 2. 380 ff. seine Bedenken hatte,[41]
während die Gestirngötter in ihrer leibhaften Gestalt offen wahrge-
nommen werden[42] – die Seelen sind in beiden Fällen nicht erfasst.

Es wird kein unehrerbietiges Wort gegen die Volksgötter laut,
und einzig ihr menschengestalteter Aspekt fordert die Skepsis
des Philosophen heraus, die sich nur in Rücksicht auf den
Nomos mit der herrschenden Vorstellung abfindet; durch diese
Zurückhaltung werden sie aber eher in ihrer Würde erhöht als
missachtend beiseitegeschoben. Es geht nicht an, diese Potenzen
im Sinne Platons von den Gestirngöttern zu isolieren: dass die
Rede des Demiurgos nur an die einen und nicht auch an die
andern gerichtet wäre, ist eine Annahme, die schon durch den
Wortlaut ausgeschlossen wird.[43] Wir bewegen uns hier in einem
Gedankengang, der für den Autor verbindlich ist: er hat die
Volksgötter nicht an einen bestimmten Platz in der Weltordnung
gestellt, um sie gleich wieder auszuschalten. Dass Ge als πρώτη
καὶ πρεσβυτάτη θεῶν bezeichnet wird, ist nicht im Hinblick auf
irgendwelche Genealogien gesagt, sondern im Geiste Platons
selber: wie soll man darin Ironie wittern! Gleichviel welchen
Grad der Sicherheit die verschiedenen Aufstellungen des εἰκὼς
λόγος beanspruchen mögen, man darf nicht kurzerhand eine einzelne Partie ausklammern, die überhaupt keine sachliche Geltung
hätte; wenn Platon sich so reserviert, wie es im Punkte des
Anthropomorphismus der Fall ist, sagt er es ausdrücklich, um

[39] Vgl. auch *Od.* 16. 161. F. Pfister, *RE Suppl.* vol. IV, col. 279, 282f.,
s.v. "Epiphanie." Andere Homerbelege führt Taylor, *op. cit.*, p. 247 an.
[40] Diese sind allesamt berücksichtigt, wenn auch nur zum kleinsten
Teil einzeln genannt (anders Taylor, *op. cit.*, p. 246).
[41] Vgl. *Epin.* 984e, 985bc.
[42] Der Gegensatz ist hier also anders als an der oben angeführten
Stelle *Soph.* 232c. Vgl. *Leg.* 931a; *Epin.* 985d.
[43] Gegen Taylor, *op. cit.*, p. 247 Cornford, *op. cit.*, p. 139. A. J. Festugière, "Platon et l'Orient," *Rev. Phil.* 73 (21) (1947), p. 30, Anm. 2.

dann den *Nomos* doch bestehen zu lassen. Es hat auch keinen Zweck, die Darstellung im *Timaios* dem Pythagoreer gutzuschreiben, denn in dem parallelen Passus wird dieselbe Anschauung von Kritias vertreten. Welchen Rang die Volksgötter einnehmen, wird allerdings nicht gefragt; denkt man an *Epinomis* 984d, könnte vielleicht auffallen,[44] dass sie als οἱ ἄλλοι δαίμονες eingeführt werden, während der Ausdruck θεοί erst ein wenig später einfliesst, nachdem die populäre Vorstellung von ihrer menschlichen Nachkommenschaft berührt ist. Jedenfalls verlangt Platon eine spirituelle Auffassung der Mächte, die sich irgendwie unter den Naturobjekten bergen. Er kann nicht ein Leben lang wie Sokrates am traditionellen Glauben festgehalten und die Götter verehrt haben, um plötzlich die alten zugunsten der neuen abzudanken. Gewiss propagiert er *Epin.* 983e ff. die Gestirnreligion, schon weil sie bisher vernachlässigt war, und sie mag seinem Herzen längst näher gelegen haben, aber auf die Volksreligion hat er darum nicht verzichtet. Er hat sie auch nicht etwa in allzu nachgiebiger Verleugnung besserer Überzeugung wie durch eine Hintertür wieder in eine Welt eingeführt, die für sie keinen Platz mehr hatte.[45] Warum sollte sie denn eigentlich nicht in sein System passen, wenn er sie so deutete, wie er es nachweislich, glaube ich, getan hat? Die Götter, von denen die Welt voll ist, gehören in seine "philosophie religieuse"[46] ebenso hinein wie der höchste Gott, auf den sich die moderne Betrachtung gerne allzu sehr konzentriert. Wie diese Mächte sich dann zu dem, was er ϑεῖα σώματα nannte, verhalten mochten, war zwar grundsätzlich klar, aber vor spezifizierten Behauptungen hat er sich weislich und ehrfurchtsvoll zurückgehalten.

Bonn

---

[44] Susemihl, *Entwickelung* II, 2, p. 388.

[45] Gegen diesen Vorwurf (G. Stallbaum, *Platonis Timaeus et Critias* [Goth. et Erf., 1838], p. 15) glaubt Steinhart, *op. cit.*, ihn nur mit der Annahme, dass er von ihnen bloss ironisch rede, schützen zu können. Diese Ironie soll sich Platon nach Apelt, Übersetzung, p. 163, Anm. 92, nur in einem für die "höher Gebildeten" bestimmten Werke erlaubt haben. Vgl. auch J. Duchemin, *Rev. Ét. Grec.* 59–60 (1946–1947), pp. 497 ff. Von andern wird aber Platons Glaube an die Volksgötter betont; s. z.B. G. M. A. Grube, *Plato's Thought* (London, 1935), pp. 150 ff., Reverdin, pp. 41, 52 ff., P. Boyancé, "La Religion de Platon," *Rev. Ét. Anc.* 49 (1947), p. 181.

[46] Vgl. z.B. J. Souilhés nachgelassene Arbeit, "La Philosophie Religieuse de Platon," *Archives de philos.* 26 (1963), pp. 227 ff., 379 ff.

PHILO VON ALEXANDRIA UND DER HELLENISIERTE TIMAEUS

WILLY THEILER

Wir haben uns kürzlich ganz zufällig im schönen Haus von Wolfgang Schmid getroffen, der nun Betrauerte und ich, während wir uns bisher nur gegenseitig rezensierten und auf Grund gemeinsamer platonischer Bemühungen über den Ozean hin eine ἐκ διεστη-κότων φιλία bestand, poseidonisch gesprochen.

Die folgenden aus äusseren Gründen nur bruchstückhaften und vorläufigen Ausführungen schliessen in gewissem Sinne an den Aufsatz: "Philo von Alexandria und der Beginn des kaiserzeitlichen Platonismus"[1] an, wo unter anderem auf eine schon vorphilonische Phaedrusexegese hingewiesen wurde, von der z.B. auch Maximus Tyrius zehrt, und wo auch der Name des Eudor von Alexandria fiel als möglicher Kommentator Platos zwischen Poseidonios – den er benutzte – und Philo. Dass der *Timaeus Locrus* stark auf Eudor beruht, hatte schon A. E. Taylor in seinem bedeutenden Timaeuskommentar (Oxford, 1928), pp. 655 ff., gesichert. Den Namen nennt einmal auch im Hinblick auf Philos Περὶ τῆς κατὰ Μωυσέα κοσμοποιίας[2] die sorgfältige, doch mit anderem Schwerpunkt versehene Dissertation von J. Horovitz, *Das platonische Νοητὸν Ζῷον und der philonische Κόσμος Νοητός* (Marburg, 1900), gleichzeitig, durch Beilagen erweitert, herausgegeben unter dem Titel *Untersuchungen zu Philons und Platons Lehre von der Weltschöpfung* (mir nicht vorliegend). Noch nicht benutzbar war, weil noch nicht ausgeliefert, das für 1967

---

[1] In W. Theiler, "Philo von Alexandria und der Beginn des kaiserzeitlichen Platonismus," *Parusia, Festgabe für Johannes Hirschberger* (Frankfurt/Main, 1965), pp. 199–218.

[2] *De opificio mundi*, abgekürzt *op.*; die andern Abkürzungen philonischer Schrifttitel nach meinem Sachweiser im 7. Band *Philo von Alexandria, Die Werke in deutscher Uebersetzung* (Berlin, 1964).

angezeigte Werk von U. Früchtel, *Die kosmologischen Vorstellungen bei Philo von Alexandrien.*

Dass Philo den platonischen *Timaeus* direkt kennt, wird man nicht bezweifeln, so wie ihm auch andere Dialoge gegenwärtig sind. Er nennt Plato (*op.* 133) mit *Menex.* 238a, spielt (*op.* 2) auf *Leg.* 719e an, (*op.* 4) auf *Phdr.* 247c und denkt wohl (*op.* 6) an das Buchstabengleichnis *Resp.* 368d, in *op.* 55 und 60 an *Epinomis* 978d, 988b (neben *Tim.* 47a6). Auch schon (*aet.* 25) zitiert er, und zwar unter Nennung des *Timaeus,* wörtlich 32c und spielt (*aet.* 74) auf die abgelegene Stelle *Tim.* 73a ἀπληστίαν ἄμουσον an mit falscher Wortkonstruktion.

Es ist nun aber merkwürdig, dass fast alle Zitate des *Tim.* (so sei der platonische *Timaeus* abgekürzt) in *op.*, der gegenüber den esoterischen allegorischen Kommentaren mehr literarische Ansprüche befriedigenden Schrift, die durch *Abr.* fortgesetzt wird (vgl. *Abr.* 3, 13, 258: ἐν τῇ κοσμοποιίᾳ), irgendwie auf eine exegetische Beschäftigung mit den betreffenden Sätzen weisen, die auf ältere Diskussion, ja Kommentierung führen kann. *Op.* 21 wird zwar scheinbar wörtlich zitiert (vgl. auch *plant.*131 ὅπερ καὶ τῶν ἀρχαίων εἶπέ τις, ἀγαθὸν εἶναι τὸν πατέρα καὶ ποιητήν) mit der Fortsetzung, dass kein Neid Gottes gegenüber der Materie bestand. Aber *Tim.* 29e spricht von der Neidlosigkeit in viel allgemeinerem Sinne, und der ποιητὴς καὶ πατήρ wird viel früher (28c) genannt, in dieser Reihenfolge, die absichtlich öfters geändert wird, auch z.B. *op.* 21 und *spec.* 3. 189 wie bei Plutarch *Quaest. Plat.* 1000e, wo das Motiv der Umstellung verständlich wird, wie in anderer Weise aus der Polemik gegen Numenios, der den "Vater" über den Demiurgen einstufte, bei Proklos *In Ti.* I, 304, 8 Diehl.[3] An der zweiten Stelle, *op.* 119, wo ausdrücklich Plato (*Tim.* 75d) genannt ist, über den Mund als Eingang des Notwendigen und Ausgang des Besten, ist die Ersetzung durch Sterbliches, die Nahrung, und Unsterbliches, der unsterblichen Seele unsterbliche Gesetze jedenfalls eine recht erhöhende Interpretation. In *op.* 12 findet sich eine zweckmässig vereinfachende Paraphrase von Tim. 28e ff. darüber, dass ὅδε ὁ κόσμος, der

---

[3] Hübsch die Differenzierung bei Chalcidius p. 179, 7 Waszink; anders bei Porphyrios nach Proklos *In Ti.* I, 300, 1. *Porphyrii in Platonis Timaeum Commentariorum Fragmenta* sind nun vortrefflich gesammelt von A. R. Sodano (Neapel, 1964).

mundus sensibilis, ein Gewordener ist. In *op.* 16 (vgl. auch *aet.* 15) könnte es scheinen, als ob Philo, wenn er den körperlichen Kosmos als den τοσαῦτα περιέξοντα αἰσθητὰ γένη ὅσαπερ ἐν ἐκείνῳ (im *mundus intellegibilis*) νοητά nennt, etwas näher als dem echten *Tim.* 30c 7, 33b 2 dem gegenüber Philo etwas älteren *Tim. Locr.* 95a steht (τέλειος δ'ἀεὶ κατὰ τὰ αἰσθητὰ ἐστιν (ὅδε ὁ κόσμος 94d), ὅτι καὶ τὸ παράδειγμα τῆνο αὐτῷ περιέχον πάντα τὰ νοητὰ ζῷα ἐν αὐτῷ). *Op.* 26 ist zwar von *Tim.* 38b über die Zeit als mit dem Kosmos entstanden angeregt wie viele anderen späteren Stellen, aber die Formulierung verrät doch auch eine daran anknüpfende Diskussion, wie das mehr singuläre ἢ μετ' αὐτόν verrät und die stoische Definition der Zeit als διάστημα τῆς τοῦ κόσμου κινήσεως (auch bei Plotin 3. 7. 8. 30). Dass Philo an den *mundus sensibilis* denkt, zeigt *op.* 27 Ende (θεῶν ... αἰσθητῶν οἶκος; ähnlich schon *aet.* 112), wenn auch 29 plötzlich zum unkörperlichen Himmel übergegangen wird, bis 36 (στερέωμα) wieder vom körperlichen Himmel gesetzt ist. Chalcidius p. 280, 9 Wz. drückt es so aus: *Origenes asseverat ita sibi ab Hebraeis esse persuasum ... initium* (ἀρχήν) *minime temporarium dici, neque enim tempus ullum fuisse ante mundi exornationem dieique et nocturnas vices, quibus temporis spatia dimensa sunt.* Man darf vielleicht erschliessen, dass nach einem vorphilonischen Dogma die Welt nicht einfach als in Ewigkeit bestehend angenommen wurde, wie es die Meinung der meisten Platoniker war, sondern dass in der Ordnung der Materie (vgl. *op.* 22 und nach *Tim.* 30a, Philo *plant.* 3) und der Einrichtung der die Zeit bestimmenden Himmelskörper der Anfang der Welt gesehen wurde, wie ein solcher Anfang der Mythus des platonischen *Timaeus* nahelegte und für Juden und Christen der mosaische Bericht. Plutarch von Chäronea und Attikos freilich, die nach Proklos *In Ti.* I, 276, 31 (vgl. 382, 7) eine ähnliche Lehre vertreten und die Entstehung der Welt angenommen haben, meinten, dass doch auch die ungeordnete Bewegung der Materie vorher mit Zeit verbunden sei. Nach Proklos *In Ti.* III, 37, 12 wurde aber des Attikos nicht geordnete Urzeit bestritten (Plutarch *Procr. an.* 1014b bringt nichts über die Zeit). Philoponos *De aet. mundi* p. 548, 16 Rabe, hält beides für möglich, den Anfang der Welt κατὰ χρόνον und das Zusammenfallen τῇ τοῦ χρόνου γενέσει. Philo lehnt die rückwärtige Ewigkeit der Welt ab; sie würde einen Schöpfer mit

πρόνοια (auch *op.* 171; *praem. 42, spec.* 3. 189) unmöglich machen.
Nach Proklos *In Ti.* I, 415, 18 hat Plutarch den Demiurgen
πρόνοια genannt, und Attikos bei Euseb. *Praep. Evang.* 15. 6.
2 sagt von Plato λογισάμενος ὅτι τῷ μὴ γενομένῳ οὔτέ τινος ποιητοῦ
οὔτέ τινος κηδεμόνος πρὸς τὸ γενέσθαι καλῶς χρεία, ἵνα μὴ ἀποστερήσῃ
τὸν κόσμον τῆς προνοίας, ἀφεῖλε τὸ ἀγέννητον αὐτοῦ. Der Platoniker
Tauros, ein Anhänger der Weltewigkeit, meint, wie Philoponos
De aet. mundi p. 187, 4 ff. berichtet, sie zu verneinen käme aus der
frommen Sorge, die πρόνοια glaubhaft zu machen.

Op. 53 handelt über das Auge als Vorbedingung der Philosophie, nach *Tim.* 47bc; bei Philo ausgenutzt zur Frage nach den
Welturschen, ja in *spec.* 1. 336 (vgl. auch *spec.* 3. 187 ff.,
Abr. 164) zur Aufzählung der drei Teile der Philosophie, ähnlich
bei Chalcidius p. 269, 20 ff. Wz., wo die Teilung Theologie (mit
Suchen Gottes)-Physik-Mathematik steht. *Op.* 72 erinnert mit
αἰτία εἰκότι στοχασμῷ πιθανή an die Ausführung *Tim.* 29c, klingt
aber mit πιθανή an nachplatonische skeptische Terminologie an.
Interessant die folgende Stufung in Pflanze (von ἀφάνταστος
φύσις durchwaltet, später Ausdruck, auch bei Plotin 3. 8. 1. 22;
vgl. 3. 6. 4. 22 f.; beidesmal φασίν)-Tier-Mensch-Gestirn. Die
Gestirne sind dabei mit grösserem Nachdruck als bei Plato im
Timaeus als ζῷα (νοερὰ) angesprochen; wir wissen zufällig durch
Achilles, *Aratea* p. 40, 25 Maass, dass Eudor die Frage, ob die
Gestirne Lebewesen sind, mit ja beantwortete. Einzig der Mensch
nun ist zur Tugend und Schlechtigkeit fähig, steht, also in einer
tragischen Entscheidungssituation. Das hat später Ammonios
Sakkas stark hervorgehoben.[4] Philo zieht darum, um Gott zu
entlasten (auch *conf.* 176), zur Schaffung des Menschen auf
Grund des ποιήσωμεν von Gen. 1 : 26 nach *Tim.* 42d Hilfskräfte
heran; eine andere Begründung für sie bei Chalc. p. 177, 20 ff.
Op. 171 wird theologisch stärker als von *Tim.* 31b 2 die Einsheit
der Welt wegen des *einen* Demiurgen betont, so auch Proklos *In
Ti.* I, 456, 20 ff. Zugleich wird nach bewährtem Interpretations-
verfahren auch die spätere Stelle *Tim.* 55c beigezogen, wobei
Philo den unendlich vielen Welten nicht wie Plato an Demokrit,
sondern an Epikur denkt. In *op.* 171 wird auch *Tim.* 32c benutzt,
um die Verwendung der gesamten ὕλη für die eine Welt hervorzu-
heben.

4 Vgl. *Forschungen zum Neuplatonismus* (Berlin, 1965), p. 25.

Die Beobachtung von Uebereinstimmungen mit Eudor, mit dem älteren von Eudor beeinflussten *Tim. Locr.*, aber gerade auch die von der Verwandtschaft in der Exegese mit Spätplatonikern, die nicht von Philo abhängig sind,[5] führt auf die Vermutung, dass Philo schon einen Timaeuskommentar benutzen konnte, den wir bei der mangelnden Kenntnis sonstiger Prätendenten vielleicht etwas voreilig allein mit Eudor in Zusammenhang bringen. Es ist tatsächlich etwas gewagt, uns nur auf Eudor zu verlassen. Wir kennen freilich sein doxographisches Interesse in der Timaeuserklärung aus Plutarch *Procr. an.* 1013b, 1020c; auch die Nennung οἱ περὶ Ποσειδώνιον (1032b) dürfte auf ihn zurückgehen und *aet.* 75 (mit poseidonischer Lehre), 76 ff. Es mag auch sein, dass die Gesamtdisposition von *op.* etwas derjenigen des eudorisch beeinflussten *Tim. Locr.* ähnelt, ungeachtet der an sich engen Verwandtschaft des echten *Tim.* mit *Tim. Locr.* Die Hauptteile des *Tim. Locr.* sind (1) Prinzipienlehre, (2) Schöpfung der Welt und Weltseele, (3) Schaffung des Menschen, (4) Gefährdung des Menschen durch körperliche und geistige Krankheiten, wogegen Heilmittel und Strafen (Seelenwanderung) anzuwenden sind. Bei Philo finden wir (1) Prinzipienlehre, (2) Schöpfung der Welt, (3) (69 ff.) Menschenschaffung, (4) (151) Lust und Liebe als Verderber des Menschen unter Hinweis auf die historische Degeneration, nicht den metaphysischen Abstiegsweg in Einkörperungen. Aber die Vergleichbarkeit ist eher vage. Es hat sich eben *Tim. Locr.* und wohl auch Eudor viel näher an den Platotext gehalten; Philo hat im Unterschied zu ihnen die mathematische Seelen- und Elementenlehre und die ganze physiologisch-medizinische Seite des *Tim.* nicht übernommen und muss sich an den Bibeltext halten. Statt der mathematischen Seelenteilung bietet Philo an anderen Anhakestellen [6] mehrfach eine hellenistische Zahlenspekulation, die freilich auch ausserhalb Philos Timaeuserklärungen gefüllt hat, bei Theo von Smyrna (und schon Adrast), Chalcidius, Macrob. *In somn. Scip.* (Transposition des Timaeuskommentars des Porphyrios). Die Zahlenspekulation ist auch

[5] Dass z.B. bei Plotin über Numenios Philonisches nachwirken kann, ist eine kaum in Rechnung zu stellende Möglichkeit.

[6] Besonders *op.* 13 f., 47–52, 89–128. Die Zusammenstellung der Stellen Philos, der ein verlorenes Werk über die Zahl verfasst hat, bei K. Staehle, *Die Zahlenmystik bei Philon von Alexandreia* (Leipzig, 1931); die Literatur dort, p. 13.

von Poseidonios aufgenommen worden, wie Theo von Smyrna zeigt; bei der Behandlung der Siebenzahl schreibt er (103. 16): ἑπόμενος δὲ τῇ φύσει καὶ ὁ Πλάτων ἐξ ἑπτὰ ἀριθμῶν συνίστησι τὴν ψυχὴν ἐν τῷ Τιμαίῳ. ἡμέρα μὲν γὰρ καὶ νύξ, ὥς φησι Ποσειδώνιος, ἀρτίου καὶ περιττοῦ φύσιν ἔχουσι. Er denkt an das lamdahafte Schema

$$
\begin{array}{ccc}
 & 1 & \\
2. & & .3 \\
4. & & .9 \\
8. & & .27
\end{array}
$$

nach *Tim.* 35b, das auch Philo *op.* 92 im Sinne hat, und wir greifen ein Stück Timaeusexegese des Poseidonios.

Kein Gewicht soll darauf gelegt werden, dass Philo (wie *Tim. Locr.*) ohne weiteres (136, 171) das Wort ὕλη braucht (nicht schon Plato). Aber zu betonen ist, dass Philo nicht als Präger bestimmter Begriffe in Frage kommt (z.B. νοητὸς κόσμος gegenüber νοητὸν ζῷον bei Plato,[7] ἀρχέτυπον für die Idee [*op.* 16. 25, 69, 78]; das Bild σφραγίς auch für die Idee [*op.* 25, 34, 129, 134]) ist durch Arius Didymus und Albin für den alexandrinischen Platonismus gesichert (Diels, *Dox. Graec.*, p. 447). Ferner zeigt sich bei *Tim. Locr.* und im späteren Platonismus – und der würde für Rückschlüsse auf vorphilonische Exegese genügen – ein Stück gleicher Prinzipienlehre (zum ersten Dispositionspunkt gehörend), indem bei *Tim. Locr.* 94c genannt sind ἰδέα τε καὶ ὕλα καὶ ὁ θεός, bei Plutarch *Quaest. conv.* 720a θεός, ὕλα, ἰδέα. Besonders aber hat die Gaiusschule die Reihe gekannt (Albin c. 8–10, z.B. p. 163, 10 Hermann und von ihr bestimmt Chalcidius c. 304 [mit c. 339]). Immer ist da die Idee als Gedanke Gottes verstanden. Philo nennt (*op.* 8) nun freilich am Anfang ausdrücklich nur zwei Prinzipien τὸ δραστήριον αἴτιον (höher als die Idee) und τὸ παθητόν, die Materie, so wie Antiochus von Askalon, den man oft als Lehrer des Eudors ansieht, bei Cicero *Acad.* 24 zusammen mit 29. Nachher (22) kennzeichnet Philo die Materie in Weiterführung von 9 ähnlich wie der Gegner von Plutarch *De Is. et Os.* 374e. Nach Seneca *Ep.* 65. 2 trennt der Stoiker *causa (ratio, artifex) et materia*; es folgt der Satz *omnis ars naturae imitatio est,*

---

[7] Horovitz, *op. cit.*, pp. 74 f. versucht ohne Ueberzeugungskraft, in Philo den Schöpfer des Terminus zu sehen.

was Philo (*op.* 78) auf das Verhältnis von archetypischer Sphärenharmonie – die auch sonst Eingang in die Timaeusexegese gefunden hat (Chalc. p. 120, 10 ff. Wz.) – und menschlicher Musikkunst anwendet. Vor allem bringt der Senecabrief nach dem Handbuch des Arius Didymus, der Eudor verpflichtet ist (*Parusia*, p. 215), die Lehre von der Idee als Gedanke Gottes. Es ist dort auch noch vom aristotelischen mit der Materie verbundenen *Eidos* als möglichem Prinzip die Rede und vom *propositum* (*propter quod*), das nachher § 10 bei Gott als *bonitas* charakterisiert wird. Philo verrät (*op.* 21) dass er auch schon in einer verhärteten Reihe ein solches Glied kennt τὸ πρὸς ἀλήθειαν ἀγαθόν ... τὴν αἰτίαν ἧς ἕνεκα. Aber vor allem erscheint bei Philo die Idee als Gedanke Gottes, als sein λόγος. Er arbeitet mit dem Architektenbild, das schon Aristoteles für sein *Eidos* angewendet hatte (*Metaph.* 1032b13 f., 1070a14): (*op.* 20) καθάπερ οὖν ἡ ἐν τῷ ἀρχιτεκτονικῷ προδιατυπωθεῖσα πόλις χώραν ἐκτὸς οὐκ εἶχεν, ἀλλ'ἐνεσφράγιστο τῇ τοῦ τεχνίτου ψυχῇ τὸν αὐτὸν τρόπον οὐδ'ὁ ἐκ τῶν ἰδεῶν κόσμος ἄλλον ἂν ἔχοι τόπον ἢ τὸν θεῖον λόγον τὸν ταῦτα διακοσμήσαντα. Entsprechend *op.* 24 im Vergleich οὐδὲ γὰρ ἡ νοητὴ πόλις ἕτερόν τί ἐστιν ἢ ὁ τοῦ ἀρχιτέκτονος λογισμὸς ἤδη τὴν πόλιν κτίζειν διανοουμένου.[8] Ein anderer Name für Demiurg ist *op.* 21 δύναμις ἡ κοσμοποιητική; auch sie fällt mit dem λόγος zusammen. Eudor (vgl. *Parusia*, p. 214) bei Stobaeus II, 49, 12 Wachsmuth, sagt ἐν θεῷ τὸ κοσμοποιὸν καὶ κοσμοδιοικητικόν[9]. An der zitierten Philostelle (*op.* 20) ist natürlich τόπος nicht im räumlichen Sinn verstanden wie am Anfang von 17 (τὸν δ'ἐκ τῶν ἰδεῶν συνεστῶτα κόσμον ἐν τόπῳ τινὶ λέγειν ... οὐ θεμιτόν). Auch Plotin 4. 2. 1. 19 betont die *inlocalitas* der intelligiblen Wesenheit (vgl. auch 6. 4. 2. 3 und mit *op.* 36 ἱδρυθεὶς ἐν τῷ θείῳ λόγῳ ist zusammenzustellen Plot. 6. 4. 8. 4 ἱδρυμένον αὐτὸ ἐν ἑαυτῷ). Alles weist auf schon vorphilonische Auslegung zurück. Hellenistisch-persönlich klingt es und steht nicht bei Plato, aber auch nicht in unserer sonstigen Ueberlieferung der Gaiusschule, wenn *op.* 16 Gott βουληθεὶς τὸν ὁρατὸν κόσμον τουτονὶ δημιουργῆσαι προεξετύπου τὸν νοητόν. Dass es vielleicht nicht erst philonische Formulierung ist, könnte man aus Attikos bei Euseb. *Praep.*

---

[8] Horovitz, p. 87 meint vielleicht richtig, dass der Ideenbereich noch über den κόσμος νοητός hinausreicht, darum (manchmal) dieser Zusatz.

[9] Der Ausdruck κοσμοποιία im philonischen Titel fehlt bei Plato, ist aber z.B. bei Proklos *In Ti.*, schon I, 3, 21 häufig.

Evang. 15. 13. 5 schliessen: Plato γνωρίζων ἐκ τῶν ἔργων τὸν τεχνίτην πρότερον νοῆσαι τοῦτο ὃ μέλλει δημιουργήσειν, εἶθ᾽οὕτω τῷ νοηθέντι κατόπιν (nachträglich) ἐπὶ τῶν πραγμάτων προσάγειν τὴν ὁμοιότητα ....

Dass der Schöpfungsakt ein momentaner ist, dass mit dem göttlichen Gedanken die Verwirklichung da ist, hebt Plato nicht eigens hervor, aber später wird das öfters erwähnt: Porphyrios bei Philoponos *De aet. mundi*, p. 148, 13; Proklos *In Ti.* I, 282, 29; III, 244, 14. Aber schon Philo drückt es wegen der biblischen Tagescheidung aus (*op.* 13, 67). Dass trotzdem eine hierarchische Ordnung gewahrt wird (*op.* 13, 28: τάξις ... ταῖς τῶν τεκταινομένων ἐπινοίαις) bemerkt später im Zusammenhang der Ueberführung der göttlichen Gedanken auf unsere Welt Hierokles in *Carm. aur.* 27. 19 ff. (Mullach[1]): ἐκεῖ ... ἡ τάξις ... οὕτω δὴ καὶ ἐν τῷδε τῷ παντὶ τὰ πρὸς τὴν πρώτην νόησιν τοῦ θεοῦ γενόμενα πρῶτα (hierarchisch) ἂν εἴη usw. Bei Philo wird übrigens (*op.* 15) der erste Tag, ἡμέρα μία nach Gen. 1 : 5, von den übrigen sozusagen sinnlichen Tagen abgetrennt und mit μονάς zusammengebracht und für den Bereich der Ideenwelt verwendet. Dass μονάς auch die Zusammenfassung der Idee sein kann, hat Eudor nach Simplicius *In phys.* 1. 181, 29 Diels behauptet (ἄλλο δὲ ἐν τὸ τῇ δυάδι ἀντικείμενον, ὃ καὶ μονάδα καλοῦσι [Pythagoreer nach der Konstruktion des Eudors]).[10]

Bis jetzt suchten wir nach vorphilonischer Kommentierung, die wir der Bequemlichkeit halber möglichst auf dem Namen des Platonikers Eudor stellten. Dass die philonische Weltschöpfung, wenn sie sich auch vielfach an den platonischen *Timaeus* anlehnt, hellenistisch modernisiert ist, überrascht nicht. Wie zu erwarten, gibt es auch stoische Formulierungen. Herausgegriffen seien die, die auf Poseidonios zurückgehen können, ohne das Problem zu berühren, ob Poseidonios in einer Sonderschrift einige Fragen des platonischen *Timaeus* behandelt hat. Dass er sie behandelt hat, ist aus dem Zitat bei Sextus Emp. *Math.* 7. 93, aus Plutarch *Procr. an.* 1023b, und aus der genannten Stelle bei Theo von Smyrna 103. 16 ff. klar. Da Eudor schon Poseidonios benutzt hat (vgl. *Parusia*, p. 212 f.), ist möglich, dass wenigstens einige der poseidoniosverdächtigen Sätze über Eudors Timaeuskommentar in den Philo hineingekommen sind. Nach *op.* 38, der

---

[10] Vgl. das Schema *Parusia*, p. 207.

Erklärung von Gen. 1 : 9, aber auch im Blick auf *Tim.* 60bc soll
für die trockene auseinanderfallende Erde die Feuchtigkeit sozusagen ein Leim sein: κόλλα γάρ τίς ἐστιν ἡ μεμετρημένη γλυκεῖα
νοτὶς τῶν διεστηκότων (poseidonischer Begriff). Ebenso poseidonisch die Wiederholung *op.* 131 ... ἵν' ὡς ἂν ὑπὸ δεσμοῦ συνέχηται
γλυκείᾳ ποιότητι κόλλης τρόπον ἐνούσης (dann ein anderes Eini-
gungsmittel: πνεύματος ἐνωτικοῦ δύναμις). K. Reinhardt hat
(*Kosmos und Sympathie*, p. 387) andere Stellen mit ähnlichen
Gedanken genannt, die auf Poseidonios weisen (Seneca *QNat.*
2. 1. 4 mit der poseidonischen Frage *alliget aquas [terra] an aquis
alligetur*; Plotin 2. 1. 6. 24 ἐπεὶ οὐδὲ τὴν γῆν ἄνευ ὑγροῦ φασι
συστῆναι δύνασθαι· κόλλαν γὰρ εἶναι τῇ γῇ τὴν ὕδατος ὑγρότητα;
eine Spur auch in der *Kore Kosmou* bei Stob. I, 468, 24: τὸ
ἐνωτικὸν τοῦ ὕδατος). Ueber κόλλα hat sich Poseidonios sonst
Gedanken gemacht. Eudor berichtet bei Achilles, *Aratea* p. 41,
2 in der Polemik gegen die falsche epikureische Seelenansicht
(und in Uebereinstimmung mit Platos *Timaeus*): αἱ ψυχαὶ τὰ
σώματα (συνέχουσι), ὥσπερ καὶ ἡ κόλλα ἑαυτὴν καὶ τὰ ἐκτὸς κρατεῖ.
Die in *op.* 38 folgende poetisch dargestellte Grundwassertheorie
durfte auch nicht unbeeinflusst von Poseidonios sein (vgl.
Seneca *QNat.* 3. 15. 2).[11] *Op.* 66 lässt eine aufsteigende Reihe der
Tiere erwarten, Sekularsierung der Deszendenz in der Metam-
psychose (*Tim.* 91 d ff.). Die Fische stehen an der untersten
Stelle (vgl. 68) ζῷα καὶ οὐ ζῷα ... πρὸς αὐτὸ μόνον τὴν τῶν σωμάτων
διαμονὴν παρασπαρέντος αὐτοῖς τοῦ ψυχοειδοῦς. Das erinnert stark
an das Poseidoniosfragment im Scholion T zu Homer M 386
δοκεῖ αὐτῷ καὶ τοῖς ὀστοῖς τὸ ψυχικὸν παρεσπάρθαι, ὡς καὶ Ποσειδώνιος
ἐν γ' Π. ψυχῆς. Dass Poseidonios zwischen Tier und Pflanze die
ζωόφυτα eingeordnet hat, ist bekannt (Nemesios 41, zusammen
mit Galen *Plac.* 457).[12] Die höchste Stelle in der Reihe der
Lebewesen nimmt der Mensch ein, und mit grösserem Eifer, als
bei Plato, wird im dritten Dispositionspunkt seine Vorzugsstel-
lung gefeiert; Plato spricht erst am Schluss 90a vom obersten
Seelenteil, dem Daimon, und der Himmelsverwandtschaft. Bei
Philo *op.* 69 ff. ist das Bild Gottes, der Mann, in allen Elementensphären heimisch, steigt zu dem Chor der Gestirne und ihrer
Musik auf, und strebt zur intelligiblen Wesenheit. Dass eine

---

11 Vgl. E. Oder, *Philologus Suppl.* 7, pp. 289 ff.
12 W. Jaeger, *Nemesios von Emesa* (Berlin, 1914), p. 116.

vorphilonische Phaedrusexegese (wie in *mut.* 179 ist verräterisch schon das Wort ἀψίς aus *Phdr.* 247e) zugrunde liegt, ist *Parusia*, p. 200 f. bemerkt worden. Aber es mischen sich auch stoische Töne in die platonische Melodie ein. Dass der Mensch in allen Elementensphären heimisch ist (*op.* 69, wie an der polyphonen Stelle Nemesios 64 Matth.), dass er ein χερσαῖον, ἔνυδρον, πτηνόν (ἀεροπόρον), οὐράνιον ist (*op.* 147), darf als poseidonisch gelten (leicht abgewandelt in einer sicheren Poseidoniosstelle[13] aus Strabo 810). In den Himmel steigt der Mensch auf nach der Darstellung der Bewältigung von Meer und Winden und des Besitzes der *terrena commoda* bei Cicero *Nat. D.* 2. 153, allem nach poseidonisch: Der Mensch gelangt zur Erkenntnis Gottes und damit zur Frömmigkeit und allen Tugenden: *e quibus vita beata existit par et similis deorum, nulla alia re nisi immortalitate ... cedens caelestibus.* Philo bemerkt (*op.* 77) vom Mensch: τὸ φιλοσοφίας ἀνεβλάστησε γένος, ὑφ'οὖ καίτοι θνητὸς ὢν ἄνθρωπος ἀπαθανατίζεται, vgl. 154 τὴν μεγίστην τῶν ἀρετῶν θεοσέβειαν, δι'ἧς ἀθανατίζεται ἡ ψυχή (135 metaphysisch gewandt). Er denkt besonders an den ersten noch nicht degenerierten Menschen Adam, den von Gott aus Erde geschaffenen und mit πνεῦμα erfüllten (*op.* 135, 140; *op.* 136 ὁ πρῶτος ἄνθρωπος ὁ γηγενής), den Menschen mit voller Geisteskraft (*op.* 150). Er heisst (op. 144) συγγενής τε καὶ ἀγχίσπορος ὢν τοῦ ἡγεμόνος, ἅτε δὴ πολλοῦ ῥυέντος εἰς αὐτὸν τοῦ θείου πνεύματος. Nach jungen Stoikern bei Sextus Emp. 9. 28 waren die ersten und erdgeborenen Menschen durch Schärfe des Verstandes durch die Erfassung Gottes ausgezeichnet (*alti spiritus viros ... et a dis recentes*, Poseidonios bei Seneca *Ep.* 90. 44). Philo sagt weiter (*op.* 144): ἑπόμενος κατ'ἴχνος αὐτῷ (Eudor bei Stob. II, 49, 14 zitiert für die ὁμοίωσις θεῷ das homerische (E 193) μετ'ἴχνια βαῖνε θεοῖο und das pythagoreische ἔπου θεῷ; *sequi deos*, Seneca *Ep.* 90. 34). Dann über die ἀρεταί und die πρὸς τὸν γεννήσαντα θεὸν ἐξομοίωσις.

Philo spricht (*op.* 140 f., 145, 148) von einer Dekadenz und Schwächung des Menschen mit der Entfernung vom ersten Menschen der im eigentlichen Sinne κοσμοπολίτης war, im Hause des Kosmos ohne künstlichen Bauten lebend und nach dem Gesetz des Kosmos (*op.* 143, vgl. 3). Auch Seneca der im 90.

---

[13] K. Reinhardt, *Poseidonios*, p. 125; I. Heinemann, *Poseidonios' metaphysische Schriften*, II, p. 82.

Briefe Poseidonios vielfach folgt, preist für eine Vielheit der ersten Menschen den ursprünglichen Allbesitz (36 ff.) und die *pulcherrima domus* der Welt (42) und weiss von der Schwächung der Zeugungskraft (44, gegenüber *mundus nondum effetus*). Philo (*op.* 79–81 und dann 167)[14] nennt als Folge der Zuchtlosigkeit der Menschen (80: τῶν ἀνθρώπων ἀνέδην ἐκκεχυμένων εἴς τε τὰ πάθη, vgl. Seneca *Ep.* 90. 6 *subrepentibus vitiis*) das Aufhören des automatischen Wachstums ohne Landbaukunst, neben dem Verlust der Freiheit der Frau das mühereiche Leben des Mannes (*op.* 167: πόνους καὶ ταλαιπωρίας ... ἕνεκα πορισμοῦ τῶν ἀναγκαίων) und bemerkt 169: τὰς δὲ τροφὰς οὐκέθ'ὁμοίως ἐξ ἑτοίμου παρασχών (Gott), ἵνα μὴ δυσὶ κακοῖς ἀργίᾳ καὶ κόρῳ χρώμενοι πλημμελῶσι καὶ ὑβρίζωσι. Vergil *G.* 1. 118 ff. ist nicht ganz so unähnlich und könnte letzlich auch Poseidonios folgen in der Schilderung des mühereichen Lebens und in den Versen 124–127: (*Juppiter*) *nec torpere gravi passus sua regna veterno;/ante Jovem* (das Nächste von Seneca *Ep.* 90. 37 zitiert) *nulli subigebant arva coloni/ ne signare quidem aut partiri limite campum/ fas erat ...* (145–146) *labor omnia vicit/ improbus et duris urgens in rebus egestas.* Als Anfang des Unheils sieht Philo (*op.* 151) ἡδονή (vgl. *Tim.* 64c, 86e, 42a und besonders auch *Tim. Locr.* 102e) und ἔρως an (im Anschluss an die Evageschichte). Der Ausdruck (*op.* 152) könnte poseidonisch scheinen ἔρως ... καθάπερ ἑνὸς ζῴου διττὰ τμήματα διεστηκότα συναγαγὼν εἰς ταὐτόν im Anschluss an die Alkibiadesrede des platonischen *Symposions* 191d ff. So ist dann ein unglückseliges Leben an Stelle des glücklichen getreten.

Sonst sei noch als Poseidonios nahe erwähnt der Gedanke der Abhängigkeit des Irdischen vom Himmlischen[15] auf Grund der Sympathie (*op.* 117). Verwandt ist auch der Hinweis auf die Sympathie und die Erscheinungen wie Ebbe und Flut, die die Aufmerksamkeit des Poseidonios auf sich gezogen haben (*op.* 113) und schliesslich auch die Nennung der Gestirnszeichen (nach Gen. 1 : 10) für atmosphärische Erscheinungen, ja auch Erdbeben (dazu Cicero *Div.* 1. 112, nach Poseidonios).

Bern

---

[14] Ueber Symposion und Theater (*op.* 78), W. Jaeger, *Nemesios von Emesa*, p. 139 unter Vergleich mit *P. hypsous* 35. 2 f.; dazu M. Pohlenz, *Die Stoa*, II, p. 121.

[15] Vgl. K. Reinhardt, *Kosmos und Sympathie*, p. 52. 2.

DIE STELLUNG PLUTARCHS
IM PLATONISMUS SEINER ZEIT

HEINRICH DÖRRIE

A

(1) Diesen Seiten ist die Aufgabe gestellt, einige der Besonderheiten, durch die sich Plutarch von den Platonikern seines Jahrhunderts abhebt, darzustellen.

Wenn diese Frage bisher kaum in Angriff genommen wurde, so liegt das daran, dass die herkömmliche Methode sachlicher Vergleiche nicht zu schlüssigen Antworten führt. Weder kann Plutarchs Philosophie von einem sonst wohl bekannten Lehrer hergeleitet werden[1] noch kann ein System Plutarchs Linie für Linie mit einem System anderer Platoniker vergleichen werden. Und drittens hat Plutarch, so sehr er sich von anderen Platonikern unterscheidet, keine derartige Polemik geführt, dass aus ihr seine eigene philosophische Entscheidung abzulesen wäre.

Denn die Wesenszüge, durch die sich Plutarch vom offiziellen Platonismus seiner Zeit (kurz benannt: Schulplatonismus) unterscheidet, entziehen sich vordergründiger Untersuchung; sie sind tiefer begründet. Sie werden nur zu einem kleinen Teil in sachlichen Diskrepanzen sichtbar (vgl. Teil B dieser Arbeit). Wesentlich mehr ergibt sich, wenn man die philosophische Absicht und das philosophische[2] Ziel Plutarchs ins Auge fasst;

---

[1] Zweifellos war Plutarchs Lehrer Ammonios ein hoch geachteter Platoniker. Doch lässt Plutarch nichts an Lehr-Entscheidungen erkennen, durch die Ammonios den Platonismus bereichert oder beeinflusst hätte. Eindrucksvoll wird die tiefe Religiosität des Ammonios geschildert; bemerkenswert ist sein Hinneigen zu mathematischer Betrachtungsweise. Doch kann von da aus keine Charakteristik gewonnen werden, die den Ammonios etwa von anderen Platonikern grundsätzlich unterscheidet.

[2] "Philosophisch" ist hier durchaus im antiken und im plutarchischen Sinne zu verstehen; danach ist "das Philosophische" ebenso sehr auf die

einer Praxis (wie er sie verstand) zu-, dem schulgerechten Theo-
retisieren aber abgewandt, erarbeitete er sich einen *Stil* philosophischen Wirksam-Werdens, der sich von der gedanklichen
Schärfe, aber lebensfremden Rigorosität der Schulplatoniker
abhebt.

(2) Freilich stösst man auf einen gravierenden Unterschied,
wenn man fragt, welches Publikum Plutarch sich zu Lesern
wünscht, und auf wen sich die Lehrschriften des Schulplatonismus beziehen. Ein Albinos in seinem *Didaskalikos*, ein Kalvisios
Tauros in seinem *Timaios-Kommentar* [3] richten sich nur an Fach-
leute, bestenfalls an den Nachwuchs; sie schliessen den nicht
fachgerecht Vorbereiteten als Leser aus. Sie vermitteln hoch-
wertige, dabei aber eindeutig rationale Information.

Plutarchs Absicht zu wirken muss sehr anders beschrieben
werden; dem, was er niederschreibt – nur die rein polemischen
Schriften sind auszunehmen – ist durchweg etwas Pädagogisches
beigemischt. Er schliesst nicht einmal die ἀμαθεῖς als Leser
durchweg aus, ist sich aber bewusst, für die zu schreiben, die
aus der Lektüre einen Gewinn zu ziehen vermögen. Gewiss ver-
gröbert der Gesamt-Titel *Moralia* das von Plutarch Gewollte
sehr. Aber diese Benennung enthält einen Kern des Richtigen.
Mit dem Ziel ethischer Besserung und Reinigung seiner Leser
ist gegeben, dass er nicht nur auf deren *ratio*, sondern ebenso
sehr auf die noblen und dabei formbaren Triebe (nach Platons
Terminologie τὸ θυμοειδές) einwirkt. Dann genügt ein diskur-
siver Vortrag über das erweisbar Richtige nicht; dann muss die
Darstellung auch im Psychagogischen eingängig sein.[4] Und eben
das hat Plutarch in hohem Masse erreicht.

Erkenntnis wie auf die Lebensführung gerichtet. Eine Unterscheidung
von Reiner und Praktischer Vernunft wäre für Plutarch unvollziehbar
gewesen.

[3] Fragmente bei Johannes Philoponos, *De aetern. mundi* 6. 8, 21
passim, 13. 15. (pp. 144–149, 186 *passim*, 520–527 Rabe).

[4] Was Gellius aus der Schulstube des Kalvisios Tauros berichtet,
zeigt mancherlei Analogie zu Plutarchs Thematik; vgl. *NA* 1. 26, 2. 2,
7. 10 *passim*, 18. 10, 20. 4; offenbar pflegte auch Kalvisios Tauros diese
Art des Unterrichtes – aber vor allem für Laien (wie Gellius) die zum
Eigentlichen nie aufsteigen würden. In den Resten des *Timaios-Kommen-
tars* zeigt sich Kalvisios Tauros als eine ganz andere Persönlichkeit; vgl.
K. Praechter in *RE* 2, IX (1934), col. 58–68, s.v. "Tauros."

Dabei ist er keineswegs einem Maximos von Tyros zu vergleichen, dem es allzu sehr auf Breitenwirkung ankam; sondern
Plutarch hat offenkundig die Mission gespürt, sein Wissen aus-
zubreiten und weithin zugänglich zu machen, weil allem Wissen
eine ethische Wirkung zukommt; παιδεία im besten Sinne war
der eigentliche Antrieb für Plutarch, sein vielschichtiges Werk
zu verfassen. Was dagegen aus dem Platonismus seines und des
folgenden Jahrhunderts erhalten ist, ist durchweg schul-intern.

(3) Die Absicht, auf weite Kreise zu wirken, erlegte Plutarch
freilich zwei wichtige Beschränkungen auf. Dass er systematische
Darstellungen platonischer Probleme fast völlig vermeidet, ist
wohl verständlich. Damals wie heute galt, dass man eine weitere
Öffentlichkeit mit Systematischem nicht langweilen darf. Zugleich aber war ein jeder Platoniker – und dazu gehörte Plutarch –
von der Gültigkeit des Axioms überzeugt, dass der Gipfel der
Philosophie – πρώτη φιλοσοφία – nicht mitgeteilt werden dürfe.
Das sei erstens unnütz, denn der nicht Vorgebildete könne das
hierzu Vorgetragene nicht verstehen; es sei zweitens gefährlich,
denn es werde mit Sicherheit Missverständnisse und Miss-
bräuche hervorrufen, und es sei drittens unfromm, weil ein
solches Reden die Würde der Gottheit zerrede.

An diese ungeschriebene Regel hat sich Plutarch durchweg
gehalten; wohl teilt er – auch das sehr selten – hier und da
θεολογούμενα mit, i.e. Aussagen über das Göttliche, die er oben-
drein gern anderen Gewährsmännern in den Mund legt. Auf keinen Fall spricht er – um hier die Terminologie des platonischen
Timaios 29b zu gebrauchen – λόγους μονίμους καὶ ἀμεταπτώτους,[5]
sondern er spricht, wie Platon, δι'εἰκότων. Um es noch deutlicher zu
sagen: er vollzieht das platonische αἰνίττεσθαι nach, womit er unter
den Platonikern schlechthin allein steht. Da alle übrigen zu Mit-
gliedern ihrer Schule, also zu εἰδότες sprechen, hat niemand sonst
diese von Platon her vorgegebene Art der Verschlüsselung gewählt.

[5] Diese Stelle im *Timaios* hat eine ganz ungemeine methodische Bedeutung gewonnen; vgl. vor allem Proklos zur Stelle, wo die wichtige
Distinktion des Gaios hierzu mitgeteilt wird. Auch Macrob. *Commentarii
in Somnium Scipionis* I. 2 (wohl aus Porphyrios) über die Legitimität
allegorischer Darstellung steht in der Nachfolge von *Ti.* 29bc. Zum
Problem im Ganzen: K. Praechter, "Zum Platoniker Gaios," *Hermes*
51 (1916), pp. 510–259; Bernd Witte, "Der εἰκώς λόγος in Platons
Timaios, Beitrag zur Wissenschaftsmethode und Erkenntnistheorie des
späten Plato," *Archiv für Geschichte der Philosophie* 46 (1964), pp. 1–16.

(4) Es wird also notwendig sein, diese αἰνίγματα so gut und
so weit das möglich ist, zu entschlüsseln, um die Möglichkeit
des Vergleichens zu gewinnen. Dabei wird sich freilich herausstellen, dass Plutarch jenes αἰνίττεσθαι nicht nur aus frommer
Ehrfurcht anwandte. Durch solche Verschlüsselung entzog er
sich zugleich den Vorwürfen, will sagen den voraussichtlich sehr
scharfen Diskussionen, die unvermeidbar gewesen wären, wenn
er seine Philosophie im Klartext – δογματικῶς – vorgetragen
hätte. Dann nämlich werden schwerwiegende Diskrepanzen vom
offiziellen Platonismus sichtbar. In diesem Punkte haben die
späteren Neuplatoniker, vermutlich unter Führung von Porphyrios,[6] sehr klar gesehen: Für den, der darin geschult war, eine
Aussage auf ihren dogmatischen Gehalt zu reduzieren, konnte
kein Zweifel sein, dass Plutarch dogmatisch am Rande des
Platonismus steht. Diesen Vorwurf, Plutarch weiche an ent-
scheidendem Punkt (Ideenlehre) von Platon ab, hat nachmals
Syrian[7] mit ernster Deutlichkeit ausgesprochen. Wohl gilt es zu
bedenken, dass im Jahrhundert Plutarchs ein Sich-Absondern
von der Lehre der Akademie anderes Gewicht und anderen Wert
hatte als hernach, da der Abwehrkampf der Platoniker Ge-
schlossenheit forderte. Voraussichtlich wird sich sogar das Motiv
bestimmen lassen, das Plutarch dazu bewog, die akademischen
Denk-Modelle zu verlassen: Plutarch kam mit pythagoreischen,
vielleicht gar mit gnostischen Gedanken von Weltentstehung und
Seelenwanderung in Berührung. Diese scheint er für wertvolle
Ergänzungen des ihm wohl vertrauten Platonismus angesehen
zu haben. Er wollte sie, ohne das bewährte platonische Funda-
ment zu verlassen, mit dem überkommenen Lehrgut vereinigen.
So wie zuvor eine Verbindung pythagoreischer Elemente mit der
Stoa fruchtbar geworden war, so ging es Plutarch darum,
Elemente pythagoreischer, vielleicht gar poseidonischer Prove-
nienz in den Platonismus einzupflanzen. Ja, es wird in Betracht
zu ziehen sein, ob Plutarch mit gnostischen Vorstellungen vom
Abstieg der fehlbaren und vom Aufstieg der gereinigten Seele

---

[6] Die schroffe Kritik an Plutarchs Lehre von der Weltentstehung im
zeitlichen Sinne, die bei Proklos mehrfach laut wird (z.B. *In Ti.* I, p. 276.
31 *passim*) geht mit Sicherheit auf Porphyrios' Einwände zurück.
[7] Vgl. Syrian, *In Arist. Metaph. M* 4, p. 105. 36 ff. Kroll (ausgeschrieben unten, p. 53).

in Berührung kam. Auf jeden Fall hat er ausser-platonischen
Elementen in viel stärkerem Masse Rechnung getragen als die
ihm zeitgenössischen Platoniker, von denen zumindest das Lehr-
gebäude des Kalvisios Tauros zu Athen und das des Albinos zu
Smyrna gut bekannt sind.

B

(1) Wollte man ganz im Groben die charakteristischen Dogmata
des frühen Mittelplatonismus umschreiben, so müsste man auf
die Lehre von den ἀρχαί und vom τέλος hinweisen. Wieder und
wieder werden als die drei Urgründe oder Prinzipien der Welt
θεός, ὕλη, παράδειγμα = Schöpfer, Materie und Vorbild bezeichnet, die man gern in der präpositionalen Umschreibung ὑφ'οῦ,
ἐξ οὗ, πρὸς ὅ wiedergibt. Als Ziel und Zweckbestimmung wird
das Axiom verkündet ὁμοίωσις θεῷ κατὰ τὸ δυνατόν – so die Formulierung Platon, *Tht.* 176ab, die in umsichtig vollzogenen
Beweisgängen als das eigentliche und unumstössliche Postulat
Platons erwiesen wird.

Was Plutarch hierzu sagt, steht zu dieser gängigen Lehre der
übrigen Platoniker nur in gebrochenem Verhältnis. Er kennt jene
im Platonismus geradezu kanonischen Formulierungen sehr wohl.
Er wendet sie aber nie in der üblichen Weise an, sondern macht
einen eigenartig preziösen Gebrauch von diesen gängigen Formeln: Er sucht dem Zwang, dem jeder unterliegt, der diese
Formeln geradlinig anwendet, zu entrinnen und bietet darum sehr
subtile Umsetzungen, ja Umdeutungen dieser Formeln an.

Nun lohnt es sich, einigen dieser Umwertungen nachzugehen,
weil an ihnen der Abstand vom zeitgenössischen Platonismus
erkennbar wird.

In den *Quaest. Plat.* 2. 1001bc gibt Plutarch in knapper Raf-
fung Einblick in seine Prinzipien-Lehre: δυεῖν ὄντων ἐξ ὧν ὁ
κόσμος συνέστηκε, σώματος καὶ ψυχῆς, τὸ μὲν οὐκ ἐγέννησε θεὸς
ἀλλά, τῆς ὕλης παρασχομένης, ἐμόρφωσε καὶ συνήρμοσε, πέρασιν
οἰκείοις καὶ σχήμασι δήσας καὶ ὁρίσας τὸ ἄπειρον· ἡ δὲ ψυχή, νοῦ
μετασχοῦσα καὶ λογισμοῦ καὶ ἁρμονίας, οὐκ ἔργον ἐστὶ τοῦ θεοῦ
μόνον ἀλλὰ καὶ μέρος, οὐδ'ὑπ'αὐτοῦ, ἀλλὰ καὶ ἀπ'αὐτοῦ καὶ ἐξ αὐτοῦ
γέγονεν.

Dies ist eine Prinzipien-Lehre, aus welcher die Idee als Vorbild verschwunden ist; der Schöpfer bedient sich der Seele, um dem materiellen Prinzip, das als das Grenzenlose bezeichnet wird, Grenze und Mass aufzuerlegen. Dabei ist die Seele keineswegs Objekt der göttlichen Schöpfung – ἔργον – sondern sie ist ein Teil Gottes; die Stellung der Seele kann nicht allein durch die präpositionale Umschreibung ὑπ'αὐτοῦ bezeichnet werden,[8] sondern die Umschreibungen ἀπ'αὐτοῦ und ἐξ αὐτοῦ gelten ebenso. Es ist also nur noch die sprachliche Form einer präpositionalen Umschreibung erhalten; diese richtet sich indes nicht auf mehrere Prinzipien, sondern allein auf die Seele, wodurch deren vielfältige Funktion, den Schöpferwillen Gottes auf die Materie zu übertragen, bezeichnet wird.

(2) Eine analoge Umdeutung der formelhaft gewordenen Drei-Prinzipien-Lehre bietet Plutarch *De an. procr.* 5. 1014ab. Dort wendet Plutarch die wohl bekannten Benennungen an:

1) τὸν μὲν κόσμον ὑπὸ θεοῦ γεγονέναι,

2) τὴν δὲ ... ὕλην, ἐξ ἧς γέγονεν, οὐ γενομένην ...

Von der Materie heisst es folgerichtig, sie sei nicht entstanden, sondern unterliege ständig dem Geordnet-Werden durch den Schöpfer (was soweit gut platonisch wäre): ὑποκειμένην ἀεὶ τῷ δημιουργῷ εἰς διάθεσιν καὶ τάξιν αὐτῆς καὶ πρὸς αὐτὸν ἐξομοίωσιν ὡς δυνατὸν ἦν ἐμπαρασχεῖν.

Das überkommene Axiom, es müsse ein Prinzip geben, nach dessen Vorbild die Welt, wenn nicht geschaffen, so doch geordnet sei, ist zwar nicht aufgegeben; aber dieses Prinzip, nach dem an dritter Stelle gefragt werden müsste, wird mit dem Schöpfer gleichgesetzt: Er selbst ist das Vorbild der Welt; er wollte, dass die Welt ihm gleichartig sei. So wird nun die wichtige Wanderstelle (aus dem *Theaetet* 176b), die eigentlich die Zweckbestimmung des Menschen bezeichnet, hierher gezogen und als eine Aussage über die Schöpfer-Absicht Gottes ausgewertet. Im Weltbild Plutarchs ist kein Raum für einen an und für sich bestehenden κόσμος νοητός der ewigen und unveränderlichen Vorbilder; wo nachmals die Neuplatoniker die drei transzendierenden Stufen des τελικόν, παραδειγματικόν, δημιουργικόν sonderten, da besteht

---

[8] Dieses ist die überlieferte Bezeichnung des schöpferischen Prinzips; die übrigen präpositionalen Bezeichnungen bietet die Überlieferung der Schule nicht.

für Plutarch eine Einheit, deren dihairetische Aufspaltung[9] er nicht zulässt. Mit grossem Nachdruck beschreibt Plutarch unmittelbar nach der soeben zit. Stelle[10] die Funktion von Seele und Körper bei der Erschaffung der Welt.

Die Absage an eine Vorstellung der Ideen als Wesenheiten vor dem Schöpfer stcht, wenn auch in sehr vorsichtiger Formulierung, *Quaest. conv.* 8. 2. 719a: οὐ γάρ τί που καὶ θεὸς δεῖται μαθήματος οἷον ὀργάνου στρέφοντος ἀπὸ τῶν γενητῶν καὶ περιάγοντος ἐπὶ τὰ ὄντα τὴν διάνοιαν· ἐν αὐτῷ γὰρ ἔστιν ἐκείνῳ καὶ σὺν αὐτῷ καὶ περὶ αὐτόν.

Damit wird ein Vorbild, nach dem sich der Schöpfer richtet, abgewertet zu einem Werkzeug; hätte der Schöpfergott eine Belehrung nötig, so wäre er nicht mehr autark. Damit wird eine Prinzipien-Lehre negiert, welche diskursiv vom Göttlichen trennen möchte, was notwendig zu seinem Wesen gehört. Dieser Gedanke, hier nur im Vorübergehen geäussert, war für Seneca, *Ep.* 65. 11 das wichtigste Hindernis gegen die Annahme einer *turba causarum*. Der göttliche Baumeister ist dem menschlichen Architekten darin unähnlich, dass er τὰ ὧν οὐκ ἄνευ nicht ausser sich, sondern in sich hat.

(3) Dem eben Gesagten scheint zu widersprechen, dass Plutarch sowohl in dem Text, der unmittelbar auf die soeben zit. Stelle folgt, wie auch *De def. or.* 35. 428f., an beiden Stellen in enger Anlehnung an Formulierungen Platons, einen Schritt auf eine Ideenlehre hin zu tun scheint. Sieht man aber genau hin, so werden – vor allem *Quaest. conv.* 8. 2. 720a–c – die Ideen verstanden als das formale Prinzip, das das Ungeformte ordnet. Die Ideen haben also eben die Funktion, die Plutarch im übrigen der Seele zuschreibt; in merkwürdiger Schematik wird den Ideen eine qualitative, dem Materiellen eine quantitative Wirkung (= Dimensionierung) zugeschrieben. Das so sich ergebende Problem versteht Plutarch als ein mathematisches. Gott setzte sich die

[9] Hierzu ist der wie ein Axiom formulierte Satz *De def. or.* 37. 430e zu stellen: οὐ γάρ ὁ θεὸς διέστησεν οὐδὲ διῴκισε τὴν οὐσίαν, ἀλλ' … ἔταξε καὶ συνήρμοσε δι'ἀναλογίας καὶ μεσότητος. Kein Wort davon, dass die Ideen als ewige Vorbilder das Mass für die "Analogie" hätten geben müssen, nach der der Schöpfer die Welt ordnet: Plutarch kennt nur eine οὐσία.

[10] Das dort Gesagte ist fast gleichlautend mit *Quaest. Plat.* 2. 1001bc. Auf diesen für Plutarch zentralen Komplex wird unten, p. 52 f. eingegangen.

Aufgabe, zu diesen beiden Gegebenheiten, dem qualitativen und dem quantitativen Prinzip, die mittlere Proportionale zu finden: Und so erschuf der Schöpfer die Welt, die dem Vorbild der Ideen ähnlich und an Quantität der Materie gleich ist (da es nichts ausserhalb der Welt geben kann). Zwar ist damit die ausdrücklich zitierte Vorstellung vom παράδειγμα = *Ti.* 28bc nachvollzogen, aber doch mit der bezeichnenden Abweichung, dass das Qualitative und das Quantitative wie zwei Seiten, nämlich wie die Katheten im Dreieck gesehen werden, zu denen die Hypotenuse gesucht wird, in denen sich beider Potenzen – δυνάμεις – addieren: $a^2 + b^2 = c^2$. Die Ideen liegen also nicht im Metaphysischen vor dem Schöpfer, sondern sie gehören zu den Gegebenheiten der mathematischen Aufgabe, die er erfüllt.[11] Das hier Gesagte wiederholt Plutarch in einer Art Kurzfassung in *De Is. et Os.* 56. 373f–374a.

Es ist eine alte *crux* im Verständnis des Plutarch, wieso er in der Polemik gegen eine Definition der Seele des Poseidonios[12] in mehreren Punkten dem bisher Gesagten zu widersprechen scheint. In dieser Zurückweisung der poseidonischen Definition kommt es dem Plutarch vor allem darauf an, dass die dem Körperlichen zugeordnete Seins-Weise des ἕτερον καὶ μεριστόν radikal von der Seins-Weise der Identität und des Qualitativ Wirksamen gesondert bleibt. Um dieser Polemik willen wiederholt Plutarch die wohl bekannten Wesensbestimmungen von den Ideen, die unbeweglich sind, und im Gegensatz dazu von der Seele, die stets in Bewegung und die Ursprung aller Bewegung ist; die Ideen sind gesondert – χωριστά – die Seele dagegen dem

[11] Im weiteren Verlauf vereinfacht Plutarch die Aufgabe, die er zuvor sehr prägnant, aber doch in virtuoser Kunstprosa dargestellt hat. Es ist die von Euklid, *Elem.* 6. 25 behandelte Aufgabe: Es soll eine Figur gezeichnet werden, die einer gegebenen Figur flächengleich, und einem gegebenen Dreieck ähnlich (also winkelgleich)ist. Plutarch führt die Lösung dieser Aufgabe gar nicht vor; sie ist durch Konstruktion zweier Parallelogramme zu lösen, die den beiden gegebenen Figuren flächengleich sind und mit dem Dreieck den grössten Winkel gemeinsam haben. Für Plutarch vereinfacht sich die gestellte Aufgabe auf die Diagonale als die mittlere Proportionale zwischen den Seiten eines Rechtecks.

[12] Plutarch, *De an. procr.* 22. 1023b τὴν ψυχὴν ἰδέαν εἶναι τοῦ πάντη διαστατοῦ κατ' ἀριθμὸν συνεστῶσαν ἁρμονίαν περιέχοντα. Seltsamer Weise kommt diese Definition derjenigen sehr nahe, die Iamblich als die Seelen-Definition Speusipps überliefert: *frg.* 40: τὴν οὐσίαν τῆς ψυχῆς ... ἀφωρίσατο ... ἐν ἰδέᾳ δὲ τοῦ πάντη διαστατοῦ Σπεύσιππος.

Körper eingefügt – συνειργμένη. Am deutlichsten wird der Widerspruch zum bisher Dargelegten in dem abschliessenden Satze 1023c: ὁ θεὸς τῆς μὲν ἰδέας ὡς παραδείγματος γέγονε μιμητής, τῆς δὲ ψυχῆς ὥσπερ ἀποτελέσματος δημιουργός.

Hier liegt eine Wiedergabe der traditionellen Drei-Prinzipien-Lehre vor, nach welcher der Demiurg die Funktion des Mittlers zwischen παράδειγμα und ἀποτέλεσμα hat. In der Abwehr einer von aussen kommenden, nicht-platonischen Lehre bietet Plutarch das Rüstzeug der herkömmlichen Systematik auf; aber die zuvor angeführten Zeugnisse lassen keinen Zweifel daran, dass Plutarch von dieser Systematik keinen konstruktiven Gebrauch macht.

(4) In der 3. der *Quaest. Plat.*, vor allem 1002bc wird erkennbar, wie sich die bisher beobachtete Widersprüchlichkeit zum Teil wenigstens auflösen lässt. Schon bei Behandlung der Frage "Wieso sagt Platon, dass Gott stets Geometrie treibt?" (*Quaest. conv.* 8. 2) war eine pythagoreische Komponente spürbar geworden. Diese pythagoreische Blickrichtung hat nun in *Quaest. Plat.* 3 entschieden den Vorrang: Hier werden die Ideen als das Mass und Ordnung Gebende, d.h. als ideale Zahlen verstanden. Freilich ist der Abstand, den diese mathematische Betrachtungsweise Plutarchs von der der Alten Akademie hat, sehr gross. Immerhin verdient dieses Textstück grosse Aufmerksamkeit (die es bisher nicht gefunden hat); denn soviel ich sehe, liegt hier der einzige ernstliche Versuch vor, die mathematische Philosophie der Alten Akademie zu erneuern. Derlei wurde hier und da – in Anlehnung an die wohl bekannten Postulate Platons – gefordert,[13] aber nie verwirklicht.

(5) Nur im Vorbeigehen kann auf das eigenartige Lehrstück verwiesen werden, mit Hilfe dessen Plutarch den Nachweis führt, dass es Ideen gibt. Er geht, ähnlich der auf den Gottesbeweis führenden *via negationis* den Weg der Depotenzierung (1001 f.) – nicht viel anders, als Albinos es forderte und als das bei Aristoteles erhaltene Modell[14] es nahelegt. Zu den drei räumlichen Dimensionen tritt (für Plutarch) als vierte Dimension die Bewegung – so namentlich der Sterne, und als fünfte Dimension die Harmonie, die Bewegungen gar hörbar macht. Geht man diesen Weg zurück, so stösst man auf die Ideen als ein-dimensio-

---

[13] So Albinos, *Did.* 7, p. 161. 10 ff. C. F. Hermann.
[14] Arist. *De an.* A 2. 404b21 ff.

nale Wesen: Hier wird das Axiom von den unteilbaren Linien erneuert (1002a). Eine Genese der Zahlen findet erst statt, wenn das Prinzip der ἀόριστος δυάς hinzu tritt; die Ideen als Monaden sind mithin nicht zählbar; sie sind gar in zwei Richtungen gar nicht unterscheidbar von einander: κατὰ τὸ ἕν καὶ μόνον νοούμενον. Als Monaden sind sie alle Manifestationen des Einen. In ihrem Bereiche gibt es daher nur ein Kriterion: ἔτι τῶν μὲν νοητῶν ἕν μὲν κριτήριον ὁ νοῦς.

Das ist ein Kriterion, das sich in den niederen Stufen der Erkenntnis analog fortsetzt: διάνοια ist das Kriterion im Bereiche der Mathematik, die das Intelligible widerspiegelt; im Bereiche der Körperlichkeit entsprechen dem die Wahrnehmungen durch die fünf Sinne.

Alles Bisherige diente dem Nachweis der These, die höheren Wesenheiten seien räumlich kleiner als die Körperwelt. Nun, da Plutarch zum Gegenbeweis ansetzt, fällt der wichtige Satz: ὁ γάρ θεὸς ἐν τοῖς νοητοῖς. Was Gott unter den νοητά eigentlich ist, präzisiert Plutarch nicht. Auf keinen Fall sind die Ideen Gedanken Gottes – von dieser Formulierung macht Plutarch niemals Gebrauch. Sondern in einem nicht näher zu bestimmenden Verhältnis befindet sich das Göttliche unter den Monaden, unter den unteilbaren Linien. Wie so oft, verschweigt Plutarch die theologische Folgerung, die nun gezogen werden müsste. Diejenigen Kriteria, durch die man die Körperwelt ergreift, gleichen Werkzeugen. Der νοῦς, der das einzige Kriterion in der Welt der νοητά ist, darf er mit einem Werkzeug verglichen werden, dessen ein menschlicher τεχνίτης bedarf? Nach dem *Quaest. conv.* 8. 2 Gesagten (oben, p. 42) wahrscheinlich nicht.

Offenbar hat sich Plutarch durch einen pythagoreischen Gewährsmann lenken und anregen lassen. Wieder und wieder ist Plutarch geneigt, auf die Formulierungen Platons, namentlich im *Timaios*, zurückzugehen und auf ihnen seine Beweisführung aufzubauen. Aber diese Beweisführung ist seltsam unorthodox. Es fehlt gänzlich eine Verwendung der auf Xenokrates[15] zurückgehenden Definition der Ideen; an ihre Stelle tritt 1001e eine in solcher Form nicht schul-platonische Anwendung des Siegel-

---

[15] Xenokrates *frg.* 30 Heinze pp. 169–170: ἰδέα ... θέμενος αἰτίαν παραδειγματικὴν τῶν κατὰ φύσιν ἀεί συνεστώτων.

vergleiches.[16] Die Konzeption, die Ideen seien Gedanken Gottes fehlt nicht nur; sie ist sogar in diesem Zusammenhang gar nicht vollziehbar. Vielmehr ist der νοῦς, nicht ausdrücklich mit θεός gleichgesetzt, eine unter vielen Monaden. Plutarch, der sich in der bezeichneten Polemik als wohlerfahren in der schulüblichen Terminologie ausweist, hat hier den Versuch gemacht, die Welt, ihre Entstehung und ihre Vielfältigkeit auf die beiden Prinzipien des Identischen und des Verschiedenen zuruckzuführen. Ihre Wirkung auf die Welt wird im Bereich des Mathematischen widergespiegelt ὥσπερ ἐν κατόπτροις (1002a). Hier hat sich Plutarch, unter entschiedener Ablehnung der offiziellen Ideenlehre, einer pythagoreischen Vulgat-Überlieferung angeschlossen. Hält man sich dies vor Augen, so wird unmittelbar einsichtig, warum Plutarch in der Lehre von der Weltenstehung vom Schulplatonismus abwich: Sein Hinneigen zum pythagoreischen Dualismus empfahl den Ansatz einer Materie, die im Zustand der Unordnung *vor* der Weltschöpfung besteht.

(6) Ähnlich der Prinzipien-Lehre und der auf Xenokrates zurückgehenden Definition der Idee lässt Plutarch auch die ὁμοίωσις – Lehre in den Hintergrund treten. Er zitiert sie *De sera* 5. 550d, zieht aber sogleich eine unorthodoxe Folgerung aus ihr: κατὰ Πλάτωνα πάντων καλῶν ὁ θεὸς ἑαυτὸν ἐν μέσῳ παράδειγμα θέμενος τὴν ἀνθρωπίνην ἀρετὴν ἐξομοίωσιν οὖσαν ἀμωσγέπως πρὸς αὑτόν, ἐνδίδωσιν τοῖς ἕπεσθαι θεῷ δυναμένοις· καὶ γὰρ ἡ πάντων φύσις, ἄτακτος οὖσα, ταύτην ἔσχε τὴν ἀρχὴν τοῦ μεταβαλλεῖν καὶ γενέσθαι κόσμος, ὁμοιότητι καὶ μεθέξει τινὶ τῆς περὶ τὸ θεῖον ἰδέας καὶ ἀρετῆς.

Gott hat sich also selbst als παράδειγμα gesetzt.[17] Mithin bietet er allen Wesen, die ihm zu folgen vermögen,[18] Beispiel und

---

[16] Dagegen spielt der Siegel-Vergleich bei Philon von Alexandreia eine ganz ungewöhnliche Rolle, so *Ebr.* 133; *Mig.* 102 ff.; *Mut.* 134 ff.; *Fug.* 13; sehr breit *Op.* 17–24. Der offizielle Platonismus hat von dieser Metapher, welche die Ideen zum Werkzeug des Schöpfers macht, nur sehr vorsichtig Gebrauch gemacht – vor allem mit Rücksicht auf die Einheit der Welt. Wäre das Vorbild der Welt einem Siegel gleich, es könnte, ja müsste viele Abdrücke geben.

[17] Vgl. oben, p. 43; es liegt die gleiche Konzeption vor, dass Gott vom Vorbild nicht getrennt sein kann.

[18] Dies die wichtige, im Platonismus immer wieder vorgetragene Einschränkung: Keineswegs haben alle, vielmehr haben nur wenige die Anlage dazu, das τέλος zu erreichen.

Anreiz zur ὁμοίωσις. Dass dies die Zweckbestimmung für den einzelnen Menschen ist, wird um des grösseren Beispiels willen sogleich verlassen: Die ὁμοίωσις-Formel gilt nicht nur für den Menschen, den Mikrokosmos – sondern eben für den Makrokosmos, für die Natur des Alls, die – nun im physikalischen Sinne – nach der Verähnlichung mit Gott strebt.

Im übrigen macht Plutarch keinen Gebrauch von der ὁμοίωσις-Formel. Dass er *De sera* 17. 560b fordert, ein jeder Mensch müsse ein προσόμοιον ἀμωσγέπως ἐκείνῳ in sich tragen; dass er *Ad princ. inerud.* 3. 780e den Herrscher für ein Abbild Gottes – εἰκὼν θεοῦ – erklart mit der näheren Bestimmung αὐτὸς αὑτὸν εἰς ὁμοιότητα θεῷ δι'ἀρετῆς καθιστάς – das alles erschüttert die eben ausgesprochene Feststellung nicht. Ja, an der zuletzt zit. Stelle 3. 781a ist gar die entscheidende Abschwächung zu lesen: τοὺς δὲ τὴν ἀρετὴν ζηλοῦντας αὐτοῦ καὶ πρὸς τὸ καλὸν καὶ φιλάνθρωπον ἀφομοιοῦντας ἑαυτοὺς ἡδόμενος αὔξει... (ὁ θεός).

Das gleiche Konvergieren auf eine ethische Bemühung findet sich ausgesprochen *De sera* 5. 550e: οὐ γὰρ ἔστιν ὅ τι μεῖζον ἄνθρωπος ἀπολαύειν θεοῦ πέφυκεν ἢ τὸ μιμήσει καὶ διώξει τῶν ἐν ἐκείνῳ καλῶν καὶ ἀγαθῶν εἰς ἀρετὴν καθίστασθαι.

Bei den im Ganzen seltenen Belegen, in denen Plutarch mit der viel diskutierten Formel spielt, bleibt er seltsam im Vordergründigen. Er stellt die Verbindung zum Problem der σωτηρία nicht her; es fehlt die schon für Platon wichtige Verbindung zum ὅσιον und damit fehlt jeder Ausblick auf eine Kathartik, die den Menschen heilswürdig macht. Warum derlei – in Verbindung mit der ὁμοίωσις-Formel für Plutarch kaum Bedeutung hatte, wird klar, wenn man sich Plutarchs Überlegungen zur Soteriologie und zur Rechtfertigung der menschlichen Seele vor Augen stellt.

C

(1) Als Zwischen-Ergebnis ist festzuhalten:
Plutarch ist mit der Fachsprache des zeitgenössischen Schulplatonismus vollauf vertraut; er ist auch damit vertraut, inwiefern wichtige Wendungen (wir nennen sie gern Wander-Zitate) aus Platon hergeleitet sind. Aber ganz offenkundig widersetzt sich Plutarch der offiziellen Verwendung dieser Wander-

Zitate. Er entzieht sich einer "Sprachregelung," die, wenn man ihr folgt, zu systematischen Ergebnissen führt. Plutarch ist "unorthodox," indem er den in der offiziellen Schule gezogenen Schlussfolgerungen geradezu planmässig ausweicht. Er ist insofern ein "besserer Platoniker" als die schulgerechten Vertreter, als er sich seinen eigenen Weg zu Platon durch keine Tradition verlegen lassen will. Sehr lehrreich hierfür ist sein Ansatz zu Beginn der Schrift *De animae procreatione in Timaeo*; dort lehnt Plutarch beide Definitionen, die zum Wesen der Seele vorgetragen sind, als unzureichend ab und nimmt sich vor, einen mittleren Weg zu gehen, der Platon besser gerecht wird (vgl. cap. 2. 1013b).

Es wäre unangemessen, von Plutarch ein Gegen-System (gerichtet gegen das offizielle System) zu verlangen; was er an verschiedenen Stellen, namentlich zur Idee, vorträgt, müsste, nähme man's als Teile eines Systems, zu einander in Widerspruch rücken. Wahrscheinlich sind derlei "Widersprüche" als Ansätze Plutarchs zu verstehen, bestimmten Konsequenzen des offiziellen Systems zu entfliehen.

D

(1) Können nun – vom eben untersuchten Detail abgesehen – die grossen Linien bezeichnet werden, in denen sich Plutarchs Konzeption grundlegend von der des Schulplatonismus unterscheidet?

Ja – das wird möglich sein, wenn man es als methodisch zulässig ansieht, die Entschlüsselung der drei Mythen,[19] die Plutarch in seine Dialoge eingefügt hat, als Beweisstück hier einzufügen.

Den Mythen liegen – zum Teil in klar erkennbarer Korrektur Platons – zwei hauptsächliche Gedanken zu Grunde:[20] *Erstens*, niemand braucht zu befürchten, dass er nach dem Tode unverdienter Qual oder namenloser Schrecknis entgegengeht. Mit den stärksten Stil-und Beweismitteln wird der Leser darauf

---

[19] Die Belegstellen: *De sera* 22. 563b–33. 568a; *De gen.* 22. 590b–23. 592f; *De fac.* 26. 940f–30. 945e.

[20] Genauer: Ein Gedanke drückt sich in zwei Aspekten aus.

hingedrängt, dass eine schlechthin unbestechliche Gerechtigkeit alle Verfügung trifft; so ist keine neidische Rache für Missetaten zu fürchten,[21] sondern wohltätige Mächte, die im Dienste von Weisheit und Gerechtigkeit stehen, wirken darauf hin, dass alles reiner und besser wird. Darum muss Unreinheit, durch böse Taten erworben, freilich in langer und schmerzhafter Reinigung abgelegt werden. Letzten Endes aber ist niemandem der Aufstieg verwehrt.

Die Emphase dieser Theodizee muss in einen Zusammenhang mit eschatologischen Vorstellungen der Gnosis gebracht werden: Dort die Angst um die völlig in Frage gestellte Existenz, die möglicherweise irrationalen oder feindlichen Mächten ausgeliefert ist; hier die bündige Versicherung, dass jedem nach seinem Verdienste geschieht. Zwar können die Strafen lang und schrecklich sein – aber sie sind niemals willkürlich oder unverdient; an ihrem Ende steht *immer* das Wieder-Rein-Werden. Insofern enthalten die Jenseits-Mythen Plutarchs eine Antwort auf die geängstigten Fragen, die in der Gnosis laut wurden.

(2) Es wäre aber falsch, Plutarch in einen diametralen Gegensatz zur Gnosis zu rücken. Seine Antwort freilich ist von einem in der Gnosis ungewohnten Optimismus; seine Konzeption von den Vorgängen des Auf- und Absteigens von Seelen hat mancherlei Analogie zu gnostischen Vorstellungen und ist gerade darum von Vorstellungen Platons weit verschieden.

Denn hierin liegt der *zweite* Aspekt des oben p. 40 skizzierten Grundgedankens: Dem Aufstieg der gereinigten Seele sind keine Schranken gesetzt; sie kann sich, wenn sie das Seelisch-Triebhafte ablegt, zum reinen νοητόν läutern, also zur Idee, und kann als solche zur Einung mit dem intelligiblen Zentralfeuer, der Sonne[22] gelangen.

Diese wichtige Vorstellung hat Plutarch nicht nur in der Verschlüsselung seiner Mythen, also αἰνιγματωδῶς gegeben; er hat sie auch im Klartext als eine der wichtigsten Erkenntnisse, ja als ein Naturgesetz formuliert, so *De def.* 10. 415b ἕτεροι (sc. φιλόσοφοι)

---

[21] Selbst Nero, wiewohl als Muttermörder mit dem scheusslichsten Makel behaftet, wird wegen des *meritum*, das er durch die Befreiung der Hellenen erwarb, zu milderer Bestrafung begnadigt.

[22] So *De fac.* 30. 944e. Auf die vielfachen Verbindungen, die zwischen Plutarchs Kosmologie und der Solar-Theologie des Poseidonios bestehen, kann hier nicht eingegangen werden.

δὲ μεταβολὴν τοῖς τε σώμασιν ὁμοίως ποιοῦσι καὶ ταῖς ψυχαῖς, ὥσπερ ἐκ γῆς ὕδωρ ἐκ δ'ὕδατος ἀὴρ ἐκ δ'ἀέρος πῦρ γεννώμενον ὁρᾶται, τῆς οὐσίας ἄνω φερομένης, οὕτως ἐκ μὲν ἀνθρώπων εἰς ἥρωας ἐκ δ'ἡρώων εἰς δαίμονας αἱ βελτίονες ψυχαὶ τὴν μεταβολὴν λαμβάνουσιν. ἐκ δὲ δαιμόνων ὀλίγαι μὲν ἔτι χρόνῳ πολλῷ δι'ἀρετῆς καθαρθεῖσαι παντάπασι θειότητος μετέσχον.[23]

Schlechtes macht schwer, Frei-Sein von Schlechtem macht leicht. Wenn dieses Axiom gilt, dann muss die Vertikal-Bewegung der Seelen dem gleichen Naturgesetz folgen, das die Stoa ihrer Kosmogonie zu Grunde gelegt hatte: Alles Leichte strebt nach oben; je leichter ein Materie-Teilchen ist, um so mehr gleicht es dem feurigen πνεῦμα. Der Aufstieg der Seelen wird also durch eine physikalische Selbstverständlichkeit mehr beschrieben als erklärt. Dem Leser bleibt kein Ausweg: er muss diese Gleichung einer Eschatologie mit einem Naturgesetz anerkennen. Es ist so! und es ist ganz einfach!

Damit tritt Plutarch in Widerspruch zu dem Stufungs-Gedanken, der alle platonischen Systeme beherrscht; es ist etwa an den Mythos im *Phaidros* zu erinnern, wonach die Seele auf die ewigen Ideen schaut; wohl ist solche θεωρία als μέθεξις vollziehbar, ja, durch sie gewinnt die Seele die Kraft, ihre Bahn auf dem Himmelsrund einzuhalten. Aber es wäre unvorstellbar, dass die Seele in das Reich der Ideen aufstiege.

Die Vorstellung von einem mehrfach gestuften Jenseits hat Plutarch in breiter Schilderung *De gen.* 22. 519b[24] ausgeführt. An sich sind diese Bereiche, die einander wie Sphären überlagern, durch scharf markierte Grenzen von einander abgeschlossen. Aber die göttliche Vorsehung hat an die Stellen, wo sich die Sphären berühren, je eine der Moirai eingesetzt mit dem Auftrage zu binden und zu lösen: Als die Schlüsselbewahrerinnen geben oder versagen diese Mächte den Auf- oder Abstieg. Mit anderen Worten, der vierfach gestufte, im Sinne des Schulplatonismus konzipierte Kosmos ist – in entscheidender Abänderung – durchlässig gemacht worden; wer dessen würdig ist, kann in diesem Gebäude auf und absteigen; das *De def. or.* 10. 415b formulierte

---

[23] Vgl. Verg. *Aen.* 6. 129–130 und E. Norden (ed.), *Publius Vergilius Maro Aeneis Buch VI* (Stuttgart, 1957), *ad loc.*

[24] Vgl. H. Dörrie, "Zur Ursprung der neuplatonischen Hypostasenlehre," *Hermes* 82 (1954), pp. 331–342.

Naturgesetz kann in dieser so geordneten Welt vollzogen werden.

Offensichtlich geht Plutarch von einer zunächst stoischen Konzeption aus; er harmonisiert diese mit der platonischen Vorstellung vom vierfach gestuften Weltgebäude, behält aber den für ihn hochwichtigen Gedanken bei, dass ein Auf- und Absteigen von Seelen (deren Qualität sich beim Auf- und Abstieg wandelt) möglich ist.

Vollzieht man diese Gedanken nach, so wird zunächst klar, warum Plutarchs Vorstellung von den Ideen so seltsam gebrochen ist: Die Welt der Ideen – κόσμος νοητός – kann ja bei solcher Konzeption keineswegs als Vorbild alles Irdischen, als παράδειγμα allein, aufgefasst werden. Die Ideen stellen keine Welt für sich – αὐτὰ καθ'ἑαυτά – mehr dar, sondern sind in das Gefüge einbezogen.

Da Plutarch die Sonderung zweier Weltseelen, die Platon vollzog,[25] nachgebildet hat,[26] wird er gern als "Dualist" bezeichnet. Das ist aber nur für jenen engen Bereich zutreffend, wo es um die Erklärung der Frage geht πόθεν τὰ κακά – nur hier ist der Ansatz einer bösen Seele sinnvoll, welche die gute Seele daran hindert, sich voll in der Welt zu verwirklichen. Blickt man auf Plutarchs Kosmologie im Ganzen, so ist er in viel höherem Sinne Monist als die meisten Platoniker. Die von Platon eindeutig gezogene Grenzlinie zwischen dem "An-und-für-sich" und dem Abgeleiteten und Bezogenen ist aufgehoben. Da jede menschliche Seele λόγος enthält, und da dieser Besitz unverlierbar und unzerstörbar ist, *muss* es Wege des Auf- und Abstieges geben. Platons Gedanke von der Teilhabe wird aufgelöst und überwunden, das μετέχειν wird zum ἔχειν, das Intelligible, zuvor Objekt der Schau, wohnt der Seele bereits inne.

Alles dieses ist von Plutarch noch keineswegs im Sinne neuplatonischer Systematik formuliert; lediglich Ansätze, die freilich deutlich in diese Richtung weisen, sind den αἰνίγματα Plutarchs zu entnehmen. Unverkennbar sind erhebliche Teile des stoischen Weltbildes: Die freie Beweglichkeit des Logos, der,

---

[25] Pl. *Leg.* 10. 896e–897e.
[26] Plutarch *De Is. et Os.* 30. 362e ff. beschreibt Typhon als das Symbol der bösen Seele; vgl. ferner *De an. procr.* 5. 1014b–e. Hier ist der Dualismus durch eine geschichtstheoretische Überlegung entkräftet: Unordnung und Unvernunft werden durch die ordnende Vernunft überwunden: οὐ γὰρ ἐκ τοῦ μὴ ὄντος ἡ γένεσις, ἀλλ'ἐκ τοῦ μὴ καλῶς μηδ'ἱκανῶς ἔχοντος.

gemäss seiner physikalischen und seiner ethischen Valenz, das
leichteste "Element" ist und darum zum Aufsteigen drängt, ist
ganz offensichtlich stoischen Vorstellungen, vielleicht gar Poseidonios selbst, entnommen und nachgebildet. Ist Plutarch darum
Eklektiker? Ganz gewiss wäre es einseitig, solchen vorgeblichen
Eklektizismus zum bezeichnenden Merkmal Plutarchs zu erklären. Jene monistische "Weltsicht" bot Plutarch die Ansatz-
punkte, um die Stufungslehre des Schulplatonismus entscheidend
zu korrigieren. Ob dieses Weltbild der stoischen Schule entstamm-
te oder nicht, durfte für Plutarch gleichgültig bleiben. Denn
er kannte Platons Schriften gut genug, um zu wissen, dass dieses
Weltbild auch aus Platon abzuleiten ist – wenn man den *Timaios*
im Wortsinne nimmt. Mögen die Einflüsse einer durch Poseidonios' Schule geformten Stoa auf Plutarch erheblich gewesen
sein – dieser durfte die subjektiv berechtigte Überzeugung hegen,
durch selbständigen Rückgriff auf einen besser (als von anderen)
verstandenen Platon die Wahrheit gefunden zu haben.

E

Diese von Plutarch gefundene und vertretene Kosmologie
hat einen rückwärts gewendeten und einen in die Zukunft weisenden Aspekt:

(1) Einerseits steht Plutarch auf dem Boden der hellenistischen
Philosophie. Dieser Kosmos, dieses Weltgebäude, das uns um-
gibt, enthält alles; Plutarchs Philosophieren "durchstudiert die
gross' und kleine Welt"[27] – aber sie dringt, beim Wortsinn genommen, nirgendwo in den Bereich der eigentlichen Transzendenz
vor: Man könnte versucht sein, von einer platonisierenden Konstruktion zu sprechen, die Punkt um Punkt mit der stoischen
Konstruktion konkurriert, ohne deren Bezug auf diese eine Welt
je zu verlassen: Tatsächlich hat ja Plutarch dieser Welt kein
von ihr gesondertes Paradigma vorgeordnet. Wenn man zu seiner
Zeit[28] den Platonismus durch die drei im Grunde gleiches be-

---

[27] J. W. Goethe, *Faust* I, Studierzimmer, v. 2012.
[28] Iustin, *Dial.* 2. 6 schildert, was ihn an dem Unterricht in der Schule
eines Platonikers faszinierte: καί με ᾕρει σφόδρα ἡ τῶν ἀσωμάτων νόησις
καὶ ἡ θεωρία τῶν ἰδεῶν ἀνεπτέρου μου τὴν φρόνησιν ... καὶ ὑπὸ βλακείας
ἤλπιζον αὐτίκα κατόψεσθαι τὸν θεόν· τοῦτο γὰρ τέλος τῆς Πλάτωνος φιλοσοφίας.

deutenden Merkmale: "Unkörperliches denken; die Ideen schauen, Gott erblicken" kennzeichnete, so trifft das nur ganz am Rande auf Plutarch zu: Sein Philosophieren gilt im Grunde nicht dem νοῦς, sondern der Seele; und alle Zugänge zum νοῦς sind nicht im absoluten Sinne, sondern nur durch das Medium der sich reinigenden Seele praktikabel.

Mit der Genauigkeit des geschulten Systematikers trifft Syrian [29] diese Abweichung Plutarchs von der Grundlinie des Platonismus. Zwar sei ihm und seinen Gesinnungsgenossen noch nicht zum Vorwurf zu machen, dass sie die Allgemeinbegriffe, die in der psychischen Substanz ewig anwesend sind, Ideen nannten (auch das sind Ideen, nur hat man damit ihre Transzendenz verkannt); sondern der an Abfall grenzende Irrtum Plutarchs bestand darin, dass man jene Trenn-Linie – χωρίζειν – nicht zog, also das Transzendente und das Immanente verwirrte und vermischte: μηδὲ Πλούταρχον καὶ 'Αττικὸν καὶ Δημόκριτον τοὺς Πλατωνικοὺς κατ' αὐτὸ τοῦτο ζηλοῦμεν, ὅτι γε τοὺς καθόλου λόγους τοὺς ἐν οὐσίᾳ τῇ ψυχικῇ διαιωνίως ὑπάρχοντας ἡγοῦνται εἶναι τὰς ἰδέας· ... ἀλλ'ὅμως οὐ χρὴ συμφύρειν εἰς ταὐτὸ τοὺς τῆς ψυχῆς λόγους καὶ τὸν ἔνυλον καλούμενον νοῦν τοῖς παραδειγματικοῖς καὶ ἀΰλοις εἴδεσι καὶ ταῖς δημιουργικαῖς νοήσεσιν· ἀλλ'ὥσπερ ὁ θεῖος Πλάτων τὸ μὲν ἡμέτερον εἰς ἕν λογισμῷ συναιρεῖσθαί φησι καὶ ἀνάμνησιν εἶναι ὧν ἐθεασάμεθά ποτε συμπορευθέντες θεῷ, τὸ δὲ θεῖον ἀεὶ κατὰ τὰ αὐτὰ ὡσαύτως ἔχειν, οὕτω καὶ αὐτοὺς διαιρεῖν, ἔστ'ἂν ἐθέλωσιν εἶναι Πλατωνικοί.

Diese harte Kritik ist berechtigt, ja sie beschreibt Plutarchs Verharren in der Diesseitigkeit richtig, wenn Plutarchs Text nur einem, d.h. wortwörtlichen Verständnis geöffnet werden soll; seiner Ambivalenzen, seiner αἰνίγματα, seines achtungsvollen Verschweigens theologischer Aussage wird dann keine Rechnung getragen:[30] Vermutlich ist sein Weltbild in den transzendenten

---

[29] Syrian, *In Arist. Metaph.* M 4, p. 105. 36 ff. Kroll.

[30] Hierzu ein Beispiel: *De fac.* 29. 944e–945b wird der Vorgang beschrieben, wie die Seele auf dem Monde ein zweites Mal "stirbt," d.h. zu wahrem Leben gelangt und nun in die Sonne eingeht. Soll man hier "physikalisch" die wahrnehmbare Sonne verstehen? Neben und hinter diesem Verständnis steht die Sonne des Platonischen Sonnen-Gleichnisses, das Zentrum des Intelligiblen: Die Seele ist ein νοητόν geworden; sie vereinigt sich nun mit den übrigen νοητά. Es liegt am Mythos, dass dies an der Reise vom Mond zur Sonne anschaulich gemacht wird.

Raum hinein geöffnet[31] – aber keines Menschen Seele hat je soweit dringen können.[32]

(2) Nun wäre es fruchtlos, in Spekulationen über Plutarchs metaphysische Spitze einzutreten: Er hat darüber nichts gesagt und nichts sagen wollen, weil es die Aussage-Möglichkeiten dessen, der es findet, und die Verständnis-Möglichkeit derer, denen es seiner mitteilen möchte, übersteigt.[33]

Wohl aber lässt sich der Grund erweisen, *warum* Plutarch jene fast archaisch anmutende Zurückhaltung übt, d.h. den Schritt in die (neu-)platonische Transzendenz absichtsvoll unterlässt. Jene Antwort (vgl. oben, p. 48 f.), die Plutarch den um ihre σωτηρία Bangenden gibt, setzt die Offenheit und die Durchlässigkeit der plutarchischen Welt voraus; wer etwa das Gebäude der gegeneinander abgeschlossenen Stufen vertrat – was in der von Justin besuchten platonischen Schule, vgl. oben, p. 52, Anm. 28 offenbar der Fall war, der könnte jene seelische Hilfe ganz zweifellos nicht bieten.

Plutarch widersetzt sich dem herrschenden System, weil es auf dem Wege ist, ein geschlossenes System zu werden. Er errichtet auf platonischer Basis, aber mit weitgehender Eigenwilligkeit, ein offenenes "System" – eine Lehre, die den grossen Vorteil hat, Lebenshilfe bieten zu können.

Nun ist es bemerkenswert, in wie hohem Masse Plutarch damit "nach vorne" weist. Gewiss ist er von dem, was für Plotin ἕνωσις bedeuten sollte, noch sehr weit entfernt; weit entfernt ist er vor allem davon, die "Eins" als den Ur-Faktor von Jenseits und Diesseits zu erweisen. Nichts ist bei ihm davon zu lesen, dass alle Vielfalt der Welt als eine "Entfaltung" der Eins zu verstehen sei – kurz, von der weit angelegten Begründung der Eins-Lehre weiss Plutarch nichts.

Dennoch gibt es für ihn eine ἕνωσις als die Erfüllung aller

[31] Das drückt Albinos, *Did.* 10, p. 164. 18 Hermann aus: ... ὅπερ ἂν ἔτι ἀνωτέρω τούτων ὑφέστηκεν.

[32] In den beiden Mythen, die die Wanderung einer Seele durch den Weltenraum schildern, wird deutlich bezeichnet, dass die menschliche Seele bis zur Sphäre des Mondes, aber nicht weiter aufsteigt. Denn auf dem Monde legt sie ihr Seelisches ab.

[33] Dies der Nachvollzug von Platons Warnungen, das ἄρρητον nicht zu profanieren; eng damit zusammenzuhalten ist Kelsos (bei Origenes) 7. 36; 39 und bes. 42; vgl. *NAG* (1967), 2, 32 ff.

Existenz nach dem Tode. Sein Jenseits transzendiert nicht den Raum, es transzendiert die Lebenszeit. In ferner Zukunft wird die Seele zum Daimon, der Daimon zum Gott;[34] dass der Grosse Pan[35] stirbt, ist nicht als seine Auflösung, sondern als seine Erhöhung zu verstehen; denn alle Seelen wandeln sich früher oder später[36] zur reinsten Substanz und steigen empor. Jedes Sterben ist Aufsteigen[37] und Annäherung an das Höchste.

Soweit Plutarch vom offiziellen Platonismus entfernt ist, so nahe steht er den Entwicklungslinien, die auf Porphyrios' Schrift *De regressu animae* hinführen; in weiter Entfernung – von Plutarch als selten verwirklicht, aber doch als möglich erwiesen – wird die als die Vereinung der Seele (oder des Wesentlichen an ihr) mit der Sonne als dem Führungs-Organ der Welt erkennbar. So weiten Abstand Plutarch von neuplatonischer Mystik hält, so wird doch der Weg sichtbar, der später zur Mystik Plotins und Porphyrios' führen sollte.

Auch Plotin hat sich, angeleitet von seinem Lehrer Ammonios, radikal über die Grenzlinien und Unterscheidungen, die der offizielle Platonismus gezogen hatte, hinweggesetzt. In diesem Schritt hatte er in Plutarch einen Vorgänger: Beide fanden in der Kosmologie der offiziellen Schule ein System vor, das den heilsnotwendigen Aufstieg der Seele schwerlich zuliess;[38] wie für Plotin (und ganz besonders für Porphyrios) wird man für Plutarch mit aller Sicherheit diese Schlussfolgerung ziehen dürfen: Der Widerspruch gegen das offizielle System ist nicht aus schul-

---

[34] Plutarch *De Is. et Os.* 362e ʿΟ ... ῎Οσιρις καὶ ἡ ῎Ισις ἐκ δαιμόνων ἀγαθῶν εἰς θεοὺς μετήλλαξαν.

[35] Plutarch *De def. or.* 17. 419b–e; alle Dämonen "sterben" derart und hören damit auf, Mittler von Orakeln zu sein.

[36] Dass der letzte Reinigungsprozess viel Zeit erfordere, deutet Plutarch mehrfach an, bes. *De fac.* 30. 944f und 945a.

[37] Darum kommt Plutarch viel auf die Berichtung der herkömmlichen Vorstellung an: Die Toten halten sich nicht unter der Erde auf; vielmehr bewegen sie sich in der Richtung des Auf-Steigens, wo der Mond ihr eigentlicher Ruhe- und Aufenthaltsort wird; so bes. *De fac.* 27. 942d. Welchen Einfluss das Buch des Herakleides Pontikos ausübte, lässt sich kaum abschätzen. Plutarch zitiert es *De lib. et aegr.* 5; VII 5. 5 Bernardakis. Vgl. im Übrigen F. Wehrli, *Die Schule des Aristoteles* (Basel, 1944–1959), VII, *frg.* 71, 72.

[38] Für Plotin bestand ein hauptsächlicher Anstoss darin, dass den Ideen eine eigene Existenz ausserhalb des νοῦς eingeräumt war; über die Kontroversen, die sich daraus dem Schulhaupte Longinos gegenüber ergaben, vgl. Porphyrios *Plot.* 18. 10–24.

internen Gründen herzuleiten; er war nicht auf theoretische Erwägungen gegründet. Sondern Plutarch hat, hierin den Begründern des Neuplatonismus vergleichbar, etwas von der drängenden Sorge, ja Beängstigung[39] seines *saeculum* verspürt. Den Auftrag, eben dazu etwas Hilfreiches zu sagen, hat er offensichtlich höher gestellt, als sich im Einklang mit dem Schulplatonismus zu wissen. Bei ihm wird etwas von einer Offenheit spürbar, die die übrigen Platoniker seiner Zeit vermissen lassen. Plutarch hielt daran fest, dass die Philosophie *magistra vitae* sein müsse, und er hat diese ihre Funktion einer Zeit gegenüber neu begründet, die "Leben" im Hinblick auf die ἔσχατα verstand. Dass Plutarch sich diese Aufgabe stellte, und dass er, fest in seinem Platon-Verständnis wurzelnd, darauf Antworten zu geben versuchte, denen die offizielle Schule sich entzog – das begründet seine besondere Stellung unter den Platonikern jener Zeit.

Münster

---

[39] Zur Charakteristik jener Zeit in diesem Fragen-Bereich hat Wichtiges zusammengetragen E. R. Dodds, *Pagan and Christian in an Age of Anxiety* (Cambridge, 1965).

ÄHNLICHKEIT UND SEINSANALOGIE
VOM PLATONISCHEN PARMENIDES
BIS PROKLOS

JOHANNES HIRSCHBERGER

In der klassischen Metaphysik gibt es ein Axiom, das häufig zitiert wird, bei den Philosophen wie bei den Theologen. Bei Nikolaus von Cues erscheint es gleich zu Beginn seiner *Docta Ignorantia* (I. 3) unter der Formel: *infiniti ad finitum proportio non est*. Cusanus meint, das Axiom sei *ex se manifestum*. Bei den Theologen wird es gerne umschrieben mit dem Satz, dass die Welt zwar Gott ähnlich sei, nicht aber sei auch umgekehrt Gott der Welt ähnlich.[1] Die Aussage wird nicht immer richtig verstanden, ja sie wird manchmal sogar auf den Kopf gestellt und damit unsinnig und unhistorisch: es gebe keine Proportion des Endlichen zum Unendlichen, ausser es ist diese Formulierung nur ein ungenauer und schlechter Ausdruck für das alte und eigentliche Axiom. Dieses selbst gehört in den Platonismus, in welchen, wird sich zeigen, und erhält von dort seinen Gehalt. Diese Herkunft ist manchmal mit Händen zu greifen, einfach schon aus der Terminologie, auch dort noch, wo man es nicht erwartet, so z.B. bei Thomas von Aquin, *De Ver*. 23, 7, *ad* 11, ganz zu schweigen von seinem Kommentar zu *De Divinis Nominibus*, etwa 9. 6, 832 Pera. Wird die Herkunft nicht durchschaut, entstehen Missverständnisse, da durch Spekulation allein die rechte Interpretation nicht zu leisten ist. Durchschaut man sie, dann erkennt man in dem Axiom einen Kernsatz der Seinsanalogie und ihrer Versuche, das Unendliche mit Hilfe des Endlichen zu fassen, wobei sich dann typischerweise das Unendliche dem Endlichen

---

[1] Vgl. R. Klibanskys Anmerkung zu I. 3. 20 in seiner Edition der *Docta ignorantia*, wobei der Verweis auf Arist. *Cael*. allerdings wohl kaum am Platze ist. Ferner J. Hirschberger, *Geschichte der Philosophie* I[8] (Basel, 1965), pp. 390 f., 486 f. Und K. Kremer, *Die neuplatonische Seinsphilosophie und ihre Wirkung auf Thomas von Aquin* (Leiden, 1966), p. 133, Anm. 208.

gegenüber als transzendent erweist. *Deus semper maior*, sagt dafür die Theologie in ihrer Sprache. Was gemeint ist, ist aber ein transzendental-logisch-ontologischer Sachverhalt. Die ganzen Gedankengänge um die Relation zwischen Endlichem und Unendlichem kreisen nun um die Ähnlichkeitsidee. Sie trat auf in der platonischen *Methexis*. Im Verfolg ihrer weiteren Durchdringung wurde erstmals ausgesprochen, dass die Ähnlichkeitsrelation nicht rein logisch-abstrakt genommen werden könne, sondern einen besonderen ontologischen Sinn habe, der aber zugleich ein transzendentallogischer ist. Sie beziehe sich nur von unten nach oben, sei aber nicht umkehrbar. Wenn A = B sei, müsse nicht auch B = A sein. Warum? Weil *infiniti ad finitum proportio non est* (wobei "gleich" als "ähnlich" verstanden wird). Das geschah zunächst, nur fragend und bloss so hingeworfen, im Platonischen *Parmenides*.

I. DER PLATONISCHE PARMENIDES ÜBER *METHEXIS* UND *HOMOIOTES*

Parmen. 132 f. ist oft erörtert worden als ein Beleg für die Annahme, dass dem späten Platon Zweifel an seiner eigenen Ideenlehre gekommen seien. Speziell noch interessierte man sich für das im Laufe der Diskussion auftauchende Argument vom τρίτος ἄνθρωπος, genauer gesagt, für eines dieser Argumente, das eben dort vorgebrachte, denn es gibt ja deren mehrere.[2] Der Gedankengang im *Parmenides* meint: Wenn die Ideen Musterbilder sind, die sich über den nach ihnen benannten Einzeldingen erheben, dann müsse sich über der Idee ihrerseits und den ihr untergeordneten Einzeldingen neuerdings eine Idee als Musterbild erheben, eine Art Superidee; über die Superidee und das ihr Untergeordnete wieder eine neue Idee, eine Supersuperidee, und so immer zu bis ins Unendliche, d.h. die Idee läuft sich in der unendlichen Iteration ihrer selbst tot und vermag also nichts zu erklären. Man hat diesen Einwand gegen Sokrates als den Vertreter der Ideenlehre gewöhnlich aufzulösen versucht mit dem Hinweis, dass das Argument die Idee als ein Ding betrachte, ein

[2] W. D. Ross, *Aristotle's Metaphysics* I (Oxford, 1924), pp. 194 ff.

"Musterding," während sie in Wirklichkeit Gedanke sei, nicht ein subjektiver Gedanke, wofür man das νόημα des Sokrates in *Parm.* 132b4 hält, sondern ein transzendentallogischer Gedanke. So, um nur einen zu nennen, die Interpretation von P. Natorp, der in der Idee "Bewusstsein überhaupt" oder "die Methode der Vereinigung des Mannigfaltigen" sieht, die aller Gegenständlichkeit vorausliegt und der nichts mehr voraus gesetzt werden könne, weder ein Gegenstand noch ein Urbild.[3] Damit ist etwas philosophisch Wesentliches getroffen, wenn es auch kantianisch serviert wird und die Gefahr besteht, dass das platonisch verstandene Objekt des νόημα,[4] wonach *Parm.* 132b7 (νόημα δὲ οὐδενός) ausdrücklich fragt, eben doch verloren geht, weil hinter der modernen Interpretation genau das verschwindet, um was man sich mit dem Eidos von Platon über Plotin und Proklos bis Cusanus immer bemüht hat, der spezielle Seinsmodus von Idee, der weder transzendentallogische Setzung noch irgendeine moderne Dialektik ist, sondern ein schwierigeres Problem aufwirft, wenngleich das Ziel der antiken Bemühung sich mit der modernen Absicht decken mag, es allerdings in einer, wie wir glauben, reineren Form erreicht als in der nach dem englischen Empirismus konstruierten, aber nicht mehr konstruierbaren modernen transzendentalen Logik. Doch das können wir hier zurückstellen, um auf einen Gesichtspunkt in der ganzen Gedankenführung hinzuweisen, der von grosser Tragweite wurde, aber immer übersehen wird. Das ist die Ähnlichkeitsidee. Über sie wird erreicht, was die Neukantianer in ihrer Weise erreichen wollten.

Die Ähnlichkeitsidee wird 132d1–5 anscheinend ganz harmlos vorgetragen: "Die eben gennanten εἴδη stehen im Sein da wie Urbilder. Alles andere gleicht ihnen und bildet ihnen gegenüber etwas Ähnliches (ἐοικέναι καὶ εἶναι ὁμοιώματα), so dass die Teilhabe an den εἴδη für alles übrige nichts anderes ist als ein Ähnlichwerden." Aber dann folgt eine Frage, die offenbar etwas aufrühren will: "Wenn etwas dem Eidos gleicht, ist es dann möglich das jenes Eidos dem Angeglichenen, soferne eben dieses gerade ein Angeglichenes ist, nicht ähnlich wäre (μὴ ὅμοιον εἶναι)?" Und nun in typisch platonischer Ironie: "Oder gäbe es

---

[3] P. Natorp, *Platos Ideenlehre*[2] (Leipzig, 1921), p. 238.

[4] Vgl. A. E. Taylor, *A Commentary on Plato's Timaeus* (Oxford, 1928), pp. 81 f.

so etwas wie, dass das Ähnliche dem Ähnlichen nicht ähnlich ist (τὸ ὅμοιον μὴ ὁμοίῳ ὅμοιον εἶναι)?'' Dass hier ein hintergründiger Gedanke lanciert werden soll, spürt man. Man erwartet geradezu: vielleicht gibt es das, und wenn, dann allerdings tut sich wohl ein interessantes Philosophem auf, und vielleicht eine neue Philosophie. Aber die ironische Frage kommt noch nicht an. Der paradoxe Gedanke wird zurückgewiesen. Es müsse so sein, dass, wenn A = B ist, dann auch B = A zu sein hat. Das führt nun allerdings dazu, dass das Argument vom Dritten Menschen wiederholt werden muss: "Es besteht also keine Möglichkeit dass etwas dem Eidos ähnlich ist, ohne dass umgekehrt nicht auch das Eidos diesem etwas ähnlich ware?[5] Wenn das aber nicht geht (sc. auch das Urbild dem Abbild ähnlich sein muss), dann erhebt sich über dem Eidos immer wieder ein anderes Eidos, und wenn dieses wieder einem anderen ähnlich ist, ein weiteres anderes und es wird überhaupt kein Ende sein, dass immer wieder ein anderes Eidos entsteht, wenn das Eidos dem Teilhabenden gegenüber auch ähnlich sein soll" (132e6–133a3). Das Ergebnis wäre dann, dass *Methexis* nicht, wie es ursprünglich geheissen hatte, Ähnlichkeit ist: "So ist es also nicht die Ähnlichkeit, worin die einzelnen Dinge an der Idee teilhaben, sondern man muss etwas anderes suchen, worin die Teilhabe bestehen könnte" (135a5 f.) Auch dieser Satz hat wieder einen ironischen Sinn, der zum Weiterdenken anreizen soll; denn dass die *Methexis* ὁμοιότης ist, hat Platon nie im Ernst bestritten. Was soll also hier die Bemerkung, man müsse nach etwas anderem suchen, worin die *Methexis* bestehen könnte? Man ist aber über diese Ironie genau so hinweggegangen wie über die herausfordernde Frage in 132d7. Nur Natorp hat etwas gespürt. Er schreibt: "Wer hier freilich am Wort hängen blieb, der musste wohl sich daran ärgern, dass er (Platon) das Sichgleichen ablehnt und doch nichts Anderes zum Ersatz anzubieten weiss. Ich glaube, dass Aristoteles eben dieses Wort im Sinne hat bei seinem Ausdruck des Ärgers: dass Plato, was eigentlich das Teilhaben sei, wenn nicht

---

[5] Die Übersetzung unserer Stelle bei Apelt, der sich anscheinend von Jowett inspirieren liess, drückt den Gedanken nicht klar genug aus: "So ist es demnach unmöglich, dass ein Einzelding der Idee ähnlich sei oder die Idee einem Einzelding." Richtig dagegen Diès in seiner Übersetzung, der unsere Stelle auch unter Berufung auf Arist. *Metaph.* 991a31 gut erläutert mit dem Wort: le même chose sera et paradigme et image.

ein Sichgleichen, 'anderen zum Suchen überlassen habe' (*Metaph.* I. 6. 987b14; ἀφεῖσαν ἐν κοινῷ ζητεῖν). Plato dachte wohl, er habe es im Phaedo zur Genüge gesagt, und wer ihn da nicht hören wolle, für den wird es auch vergeblich sein, was etwa noch weiter sich darüber hätte sagen lassen." [6] Es ist aber nicht ganz so, wie Natorp sich das vorstellt. Er hat das Ganze von seiner neukantianischen Erfahrungsphilosophie her beurteilt, was man sofort besonders deutlich sieht, wenn man unmittelbar darnach liest: "Der mächtigste Einwurf gegen die Ideenlehre ... wie das Reich der Erfahrung in der ganzen Unendlichkeit ihrer Relativität, der Methode der Ideen zu unterwerfen sei." Aber es geht hier eben nicht um eine "Erfahrung" im nachempirischen Sinn, sondern um ein Seinsdenken auf dem Wege einer viel radikaleren Apriorität als der Kantischen, nämlich ein Seinsdenken über die Ähnlichkeitsidee, wie sie 133a5 klar angesprochen wird, und das hat Natorp ebenso übersehen, wie er auch über 132d7 hinweggegangen ist.

Die Neuplatoniker jedoch haben die Hintergründigkeit der beiden Äusserungen des platonischen *Parmenides* durchschaut und in ihrer Interpretation aufgegriffen. Proklos schreibt von 132d7 ausdrücklich, dass Sokrates durch diese Frage hätte aufgeweckt werden sollen,[7] und zu der Aufforderung von 133a5 f., in etwas anderem als in der ὁμοιότης das Wesen der *Methexis* zu suchen, gibt er die förmliche Antwort: Es ist tatsächlich nicht die ὁμοιότης die Ursache der *Methexis*, sondern die μία κυριωτάτη αἰτία, die über allem steht, auch noch über den νοερὰ εἴδη, so dass grundsätzlich nichts Empirisches mehr in den Bestand der ὁμοιότης eingehen kann und ihre transzendentallogische Apriorität wirklich gesichert ist. Die Neuplatoniker entwickeln im Anschluss an solche Überlegungen eine ganze Philosophie der ὁμοιότης, gerne innerhalb ihrer Kommentare zu der Kategorie der ποιότης. So Proklos,[8] Damascius,[9] Ps.-Dionysius,[10] Elias,[11]

---

[6] Natorp, *Platos Ideenlehre*[2] (Leipzig, 1921), p. 239.
[7] Proc. *In Parmen.* 914, 39 f. Cousin[2].
[8] *Ibid.* 914 ff.
[9] *Damascii successoris dubitationes et solutiones de primis principiis*, in *Platonis Parmenidem* II (Paris, 1889), pp. 1 ff., 199 ff. Ruelle.
[10] *De Div. Nom.* 9. 6.
[11] Elias, *In Isagog.* 17, 22–35. *Comment .in Arist. gr.* XVIII, 1 Busse.

David.[12] Den Auftakt dazu gab Plotin mit seiner Unterscheidung einer doppelten ὁμοιότης in seiner Abhandlung über die Tugenden (*Enn.* I. 2. 2). Da er die Unterscheidung nicht förmlich einführt, lässt sich vermuten, dass er schon bekanntes Schulgut aufgegriffen hat, was ja nahe liegt.

Dass in der modernen Platonforschung unser Parmenidesproblem nicht weiter beachtet wurde, mag vielleicht damit zusammenhängen, dass man die Neuplatoniker für unkritische Metaphysiker hielt, während man Platon doch von Kant her verstehen wollte. So verzichtete man auf ihre Hilfe für die Platon-Interpretation. Dass die Metaphysik der Neuplatoniker transzendentalphilosophisch von Belang sein könnte, ist eine Annahme, die ausserhalb der herrschenden Vorstellungen lag. Sie soll im folgenden einsichtig gemacht werden.

II. PLOTINS DOPPELTE *HOMOIOSIS*

Von den soeben berührten Vorurteilen nicht beschwert, konnte ein Kenner wie E. Bréhier ohne weiteren Beleg sagen, dass Kapitel 2 in Plotins Abhandlung über die Tugenden sich auf *Parmenides* 132d ff. beziehe.[13] Er dürfte damit recht haben, obgleich sich im Texte Plotins kein direkter Verweis vorfindet. Die Unterscheidung zwischen zwei wesentlich verschiedenen Formen von ὁμοίωσις greift eben tatsächlich die Frage auf, die im *Parmenides* angerissen wurde. Faktisch knüpft Plotin schon im 1. Kapitel an Platon an, wenn er dort den Tugendbegriff als ein Ähnlichwerden gegenüber der höheren Welt erläutert. Das ist die ὁμοίωσις θεῷ κατὰ τὸ δυνατόν aus *Theätet* 176b. Dazu brauchte nicht zitiert zu werden. Neu aber ist, und das ist jetzt neuplatonische Weiterbildung, dass Plotin erklärt, aus der Rede vom Ähnlichwerden folge nicht, dass es auch "dort oben" Tugend gebe.[14] Das Urbild (ἀρχέτυπον) der Tugend, heisst es Kap. 2. 4, ist nicht auch selbst Tugend. Man kann da wohl mit Bréhier auf Aristoteles, *Eth. Nic.* 10. 8. 1178b10 f. verweisen; aber, was bei Plotin auftritt, ist nicht mehr der Mythos, sondern typisch neu-

---

[12] David, *Prol. philos.* 35, 8–19. *Comment. in Arist. gr.* XVIII, 2 Busse.
[13] Plotinus, *Ennéades* I (Paris, 1924), 50[1].
[14] Kap. 1, 46–51.

platonische Spekulation, vielleicht in Anlehnung an das κατὰ τὸ δυνατόν in *Tht.* 176b. Die *Homoiosis* sei nämlich eine doppelte. Sie sei entweder von der Art, dass bei den zwei verglichenen Dingen ein Selbiges (ταὐτὸν εἶδος) vorausgesetzt werde, was immer dann der Fall wäre, wenn die beiden Dinge, auf derselben Stufe stehend, dasselbe Vorbild nachahmen, oder aber von der Art, dass ein Urbild-Abbild-Verhältnis vorliege, so dass die selbige Vergleichsbasis verlassen werde und über die selbe species hinaus sich eine Über- und Unterordnung, ein Erstes und Zweites ergebe, die nichts Gleichrangiges mehr seien. Die Über- und Unterordnung bedeute sogar ein seinsmässiges Abhängigkeitsverhältnis und damit entstehe eine ganz neue Situation. In dieser zweiten Form von Ähnlichkeit würden nämlich nicht mehr zwei Gegenstände innerhalb ein und desselben Eidos verglichen – Proklos spricht da von Gegenständen, die zu einander ein σύζυγον und ἀδελφόν sind[15] – sondern ein bestimmtes Eidos mit einem anderen Eidos. Das ταὐτόν sei hier zugleich ein ἕτερον.[16] Eben darin aber liege eine neue Art von ὁμοίωσις (Kap. 2. 5–11). Am Schlusse der Abhandlung werden die zwei Arten von ὁμοίωσις kurz und bündig mit dem Satz unterschieden: "Die eine Gleichwerdung, jene nämlich mit guten Menschen, ist die Gleichheit eines Abbildes mit einem anderen Abbild, beide nämlich stammen vom selben Urbild; die andere Gleichwerdung aber (sc. mit den Göttern) richtet sich auf ein anderes,[17] auf ein Urbild (παράδειγμα)."[18] Und wegen dieser anders gearteten Gleichheit gibt es hier keine Umkehr der Relation (ἀντιστρέφειν), so dass, auch wenn das Nachgeordnete dem Übergeordneten gleich ist, deswegen nicht auch das Übergeordenete dem Nachgeordneten gleich sein müsse.[19] Wenn A = B ist, sagten wir, müsse nicht auch B = A sein.

Hier setzt im Neuplatonismus jene Entwicklung ein, die im christlichen Denken zu dem schon zitierten Satz führt, dass zwar die Welt Gott ähnlich sei, nicht aber auch Gott der Welt, denn *infiniti ad finitum non est proportio.* Es ist ein Satz, der in der

---

[15] Procl. *In Parmen.* 912, 32; 913, 37 Cousin².
[16] *Ibid.* 912, 35 f.
[17] Ich möchte I. 30 doch lieber ἄλλο statt ἄλλον lesen.
[18] I. 2. 7. 28–30 Bréhier.
[19] I. 2. 2. 8 Bréhier.

aristotelischen, oder sagen wir besser, in der mathematischen Logik keinen Sinn hätte. Bei den Neuplatonikern hat er einen Sinn und es ist ein sehr charakteristischer Sinn, den er hat. Unsere Formel "Wenn A = B, dann auch B = A" vermag ihn nicht auszudrücken. Er ist in dieser Formelsprache gar nicht zu fassen, sondern muss in eine andere Sprache übersetzt werden, in die Sprache der Kausalrelation, und zwar jener Relation, die das platonische ἐπέκεινα τῆς οὐσίας πρεσβείᾳ καὶ δυνάμει meint, womit alles Seiende gesehen wird auf Grund seiner Genesis aus dem Einen, das das Sein ist und auch bewertet wird nach seiner mehr oder weniger grossen Nähe zum Ursprung des Seins aus dem Guten oder Einen. Wenn man diese Art von Seinsverständnis nicht annehmen will, weil sie metaphysich oder axiologisch bestimmt ist, in der Sprache Plotins gesprochen, wenn man die zweite Art von Ähnlichkeit nicht annehmen möchte, sondern nur die erste, weil nur sie, als von wesensmässig Gleichem ausgehend, ein Vergleichen zulasse, muss man bedenken, dass die *Homoiotes* der ταὐτά nur über einen logisch-denkökonomischen Kunstgriff erreicht wird, über die Abstraktion, die immer eine gewisse Willkür ist, weil von unserem Interesse abhängig. Die ganze moderne Wissenschaft beruht auf solchen abstraktiven Setzungen, wofür man dann Gesetz sagt. In Wirklichkeit gibt es überhaupt nichts Selbiges, sondern alles ist mit dem ἕτερον vermischt. Damit aber rechnet die zweite Art der Plotinischen *Homoiotes*, und darin beruht das Recht der anders gearteten Erfassung des Seienden durch den Platonismus. Er sieht, wenn ich so sagen darf, auf den Grund der Dinge, auf den hin alles orientiert wird, weil alles von dort kommt und darum auch von dort her verstanden werden und benannt werden muss als ὁμοίωμα und ὁμώνυμον und μέθεξις, oder wie man es sonst heissen will, um mit *Parm.* 133d zu sprechen. Es ist die Sprache der Seinsanalogie, bei Aristoteles die πρὸς ἕν – oder ἀφ᾽ἑνός – Benennung.[20] Bei Plotin drückt das ganze System diesen Gedanken aus. Ich kenne dort allerdings keine direkte Behandlung unserer Frage in Form einer Interpretation unserer Parmenidesstelle. Das geschieht jedoch

---

[20] Vgl. J. Hirschberger, "Paronymie und Analogie bei Aristoteles," *Philos. Jahrb.* 68 (1960), p. 203. Analogie als ἀφ᾽ ἑνός Aussage bei Proklos, *Stoich. prop.* 100.

in ausführlicher Weise nach Plotin, vor allem bei Proklos, und dessen Gedanken sind nun zu analysieren.

III. PROKLOS ÜBER DIE REDUKTION DER ÄHNLICHKEIT AUF DIE EINE, OBERSTE URSACHE

Proklos bietet zu *Parm.* 132d–133a einen ausführlichen Kommentar.[21] Der Gedankengang lässt sofort sichtbar werden, worauf Proklos hinaus will, auf Ideen, die nicht nur Urbilder sind, also logische Denkgestalten, die man nach Gesichtspunkten wie Identität, Verschiedenheit, Ähnlichkeit vergleichen könnte, sondern auf Ideen, die zeugend sind, vollendend und bewahrend, anderem Seienden gegenüber also Kausalität besitzen (αἰτία) und insoferne ein stärkeres und volleres Sein (κρείττων εἶναι) darstellen, schliesslich und letzlich aber auf eine allererste vollkommene Ursache (πρωτουργὸς καὶ ὁλικὴ αἰτία),[22] von der dann anderes als von seinem Grunde abhängig ist, weil es davon gesetzt, gewirkt, gegründet ist.[23] Der Weg, der zu einer solchen Fassung von Eidos führt, ist eine Analyse des Ähnlichkeitsbegriffes. Sie will ausführen, was im platonischen *Parmenides* 133a5 f. gefordert wurde, etwas anderes zu suchen als die Ähnlichkeit, um *Methexis* erklären zu können.

Der Athener macht sich sofort zu Nutze, was Plotin schon herausgestellt hatte, die Unterscheidung zweier Formen von Ähnlichkeit, einer solchen zwischen gleichgestaltetem Seienden (σύζυγον-ἀδελφόν)[24] und einer solchen zwischen Urbild und Abbild, wo ein Seiendes von einem ἀρχέτυπον stamme, weil es von dessen Eidos (ἀπ' ἐκείνου) hat, was es ist, ohne doch mit ihm (μετ' ἐκείνου) auf gleicher Seinsstufe zu stehen. Auf diesen Unterschied, meint er, hätte Sokrates hinweisen müssen, als Parmenides ihn mit dem Argument vom Dritten Menschen in die Enge trieb.[25] Das *participans* sei nämlich zwar dem *participatum*

---

21 Proklos, *In Platonis Parmenidem* (Paris, 1864), pp. 911–919, ed. V. Cousin[2].
22 *Ibid.* 912, 16 f.
23 *Ibid.* 911 f.
24 Vgl. oben Anm. 15.
25 Procl. *In Parmen.* 912, 31 f. Cousin[2].

ähnlich, aber nicht umgekehrt. Das Abbild schliesse neben der ταὐτότης mit dem Urbild, an dem es teilhat, auch noch das ἕτερον ein, und deswegen gäbe es nicht die Reziprozität einer Gleichheit von unten nach oben und von oben nach unten. Die Vorschrift heisst darum μὴ ἀντιστρέφειν. Die Gleichheit des Abbildes gegenüber dem ἀρχέτυπον bedeutet also zugleich eine Differenz zwischen ἀρχέτυπον und ὅμοιον, παράδειγμα und εἰκασθέν, μεθεκτόν und μετέχον.[26] Und darin bestehe die zweite Art von ὁμοιότης. Die Differenz aber sei gegeben mit der Ursächlichkeitsrelation. Darüber ist nun Näheres zu sagen.

Proklos hat nämlich die Ähnlichkeitsanalyse noch weiter getrieben als Plotin, so weit, bis sich die Reduktion der Ähnlichkeit auf das Grund-Folge-Verhältnis herausgestellt hatte. Es gäbe nicht nur die zweifache Ähnlichkeit Plotins. Wir müssten noch genauer unterscheiden, entsprechend den Rängen der Seins-modi: Etwas anderes sind die εἴδη φυσικά, die über den αἰσθητά stehen, wieder etwas anderes die ψυχικὰ εἴδη und nochmals etwas anderes die νοερὰ εἴδη. Diese letzteren seien nun aber auch das Letzte. Über ihnen steht nichts mehr. Sie sind jenes wirkliche παράδειγμα, von dem eigentlich und im letzten Sinne allein gilt, dass es niemals dem ähnlich ist, was nach ihm kommt. „Die psychischen Species also sind sowohl Urbilder wie auch Abbilder. Soferne sie Abbilder sind, sind sie unter sich einander ähnlich, wie auch dem, was nach ihnen kommt, weil das alles sein Sein besitzt auf Grund der νοερὰ εἴδη. Ebenso verhält es sich mit den φυσικὰ εἴδη. Sie stehen in der Mitte zwischen den psychischen und sinnlichen Species und sind den sinnlichen Species ähnlich, nicht soferne sie Urbilder dafür sind, sondern insoferne beides (Physisches und Sinnliches) Abbild des über ihnen Stehenden ist. Das aber, was nur Urbild ist, ist nicht mehr seinem Abbild ähnlich. Ähnlich nämlich ist, was durch das Selbige geprägt wurde. Jenes aber (sc. die echten und einzigen Urbilder) ist durch nichts mehr geprägt, es ist ja das Erste.[27] Mit den πρῶτα, die durch kein ταὐτόν mehr geprägt sind, dem sie ähnlich sein könnten (οὐδὲν πέπονθε: 913, 14), die also ein Absolutum sind, weder in einer Abstraktion zusammengefasste Erfahrung noch von einer Ursache gewirkt, die also noologisch in sich selbst ruhen, reine und absolute παραδείγματα

[26] *Ibid.* 912.
[27] *Ibid.* 913, 4–14.

sind, hat Proklos erreicht, was er wollte, jenes Transzendente, das schlechthin ἐπέκεινα ist, der Welt gegenüber weder selbig noch ähnlich, dem aber die Welt wenigstens immer noch ähnlich ist,[28] aber im Sinne der zweiten ὁμοίωσις des Plotin, die das ταὐτόν, das zur Ähnlichkeit gehört, zugleich als ein ἕτερον erkennt.

Sieht man sich aber die neuen Formen von Ähnlichkeit, die Proklos einführt, näher an, dann zeigt sich, dass sie eigentlich doch nichts Neues sind. Jenes Ähnliche nämlich, das sich im Individuellen, in der Art, der Gattung, der Übergattung u.s.w. finden könne, also eine Ähnlichkeit auch in der Vertikale sein möchte, beruht auf der ταὐτότης der höchsten zu Grunde gelegten Gattung, die sich natürlich von oben nach unten im gleichen logischen Sinne durchhält. Wir haben also immer noch das erste ὅμοιον Plotins vor uns, die, wenn ich so sagen darf, horizontale Ähnlichkeit auf dem Grunde des selben Allgemeinen, nur dass es jetzt eine Übergattung ist, auf deren Grund die Species und Genera jetzt einander auch σύζυγα und ἀδελφά sind. Alles, was unter dem Ersten steht, ist dann in dieser Letztbeziehung ein immer selbiges εἰκών.[29] Und auch das zweite ὅμοιον Plotins bleibt, denn Proklos bemerkt ausdrücklich, dass jene Ähnlichkeit, die er über alle Stufen hin sehen will, die also umkehrbar ist, wir nannten sie die vertikale, nicht die von Urbildern zu Abbildern sei.[30] Obwohl er eigentlich nur in den obersten αἰτίαι die wahren παραδείγματα erblickt, gilt das Gesetz der Nichtumkehrbarkeit auch weiter unten, von jeder höheren zu jeder niederen Stufe als eine Art Ausstrahlung und Fortwirkung der obersten Ursache, die nie und nirgends verkehrt werden dürfe. Der Scholastiker Proklos hatte aber sehr wohl gesehen, dass trotz der durchgehenden und alles differenzierenden Macht des Ersten sich Gleichheiten finden, die auch vertikal durch alle Species gehen. Sie sind anderer Seinsmodalität, entstehen durch Abstraktion, sind also logische Setzungen, wie wir oben schon sahen, sind aber auch dann noch von grösster Bedeutung, denn sie bilden die Ermöglichung wissenschaftlicher Begriffs- und Gesetzesbildung. Indem er aber gleichzeitig seine Maxime μὴ ἀντιστρέφειν

---

[28] Aus dem Gesagten ergibt sich, dass "gleich" im Sinne von "ähnlich" gebraucht werden kann (ὅσον = ὅμοιον), aber auch im Sinne von Selbigkeit (ταὐτόν).

[29] Procl. *In Parmen.* 913, 10 f.

[30] *Ibid.*

festhält, wahrt er die Transzendenz der Urbilder, letzlich aber des Einen, dem alles ähnlich ist in einer unendlichen Analogie von der untersten Tiefe aufsteigend über die Ordnungen der εἴδη bis zur unmittelbaren Nähe des Einen,[31] denn es ist auch bei Proklos so, wie Plotin gesagt hat: "Das Eine ist Ursprung des Wieviel, welches gar nicht zur Existenz gelangt wäre, wäre nicht zuvor das Sein und das, was vor dem Sein ist; nicht hieran also (sc. das Eine als Punkt und Zahl) soll man bei der Bezeichnung Eines denken, sondern diese Dinge sind jenen höheren immer nur ähnlich im Sinn der Analogie in Bezug auf ihre Einfachheit und ihr Freisein von Vielheit und Teilbarkeit."[32] Proklos ist in unserer Frage ein treuer Schüler Plotins.

Man könne nun, meint Proklos, dasselbe Ergebnis auch auf "theologischem Wege" erreichen.[33] Das bisher Gesagte, sei der "philosophische Weg" gewesen. Sachlich unterscheidet sich aber der theologische Weg in nichts vom philosophischen. Nur einige Termini aus der hieratischen Sprache tauchen auf und verraten, dass man sich in einem anderen Hörsaal befindet, so z.B. die ἔνθεος φήμη, die θέμις, die εἴδη als Demiurgen und als Götter. Dazu kommt, dass in der Rede von dem hyperkosmischen Nus und dem ἀμέθεκτον eine religiös empfundene Weltanschauung mitspricht. Proklos hatte ja im Eifer für die Transzendenz des Weltgrundes etwas getan, was dem genuinen Platonismus und auch noch Plotin fremd ist, er hatte die *Methexis* am ἀμέθεκτον aufgehängt und dann, um die Paradoxie wieder zu überbrücken, ein μετεχόμενον dazwischen geschoben, als ob damit etwas gedient wäre, denn das Problem wird ja nur zurückgeschoben. Hier hatte sich der Trend der Schulbegriffe vom Sinn der Sache gelöst und sich in Worten überschlagen.[34] Aber des Proklos Übereifer lässt immerhin noch erkennen, dass der theologische Weg nichts anderes ist als jene "erste Philosophie," die seit Aristoteles, richtiger aber seit Platons ἱκανόν aus dem Symposion bis zu Leibnizens *ratio sufficiens* nach dem fragt, was allem Seienden das zureicht, was es braucht, um überhaupt als Seiendes gedacht

---

[31] *Ibid.* 912, 41.
[32] Plotinus, *Enn.* 6. 9. 5. 40–46 Bréhier.
[33] Procl. *In Parmen.* 913, 15 ff. Cousin².
[34] Vgl. K. Kremer, *Die neuplatonische Seinsphilosophie und ihre Wirkung auf Thomas von Aquin* (Leiden, 1966), pp. 212 f.

werden zu können. Immer hängt hier alles an einer Voraussetzung (ὑπόθεσις) vom ἄτομον εἶδος über Hypothesis und Hypothesis bis hinauf zum Anhypotheton. Es ist der letzte Sinn aller Diairesis und aller Dialektik.

Bedenkt man nun die Termini, die im Laufe unserer Überlegungen immer wieder gebraucht wurden, die Worte also vom "Stärker-sein" (κρείττων εἶναι), vom "Ins- Werk-Setzen" (δημιουργεῖν), von der "Ähnlich-machenden-Ursache" (ἀφομοιωτικὴ αἰτία), von der "Seinswerdung" unmittelbar nach dem ἀμέθεκτον (ἰδέαι ... περὶ τὸν ἀμέθεκτον νοῦν λαχοῦσαι τὴν ὑπόστασιν), vom "Erzeugen," "Vollenden" und "Bewahren," dann ist klar, was geschehen ist: Proklos hat die Ähnlichkeitsidee zurückgeführt auf ihren Ursprung, auf ein seinssetzendes, schaffendes Prinzip, kurz, auf die Idee der Kausalität, der Verursachung und des Grundes: "Auf der Suche nach der einen, höchsten Ursache der *Methexis* nennen wir jetzt nicht mehr die Ähnlichkeit, sondern eine noch über den νοερὰ εἴδη stehende Ursache. Diese εἴδη sind stärker als jene, die im Bereiche des Ähnlichen und Nichtähnlichen auftreten, da sie nicht bloss denkerische εἴδη sind, die den psychischen, physischen und sinnlichen Logoi konstitutiv vorangehen, sondern dem nicht mehr partizipierbaren Nus und den im eigentlichen Sinne noetischen Göttern zugehören. Bis hierher führt unsere dialektische Überlegung."[35] Dass der dialektische Weg zum Ziel gekommen ist, leuchtet ein. Es wurde ein Prinzip gefunden, das nicht mehr bloss Ähnlichkeit ist und so im Gleichrangigen verlaufen könnte, sondern Ursache ist und als solche gerade auch die höhere Wertigkeit, die Nichtumkehrbarkeit der zweiten Art von Ähnlichkeit bei Plotin erklären kann, weil Ursache und Wirkung eben nicht umkehrbar sein können. Daher dann auch die absolute Transzendenz der ersten Ursache.

IV. PARADEIGMA ALS URSACHE ODER GRUND?

Was meint Proklos mit seiner πρώτη αἰτία nun aber eigentlich? Wir gaben den Begriff bisher bald mit Ursache bald mit Grund wieder. Das ist aber doch zweierlei. Was Platon in der zweiten

---

[35] Procl. *In Parmen.* 918, 26–35.

Fahrt des *Phaidon* gegenüber den materiellen Ursachen der Vorsokratiker eingeführt hat, das Eidos, war "Grund," weil ein Ideelles das tat, was nach den Vorsokratikern die Materie, Muskel, Fleisch und Blut tun sollten. Was Aristoteles mit seinem ὅθεν ἡ κίνησις anzielte, war "Ursache," weil die Energeia Verwirklichung körperlicher Vorgänge war, Wirkursache, *causa efficiens* war, wie das Mittelalter, Druck und Stoss, wie die Neuzeit sagte. Bei Proklos ist αἰτία wieder Grund im platonischen Sinne, weil die obersten Paradeigmata, die schliesslich in einem einzigen obersten Urbild zusammengefasst werden, den Seinsprozess als ein ideelles ἱκανόν in Bewegung setzen. Die Bewegung kommt nicht von einem anderen Seinsmodus als einem ideellen, dem Eidos oder der Idee. Proklos sieht auch in der Bewegung einen Vorgang im Wesen (οὐσιώδης), einen Formenwechsel, der formhaft entsteht, aus dem Eidos, das sich und sein Wesen entfaltet, wo immer sich etwas bewegt. Alles ist Diairesis und Dialektik. Auch die *causa efficiens*, die *causa movens*, der Akt gegenüber der Potens, Druck und Stoss gegenüber der trägen Masse sind Vorgänge innerhalb des Prozesses des Einen zum Vielen und umgekehrt. Ohne weiteres wird in der von uns behandelten langen Passage aus dem Parmenideskommentar der Übergang vom Was auf das Dass vollzogen. Es ist nicht so, dass die Ähnlichkeitsrelation auf ein Tun, ein *agere*, reduziert würde, sie wird auf eine erste und oberste αἰτία reduziert, die ein Eidos ist, das als Eidos auch schon *actio* und *creatio* ist. Proklos sieht im Eidos nicht etwas Statisches, so wenig wie Plotin oder Platon. Erst in der neuzeitlichen Platoninterpretation wird dieses Missverständnis der Idee bis zur Ermüdung wiederholt. Allerdings nicht nur in der Neuzeit. Als die neuplatonische αἰτία dem Mittelalter bekannt wurde, hat man sie unter dem Einfluss der stoischen[36] und dann der aristotelischen Philosophie kurzerhand als *causa movens* oder *efficiens* verstanden. In die gleiche Richtung wurde die Interpretation von αἰτία auch noch durch eine unreflektierte Deutung des Genesisberichtes über die *creatio* gedrängt. Diese erschien als ein freies Handeln (*agere*) und Wirken Gottes, weswegen man

---

[36] Bezeichnend, was Seneca in den Briefen an Lucilius sagt (Über Ursache und Materie): "Wir suchen eine erste und allgemeine Ursache. Diese muss einfach sein, denn auch der Stoff ist einfach .... Sie hängt von einer einzigen, nämlich der wirkenden ab."

glaubte, sich gegen die Emanation wenden zu müssen, die man, über Avicenna, als einen notwendigen und automatischen Prozess verstand,[37] obwohl weder durch den Teilhabe– noch durch den Grundbegriff darüber etwas präjudiziert war. Mit Teilhabe, Begründung, und Emanation war nur gesagt, dass alles Seiende das Eine darstelle, ein Abbild des einen Urbildes sei, das sich im Nus diairetisch entfaltet und zu dem man auf dialektischem Wege wieder zurückfinden könne, einfach deswegen weil in jeder Wesenheit und Wirkursächlichkeit, wenn man sie denken will, und das heisst zugleich, wenn sie sein sollen, unendliche Voraussetzungen und Gründe als Bedingungen mitgedacht werden müssen, die letzlich alle in einem Grundlosen gründen, einem Anhypotheton, das "nichts mehr erleidet" und darum ἐπέκεινα, welttranszendent ist, "unumkehrbar" transzendent. Da man aber nicht mehr wusste, dass das Eidos selbst schon Energeia ist, wiederholte man, was Aristoteles schon gegen Platon gesagt hatte, dass man mit Ideen allein keine Häuser bauen könne, und dass darum zu der Potenz, wofür man das Eidos allein hielt, noch der Akt kommen müsse. Bei Proklos wird aber schon in der Einleitung zu seinem Kommentar evident, dass das oberste Eidos als oberstes Paradeigma ein ἱκανόν in jeder Hinsicht sei, also auch das sei, was man Wirkursache heissen möchte. Keine Rede von κίνησις oder einer eigenen *causa movens*. Diairesis und Dialektik sind kein Operieren mit blossen Begriffen, denen man noch die Existenz als ein Eigenes hinzufügen müsste. Die Unterscheidung von Möglichkeit und Wirklichkeit liegt in ihnen selbst. Darum ist nach Proklos die sokratische Dialektik, die vom obersten ἀληθές ausgeht und zu ihm zurückkehrt im Unterschied zur Scheinwelt der sophistischen Begriffsakrobatik Wirklichkeit (ἐνέργεια). Das Eine und Viele des eleatischen Weisen seien darum Realität, aber eine Realität, deren *modus essendi* durch das ἱκανόν und das ἀνυπόθετον ἀληθές bestimmt und "gegründet" ist.[38] Unter den genannten Einflüssen hat das Mittelalter dem Eidos

[37] Thomas, *S. T.* 1. 47. 1. In 1. 44. 1 kann man in lehrreicher Weise sehen, wie neuplatonisches und aristotelisch-stoisch-christliches Denken sich überlagern. Vgl. J. Hirschberger, *Geschichte der Philosophie* I⁸ (Basel, 1965), pp. 479–486.

[38] Procl. *In Parmen.* 655, 12–656, 8 Cousin². W. Beierwaltes, *Proklos, Grundzüge seiner Metaphysik* (Frankfurt, 1965), p. 117 hat dafür den treffenden Ausdruck "Sinnkausalität" geprägt.

eine Existenz von aussen zuführen zu müssen geglaubt. Das Losungswort war immer die Unterscheidung von Wesenheit und Dasein. Der Gedanke hat sich allerdings keineswegs auf das Mittelalter beschränkt. Die alte Unterscheidung lebt weiter in der Kritik des ontologischen Argumentes durch Kant und überall dort, wo man ihm sein Missverständnis dieses Argumentes abgenommen hat. Nur am Anfang und am Ende des Mittelalters stehen zwei Männer, die den Seinsmodus des neuplatonischen Eidos als einer αἰτία im Sinne des Grundes noch verstanden haben, Eriugena und Nikolaus von Cues, ersterer in *De Divisione Naturae*, letzterer in *De Principio*.

V. ABSOLUTER GRUND?

Eine ähnliche Verkennung der proklischen Philosophie wie in der Deutung seiner αἰτία als einer *causa efficiens* liegt vor, wenn man sein Eidos als metaphysischen Gegenstand betrachtet und dabei unter Metaphysik das versteht, was Kant mit "alter" Metaphysik gemeint hat. Er hatte ja metaphysische Gegenstände als hypostasierte Begriffe bezeichnet und in diesen Hypostasen eine neue Gegenstandswelt erblicken wollen, die uns auf einem Umweg auch wieder auf eine Erfahrungswelt festlegt. Nur Fichte und Hegel hätten sich um eine absolute Reflexion bemüht, um endgültig die Macht der Erfahrung zu brechen. Die Reduktion der Ähnlichkeiten (ὅμοια) auf eine oberste αἰτία, die sich uns als Grund enthüllte oder als ἱκανόν und ἀνυπόθετον [39] entbindet uns der Aufgabe, eine absolute Reflexion zu suchen. Sie ist selbst die absolute Reflexion, weil das Eidos kein Gegenstand im Sinne der Kantischen Erfahrungsphilosophie ist, auch nicht eine erfahrbare Hypostase. Insoferne species und genera Washeiten sind, könnte man immerhin an Gegenständlichkeit denken, wenn auch nicht an Gegenstände, weil sie weder begriffliche Zusammenfassungen von Vorstellungen sind noch etwas nur Gegebenes. Sie sind eigentlich immer etwas Aufgegebenes. Sie werden auch nicht aus der Erfahrung gewonnen, obgleich sie nicht ohne Sinnlichkeit zustande kommen und auch an der Sinnlichkeit verifiziert werden

[39] Procl. *In Parmen.* 655, 31 ff. Cousin[2].

können, wie das schon Platon in dem Phaidon-Abschnitt über
die Hypothesis erläutert hat,[40] auf den sich Proklos, wie zu
erwarten, ausdrücklich bezieht.[41] Aber in dieser Verifikation
wirft die Erfahrung nicht das Eidos ab, wie etwa eine Abstraktion den Begriff abwirft, sondern mit Hilfe der Sinneserfahrung
soll das immer schon mit sich selbst identische Eidos in seinem
Ansich besser und genauer getroffen werden.[42] Das Eidos ist
nicht durch die Erfahrung als was wir es denken, wohl aber
nicht ohne sie. Das οὗ οὐκ ἄνευ ist weniger als eine αἰτία. Das hat
auch Aristoteles genau auseinander gehalten. Voll sichtbar aber
wird die Apriorität des Eidos in der obersten Ursache, dem was
bei Aristoteles das εἶδος εἰδῶν ist, bei Cusanus der Grund aller
Gründe. Dieses Eidos erscheint in aller Form als ἱκανόν und
ἀνυπόθετον, schon in der soeben zitierten Stelle aus der Einleitung
zum Parmenideskommentar, so dass man da schon weiss, was
Proklos anzielt. Das oberste Eidos ist das Absolute schlechthin,
frei von aller gegenständlichen Eingrenzung, ist darum die Fülle
und als Fülle die Existenz, wenn man schon die Existenz von der
Usia schlechthin trennen will, was bei Proklos nicht der Fall ist.
Die Trennung von Wesenheit und Existenz ist ja eine spätere
Fragestellung. Es ist der tiefste Sinn des μὴ ἀντιστρέφειν, klar zu
machen, dass der Ursprung alles Seins und Denkens, eben weil er
wirklich Ursprung ist, durch nichts mehr bedingt ist. Die Absolut-
heit der proklischen obersten αἰτία ist rein. Sie braucht keinen
empirischen Einschuss mehr zu annullieren.

In der *prop.* 32 der *Stoicheiosis* erklärt Proklos, dass die
ὁμοιότης alles zusammenbindet. Platon hatte im *Menon* gesagt, dass das ganze Sein συγγενής sei.[43] Es wird bei ihm durch
das Gute zusammengebunden. Und Plotin sah in der Ähnlichkeit
die Analogie alles Seienden zum Einen. Proklos schaut die Welt
ebenso an. Die echten Paradeigmata sind nicht umkehrbar, halten
aber alles in Einheit zusammen. Es ist ein und derselbe Gedanke,
den die drei Platoniker meinen: das Absolute, das früher ist als

---

[40] Pl. *Phd.* 99d ff.
[41] *Ibid.*
[42] Daher das Wort des Cusaners, dass es in dieser unserer Welt nichts
gibt, was man nicht noch genauer fassen könnte.
[43] Pl. *Meno* 81c9 f.

das Endliche, auch im Menschen und seinem Denken. Mit ihm steht er immer über der Welt, wie sehr er auch in der Welt existieren mag.[44]

Johann Wolfgang Goethe Universität,
Frankfurt am Main

---

[44] R. E. Allan hat in den von ihm herausgegebenen *Studies in Plato's Metaphysics* (London, [2]1967) mehrere, für unsere Thematik wichtige Abhandlungen von G. Ryle, W. G. Runciman, G. Vlastos, P. T. Geach veröffentlicht. Die Auseinandersetzung damit konnte hier nicht mehr durchgeführt werden. Ich möchte sie andern Orts geben.

SUR LA COMPOSITION ONTOLOGIQUE DES SUBSTANCES SENSIBLES CHEZ ARISTOTE (*METAPHYSIQUE Z* 7-9)

SUZANNE MANSION

Le livre Z de la *Métaphysique*, consacré à l'étude de la substance et en particulier de la substance sensible, est un des plus obscurs du traité aristotélicien. Sa structure est malaisée à percevoir. Certains chapitres paraissent difficiles à insérer dans la ligne générale de l'argumentation. Sir David Ross, après avoir rappelé le dépeçage auquel s'était livré Natorp et tenté de reconstituer autant que faire se peut l'unité du livre, concède à son prédécesseur que les chapitres 7-9 rompent l'enchaînement des idées perceptible dans la suite des chap. 1-6, 10-12. Il note que les résumés de Z 11. 1037a21–b7 et H 1. 1042a4–22 ne font pas mention du contenu de Z 7-9, mais ajoute qu'Aristote se réfère cependant à celui-ci en Z 15. 1039b26.[1]

Que les 17 chapitres de Z, tels qu'ils apparaissent dans nos éditions, ne forment pas une suite logiquement bien ordonnée, tout lecteur attentif le reconnaîtra sans peine. Mais ce manque de cohérence lui-même, joint au fait que des rappels de discussions antérieures apparaissent là où on ne les attend pas et sont absents des résumés systématiques, semble bien exclure l'hypothèse d'un remaniement quelque peu poussé des notes d'Aristote par quelque éditeur. Comme l'a bien vu Jaeger, on se trouve plutôt, ici comme ailleurs, en présence d'un texte retravaillé par son auteur. Celui-ci est un penseur qui chemine péniblement, qui se reprend, qui insère peut-être dans des exposés anciens des développements qui existaient jusque-là à l'état séparé. Ce dernier cas pourrait bien être celui des chapitres 7-9, qui traitent du devenir et forment un tout.

Mais notre intention n'est pas de creuser plus avant le problème

---

[1] W. D. Ross, *Aristotle's Metaphysics*, Vol. II (Oxford, 1953), p. 181.

de critique littéraire que pose l'insertion de ces chapitres dans le livre Z. Partant de l'hypothèse que ceux-ci ne se trouvent à la place qu'ils occupent ni par l'effet du hasard, ni par l'opération d'un éditeur postérieur à Aristote, nous voudrions nous demander dans les pages qui suivent, comment ils contribuent, fût-ce à la manière d'une digression, à l'éclairage du thème central du livre Z.

Ce thème se déploie dans ses grandes lignes de la manière suivante. Nous cherchons ce qu'est la substance, dit Aristote, non seulement ce qui a droit au nom de substance, mais ce qui fait en quelque sorte la substantialité de la substance.[2] Quatre sens principaux du terme *ousia* sont retenus comme réponses possibles à cette question. L'*ousia* peut en effet être entendue comme la quiddité (τὸ τί ἦν εἶναι), comme l'universel, comme le genre et enfin comme le sujet.[3] Un examen rapide de la substance comme sujet, au chap. 3, aboutit à une conclusion jugée inadmissible par Aristote: la substance serait la matière sans détermination.[4] L'étude de l'ὑποκείμενον est abandonée, au moins provisoirement.[5] Celle de la substance comme universel est faite aux chapitres 13 et 14. Quant au genre, ses titres à la substantialité ne paraissent pas faire l'objet d'un examen distinct de celui qui est consacré à la substantialité de l'universel.[6] Reste alors la quiddité ou essence. C'est à élucider ce sens de la substance qu'Aristote apporte le plus de soins et d'efforts. Trois chapitres, parmi les plus difficiles du livre (ch. 4–6), élaborent péniblement la notion de quiddité et arrivent à deux conclusions principales: seules les substances ont une quiddité au sens propre;[7] cette quiddité, même pour les substances sensibles, fait un avec leur être.[8]

Bien que les chapitres 10–12 ne prolongent pas directement l'argumentation des chapitres 4–6, il est facile de voir qu'ils

[2] M. R. Boehm, dans son récent ouvrage: *Das Grundlegende und das Wesentliche. Zu Aristoteles' Abhandlung "Über das Sein und das Seiende" (Metaphysik Z)* (La Haye, 1965), a bien mis en lumière ce double sens de la question τίς ἡ οὐσία; en Z 1. 1028b4, voir pp. 55 sq.

[3] Z 3. 1028b33–36.

[4] *Ibid.*, 1029a26–28.

[5] En fait Aristote n'y reviendra plus qu'en passant dans le livre Z; voir chap. 13. 1038b2–6. Voir aussi le résumé de Z en H 1. 1042a26–31.

[6] Cf. W. D. Ross, *op. cit.*, p. 164 *ad* 1028b34–36.

[7] Z 5. 1031a12–14.

[8] Z 6, surtout 1031b18–20 et 31–32.

traitent de questions connexes à celle de la quiddité. Ils s'occupent en effet de la définition, expression de l'essence, et de ses parties, dans leurs rapports avec la chose définie et ses parties (parties de la matière, de la forme et du composé des deux).

Tel est donc le cadre où vient s'insérer l'excursus concernant le devenir des chapitres 7–9.

Le contenu de ceux-ci est difficile à résumer. C'est une suite de considérations dont le lien le plus apparent entre elles est qu'elles ont toutes trait au devenir et à ses principes, la matière et la forme, notions supposées familières au lecteur. L'exposé s'appuie visiblement sur celui de la *Physique*, livre I. La distinction classique est faite entre devenir naturel, artificiel et fortuit, mais l'attention se concentre d'abord sur les deux premiers. C'est au chapitre 9 seulement qu'Aristote tente d'assimiler tant bien que mal le cas du devenir fortuit aux deux précédents. Les points principaux qu'il paraît vouloir mettre en lumière dans l'ensemble de ces chapitres, sont l'identité qui existe, dans les productions naturelles entre générateur et engendré,[9] le fait que les principes du devenir, forme aussi bien que matière, sont inengendrés,[10] enfin le caractère actif ou efficient de la forme des substances sensibles et en conséquence l'inutilité de poser des Formes platoniciennes séparées pour expliquer le devenir.[11]

Ces conclusions ont-elles quelque rapport avec l'étude de la substance comme quiddité et, plus généralement, éclairent-elles la notion de substance, sur laquelle s'acharne Aristote dans tout le reste du livre Z ? Il nous semble que oui, par l'intelligence plus profonde qu'elles nous donnent des rapports entre matière et forme.

Pour le voir, il faut se reporter au début du livre et tâcher de pénétrer plus avant dans la problématique d'Aristote. Celui-ci, avons-nous dit, a écarté au chapitre 3 une conception selon la-

[9] Z 7. 1032a24–25; 8. 1033b29–32. Le principe est universel pour la génération des substances naturelles, malgré certaines exceptions apparentes (le mulet): 1033b33–1034a2. Il s'applique aussi dans une certaine mesure aux productions artificielles: Z 9. 1034a21–24, mais il n'est pas valable pour le devenir naturel dans les catégories autres que la substance: 1034b16–19.

[10] Z 8. 1033a24–b19; 9. 1034b7–19.

[11] Z 7. 1032a24–25; 8. 1033b20–1034a5; 9. 1034a31–32, où οὐσία est pris au sens de substance formelle.

quelle l'*ousia* tiendrait toute sa substantialité de la matière. Il manque en effet au substrat dernier, au support ontologique de la forme, d'être un être "séparable," capable d'exister seul, et d'être une chose déterminée.[12] Ce double caractère appartient, pense-t-on, davantage à la forme et au composé, de sorte que ceux-ci méritent à meilleur titre le nom de substance. Mais, puisque le composé est postérieur à ses parties, c'est la substantialité des composants qu'il faut examiner. Non plus celle de la matière – on a déjà vu que c'est comme substrat qu'elle a des titres, du reste insuffisants, à la substantialité – mais celle de la forme, car, dit Aristote, c'est elle qui présente le plus de difficulté. L'examen commencera par la forme des substances sensibles, poursuit-il, parce qu'il s'agit là de substances que tout le monde reconnaît.[13]

La question étant ainsi posée, il est naturel que l'investigation d'Aristote procède comme elle le fait, en prenant pour fil conducteur la notion d'essence (τί ἦν εἶναι). Si, en effet, Platon a déclaré que les êtres véritables (les vraies substances, par conséquent) sont les Formes intelligibles, c'est parce que ce sont des choses en soi, des essences, auxquelles les choses d'ici-bas ne font que participer, mais dont elles tiennent les caractères par lesquels on les reconnaît et on les nomme. La substantialité est-elle donc l'"essentialité," le fait d'être une forme en soi? Comme on sait, la réponse d'Aristote à cette question consiste à accepter cette idée tout en refusant la séparation platonicienne

---

[12] Littéralement: un "ceci" (τόδε τι), non pas un individu, mais une substance possédant une détermination. Sur le sens de l'expression τόδε τι cf. J. A. Smith, "τόδε τι in Aristotle," *Classical Review* 35 (1921), p. 19, et E. Tugendhat, *TI KATA TINOΣ Eine Untersuchung zu Struktur und Ursprung aristotelischer Grundbegriffe* (Freibourg en Brisgau, 1958), p. 25, n. 22, et notre étude: "Notes sur la Doctrine des Catégories dans les Topiques," in *Aristotle on Dialectic. The Topics* (Oxford, 1968), p. 194, n. 3.

[13] Z 3. 1029a26–34. La restriction contenue dans cette phrase indique qu'Aristote pose la question de la substantialité de la forme dans toute sa généralité et pense à d'éventuelles substances immatérielles, qui seraient de pures formes.

Nous ne pouvons songer à discuter ici la manière dont cette problématique du début de Z est présentée par M. R. Boehm dans son ouvrage déjà cité. Même si les conclusions de l'auteur nous paraissent difficiles à accepter en bien des cas, ses analyses pénétrantes jettent souvent un jour nouveau sur d'anciens et complexes problèmes.

des formes. Il accorde donc que les substances sont substances en vertu de leur forme, ou au moins que la possession d'une forme essentielle distingue la substance de tout mode d'être secondaire (qualité, quantité, etc.). Mais il pense que cette identité entre une chose et sa quiddité, caractéristique des sujets subsistants, se réalise ici-bas et qu'il est donc inutile de poser separées des substances sensibles, des Essences qui n'en seraient que les doublures.[14] Le problème de la substance n'est cependant pas résolu dans sa généralité par cette réponse, si importante soit-elle. Car les substances dont on affirme l'existence dans le monde sensible, sont composées dans leur être même. Or, en mettant la substantialité du côté de la forme, même immanente dans le sensible, on risque fort de ne plus apercevoir le rôle de la matière dans la constitution de la substance. Quelle est, en effet, la nécessité pour la forme des substances sensibles de résider dans une matière? Comment faut-il concevoir ce principe formel pour comprendre qu'il ne subsiste pas par lui seul, mais ait besoin d'informer une matière pour constituer une substance? Si l'on ne parvient pas à résoudre ce nouveau problème, vaine aura été la réfutation du platonisme et on continuera à osciller sans pouvoir choisir entre une conception "formaliste" de la substance (l'*ousia*, c'est l'essence) et une conception matérialiste (l'*ousia*, c'est le substrat concret), aussi peu satisfaisantes l'une que l'autre.

Sans proposer directement de réponse à cette question, les chapitres 7–9 nous paraissent y jeter quelque lumière. C'est ce qu'il nous faut maintenant tenter d'expliquer.

C'était pour sortir des apories du devenir que les notions de matière et de forme ont été élaborées par Aristote au premier livre de la *Physique*. Il n'est pas étonnant dès lors qu'une analyse plus poussée du rôle de ces principes dans le devenir apporte de nouvelles précisions quant à leur relation mutuelle.

Selon une méthode qui lui est habituelle, Aristote compare ici le devenir naturel au devenir artificiel, comparaison légitime,

---

[14] La longue et subtile analyse qui commence en Z 4 culmine au chap. 6, lorsqu'Aristote retourne contre Platon l'argument qui établissait les Idées: si c'est une nécessité pour les Formes en soi, parce qu'elles sont des essences pures, que leur être soit identique à leur quiddité, sous peine de voir le processus de séparation se poursuivre à l'infini, pourquoi ne pas admettre que dès ici-bas cette identité existe pour les êtres "par soi et premiers." Voir surtout 1031b31–1032a11.

puisque "l'art imite la nature," et qui a l'avantage de nous faire comprendre la nature au moyen d'un modèle qui nous est plus accessible.[15] Si notre vue du chapitre 7 est exacte, en effet, la description assez étendue qui y est faite d'une production artificielle (rétablissement de la santé d'un malade par le médecin) est destinée à nous faire saisir le rôle des différents facteurs du devenir dans la génération des substances.

Après avoir posé que toute production, qu'elle soit naturelle, artificielle ou fortuite, s'opère sous l'effet d'une cause, à partir de quelque sujet et aboutit à quelque chose de déterminé,[16] Aristote note que, dans la génération d'une substance, la cause efficiente est nature – comme la matière et le produit – mais nature au sens de forme, et est formellement identique à l'être engendré: l'homme engendre l'homme.[17] Il passe ensuite aux productions artificielles et démontre que, là aussi, le principe efficient est de même espèce que la chose produite. Si, en effet, le médecin est capable de produire la santé dans un corps malade, c'est qu'il a dans l'esprit la forme ou essence de la santé, qui lui permet de juger de ce qui est défectueux dans l'état de son malade, puis de chercher le moyen concret de remédier à cet état. Supposons par exemple que la santé réside dans un équilibre du chaud et du froid et que cet équilibre ait été rompu par la maladie au profit du froid. Il faudra donc échauffer le corps du malade, ce que l'on peut obtenir par la friction. Arrivé à cette conclusion, le médecin n'aura plus qu'à appliquer cette thérapeutique pour produire la guérison. L'analyse, on le voit, a fait apparaître deux étapes dans ce processus: la *conception* du but à atteindre et des moyens pour y parvenir et la *réalisation*, le dernier terme conçu étant le point de départ de l'exécution.[18]

Dans la perspective que nous avons adoptée, c'est le rôle précis dévolu ici à la forme qui doit retenir notre attention.

---

[15] De même dans le *De anima*, pour faire saisir ce qu'il veut dire en affirmant que l'âme est la forme du corps, Aristote se sert d'une comparaison avec un objet fabriqué: la hache. Comme la hache est un outil destiné à exécuter une tâche déterminée, il est facile de savoir ce qu'elle est, de comprendre que c'est son adaptation à son but qui en fait-formellement une hache (2. 1. 412b10–17). Cf. *Part. An.* 1. 5. 645b14–20.

[16] Z 7. 1032a12–14.

[17] *Ibid.*, 1032a16–25.

[18] *Ibid.*, 1032a32–b30. Pour les difficultés accessoires que soulève ce passage, nous renvoyons au commentaire de Ross (pp. 184–185) et à la

Remarquons tout d'abord l'identification qui est faite entre la forme et l'essence. C'est bien de l'essence de la santé qu'il s'agit, car c'est l'essence de la santé qui est supposée connue par le médecin. Or cette essence est expressément identifiée à la forme.[19] Ceci n'a rien d'exceptionnel, puisqu'Aristote définit habituellement la cause formelle comme étant la quiddité.[20] Mais le Stagirite s'exprime ici d'une manière pour le moins ambiguë: la santé qui est dans l'esprit du médecin (de même que la maison qui est dans l'esprit de l'architecte), c'est la santé (ou la maison) *sans matière*.

En un certain sens, écrit-il, c'est de la santé que vient la santé, de la maison, la maison, de celle qui est sans matière, celle qui en possède une, car la médecine et l'art de bâtir sont la forme de la santé et de la maison, et par "essence sans matière," j'entends leur quiddité.[21]

Que faut-il comprendre par là? Il est bien évident que la santé et la maison ne sont pas présentes réellement dans l'esprit de ceux qui les pensent et que ces derniers n'en possèdent qu'une représentation. Mais, si c'était seulement cela qu'Aristote voulait dire, on aurait ici une confusion grossière entre l'ordre de la pensée et celui de la réalité, une assimilation indue entre la forme, principe réel de la chose, et l'idée qui la signifie. Sans oser affirmer qu'Aristote évite totalement cette confusion, nous pensons cependant pouvoir dire qu'il y a un autre sens à retirer de ses paroles. En effet, ce qu'il analyse, c'est le passage de l'acte de poser consciemment un objectif à atteindre, à la réalisation de cet objectif. Or il nous semble que ce qu'il veut souligner, c'est que cet acte est dynamique (puisqu'il commande la réalisation) et

note 4, p. 383 de la traduction Tricot. Après avoir expliqué que dans la production artificielle, c'est la forme (la santé) qui est la cause efficiente, Aristote est quelque peu embarrassé par les cas où le même résultat est produit par le hasard. Sa réponse à la difficulté est que le point de départ de la production fortuite est identique au premier terme de la phase d'exécution dans l'action du technicien (l'échauffement, que le médecin décide de provoquer). Ainsi on peut dire que ce point de départ, par le lien qui le rattache au résultat qu'il produit, est homogène à celui-ci: l'échauffement est une partie de la santé, la partie à produire dans le cas considéré. Mais, comme le remarque Ross, Aristote a tort d'assimiler le rapport θερμότης-ὑγιεία au rapport λίθοι-οἰκία (1032b29–30).

[19] εἶδος δὲ λέγω τὸ τί ἦν εἶναι ἑκάστου καὶ τὴν πρώτην οὐσίαν, 1032b1–2.

[20] Voir *Metaph.* A 3. 983a27–28; 2. 1013a26–27; 1013b22–23; 8. 1017b21–26; Z 10. 1035b32; H 4. 1044a36.

[21] 1032b11–14.

qu'il l'est parce qu'il possède, par rapport au processus qu'il
dirige, le caractère d'un schéma où d'une forme qu'une matière
viendra remplir. Ce double caractère, dynamique et formel,
apparaît d'ailleurs à chacune des deux étapes de la production
(conception et exécution), comme on va le voir.

Soit donc posé comme but de rétablir la santé de tel malade
déterminé. La position de ce but, ainsi que le remarque Aristote,
entraîne tout un travail de recherche intellectuelle par lequel
le médecin tentera de préciser les moyens à employer. Le but est
sans doute connu au départ, mais pas d'une façon telle que les
moyens pour y parvenir soient du même coup présents à l'esprit :
ceux-ci auront à être découverts. Mais on voit bien que c'est la
connaissance du but qui sert de norme à la découverte des
moyens. Poser le but, c'est poser une exigence de recherche des
moyens, ce qui implique que la connaissance du but est dynamique
parce qu'elle est schématique ou formelle. Lorsqu'on sera arrivé
à déterminer de proche en proche, dans la série des moyens,
le premier terme qu'il est au pouvoir du technicien de réaliser,
la phase d'exécution commencera. Elle présentera les mêmes
caractères que la phase précédente. Elle sera, elle aussi, dominée
par le but à atteindre, dont le dynamisme vient pareillement de
ce qu'il est exigence de réaliser quelque chose qui n'existe pas
encore. Comme schème directeur du travail de réalisation, le
but peut, ici encore, s'appeler une forme, l'exécution étant alors
l'imposition de cette forme à une matière préexistante.

L'analyse de l'activité intelligente du technicien aboutit donc
à faire voir que la production artificielle est tout entière dominée
par la visée intentionnelle de la chose à produire. À la fois parce
que cette visée est une représentation *schématique* de l'essence
de la chose et parce qu'elle est vouloir d'un but *à atteindre,* on
peut dire que ce qui commande la conception et l'exécution de
l'action est une forme.[22]

Dans quelle mesure les résultats auxquels a conduit l'analyse
de la production artificielle peuvent-ils être appliqués à la

[22] En rigueur de termes, cette forme est une forme mentale, c'est la
chose pensée et voulue. Mais, puisque l'idée est pour Aristote visée d'une
essence réelle, il paraît tout de même juste de dire en dernière analyse que
cette essence exerce une causalité – réelle aussi – sur le processus tout
entier. Il est clair pourtant qu'Aristote ne distingue pas nettement ces
deux plans.

production naturelle? Aristote ne le dit pas, bien que son intention soit sans nul doute de faire pareille application. Il s'est contenté d'affirmer en commençant la similitude qui existe entre les deux sortes de production: pour toutes deux, le point de départ et le point d'arrivée ont même essence, l'homme engendre l'homme comme la santé engendre la santé. La différence, c'est que, pour l'art, il s'agit d'une essence représentée,[23] ce qui ne saurait être le cas dans le génération naturelle.[24] Mais, compte tenu de cette différence, le schème technique reste très éclairant pour comprendre les processus naturels.

En effet, la mystérieuse transmission de la forme du générateur à l'engendré peut être conçue, à l'instar de ce qui se passe dans le domaine de la technique, comme la disposition d'une série de moyens en vue d'une fin. Le dynamisme de la forme consiste en son pouvoir d'organiser des matériaux de telle sorte qu'un résultat déterminé se produise. Et si ce résultat peut être la venue à l'existence d'un individu semblable à son générateur, c'est justement parce que la détermination à reproduire existe déjà d'une certaine façon dans celui-ci.[25]

Ces points étant acquis, examinons ce que le chapitre 8 apporte de neuf quant à la conception des rapports entre matière et forme. Deux thèses y ont de l'importance pour notre propos.

La première, c'est que, dans le devenir, ni la matière ni la forme ne sont engendrées. Pour la première, c'est évident. La matière est le substrat dont l'existence préalable est nécessaire pour que le devenir puisse avoir lieu. Pour la forme, la chose est moins claire. La raison donnée par Aristote est que, si la forme était engendrée, elle aurait besoin, elle aussi, d'un substrat

---

[23] εἶδος ἐν τῇ ψυχῇ, 1032b1.

[24] Dans un parallèle établi par Aristote entre l'art et la nature, νοῦς est opposé à φύσις: ὥσπερ γὰρ ὁ νοῦς ἕνεκά του ποιεῖ, τὸν αὐτὸν τρόπον καὶ ἡ φύσις, καὶ τοῦτ'ἔστιν αὐτῆς τέλος, *De An.* 2. 4. 415b16–17.

[25] Pour pouvoir affirmer que le résultat de la génération a le caractère d'une fin, c'est-à-dire d'un bien, poursuivie inconsciemment par la nature, d'autres considérations sont encore nécessaires, qu'Aristote ne fait pas ici. Il explique dans le *De anima* la fonction de reproduction des êtres vivants par leur tendance à participer au divin et à l'éternel autant qu'ils le peuvent (2. 4. 415a26–b2). Cette justification n'importe pas au problème traité en *Metaph.* Z, où on examine seulement le "comment" de la génération et son rapport à la forme.

préexistant et on irait à l'infini.[26] Il est du reste manifeste que l'artisan qui fabrique une sphère d'airain, ne fait ni l'airain ni la sphère, il se contente d'imposer la forme sphérique à une matière donnée.

Mais alors, se demande Aristote, si la forme ou essence de la sphère n'est pas sujette à la génération, ne faut-il pas en conclure qu'il existe "quelque sphère séparée des sphères sensibles, ou quelque maison en dehors des briques?"[27] Sa réponse négative est la deuxième thèse qu'il nous faut retenir. La justification en est donnée dans un paragraphe extrêmement dense, dont voici la teneur. Toute génération consiste dans l'imposition d'une qualification à un substrat donné.[28] Or,

> toute substance individuelle, Callias ou Socrate, est comparable à telle sphère d'airain particulière; tandis que "l'homme" ou "l'animal" est comme la sphère d'airain en général. Il est donc évident que la cause qui consiste dans les Formes (au sens où certains ont l'habitude d'en parler, comme de Formes existant en dehors des individus), n'est d'aucune utilité, au moins pour les générations et pour les substances.[29]

Sous ces affirmations, obscures par leur concision, voici, nous semble-t-il, ce qu'il faut entendre. Ce qui se communique par la génération, ce n'est pas la substantialité tout entière, mais seulement son aspect formel. Or cet aspect n'est pas isolable de la matière, quoi qu'en pensent les partisans des Idées. Les Formes platoniciennes, en effet, étant supposées être les essences des choses sensibles, répondent à ce qui est pensé dans le concept de ces choses sensibles: l'homme, l'animal. Mais le concept général d'homme est, par rapport à l'individu, dans la même relation que le concept de "sphère d'airain" par rapport à telle sphère d'airain particulière: c'est le concept d'un être essentiellement matériel, d'une forme dans une matière. La Forme platonicienne, si elle est vraiment l'essence de la chose sensible, n'en est pas le principe formel, posé à part de cette chose, et elle ne peut avoir le rôle

---

[26] Z 8. 1033a24–b19. L'exemple dont il se sert, dans ce cas-ci encore, emprunté à l'art et pour les mêmes raisons que précédemment: le domaine de l'activité humaine est plus clair pour nous et la transposition au domaine de la nature, facile à faire.

[27] *Ibid.*, 1033b20–21.

[28] *Ibid.*, 1033b21–24.

[29] *Ibid.*, 1033b24–28. À la ligne 28, nous adoptons la leçon πρός γε τὰς γενέσεις du ms. Aᵇ (au lieu de πρός τε) avec Ross et Jaeger.

informant qu'on voudrait lui faire jouer. Ce n'est pas *une substance qui ne serait que forme* qui peut être le principe actif de la génération des substances sensibles, mais bien un être dont l'action physique transforme une matière dans un sens déterminé.

Où trouver cet être, sinon dans l'ordre sensible lui-même, dans une substance composée de matière et de forme, capable de reproduire dans une autre matière l'organisation qui fait sa constitution propre? C'est à cette conclusion que s'arrête Aristote, en posant comme cause de la production des substances naturelles un générateur concret, de même espèce que l'engendré.[30]

Si l'on veut jeter un regard en arrière sur le chemin parcouru, on pourra résumer ainsi les résultats auxquels on est arrivé.

L'examen du rapport matière-forme dans la génération a fait apparaître sous un jour nouveau l'inséparabilité de ces principes dans la substance sensible. La seule substance complète dans l'ordre sensible est une matière déterminée par une forme, ces deux principes étant corrélatifs et donc insuffisants l'un sans l'autre pour fonder la substantialité, non toutefois pour les mêmes raisons. La forme est la détermination essentielle *de* quelque chose; la matière est le *quelque chose* à déterminer, à organiser. La forme étant détermination essentielle, peut être dite en quelque sorte la substance sans matière. La comparaison du devenir naturel avec l'art a fait voir, en effet, en quel sens la forme du générateur est une sorte de schème directeur d'action, qui tend à organiser une matière suivant sa propre détermination, de manière à s'imprimer dans un individu nouveau.

Aristote a bien vu que cette manière de comprendre les choses limite la génération à la production de la substance composée comme telle et ne s'étend pas à celle de ses composants. Mais il a aperçu aussi que cela exclut toute existence séparée de la forme, car celle-ci ne peut pas plus exister à part de la matière que l'ordre ou la composition d'éléments ne peut exister à part des touts ordonnés ou composés, ou qu'une fin ne peut se réaliser à part des moyens qui y mènent.

---

[30] *Ibid.*, 1033b29–32; 1034a2–8. Le chapitre 9 examine les restrictions apparentes ou réelles à mettre au principe de la génération du même par le même. Il n'apporte aucun élément théorique nouveau dont il faille tenir compte dans la question qui nous occupe.

Il est toutefois une conséquence extrêmement importante qu'il ne semble pas avoir tirée explicitement de sa propre doctrine, c'est que la forme des substances sensibles ne saurait plus être simplement identifiée à leur quiddité.[31] Ce qu'une substance sensible est par soi (sa quiddité) n'est pas seulement sa détermination, c'est sa détermination en tant qu'elle informe une matière, car on vient de voir qu'il est essentiel à une substance sensible d'être une forme incarnée. En un sens donc, la matière entre dans l'essence des substances d'ici-bas et doit être présente dans le concept qui exprime cette essence. Aristote l'a reconnu lorsqu'il a dit que le concept d'homme est comparable à celui de la sphère d'airain, mais il n'en a pas conclu ce qui s'ensuit logiquement, à savoir, que la forme est, non pas l'*essence*, mais le *principe* qui donne à une chose sa détermination essentielle.

Une autre conséquence de sa théorie ne lui a cependant pas échappé: c'est que, si la matière entre dans l'essence de la substance sensible, ce n'est pas en se transformant en quelque sorte en note formelle, c'est en gardant au contraire son opposition à la forme et pour conférer à la substance ce que la forme ne peut lui donner, à savoir, l'unité numérique.[32]

On le voit donc, les résultats de l'analyse du devenir en Z 7–9 sont loin d'être négligeables pour la conception métaphysique de la substance sensible. Une étude de la suite du livre Z montrerait du reste qu'ils sont mis à profit, notamment dans les chapitres 10–12. Mais c'est leur portée théorique que nous voudrions souligner en terminant. Non seulement ces conclusions font apparaître les rôles respectifs de la matière et de la forme dans la substantialité des substances d'ici-bas, mais elles préparent même la réponse à la question ultime de la métaphysique aristotélicienne: y a-t-il des substances au delà du sensible?[33] Car, prenant conscience qu'il n'est pas possible d'abstraire réellement la forme des substances sensibles de leur matière,

---

[31] Aristote continue pourtant à le faire dans ces chapitres et plus loin. Cf. Z 7. 1032b1–2; 1032b14; 8. 1033b5–7; 10. 1035b32; H 4. 1044a36.

[32] Z 8. 1034a5–8: "Le tout qui est engendré, c'est telle forme dans telles chairs et tels os, Callias ou Socrate, et c'est autre chose (que le générateur) à cause de la matière, qui est autre, mais c'est identique quant à la forme, car la forme est indivisible."

[33] Cf. Z 11. 1037a10–16; 17. 1041a6–9.

on s'apprête à comprendre que la différence entre ces dernières et d'éventuelles substances immatérielles, ne tient pas au statut – non-séparé ou séparé – de la forme, mais à la nature même de celle-ci.

Louvain

EXPLICATION D'UN TEXTE D'ARISTOTE:
DE PARTIBUS ANIMALIUM I. 1. 641a14–b10

JOSEPH MOREAU

Le livre I du *De partibus animalium* est une introduction à l'étude
de la biologie, à l'usage non des spécialistes, mais des gens
cultivés (πεπαιδευμένοι). Le chapitre 1, notamment, traite de la
méthode qui convient à cette étude, et se demande si, dans l'explication de la genèse des êtres vivants, il faut invoquer de
préférence la cause mécanique ou la cause finale (639b11–14),
en d'autres termes si le point de départ de l'explication doit être
la considération de la raison (λόγος), de l'essence (οὐσία), ou celle
des éléments: un être est-il ce qu'il est devenu, le résultat d'un
devenir aveugle et purement mécanique, ou est-il une essence
qui commande son devenir? Est-il devenu ce qu'il est? Aristote
prend le second parti, celui de la priorité de l'essence sur le
devenir, de la finalité sur le mécanisme: ἡ γὰρ γένεσις ἕνεκα τῆς
οὐσίας ἐστίν, ἀλλ'οὐχ ἡ οὐσία ἕνεκα τῆς γενέσεως (640a18–19; cf.
Pl. *Phlb.* 54a). C'est au nom de ce principe qu'il combat les
explications qui font seulement appel à la matière et à la nécessité, aux propriétés des éléments et à leurs actions réciproques,
leurs effets mécaniques. Dans l'explication des choses naturelles,
et en particulier des êtres vivants, comme dans celle des produits
de l'art, il faut tenir compte de la matière et de la forme, et
accorder le rôle prépondérant à la forme. L'analogie de la production naturelle et de la production artificielle, de la nature et
de l'art, est un trait fondemental de la physique aristotélicienne
(*Ph.* 2. 8. 199a8–15, 17–18, 199b30, et ici-même 639b15–16, 20–21).
    Cette introduction à la biologie fait donc intervenir les concepts
fondamentaux de la science aristotélicienne: les quatre causes, la
notion de nature et d'âme, mais afin de résoudre un problème
précis: celui de l'explication des organismes vivants, de leur
genèse et de leur développement. Ces concepts ne sont pas

exposés abstraitement, mais présentés dans leur application et leur usage, ce qui permet d'en mieux saisir la signification.

Le passage qui nous occupe particulièrement fait intervenir la notion d'âme, considérée comme principe d'explication des organismes vivants, comme concept biologique. Il éclaire par là d'une vive lumière la doctrine du *De anima* et le rôle de ce traité, de caractère principalement biologique. Il pose du même coup le problème des fonctions de l'âme, qui ne se réduisent pas à des fonctions biologiques; il soulève la question des rapports de l'intellect et de l'âme, et par là celui des rapports de la psychophysiologie et de la noétique, de la physique et de la métaphysique. Il est difficile de décider si les remarques contenues dans ce passage sont une préparation à la doctrine du *De anima*, ou si elles en sont seulement l'écho. Elles ont du moins le mérite de présenter un raccourci saisissant des problèmes soulevés par le *De anima*, et d'en préciser le sens en les reliant à leur contexte biologique.

I. LE PROBLÈME DE MÉTHODE

641a14–17: Δῆλον τοίνυν ὅτι οὐκ ὀρθῶς λέγουσι, καὶ ὅτι λεκτέον ὡς τοιοῦτον τὸ ζῷον, καὶ περὶ ἐκείνου, καὶ τί καὶ ποῖόν τι, καὶ τῶν μορίων ἕκαστον, ὥσπερ καὶ περὶ τοῦ εἴδους τῆς κλίνης.

Il est clair, dès lors, qu'ils ne s'expriment pas correctement (sc. ceux qui se contentent d'explications mécanistes) et qu'il faut dire que l'être vivant est de telle sorte (i.e., comparable à un ouvrage de l'art; cf. 641a10–14); il faut expliquer à son sujet ce qu'il est (*quid*) et de quelle sorte il est (*quale quid*), lui et chacune de ses parties, ainsi qu'on l'explique pour la forme du lit.

La comparaison finale éclaire le sens de la phrase. Pour expliquer ce qu'est un lit, comment est produit un lit, il ne suffit pas d'en considérer la matière, le bois; il faut tenir compte de la forme qu'a voulu réaliser l'artisan. Un lit, c'est une forme réalisée dans une matière, un *ceci* dans un *cela*, ou mieux un *cela* façonné de telle façon (κλίνη γὰρ τόδε ἐν τῷδε ἢ τόδε τοιόνδε. 640b26). D'où la nécessité, dans l'explication du lit, de tenir compte de la figure (σχῆμα), de la qualification de son contour visible (ποῖον τὴν ἰδέαν. *Ibid.*, 27–28). De même, au sujet de l'être vivant, il ne suffit pas de dire ce qu'il est (τί), i.e., de quoi il est fait, de chair et de sang, de terre et d'eau, mais ce qui le qualifie essentiellement (ποῖόν τι).

641a18–25: Εἰ δὴ τοῦτό ἐστι ψυχὴ ἢ ψυχῆς μέρος ἢ μὴ ἄνευ ψυχῆς (ἀπελθούσης γοῦν οὐκέτι ζῷόν ἐστιν, οὐδὲ τῶν μορίων οὐδὲν τὸ αὐτὸ λείπεται, πλὴν τῷ σχήματι μόνον, καθάπερ τὰ μυθευόμενα λιθοῦσθαι), εἰ δὴ ταῦτα οὕτως, τοῦ φυσικοῦ περὶ ψυχῆς ἂν εἴη λέγειν καὶ εἰδέναι, καὶ εἰ μὴ πάσης, κατ'αὐτὸ τοῦτο καθ'ὃ τοιοῦτο τὸ ζῷον, καὶ τί ἐστιν ἡ ψυχή, ἢ αὐτὸ τοῦτο τὸ μόριον, καὶ περὶ τῶν συμβεβηκότων κατὰ τὴν τοιαύτην αὐτῆς οὐσίαν, . . .

"Si donc cette qualification essentielle est l'âme, ou une partie de l'âme, ou si elle n'est pas sans l'âme" (...), il s'ensuit que dans l'explication des organismes vivants (qui ne peut écarter la considération de la forme, de la qualification essentielle) il faut tenir compte de l'âme.

Tel est le sens général de cette phrase: Supposé que l'âme soit la qualification essentielle de l'être vivant, l'explication en biologie ne pourra faire abstraction de l'âme. La supposition (ou hypothèse) d'où se tire cette conclusion, l'hypothèse selon laquelle l'âme est la forme, la détermination essentielle de l'être vivant, est justifiée dans une parenthèse:

> Ce qu'il y a de sûr, c'est que l'âme une fois partie, il n'y a plus d'être vivant, et aucune de ses parties ne demeure la même, excepté par la figure seulement, comme dans la légende des êtres changés en pierre.

Un double enseignement est contenu dans cette parenthèse: 1: Du moment que l'âme est ce dont le départ marque la cessation de la vie, on peut regarder l'âme comme la détermination essentielle, la forme de l'être vivant; 2: La forme, dans le cas de l'être vivant, ne se réduit pas à la figure, comme dans le cas de la statue; l'âme est une forme dynamique, l'aptitude à exercer certaines fonctions, un entéléchie première (640b34–641a5; cf. _De An._ 2. 1. 412b20–22). L'âme, ou entéléchie première, est pour le corps ce qu'est pour l'oeil la vue (ὄψις), par opposition à la vision (ὅρασις); elle est la fonction ou l'ensemble des fonctions, par opposition à l'exercice (_De An._ 2. 1. 412b18–413a1).

> De cette hypothèse (εἰ δὴ ταῦτα οὕτως), (i.e., de la définition de l'âme comme principe des fonctions vitales), il s'ensuit qu'il appartient au physicien (au naturaliste, au biologiste, par opposition au métaphysicien,

au philosophe) de traiter de l'âme et d'en connaître, sinon de l'âme tout entière (i.e., considérée dans toutes ses fonctions), sous cet aspect du moins selon lequel l'être vivant se qualifie comme tel (i.e., selon lequel l'âme est principe des fonctions vitales); il devra savoir ce qu'est l'âme, ou du moins cette partie précisément (l'âme animale, principe vital) et traiter des attributs (des fonctions) correspondant à cet aspect de son essence (à son essence considérée de cette manière, comme principe des fonctions vitales).

641a25–32: ... ἄλλως τε καὶ τῆς φύσεως διχῶς λεγομένης καὶ οὔσης τῆς μὲν ὡς ὕλης τῆς δ'ὡς οὐσίας. Καὶ ἔστιν αὔτη καὶ ὡς ἡ κινοῦσα καὶ ὡς τὸ τέλος. Τοιοῦτον δὲ τοῦ ζῴου ἤτοι πᾶσα ἡ ψυχὴ ἢ μέρος τι αὐτῆς. Ὥστε καὶ οὕτως ἂν λεκτέον εἴη τῷ περὶ φύσεως θεωρητικῷ περὶ ψυχῆς μᾶλλον ἢ περὶ τῆς ὕλης, ὅσῳ μᾶλλον ἡ ὕλη δι'ἐκείνην φύσις ἐστὶν ἤ περ ἀνάπαλιν. Καὶ γὰρ κλίνη καὶ τρίπους τὸ ξύλον, ὅτι δυνάμει ταῦτά ἐστιν.

À ces raisons particulières, tirées de la nature propre de l'objet de la biologie, s'ajoutent des raisons générales pour le physicien, le naturaliste, de tenir compte de l'âme dans l'étude et l'explication des êtres vivants:

D'autre part, il faut considérer aussi que la nature (objet du physicien) se dit en plusieurs sens; elle est, d'un côté, en tant que matière, de l'autre en tant que forme (cf. *Ph.* 2. 1. 193a28–31; 194a12–13); et elle est aussi en tant que motrice et en tant que fin (le moteur et la fin se ramènent, en effet, à la forme. *Ph.* 2. 2. 198a24); or, c'est un principe de cette sorte (forme, moteur et fin) qu'est l'âme de l'être vivant, ou bien tout entière, ou en quelqu'une de ses parties. De sorte que, de cette façon encore, il appartiendrait à celui qui étudie la nature de traiter de l'âme plutôt que de la matière, pour autant que c'est par elle (par la forme, et dans ce cas particulier par l'âme) que la matière est nature, et non inversement.

En quel sens, en effet, dit-on que la matière est nature? La remarque suivante l'explique: "En effet, lit ou trépied, le bois l'est déjà, en ce sens qu'il est ces objets (cette nature) en puissance." Cette remarque est de sens tout opposé à celle du sophiste Antiphon, pour qui, dans un objet artificiel, comme le lit, ce qui est nature, c'est le bois; ce qui signifie que tout ouvrage de l'homme est fait de matériaux empruntés à la nature (*Ph.* 2. 1. 193a13–15).

II. LE PROBLÈME DES FONCTIONS DE L'ÂME

641a32–34: Ἀπορήσειε δ'ἄν τις εἰς τὸ νῦν λεχθὲν ἐπιβλέψας, πότερον περὶ πάσης ψυχῆς τῆς φυσικῆς ἐστι τὸ εἰπεῖν ἢ περί τινος.

"On pourrait se demander, en considérant ce qui vient d'être dit, si c'est de toute âme qu'il appartient au physicien de traiter, ou d'une certaine âme" (de l'âme tout entière ou d'une partie seulement, de toutes ses fonctions ou de quelques-unes seulement de ses fonctions).

Aristote répond à la question par une considération épistémologique:

641a34–36: Εἰ γὰρ περὶ πάσης, οὐδεμία λείπεται παρὰ τὴν φυσικὴν ἐπιστήμην φίλοσοφία.

"Si c'est de toute l'âme que traite le physicien, il ne reste plus, à côté de la science physique, d'autre philosophie." La physique n'est plus la philosophie seconde; elle devient la philosophie première (*Metaph.* E1. 1026a27–30; Z11. 1037a14–16). Si la psychologie tout entière est absorbée dans la science, il n'y a plus de philosophie. Conséquence inacceptable pour le philosophe; mais comment s'ensuit elle de l'hypothèse? C'est ce que montre le raisonnement suivant:

641a36–641b4: Ὁ γὰρ νοῦς τῶν νοητῶν. Ὥστε περὶ πάντων ἡ φυσικὴ γνῶσις ἂν εἴη· τῆς γὰρ αὐτῆς περὶ νοῦ καὶ τοῦ νοητοῦ θεωρῆσαι, εἴπερ πρὸς ἄλληλα, καὶ ἡ αὐτὴ θεωρία τῶν πρὸς ἄλληλα πάντων, καθάπερ καὶ περὶ αἰσθήσεως καὶ τῶν αἰσθητῶν.

L'intellect a pour objet les intelligibles. En conséquence, tous les objets tomberaient sous la connaissance physique (rentreraient dans la connaissance de la nature); c'est à la même science, en effet, qu'il appartient d'étudier l'intellect et l'intelligible, s'ils sont corrélatifs, et si c'est d'une même étude que relèvent toujours les corrélatifs, comme c'est le cas de la sensation et des sensibles.

En somme, si l'étude de l'intellect (de la fonction intellective de l'âme) relève de la science, de la physique, celle de l'intelligible en relève aussi; et il n'y a plus d'objet pour la métaphysique. La métaphysique a pour objet, en effet, les substances immatérielles (*Metaph.* Λ 6. 1071b20–21).

Comment échapper à cette condamnation de la métaphysique? En rejetant l'hypothèse qui inclut l'âme entière dans l'objet de la physique, qui fait rentrer toutes ses fonctions dans la psycho-physiologie.

641b4–7: Ἢ οὐκ ἔστι πᾶσα ἡ ψυχὴ κινήσεως ἀρχή, οὐδὲ τὰ μόρια ἅπαντα, ἀλλ'αὐξήσεως μὲν ὅπερ καὶ ἐν τοῖς φυτοῖς, ἀλλοιώσεως δὲ τὸ αἰσθητικόν, φορᾶς δ'ἕτερόν τι καὶ οὐ τὸ νοητικόν·

Ou bien (autre hypothèse, qui permet d'échapper à la conséquence précédente) ce n'est pas l'âme tout entière qui est principe de mouvement, ni la totalité de ses parties; mais principe d'accroissement est cette partie qui se trouve aussi dans les plantes, d'altération la partie sensitive, de locomotion une autre partie, mais qui n'est pas la partie intellective.

L'âme, en tant que forme de l'organisme, en tant que principe des fonctions vitales, peut être dite principe de mouvement dans l'acception générale de ce terme, qui comprend plusieurs espèces; et en ce sens elle est proprement nature (cf. *Ph.* 2. 1. 192b20–23, la définition de la nature comme principe immanent de mouvement et de repos). Mais l'âme en sa totalité n'est pas toujours principe de mouvement. L'accroissement, l'altération, le transport, qui sont les trois formes de mouvement observables chez les êtres vivants, ont respectivement pour principe l'âme nutritive, sensitive, locomotrice. La locomotion ne se rencontre que chez les animaux, doués de sensation, par opposition aux plantes, mais non chez tous (*De An.* 2. 2. 413a33–b4); cependant, elle n'est pas le propre des êtres intelligents:

641b7–8: ὑπάρχει γὰρ ἡ φορὰ καὶ ἐν ἑτέροις τῶν ζῴων, διάνοια δ'οὐδενί.

"La locomotion, en effet, se rencontre chez d'autres animaux que l'homme; mais l'entendement n'appartient à aucun autre." L'activité intellectuelle suppose donc dans l'âme un principe distinct de ceux qui s'expriment dans les diverses formes de mouvement; l'âme, par conséquent, ne se réduit pas entièrement à un principe de mouvement, n'est pas entièrement *nature*. L'âme, sous cet aspect, n'est plus un objet pour le physicien:

641b8–10: Δῆλον οὖν ὡς οὐ περὶ πάσης ψυχῆς λεκτέον· οὐδὲ γὰρ πᾶσα ψυχὴ φύσις, ἀλλά τι μόριον αὐτῆς ἕν ἢ καὶ πλείω.

"Il est évident, dans ces conditions, que ce n'est pas de l'âme entière (de toute sorte d'âme) qu'il fera son objet; c'est que non plus toute âme n'est point nature; elle ne l'est qu'en partie, que cette partie soit une ou multiple."

On voit l'intérêt philosophique de cette conclusion: il est de préciser la relation de l'âme et de la nature, et de réserver la transcendance d'une partie de l'âme, l'âme intellectuelle. L'âme, en tant que principe des fonctions vitales est nature, entéléchie première, forme dynamique, principe immanent de mouvement et de repos.

Cependant, toute nature n'est point âme: les éléments, l'air, le feu, etc. ont une nature (*Ph.* 2. 1. 192b9–12, 32–36), une forme dynamique, mais trop élémentaire, trop simple, pour constituer une âme; une âme est une nature plus complexe, la forme non d'un corps simple, mais d'un corps organisé (*De An.* 2. 1. 412b5–6).

Mais, réciproquement, toute âme n'est point nature; il y a dans l'âme humaine une activité qui passe la nature, qui ne se réduit pas à une fonction, dont l'exercice n'est pas lié directement au fonctionnement d'un organe (*De An.* 3. 4. 429a24–25, b4–5), une activité par laquelle l'âme est ouverte à la transcendance, est en union avec l'Absolu.

Bordeaux

ARISTOTELES, *DE INTERPRETATIONE* 3. 16b19–25

HANS WAGNER

Philip Merlan schenkt uns neben seinen grossen Untersuchungen immer wieder auch kurze Studien und kritische Hinweise, die sich mit Vorliebe auf solche Punkte beziehen, über die
wir eigentlich im reinen zu sein glauben, aber, wie er uns dann
schnell belehrt, es in Wahrheit keineswegs sind und es auch
nicht sein können, weil uns lediglich Vorurteil und Gewöhnung
mit Scheinlösungen zufrieden sein liessen. Nicht selten trifft er
dann schon beim ersten Schlag den Nagel auf den Kopf.

Im folgenden möchte auch ich einen Nagel auf den Kopf
treffen. Vielleicht misslingt es. Ich werde deshalb gleichzeitig zu
beweisen versuchen, dass jedenfalls bisher kein Hammer den
betreffenden Nagelkopf getroffen hat.

Der Nagelkopf steckt im letzten Drittel des 3. Kapitels der
aristotelischen Schrift *De Interpretatione*, in dem Abschnitt
16b19–25. Ich versuche im folgenden dreierlei: (1) den Nachweis,
dass die Stelle schwer zu interpretieren ist; (2) den Nachweis, dass
die sonst so ehrwürdige Erklärertradition diese Stelle einhellig
erläutert, aber dabei auf dem Holzweg ist, da sie den Text nicht
verständlich machen kann; (3) eine Erklärung der Stelle, die ihr
einen Sinn, und sogar einen guten Sinn, gibt.

*

Ich gebe zunächst eine Reihe neuerer Übersetzungen:

a) E. Rolfes (1925): Die Verba sind, für sich allein ausgesprochen,
Nomina und zeigen etwas an – denn wer sie spricht, bringt seine Aufmerksamkeit zum Stehen, und wer sie hört, lässt seine Aufmerksamkeit zum
Stehen bringen – aber sie zeigen noch nicht an, ob das Bezeichnete ist
oder nicht. Denn auch wenn man sagt: sein, oder: nicht sein, wird kein
wirkliches Ding damit bezeichnet, so wenig wie wenn man bloss für
sich sagt: seiend. Denn dieses ist an sich nichts, zeigt aber eine Verbindung
mit an, die man ohne die verbundenen Stücke nicht denken kann.

b) H. P. Cooke (Loeb-Ausgabe): Verbs by themselves, then, are nouns, and they stand for or signify something, for the speaker stops his process of thinking and the mind of the hearer acquiesces. However, they do not as yet express positive or negative judgements. For even the infinitives "to be," "not to be," and the participle "being" are indicative only of fact, if and when something further is added. They indicate nothing themselves but imply a copulation or synthesis, which we can hardly conceive of apart from the things thus combined.

c) Ross/Edghill (Oxford-Übersetzung): Verbs in and by themselves are substantival and have significance, for he who uses such expressions arrests the hearer's mind, and fixes his attention; but they do not, as they stand, express any judgement, either positive or negative. For neither are "to be" and "not to be" and the participle "being" significant of any fact, unless something is added; for they do not themselves indicate anything, but imply a copulation, of which we cannot form a conception apart from the things coupled.

d) J. Tricot (1946; 1959): En eux-mêmes et par eux-mêmes ce qu'on appelle les verbes sont donc en réalité des noms, et ils possèdent une signification déterminée (car, en les prononçant, on fixe la pensée de l'auditeur, lequel aussitôt la tient en repos), mais ils ne signifient pas encore qu'une chose est ou n'est pas. Car *être* ou *ne pas être* ne présente pas une signification se rapportant à l'objet, et pas davantage le terme *étant*, lorsqu'on se contente de les employer seuls. En elles-mêmes, en effet, ces expressions ne sont rien, mais elles ajoutent à leur propre sens une certaine composition qu'il est impossible de concevoir indépendamment des choses composées.

e) G. Colli (o.J.; 1955): I verbi, come tali, detti per sé, sono dunque nomi e significano qualcosa (chi li dice arresta infatti il suo animo, e chi ascolta acquieta il proprio), ma non significano ancora se questo qualcosa è o non è. In effetti, l'essere o non essere non costituisce un segno dell'oggetto, neppure quando tu dica per sé, semplicemente come tale: ciò che è. Ciò che è difatti, in sé non è nulla, ma esprime ulteriormente una certa congiunzione, che non è possibile pensare senza i termini congiunti.

f) J. L. Ackrill (1963; 1966):[1]When uttered just by itself a verb is a name and signifies something – the speaker arrests his thought and the hearer pauses – but it does not yet signify whether it is or not. For not even "to be" or "not to be" is a sign of the actual thing (nor if you say simply "that which is"); for by itself it is nothing, but it additionally signifies some combination, which cannot be thought of without the components.

Vergleicht man nun diese sechs neueren Übersetzungen miteinander, so stimmen sie zwar nicht bis in alle Einzelheiten hinein miteinander überein. Mit Bezug auf eine nicht gänzlich irrelevante Textfrage gehen sie sogar auseinander: am Anfang des Satzes 16b22–23 lesen Rolfes, Cooke und Ackrill offenbar οὐδὲ γὰρ, während Ross/Edghill, J. Tricot und Colli offenbar οὐ γὰρ

---

[1] *Aristotle's "Categories" and "De Interpretatione,"* translated with notes by J. L. Ackrill (Oxford: At the Clarendon Press, 1963; 1966).

lesen, wofür sich auch (und wohl mit Recht) Minio-Paluello in seiner kritischen Ausgabe (1949; 1956) entschieden hat. Andererseits aber besteht volle Einhelligkeit der Textdeutung unter allen sechs neueren Übersetzern mit Bezug auf das Textstück: ἀλλ'εἰ ἔστιν ἢ μὴ οὔπω σημαίνει (16b21–22). Und was noch mehr ist, sie haben dabei gleichzeitig auch die lange und ehrwürdige Erklärertradition seit der Antike auf ihrer Seite. Nun will es das Unglück, dass mir gerade diese alte und ehrwürdige Deutung des Textstücks 16b21–22 als unmöglich erscheint. —

Es ist wohl notwendig, zunächst einmal das der Deutung gestellte *Problem* zu entwickeln. Und dazu wiederum ist es wohl unerlässlich, einen Blick auf den Gesamtzusammenhang zu werfen, innerhalb dessen die nun zum Problem gemachte Textstelle steht. Damit also ist zu beginnen.

Um zu seinem eigentlichen Thema, zum Behauptungssatz (dem sprachlichen Ausdruck des logischen Urteils), zu kommen, erörtert Aristoteles zunächst einige ihm wichtig erscheinende Tatsachen, welche die beiden Fundamentalglieder eines solchen Behauptungssatzes (künftig als Urteilssatz bezeichnet) betreffen: den Subjekts- und den Prädikatsausdruck. Dabei geht er – offenbar guten Gewissens, aber sicher auch der Einfachheit halber – so vor, dass er als Modell einen Satz ansetzt, bei dem der Subjektsausdruck ein (einziges und einfaches) Substantiv und der Prädikatsausdruck ein (einziges und einfaches) Verb ist – etwa: ἄνθρωπος ὑγιαίνει. Dieser Ansatz bietet einen Vorteil (für Aristoteles, nicht für uns Erklärer): Der Terminus ὄνομα lässt sich für "Substantiv" wie für "Subjektsausdruck," der Terminus ῥῆμα für "Verb" wie für "Prädikatsausdruck" im gleichen Masse verwenden.

Laute sind noch keine Wörter, Wörter sind nicht notwendig ὀνόματα; der blosse Schmerzenslaut, eines Tieres etwa, ist zwar Äusserung, Äusserung eines Inneren, und so verrät er denn auch etwas (δηλοῖ τι; vgl. 2. 16a28); aber er ist kein ὄνομα; und er ist kein ὄνομα, weil er kein σύμβολον ist.

Wenn nun Aristoteles das σύμβολον auch primär dadurch charakterisiert sein lässt, dass es κατὰ συνθήκην (2. 16a26–28) sei, so ist doch klar, wie er sich die Dinge genauer denkt: Ein ὄνομα ist zunächst einmal ein (gesprochenes oder hingeschriebenes) Lautgebilde; aber nur eine φωνὴ σημαντική ist ein ὄνομα; d.h.:

entscheidendes Definitionsstück ist der Bezeichnungs- und Verweisungsbezug. Es mag Laute geben, die gar nichts bezeichnen und auf gar nichts verweisen (οὐδὲν σημαίνειν); es mag Laute geben, die zwar etwas verraten (b28) (sogar verkohltes Holz am Waldrand kann etwas verraten), aber eben doch keine echte Verweisungs- oder Bezeichnungsfunktion (σημαίνειν) besitzen; wir wissen (oder sollten doch wissen), dass Verweisungs- oder Bezeichnungsfunktion innerhalb blosser Natur, d.h. ohne die eine Verweisungs- oder Bezeichnungsrelation begründende *Leistung des Subjekts*, nicht möglich ist. Wenn Aristoteles σημαίνειν, σύμβολον–Sein und ὄνομα–Sein auf συνθήκη zurückführt, so ist nicht der Konventionscharakter solcher συνθήκη, sondern jene einzel- wie intersubjektive *Leistung des Verweisungs- oder Bezeichnungsbezugs* dasjenige, worauf es ihm letzlich ankommt. Diese Tatsache wird übrigens auch durch die aristotelische Bemerkung deutlich, dass ein Wort auch dann sehr wohl eine Verweisungs- oder Bezeichnungsfunktion haben könne, wenn diese schon deshalb nicht ein blossnatürlicher Bezug sein kann, weil das eine Bezugsglied in der Natur überhaupt nicht vorkommt: das eine blosse Fiktion bezeichnende Wort (wie etwa τραγέλαφος) bezeichnet gleichwohl etwas: nämlich im *Rückbezug* auf das fingierende Subjekt und sein fingierendes νόημα (vgl. 1. 16a16 f.); dieser Rückbezug auf das Subjekt ist eben neben dem Gegenstandsbezug niemals zu vergessen, wenn die Struktur eines ὄνομα, eines σύμβολον und ihres σημαίνειν, zur Frage steht.

Wie wir οὐδὲν σημαίνειν und σημαίνειν τι zu unterscheiden haben, so freilich auch σημαίνειν τι und ἀληθεύειν/ψεύδεσθαι, Verweisungscharakter und Wahrheitsdifferenz. Kein einzelnes Wort kann über seinen Verweisungscharakter hinaus auch Wahrheitsdifferenz haben; erst ἄνθρωπος κάμνει, ἔστι τραγέλαφος, ἔστι Φίλων sind Gebilde, die die Ebene der Geltungsalternative wahr/falsch erreichen (übrigens: ist statt des echten ὄνομα bloss eine seiner πτώσεις gegeben, so reicht das Prädikat ἔστιν für Geltungsdifferenz des Gebildes *nicht* aus: Φίλωνός ἐστιν ist ein unvollständiges Gebilde, das weder falsch noch wahr zu sein vermag; vgl. 2. 16b2–5).

Mit dem Prädikatsausdruck – und zwar, wie es jedenfalls zunächst zu sein scheint, nur mit dem Prädikatsausdruck, der gleichzeitig Verbum ist (ὑγιαίνει; κάμνει) – beschäftigt sich das

3.Kapitel. Kein Zweifel, dass das ῥῆμα nicht weniger als das ὄνομα Verweisungs- und Bezeichnungscharakter besitzt; σημαίνει τι; σημεῖόν ἐστιν. Näherhin: es ist σημεῖον τῶν καθ'ἑτέρου λεγομένων; τῶν καθ'ὑποκειμένου ὑπαρχόντων (vgl. 16b7; 10). Etwas erstaunlich ist, dass ein negativer Prädikatsausdruck (wie οὐχ ὑγιαίνει) oder auch ein nicht-präsentischer Prädikatsausdruck (wie ὑγιανεῖ) kein ῥῆμα sein soll (vgl. 16b11–18). Sieht man von diesen einschränkenden Festlegungen ab, so lässt sich für das ῥῆμα folgendes eindeutig festhalten: (a) Es ist Träger des Verweisungs- und Bedeutungsbezugs *auf die Bestimmtheit*, die dem Urteilssubjekt eigen ist (sei einem ἄνθρωπος die *Bestimmtheit* ὑγιαίνει eigen; dann bezeichnet das Prädikatsverb ὑγιαίνει diese Bestimmtheit ὑγιαίνει, die dem Subjektsgegenstand ἄνθρωπος eigen ist); (b) Ist das ὄνομα ein σημεῖον, insofern es auf den *Gegenstand* des Urteils bezeichnend verweist, so ist das ῥῆμα ein σημεῖον, insofern es auf die *Bestimmtheit* dieses Gegenstands bezeichnend verweist; (c) Ein spezifisch differenzierendes Novum gegenüber dem ὄνομα besitzt das ῥῆμα darin, dass es stets einen *Zeitbezug* mitbezeichnet (sogewiss es in einem Tempus steht): προσσημαίνει χρόνον (vgl. 16b6; 8–9; 17–18).

Damit nun sind wir bis unmittelbar vor die kritische Textstelle (b21) gelangt, die das Thema unserer Untersuchung ist. Aristoteles erklärt in b19–20: Spricht man ein ῥῆμα allein (ohne Zusammenhang mit einem Satzsubjekt) aus, sagt man also beispielsweise lediglich ὑγιαίνει („ist gesund"), so ist es – statt ein ῥῆμα zu sein, vielmehr nur – ein ὄνομα (ein Wort, das etwas bestimmtes bedeutet); ein ῥῆμα ist es offenbar deshalb nicht, weil es nicht eine Bestimmtheit auf einen Gegenstand als diesem eigen bezieht (dies aber wäre gerade die Funktion eines ῥῆμα, wie wir aus 3. 16b7–10 wissen); aber, wie gesagt: es ist immerhin ein ὄνομα und bedeutet und bezeichnet etwas (σημαίνει τι; b20); *aber*, so fahren nun die Interpreten und Übersetzer fort, *es bedeutet und bezeichnet noch nicht, ob es ist oder nicht* (b21–22).

Der Ausdruck: ἀλλ'εἰ ἔστιν ἢ μὴ οὔπω σημαίνει wird also für gleichbedeutend gehalten etwa mit dem Ausdruck: ἀλλὰ πότερον ἔστιν ἢ οὐκ οὔπω σημαίνει. Ich will schon jetzt vorneweg sagen, dass diese Annahme sprachlich-grammatikalisch durchaus möglich ist[2] (wenn sie auch vielleicht nicht ganz so natürlich ist, wie anscheinend angenommen wird). Es sollen nochmals die Übersetzungen unseres Satzes folgen:

Rolfes: aber sie zeigen noch nicht an, ob das Bezeichnete ist oder nicht. *Cooke*: However, they do not as yet express positive or negative judgements. *Ross/Edghill*: but they do not, as they stand, express any judgement, either positive or negative. *Tricot*: mais ils ne signifient pas encore qu'une chose est ou n'est pas. *Colli*: ma non significano ancora se questo qualcosa è o non è. *Ackrill*: but it does not yet signify whether it is or not.

Es wäre nach diesen Übersetzungen und Deutungen also wohl so: Das alleinstehende[3] ῥῆμα (etwa: ὑγιαίνει) hat zwar Bedeutung, Verweisungs- und Bezeichnungscharakter, aber es bezeichnet "noch nicht"[4], ob "es" ist oder nicht ist. Was soll dies letztere heissen? "läuft" (oder: "ist gesund") bezeichnet noch nicht, ob "läuft" (oder "ist gesund") ist oder nicht ist. Ob also diese sachliche *Bestimmtheit* ("läuft"; "ist gesund") ist, statthat. Da bleibt aber doch wohl keinerlei sinnvolle Alternative (εἰ ἔστιν ἢ μὴ) offen!

Oder soll die offengelassene Alternative die sein, ob es einen *Gegenstand* gibt oder nicht, der läuft bzw. gesund ist? Dies bleibt zwar sicherlich offen, aber es wäre doch wohl eine mehr als triviale Feststellung, dass das noch ausdrücklich als alleinstehend angesetzte ῥῆμα nichts über Sein oder Nichtsein eines *Gegenstands* besagt; denn es ist mehr als trivial, dass ein Ausdruck, in dem die Gegenstandsstelle ausdrücklich getilgt ist, über Gegenstände *nichts* sagt – auch nicht über deren Sein oder Nichtsein.

Dass *in concreto* bei solcher Auffassung des Satzes nichts Vernünftiges herauszuholen ist, muss man sich insbesondere

---

[2] εἰ ... ἢ μή kann in abhängiger disjunktiver Satzfrage, gleichbedeutend mit εἰ ... ἢ οὐ, "ob ... oder nicht" heissen; vgl. Kühner-Gerth[3], II. 2 (Hannover, 1904), p. 191. εἰ in der Bedeutung "ob" (statt πότερον) in indirekten Satzfragen, und zwar eigentlich in Doppelfragen, vgl. *ibid.*, p. 533.

[3] Eine mindestens seit Platon übliche, von Aristoteles voll übernommene Bedeutung von καθ᾽ αὐτό, καθ᾽ αὐτά u. dergl. ist "für sich stehend, für sich genommen, allein für sich, für sich selbst seiend"; siehe auch καθ᾽ αὐτό in 2. 16a21.

[4] "noch nicht," d.h. im Unterschied zu einem volleren Ausdruck (hier: zu einem vollen Satz mit ὄνομα und ῥῆμα); vgl. οὔτε ... πω in 1. 16a15–16; οὔπω in a17; οὐδὲν ... πω in 2. 16b4.

auch deswegen vor Augen halten, weil es *in abstracto* ein Moment
gibt, das tatsächlich verführerisch wirken kann: überlässt man
sich diesem abstrakten Moment, dann kann es tatsächlich so
aussehen, als ob es sich um den auch sonst immer wieder präsen-
ten Gegensatz zwischen σημαίνειν τι einerseits und ἀληθεύειν/
ψεύδεσθαι andrerseits handle, sodass der Sinn also der wäre:
"läuft" ("ist gesund") bedeutet und bezeichnet zwar etwas, aber
es gibt "noch nicht" Auskunft über (seine eigene!) Wahrheit oder
Falschheit. Aber kein *in abstracto* noch so vertrauter und noch so
wesentlicher Gegensatz kann in einem bestimmten Satz sinnvoll
sein, wenn er nicht eben auch in diesem bestimmten Satz konkreten Sinn haben kann. Der obige Gegensatz kann jedoch in
unserem Satz einen solchen Sinn nicht haben. Der einfachste
Beweis ist der: auch ein *voller* Satz (z.B. "Sokrates läuft"; "ist
gesund") *bezeichnet* niemals, ob das Behauptete "ist oder nicht
ist"; er *fällt* zwar *unter die Alternative* wahr/falsch (ἢ ἀληθεύει ἢ
ψεύδεται), er mag auch Wahrheit prätendieren; aber gerade auch
von ihm würde gelten: εἰ ἔστιν ἢ μὴ οὔπω [καὶ οὐδέποτε!] σημαίνει.

Aber setzen wir gleichwohl (so als hätten wir wirklich noch
keinen Grund zum Zweifel) einmal an, unser Satz sei in der ange-
gebenen Weise richtig verstanden und richtig übersetzt, und
sehen wir nun zu, wie das im Text *Folgende* (b22–25) sich zu ihm
verhält. Es stellt, so gewiss die Verbindungspartikel γὰρ heisst,
eine *Begründung* für das Vorausgegangene dar, sei es für den
ganzen Satz b19–22, sei es für den letzten Satzteil b21–22. Aber
es ist schwer einzusehen, *wieso* es eine Begründung soll darstellen
können – und zwar gleichgültig, ob man οὐδὲ γὰρ oder οὐ γὰρ
liest. Das alleinstehende ῥῆμα soll *etwas* bezeichnen, soll andrerseits freilich "noch nicht" bezeichnen, ob jenes bezeichnete Etwas
statthat oder nicht statthat, *weil* (selbst) "sein" oder "nicht sein"
keinerlei Bedeutungs- und Bezeichnungsfunktion besitzt mit
Bezug auf die (welche?) Sache (den Gegenstand?). Nochmals:
"läuft" bezeichnet immerhin etwas, "sein" oder "nicht sein"
bezeichnet *nicht* etwas; da es sicher nicht so sein kann, dass
"läuft" deswegen etwas bezeichnet, weil (selbst) "sein" oder
"nicht sein" die Sache *nicht* bezeichnet, steht fest, das der
γὰρ-Satz nicht auch die erste Hälfte unseres Satzes 16b19–22
mitbegründet, dass er nur die zweite Hälfte, wenn überhaupt etwas, begründet. Dann wäre es also so: "läuft" bezeichnet des-

wegen "noch nicht," ob "läuft" (Laufen, etwas Laufendes) ist oder nicht ist, weil (selbst) *"sein"* oder *"nicht sein"* die Sache nicht bezeichnet. Ist es aber nicht ein Widersinn zu sagen, das alleinstehende ῥῆμα (z.B. "läuft") sei deswegen in seinem σημαίνειν eingeschränkt, weil (selbst) *"sein"* oder *"nicht sein"* die Sache (überhaupt) nicht bezeichnet? Weil (selbst) *"sein"* oder *"nicht sein"* die Sache nicht bezeichnet, soll das alleinstehende ῥῆμα zwar etwas bezeichnen, aber nicht das Statthaben oder Nicht-statthaben jenes Etwas?

Niemand wird damit einen Sinn verbinden können. Es hilft auch nicht, das Schema eines *a-fortiori*-Schlusses hineinzulesen:[5] Was dem εἶναι und μὴ εἶναι nicht gegeben sei, sei *a fortiori* einem alleinstehenden ῥῆμα versagt. Aber abgesehen davon, dass man dabei dem εἶναι (und μὴ εἶναι?) (und ὄν; b23) – trotz der entgegengesetzten aristotelischen Feststellung: αὐτὸ μὲν γὰρ οὐδέν ἐστιν (b23–24) – in neuplatonischer Art einen über jede *bestimmte* mögliche Gegenstandsbestimmtheit (wie "läuft," "ist gesund") hinausgehenden metaphysischen Rang einräumen müsste, ergäbe sich ja: weil (selbst) dieses Sein die Sache nicht bezeichnet, bezeichnet das alleinstehende ῥῆμα zwar etwas, aber nicht das Sein oder das Nichtsein jenes bezeichneten Etwas. Auch dies wird aber niemand für ein vernünftiges Argument halten.

Solange wir unser problematisches Satzstück b21–22 so verstehen, wie wir es bisher zu verstehen pflegen, liefert der γὰρ-Satz b22–23 nichts, was man als eine vernünftige Begründung ansehen könnte: es führt kein Weg der Begründung von dem, was in b22–23 über "sein" und "nicht sein" gesagt wird, zu dem, was in b19–22 über σημαίνειν und οὔπω σημαίνειν des allein-stehenden ῥῆμα gesagt worden ist.

Aber darüberhinaus: Ist denn nicht überhaupt ein Thema-wechsel eingetreten? Ist nicht in b22–25 (statt von solchen alleinstehenden ῥήματα wie ὑγιαίνει) vielmehr von εἶναι, μὴ εἶναι, ὄν, und nur noch von diesen, die Rede? Und die Rede ist sogar sehr interessant: "sein," "nicht sein," sogar "seiend" entbehren der Fähigkeit, die Sache, den Gegenstand, von dem etwa die Rede

---

[5] Das folgende wurde tatsächlich auch versucht: vgl. Kommentar des Ammonios Hermeiou zu *De Interpretatione*, 55, 11 ff., ed. Busse; die Verzerrung des Gedankens, ohne welche der Versuch ganz unmöglich gewesen wäre, wird gleichzeitig ebenfalls deutlich.

sein soll, zu bedeuten und zu bezeichnen. Und b23–24 gibt den Grund dafür an: "sein" ist nämlich selbst nichts (und was selbst *nichts ist*, kann begreiflicherweise weder einen Gegenstand noch eine Bestimmtheit an einem Gegenstand bezeichnen oder bedeuten)[6].

Aber, wenn es auch wahr ist, dass εἶναι kein σημεῖον τοῦ πράγματος ist und ihm kein σημαίνειν τὸ πρᾶγμα eignet, so eignet ihm doch andrerseits ein προσσημαίνειν, und zwar das προσσημαίνειν σύνθεσίν τινα: es bedeutet/bezeichnet den Urteilsgegenstand (z.B. Sokrates) nicht, es bedeutet/bezeichnet auch keine der dem Urteilsgegenstand zugesprochenen Bestimmtheiten (keines der καθ'ἑτέρου λεγομένων; 16b7; keines der ὑπαρχόντων, οἷον τῶν καθ'ὑποκειμένου; 16b10), aber es drückt eine bestimmte σύνθεσις aus (προσσημαίνει; ganz ähnlich, wie das ῥῆμα, über seinen σημεῖον–Bezug auf den Gegenstand hinaus, zusätzlich auch das Zeitverhältnis ausdrückt: προσσημαίνει χρόνον in 16b6 und 18). Diese σύνθεσις ist die Urteilssynthesis. "sein" übernimmt diese Aufgabe, die Urteilssynthesis auszudrücken, in Urteilssätzen vom Schema: S ist P.

Erstaunlicher, aber gleichzeitig auch überzeugenderweise sagt nun Aristoteles abschliessend, unter dieser Synthesis lasse sich nichts denken (oder: sie selbst lasse sich gar nicht denken) ohne die in ihr und durch sie verbundenen beiden Glieder S und P.[7] Offenbar entsprechen sich die Leerheit von "sein" und die Leerheit der abstrakt genommenen Urteilssynthesis: "sein" stiftet von sich aus nicht mehr als eine bloss leere Urteilssynthesis, und

---

[6] Woran bei αὐτὸ in b23 zu denken (oder doch vor allem zu denken) ist, ergibt sich erst aus προσσημαίνει σύνθεσίν τινα; μὴ εἶναι (b22) scheidet (mindestens im eigentlichen Sinn) aus, weil es nur die *negative* Urteilssynthesis (S ist *nicht* P) ausdrückt, die Aristoteles bekanntlich nicht als σύνθεσις, sondern als διαίρεσις bezeichnet (auch durchwegs in unserem Büchlein; so schon 1. 16a12); ὄν scheidet aus (wiederum mindestens im eigentlichen Sinne), weil es, als Partizip, höchstenfalls mittelbar eine (affirmative) Urteilssynthesis ausdrückt; unmittelbar und voll bezieht sich αὐτὸ in b23 also nur auf εἶναι in b22 zurück.

[7] Dieses Theorem vom leeren "sein" und von der an und für sich leeren Urteilssynthesis hat seine bedeutsamen und hochinteressanten Hintergründe; es steht auch in einem wohldefinierten Zusammenhang mit dem Theorem von der Mehrdeutigkeit des Terminus "seiend." Darüber habe ich einiges gesagt gegen Ende meines Aufsatzes "Über das aristotelische πολλαχῶς λέγεται τὸ ὄν," *Kant-Studien* 53 (1961–1962), pp. 75–91, s. bes. pp. 89 f.

zwar, weil es selbst bloss leer ist; andrerseits verlangt die Leerheit der abstrakt genommenen Urteilssynthesis als Voraussetzung
für sich diese Leerheit von "sein"; und offenbar muss die abstrakt
genommene Urteilssynthesis deswegen ihreseits leer sein, damit
sie in strenger Abhängigkeit von den zu verbindenden Gliedern
(S und P) jeweils ihre besondere Gestalt, ihren besonderen Modus
und ihren besonderen Rang zugewiesen erhalten kann.

Wir können die Interpretationsproblematik in vier Fest-
stellungen und vier zugehörige Fragen zusammenfassen:

(1) War mindestens noch in 16b19–20 vom isolierten ῥῆμα die
Rede, so ist spätestens ab b22 von "sein," "nicht sein" und
"seiend" die Rede. Ist auch noch in unserem problematischen
Satzstück b21–22 vom isolierten ῥῆμα die Rede, oder von
etwas anderem, etwa bereits von dem, wovon auch in folgenden b22–25 die Rede ist?

(2) Solange wir b19–22, insbes. b21–22, so auffassen, wie es bisher
geschieht, ergibt das folgende b22–25, insbes. das unmittelbar
folgende b22–23 keine verständliche Begründung. Ergibt sich
eine verständliche Begründung, wenn wir b19–22, insbes. aber
b21–22, anders als bisher auffassen und deuten?

(3) Solange wir bei der bisherigen Deutung von b19–22, insbes.
von b21–22, bleiben, folgt auf den relativ kurzen Satz b19–22
über die Bedeutungskraft des isolierten ῥῆμα ein unver-
ständlicherweise mit γὰρ eingefügter *Exkurs* über etwas ganz
anderes, nämlich über die fehlende Bedeutungskraft von
"sein," "nicht sein" und "seiend." Wird aus b22–25 sowohl
ein in sich selbst verständlicher Begründungszusammenhang
wie auch insbes. ein verständliches Argument für das Voraus-
gehende, wenn wir an die Stelle der bisherigen Deutung von
b19–22, insbes. von b21–22, eine andere Deutung setzen?

(4) Selbst wenn man den Satz b19–22 bloss ganz für sich, noch
ohne jede Rücksicht auf den Rest des Kapitels, betrachtet,
erheben sich Zweifel über seine Sinnhaftigkeit, solange man
ihn wie bisher deutet. Lässt er sich anders deuten, und zwar
gleichzeitig so, dass über seine Sinnhaftigkeit kein Zweifel
mehr übrig bleiben muss?

*

Es ist eine eigenartige Sache, die ehrwürdige, von den relativ frühen Anfängen durch die Jahrhunderte bis auf unsere Tage herauf gehende Erklärungstradition. Sie hat etwas Grosses an sich, und sie trägt uns und hilft uns. Aber, es lässt sich nicht leugnen, zuweilen verführt sie uns auch. Es geschah natürlich niemals zufällig, wenn sie selbst auf einen Holzweg geriet; es waren immer bestimmte Anlässe dafür da, sei es in einem vederbten, sei es in einem guten, aber schwierigen oder etwas rätselhaften Text. Mit dem Text gleichwohl fertig zu werden, dieses Bemühen führte auf den Holzweg. Und zusammen sei es mit der Autorität des Vorgängers und der Vorgänger, sei es mit der jeweiligen Hilflosigkeit der Nachfolgenden, sei es mit beiden zugleich, verleitete es dazu, auf dem einmal eingeschlagenen Holzweg zu verbleiben. Meistens ziehen wir Heutige eine Bahn, die Könige gebaut haben; aber zuweilen ziehen wir in einem Zug von Blinden, die einem Anführer folgen, der auch selbst blind war.

Ob sie es eingestehen oder nicht, was *unsere* Stelle anlangt, so verraten unsere Vorgänger zum mindesten mit dem, was sie *tun*, seit den uns zugänglichen Anfängen, dass sie sich der Schwierigkeit der Stelle bewusst sind: sie versuchen allerlei, um mit ihr zurecht zu kommen; zuletzt scheuen sie selbst arge (mit merklichen Sinnverschiebungen und Sinnverzerrungen verbundene) Auskunftsmittel nicht. Gleichzeitig besteht kein Zweifel, dass ihre Notlage eindeutig durch ihre, von ihnen nicht in Frage gestellte, Deutung unseres problematischen Satzstücks 16b21–22 verursacht ist. In beidem nun, in der unangetasteten Deutung von 16b21–22 wie in der Notlage bezüglich der anschliessenden Zeilen 16b22–25, bleiben die Nachfolgenden auf der Bahn der Vorausgegangenen. Aber kaum einer ist unter ihnen, von dem man den Eindruck haben könnte, er fühle sich wohl und behaglich dabei.

Von *Ammonios Hermeiou* haben wir zu 16b19–25 vier volle Seiten Erläuterungen (pp. 54–57); der Autor zieht auch Porphyrios (56, 16 ff.) und Alexandros (57, 18 ff.) bei.

Sofort behauptet der Autor, es gehe Aristoteles um den Nachweis, dass das isolierte ῥῆμα zwar mögliche Gegenstandsbestimmtheiten bezeichne, aber keinesfalls Wahrheit oder Falschheit (vgl. 54, 14–16; 20–22). Und so interpretiert er denn auch εἰ ἔστιν ἢ μὴ als Alternative wahr/falsch (55, 11–13) und sagt entsprechend:

ἀλλὰ ἀλήθειαν ἢ ψεῦδος οὐδέπω σημαίνει (55, 15–16); und der folgende Satz soll die Begründung dafür geben: denn auch 'sein' sei kein Zeichen...; und wenn nicht einmal dieses fundamentalste und allgemeinste ῥῆμα 'sein' als isoliertes Wort *wahrheitsdifferent* sein könne, dann könne es irgendein anderes ῥῆμα noch viel weniger (55, 19 ff.).

Wenn der Autor dann (ab 56, 16) *Porphyrios* mit ins Spiel zieht, wird die Sache nicht besser: vielmehr wird nun gar unser Satz: οὐ γὰρ τὸ εἶνα ... σημεῖόν ἐστι τοῦ πράγματος *gleichgesetzt* mit einem Satz, nach welchem das isolierte ῥῆμα keinen Bedeutungsbezug habe auf das *Sein oder das Nichtsein der Sache*, sodass aus unserem Satz: τὸ εἶναι οὐ σημεῖον τοῦ πράγματος der Satz wird, das isolierte ῥῆμα sei nicht σημαντικὸν τοῦ εἶναι τὸ πρᾶγμα (56, 28–32; τοῦ ὑπάρχειν τὸ πρᾶγμα in 56, 23–25). Nicht zweifelt der Autor (mit seinem Gewährsmann) daran, dass b22–23 noch vom isolierten ῥῆμα (z.B. περιπατεῖ; 56, 25–28) spricht, und verrät dies auch ausdrücklich in 57, 1.

Kommt er zur Erläuterung von αὐτὸ μὲν γὰρ οὐδέν ἐστιν, so bedeutet ihm dieses οὐδέν wiederum bloss dies eine, dass "sein" und "seiend" weder wahr noch falsch sein könne (οὐδὲν = οὔτε ἀληθὲς οὔτε ψεῦδος; 57, 8).

Und nun wird im folgenden aus προσσημαίνει σύνθεσίν τινα: μέρος γίγνεται συνθέσεως (und als Beispiel für eine Urteilssynthesis wählt der Autor gerade hier τὸ ὂν ἔστι;) (57, 9 ff.) und, insofern nun "ist" (statt Ausdruck für die Urteilssynthesis zu sein) zum Bestandteil der Urteilssynthesis wird, wird schliesslich dieses "ist" zum *Träger* der Wahrheitsdifferenz, weil ja σύνθεσις als δεκτικὴ ψεύδους τε καὶ ἀληθείας zu verstehen ist (57, 13–18).

Wie ernsthaft sich auch Ammonios Hermeiou bemüht, weder seine Bemühungen noch seine Auskunftsmittel und Sinnverschiebungen können ihn an das Ziel eines vernünftigen Verständnisses bringen. Was ihm den Erfolg grundsätzlich versperrt, das sind zwei Dinge vor allen anderen: seine Annahme, der ganze Abschnitt 16b19–25 spreche vom isolierten ῥῆμα des Typus περιπατεῖ, sowie seine Deutung des Ausdrucks εἰ ἔστιν ἢ μὴ (b21) als Wahrheitsdifferenz des Urteils (ἀληθές/ψεῦδος).

Stephanos hat ebensowenig einen Zweifel darüber, dass εἰ ἔστιν ἢ μὴ in Wahrheit εἰ ἔστιν ἀληθὲς ἢ μὴ bedeute, und meint, so hätte Aristoteles auch sagen sollen; das isolierte ῥῆμα gebe noch keinen Urteilssatz und erreiche damit auch nicht die Ebene möglicher Wahrheitsdifferenz (14. 33–37); und dasselbe gelte vom isolierten "ist"; wenn es heisse, es sei nichts, so bedeute das, es ergebe noch nichts Wahres und keinen Urteilssatz (14. 38–15. 4).

Was *Boëthius* angeht, so lässt sich aus seiner Übersetzung wenig erschliessen (*sed si est vel non est nondum significat*). In seinem kürzeren Kommentar (*Editio prima*) sagt er zu unserer Stelle: das isolierte Verbum bezeichne zwar etwas in bestimmter Weise, ergebe aber keinen Urteilssatz und konstituiere nichts Wahres oder Falsches (p. 64, 15 ff. Meiser); und wenn er sagt: *non designat esse ipsam rem vel non esse*, so kehrt einfach jenes σημαντικὸν τοῦ εἶναι τὸ πρᾶγμα wieder, das bei Ammonios Hermeiou steht; aus "*esse non est signum rei*" wird: "ein isoliertes *Verbum*, wie *currit, non designat esse rem*" (p. 64, 29–65. 1 Meiser).

In seinem längeren Kommentar (*Editio secunda*) hält sich Boëthius im schon festgelegten Rahmen: durch das isolierte Verbum *nulla negatio affirmatiove perficitur* (p. 75, 5 Meiser) – wieder soll dies der Sinn unseres problematischen Satzstückes b21–22 sein; aus: "*esse non est signum rei*" ist inzwischen eindeutig geworden: "das isolierte *Verbum non est signum rei esse vel non esse*" (p. 76, 10 ff. Meiser; vgl. pp. 400–402).

Michael Psellos (Byzanz) folgt ganz den Spuren, die uns schon Ammonios Hermeiou hinterlassen hat (Ausgabe seines Kommentars, Venetiis apud Aldum, MDIII). Seine unmissverständliche Paraphrase zu unserem kritischen Satz 16b19–22: πλὴν εἰ καὶ ὕπαρξιν δηλοῦσιν ἔστιν ὅτε τὰ ῥήματα, ἀλλ'οὔπω καὶ τοῦ εἶναι ἢ μὴ εἶναί ἐστι σημεῖα· τουτέστι καταφάσεως ἢ ἀποφάσεως ἢ ἀληθείας ἢ ψεύδους. Und bezüglich des Satzes, dass "ist," "sein," "seiend" nichts sei, sagt der Autor: οὐδέν ἐστιν ὅσον πρὸς ψεῦδος καὶ ἀλήθειαν.

Auch die Interpretation des Metropoliten *Magentenos von Mitylene* bleibt völlig in dieser Bahn (Ausgabe ebenfalls Venetiis, apud Aldum, MDIII).

Wilhelm von Moerbeke hat in der ersten Satzhälfte nach dem Subjekt *ipsa secundum se dicta verba*, den Plural: *nomina sunt et significant aliquid*, in der zweiten Satzhälfte (wie schon Boëthius) den Singular: *sed si est aut non est, nondum significat* (p. 43, 5–7). Das müsste an sich darauf schliessen lassen, dass

ein Subjektwechsel von der ersten zur zweiten Satzhälfte erkannt worden ist.

Thomas v. Aquino legt seinem Kommentar zur Stelle einen
Text zugrunde, der in allen wesentlichen Punkten mit dem von
Boëthius und Wilhelm übereinstimmt; doch gibt er eigens an,
dass im *griechischen* Text unser τὸ ὄν ... ψιλόν steht: *neque si*
ens *ipsum dixeris nudum.*

Im entscheidenden Ausgangspunkt bleibt Thomas ganz innerhalb der Tradition: auch nach ihm besagt unser problematischer
Satz, dass das isolierte Verbum nichts bedeuten und bezeichnen
könne hinsichtlich einer Urteilssynthesis oder der Wahrheitsdifferenz; der folgende Satz enthalte dann ein Argument *a potiori
ad minus*: wenn nicht einmal das Verbum "sein" das könne,
umso weniger dann jedes andere. Gar nicht zufrieden ist Thomas
aber mit der Tradition bezüglich des ὄν (in b23) und des abschliess-
senden Satzes (b23–25): er verwirft die Deutung des Alexandros
(der die aristotelische Aussage, "sein" selbst sei leer, mit einem
Hinweis auf die Äquivozität dieses Terminus begründen wollte),
des Porphyrios (der sie damit begründen wollte, sie bedeute
lediglich die blosse Urteilssynthesis) und des Ammonios (der sie
einfach damit begründete, dass "sein" noch nicht die Wahrheitsdifferenz bezeichne – was doch eben von jedwedem isolierten
Verbum, nicht aber speziell von "sein" gelte). Und positiv: ganz
und gar ist Thomas davon überzeugt, dass eben dieses *ens nudum*,
von dem Aristoteles sage, es sei nichts, identisch sei mit dem
schlechthin Höchsten, dem *ipsum esse, fons et origo ipsius esse.*
Was also, wenn gleichwohl im Text steht: *nec ipsum* **ens** *significat rem esse vel non esse* und **nihil** *est*? Nun, es bezeichne eben
nicht, meint Thomas, dass irgendein *Bestimmtes* nun gerade sei
(*non significat* **aliquid** *esse*); es bezeichne auch nicht lediglich
die Urteilssynthesis – es bezeichne ja in Wahrheit gerade das
Höchste: das *in actu esse*, die *actualitas*; nur sei davon, meint
Thomas, eben gerade im Text nicht die Rede; es sei nicht die
Rede von seinem *significare* und *significatum*; wovon allein die
Rede sei, sei sein con*significare* (προσσημαίνει; b24), und dies gelte
tatsächlich nur der Urteilssynthesis; damit aber stehe es noch
unter der Ebene der Wahrheitsdifferenz und *insofern* sei dieses
"sein" als *nihil* bezeichnet und bezeichenbar.

Was Thomas bietet, ist ein Muster philosophischen Scharfsinns und kritischer Selbstständigkeit gegenüber der Einförmigkeit langer Erklärertradition. Und doch kommt er zu keiner befriedigenden Erklärung. Zwei Dinge verhindern es: einmal dies, dass er mit Bezug auf unseren problematischen Satz bei der *communis opinio* bleibt; sodann dies, dass er aufgrund seiner systematischen Überzeugung vom *ens* als *fons et origo ipsius esse* das αὐτὸ μὲν γὰρ οὐδέν ἐστιν (b23/24) nicht wahrhaben will und seine Zuflucht zur Unterscheidung zwischen einem *principaliter significare* von "sein" und einem blossen *consignificare* von "sein" nimmt, mit der Behauptung, ersteres stehe eben hier nicht in Rede.

Von *Julius Pacius* haben wir eine Ausgabe des griechischen Textes mit lateinischer Übersetzung und kurzen Anmerkungen (2. Aufl., Frankfurt, 1597) sowie einen *Commentarius Analyticus* (ebenfalls Frankfurt, 1597). Zwar bleibt Pacius hinsichtlich unseres kritischen Satzes in den Spuren der Tradition: das *Verbum*, meint auch er, *quamdiu solum et per se accipitur, nondum affirmat aut negat* – dies sei der Sinn unseres kritischen Satzes. Aber klug erfasst er den Sinn des Weiteren: Aristoteles gehe b23 zur *copula verbalis* über und sage von dieser: *nullam rem significat*; das kopulative *est* und *non est* seien so wenig wahrheitsdifferent, *ut ne quidem sint verba* und *ut ne quidem significent ullam rem simplicem*. Das ψιλόν (b23) fasst er als *purum vocabulum et pura copula*, unterscheidet ein alleinstehendes Partizip ὄν des *Verbums* εἶναι (*esse existentiae*) und ein alleinstehendes Partizip ὄν der *Kopula* εἶναι und sagt, nur von letzterem Partizip sei die Rede und dieses bezeichne keinerlei Sache. Das sei auch der Sinn von οὐδέν ἐστιν (b24). Andrerseits sei es die Aufgabe des *esse copulae*, Bestimmung und Subjekt miteinander zu verbinden: *"adsignificat" hanc compositionem*.

Viele Nebel verschwinden mit alledem. Aber nicht alles wird klar und hell. Noch bleibt die alte Deutung unseres kritischen Satzstücks b21–22; damit auch die Überzeugung, dass dieses Satzstück noch vom isolierten Verbum weiterspreche, dass also erst der οὐ(δὲ) γὰρ-Satz vom isolierten Verbum zur isolierten Kopula übergehe. Pacius nimmt die Tatsache dieses Themawechsels deutlich wahr; er erkennt auch klar, dass es sich um eine absteigende Klimax handelt: ein Urteilssatz bezeichnet nicht nur, er ist auch zusätzlich wahrheitsdifferent; ein isoliertes

Verbum ist nicht wahrheitsdifferent, aber es bezeichnet; die isolierte Kopula hat nicht einmal mehr dies, dass sie irgendwie eine Sache bezeichnete. Pacius fragt auch nach dem Grund für den Themawechsel. Obwohl er οὐδὲ γὰρ am Anfang von b22–23 liest, lässt er sich nicht mehr zu jenem Schluss *a potiori ad minus* verführen; er nimmt einen anderen Grund für den Themawechsel an: im Anschluss an b19–22 könnte jemand sagen: Gut, das isolierte *Verbum* mag also nicht bezeichnen *"utrum sit aut non sit"*; aber bezeichnet nicht ein (isoliertes) "ist" und "ist nicht" das Sein und das Nichtsein? Und einer solchen Einwandfrage begegne Aristoteles mit der Erklärung b23 ff.: "ist" und "ist nicht" seien nicht einmal Verba, sie bezeichneten noch *weniger*, als was ein Verbum bezeichnet, sie bezeichneten überhaupt keinerlei Sache.

Was Theodor *Waitz* in seiner mit Scholien und Anmerkungen versehenen Ausgabe des *Organon* (Leipzig, 1844; Neudruck Aalen, 1965) zu unserem Abschnitt sagt (p. 330), darf ich übergehen.

G. *Colli* (pp. 759 ss.) nimmt unsere Stelle zum Anlass zu längeren Ausführungen allgemeinerer Art über die Bedeutung von τὸ ὄν und εἶναι bei Aristoteles, spez. in dessen *Organon*: "Sein" sei das allgemeinste Verbum; das isolierte Verbum "ist" sei zwar ein ὄνομα, aber dieses ὄνομα bezeichne keinen Gegenstand, es sei eine "einfache Bestimmung," die wir nicht zu einem Gegenstand machen dürften; es sei ganz verkehrt, ihm einen gegenständlichen Sinn zuzusprechen, wie das auch H. Maier getan habe (p. 759); den Unterschied zwischen *esse copulae* und *esse existentiae* kenne Aristoteles nicht (pp. 761–763); "ist" drücke die schlechthin universale Bestimmung aus, nur sekundär und vermittelt spiegle es dann auch die Verbindung zwischen der Subjekts- und der Prädikatsgegenständlichkeit (p. 764).

Was diesen ausholenden und z.T. überraschenden allgemeineren Ausführungen als Erläuterung zu unserer Stelle selbst gegenübersteht, ist knapper: b21–22 besage, dass das isolierte Verbum zwar ein ὄνομα sei, aber was es bezeichne, sei nicht schon ein Gegenstand, sondern nur eine Gegenstandsbestimmtheit, denn "ist" verrate noch nicht, ob dieses "ist" auch sei, falls man es als Gegenstand setzen wollte (p. 759); weder "ist" noch "Seiendes" bezeichne einen Gegenstand (*ibid.*).

J. L. *Ackrill* gibt scharfsinnige und nützliche Anmerkungen zu unserer Stelle, m.E. das Beste, was wir bisher haben (pp. 121–124). Wie er unseren kritischen Satz übersetzt, wissen wir bereits: Übersetzung und Deutung bleiben hier im Rahmen der ehrwürdigen Tradition. Aber sofort wendet sich sodann des Verfassers Scharfsinn der tatsächlich drängenden Frage zu: "How does the second sentence of the passage (= b22 ff.) support the first (b19–22)"? *Dass* ein Begründungsverhältnis vorliegt, ist durch γὰρ erwiesen; *wieso* eines vorliegt, ist tatsächlich eine grosse Frage. Ackrill hält zunächst zwei verschiedene Deutungen für möglich, und zwar jenachdem, ob man οὐ γὰρ oder οὐδὲ γὰρ lese.

Die *erstere* Deutung wäre danach die: Um die Behauptung, das isolierte Verbum bezeichne nicht, ob der mit dem Verbum (z.B. "läuft") ausgedrückte Umstand auch wirklich statthabe oder nicht, gegen den Einwand zu verteidigen, "läuft" bedeute doch so viel wie "*ist* laufend" (vgl. 12. 21b9–10; auch sonst öfters bei Aristoteles) und drücke somit doch ein *Statthaben* des Umstands aus – um jene Behauptung gegen genau diesen Einwand zu verteidigen, sage Aristoteles nun, dass jedes solche "ist," "ist nicht," "sein," "nicht sein," "seiend" u. dergl. unfähig sei, ein Statthaben von etwas zu bezeichnen, dass jeder solche Ausdruck vielmehr allein die Urteilssynthesis bezeichnen könne.

Nun, wir wissen aus dem Früheren, dass Ackrill diese erstere Deutungsmöglichkeit nicht geradezu erst erfinden musste. Und er tut recht, wenn er sie nicht für sich akzeptiert. Die *zweite* Deutungsmöglichkeit bindet der Verfasser an die Lesart οὐδὲ γὰρ; sie besagt, dass Aristoteles in dem Satz nicht mehr vom isolierten Verbum, sondern von etwas Neuem, nämlich vom alleinstehenden "ist," spreche, und dies tue, um von ihm zu sagen, dass auch es (nicht anders als etwa "läuft") kein Statthaben von etwas behaupte, was vielleicht jemand annehmen könnte (wenn er gerade das alleinstehende "ist" als existenzbezeichnend versteht). – Sodann stellt sich Ackrill die Frage, wie nun der *letzte* Teil des Abschnitts (b23–25) zu verstehen ist. Wiederum zwei Möglichkeiten (den obigen zugeordnet): Es kann einmal so sein, dass er das kopulative "ist" erläutern soll: das "ist" habe nur die Fähigkeit, die Urteilssynthesis zu bezeichnen. Es kann auch sein, dass das existentiale "ist" erläutert werden soll; dann bedeutet die Behauptung, es sei selbst nichts, lediglich dies, dass dieses "ist" genau so wie jedes andere Verbum von sich aus nichts behaupte, freilich etwas bezeichne und auch die Urteilssynthesis ausdrücke. Von ersterer Möglichkeit ist der Verfasser nicht recht überzeugt; zuletzt lässt er die Alternative überhaupt offen. –

Wenn wir die lange Interpretationsgeschichte überblicken, so können wir folgendes feststellen: Der Absatz wurde immer als schwierig empfunden, immer rang man um eine brauchbare Deutung, weil keine befriedigte; derartiges offen zuzugeben, ist freilich erst Sache unserer heutigen Denkweise. Mit der aristotelischen Behauptung in b23–24, dass das "ist" für sich selbst nichts sei, hat eigentlich nur Alexandros etwas rechtes anzufangen gewusst (Bericht des Ammonios); er brachte sie mit der Äquivozität des Terminus ὄν in Verbindung – mit Recht offenbar, wenn es auch genügt hätte, von Analogizität dieses mehrdeutigen Terminus zu sprechen. Pacius bedeutete in manchen Punkten einen merklichen Schritt vorwärts. Aber weder er noch jemand vor oder nach ihm hat daran gerüttelt, dass unser kritischer Satz b19–22 durchwegs vom isolierten Verbum ("läuft") handle und dass das letzte Stück dieses Satzes dies eine zum Ausdruck bringe, dass das isolierte Verbum nicht in der Lage sei, eine Wahrheitsdifferenz (*utrum verum sit an non*) zu bezeichnen.

An dieser ehrwürdig langen Einhelligkeit wollen wir im letzten Abschnitt nun gerade rütteln und dann zusehen, ob nicht anschliessend alle Dunkelheiten wegfallen.

*

Eine einzige kurze Klärung dürfte vor dem letzten Schritt noch wünschenswert sein. Was haben – laut *De Int.* – ῥῆμα und ἔστιν (εἶναι u. dergl.) eigentlich miteinander zu tun? Was bedeutet hier ῥῆμα genau? Insbesondere: Wie ist das Verhältnis zwischen diesem ῥῆμα-Begriff und dem allgemeinen urteilslogischen Prädikatsbegriff?

De Int. c. 10 belehrt uns, dass jedes Urteil (ob affirmativ oder negativ) etwas (= P) mit Bezug auf etwas (= S) zum Ausdruck bringt (σημαίνει τι κατά τινος) und folglich aus ὄνομα und ῥῆμα bzw. aus ἀόριστον ὄνομα und ῥῆμα besteht (19b5–12). In diesem Zusammenhang erfahren wir auch, dass das alleinstehende (d.h. existentiale) ἔστιν und γίγνεται ῥήματα sind, weil sie die (in c. 3)

angegebene Definition erfüllen, insbesondere Zeitverhältnisse
mitausdrücken (19b13–14). C. 3 selbst belehrt uns dahingehend,
dass jedenfalls solche Verbalausdrücke wie ὑγιαίνει, κάμνει als
ῥήματα zu gelten haben (die Limitativ-ῥήματα, die wir natürlich
nicht mit den in einem Urteil *negierten* ῥήματα verwechseln dürfen
[*non-valet* mit *non valet*] können wir für unsere Zwecke ausser
Acht lassen). Legen nun die Beispiele von c. 3 nahe, nur an das
verbale Prädikat (ὑγιαίνει) zu denken, so steht doch fest, dass wir
in Wahrheit nicht allein an dieses denken dürfen. Mindestens einmal sagt uns schon der bare Text, dass auch adjektivische Ausdrücke ῥήματα sind (λευκὸς als ῥῆμα in 10. 20b1–2; dasselbe sicher
erschliessbar aus 20a31 ff. und mindestens vermutbar aus 1.
16a13–15). Kein Zweifel, λευκὸς γὰρ Σωκράτης ist ein voller Satz
und λευκός ist sein Prädikatsausdruck.

Wie steht es schliesslich mit der Kopula? Befriedigende Auskunft gibt uns 10. 19b19 ff. Sie tritt als drittes Element (τρίτον;
b19) in den entsprechenden Sätzen auf (S ist P); sie ist ein
προσκατηγορούμενον (aus b19–20) und προσκείμενον (aus b25; 30);
obwohl drittes Element, *gehört sie zum Prädikatsnomen* (προσ-
κεῖται) – auch wenn sie selbst negiert ist (οὐκ ἔστιν), und auch
wenn das Prädikatsnomen (limitativ) negiert ist (οὐ δίκαιος)
(b24–30).

Resultat: Sehen wir von Existentialprädikaten wie ἔστιν oder
γίγνεται ab (weil sie unser Absatz aus c. 3 sicher nicht mitbe-
rücksichtigt), sehen wir weiterhin auch von der Problematik des
ἀόριστον ῥῆμα ab (die unser Absatz aus c. 3 nur im Hinblick auf
spätere Zwecke einführt) und halten wir uns zunächst nur an das
affirmative Urteil, so ergeben sich drei Urteils- und drei ῥῆμα-
Typen:

Σωκράτης ὑγιαίνει; Σωκράτης ὑγιής; Σωκράτης ὑγιής ἐστιν. Als
ῥῆμα-Typen also: ὑγιαίνει; ὑγιής; ὑγιής ἐστιν.

Damit stehen wir, endlich, vor der Auflösung der Schwierigkeiten, die uns der Absatz 3. 16b19 ff. macht. Aristoteles erwägt
das isolierte, für sich genommene, ῥῆμα (sei es ὑγιαίνει, ὑγιής,
ὑγιής ἐστιν) und sagt: Nimmt man die ῥήματα für sich, losgelöst
aus dem Urteilssatz, so sind sie ὀνόματα und haben (als solche
auch) jeweils eine bestimmte Sachbedeutung; treibt man jedoch
das Isolieren so weit, dass (bei einer Zerlegung etwa des Prädi-
kats ὑγιής ἐστιν) nur noch allein "ist" oder auch (im negativen

Urteilssatz) "ist nicht" dasteht, *so hat dieses Bruchstück überhaupt noch keine Sachbedeutung.*[8]

Und nun schliesst das folgende (b22–25) völlig logisch und völlig verstehbar an: "denn 'sein' oder auch 'nicht sein' ist kein Wort, das die Sache (den Gegenstand) bezeichnen würde" (d.h. es sagt überhaupt *nichts* von Sache und Gegenstand – was auch sollte das *esse copulae* davon sagen?) "und es bezeichnet auch keine Sache in der alleinstehenden Partizipform 'seiend.' Denn es selbst ist gar nichts, bezeichnet aber eine bestimmte Synthesis (nämlich die Urteilssynthesis von S und P), unter der sich freilich nichts denken lässt, solange man von ihren beiden Gliedern (S und P) absieht."

Es ist ganz klar: Von "sein," "nicht sein," "ist" und "ist nicht" ist nicht erst in b22 ff., sondern schon in unserem problematischen Satzstück b21–22 die Rede. Und klar ist auch, wie es dazu kommt. Einer der Schritte, die Aristoteles sowohl mit dem ὄνομα (in c. 2) wie mit dem ῥῆμα (in c. 3) macht, ist der einer Isolierung der Stücke, verbunden mit der Frage, ob das jeweils isolierte Stück noch Sachbedeutung haben kann (vgl. nochmals 2. 16a21–26). Dass nur ein *ganzer* Urteilssatz unter die Alternative wahr/falsch fallen kann, steht schon fest (vgl. 1. 16a12 ff.); dass selbst er nicht *bezeichnet*, ob das statthat oder nicht, was er aussagt, die Wahrheitsalternative (ἢ ἀληθεύει ἢ ψεύδεται) also zwar eröffnet, aber nicht selbst zu entscheiden vermag, sollten wir nicht vergessen; es wäre ganz sinnlos, wenn Aristoteles in unserem Satz 3. 16b19–22 nun gar für das isolierte Verbum feststellen wollte, dass es nicht Wahrheit oder Falschheit *bezeichne.* Hat also weder das isolierte ὄνομα noch das isolierte ῥῆμα eine Fähigkeit zur Wahrheitsdifferenz, so hat doch jedes von ihnen Sachbedeutung. Treibt man aber die Isolierung so weit, dass schliesslich vom ῥῆμα nur noch *die Kopula* ("ist"; "ist nicht") allein ins Auge gefasst ist, so fällt selbst die Sachbedeutung noch weg.

Ist die traditionelle Auffassung unseres problematischen Satzstücks nach der griechischen Grammatik möglich, so lässt die

---

[8] Nicht nur σημαντικός wird von Aristoteles gelegentlich absolut gebraucht (mehrmals in *De Int.*, z.B. 16a19; 20; b26; 31; 17a1), sondern auch σημαίνειν, so (neben unserer Stelle) ganz zweifellos in dem überhaupt vergleichenswerten Satz 16b32 f..

zutreffende Auffassung darüberhinaus auch eine nicht eben seltene Eigenart aristotelischer Ausdrucksweise zur Geltung kommen.

Nach Pedantenweise soll zu guter Letzt unser Satz 16b19–22 eine erläuternde Einfügung erhalten – und zwar erst deutsch, dann griechisch:

Isoliert (wenn z.B. nur gesagt wird "kränkelt," "kränkelt nicht," "weiss," "nicht weiss," "ist weiss" oder auch "ist nicht weiss") sind die Prädikatsausdrücke (lediglich) Sachwörter und haben (als solche) eine Sachbedeutung ... aber wenn (lediglich) "ist" oder "ist nicht" gesagt wird, so hat das noch keine Sachbedeutung; αὐτὰ μὲν οὖν καθ'αὑτὰ λεγόμενα (οἷον εἰ κάμνει ἢ μὴ κάμνει ἤτοι εἰ λευκὸς ἢ μὴ λευκὸς ἤτοι εἰ λευκός ἐστιν ἢ μή) τὰ ῥήματα ὀνόματα ἐστι καὶ σημαίνει τι, ... ἀλλ'εἰ ἔστιν ἢ μή, οὔπω σημαίνει.

Und *so* wäre unser Abschnitt eine in sich vernünftige und im sachlichen Zusammenhang des Textes sogar eine notwendige Feststellung des Aristoteles!

Hat mein Hammer den Nagel auf den Kopf getroffen, so sollen Hammer und Nagel fortab Philip Merlan gehören.

Bonn, z.Zt. Yale University

ON THE CHARACTER OF ARISTOTLE'S ETHICS

C. J. DE VOGEL

What was the actual basis – or, say, the ultimate norm – of Aristotle's ethics?

It must seem strange that such a question has still to be raised after generations of scholars have discussed the *Nicomachean Ethics* in centers of Aristotelian studies like that at Oxford; after a voluminous commentary on the *Ethics* has recently been published at Louvain;[1] after new German translations have appeared, of which one (the Dirlmeier translation published in Berlin[2]) is accompanied by an introduction and an extensive commentary; and after a whole volume has been dedicated at Princeton to the subject of Aristotle and the problem of value.[3] Yet for all of this, it still becomes necessary to inquire into the basic principles of Aristotle's moral philosophy and to ask what its real character is.

Certainly the comments which have been made in the last ten or twelve years give me reason to believe that my initial question needs to be considered anew. Dirlmeier suggested in 1956 that Aristotle leaves the modern reader remarkably uncertain about what the ultimate norm of Aristotelian ethics is.[4] In the Introduction and Summary to the first volume of his *History of Greek Philosophy*, W. K. C. Guthrie pointed to the momentous consequences which followed from the abandonment of Plato's transcendent forms by Aristotle: for Plato, questions of conduct were bound up with metaphysical knowledge of the transcendent

---

[1] R. A. Gauthier and J. Y. Jolif, *L'Ethique à Nicomaque*, Introduction, traduction et commentaire (3 vols.; Louvain, Paris, 1959).

[2] Aristoteles, *Nikomachische Ethik*, übersetzt von F. Dirlmeier (Berlin, 1956).

[3] W. J. Oates, *Aristotle and the Problem of Value* (Princeton, 1963).

[4] Dirlmeier, *op. cit.*, p. 246.

world of the ὄντως ὄν; for Aristotle, who denied the existence of such a transcendent reality, nothing but the contingent world remained. What else could happen but that moral virtue and rules of conduct came to lie entirely within this realm for him? [5]

It is precisely the aim of W. J. Oates' work, cited above, to establish that Aristotle, after rejecting the theory of the Ideas, was not able to give a metaphysical foundation to his ethics, and hence, never did construct a coherent and adequate theory of value. What we find when we analyze his works is that his attitude towards problems of value was shifting, that his ethics (which are dominated by the ultimate goal of *eudaemonia*) have essentially a subjective character, that his politics share much the same principles as the ethics, and that the rhetoric (though Aristotle did give it its legitimate place as a τέχνη) shows an amoral, and not seldom, an immoral character. Rather frequently Aristotle uses the opinions of the majority of men as a criterion of value. Purely conventional views are often accepted as a standard, and now and then things appear which, according to a Christian point of view, are absolutely abject and repulsive.

Now I am not going to defend Aristotle on these last mentioned points. It is true that there are some things in the *Ethics* itself which are far from edifying. Professor Oates is absolutely right, for example, when at the end of the picture of the μεγαλόψυχος he exclaims: "What a portrait this is, even down to the details of his deliberate motion, his deep voice, and level utterance!" This does give a somewhat peculiar view of Aristotle's value thinking in the realm of ethics. For after all, μεγαλοψυχία was for Aristotle "the crown of virtues."

Oates is perfectly right as well, when he draws our attention to Aristotle's statement in the *Politics*, that war is "a natural art of acquisition, for the art of acquisition includes hunting, an art which we ought to practice against wild beasts, and against men who, though intended by nature to be governed, will not submit; for war of such a kind is naturally just." [6] Aristotle's argument in favor of the view that it is justified, and even necessary, to

---

[5] W. K. C. Guthrie, *A History of Greek Philosophy* (Cambridge, 1962), I, pp. 13 ff.
[6] *Pol.* 1. 8. 1256b23–26; Oates, pp. 324 f.

kill the innocent children of your enemies,[7] does not escape Oates'
attention either. And who would wish to contradict him when
he says: "Perhaps we may be wrong to expect moral elevation in
a practical handbook on rhetoric, but it does not seem un-
reasonable to ask that Aristotle exhibit a little more ethical
sensitivity than he does in this passage."?

Another fully justified point against Aristotle is the way in
which he discriminates between men, women, children and slaves.
This Oates does not fail to notice, commenting on it with his
usual sober and reserved indignation.

As to the metaphysical background, Professor Oates is entirely
right when he observes that Aristotle's God, the Prime Mover,
as described in *Metaph.* Λ 7 and 9, cannot serve as a sanction of
moral values. In fact, it is quite true that the Prime Mover has
no direct relations whatsoever with our world or with human
affairs. The only effect He has – not as a deliberate action but,
as it were, in spite of Himself – is that He moves the outermost
heaven, a motion which is effected by some kind of attraction
which goes out from Him to that which is directly inferior to
Him. It cannot even be said that He indirectly causes all other
motion in the universe – that of the lower heavenly spheres,
each of them successively, and finally the motion in our world –
since everything and every kind of being ultimately desires the
ultimate Good, i.e., the supreme Being, the Prime Mover. To a
modern mind this might seem to be a satisfactory explanation,
one in accord with the spirit of Aristotle himself, who in fact
makes everything desire its ultimate good and can hardly be
supposed not to have admitted that the supreme Being is the
supreme Good. Yet, however acceptable this might seem, it is
not what Aristotle taught. It is even formally excluded by his
conception both of the unmoved Movers of the lower heavenly
spheres, and of the natural beings of our world. For every
unmoved Mover is a self-sufficient Being, having its "end"
within itself, and as such not able to strive after any other "end"
external to it. And likewise all natural things in our world have
their particular "end" within themselves, this being "the good"
after which they naturally strive. Once they have attained that

---

[7] *Rh.* 2. 21. 1395a17–18; Oates, p. 350.

end, they have reached their own perfection, so that it is contradictory to posit that they would still "strive" after some transcendent ἀγαθόν, beyond this world. Such an explanation – which has been proposed only too frequently, by several modern interpreters – would, in fact, involve *correcting* Aristotle, so as to make him support a unitary world order, which, in theory at least, he himself required, but which he was actually not able to conceive since he was kept from it by his own explicit principles.

In all this, then, I find myself in perfect agreement with the views and statements of Professor Oates. There is one side of Aristotle's physics (which we would rather call metaphysics), however, on which I think something must be added to his valuable work – something which might alter to some extent the whole picture of Aristotle's ethics. This is what I wish to explain.

I take the following observation as my starting-point: When a modern philosopher states that in one system of ethics or another there is a total lack of transcendent principles, this statement means to him and to his audience that the system of ethics referred to is built on merely contingent views or facts, which, as a matter of fact, cannot be admitted as "principles" at all. This is the way in which both Guthrie and Oates consider Aristotle's ethics. We might state the matter thus: as soon as the transcendent World of Forms has fallen away, nothing but contingent things is left.

But is this not saying too much – or rather, if we take it from the positive side, not saying enough? For is there not the thinking mind of man, the intellect or *noûs*, which Aristotle says is "the divine in us"? Well, then, could it not be that, once the transcendent World of Ideas has disappeared, a "humanistic" system of ethics comes into being, i.e., an ethics in which actually *it is man who creates the values*?

"C'est l'homme qui crée les valeurs." In our day, this is for J. P. Sartre the unavoidable consequence of the thesis of the non-existence of God: if God does not exist, he remarks very rightly, we cannot go on as if there were eternal values in an objective order, independent of our mind. Such values cannot exist. We are here, left to ourselves, and it is we ourselves who, by our individual act of thinking, create the notions of good and evil. *C'est l'homme qui crée les valeurs.*

Is this what happens in Aristotle's ethics?

Perhaps one feels inclined to reply that, in fact, in Aristotle's ethics the φρόνιμος, or even, more generally speaking, the σπουδαῖος does appear as a kind of norm, since he is able to determine what is "the mean between the extremes," which is virtue. And does that not actually say that it is man – not, of course, *any* man, but at least *the wise* man – who "creates" the values?

A desperate situation, indeed! Does it not seem like a circle: "virtue is needed in order to find out what virtue is"?

Of course, we cannot deny that, in a sense, man – viz. the wise man – functions as a norm in Aristotle's ethics. But the following point is basically much more important.

It is not the case that for Aristotle, since he had abandoned the theory of transcendent Ideas, nothing but contingent things and facts was left. Aristotle's view of Nature was different. To him, Nature was not "just what happens," which, as such, cannot provide us with anything like a norm. On the contrary, for him the processes of Nature are dominated by *intelligible principles*, which are primary and eternal. These principles, the "forms," are, so to speak, the higher aspect of Nature. They are *Nature as the Divine*: Nature which "creates nothing without a reasonable ground," or, "without a purpose." [8]

In the famous formula at the end of the fourth chapter of the *De caelo*, the words ὁ θεὸς καὶ ἡ φύσις do not denote two different beings: they are a kind of hendiadys, indicating one and the same being, viz. *Nature which is divine*. For to Aristotle, Nature in its higher aspect *is* the τέλος and the οὗ ἕνεκα. [9]

Now, two points have to be noted. First, that "God" in this sense has nothing, of course, to do with the Prime Mover. It is only the theist – either Christian or Muslim – who, as soon as the name of God is mentioned, is inclined to make the identification with the supreme Being which from his point of view can only be called by that name. For Aristotle it was not so, nor was it so for Plato. Both of them used to speak of "God and the Divine" on different levels. Plato, for instance, called the creator of the visible world, the Demiurge, who obviously was a transcendent

---

[8] *Cael.* I. 4. 271a34: ὁ δὲ θεὸς καὶ ἡ φύσις οὐδὲν μάτην ποιοῦσι.
[9] *Ph.* 2. 2. 194a28.

Noûs, "God"; but he also called the divine souls of the heavenly bodies, created by the Demiurge, "gods," and the World-soul that contained and permeated the visible world, the direct cause of its beautiful order, "god." Next, those souls of men who live on the level of philosophical insight were called "gods" by Plato more than once.[10] Furthermore, it would be a definite "theist's" error to think that "God," the Demiurge, who is the transcendent cause of the cosmic order, is to be identified as such with the supreme Principle of all, the Good. The Good is on a level beyond Noûs and Being.[11] Intelligible Being springs directly from it, and is on the level of transcendent Noûs, which in its turn creates the superior intellects of the heavenly bodies, the intellect of the visible world, and the intellects of men.

Such was the hierarchy of the Divine for Plato. Aristotle, too, knew such a hierarchy: under his Prime Mover he placed the series of 47 or 55 "Intellects" of the heavenly spheres, which he explicitly declared to be "gods."[12] Next, there is the noûs in man, which he repeatedly called "god" or "the Divine in us,"[13] definitely declaring that this part of us alone is immortal and "impassible" (ἀπαθής),[14] and takes its origin not in the world of man as a physical being but enters from without.[15]

The second point to be noticed is that for Aristotle Nature was by no means essentially the contingent which, as such, could not provide us with anything like a norm. On the contrary, for him Nature contained true "principles": πρῶτα καὶ αἴτια, viz. *the eternal and immutable forms* by which its processes are ruled and concrete things come to be the determined and qualified beings that they are.

Thus, for Aristotle *Nature did contain norms.* For by becoming that which is implied in its λόγος (its definition or intelligible form) each particular thing reaches its perfection. Plato and Aristotle define ἀρετή, in its most general sense, in such terms: the "virtue" (excellency) of a thing is that it fulfill its particular

[10] *Phd.* 82bc; cf. *Phdr.* 248a; *Tim.* 41c–42a.
[11] *Resp.* 6. 509b.
[12] *Metaph.* Λ 8. 1074a38–b10.
[13] *Protrept. frg.* 10c Ross; *Eth. Nic.* 10. 7. 1177b26–31; cf. 1178a2–4, *Metaph.* Λ 3. 1070a26–28.
[14] Besides the above-cited passages *De An.* 3. 5. 430a17–18, 22–25.
[15] *Gen. An.* 2. 3. 736b22–29.

function well, e.g., of the eyes, the function of seeing; of the ears, that of hearing.[16] A circle, says Aristotle, is then most perfect, when it realizes as perfectly as possible that which is implied in its definition.[17] Thus man possesses his particular virtue, when he realizes in the highest degree that which is his essence, which implies his proper function: his "essence" or "form" which is "a living being endowed with reason," his proper function which is that of thinking.[18]

It is an essential feature of man, too, that he is a *social* being (πολιτικὸν ζῷον).[19] Not every essential quality is expressed in the definition of a being; yet, it is *implied* in it, for it belongs to the essence itself. So it is with the aspect of man as πολιτικὸν ζῷον: his *social* character, we might say, is implied in his character as a *rational* being. That is to say, the thinking function of man is his first and dominating characteristic, and hence, rightly exercising this function is man's first and most particular virtue. But the social aspect is implied in it, and so the practice of the *social* virtues (justice, courage, self-control and many others, designated as "moral virtues" by Aristotle) does belong to man's essential being. Thus, here again we see that Nature *does* provide us with a norm.

All of this is obviously not new to those who are familiar with the works of Aristotle. It must, of course, be well-known to scholars such as Professors Guthrie and Oates. Yet, it happens that, when a man is strongly impressed by the tremendous loss of transcendent principles caused by the rejection of the theory of Ideas, it seems to him that, as a matter of fact, in this situation nothing but the contingent is left. And so when he expresses this view in this way, it may happen that he introduces his own view of nature – the modern view – instead of Aristotle's. Professor

---

[16] Pl. *Lach.* 190a ff.; *Resp.* 353b.

[17] Aristotle, *Ph.* 7. 3. 246a13–17.

[18] *Eth. Nic.* 1. 7. on the ἔργον τοῦ ἀνθρώπου, 1097b24–1098a18. On the definition of virtue as a *perfectio naturae* see also St. Augustine, *De libero arbitrio* 3. 13. 38; on the definition of the *bonum hominis* as *secundum rationem esse*: Thomas Aquinas, *S. Th.* II 1, qu. 71., Art. 2; C. J. De Vogel, *Greek Philosophy, A Collection of Texts*[2], selected and supplied with some notes and explanations III (Leiden, 1964), nr. 1003 with n. 1.

[19] *Pol.* 1. 2. 1253a2–4. a7–18.

Oates is perfectly right when he says (towards the end of his concluding chapter) "that a metaphysician would be well advised to keep always before him Being and Value as tightly conjoined." We must reply on behalf of Aristotle that he *did* keep these two conjoined in his theory of Nature.

I am not thinking at all at this point of such a passage as the beginning of *Metaph.* Λ 10, where Aristotle raises the question of whether the Nature of the Universe has the principle of its order dwelling in it, or as an external ἀγαθόν which transcends it; or perhaps both, as it is in an army, where "the good" is in the existing order, while at the same time there is the general who is the cause of the order.[20] Oates comments excellently on these and the following lines.[21] He is entirely right in observing that "sometimes" enthusiastic admirers of Aristotle "may make too much of the image"; for in fact, a theistic interpretation of the army simile does not square at all with Aristotle's concept of the Prime Mover; nor can the image of the house [22] contribute very much towards solving the problems that are left open in Aristotle's theology. Oates' criticism of Ross's interpretation of this passage in Aristotle is entirely justified. What might be added is, first, that in the image of the army Aristotle does not opt for the existence of a transcendental cause; he only suggests the possibility, and he seems to do so more or less by the way: he leaves the matter undecided. Secondly, if he had assumed a transcendent Cause of the order in this world at all, we should ask ourselves *where* in the framework of Aristotle's metaphysics such a Principle could have been placed. It is clear that its transcendence had to be that of the first degree in relation to our world. That is to say, it should have been a Noûs immediately superior to the earthly sphere, either inferior to the Unmoved Mover of the undermost sphere of the moon or identical with that lowest of Unmoved Movers.[23]

[20] *Metaph.* Λ 10. 1075a11–15.
[21] Oates, *op. cit.*, pp. 253–259.
[22] *Metaph.* Λ 10. 1075a19–23.
[23] I made a similar suggestion in my comments on the introductory chapters of *Metaph.* A, given as a contribution to the second Symposium Aristotelicum at Louvain, 1960, "La méthode d'Aristote en métaphysique d'àpres Métaphysique A 1–2," *Aristote et les Problèmes de Méthode* (Louvain, Paris, 1961), pp. 147–170, especially 162–164. In that paper I also dealt with the problem of the πρῶτα καὶ αἴτια indwelling in Nature.

Neither my remarks about Aristotle's view of Nature as containing first Principles, nor the attempt at a more precise explanation of what an assumed transcendent cause of the physical world-order might have been for Aristotle are meant to detract from the very valuable work of Oates. On the contrary, I wish to express my high esteem and my gratitude for this work, which is something more than a clear analysis of, and comment on, many interesting passages in Aristotle; it is a work of a noble spirit and of true philosophical insight. I enjoyed reading it.

Utrecht

ARISTOTLE'S DEFINITION OF SOUL

JOSEPH OWENS

I

On account of both its worth and its accuracy, Aristotle at the beginning of the *De Anima* (I. I. 402a1–7) ranks knowledge of soul among the topics that enjoy the highest priorities. He regards it as making great contribution towards the acquisition of truth in general, and in particular towards the philosophy of nature. Against this background he may be expected to show keen interest in working out a correct and penetrating definition of soul. According to the norms of his own logic, the nature of a thing as expressed in its definition is the starting point of every demonstration in scientific procedure;[1] and where, as in the present case, the subject is introduced as offering an especially high degree of accuracy, the enticement to spend sufficient time on the basic definition involved could hardly help but make itself felt.

The definition that Aristotle (I. I. 402a7–b26; 403a25–b13) requires, then, is clearly one that will make manifest the substantial nature of soul. This type of definition is contrasted with a mathematical definition and a metaphysical definition (403b14–16). Yet its function is thought out on the lines of the basic mathematical notions that make geometrical reasoning possible (402b16–25), even though the contribution made by prior

---

[1] "... in all demonstration a definition of the essence is required as a starting-point, so that definitions which do not enable us to discover the derived properties, or which fail to facilitate even a conjecture about them, must obviously, one and all, be dialectical and futile." *De An.* I. I. 402b25–403a2 (Oxford tr.). Cf. *An. Post.* I. 4. 73b26–74a3 for the geometrical model, the demonstration of the attribute of equality to two right angles for the angles of a triangle.

knowledge of the attributes is cautiously emphasized and the possibility of encountering metaphysical considerations is suggested. Further, Aristotle sounds a warning, necessary in his own day as well as in ours, against restricting the inquiry to "the human soul,"[2] since the scope of the investigation is much wider.

In accord with this project, the first book of the *De Anima* surveys the rich literature of preceding Greek thought about the nature of soul. It discusses the philosophical notions at considerable length, with mention (5. 410b28–30) of the Orphic religious traditions. The overall tendency of Greek tradition is found to interpret soul in terms of movement and sensation and knowledge, as though soul were somehow the source of these activities (2. 403b25–404b30). In that setting the following book in its two opening chapters (2. 1–2. 412a3 ff.) undertakes directly to elaborate a satisfactory definition. The aim expressly is "to give a precise answer to the question, What is soul? i.e. to formulate the most general possible definition of it."[3]

Returning to grass-roots considerations after the discussion of the preceding philosophical views, Aristotle notes (412a13–15) that of natural bodies some have life and some do not, and that by "life" people mean self-sustenance together with growth and wasting away. Explaining this in terms of his own philosophical notions, he shows that a living body is to be located in the category of substance as a composite of matter and form. Form is entelechy, and this has two senses, illustrated by the relation to each other of knowledge and thinking.[4] The first conclusion

---

[2] *De An.* 1. 1. 402b3–5. The expression "human soul" is used also at *Pol.* 3. 15. 1286a19. "Nutritive soul," "sensitive soul," and "intellective soul" occur more frequently; see Hermann Bonitz, *Index Aristotelicus*[2] (Berlin, 1870), 865a3–35.

[3] *De An.* 2. 1. 412a4–6 (Oxford tr.). The role of definition, accordingly, is to express the essence – in this case what soul in general is.

[4] *De An.* 2. 1. 412a9–11; cf. a22–26. Cf. "change from not-working to working" at 4. 416b2–3 (Oxford tr.). The notion of "actuality" (ἐνέργεια) in this context seems to imply operation, in such a way that something can be an entelechy without "actualizing" itself. Accordingly it is safer here to use the word "entelechy" or "perfection" to translate *entelecheia*, and to leave "actuality" for rendering "*energeia*," even though elsewhere the two words may be found used interchangeably as noted by George A. Blair, "The Meaning of 'Energeia' and 'Entelecheia' in Aristotle," *International Philosophical Quarterly*, 7 (1967), pp. 101–117. See especially the reference on p. 102, n. 4. At *De An.* 2. 2. 414a8–10, in a context in

drawn is that such a composite living body cannot be soul. The reason is that a body is not an attribute, but functions rather as subject and matter. The second conclusion follows immediately. The soul has to be substance in the sense of the form of a natural body that potentially has life (412a16–21). In this way the first formulation of the definition of soul is reached. The notion "natural body" is later (412b11–17; cf. *Ph.* 2. 1. 193b3–12) contrasted with artifact, and not with geometrical solid, in this context. Since form is entelechy, the second version of the definition presents soul as the "entelechy of the kind of body just described" (412a21–22).

What is to be thought of this reasoning? The attributes in question are apparently those of "living" and "non-living," as they bring about the basic distinction just mentioned between the two kinds of bodies. "Life" seems regarded as the distinguishing attribute that has to be explained, and, in the light of the philosophic discussions already surveyed, it has to be explained by soul. Soul, then, will not be the body, since body can also be characterized by the attribute of "non-living," and accordingly can exist without the requirement of soul. Rather, soul will have to be the feature that characterizes a living body in the category of substance.[5] This will make it formal in nature, and locate it in the category as form in contrast to matter. Aristotle's reasoning, though elliptic, is cogent enough. The obvious objection is that it uses logical distinctions to attain the real distinction between form and matter. "Body" is already a genus with its own identifiable characteristics, unlike matter that in itself has no distinguishable traits.[6] The further differentiae "living" and "non-living" cannot be regarded as really distinct from "body" in the way form is distinct from matter. Yet here Aristotle passes lightly from the order of logic to the

which knowledge and health are viewed as the actuality of an efficient cause (a11–12), the qualification "and, as it were, an actuality of the recipient" is used.

[5] Both generic and specific traits signify the *kind* of substance, and to that extent are qualitative within the category of substance. See *Cat.* 5. 3b18–21.

[6] A discussion of this topic may be found in my paper, "Matter and Predication in Aristotle," in *The Concept of Matter*, ed. Ernan McMullin (Notre Dame, Ind., 1963), pp. 99–113.

order of reality. He seems to feel no inconvenience in this process. In the *Metaphysics*[7] the ultimate differentia is what best expresses the form in a definition. Here the differentia is "life." If "life" is the feature that entails soul in the bodily substance, why should it not be used in the foregoing way to show that soul has to be the formal element in the living substantial composite?

In Aristotelian procedure, then, there seems to be no strenuous objection to this way of passing from the differentia "life" to the real soul. It does, however, require further explanation of the relation between soul and life, and Aristotle at once obliges. Since entelechy or perfection has two senses, comparable respectively to knowledge and thinking, he explains that soul is entelechy in the way in which knowledge is a perfection even when no thinking is being done. The reason is that soul is present in both sleeping and waking. Accordingly the waking state may be compared to thinking, while sleep is like having knowledge without actualizing[8] it. In the same individual the process is from knowledge that is first there, and then exercised. This prior status of knowledge from the viewpoint of process results in a further amelioration of the definition. The third formulation is that soul is the first entelechy of a natural body potentially having life (412a22–28).

The only addition made has been the insertion of "first" before "entelechy." The explanation is clear enough if the illustration is kept within its Aristotelian setting. The difference between sleeping and waking in regard to the possession and exercise of knowledge shows how one can have a perfection without actually exercising it. So one can have the perfection that constitutes a living body without actually performing the vital operations for which one is thereby equipped. Since from this viewpoint having is prior to actualizing, soul has to be defined as the first entelechy. In the illustration two dangers are to be avoided. One would be to press the illustration of "sleep" to the point where it would have to mean no activity at all. This would be impossible, since sleep is a vital activity in its very

[7] Z 12. 1038a19–26. The ultimate differentia is regarded as containing all the other differentiae, just as "two-footed" contains "endowed with feet" (a32–33).
[8] See *supra*, n. 4.

nature. The analogy resides merely in the role of sleep as impeding the exercise of thought, in contrast to the actualizing of thought that takes place in the waking state. For Aristotle anyone who has knowledge exercises it in actual thinking, unless something is impeding this exercise.[9] Similarly, the second danger would be to regard the activity as a really distinct actuality superadded in the manner of a Scholastic "second actuality."[10] The latter expression is not used by Aristotle. His use of "first" in this respect is explained solely in terms of the priority of having to exercising in a knowing process that takes place in the one and the same individual.

Finally, the kind of body that potentially has life is shown to be organic body. The fourth version of the definition, consequently, is that every soul is the first entelechy of a natural organic body (412b1–6).

A few concluding and enlightening observations are added. The composition of matter with form is such that the unity is found dominantly in the form in a way that renders superfluous any question about the composite's unity.[11] Accordingly a body apart from soul does not qualify as a potentially living body. A dead body is not the subject of which Aristotle has been speaking. He has been speaking throughout of a living body, and distinguishing in it the first entelechy that plays a role analogous to sleep in respect of a waking state. Yet the possibility that parts of the soul, on the other hand, may have separate existence looms large.[12] Even the question of a relation of soul to body in the manner of sailor to ship is raised in this context.[13] But in

---

[9] *Ph.* 8. 4. 255b3–4; b21–23.

[10] E.g., *"actus autem secundus est operatio,"* Aquinas, *ST.* 1. 48. 5c. However, Aquinas uses *"perfectiones secundae"* to mean acquired or infused habits, such as virtues. See *In I Sent.*, d. 39, q. 2, a. 2, ad 4m (ed. Mandonnet, 1. 934–935). But in both uses really distinct accidents are meant, as superadded entities in contrast to the first actuality or the first perfection. Aquinas' existential approach requires new being for a previously non-existent operation.

[11] *De An.* 2. 1. 412b6–9. Cf. *Metaph.* H 6. 1045a7–b24.

[12] *De An.* 2. 1. 413a5–7. Cf. 2. 413a31–32; b24–27.

[13] *De An.* 2. 1. 413a8–9. In 3. 5. 430a12–15, an intellect that seems to act as an efficient cause is introduced. But the theme is not developed. Alexander, *In De An.*, ed. I. Bruns (Berlin, 1897), pp. 15, 9–26 and 20, 26–21, 12, rejects the notion of soul as pilot. Themistius, *In De An.*, ed. R. Heinze (Berlin, 1899), p. 43, 27–30, sees, however, the separate

130   *Joseph Owens*

regard to the notion of "potentially living body" or "organic body," the text leaves no doubt that it means a composite already endowed with form as first entelechy, yet considered on the generic level on which "body" does not express the differentiae of "living" and "non-living." The addition of the differentia "non-living," as in "dead body," would disqualify the body from having a place in the definition of soul.[14]

The chapter ends by offering the formula now reached as "sketching a rough model"[15] for the further and exact elaboration of the soul's definition.

II

In what way is the elaboration of the definition to take place? Not only the fact (τὸ ὅτι) but also the cause (τὴν αἰτίαν), Aristotle suggests at the beginning of the second chapter (*De An.* 2. 2. 413a13–16), should be present and manifest in the definition. A mathematical instance is used to illustrate the point. The squaring of a rectangle could be defined as the construction of

intellect in the comparison of pilot with ship. Philoponus, *In De An.*, ed. M. Hayduck (Berlin, 1897), p. 225, 29, allows it to be understood in the same way regarding "parts of the soul" in the plural, the "parts" being the intellective powers (p. 225, 31; cf. p. 227, 29–32). For Simplicius, *In De An.*, ed. M. Hayduck (Berlin, 1882), p. 95, 26–27, the "parts" are the theoretical and practical powers. A discussion may be found in R. D. Hicks, *Aristotle, De Anima* (Cambridge, 1907), pp. 319–321.

[14] *De An.* 2. 1. 412b25–26. In this respect organic compounds synthesized in a laboratory, at least as at present understood, would not meet Aristotle's description of "organic body." On the tenet that what is potentially something is the material that is immediately disposed for it, as brass for a statue and wood for a casket, see *Metaph.* Θ 7. 1049a8–24.

[15] *De An.* 2. 1. 413a9–10. "Sketch" is from painting, "rough model" from sculpture. On the mixed metaphor, see J. A. Stewart, *Notes on the Nicomachean Ethics* (Oxford, 1892), I, p. 17. A longer discussion of the situation may be found in H. Cassirer, *Aristoteles' Schrift "Von der Seele"* (Tübingen, 1932), pp. 21–47. The project implied seems to be the working out of the definition from the dull, lifeless, inexpressive stage of the clay model to the vigor and verve that was wrought into the finished marble by the Greek sculptors, and that has been eulogized in Macauley's lines:
The stone that breathes and struggles,
The brass that seems to speak; –
Such cunning they who dwell on high
Have given unto the Greek (*The Prophecy of Capys*, 28).

an equilateral triangle equal in space to the oblong figure.[16] That would state the conclusion of the geometrical process. Or it could be defined as the finding of the mean proportional that is the line upon which the square is to be constructed. In that case the definition exhibits the cause (τὸ αἴτιον) of the object in question (413a16–20).

What logical framework is being invoked here? It seems unmistakably that of the *Posterior Analytics* (1. 13. 78a22 ff.). There the distinction is established between an intellectual process that establishes a fact (τὸ ὅτι) and one that makes apparent the immediate cause of the fact (τὸ διότι). For scientific knowledge and demonstration a conclusion can be established in different ways. One way is through the thing's immediate cause, the cause that may be called the *first* cause in the sense of the immediately proximate cause. In this case there is no intermediate factor whose absence could prevent the issuing of the effect from the cause. Effect and cause are here reciprocal. To posit the one is to posit the other. What is given is therefore *the* reason why, in the sense in which the Oxford translation finds itself obliged to insert an adjective and render "*the* cause" (τὸ αἴτιον – 78b15) as "the strict cause."[17] The illustrations given are nearness as the reason why the planets do not twinkle, and spherical figure as the reason why the moon waxes (78a40–b7). In this context *the* cause in the *De Anima* (2. 2. 413a20; cf. a15) text, used in explicit contrast to the *fact* (τὸ ὅτι), can hardly mean anything else than what the Oxford translation renders as "the strict cause" (*An. Post.* 1. 13. 78b15) in the sense of *the* reason why (τὸ διότι) of the *Analytics*.

---

[16] See Euclid 6. 13; cf. 2. 14. Euclid need not be put back far enough in the century to allow Aristotle to have read his work. The common heritage of Greek mathematics would suffice for the use of this example.

[17] The remote cause is nonetheless named a "cause" (*An. Post.* 1. 13. 78b24; b28–29) in this context. The neuter and feminine forms of "cause" in the Greek are used interchangeably, in accord with the gender of the noun to which they refer; see 78b17. On the requirement that the "strict cause" fit exactly, cf. "On the other hand, any isoceles triangle has its angles equal to two right angles, yet isoceles triangle is not the primary subject of this attribute but triangle is prior." *An. Post.* 1. 4. 73b38–39 (Oxford tr.). For a discussion of the *De Anima* framework in terms of ὅτι versus διότι, see Philoponus, *In De An.*, p. 225, 37–227, 26; F. A. Trendelenburg, *Aristotelis De Anima*[2] (Berlin, 1877), pp. 276–279.

As regards the contrasted knowledge of the fact, the *Analytics* gives two ways in which such knowledge may be had. A conclusion may be demonstrated on the strength of an effect. For instance, planets may be shown to be near because they do not twinkle, and the moon to be spherical because it waxes. Though the effect and the cause reciprocally involve each other, as in these examples, the demonstration now is through the effect, not through the cause. Here the effect is better known to *us*, and can therefore serve as a starting point for the reasoning process.[18] Once one knows on other grounds (78a33–35) that great distance from the observer causes the phenomenon of twinkling, the failure to twinkle gives *a* reason why the planets must be close. It is *a* reason for the conclusion, but not the full-fledged reason in the sense of providing the exactly fitting cause for the relative nearness of the planets. Unlike the first type, namely through "the strict cause," this second method of demonstrating is not restricted to cases where cause and effect are reciprocal (78b11–13). Any effect indicates in some way its cause, one may add to complete the picture, and the occurrence of an effect may well imply a number of remote causes besides the immediate cause.

The other way in which knowledge of the fact may be had is by demonstration through a remote cause (78b29). The example given is that a wall does not breathe because it is not an animal, with illustration by the claim that the Scythians have no flute-players because they have no vines. This way demonstrates a negative conclusion cogently enough. It gives *a* reason, and a convincing reason. But it does not give *the* reason, in the sense of "the strict cause." To be an animal does not immediately require ability to breathe. To be an animal and to breathe do not reciprocally entail each other, in the way "the strict cause" reciprocally entails its effect. A kind of cause (78b23–24; b28) is given, but not the "strict" or exactly fitting cause that would unavoidably give rise to the effect.

What bearing do these directives from the *Analytics* have upon the problem faced by the *De Anima* in elaborating the definition of soul? "Potentially living body," or "organic body"

[18] *An. Post.* I. 13. 78b12–13. Cf. *De An.* 2. 2. 413a11–13; *Ph.* I. 1. 184a10–23; *Metaph.* Z 4. 1029b3–8.

would be the effect of which soul is the formal cause. Further, form in general would have the role only of a remote cause, since it is a cause of both living and non-living bodies, and not immediately determined to either. What is required to make it *the* cause of a living body, in the sense of "the strict cause," is a differentia that would restrict it to living bodies. The differentia is not to be explained merely by relating the general notion of form to "living body," for in that case the explanation would be through the effect, and not genuinely in terms of cause. Just as the notion of form in general comes directly from the intelligible content met with in things, so a notion of "vital form," as differentiated from non-vital form, will have to be isolated as something immediately intelligible in the data that confront human cognition. Nothing less will satisfy the norms of "the strict cause" indicated by the background of the *Analytics* to which the reference here seems unavoidable.

In the mathematical illustration, the construction of the square would be the effect or conclusion. "Line" in general would be a remote cause for the construction, while the line that is the mean proportional would as a parameter be the "strict" or exactly fitting cause. The parallel is exact, and there is no doubt that the procedure works in the mathematical realm. But can it do so in the case of the soul? At least, the attempt can be made.

III

The formulation reached in the first chapter of *De Anima* 2 (412b5–6), then, will have to be elaborated in a way that will change it from a definition given in terms of the fact to one given in terms of "the strict cause." How is this to be accomplished? The wording "first entelechy of a natural organic body" gives a remote cause, "entelechy," that can exercise the role of formal cause in regard to both living and non-living bodies. To restrict it to the notion of "soul," the effect "organic body" is inserted into the definition. The definition, accordingly, makes plain the fact without giving the immediate cause. In order to formulate the definition in terms of immediate cause, the formal aspect that differentiates the form of an organic body from the form of an inorganic body will have to be brought to light. In a word, the differentia of organic body has to be isolated solely in terms of formal aspect, and not in terms of the composite living body that is its characteristic effect.

The procedure indicated, consequently, is a closer look at the notion of "living," to see if just in itself it makes manifest a formal differentia. A return to the starting point recalls that what has soul is distinguished from what has not by the characteristic of living. Living, however, is spread through various senses, in mind, sensation, local movement and rest, and in the nutritional processes and growth and wasting away. Nutrition is obviously basic for all these instances of life. Sensation characterizes animal life, with touch the fundamental sense. Where local motion follows, there will be imagination, appetite, pleasure, and pain (413a20–b24).

When intellection is scrutinized, however, it gives rise to a difficulty that at first sight seems to keep bothering Aristotle unduly.[19] Intellection conjures up the problem of its own separate existence (413b13–16; b26–27), a problem that Aristotle had in mind at the end of the preceding chapter (1. 413a6–7). Intellectual activity seems to indicate "a widely different kind of soul, differing as what is eternal from what is perishable."[20] At least, it would imply a part (2. 413b13–14; b27–28) of the soul that has this characteristic. Nevertheless the unity of the soul is not for a moment called into question. As the form of the living body the soul is the origin (ἀρχή) of all the vital activities just mentioned (b11–13), fully in accord with the tenet of the *Physics* (2. 1. 192b13–193b5) that the form is the active principle (ἀρχή) of motion in all natural bodies. Further, these "parts" or capacities of soul are distinguished from one another on the basis of the differences between their immediately known

---

[19] See *supra*, n. 12. The problem is faced in *De An*. 3. 5. 430a10–25, but without satisfactory solution, and has caused unending difficulty in the Aristotelian tradition.

[20] *De An*. 2. 2. 413b26–27 (Oxford tr.). This way of speaking lends color to the charge by Plotinus, *En*. 4. 7. 8[5]. 15–16, that the Peripatetics are forced to introduce another soul or mind to enable a man to think, since the first soul enabled him only to have a living body.

activities.[21] This general principle is of prime importance for the interpretation of the whole chapter.

Life, the survey shows, is at its minimum the vegetative. Upon the vegetative follows the sensitive, and then the intellective. With "life" in its minimum sense used to denote the vegetative activity, the distinguishing characteristic of soul may now, on the basis of vital operations immediately known, be expressed as "that whereby we live and perceive" (414a4) and also as "that whereby we know" (a5). All reference to the effect, namely the living body or organic body, has been eliminated from this formulation. The characterization is given solely in terms of reflexively or internally known activities. In the source whose specific character is reached through knowledge of these activities, Aristotle's concern for the moment is to distinguish two grades. Just as "that whereby we know" may mean either knowledge (a quality) or soul, so "that whereby we live and perceive" may have the two corresponding senses. As a parallel, "that by which we are healthy" is health on the one hand and body on the other. Knowledge and health are viewed in this respect as form and, as it were, actuality of the two different recipients, a recipient capable of knowing and a recipient capable of being healthy.[22] Since soul, then, is that "by or with which primarily we live, perceive, and think "(414a12–13; Oxford tr.), the conclusion is that it has to be form, and not matter or subject (414a14).

But is this conclusion justified by its immediate premises? And what is the exact force of the emphatically placed "primarily" in the context? True, the conclusion that soul is form coincides with its function as primary entelechy in the preceding chapter (1. 412a19–21). Moreover, the passage goes on (414a16–27) to show that soul requires a body specifically adapted to it, an appropriate kind of matter.[23] The burden of the discussion,

---

21 *De An.* 2. 2. 413b29–31. Cf. 4. 415a16–22, where the order of this knowledge is shown to be from objects to functions to faculties.

22 *De An.* 2. 2. 414a7–10. The ᾧ of the traditional text at a7, though bracketed by Hett and Ross after Bywater, is retained by G. Rodier, *Aristote, Traité de l'Ame* (Paris, 1900), and P. Siwek, *Aristoteles, Tractatus de Anima* (Rome, 1965). On the question, see R. D. Hicks, *Aristotle, De Anima* (Cambridge, 1907), p. 328.

23 On this notion, see *supra*, n. 14.

then, tends towards explaining the kind of body in terms of the
formal element, rather than explaining soul in terms of the composite effect, the living body. If this is what has been accomplished, will not the new elaboration of the definition of soul meet
the requirement of exhibiting "the strict cause," as envisaged
at the beginning of the present chapter?[24] To this extent the
conclusion would seem to fit neatly enough into the overall
framework of the chapter. Yet if in the immediate parallel the
recipient is body, and the form received is health, should not soul
as the recipient[25] of knowledge and in general of life appear
rather in the role of a quasi-matter on the strength of this
reasoning, as Sir David Ross suggests?[26] Should not soul function as the subject that receives the qualities of knowledge and
life? Yet from the premises Aristotle draws the opposite conclusion. The soul, by which we *primarily* live and perceive and
know is not matter or subject, but form. In this respect it would
seem to have the same function as that of first entelechy in the
preceding chapter.

· Certainly there is a difficulty here. To illustrate the notion
of first entelechy in the opening chapter, Aristotle had contrasted knowledge with thinking, and in that framework had
explained soul as first entelechy after the model of knowledge

[24] *De An.* 2. 2. 413a15. Cf. *supra*, n. 17.
[25] *De An.* 2. 2. 414a10. The same Greek term for "recipient" is used in
a context in which the soul may remain impassive while receiving a form
in cognition: "The thinking part of the soul must therefore be, while
impassible, capable of receiving the form of an object; that is, must be
potentially identical in character with its object without being the object."
De An. 3. 4. 429a15–16 (Oxford tr.). The notion of "recipient," accordingly, should not be too facilely identified with that of "matter" or of
"subject" in this context. The traditional Scholastic explanation of
cognition, in fact, was that the things known were received by the faculty
immaterially and *objectively*, in contrast to materially and subjectively,
and therefore were received as forms into form, and not as forms into
matter. See Josef Gredt, *Elementa Philosophiae Aristotelico-Thomisticae*[7]
(Freiburg i. Breisgau, 1937), I, pp. 356–360. At the same time there is the
other sense (*De An.* 3. 5. 430a10–24) in which intellect is passive and like
matter.
[26] *Aristotle, De Anima* (Oxford, 1961), p. 220. Ross correctly states that
Aristotle's "real way out" is to class soul as a first entelechy. This con-
trasts it with "matter," but not necessarily with "recipient," in accord
with what has been said in the preceding note. Ross, however, considers
that "first entelechy" would contrast it with "recipient" as well as with
"matter."

(1. 412a22–28). Now, however, knowledge is contrasted with soul (2. 414a5–6) as form with recipient. But is there anything impossible in this shift in the role of knowledge for the two different illustrations? As a learner a man can be in potentiality to knowledge, and after he has learned, he can still be in potentiality to thinking, as the *Physics* (8. 4. 255a33–35) asserts. May not knowledge, accordingly, be used on the two different occasions respectively to illustrate the soul's relation to its activities and to elucidate the formal element in the knowing subject? Can it not first, in the opening chapter, illustrate the function of soul as basic entelechy in contrast to subsequent vital operations? From that viewpoint soul as primary entelechy informs matter within the category of substance. Secondly, may not knowledge in its role of a qualitative form received by the knowing subject aptly clarify the more basic but less known formal principle of the substance in which it inheres? In this way knowledge as an illustration focuses attention on the function of soul as the basic *formal* capacity for living, perceiving, and knowing – a formal character that can be grasped through the regular way of object, activity, and faculty. In the present perspective is not knowledge as a qualitative form geared to explain the formal side of its recipient substance, and consequently to establish soul as a form, and not as matter or subject in the first of the categories?

How, in fact, could this other substantial principle, matter, be ranged for Aristotle under "that by which we know," since for him matter is unknowable in itself and an impediment to cognition? Rather, just as knowing requires knowledge as a formal principle on the qualitative level, so on the substantial level it requires a corresponding formal principle, a principle that has to be contrasted with matter. The conclusion indicated by the framework, then, is that in accord with the illustration, soul is the *form* by which basically we live and perceive and think, and not the matter or ultimate subject. As in the opening chapter, soul still appears as the primary entelechy, the entelechy in the category of substance. The backward reference ("as we said," 414a15) in giving the reason why soul is form throws the discussion squarely into the context of the preceding chapter where form in a twofold sense of entelechy was contrasted with matter (1. 412a6–11). The result, accordingly, is that while knowledge as a form and, as it were, an actuality is received in the knowing subject, the soul even as a component of the recipient is similarly an object with intelligible content (*logos*, 414a9) and a form.

Is not that precisely the conclusion one would expect from the illustration through knowledge in the two contexts? The abrupt change from one role of knowledge (potentiality for thinking, as at *Ph.* 8. 4. 255a34) to the other (entelechy of a recipient) is confusing, but is it not possible enough against the background of Aristotle's double relation of knowledge, in the one case to thinking, in the other to the knowing substance? Even though Aristotle in the preceding chapter ranged knowledge with having and not actualizing (1. 412a22–26), he seems to balance this out now (2. 414a9–10) by recalling in a parenthesis that knowledge is "as it were an actuality," since the actuality of an efficient cause is in the passum. Learning and health, in fact, are elsewhere (*Ph.* 3. 1. 201a18; 3. 202a32–b22; *Metaph.* Θ 7. 1049a3–8; K 9. 1065b19) viewed as actualities produced by efficient causes. The subsequent actuality that is the activity of thinking takes place therefore through knowledge and through soul, both of which are forms. Correspondingly, we perform the other vital operations through the informing qualities and soul. Does not the situation itself, then, call for the stated result clause: "it follows that soul must be a ratio or formulable essence, not a matter or subject"?[27]

---

[27] *De An.* 2. 2. 414a13–14 (Oxford tr.). Cf. "the body is the subject or matter" at 1. 412a18–19. I had completed this paper before reading the illuminating article of Rosamond Kent Sprague, "Aristotle *De Anima* 414a4–14," *Phoenix* 21 (1967), pp. 102–107. Mrs. Sprague's norm for interpreting Aristotle here seems unquestionable, that it is "*prima facie* unlikely that he would prepare the way by means of illustrations implying the opposite of what he intended to say" (p. 102). However, looking forward to lines a14–28, can one really have "no doubt that Aristotle would have completed the scheme" (p. 103) in a way that would parallel soul with the context's acceptance of knowledge and health (p. 104)? This inference seems to presume that "recipient" has to be equated with "matter" or "body". But in establishing the emphatic position of πρώτως (*in the most primary sense* (p. 104), and its backward reference to the definition worked out in the preceding chapter ("that the soul is actuality," p. 106), and in exploring the Platonic background, Mrs. Sprague's study is an exceptionally welcome contribution to the understanding of this difficult problem.

The reason why soul cannot be matter or subject is immediately introduced with the conjunction γάρ (414a14). As an entelechy the soul has been already established as form, and therefore can be neither matter nor body. In this way it is something of the body, in the sense of the form of a body. But as the basic form it cannot be fitted to an already constituted body. Rather, it itself determines the appropriate kind of body or matter.[28] From all this, Aristotle asserts, it is *clear* that soul is an entelechy of that which has the potentiality to be of this kind (414b14–28). "Of this kind" seems to mean the special type of body that is specified by soul, as at a22, in the context in which the kind of body is determined by the form, here the soul. But the differentia that makes manifest the specific type of form has now been explained on the basis of the formal notions of life, sensation, and knowledge.[29] The specification is given entirely in formal

Against Ross and Sprague, T. M. Robinson, in an as yet unpublished paper "Soul and Definitional Priority: *De An.* 414a4–14," suggests that "primarily" at 414a13 may have no particular reference to the sense involved in the expression "first entelechy." After examining the various senses of priority in Aristotle, Robinson finds abundant signposts that "priority from the point of view of strict definition" fits the situation. Since the object of definition is form, the (ontological) conclusion is allowed that soul be a form. This interpretation keeps the relation of soul to knowledge at 414a5–6 from looking "like an odd man out," but it involves Aristotle in the witting or unwitting "exploitation of the ambiguity between ontological and definitional priority" embedded in the notion "primarily." For the bearing on my own interpretation, see *infra*, n. 30.

Greek commentators tend to understand "primarily" here as applying to form in relation to the secondary role played by matter in the constitution of the physical thing. See Alexander, p. 31, 10–22; Philoponus, p. 245, 28–32; Sophonias, *In De An.*, ed. M. Hayduck (Berlin, 1883), p. 50, 11–12.

[28] *De An.* 2. 2. 414a17–27. On the notion "appropriate matter," see *supra*, n. 14. On the difficulty in placing matter under the notion "that by which we live," see Simplicius, p. 104, 3–13. On the general progress made in the definition, see Rodier, *op. cit.*, II, p. 208, *ad* 414a18.

[29] Hicks, *op. cit.*, p. 331, sees a "logical flaw" in this formulation. Just as "such as we have described" (p. 312) at *De An.* 2. 1. 412a21, meant "a natural body potentially having life," so, Hicks maintains, the Greek term should have the same reference at 2. 414a28. But this seems to take for granted that no progress has been made in the elaboration of the definition throughout chapter two of the second book. If "such as we have described" now means the potential or material component required by the formal principle through which we primarily live and perceive and think, the description has taken place in terms of notions

terms, and no longer in terms of the relation of form in general to an already constituted living body.

If this is admitted, the structure of the second chapter of *De Anima* 2 becomes intelligible. A definition through "the strict cause," as outlined in the *Analytics*, is envisaged and allegedly reached. The burden of the chapter is to show that as a special kind of body, "living body" is determined by its first entelechy and is not made "living" by the insertion of a soul into the already constituted body. The notions of life, as made known through nutrition and growth, and of sensation and intellection, are therefore the determining notes of the definition. But these notions more obviously belong to the categories of quality or action and passion. They have to be read back into the category of substance. Hence arises the use of the illustration of soul in contrast to knowledge and body in contrast to health, with the preoccupation of throwing the considerations into the category of substance (414a15) as described earlier (1. 412a6–21) in working out the initial definition of soul as first entelechy. This preoccupation would amply justify the use of "primarily" in the emphatic position in the formulation "with which primarily we live, perceive, and think" (414a12–13).

A suggestion that the "primarily" refers to the order in which the two alternatives are mentioned seems entirely untenable. In the twofold sense of entelechy illustrated in the first chapter (412a10; a22), the soul does come under the first-mentioned sense. But in the illustration in the second chapter, soul is expressly contrasted with the first-mentioned sense of vital principle, now illustrated by knowledge (414a5–6); and the contrast seems continued by the repetition of the same particles μέν with knowledge and δέ with soul at lines a8 and a12. Here soul is unmistakably kept in the second-mentioned of the two senses.

grasped reflexively in internal experience, and not through externally observed living bodies. Instead of "that which has the capacity to be endowed with soul" (Hicks, p. 59), the notion referred to would be "the type required by the primary capacity to vegetate, perceive, and think," insofar as each of these activities is a specific instantiation of the general notion of life.

Another suggestion is that the "primarily" means "prior from the point of view of definitional precision,"[30] in the sense that life and sensation and knowledge are the formal characteristics of which soul is the strictly appropriate recipient. This suggestion is attractive. It focuses sharply on the requirement of defining soul in terms of the exactly fitting differentia. But it seems hard to accommodate with the immediately following explanation (a14–28) that the soul is form in the sense of one of the elements in the category of substance. For the same reason it is difficult to understand the "primarily" as implying "the first cause" in the sense of the immediate or "strict" cause in the *Posterior Analytics* (1. 13. 78a25), even though this might be suggested by the aims of the present article. Aristotle does not use this characteristic of "first" in outlining the framework of "the fact" and "the cause" at the beginning of *De Anima* 2. 2. A reference to it as used in the *Analytics* would seem farfetched. A reference to the "first entelechy" of *De Anima* 2. 1, on the other hand, seems entirely normal.

IV

But with this overall interpretation of the chapter granted, does Aristotle's reasoning actually achieve a definition in terms of "the strict cause" of the *Analytics*? An obvious objection, that receives no satisfactory answer in the Aristotelian setting, is that the formal notion used is too wide. The formal notion is life in its various senses (*De An.* 2. 2. 413a22–25). That notion

---

[30] T. M. Robinson, *op. cit., supra*, n. 27. Robinson's careful study of the various senses of "primary" in Aristotle, and of Aristotle's own attitude towards the multisignificant notion, reveals a setting in which the term in a given instance could do double duty. That the main intention here is "definitional priority" does not rule out, in Robinson's view, the insertion of "ontological priority" to suit Aristotle's purposes in the given situation. By the same token, "primarily" could here express definitional priority and at the same time imply the notion of "immediate cause" as in "primary" at *An. Post.* 1. 13. 78a25–26. Likewise, backward reference to "first entelechy" at *De An.* 2. 1. 412b5–6, would be compatible with an implication of the sense of "primary" in the *Analytics*. But in both cases some pertinent indications in the text would be required to establish the presence of the additional sense. Such indications, however, are lacking.

extends to separate forms, to substances that are not forms of
bodies. This tenet is abundantly clear in the *Metaphysics*, and
keeps bothering Aristotle in the present discussion in the *De
Anima* (1. 413a6–7; 2. 413b24–27). But a soul has to be the form
of a body, of matter (414a20–21). Life, accordingly, is a notion
that ranges wider than soul, just as "animal" in the *Analytics*
(1. 13. 78b15–31) is too wide to entail the conclusion that
something breathes. A remote cause is given, but not "the
strict cause," Definition of soul with "life" as the specific
differentia does not meet the terms of the requirement set up
at the beginning of *De Anima* 2. 2.

What has been happening? Aristotle, in full accord with the
spirit of Greek intellectual optimism, seems to have had no
doubt about the power of the human mind to penetrate the
specific differentiae of natural things.[31] In the present instance he
is encountering a privileged case. One is aware of one's own
vegetative life, sensation, and intellection in an intimate way
quite other than the quantitative and qualitative observation
by which one knows external things. One is aware of the waving
of one's own hand in a markedly different way from the perception of the waving of a friend's hand as the train pulls out.
One experiences, moreover, the differences between the grades
of vegetative, sentient, and intellectual life, and the hierarchical
orientation (see *Pol.* 1. 8. 1256b15–22) of one to the other. But
does this reflexive awareness provide the type of insight that
can be communicated in definition?

There is, of course, no question of leveling a charge of subjectivism against Aristotle. His conception of specific form as the
basis of universality[32] involves a specific unity of human experience in all individual men. What one man experiences in
regard to life, sensation, and intellection will be specifically the
same as the corresponding experiences in other men as made

[31] See *Part. An.* 1. 1. 640a33–b4; cf. 639b14–30. Aristotle, however,
was aware of the difficulties of determining in practice what the form
actually is in a particular case, as is apparent from *Mete.* 4. 12. 389b28–
390a20. On human ignorance of real essences, see Locke, *Essay*, III, 6,
2–27.
[32] A discussion of this topic may be found in my paper "The Grounds of
Universality in Aristotle," *American Philosophical Quarterly*, 3 (1966),
pp. 162–160.

known through conversation and writing. The specific unity of human nature provides a solid basis for objective communication. The present difficulty does not lie there. Rather, the difficulty is located in the failure of human intellection to penetrate this awareness of life, sensation, and intellection in a way that would allow reasoning from a "strict cause" to effects. The notions of life, sensation, and intellection, no matter how certainly they are experienced through internal awareness, do not give the clarity and penetration that would allow a science of the soul to be developed in the way a science of geometry is built up from the geometrical differentiae.[33] One may be conscious of the graded hierarchy in life, sensation, and intellection, conscious of it with unshakable certainty. But one does not penetrate this knowledge in a way that yields specific premises for scientific conclusions. The privileged knowledge establishes the *fact* of specific difference between the living and non-living, and between the sentient and the intellective. But it does not make manifest the differentia in the way required for functioning as "the strict cause" in the definition. The trouble does not stem from a failure in objective communication. Not the medium but the message is at fault.

Aristotle is unhesitant in maintaining the fundamental unity of the human agent,[34] and in seeing in soul a unifying principle "with which primarily we live, perceive, and think." He realizes that our privileged awareness of life as specifically differentiated is on the operational level, and has to be read back into its

---

[33] Malebranche, reacting against the Cartesian fundamental tenet that the mind has a clear and distinct idea of itself and its activity, showed (*De la Recherche de la Verité*, III, 2e partie, c. 7, no. 4; *Entretiens sur la Metaphysique et sur la Religion*, II, 10) that in this respect it has only an interior sentiment that gives but imperfect knowledge. An idea of the soul would allow psychology to be done *more geometrico*: "Mais si nous voyions en Dieu l'idée qui répond à notre âme, nous connaîtrions en même temps ou nous pourrions connaître toutes les propriétés dont elle est capable; comme nous connaissons (ou nous pouvons connaître) toutes les propriétés dont l'étendue est capable, parce que nous connaissons l'étendue par son idée." *Recherche, loc. cit.* For Aristotle, *Metaph.* Λ 9.1074b35-36, human knowledge and sensation are only concomitantly of themselves. Knowledge of the self and its activities, according to this tenet, should be parasitical upon the knowledge of the external sensible object, and open to clear analysis only in terms of sensible things.

[34] Strictly speaking, it is the *man* who feels and perceives and thinks, and he does so through the soul – *De An.* 1. 4. 408b1-15.

qualitative and its substantial source. In this twofold source, the substantial as the more basic may be called "primary." Hence Aristotle insists on the notion "primary" in the definition of soul. He drives his effort as far as possible in the direction of defining soul in purely formal terms, instead of through reference to its matter, the organic body. But does he not meet frustration in the failure of the internally experienced differentia to make manifest the "strict cause" of the vital effects? The differentia does not explain, for instance, how intellection can be separately existent and yet be an activity of the one agent that grows and perceives. Nor in general does it give knowledge from which the specific properties can be deduced.

Aristotle's insights are too keen to be victimized by any temptation towards facile systematization. But the penalty is that key issues have to remain in a state of *aporia*.[35] Among these is the substantial nature that the definition of soul tries to express. A definition that will "enable us to discover the derived properties" (text *supra*, n. 1), in accord with the geometrical model of a demonstrative premise, has not been reached. Nor, insofar as soul is an object of human cognition, is a definition of this type available. Psychology as a special science requires development through the experimental methods of modern research, while knowledge of the spiritual falls within the scope of metaphysics. To sum up, the nature of soul cannot be grasped in a way that would furnish a satisfactory definition within an Aristotelian philosophy of nature.

The direction taken by the work on the definition of soul in the first two chapters of *De Anima* 2, however, seems clear enough. The first chapter describes soul in terms of the general notion of form in relation to a special effect, the living body.

---

[35] For an interpretation of Aristotle's metaphysics as thoroughly aporematic, see Pierre Aubenque, *Le Problème de l'Etre chez Aristote* (Paris, 1962). The topic of the agent intellect in *De Anima* 3. 5. 430a10–25, so important for the considerations of the present article, is an undoubted instance of a key problem left in the state of *aporia*. But one should be careful about drawing generalizations from this and a few other instances, no matter how great the overall importance of these latter may be.

The present paper has benefited greatly from seminar discussions held by the Classics and Philosophy departments of the University of Toronto during the winter term of 1967–68, especially from the contributions of J. A. Philip, T. M. Robinson, D. Gallop, and A. C. Pegis.

Against the background of the *Analytics*, the second chapter strives to elaborate the definition in terms of soul as "strict cause" of the living body. It reaches its notion of soul through the features of life more readily known first on the operational and then on the qualitative levels, reading them back to the substantial level, and showing that the type of form so reached requires a living body as its appropriate matter. The procedure is from immediate cause to effect, and not from effect to cause as in the preceding chapter. But success eludes its grasp.

Pontifical Institute of Mediaeval Studies
Toronto

PER L'INTERPRETAZIONE DI ARISTOTELE,
DE AN. 404b18 SGG.

MARGHERITA ISNARDI PARENTE

Su *De An.* 1. 404b sgg. moltissimo è stato scritto. Le alternative offerte dalla critica più recente alla tendenza tradizionale all' attribuzione a Platone,[1] ancor oggi diffusissima, sono una

---

[1] Questa attribuzione ha una lunga storia; *status quaestionis* della critica ottocentesca in L. Robin, *La théorie platonicienne des Idées et des Nombres d'après Aristote* (Paris, 1908), n. 273, III, pp. 304 sgg. (per il quale è stata importante la di poco precedente interpretazione di G. Rodier, *Aristote, Traité de l'âme*, Vol. II [Paris, 1900], pp. 55-58). Robin non solo interpreta il passo alla luce della sua visione della più tarda dottrina platonica come dottrina degli intermediari, ma anche nel presupposto dell'attribuzione a Platone della definizione dell' anima come τόπος εἰδῶν, *De An.* 429a27 (contro cui H. F. Cherniss, *Aristotle's Criticism of Plato and the Academy*, Vol. I [Baltimore, 1944], p. 565; W. D. Ross, *Aristotle, De Anima* [Oxford, 1961], p. 292: la dottrina ivi contenuta non è dottrina platonica, ma riporta un'interpretazione della dottrina delle idee rifiutata da Platone in *Parm.* 132b3-6). A Platone attribuiscono il passo E. Frank, *Platon und die sogenannten Pythagoreer* (Halle, 1923), pp. 113-114, 116 sgg.; A. E. Taylor, *Plato* (London, 1926, 1927²), p. 514, e (con qualche esitazione circa la seconda parte del passo, cf. *infra*) *A Commentary on Plato's Timaeus* (Oxford, 1928), pp. 110-111; W. D. Ross, *Aristotle's Metaphysics* (Oxford, 1924, 1948²), p. LXX; Ross, *Plato's Theory of Ideas* (Oxford, 1951), pp. 214-215; Ross, *Aristotle's De Anima*, pp. 177-179; P. Merlan, "Beiträge zur Geschichte des antiken Platonismus, II," in *Philol.* 89 (1934), pp. 197-214 (p. 210); C. J. de Vogel, "Problems Concerning Later Platonism, II," in *Mnemos.* 4. 2 (1949), pp. 299-318 (pp. 304 sgg.); H. D. Saffrey, *Le ΠΕΡΙ ΦΙΛΟΣΟΦΙΑΣ d'Aristote et la théorie platonicienne des Idées nombres* (Leiden, 1955); W. Burkert, *Weisheit und Wissenschaft. Studien zu Pythagoras,Philolaos und Platon* (Nürnberg, 1962), pp. 23-25; F. Lasserre, "Nombre et connaissance dans la préhistoire du Platonisme," in *Mus. Helv.* 15 (1958), pp. 11-26 (p. 25, n. 27); H. J. Krämer, *Arete bei Platon und Aristoteles. Zum Wesen und zur Geschichte der platonischen Ontologie* (Heidelberg, 1959), p. 414, n. 68, p. 431, n. 191, e ancor più decisamente *Ursprung der Geistmetaphysik* (Amsterdam, 1964), pp. 202-207; K. Gaiser, *Platons ungeschriebene Lehre* (Stuttgart, 1963), pp. 44 sgg.; M. Untersteiner, *Aristotele. Della filosofia* (Roma, 1963), pp. 147-162, con amplissimo commento, *Platone, Repubblica libro X* (Napoli, 1965), pp. 189 sgg.

l'attribuzione a Senocrate, difesa da H. Cherniss con critica stringente,[2] e l'altra, che peraltro non ha avuto finora un seguito rilevante nonostante alcune accoglienze favorevoli, l'attribuzione all'antico Pitagorismo:[3] Aristotele, dopo un rapido accenno al *Timeo* (404b15–16), sarebbe passato a citare una sua precedente esposizione di dottrine pitagoriche, prima di passare poi (in b27) a Senocrate.

L'attribuzione a Platone si basa anzitutto sulla convinzione, che anch'essa torna oggi a riscuotere largo credito, che sia da attribuirsi a Platone la dottrina delle idee-numeri,[4] dottrina che si crede appunto di poter riconoscere con sicurezza nel passo in questione. Si basa, in secondo luogo, sulla lettura delle linee 19–21 (αὐτὸ μὲν τὸ ζῷον ἐξ αὐτῆς τῆς τοῦ ἑνὸς ἰδέας καὶ τοῦ πρώτου μήκους καὶ πλάτους καὶ βάθους) alla luce della dottrina dello αὐτὸ ὅ ἐστι ζῷον del *Timeo*:[5] noi leggeremmo cioè qui una definizione dell'idea del

---

[2] È, questa, l'interpretazione difesa da H. Cherniss contro Robin, Frank, Taylor ecc. in *Aristotle's Criticism Pl. Acad.*, pp. 565 sgg., e poi contro Saffrey, in *Gnomon* 31 (1959), pp. 36–51. Propende ad aderire alla tesi del Cherniss, in un primo tempo, E. de Strycker, in *Ant. Class.* 18 (1949), p. 106; ma cf. poi la diversa opinione da lui espressa, con adesione alla tesi del Saffrey, in "On the First Section of fr. 5a of the *Protrepticus*," *Aristotle and Plato in the Mid-Fourth Century*, I. Düring, G. E. L. Owen, edd. (Göteborg, 1960), pp. 76 sgg. Per l'attribuzione a Senocrate sono invece W. Theiler, *Aristoteles. Ueber die Seele* (Berlin, 1959), pp. 93–95; E. Dönt, Platons Spätphilosophie und die Akademie, *Österr. Ak. d. Wiss. SB* 251, 4, pp. 74–75.

[3] P. Kucharski, *Étude sur la doctrine pythagoricienne de la tétrade* (Paris, 1952) e "Aux frontières du Platonisme et du Pythagorisme," in *Archives de Philosophie* 19 (1955–1956), pp. 7–43. Cf. le recensioni favorevoli di Van der Waerden in *Gnomon* 25 (1953), p. 420, e Wolf, in *AAHG* 9 (1956), p. 44. Già F. Solmsen nella rec. a Cherniss, *Riddle of the Early Academy*, in *CW* 40 (1947), pp. 164–168, ritiene che nel passo si parli solo di numeri come forme fondamentali e prime delle cose e non propriamente di idee-numeri.

[4] Quella che vede nel passo le idee-numeri è l'interpretazione più tradizionale; cf. Robin, *Th. plat. Idées, Nombres*, n. 274, I, pp. 308 sgg. Per l'affermazione che nel passo del *De An.* si legge la stessa teoria esposta da Aristotele in *Metaph.* 1090b20–32, e che questa teoria si riferisce a Platone, cf. Ross, *Plato's Theory of Ideas*, pp. 208–209 (ma cf. Ross, *Aristotle's Metaphysics*[2] II, p. 481, con propensione ad attribuire il passo a Senocrate; diversamente invece in *Aristotle, De Anima*, p. 178). Della stessa opinione, Saffrey, *Le ΠΕΡΙ ΦΙΛ. d'Arist.*, pp. 20, 25 n. 2, 29 sgg.; e già prima, in polemica con Cherniss, cf. de Vogel, "Later Platonism, II," p. 304.

[5] Cf. in proposito l'ampio *status quaestionis* di M. Untersteiner, *Aristotele. Della filosofia*, pp. 154 sgg. Che tale fosse l'interpretazione antica, che cioè i commentatori neoplatonici abbiano interpretato l'αὐτὸ τὸ ζῷον

vivente (o del κόσμος νοητός come grande vivente, a seconda che si sia propensi ad accettare l'una o l'altra della due interpretazioni proposte dai commentatori antichi)[6] come formato dei primi quattro numeri ideali, esprimenti l'idea della unità, della lunghezza, della larghezza, e della profondità.

L'attribuzione a Senocrate si basa analogamente sulla convinzione che in *De An.* 404b18 sgg. sia chiaramente ravvisabile la dottrina delle idee-numeri; il che conduce a polarizzarsi sul nome di Senocrate qualora si neghi la platonicità di tale dottrina.[7] Dà inoltre molta importanza al fatto che la successione νοῦς-ἐπιστήμη-δόξα-αἴσθησις sembra corrispondere a quella riportataci da Sesto Empirico, *Math.* 7. 147 sgg. (= *frg.* 5 Heinze) appunto

del *De Anima* sulla scorta di *Ti.* 39e8, è osservazione di Saffrey, *Le ΠΕΡΙ ΦΙΛ. d'Arist.*, p. 48. Richiami al *Timeo* per il passo del *De Anima*, a partire de F. A. Trendelenburg, *De anima libri tres* (Berlin, 1834, 1877[2]; rist. Graz, 1957), p. 188, e Zeller, *Phil. d. Gr.* II, 1[5], pp. 758 sgg., n. 4, poi in R. D. Hicks, *Aristotle's De Anima* (Cambridge, 1907), p. 222; Robin, *Th. plat. Idées, Nombres*, p. 311; de Vogel, "A la recherche des étapes précises entre Platon et le neoplatonisme," in *Mnemos.* 4. 7 (1954), pp. 111–112, in part. p. 117; Ross, *Aristotle, De Anima*, p. 179.

[6] Le due interpretazioni differenti che di αὐτὸ δ ἔστιν ζῷον danno i commentatori sono νοητὸς κόσμος (Simplicio, *In De An.* p. 29, 15–20 Hayduck) e idea di essere vivente (Filopono, *In De An.* pp. 77, 5–11; 79, 13–16; 81, 9–11 Hayduck). Cf. Cherniss, in *Gnomon* 31 (1959), p. 39, n. 2. Accettazione dell'interpretazione di Filopono in Zeller, *Phil. d. Gr.* II, 1[5], pp. 758 sgg., n. 4; P. Shorey, "Recent Platonism in England," in *AJPhil.* 9 (1888), pp. 274–309 (p. 294) e "Recent Interpretations of the *Timaeus*," in *CPhil.* 23 (1928), pp. 343–362 (p. 344); Cherniss, *Aristotle's Criticism Pl. Acad.*, pp. 309–310, n. 211; A. H. Armstrong, *An Introduction to Ancient Philosophy* (London, 1947), p. 49; Ross, *Plato's Theory of Ideas*, p. 129; Saffrey, *Le ΠΕΡΙ ΦΙΛ. d'Arist.*, pp. 46–50; Untersteiner, *Aristotele. Della filosofia*, pp. 154–155. Propensione, invece, ad accettare l'interpretazione di Simplicio in J. Horovitz, *Das platonische νοητὸν ζῷον und der philonische κόσμος νοητός* (Marburg, 1890), pp. 16 sgg.; Robin, *Th. plat. Idées, Nombres*, p. 305, *Étude sur la signification et la place de la physique dans la philosophie de Platon* (Paris, 1919), p. 57 (= *La pensée Hellenique* [Paris, 1942, 1967[2]], p. 309); J. Moreau, *L'âme du monde de Platon aux Stoiciens* (Paris, 1939), pp. 38–39; V. Goldschmidt, *La religion de Platon* (Paris, 1949), p. 51, n. 1, pur con qualche incertezza; de Vogel, "A la rech. des étapes pr.," p. 117; Gaiser, *Platons ung. Lehre*, p. 45.

[7] Cherniss, *Aristotle's Criticism Pl. Acad.*, pp. 567–568, e *Gnomon* 31 (1959), pp. 44 sgg., rifiuta l'attribuzione a Platone di *Metaph.* 1090b20 sgg., oltre che di 1036b13–17, passi solitamente addotti a spiegazione di *De An.* 404b18 sgg. In 1036b13 sgg. noi avremmo la contrapposizione di una dottrina ortodossa delle idee, quella di Platone, che identifica la αὐτογραμμή con lo εἶδος τῆς γραμμῆς (1036b15), a una eterodossa, quella di Senocrate, che identifica la αὐτογραμμή con la δυάς (1036b14), (contro l'interpretazione del Ross, *Arist. Metaph.*[2] II, p. 203, ribadita in *Plato's Theory of Ideas*, p. 207); in 1036b20–32 la dottrina di Senocrate viene

per Senocrate.[8] E trova infine una conferma nella testimonianza di Temistio (*In De An.*, p. 11, 20–27 Heinze [= *frg.* 39 Heinze]) che si richiama, parafrasando il passo aristotelico, al περὶ φύσεως di Senocrate stesso.[9]

Per ciò che riguarda l'attribuzione a Platone, occorre dire che molte ne appaiono le difficoltà. Se noi assumiamo momentaneamente per dimostrato, in via di pura ipotesi, il fatto che nel passo del *De Anima* sia ravvisabile la teoria delle idee-numeri, non possiamo non chiederci successivamente se ciò possa costituire veramente una prova a favore della platonicità del passo stesso. Ma è chiaro che per questo occorrerebbe una sicurezza ben maggiore, nell'attribuzione di tale dottrina a Platone, che non quella di cui ci troviamo a disporre. Tutto ciò su cui possiamo basarci, infatti, è una serie di testimonianze, tra le quali possiamo attribuire solo a quelle di Aristotele, e tutt'al più a quelle di Teofrasto, una certa validità, le altre, quelle dei commentatori, essendo passate attraverso il filtro della tradizione stabilita già ormai da secoli intorno al nome di Platone;[10] e sono, queste

distinta da quella precedente di Speusippo (b13–20) e da quella di Platone esplicitamente citata più oltre, in b32. Quanto alla teoria dell'anima, specificamente, Cherniss vede l'impossibilità di attribuire a Platone una dottrina matematizzante in base a *Top.* 140b2–6, ove Aristotele sembra dirci chiaramente che la teoria di Platone è incompatibile con quella dell'anima-numero (cf. anche *Aristotle's Criticism Pl. Acad.*, p. 12).

[8] Cherniss, *Aristotle's Criticism Pl. Acad.*, p. 570; Theiler, *Arist. Ueber die Seele*, p. 94; ma per la complicatezza della spiegazione del Theiler, cf. Burkert, *Weish. u. Wiss.*, p. 24, n. 61 e n. 64. Per il Krämer, *Arete*, p. 414, n. 68, pur se la sostanza della dottrina è platonica, la forma tradisce una certa coloritura senocratea proprio nella successione delle facoltà conoscitive.

[9] Oltre ad *Aristotle's Criticism Pl. Acad.*, p. 567, cf. la difesa dell'importanza di Temistio compiuta dal Cherniss contro il Saffrey, *Gnomon* 31 (1959), pp. 41–43. Per una nuova favorevole valutazione della testimonianza di Temistio, in ordine non al passo del *De Anima* ma alla dottrina delle idee-numeri in generale, cf. S. Pines, "A New Fragment of Xenocrates and its Implications," in *Trans. Amer. Philosoph. Society* (1961), pp. 3–33, pp. 14 sgg.

[10] Cf. per le punte più decisamente negative della critica circa le idee-numeri, P. Shorey, sia in *De Platonis idearum doctrina atque mentis humanae notionibus* (München, 1884), sia in *The Unity of Plato's Thought* (Chicago, 1903); J. Cook Wilson, "On the Platonist doctrine of the ἀσύμβλητοι ἀριθμοί, in *Class. Rev.* 18 (1904), pp. 247–260; Cherniss, *Aristotle's Criticism Pl. Acad.*, *passim* (di cui però soprattutto il II volume dovrebbe riguardare esplicitamente il problema) e *Riddle of the Early Academy*, in part. *Lecture* II, pp. 31–59. L'attribuzione a Platone della

aristoteliche e teofrastee, testimonianze spesso oscure e contro-
verse, echi di polemiche in cui difficile è spesso individuare
l'esatto bersaglio e distinguere con esattezza i riferimenti, tali
non di rado da offrirci contraddizioni insuperabili per la nostra
impossibilità di adeguati riscontri.[11] Tutto questo è una vecchia
crux interpretativa della critica platonica, questione destinata
a non trovare soluzione definitiva, ma appunto per ciò inadatta
a costituire punto di partenza per ulteriori ipotesi. Tanto più
che ciò che in definitiva continuiamo a possedere di più sicuro
intorno a Platone, gli stessi suoi scritti, la dottrina da lui espli-
tamente professata nei dialoghi, non conferma, ma anzi non di
rado (mentre offre qualche appiglio per la possibile attribuzione a
Platone di almeno qualche spunto della dottrina dei principi)

dottrina, che ebbe grande supporto dall'autorità di Robin, *Th. plat.
Idées, Nombres*, e J. Stenzel, *Zahl und Gestalt bei Platon und Aristoteles*
(Leipzig, 1924) (cf., per un ampio *status quaestionis* circa i tentativi di
ricostruire la deduzione platonica degli ἀσύμβλητοι ἀριθμοί dai principi,
Ross, *Plato's Theory of Ideas*, pp. 176–205) ha avuto oggi nuovamente
fortuna negli scritti di H. J. Krämer, *Arete* e *Ursprung d. Geistmetaphysik*, K. Gaiser, *Platons ung. Lehre*, W. Burkert, *Weish. u. Wiss.*,
cf. *supra*; la cultura tedesca sembra dunque in prevalenza orientata in
questo senso (cf. però, contro l'interpretazione del Krämer, H.-D. Voigt-
länder, in *Archiv f. Gesch. d. Philos.* 45 [1963], pp. 194–211; parallelamente
alla critica di G. Vlastos, in *Gnomon* 35 [1963], pp. 641–655). Un tentativo
d'interpretazione epistemologica della dottrina in Lasserre, "Nombre et
connaissance," p. 24. L'interpretazione del Robin continua a essere
seguita e svolta da P. M. Schuhl, *L'oeuvre de Platon* (Paris, 1954), pp. 197
sgg., pp. 206–207; da C. J. de Vogel, a partire da "La dernière phase du
Platonisme et l'interpretation de M. Robin," in *Studia Vollgraf* (Amsterdam, 1948), pp. 165–178, per tutta una serie di studi che si avrà di volta in
volta occasione di citare. In realtà la demolizione della validità obiettiva
della testimonianza aristotelica su questo punto, soprattutto nella forma
datale da H. Cherniss, non è stata mai veramente confutata.

[11] Cf. ad esempio la discordanza fra Aristotele, *Metaph.* 991b9, 992b16,
1073a18 (le idee sono numeri) e Teofrasto, *Metaph.* 6b, Ross-Fobes, p.
14 (i numeri sono al di sopra delle idee), che si ripercuote nelle interpretazioni contemporanee: così Robin, *Th. plat. Idées, Nombres*, pp. 454–461,
e *passim*, ha creduto di dover preferibilmente aderire all'interpretazione di
Teofrasto, ponendo i numeri ideali al di sopra delle idee; di contro,
rivalutando la testimonianza di Aristotele, Ross, *Arist. Metaph.*[2] I,
pp. LXVIII sgg. (ma il Ross finisce poi con l'adeguarsi, *Plato's Theory of
Ideas*, p. 218, n. 1, alla più coerente interpretazione del Robin; cf. i
tentativi per sfuggire alla contraddizione in P. Wilpert, *Zwei Aristotelische
Frühschriften über die Ideenlehre* (Regensburg, 1949), pp. 145 sgg.; in
Krämer, *Arete*, pp. 250–256). Cf., per un'abbondante denunzia delle contraddizioni col testo platonico dei dialoghi in primo luogo, e delle stesse
testimonianze fra loro, soprattutto Cherniss, *Riddle, Lecture II, passim*.

smentisce e contraddice le testimonianze circa le idee-numeri, essendo alla dottrina dei dialoghi assolutamente estranea la concezione del numero come genere supremo cui può ridursi ogni altro εἶδος.[12]

Il problema dell'interpretazione dello αὐτὸ ὅ ἔστι ζῷον (o, altrove, παντελὲς ζῷον) del *Timeo* è strettamente legato a questo più generale problema interpretativo. Riconoscere senz'altro nello αὐτὸ τὸ ζῷον di cui qui parla Aristotele l'entità trascendente, il Vivente in sé o Vivente assoluto, di cui là parla Platone, risolverebbe certamente l'interpretazione del *Timeo* nel senso dell'attribuzione a Platone della teoria delle idee-numeri. Tuttavia il confronto col *Timeo* non porta elementi a favore della liceità di questa attribuzione, solo che si pensi ad esempio a *Ti.* 39a–40a, ove Platone ci parla del vivente in sé (αὐτὸ ὅ ἔστιν ζῷον) come divisibile in quattro forme, ma secondo uno schema divisorio che non è quello della tetractide, secondo cioè le forme delle diverse specie di viventi rispondenti ai quattro elementi del τετράστοιχον;[13] forma di divisione tradizionale che non offre di

[12] In realtà l'interpretazione del Robin, che fa i numeri superiori alle idee qualitativamente determinate (cf. oggi Schuhl, *L'oeuvre de Platon*, pp. 206–207) è la sola cocrente alla dottrina platonica: se le idee hanno struttura matematica, ciò non può essere se non perchè imitano un'entità che le trascende; Platone non conosce un problema di interna struttura di un fenomeno se non nella forma della mimesi o della metessi. Ma tale interpretazione non trova riscontro nei dialoghi, che non conoscono questa concezione del numero (cf. ancora Cherniss, *Riddle*, pp. 34 sgg.; per la posizione della matematica nell' orizzonte filosofico di Platone, Cherniss, "Plato as Mathematician," in *Rev. of Metaph.* 4 [1951], pp. 395–435). Ross è andato sempre più adeguandosi a un tipo d'interpretazione che vede nel numero il "genere," più estensibile e quindi superiore, dell' εἶδος qualitativamente determinato; il quattro ad esempio è lo schema ideale del quadrato e della giustizia, che risponde anch'essa a tale numero in quanto ἰσότης (cf., oltre al già citato, Ross-Fobes, *Metaph. of Theophr.* [Oxford, 1929], p. 58). Ma per questo occorre attribuire a Platone una distinzione in εἴδη e γένη preludente già ad Aristotele; accedere in sostanza a una interpretazione della διαίρεσις sul tipo di quella già a suo tempo avanzata da J. Stenzel, *Zahl und Gestalt*, che giunse fino a vedere nello schema diairetico lo schema stesso della deduzione trascendentale delle idee-numeri. Quanto tale interpretazione sia legittima, è cosa che non è qui possibile approfondire, ma di cui si può porre in rilievo la problematicità.

[13] Non dal *Timeo*, ma dalla "dottrina orale," cioè dalla testimonianza aristotelica, è desunta la teoria secondo cui Platone avrebbe definito lo αὐτὸ ὅ ἔστιν ζῷον come risultante dall'uno e dalle idee delle dimensioni; cf. Robin, *Th. plat. Idées, Nombres*, pp. 484 sgg., 491 sgg., il quale si

per sé appigli per un'interpretazione matematico-dimensionale del Vivente in sé. Il *Timeo* non offre elementi decisivi nemmeno per l'attribuzione a Platone di una teoria dell'anima in quanto tale in termini matematici: dalla descrizione di *Ti.* 35a sappiamo che il demiurgo foggia l'anima con divisibile e indivisibile, altro e medesimo, formando di tutti questi elementi un'essenza composta,[14] ma non possiamo attribuire a questi elementi valore matematico o geometrico-spaziale fino a che, dalla considerazione dell'essenza pura dell'anima alla luce di concetti metafisico-ontologici suoi propri, Platone non passi alla descrizione della funzione dell'anima, ch'è quella di ordinare numericamente e geometricamente il corporeo.[15] Ciò è coerente a tutta la seconda

appoggia peraltro proprio su ciò la cui platonicità è da provare, *De An.* 404b18 sgg.; si tratta di un autentico circolo vizioso. Fra gli interpreti più recenti il Gaiser è quello che ha dato la maggior importanza, nel "sistema" platonico, alla teoria delle dimensioni, fino a incentrare attorno a questa tutta la dottrina di Platone, ridotta a una sorta di matematica ontologica di tipo neopitagorico; per l'esegesi del *Timeo* cf. *Platons ung. Lehre*, pp. 41 sgg., ove, come già in Robin, l'interpretazione della cosmologia platonica sulla base della tetrade une-due (linea)-tre (superficie)-quattro (corpo) si basa sulla preliminare attribuzione a Platone del passo del *De Anima* (cf. pp. 44–47). Passi come *Leg.* 10. 894a, 7. 819d–820c, sono stati dal Gaiser forzati a indici di un'interpretazione sistematica che essi in realtà non giustificano, pur denotando l'interesse di Platone a problemi geometrico-spaziali (*Platons ung. Lehre*, p. 50, pp. 187–188, con ripresa dello schema, ben noto alla critica tedesca di Platone, della "Entfaltung"; cf. già, per gli stessi passi, Frank, *Plato u. d. sog. Pyth.*, p. 371, n. 282).

[14] Per l'interpretazione del passo, cf. soprattutto, dopo G. M. A. Grube, "The Composition of the World-Soul in *Timaeus* 35ab," in *CPhil* 27 (1932), pp. 80–82, F. M. Cornford, *Plato's Cosmology* (London, 1937), pp. 59 sgg.; i quali fanno entrambi valere l'interpretazione di Proclo (*In Ti.* 187d, II, p. 155 Diehl), contro la sottovalutazione di questa da parte di Taylor, *A Commentary on Plato's Timaeus*, pp. 109 sgg. (prezioso su questo punto soprattutto per l'ampia rassegna delle interpretazioni accademiche e neoplatoniche). Cf. poi Cherniss, *Aristotle's Criticism Pl. Acad.*, p. 409, n. 337, p. 410, n. 339; B. Skemp, *The Theory of Motion in Plato's Later Dialogues* (Cambridge, 1942, 1967²), p. 68; R. Hackforth, "Timaeus 35a 4–6," in *CR*, N. S. 7 (1957), p. 197.

[15] Saffrey, *Le* ΠΕΡΙ ΦΙΛ. *d'Arist.*, pp. 5–6, 46 sgg., si serve della definizione dei principi Uno e diade indefinita come ἀδιαίρετον ... διῃρημένον in Alessandro d'Afrodisia, *In Metaph.*, p. 56, 13 Hayduck, per l'interpretazione di *Ti.* 35ab, e successivamente di *De An.* 404b18 sgg. Cf. Gaiser, *Platons ung. Lehre*, pp. 51 sgg., p. 347, n. 41, per l'interpretazione matematica dei principi e degli elementi ἀμέριστον e μεριστόν di cui l'anima è composta: tutto l'intero passo 35ab appare al Gaiser come esposizione di una teoria dell'anima quale misto foggiato per fare da

parte del *Timeo*, in cui la struttura matematica dell'universo fisico appare come il riflesso dell'ordinamento eidetico trascendente nel sensibile, la forma cioè che la μίμησις delle idee assume in particolare nel campo della natura fisico-spaziale: il "luogo" indefinito e bruto, assurgendo all'ordine, si fa spazio geometrico, suddiviso in forme geometriche delimitate.[16] Ma che la

μεταξύ fra gli estremi, che sono il puro indivisibile di per sè (le idee-numeri) e il puro divisibile (la corporeità tridimensionale), mentre l'essenza dell'anima consiste nell'unione degli intermedi indivisibile-lineare (le ἄτομοι γραμμαί sono da attribuirsi non solo a Senocrate ma anche a Platone; Gaiser, *ibid.*, p. 375, n. 136) e divisibile-superficiale. Questa presentazione sistematizza in rigida forma simmetrica la dottrina robiniana dell'anima come μεταξύ matematico. Ma un'interpretazione di questo genere è possibile solo se si dia valore di esegesi storicamente esatta a quella esegesi di *Tim.* 35a sgg. che è stata compiuta dalla prima Accademia, secondo cui nell'antitesi ἀμέριστον-μεριστόν è da riconoscersi la dottrina dei principi, quella appunto cui, come abbiamo visto, si rifà Alessandro d'Afrodisia; esegesi di cui *De An.* 404b15–18 è uno dei saggi (Πλάτων ἐν τῷ Τιμαίῳ τὴν ψυχὴν ἐκ τῶν στοιχείων ποιεῖ) e che era sviluppata soprattutto da Senocrate, stando a Plutarco, *De procr. an.* 1012de. Per poter compiere una esegesi di questo tipo occorre attribuire a Platone una teoria della ἀόριστος δυάς come genere ultimo del reale, e tale da costituire anche principio (il secondo principio) del mondo delle idee, di una realtà incorporea come l'anima, ecc. Ora, quanto ciò sia in accordo col testo del *Timeo*, dà adito per lo meno a dubbi: nel *Timeo*, se vi è uno spunto di dottrina del secondo principio, questo è da ravvisarsi nel problema, del tutto estraneo a quello dell' anima, della χώρα o ὑποδοχή, che riguarda solo ed esclusivamente la genesi del mondo fisico; il Festugière, un autore che pure indulge anch'egli all'attribuzione a Platone della dottrina dei principi, ha chiarito bene la fondamentale ambiguità di questo concetto nel *Timeo*, oscillante com'esso è fra il significato di principio attivo e di condizione delimitante (*La Révélation d'Hermès Trismegiste*, II, *Le dieu cosmique* [Paris, 1949], pp. 113 sgg.) Quanto al problema del valore matematico degli στοιχεῖα formanti l'essenza dell' anima, è significativo che Platone cominci a esprimersi in termini matematici in 36a, quando cioè, lasciato da parte il problema della composizione dell'anima nella sua essenza, passa a rappresentarsi il demiurgo nell'atto di predisporre l'anima alla sua funzione nel sensibile, funzione che si esplica per l'appunto nell'ordinamento spaziale e temporale a base di numeri.

[16] Nel *Timeo* meglio che altrove può certo trovare un appiglio l'attribuzione a Platone, da parte di Aristotele (*Metaph.* 987b14 sgg. e altrove) di una teoria degli intermediari matematici; cf. recentemente P. Merlan, "Greek Philosophy from Plato to Plotinus," in *The Cambridge History of Later Greek and Early Medieval Philosophy* (Cambridge, 1967), p. 17 (ma per la struttura geometrica dei sensibili quale è rappresentata nel *Timeo* cf., significativamente, le due diverse opinioni espresse dal Ross, *Arist. Metaph.*[2] I, p. 168, ove si afferma la natura ed essenza "intermediaria" degli εἰσιόντα καὶ ἐξιόντα di *Ti.* 50c, e *Plato's Theory of Ideas*, pp.

funzione cosmica dell'anima, a destinatareggere i cieli secondo rapporti di spazio e di tempo misurabili in numeri, sia matematizzante, non significa che l'anima debba ricondursi a valori numerici nella sua stessa essenza: i valori numerici non appaiono primari, ma sempre derivati.

Ma è opportuno ritornare al testo di Aristotele per chiarire se, a parte quella che può essere la nostra esegesi del *Timeo*, in esso sia da leggere, da b18 a b27, una unitaria esegesi di questo alla luce della dottrina dei principi e delle idee-numeri. Stando a una traduzione puramente letterale del passo, possiamo affermare che qui Aristotele ci dice che il Vivente in sè, o l'autentico vivente, è formato dalla "idea" dell'uno e dalla prima lunghezza, larghezza e profondità, e "le altre cose" sono formate in modo simile; e che ciò si può esprimere anche (ἔτι δὲ καὶ ἄλλως) dicendo che l'intelletto equivale all'uno, la scienza al due, l'opinione al tre, la sensazione al quattro. Fin dall'inizio di questa argomentazione, vediamo subito la difficoltà di spiegare τὰ δ' ἄλλα ὁμοιοτρόπως una volta che a αὐτὸ τὸ ζῷον si sia dato il significato di idea del vivente o di mondo delle idee come grande vivente.[17] Anche il valore dell'espressione ἔτι δὲ καὶ ἄλλως va

---

223–224, ove le stesse forme gli appaiono in realtà cangianti e transeunti come i sensibili stessi cui danno esistenza). Cf. Gauss, *Philos. Handkomm. z. d. Dialoge Platons* III, 2 (Bern, 1961), p. 152: il carattere intermediario del numero sta nell'essere questo, per Platone, una sorta di condizione dell'ordinamento del sensibile molteplice da parte dell'idea, distinto logicamente da questa. In realtà Platone non sembra aver dato mai, nè nel *Filebo* nè nel *Timeo*, alle forme geometriche o alla misura matematica uno *status* di entità indipendente nell'ambito di una ipotetica gerarchia ontologica, ma sembra avere semplicemente sottolineato il carattere matematizzante della forma in cui si verifica il processo della μέθεξις. L'ordinamento matematico, in definitiva, può dirsi intermediario, e può essere stato da Aristotele e dagli accademici interpretato (ed "entificato") come tale, in quanto è in forma matematica, di intervalli spaziali o temporali e di strutture figurative, che il sensibile riesce ad assurgere a una τάξις, a superare la ἀπειρία e determinarsi, a trovare un ordine che non è quello ideale, ma ne partecipa e gli somiglia.

[17] Le soluzioni variano, naturalmente, a seconda dell'interpretazione data ad αὐτὸ τὸ ζῷον. Cf. la proposta di E. Zeller, *Phil. d. Gr.* II, 1⁵, p. 758, n. 4, di sottintendere ⟨ζῷα⟩, seguita da Rodier, *Traité de l'âme*, II, p. 56; l'accettazione della spiegazione di Simplicio, che era apparsa invece sospetta al Trendelenburg, *Arist. de an.*², pp. 188 sgg., da parte di Robin, *Th. plat. Idées, Nombres*, pp. 305–306, che cioè τὰ δ' ἄλλα significhi le varie divisioni e sezioni del conoscibile, νοητά, δοξαστά, αἰσθητά; Cherniss, *Aristotle's Criticism Pl. Acad.*, p. 578, "le altre idee";

almeno in parte perduto; per quanto se ne possano ben comprendere le ragioni grammaticali e sintattiche, o l'economia nella struttura retorica della frase,[18] non si coglie adeguatamente il legame ch'esso sembra porre fra le due proposizioni, indicando una sorta di loro convertibilità: indicando cioè che la frase che riguarda il "vivente in sé" si può diversamente esprimere nella forma del carattere tetradico delle facoltà psichiche. Il testo di Aristotele sembra avere una sua rigida simmetria, che risalta in pieno solo se noi lo leggiamo in questa forma:

αὐτὸ μὲν τὸ ζῷον ἐξ αὐτῆς τῆς τοῦ ἑνὸς ἰδέας καὶ τοῦ πρώτου μήκους καὶ πλάτους καὶ βάθους, τὰ δ'ἄλλα ὁμοιοτρόπως	νοῦν μὲν τὸ ἕν, ἐπιστήμην δὲ τὰ δύο... τὸν δὲ τοῦ ἐπιπέδου ἀριθμὸν δόξαν, αἴσθησιν δὲ τὸν τοῦ στερεοῦ... εἴδη δ' οἱ ἀριθμοὶ οὗτοι τῶν πραγμάτων

Se proviamo a leggere secondo questo schema tutto il ragionamento, noi apprendiamo che: (a) il vero vivente è formato dagli εἴδη dell'uno e dalle dimensioni (b) in altri termini l'anima è quadruplice, o tetradica (l'intelletto è unitario, la scienza corrisponde al due perché va da un principio a una conclusione, μοναχῶς γὰρ ἐφ᾽ ἕν, l'opinione al tre e la sensazione al quattro) (c) tutte le altre cose sono strutturate come il vero vivente (d) tutte le altre cose si conoscono per mezzo delle facoltà della tetrade-anima proprio perché questi quattro numeri sono le forme di tutto il resto della realtà, così come lo sono dell'anima. Alla base poi dei numeri, e successivamente dell'anima e di tutte le altre cose, ci sono gli στοιχεῖα o principi. Tutto ciò ha avuto

Ross, *Plato's Theory of Ideas*, p. 212, "ogni essere costituito in modo simile"; Saffrey, *Le* ΠΕΡΙ ΦΙΛ. *d'Arist.*, p. 21, e cf. p. 49, n. 4, come τὰ ὑποκείμενα, sulla scorta di H. Bonitz, *Aristotelis Metaphysica* (Bonnae, 1849), p. 48; Untersteiner, *Aristotele. Della filosofia*, p. 158, il quale ritiene ci si debba rifare soprattutto a *Ti.* 30c7, 39e3, per spiegare il meglio possibile il significato dell'espressione.

[18] Cf. soprattutto Cherniss, *Aristotle's Criticism Pl. Acad.*, p. 574, e *Gnomon* 31 (1959), p. 50, n. 3, per la cura di sottolineare la stretta relazione fra le due espressioni legate da ἔτι δὲ καὶ ἄλλως (al contrario Taylor, *Comm. Tim.*, p. 111, ritenne che potesse trattarsi di due differenti dottrine, di cui forse la seconda potrebbe essere attribuita a Senocrate). Tuttavia, se noi continuiamo a dare a αὐτὸ τὸ ζῷον il significato di oggetto intelligibile e alla frase seguente il valore di una descrizione del soggetto intelligente, la convertibilità delle due concezioni e la simmetria perfetta del passo vengono meno.

spiegazione più ampia nel Περὶ φιλοσοφίας,[19] sì che Aristotele non ritiene qui necessario offrire riferiménti più precisi.

Un'interpretazione di questo tipo richiede che si dia ad αὐτὸ τὸ ζῷον il significato di soggetto del conoscere.[20] Sono certo da accogliersi con cautela le testimonianze neoplatoniche di αὐτοζῷον per anima.[21] Ma c'è da chiedersi se in Aristotele stesso non sia dato cogliere almeno le tracce di un possibile uso accademico del termine in questo stesso senso. In un passo della *Metafisica* (1043a34–35), Aristotele si pone, nell'ambito del più generale problema della definizione di οὐσία o di forma, il problema specifico se ζῷον sia tutto il composto animale, anima e corpo, o solo l'anima (πότερον ζῷον ψυχὴ ἐν σώματι ἢ ψυχή); e altrove, in *Top.* 137b11, abbiamo in certo modo la soluzione di questo stesso problema: ἐπεὶ ὑπάρχει τῷ αὐτοζῴῳ τὸ ἐκ ψυχῆς καὶ σώματος συγκεῖσθαι. Αὐτοζῷον qui, è evidente, vale per ζῷον ἢ ζῷον, per ἔμψυχον in quanto tale o autentico o veramente tale; non è

[19] Per l'incertezza regnante fra i critici del secolo scorso, cf. F. Ravaisson, *Essai sur la Metaphysique d'Aristote* (Paris, 1837–1846), I, p. 56, il quale attribuisce il passo al Περὶ φιλοσοφίας, insieme rimandando a Trendelenburg, *De An.*; questi a sua volta rimanda (*De An.*[2], pp. 182–183) all'opera di Ch. A. Brandis dal significativo titolo *De perditis Aristotelis libris de ideis et de bono sive philosophia* (Bonnae, 1823). L'attribuzione agli ἄγραφα δόγματα di Platone ha ricevute notevole sostegno dall'autorità del Robin, *Th. plat. Idées, Nombres,* pp. 307–308, e ancora pesa sui critici, anche se oggi la tendenza prevalente è ad ammettere, da parte di quanti rivendicano a Platone il contenuto del passo, che Aristotele nel Περὶ φιλοσοφίας si rifacesse alla dottrina orale di Platone già esposta nel Περὶ τἀγαθοῦ. Cf. ad esempio Saffrey, *Le* ΠΕΡΙ ΦΙΛ. *d'Arist.*, pp. 51 sgg., e le osservazioni di Cherniss, *Gnomon* 31 (1959), pp. 37–38, e Untersteiner, *Aristotele. Della filosofia,* pp. 153–154, circa le difficoltà del Saffrey a giustificare la forma della citazione aristotelica.

[20] Cf. già Kucharski, *Étude doctr. pythag. tétrade,* p. 37, n. 1; e "Aux frontières du Platon," pp. 30 sgg. (ove egli nota che una tale maniera di prospettarsi l'identità di struttura fra soggetto conoscente e oggetto conosciuto può sembrare eccessivamente semplicistica, ma non ha in realtà in sè maggiori elementi di arcaismo che non l'identificazione delle facoltà conoscitive con i primi quattro numeri).

[21] Saffrey, *Le* ΠΕΡΙ ΦΙΛ. *d'Arist.*, p. 48, n. 1: Aristotele dice qui, e preferibilmente anche altrove, αὐτὸ τὸ ζῷον anziché αὐτοζῷον; la parola αὐτοζῷον nel senso di κόσμος νοητός fu probabilmente evitata per non creare confusione con l'espressione αὐτοζῴον, presumibilmente foggiata su αὐτοκίνητον, che Filopono, *In De An.*, p. 165, 18–28 Hayduck, ci dice usata da Senocrate per anima. Cf. di contro Cherniss. *Gnomon* 31 (1959), p. 41, n. 3, secondo il quale la parola è assai genericamente usata in ambito neoplatonico, si che non possiamo trarne alcuna argomentazione valida per ciò che riguarda Senocrate.

usato in senso platonico di "idea," anche se poco più oltre nello stesso libro dei *Topici* abbiamo saggi di uso platonico dello stesso termine.[22] L'uso di αὐτός soprattutto nelle opere giovanili di Aristotele è, com'è noto, questione dibattuta lungamente, e che oggi, se si pensa ai più recenti studi sul *Protrettico* ad esempio, si tende a risolvere in senso alquanto diverso da quello che Jaeger fece cinquant'anni fa largamente valere, fondando su questa sua interpretazione parte della sua ricostruzione del platonismo del primo Aristotele.[23] Ma, a parte questo, i due passi combinati della *Metafisica* e dei *Topici* fanno nascere un altro problema: se Aristotele non contrapponesse cioè la sua convinzione che lo αὐτοζῷον, lo ζῷον ἧ ζῷον, risulta constare di entrambe le parti del composto umano, anima e corpo, di contro a una asserzione dei suoi avversari platonici che lo αὐτοζῷον è in realtà solo e semplicemente l'anima. Potrebbero insomma sorgere dei dubbi se veramente l'uso di ζῷον o αὐτὸ τὸ ζῷον per l'anima dell'uomo, ch'è il vero αὐτοζῷον secondo la dottrina del *Fedone*, partecipante essenzialmente alla idea della vita, sia da ascriversi solo alla tradizione neoplatonica più tarda, o abbia già nella prima scuola di Platone la sua radice.[24]

Se cade l'identificazione di αὐτοζῷον con idea del Vivente o con cosmo intelligibile come grande vivente, anche le espressioni

[22] *Top.* 143b33. Kucharski, "Aux frontières du Platon," p. 31, n. 1, cita *Metaph.* 1043a34 sgg.; ma senza trarne tutte le conseguenze implicite.

[23] Basti rimandare a I. Düring, *Aristotle's Protrepticus. An Attempt at Reconstruction* (Göteborg, 1961), pp. 217-219.

[24] È da notarsi che in *Anal. Post.* 2. 91a37, Aristotele, riferendosi alla definizione senocratea (*frg.* 60 Heinze) parla, se non esplicitamente di αὐτοζῷον, di τὸ αὐτὸ αὐτῷ αἴτιον τοῦ ζῆν, formula assai vicina allo αὐτοζωόν o αὐτοζωή di Filopono (αὐτοζωὴ γάρ ἐστιν). Per l'identificazione dell'uomo, del vivente umano in quanto tale, con la pura ψυχή, cf. il probabilmente accademico *Alcibiade* I. 130abc (da Schleiermacher in poi l'autenticità del dialogo è stata fortemente sospettata soprattutto dalla critica tedesca; cf. W. Jaeger, *Aristoteles* [Berlin, 1923], p. 169, n. 1; un rapido *status quaestionis* in P. Friedländer, *Platon²*, II, p. 317, peraltro propenso all'autenticità. La cronologia, fondata sulla supposizione dell' accademicità del dialogo, si trova fissata in H. Dittmar, *Aeschines von Sphettos* [Berlin, Leipzig, 1912], p. 174, fra il 340 e il 330). Un'eco di questo modo di concepire l'anima come "vivente autentico" nello pseudoplatonico *Assioco*, 365e, ζῷον ἀθάνατον. Ancora Saffrey, p. 48, n. 1: la parola esprimerebbe "dans les raccourci d'une formule, une doctrine purement platonicienne"; niente in realtà vieta di pensarla foggiata nell' ambito dell'Accademia antica.

158   *Margherita Isnardi Parente*

ἐξ αὐτῆς τῆς τοῦ ἑνὸς ἰδέας καὶ τοῦ πρώτου μήκους κτλ. acquistano una nuova luce. ᾽Ιδέα è parola che la tradizione ci dice usata anche da Speusippo, che rifiutò la dottrina delle idee: sulla definizione resaci per questo discepolo di Platone da Giamblico, che l'anima è ἰδέα τοῦ πάντη διαστατοῦ (Stob. *Ecl.* 1. 49. 32, p. 363, 26 Wachsmuth = *frg.* 40 Lang) dovremo tra poco tornare più ampiamente.[25] Quanto alla parola πρῶτος, il suo uso pitagorico, non nel senso di idea, ma di realtà genetica e causale, è stato già abbondantemente rilevato nella storia della critica: πρῶτος non significa di per sé trascendenza della forma.[26] Sempre per lo stesso Speusippo, vediamo da Aristotele usato spesso il termine πρῶτος, a volte nello stesso contesto in cui egli ci dice anche che Speusippo rifiutò la dottrina delle idee; cf. *Metaph.* 13. 1083a20 sgg. (*frg.* 42d Lang): τὰ δὲ μαθηματικὰ καὶ τοὺς ἀριθμοὺς πρώτους τῶν ὄντων); *Metaph.* 13. 1080b11 sgg. (42c Lang). Nel passo a noi rimasto del Περὶ πυθαγορικῶν ἀριθμῶν[27] vediamo Speusippo sostenere che vi sono

[25] P. Merlan, "Beiträge zur Geschichte d. ant. Platonismus II," pp. 198 sgg.; a proposito della parola ἰδέα contenuta nella definizione, cf. Cherniss, *Aristotle's Criticism Pl. Acad.*, p. 511, che suppone trattarsi di una esegesi del *Timeo* in polemica con Aristotele, *De An.* 407a2–3, in cui Speusippo difenderebbe Platone dall'accusa di aver inteso l'anima come una grandezza affermando invece che la intese come ἰδέα ὁ εἶδος di una grandezza. Ma cf. di contro ancora P. Merlan, *From Platonism to Neoplatonism*, (The Hague, 1953, 1960²), pp. 40 sgg., in difesa di un probabile uso speusippeo del termine εἶδος in senso non trascendente e non platonico, di εἶδος matematico. Cf., a proposito di *De An.* 404b, Kucharski, "Aux frontières du Platon," p. 29, contro il pericolo di "s'hypnotiser" sulla parola ἰδέα. Circa la πρώτη μονάς dei Pitagorici cf. J. E. Raven, *Pythagoreans and Eleatics* (Amsterdam, 1948, 1966²), pp. 112–125 (l'intero capitolo *The One*) cui Kucharski rimanda.

[26] Kucharski, "Aux frontières du Platon," p. 28 e n. 1 *ibid.*, fa osservazioni sul diverso uso che il termine πρῶτος può avere in Aristotele nello stesso contesto: cf. 1083a21 sgg., ove si rimprovera presumibilmente a Speusippo di porre i numeri πρῶτοι (l'uno πρῶτον τῶν ἑνῶν) e a 32–33, ove si parla esplicitamente di Platone, che pone δυάδα πρώτην καὶ τριάδα. Per le espressioni di πρώτη μονάς, τριάς, ecc. in senso pitagorico e non platonico, cf. la *Expositio rer. math.* di Teone di Smirne (πρώτη τετρακτύς, fra l'altro, in *Exp.*, p. 98 Hiller; ancora Kucharski, "Aux frontières du Platon," p. 28). Per una testimonianza meno sospetta cf. Aristotele, *Metaph.* 985b23 sgg. (οἱ ἀριθμοὶ φύσει πρῶτοι ... τὰ τῶν ἀριθμῶν στοιχεῖα τῶν ὄντων στοιχεῖα ὑπέλαβον εἶναι).

[27] Molto discussa l'attribuzione a Filolao con cui l'opera ci vien data dalla tradizione, secondo cui Speusippo avrebbe rielaborato materiale già filolaico; cf. la radicale negazione del Frank, *Plato und die sog. Pythag.*, pp. 140 sgg., riecheggiante in Burkert, *Weish. u. Wiss.*, pp. 310, 312; cf. Cherniss, *Aristotle's Criticism of Presocratic Philosophy* (Baltimore,

quattro ἀρχαί della grandezza, ciascuna "prima" nel suo ordine, punto, linea, superficie, e solido, rispondenti ai quattro numeri fondamentali uno, due, tre e quattro: ταῦτα δὲ πάντα ἐστὶ πρῶτα καὶ ἀρχαὶ τῶν καθ' ἕκαστον ὁμογενῶν (*Theolog. Arithm.* p. 61, 8 sgg. Ast = *frg.* 4 Lang). E', questo, un altro modo di dire che gli ἀριθμοί, cioè i quattro numeri della tetractide pitagorica, sono εἴδη τῶν πραγμάτων.[28] Che poi i numeri siano sì ἀρχαί e πρῶτα, ma che derivino anch'essi da στοιχεῖα assolutamente primi, come qui ci dice Aristotele, è anche un tratto di dottrina speusippea (cf. *Metaph.* 14. 1087b4 sgg. = *frg.* 48b Lang: γεννῶνται γὰρ οἱ ἀριθμοί ... τῷ δ' ἐκ τοῦ πλήθους, ὑπὸ τῆς τοῦ ἑνὸς δὲ οὐσίας ἀμφοῖν, ove, se il principio della derivazione dalla οὐσία dell'uno è dichiarata comune, Speusippo sembra differenziarsi per il modo particolare di concepire il secondo principio [*Metaph.* 13. 1085b5 sgg. = *frg.* 48c Lang]). Si direbbe, in sostanza, che il passo del *De Anima* ci porti piuttosto di fronte a un tipo di concezione pitagorico-speusippea che non a dottrina platonica.

1935), p. 390. La tendenza a denunciare una costante deformazione accademica del pitagorismo, per l'uso costante di presentare la dottrina di Platone e la propria come "antica rivelazione" pitagorica (mentre la tradizione più fededegna intorno al pitagorismo sarebbe rappresentata dalla testimonianza aristotelica) è accentuatissima nelle pagine del Burkert; cf. *Weish. u. Wiss.*, pp. 55–57, 63 sgg., 70–73. Cf. invece la tendenza all'attribuzione ad ambito pitagorico della teoria della tetractide come ci è presentata dal Περὶ πυθαγορικῶν ἀριθμῶν in Raven, *Pythagoreans and Eleatics*[2], p. 105; e Saffrey, *Le* ΠΕΡΙ ΦΙΛ. *d'Arist.*, p. 40, n. 2, che giunge a dubitare dell'autenticità speusippea (assai più cauto nelle sue conclusioni era stato Lang, *De Sp. Acad. Scr.*, pp. 27–28). Riporti o no l'opera, almeno in parte, materiale preesistente, non c'è ragione evidente di rifiutare l'attribuzione a Speusippo almeno di una sistematica rielaborazione di esso.

[28] Ancora Kucharski, "Aux frontières du Platon," p. 33, per l'osservazione che, se da 404b24 potremmo avere l'impressione di trovarci di fronte a una teoria generale dei numeri ideali, b27 ci riporta invece strettamente ai quattro numeri della tetractide: οἱ δ' ἀριθμοὶ εἴδη οὗτοι τῶν πραγμάτων. Cf. anche la citazione del passo del Περὶ πυθαγορικῶν ἀριθμῶν di Speusippo che il Kucharski fa, seppur fuggevolmente, a p. 34, n. 1, come esempio della stessa dottrina con diversa terminologia. Untersteiner, *Aristotele. Della filosofia*, pp. 161–162, afferma che la tesi del Kucharski potrebbe trovare supporto dalla prova, peraltro impossibile ad ottenersi, che l'omissione di αὐτά accanto a εἴδη alla linea 24 da parte di tre codici (cf. apparato critico di Trendelenburg e Ross) ci riporta il vero testo originale di Aristotele. Ma l'uso di αὐτός in Aristotele non sembra così decisivo; cf. quanto già si è osservato sopra, alla n. 23.

Si può obiettare ragionevolmente a questo punto che la dottrina della derivazione del reale dalla tetractide sembra essere stata, con una più decisa coloritura di ortodossia platonica, sostenuta anche da Senocrate e non dal solo Speusippo. Senocrate è anch'egli autore di un'opera Πυθαγόρεια; ha adottato la parola ἀέναον dal verso pitagorico sulla tetractide (Stob. *Ecl.* 1, p. 123 Wachsmuth = Heinze *frg.* 28; cf. per il passo pitagorico 58 B 15, Diels, *Vorsokr.*⁹ 1, p. 455. 10); oltre a ciò, una testimonianza di Temistio sembra attribuirgli espressamente la dottrina della derivazione del tutto dalle idee dei quattro numeri sulla scorta proprio del nostro passo (Temistio, *In De An.* p. 11, 18 sgg. = *frg.* 39 Heinze).[29] Quanta importanza debba darsi a questa ultima testimonianza è dubitevole, come è dubitevole tutta la tradizione

---

[29] Cf. già sopra per la polemica riaccesasi recentemente fra Cherniss e Saffrey soprattutto (cf. anche Kucharski, "Aux frontières du Platon," pp. 35 sgg.) a proposito del passo di Temistio. Circa l'incertezza, in generale, di tutti i riferimenti all'opera di Senocrate (essendo presumibilmente la maggior parte della produzione di questi, non pubblicata ma costituente un fondo scolastico, andata perduta nell'incendio sillano di Atene) cf. Dörrie, in *RE*, Vol. IX A 2 (1967), coll. 1511–1528, s.v. *Xenokrates* (1517). Il carattere dossografico della citazione, da Andronico, toglie ad essa buona parte del suo valore secondo il Saffrey; cf. di contro Cherniss, *Gnomon* 31 (1959), pp. 41–42, secondo il quale passi come *De An.* 31. 1–5 e 32. 20–34 sembrano attestare una differenziazione netta di Temistio sia da Andronico sia da Porfirio, quindi una presumibile conoscenza diretta del Περὶ φύσεως. Ciò non cambia peraltro molto le cose. Temistio inizia parlando del *Timeo* sulla scorta di Aristotele; interpreta fedelmente lo αὐτὸ τὸ ζῷον come κόσμος νοητός formato dalle idee delle dimensioni, citando οἱ ἄνδρες ἐκεῖνοι e conclude con riferimento generico al Περὶ φύσεως di Senocrate. Continua poi l'esame delle facoltà psichiche sempre apparentemente riferendosi agli stessi ἄνδρες, ma conclude poi (p. 12, 28 sgg.) tutto il ragionamento tornando a ὁ παρὰ Πλάτωνι Τίμαιος καὶ αὐτὸς Πλάτων e cita alfine Senocrate con una differenziazione netta, ἦσαν δ' ἕτεροι κτλ. Che οἱ ἄνδρες ἐκεῖνοι possa essere espressione tale da non suscitare problemi, per l'uso costante di usare il plurale per indicare un autore singolo, è osservazione ragionevole di Cherniss, *ibid.*, p. 40, n.2 (contro Kucharski, "Aux frontières du Platon," p. 35, che vorrebbe vedere nella frase un'allusione ai Pitagorici). Ma è anche da osservare che nel passo Temistio passa da Platone a Senocrate e poi da Senocrate di nuovo a Platone e alla dottrina del *Timeo* in Platone stesso, e poi alla fine nuovamente a Senocrate. C'è da chiedersi se qui Temistio, interpretando, com'era propensione dei commentatori, tutta la dottrina contenuta nel passo fino a b27 come platonica, non abbia voluto con la citazione di Senocrate addurre quella che gli sembrava una esegesi ortodossa di Platone (sull'ortodossia, o pretesa tale, senocratea, cf. lo stesso Cherniss incisivamente, *Riddle*, p. 44); e, con οἱ ἄνδρες ἐκεῖνοι, dire esattamente lo stesso che Aristotele con οἱ τὰ εἴδη τιθέμενοι.

commentatoria neoplatonica. Noi vedremo più oltre come i commentatori abbiano tutti frainteso, in una forma o in un'altra, il passo del *De Anima* per la confusione dell'ἐν τοῖς περὶ φιλοσοφίας λεγομένοις con le lezioni orali di Platone, col Περὶ ταγαθοῦ;[30] Temistio, che non sfuggiva alla regola, ha certamente cercato di interpretare il passo del *De Anima* sulla base di quella che doveva essere l'interpretazione pitagorizzante data da Senocrate di possibili spunti matematizzanti contenuti nella dottrina del maestro. Ora, la versione del Περὶ φύσεως di Senocrate, nei confronti della dottrina dello speusippeo Περὶ πυθαγορικῶν ἀριθμῶν, doveva consistere in una trascendentizzazione della teoria della derivazione numerico-tetradica del reale, ottenuta sostituendo ai numeri-ἀρχαί le idee dei numeri, gli εἰδητικοὶ ἀριθμοί; se Temistio ha, come altri commentatori, inteso il riferimento di Aristotele a discorsi e lezioni orali di Platone nell'Accademia (che egli veda nello αὐτοζῷον l'insieme del cosmo intelligibile, cioè l'insieme delle idee, lo dice chiaramente la sua spiegazione del termine, τουτέστι τοῦ κόσμου τοῦ νοητοῦ)[31] non è strano ch'egli abbia scelto a parafrasi quella fra le versioni esegetiche della dottrina platonica che gli sembrava più fedele a questa, quella senocratea che costituisce un tentativo di combinazione fra la dottrina pitagorica della tetractide e la dottrina platonica delle idee. Ma questo non ci dice niente di decisivo circa l'interpretazione specifica del passo.

C'è un motivo che, se si accetti l'interpretazione da noi sopra tentata di αὐτὸ τὸ ζῷον, rende difficile l'attribuzione della dottrina qui riportata a Senocrate; ed è che noi ci troviamo, in questo caso, di fronte a una dottrina dell'anima in termini geometrici, quella che Senocrate sembra aver rifiutato, in probabile polemica con Speusippo (cf. Cic. *Tusc.* I. 10. 20 = *frg.* 67 Heinze: *Xenocrates animi figuram et quasi corpus negavit esse, verum numerum dixit esse.*[32] Siamo invece ricondotti, per una concezione dell'anima in

---

[30] Cherniss, *Gnomon* 31 (1959), pp. 38–39.

[31] Cf. la spiegazione che Cherniss, *ibid.*, p. 41, dà di questa interpretazione nel brano di Temistio (contro Saffrey, p. 49, n. 1). Ma essa ha probabilmente una sua spiegazione in coerenza con tutto il passo: Temistio cita Senocrate per parafrasare Platone, che rimane il suo obiettivo di fondo.

[32] Circa la testimonianza di Cicerone cf. Cherniss, *Aristotle's Criticism Pl. Acad.*, p. 399, n. 325, contro Merlan, "Beitr. Gesch. ant. Plat. II,"

termini geometrici, ancora una volta alla dottrina speusippea:
la già vista definizione dell'anima come ἰδέα τοῦ πάντῃ διαστατοῦ
sembra trovare riscontro in altre testimonianze, quella di Giamblico (*De comm. math. sc.*, pp. 40–42 Festa), di Proclo (*In pr.
Eucl. elem. lib.*, pp. 16–18 Friedlein), per non dire della prosecuzione della dottrina in Posidonio[33] e del curioso riferimento
dossografico di essa, passato attraverso Posidonio, di Diogene
Laerzio.[34] Proclo, in particolare, sembra riportarci gli echi di una
polemica interaccademica sulla composizione aritmetica o geometrica dell'anima, con l'insistenza polemica sul carattere di
πλήρωμα di questa, comprendente in sé un compendio di tutte le
forme matematiche;[35] il che ci dice che nella tradizione platonica
la καλλίστη σύνθεσις dell'anima doveva essere oggetto di dis-
cussioni e interpretazioni contrastanti. Ora, le testimonianze
circa la prima Accademia sembrerebbero ricondurci a Speusippo
per la convinzione che l'anima sia "forma dell'estensione," compendio delle dimensioni spaziali, e non a Senocrate, che avrebbe
al contrario difeso la sua interpretazione dell'anima come puro
ἀριθμός, non contaminato con lo spazio.

pp. 204–205: Senocrate oppone qui recisamente la sua concezione dell'
anima a una concezione matematico-geometrica (per la spiegazione della
definizione ἀριθμὸς κινῶν ἑαυτόν anch'essa come esegesi del *Timeo, ibid.*,
pp. 511–512). Merlan, *From Platonism to Neoplatonism*[2], p. 47, obietta
che nel passo di Cicerone non vi è contrapposizione radicale, ma solo
distinzione: benchè l'anima non possa dirsi una grandezza, *tuttavia* può
dirsi numero.
[33] Per la dimostrazione del carattere geometrico della concezione
speusippea dell'anima, cf. il già citato "Beitr. Gesch. ant. Plat. II" del
Merlan, e successivamente, con richiamo a Giamblico e alla tradizione
neoplatonica, *From Platonism to Neoplatonism*[2], pp. 11–34; 35 sgg. per
Posidonio. Cf. anche, per un'analogia fra uno spunto del *corpus Hermeticum*
e un passo di Sesto Empirico che ci riporta la dottrina posidoniano-
speusippea, "Die Hermetische Pyramide und Sextus," in *Mus. Helv.* 8
(1951), pp. 100–105. Ribadimento dell'importanza della tetractide per la
concezione speusippea dell'anima in Krämer, *Urspr. d. Geistmetaphysik*,
p. 218 (ma con tendenza ad attribuire a Speusippo una teoria di tipo
medio o neoplatonica dell'intelletto sede della tetractide come modello
del reale, che non è giustificata dai testi).
[34] Per questo (Diogene Laerzio 3. 67), cf. Merlan, "Beitr. Gesch. ant.
Plat. II," p. 209, n. 31, a proposito dell'espressione stoica πνεῦμα.
[35] Procl. *In pri. Eucl. lib.*, p. 17, 7 sgg. Friedlein; *In Ti.* 213de, II,
238–239 Diehl. Merlan, *From Platonism to Neoplatonism*[2], pp. 19 sgg.,
pone a confronto questi passi con Giamblico, sia in *De comm. math.
scientia*, sia nei passi del *De Anima* resici da Stobeo, 1. 49, pp. 363–364
Wachsmuth.

Né per Speusippo né per Senocrate la tradizione ci parla di una riduzione delle facoltà conoscitive dell'anima ai numeri della tetractide. Conosciamo questa riduzione solo per la tradizione pitagorica: Aezio, *Plac.* I. 3. 8 (Diels, *Dox. Graec.*, pp. 282–283) e Teone di Smirne (*Exp. rer. math.*, pp. 97–98 Hiller) il quale ultimo, in particolare, ci riporta, in una lunga serie di tetractidi, una tetractide νοητή, in cui figurano appunto i quattro termini di νοῦς, ἐπιστήμη, δόξα, αἴσθησις.[36] È ben difficile fare ipotesi sull'antichità di questa formulazione, che può facilmente pensarsi, come tanto altro materiale neopitagorico, di derivazione platonico-accademica. Che i commentatori neoplatonici, parafrasando il passo del *De Anima*, siano in parte propensi ad attribuire ai pitagorici la dottrina in esso contenuta, non significa in verità molto, data la confusione fra platonismo e pitagorismo operata dalla tarda antichità, e le cui radici stanno del resto nella stessa prima Accademia;[37] fra i commentatori vediamo in realtà regnare la più grande confusione circa l'attribuzione del nostro passo (mentre Temistio, come abbiamo visto, lo parafrasa con un tratto della *Fisica* senocratea, Simplicio [*In de An.*, p. 28, 12 sgg. Hayduck] accenna a una dottrina esoterica rivestita esteriormente di formule matematiche che sembra, da alcune espressioni,[38] identificarsi con quella pitagorica; di Platone e dei Pitagorici insieme parla Filopono [*In De An.*, p. 74, 30–p. 81, 31 Hayduck]; di Platone parla decisamente Giamblico [in Stob. *Ecl.* I, p. 364, 13 Wachsmuth]). D'altronde le quattro facoltà conoscitive di cui si parla sembrano aver colorito decisamente platonico. Che esse siano però esclusivamente rispondenti a una

---

[36] Kucharski, *Étude doctr. pythag. tétrade*, pp. 37 sgg.; "Aux frontières du Platon," pp. 13 sgg. Cf. le riserve sull' importanza di questa così tarda testimonianza in Saffrey, *Le ΠΕΡΙ ΦΙΛ. d'Arist.*, pp. X sgg; negazione recisa che possa trattarsi di autentica dottrina pitagorica antica in Burkert, *Weish. u. Wiss.*, p. 62, n. 110, coerentemente del resto all'assunto di tutto il libro. La testimonianza più valida circa i rapporti fra facoltà conoscitive e numeri, per il Burkert, è quella che si riferisce ad Aristotele, Alessandro, *In Metaph.*, p. 39, 13 sgg. Hayduck (Νοῦν δὲ καὶ οὐσίαν ἔλεγον τὸ ἕν ... δόξαν δὲ τὰ δύο; cf. *frg.* 13, p. 139, 2 sgg. Ross). Tutto ciò può infirmare la derivazione pitagorica del passo del *De Anima*; ma non quella dal pitagorizzante Speusippo.

[37] Ancora Burkert, *Weish. u. Wiss.*, pp. 55–56 e altrove.

[38] Cf. per queste Saffrey, *Le ΠΕΡΙ ΦΙΛ. d'Arist.*, p. 43; ma cf. anche il giudizio negativo sulla testimonianza di Simplicio come su quella di Filopono, pp. 45–46.

partizione senocratea, non potrebbe dirsi. Sesto Empirico, *Math.* 7. 147 sgg. (= *frg.* 5 Heinze) ci attesta per Senocrate una divisione del reale conoscibile in oggetti del νοῦς o νοητά, esistenti in una sorta di τόπος ὑπερουράνιος, con evidente richiamo al *Fedro*, oggetti della δόξα, δοξαστά, che sussistono nei cieli stessi, oggetti della αἴσθησις, αἰσθητά, sussistenti al di sotto dei cieli.[39] Ma per Speusippo lo stesso Sesto appena più sopra (*Math.* 7. 145 [*frg.* 29 Lang]) parla di una distinzione in νοητά e αἰσθητά che è poi completata da una testimonianza di Proclo (*In prim. Eucl. elem. lib.*, p. 179, 8 Friedlein [= *frg.* 30 Lang]): in essa troviamo fatta una distinzione fra il νοῦς che coglie immediatamente gli oggetti, con una ἐπαφὴ ἐναργεστέρα rispetto alla stessa ὄψις τῶν ὁρατῶν, e una successiva forma di deduzione dai principi con μετάβασις a una determinata conclusione, che ricorda sensibilmente la ἐπιστήμη e il μοναχῶς γὰρ ἐφ' ἕν del passo del *De Anima*. Se quindi per Senocrate abbiamo la successione νοῦς-δόξα-αἴσθησις, per Speusippo sembra di poter formulare la successione νοῦς-ἐπιστήμη-αἴσθησις; senza contare che quella della δόξα è teoria parmenideo-platonica assai generica, condivisa probabilmente da tutti i discepoli accademici.[40]

L'identificazione che sappiamo essere stata fatta da Senocrate fra νοῦς e μονάς potrebbe forse costituire un punto a favore dell'attribuzione a Senocrate: ci è riportata come senocratea una dottrina che identifica μονάς e δυάς con νοῦς e ψυχή cosmica, facendo del νοῦς il πρῶτος θεός, detto anche μονάς, e della ψυχὴ τοῦ παντός una divinità inferiore e subordinata.[41] Questa dottrina,

---

[39] A proposito di questo passo Dörrie, *op. cit.*, s.v. *Xenocrates*, coll. 1520–1521, che lo vede come la contropartita su piano conoscitivo dell'altro, *frg.* 26 Heinze, da Teofrasto, *Metaph.* 6a: in esso sono citati αἰσθητὰ καὶ νοητὰ καὶ μαθηματικὰ καὶ ἔτι δὴ τὰ θεῖα (cf. la trad. di Ross-Fobes, p. 13, "or mathematicals"; contro cui Merlan, *From Platonism to Neoplatonism*[2], p. 44, n. 2).

[40] Cf. ad esempio, per la frequenza del termine nell'*Epinomide*, probabile opera di Filippo di Opunte, 976a5, b3, 978b4, ecc. Per la presenza della successione νοῦς – ἐπιστήμη – δόξα – αἴσθησις nello stesso Aristotele, *De An.* 428a4 sgg. e, in forma analoga, *Metaph.* 1075b35 sgg., cf. lo stesso Theiler, *Arist. Ueber die Seele*, p. 94.

[41] Cf. *frg.* 15 Heinze, da Aezio, 1. 7. 30 (Stobeo 1, p. 36 Wachsmuth). In proposito recentemente Krämer, *Urspr. d. Geistmetaphysik*, pp. 56 sgg., 99 sgg., 119 sgg., 371 sgg.; con tendenza, anche qui, ad attribuire già a Senocrate una dottrina del νοῦς come sede delle idee, contenente in sè i modelli eterni del reale, che sembra in realtà possibile solo dopo la

che rappresenta un saggio dello sforzo di Senocrate di offrire un travestimento teologico da un lato, cosmologico dall'altro, dei concetti ontologico-metafisici, ha comunque certo ben poco a che fare con la dottrina che identifica con un determinato numero il νοῦς come facoltà dell'anima; in questa formulazione il νοῦς appare non come uno dei costituenti dell'anima stessa, ma come trascendente ad essa e ad essa contrapposto, con una evidente ipostatizzazione di concetti del *Timeo*.[42] Analogamente, sembra aver poco o niente a che fare con la dottrina del νοῦς come facoltà conoscitiva il rifiuto di Speusippo di identificare l'uno o il bene con l'intelletto, che è una probabile risposta a tale identificazione compiuta da Senocrate e, in altra forma, da Aristotele: quando Speusippo (Aezio, in Stob. *Ecl.* 1. 1, p. 35 Wachsmuth = *frg.* 38 Lang) afferma che il νοῦς è dio, ma non si identifica nè con l'uno nè col bene, essendo ἰδιοφυής, egli intende anzitutto salvaguardare la peculiarità della sua concezione dell' uno come anteriore all'antitesi bene-male e alla stessa οὐσία, affermare una volta di più che l'uno, ἀνούσιος, non è passibile di qualificazioni che competono solo a ulteriori determinazioni del reale; e forse con νοῦς-θεός, stando almeno ai termini della testimonianza di Aezio, intende lo stesso principio psichico-

contaminazione con dottrine stoiche (A. Schmekel, *Die Philosophie der mittleren Stoa* [Berlin, 1892], pp. 430 sgg.; W. Theiler, *Die Vorbereitung des Neuplatonismus* [Berlin, 1930), pp. 16 sgg., 39 sgg.; G. Luck, *Der Akademiker Antiochos von Askalon* [Bern-Stuttgart, 1953], pp. 28 sgg.).

[42] Sia in Speusippo che in Senocrate va distinta la trattazione dello ἕν come supremo principio dal riconoscimento del carattere unitario dell'intuizione intellettiva. Quando gli accademici contrappongono lo ἕν come principio ad altre realtà, la contrapposizione si attua nei termini di ἕν – δυάς, ο ἄνισον, ο πλῆθος. Così, in Senocrate, il νοῦς – μονάς, concepito come supremo principio cosmico a somiglianza e proiezione cosmologica del supremo principio ontologico, viene contrapposto alla δυάς – anima del mondo, anch'essa sorta di proiezione cosmologica del secondo principio ontologico-metafisico (su questa dottrina cf. R. Heinze, *Xenokrates* [Leipzig, 1892], pp. 35 sgg., che distingue questa seconda δυάς dalla δυὰς ἀόριστος, contro l'identificazione fattane da Zeller, *Philosophie der Griechen* II, 1⁵, p. 1014, n. 3. Cf. il rilievo dato alla dottrina della diade-ψυχὴ τοῦ κόσμου dal Krämer, *Urspr. d. Geistmetaphysik*, p. 35 e *passim*). In ogni caso, tornando a Speusippo, è probabile che il *frg.* 38 Lang sottolinei semplicemente la distinzione del νοῦς come forza cosmica dall'Uno come principio, forse in polemica con Senocrate che ha fatto dell'Uno-forza cosmica la proiezione dell'Uno supremo (cf. Teofrasto, *Metaph.* 6a, Ross-Fobes, p. 12: ἅπαντά πως περιτίθησιν περὶ τὸν κόσμον, e l'importanza data a questa notizia dal Dörrie, *op. cit.*, s.v. *Xenokrates*, coll. 1517–1518).

cosmico nella sua interezza, se possiamo concedere credito alla testimonianza di Cicerone, *Nat. D.* 1. 13. 32 (= *frg.* 39a Lang), che Speusippo avrebbe cioè detto dio *vim quandam ... qua omnia regantur, eamque animalem*. Siamo di fronte a due tarde testimonianze che sembrano offrirci due diverse visioni, in Senocrate e in Speusippo, del divino, l'una in forma trascendente, subordinante la ψυχή a un superiore νοῦς ch'è anche monade suprema, l'altro immanente; in entrambe queste due concezioni il problema dell'uno o della μονάς è trattato del tutto indipendentemente dall'analisi di facoltà conoscitive, nell'ambito di una valutazione cosmologica e ontologica generale.

Detto tutto questo, occorre porsi nuovamente di fronte al capitolo del *De Anima* nel suo insieme, per studiare l'esatta collocazione in esso del nostro passo. L'argomentazione di cui questo fa parte si può considerare iniziantesi a 403b20: essa vuole essere anzitutto una presentazione di δόξαι dei predecessori di Aristotele nell'indagine intorno all'anima, che hanno creduto di poter definire l'anima stessa in base alle caratteristiche del movimento e della conoscenza (403b26, κινήσει καὶ τῷ αἰσθάνεσθαι), presentazione che passa alternativamente dall'esposizione delle teorie in cui prevale l'uno a quelle in cui prevale l'altro elemento. Platone, in questa rassegna, è richiamato una volta implicitamente, in 404a20 sgg., ove viene esposta la dottrina platonica del *Fedro* (l'anima è αὐτὸ κινοῦν) e delle *Leggi* (l'anima è la sola realtà capace di muovere se stessa e di comunicare alle altre il movimento) una seconda volta, esplicitamente, per l'altro aspetto della dottrina, quello della composizione dell'anima da στοιχεῖα che le permette (per il principio empedocleo che il simile può conoscere il simile, 404b11 sgg.) di comprendere il reale, anch'esso formato di στοιχεῖα: τὸν αὐτὸν δὲ τρόπον καὶ Πλάτων ἐν τῷ Τιμαίῳ τὴν ψυχὴν ἐκ τῶν στοιχείων ποιεῖ (404b16–17). Subito dopo viene esposta la dottrina già più ampiamente presentata altrove, nel Περὶ φιλοσοφίας, dottrina che riguarda la composizione dell' anima in base a στοιχεῖα: secondo questa dottrina l'anima, ch'è l'autentico essere vivente, compendia in sè le proporzioni dell' universo spaziale e insieme le facoltà del conoscere che sono esprimibili mediante gli stessi numeri di quelle; i numeri sono poi a loro volta formati da elementi primi, στοιχεῖα; secondo gli στοιχεῖα e secondo i numeri, così come l'anima, sono formate tutte le cose dell'universo sensibile. Ma a 404b27 Aristotele, riallacciandosi all'altro aspetto lasciato momentaneamente in disparte, quello dell'anima come principio di movimento autonomo, afferma che "alcuni" hanno sentito il bisogno di fare di questi due aspetti un'unica definizione, dichiarando l'anima essere un numero che muove se stesso.[43]

Sembra, a chi scrive, di poter affermare che ci troviamo di fronte a: (1) Platone (2) un'esegesi di Platone che pone in rilievo la teoria della formazione dell'anima in base agli stessi στοιχεῖα dell'universo (3) una seconda esegesi di Platone che intende far valere, unendoli (συνέπλεξαν), ambedue i momenti fondamentali della teoria platonica dell'anima, l'autocinesi e la formazione in base ad elementi, intesa in senso schiettamente matematico.

Non ci sembra che la logica di tutto il discorso porti ad attribuire le due esegesi alla stessa persona, Gli ἔνιοι che intervengono alla fine dell'esposizione non sono posti in contrapposizione ai sostenitori delle dottrine precedenti perchè non si tratta qui tanto di far rilevare una differenziazione quanto quella che appare ad Aristotele una prosecuzione a partire da posizioni date; ma non si saprebbe identificarli con il non nominato sostenitore della dottrina dell'anima che precede. E questi ἔνιοι autori della seconda esegesi non possono non essere Senocrate e la sua cerchia, per la peculiarità della dottrina dell'anima come ἀριθμὸς κινῶν ἑαυτόν così largamente riportataci dai commentatori come senocratea, se solo si guardi alla lunga serie delle testi-

---

[43] In questo senso sembrano ragionevoli le osservazioni di quanti vedono nelle linee 27–30 intervenire la citazione di una nuova e diversa dottrina; anche se la spiegazione offerta dal Cherniss (che cioè qui abbiamo solo la conclusione di un ragionamento precedente in cui Aristotele combina insieme due differenti aspetti della dottrina senocratea dell'anima, citando a sua giustificazione l'opera in cui ha fatto del problema una più ampia trattazione secondo questo schema combinatorio) è, come sempre, saggio di sottile perizia interpretativa. In realtà ciò che conferisce novità alla citazione di Senocrate in 27–30 è il significato generale del passo nel contesto del capitolo del *De Anima*; Aristotele, dopo essersi dilungato su definizioni in cui non è presente l'elemento cinetico (cf. de Vogel, "Later Platonism II," p. 304), conclude infine con la citazione di un autore che ha voluto unire nella stessa definizione elemento matematico ed elemento cinetico, "riunendo" ciò che trovava diviso altrove, cioè, se si guarda 404a20 sgg. e 404b15–18, nell'opera di Platone. La stessa "combinazione di due diversi aspetti della dottrina senocratea" viene meno se si dà a ἔτι δὲ καὶ ἄλλως il significato proposto sopra.

monianze raccolte nel *frg.* 60 Heinze. L'uso poi di citare insieme, senza un ordine ben fisso, Platone, Speusippo, Senocrate, è corrente in Aristotele, com'è fin troppo noto; si pensi, per la sola *Metafisica*, alla presumibile successione Platone-Senocrate-Speusippo in 1076a19 sgg., 1069a33 sgg.,[44] a quella Platone-Speusippo-Senocrate in 1028b18 sgg., 1080b22 sgg., e altrove;[45] serie talvolta complicata dall'inserzione dei pitagorici, talvolta da quella di altri platonici di impossibile identificazione, come l'ἄλλος τις di 1080b21;[46] ma costituita il più delle volte proprio dalla citazione di Platone e dei suoi due principali discepoli accademici. C'è quindi da chiedersi se anche qui non ci troviamo di fronte a un fatto di ordine analogo: se, non credendo di poter ammettere nè l'identificazione di Platone con l'autore della teoria della struttura geometrica dell'anima e della identificazione delle facoltà conoscitive con i numeri della tetractide, nè l'identificazione di questo col successivo autore di una definizione sintetica abbracciante l'aspetto matematico e l'aspetto cinetico della dottrina, non possiamo ragionevolmente supporre (sempre con il largo margine di ipoteticità che comporta ognuna di queste attribuzioni) di trovarci di fronte a una citazione di Platone seguita da una di Speusippo e successivamente da una di Senocrate.[47]

In questo caso, avremmo forse la spiegazione più precisa del significato della definizione speusippea di anima come ἰδέα τοῦ πάντῃ διαστατοῦ: esegesi del *Timeo*, certo, come qui Aristotele indica chiaramente,[48] ma insieme anche, per l'impossibilità di

[44] Cf. Ross, *Metaph.*[2] II, p. 408, p. 350.

[45] *Ibid.*, p. 163, p. 430, ecc.

[46] Ross, *Metaph.*[2] II, p. 429; cf. già le congetture di Zeller, *Phil. d. Gr.* II, 1[5], p. 1033, n. 3.

[47] Che Giamblico, nello stesso contesto in cui ci riporta la teoria di *De An.* 404b18 sgg., ci riporti anche la teoria di Speusippo come distinta e separata da questa, ch'egli attribuisce invece a Platone, può non avere molto significato; per i limiti della testimonianza di Giamblico e la sua pura dipendenza dal *De Anima* cf. Cherniss, *Gnomon* 31 (1959), p. 43 (contro Saffrey, pp. 34–37). Convinto dalla tradizione commentatoria all'attribuzione del passo a Platone, Giamblico può semplicemente non aver riconosciuto in questo riferimento una esegesi ispirata a quei criteri di costruzione geometrica, tetradico-piramidale, dell'anima che varie altre fonti gli indicavano per Speusippo.

[48] Ciò in appoggio a Cherniss, *Aristotle's Criticism Pl. Acad.*, pp. 509–511; ma senza infirmare con ciò la interpretazione del Merlan.

creare una divisione nettissima fra esegesi e dottrina in questi primi seguaci di Platone (essi inaugurano con ciò, del resto, una metodologia che sarà in ambito neoplatonico larghissimamente seguita), esposizione di una propria convinzione teoretica. Il carattere geometrico-spaziale dell' anima, che doveva sembrare a Speusippo garantito da passi quali *Ti.* 36de (ἡ δ' ἐκ μέσου πρὸς τὸν ἔσχατον οὐρανὸν πάντῃ διαπλακεῖσα κύκλῳ τε αὐτὸν ἔξωθεν περικαλύψασα κτλ.), doveva trovare per lui la sua spiegazione nell'identità fra i numeri cui sono riducibili l'uno e le dimensioni spaziali e i numeri cui sono riducibili le fondamentali facoltà conoscitive: l'identità di essenza numerica di queste con le caratteristiche fondamentali del corporeo doveva garantire ai suoi occhi in ultima analisi la possibilità di sostenere la struttura geometrica dell'anima.[49] L'intento di spiegare Platone per mezzo di Pitagora, di accettare Platone traducendolo in linguaggio pitagorico, quadra perfettamente con ciò che da altre fonti e per altri problemi conosciamo della dottrina di Speusippo; così come da ciò che conosciamo per altre vie della dottrina di Senocrate possiamo essere giustificati nel ritenere che, di fronte a questa esegesi speusippea, Senocrate sia stato portato ad affermare una esegesi di più integrale adesione a quella del maestro, un'esegesi e una dottrina che potesse, delle sparse espressioni di Platone nei dialoghi, fornire una sintesi e un compendio.

Università di Cagliari

---

[49] Cherniss ha visto, *ibid.*, p. 510, un contrasto fra questa attribuzione di teoria geometrica dell'anima a Speusippo, e *Metaph.* 1028b21–24, 1090b13–20, in cui Aristotele sembra attribuire a Speusippo un principio per le grandezze spaziali e uno diverso per l'anima. Cf. il tentativo d'interpretazione fatto recentemente da Krämer, *Urspr. d. Geistmetaphysik*, pp. 209–210, dell'anima in Speusippo come "bewegte Figuren," come "ἰδέα τοῦ πάντῃ διαστατοῦ ... mit κίνησις", e la giustificazione data di ciò a p. 209, n. 48: la qualificazione di "in movimento" si ricava sufficientemente dalla posizione cosmica immanente dell' anima del mondo e dal paragone col *Timeo* di Platone e con la definizione di Senocrate. Ciò è saggio di esegesi combinatoria che prosegue veramente il metodo esegetico dei commentatori neoplatonici; le differenze fra Platone, interpretato sulla base dell'attribuzione di *De An.* 404b18 sgg., Senocrate e Speusippo sfumano nel nulla. E'del tutto probabile che Speusippo non inserisse nella definizione dell'anima alcun elemento cinetico, almeno in forma esplicita, contentandosi di quello implicito nella connessione fra anima e ζωή o ζῷον. Ma il passo di Aristotele ἄλλην μὲν ἀριθμῶν ἄλλην δὲ

μεγεθῶν, ἔπειτα ψυχῆς (1028b21 sgg.) potrebbe essere interpretato come forzatura, da parte di Aristotele stesso (interessato a rimproverare a Speusippo la concezione episodica e non unitaria dell'essere), di una teoria che pone come ἀρχή del numero lo ἕν e il πλῆθος, come ἀρχή delle grandezze spaziali la tetractide nella forma punto-dimensioni, come ἀρχή dell'anima la tetractide nella forma delle quattro facoltà conoscitive, riducibili nella loro essenza a numeri, strutturate nel loro insieme come figura. Cherniss stesso ci ha insegnato a diffidare delle forzature aristoteliche, ed è probabile che qui ci troviamo di fronte a una di queste, che non può perciò valere a infirmare le testimonianze che ci giungono da altre parti, da Posidonio, Plutarco, Giamblico.

PLATO'S FIRST MOVER IN THE EIGHTH BOOK
OF ARISTOTLE'S *PHYSICS*

FRIEDRICH SOLMSEN

For Plato the ἀρχὴ κινήσεως in the physical world is the self-moving principle, which he identifies with Soul. A most carefully wrought proof for this doctrine is incorporated in the *Phaedrus*, and in Book X of the *Laws* the supremacy of ψυχή is established on an even broader basis.[1] Aristotle, as is well known, entertains a very different conception of the First Mover. The last Book of his *Physics* deduces the existence of an ἀκίνητον as the necessary "first" in the series of movents and clarifies its place in the scheme of cosmic movements, leaving it to the *Metaphysics* (Λ) to secure for the Unmoved Mover a corresponding position in the ontological hierarchy and to become somewhat more outspoken about his divine qualities. Since this Mover as ἀρχὴ κινήσεως succeeds to the place of the Platonic World Soul, it would seem to be no more than natural that Aristotle should in *Physics* VIII make clear why he disapproves of Plato's doctrine; in fact, one might almost expect this. Actually Aristotle does state – and substantiate – his adverse opinion about soul in the role of a first movent, yet the polemical character of the section written for this purpose has often eluded his modern students – understandably enough, because neither Plato's name nor the word ψυχή occurs in it. The section extends from 259b1 to b28. Jaeger [2] was cer-

---

[1] *Phdr.* 245c5–246a1; *Leg.* 10. 891e4–899c4, esp. 894c3–896b3. On the argument in the *Laws*, see my comments in *Plato's Theology* (Ithaca, N.Y., 1942), p. 131; on *Timaeus, ibid.*, p. 115. For a bibliography of studies dealing with "Soul as autokinetic cause" in Plato, see Cherniss, *Lustrum* 5 (1960), pp. 371 ff. Cf. also Julius Stenzel, *Kleine Schriften zur Griechischen Philosophie*[2] (Darmstadt, 1957), pp. 1 ff., 13 ff.

[2] W. Jaeger, *Aristoteles*[2] (Berlin, 1955), pp. 385 f. (Eng. translation, p. 360). Jaeger refers specifically to 259b1–20 but from his comments it appears probable that he thought of b20–28 as well.

tainly right in thinking that Plato and his theory of soul are in Aristotle's mind here. Inasmuch as Aristotle has just prior to 259b1 set forth the basic arguments in support of his own ἀκίνητον, a polemical digression against the rival principle would seem to be entirely in place at this point; yet it is better not to take this view with too much determination before the text has been scrutinized as closely as is necessary if we wish to understand Aristotle's intentions and his rather peculiar procedure. The subject of 259b1–28 [3] is the movement not so much of ψυχή as of living things, ἔμψυχα. The same subject engages Aristotle also in earlier passages of Book VIII, and it may be well to preface our analysis of 259b1–28 by a brief consideration of these other passages. [4]

At 252b16–28, where for the first time account is taken of ἔμψυχα, they require attention because their seemingly spontaneous movements could be used to argue against the eternity and uninterrupted continuation of movement in the physical world [5] (Aristotle's fundamental thesis which has been established in ch. 1). For if living beings are sometimes completely at rest, and then again begin to move, movement in the Cosmos, too, need not go on without interruption, and it would be conceivable that conditions of rest should alternate with those of movement. In brief what the ἔμψυχα suggest would be the following: ἐγγίγνεται κίνησις πρότερον οὐκ οὖσα (cf. 253a8). [6] Aristotle himself tells us plainly that the significance of such spontaneous origin of movement in living beings, if the idea as such is correct, lies in its possible application (by analogical reasoning) to the Cosmos:

---

[3] As for 259b28–31, Jaeger, *ibid.*, pp. 389 f. (Eng. translation, p. 364) and Ross, *Aristotle's Physics* (Oxford, 1936), p. 102 agree in considering it a later addition. See also on this passage Philip Merlan, "Aristotle's Unmoved Mover," *Traditio* 4 (1946), pp. 1–30, esp. p. 26. Among the many studies devoted to Platonic antecedents of Aristotle's theology this paper is distinguished by its independent and highly original approach.

[4] I have not included an examination of *De An.* I. 3 in this paper; for while this chapter offers interesting parallels to individual steps made in the arguments of *Physics* VIII, there is something unique about Aristotle's purpose and conclusion in this Book.

[5] Lifeless objects (ἄψυχα) present a similar, if less serious ἔνστασις (Arist. *Ph.* 252b12 ff.).

[6] Cf. the first words of Book VIII (250b11) where this thought is formulated as the antithesis of what Aristotle himself is setting out to prove. See also 252b7 ff., 252b16, 259b3.

εἰ δ'ἐν ζῴῳ τοῦτο δυνατὸν γενέσθαι, τί κωλύει τὸ αὐτὸ συμβῆναι καὶ κατὰ τὸ πᾶν; εἰ γὰρ ἐν μικρῷ κόσμῳ γίγνεται, καὶ ἐν μεγάλῳ· (252b24–27). For the problem we may compare Plato's question in the *Laws*: εἰ σταίη πως τὰ πάντα ὁμοῦ γενόμενα (as most of the physicists "dare" to say), τίν'ἄρα ἐν αὐτοῖς ἀνάγκη πρώτην κίνησιν γενέσθαι...; To which his answer is τὴν αὐτὴν ἑαυτὴν δήπου κινοῦσαν (895a6 ff.; Plato is on the way toward identifying this movement as that of soul).

To return to Aristotle, he recognizes the evidence presented by living beings as his greatest ἀπορία (253a7) but meets it even here by arguments essentially of the same type as those employed later (259b20 ff.) in the decisive confrontation of alleged self-movers with his own Unmoved Mover. The arguments in the earlier passage (253a7–21) may be summarized as follows: (1) Some kind of movement (in the sense of physiological process) is coming to pass all the time in the body of living beings; this is true even while they are asleep, and eventually the movement reaches διάνοια or ὄρεξις, causing such beings to wake up and to start the more characteristic movement of ἔμψυχα, which is locomotion;[7] (2) The actual origin of animal motion is in the environment (τὸ περιέχον); influences from it work on the animal body [8] and produce the movements taking place in it. Thus the origin is "outside" (ἔξω), not ἐξ αὐτῶν; (cf. 252b20, 24) and this would knock out an important distinction made by Plato;[9] (3) Self-motion (as we speak of it) in ἔμψυχα materializes only in the form of one *genus* of movement, namely, locomotion. Once more the target must be Plato, whose definition of soul as ἑαυτὴν κινοῦσα was evidently too sweeping and is considered in need of restrictions. However, Aristotle's argument as a whole is not directed against Plato but against those Presocratics who (as Aristotle reads them) deny the eternity of movement in the physical world, holding that movement may cease and later

[7] 253a11 ff., 15–20.
[8] 253a12 f., 15 ff. In the later discussion of living entities Aristotle illustrates this contention by using food as an example (259b11 ff.).
[9] *Phdr.* 245e4: πᾶν σῶμα ᾧ μὲν ἔξωθεν τὸ κινεῖσθαι ἄψυχον, ᾧ δὲ ἔνδοθεν αὐτῷ ἐξ αὐτοῦ, ἔμψυχον...κτλ.
Cf. Cherniss, *Aristotle's Criticism of Plato and the Academy* (Baltimore, 1944), p. 389, n. 309.

again arise.[10] The facts about ἔμψυχα, if correctly stated as Aristotle here endeavors to do, lend no support to such views.

As for Plato, when he called soul ἀρχὴ κινήσεως, he had in mind something more fundamental: a spiritual principle as the cause of life in man and Cosmos, nor did he use the word ἀρχή with reference to the empirical fact that a living being after a time of rest or sleep again begins to move. Even the argument quoted above from *Leg.* 10. 895a6 ff. does not rely on analogical conditions in living beings and is, moreover, purely hypothetical, involving an assumption which Plato himself condemns. Thus if Plato's definition of soul as ἀρχὴ κινήσεως is present to Aristotle during this disquisition (and this seems to me hardly open to question),[11] its meaning has been twisted and it is discussed with reference to the issue: is it possible for cosmic movement to cease and later to begin again? – which surely was not Plato's primary concern. Moreover, the fact that Plato focuses on ψυχή, Aristotle on ἔμψυχα is bound to make a difference.[12]

The second discussion of living beings is found in ch. 4. Here Aristotle has set up a classification of movements based on several criteria of differentiation. Movement, or more precisely "to be moved," καθ'αὑτά, is to be distinguished from κατὰ συμβεβηκός, motions φύσει, from motions βίᾳ.[13] Still the thesis in which this chapter culminates applies to all varieties: in each of them there must be a κινοῦν, an agent of movement: ἅπαντα ἂν κινούμενα ὑπό τινος κινοῖτο (see 256a2 f.). In the context of his classifications, Aristotle treats living beings as moved ὑφ'αὑτῶν and φύσει (254b14 ff.); he affirms: κινεῖται γὰρ τὸ ζῷον αὐτὸ ὑφ'αὑτοῦ (254b15), accepting it as self-mover at least as far as the being as a "whole" is concerned (τὸ. ζῷον ὅλον b17; within the

[10] Cf. 250b24 ff., 252a5 ff.

[11] It was, after all, Plato who had emphasized the ἑαυτὸ κινεῖν of living beings and used the argument εἰ σταίη πως τὰ πάντα ὁμοῦ γενόμενα...κτλ. Moreover the corresponding argument in 259b1–28 has Plato for its target.

[12] Regarding the larger issues which for Plato are associated with his conception of soul as originator of all movements (and which Aristotle ignores), a brief reminder must suffice here. In the proof of *Laws* X the primacy of Soul guarantees the presence of order (τάξις) in the physical world as well as the priority of mental and moral values over what is purely physical (892b, 896c f.; cf. *Plato's Theology*, pp. 142 ff.).

[13] 254b7 ff., 12 ff. In the latter passage Aristotle also distinguishes between movement ὑφ'ἑαυτοῦ and ὑπ'ἄλλου.

ζῷον an active and a passive factor are to be distinguished, 27–33).[14] This view may cause us a slight surprise, since the earlier section introduced qualifications for the ἐξ αὐτοῦ movement of living beings. Was the classification of ch. 4 worked out before closer examination of the subject had convinced Aristotle how problematic the concept of a living being as "moved by itself"[15] is? While I should not rule out this possibility, it probably is better to acquiesce in the explanation that since Aristotle's concern in ch. 4 is to make sure of his generalization: "everything in motion is moved by something," he sees no harm in operating with a rather inaccurate and no longer quite up-to-date definition of living beings. The ὑπό τινος κινεῖσθαι holds good for living entities in any case, even if the ἀρχή has on closer analysis to be sought "outside," not within the being. Actually even though Aristotle emphasizes this "outside," he may never have entirely renounced the (Platonic) definition of living beings as self-movers.

Turning now to the section in which we are especially interested (259b1–31), we may begin by summarizing the thought of 259b1–20: Various movements that materialize in a living being are not δι'αὐτῶν (b9), and even that by which they move themselves (αὐτά b7), locomotion – their characteristic movement, as we know – has its origin outside: οὐ γὰρ ἐξ αὐτοῦ τὸ αἴτιον (b7 f.). The specific theories which support these assertions are of the same type as those embodied in the pertinent section of ch. 2. The movements originate in the environment. Food enters from the outside, and when it has been digested, the being wakes up and begins its locomotion again, after a period of ἠρεμεῖν.[16] It does not matter that on Aristotle's own showing some kind of movements would continue even while the living being is asleep; he still feels entitled to assert οὐκ ἀεὶ κινοῦνται συνεχῶς ὑφ'αὐτῶν (b14 ff.). Here ἀεί and συνεχῶς have no less emphasis than ὑφ'αὐτῶν; in effect, all of these concepts are negated for the living being. The next sentence places the κινοῦν once more in the

[14] See 254b27 ff., esp. 30–33. One would think that the active factor must be ψυχή, but Aristotle here, as elsewhere in Book VIII, does not commit himself to this concept.
[15] Note also 255a5–7.
[16] See b7–14 (ἠρεμεῖν b10).

environment.[17] After it Aristotle continues: "In all these (sc. self-movers) the first movent and cause of self-movement is moved by itself but κατὰ συμβεβηκός. For the body changes its place, and as a result, also, that which is in the body and which by means of leverage moves itself." The explanation for this at first glance enigmatic sentence is supplied by Simplicius and Sir David Ross, whom we may quote: "If a lever is to continue to lift a weight, it must keep in contact with the weight as the latter moves. Aristotle's thought is that similarly the soul as it moves the body must keep in contact with the body, and thus by moving the body incidentally moves itself." Presumably the movement of soul is "incidental" because it is a part of,[18] or has its place in, the body so that it is moved by the movement of the body.

Aristotle never in this section (or in those of chs. 2 and 4 previously examined) uses the word ψυχή. Still there can be no doubt that the words τὸ αἴτιον τοῦ αὐτὸ ἑαυτὸ κινεῖν...κατὰ συμβεβηκός and again τὸ...τῇ μοχλείᾳ κινοῦν ἑαυτό refer to soul and that the interpreters have correctly accepted the words in this meaning.[19] Compared with the exalted position which Plato had given it in the scheme of movements, ψυχή is clearly now much reduced in status. It is no longer an ἀρχὴ κινήσεως, for the πρώτη ἀρχή is, as we read b13 f., outside; and it is "moved by itself" only incidentally. If it still is called αἴτιον τοῦ αὐτὸ ἑαυτὸ κινεῖν (b17), this description, while apt to recall former glories, means much less than it used to; for Aristotle insists that self-movement in the living being is nothing continuous. Is the soul itself still an ἀεὶ κινοῦν? Our section includes no clear-cut decision of this question; for Aristotle says only of the ἔμψυχον, not of ψυχή, that it is "sometimes unmoved" or "at rest" [20] and then again moved. Growth, decrease, and respiration which come to pass in the animal while it is at rest (b9) may not qualify as movements of

[17] ἄλλο γὰρ τὸ κινοῦν (b15). κίνησις or μεταβολή in the environment has its effect on the living being.
[18] Cf. the definition of "incidental" at 254b8 ff. For the quotation, see Ross, *op. cit.* (n. 3 above), p. 707.
[19] See Simpl. 1259. 8 ff.; Ross (*op. cit.* [n. 3 above]) *ad* b19; Cornford *ad loc.* (in *Aristotle, The Physics with an Engl. Transl.* by Philip H. Wicksteed and Francis M. Cornford, Loeb Classical Library, 2 vols., 1932–34).
[20] 259b5, 10.

soul, but since digestion takes place during the sleep (b12), Aristotle could, if he had wished to, have considered the nutritive soul as operating also during the sleep, while the other soul functions would become active when the living being wakes up. Yet nothing to this effect can be extracted from the section, and the implication of Aristotle's reasoning would rather seem to be that soul is no more an ἀεὶ κινούμενον than the entity in which it finds itself.

In the next sentences Aristotle proceeds to draw a conclusion from this inquiry into self-movement in living beings (it was probably for the sake of this conclusion that the inquiry was undertaken). Now what he does is to confront an incidental self-mover with the Unmoved Mover of his own system. Bearing in mind what we have learned in the preceding statements about ἔμψυχα and about ψυχή, we may ask which of them actually figures in this confrontation. Again Aristotle does not use the word ψυχή. He refers to the entity in question as something τῶν ἀκινήτων μὲν, κινούντων δὲ καὶ αὐτὰ κατὰ συμβεβηκός.[21] Since the last six words evidently echo the description just given of the movement of soul, soul must be the "something" (τί) of which Aristotle speaks.[22] Indeed, an ἔμψυχον, i.e., an entity having body as well as soul, could, in this context where the eternal movement of the physical world is the issue, only be an anthropomorphic deity, whose appearance at this juncture would be not only unexpected but also pointless. And it is after all only soul, not

---

[21] 259b21 ff. The textual tradition is not unanimous with regard to this reading (see the apparatus in Ross' edition). I do not doubt that Ross has made the right decision; for the alternative reading, present in most of the Mss. and introduced by the second hand also in Paris, 1853: κινούντων δὲ καὶ αὐτῶν κινουμένων (instead of κινούντων δὲ καὶ ἑαυτά with minor variations in the last word) does not bring out the "self-moving" quality on which the preceding description of soul and living beings focused.

[22] Cf. Jaeger, *op. cit.*, pp. 385 f., 389 (Eng. translation, pp. 360 f., 364). Here the "intelligences" or rulers of the planetary spheres are out of the question, since in b28 ff. (cf. n. 34) they are explicitly set apart from the entities under discussion. I admit that the expression in the sentence b20–22 is rather imprecise. What we might expect would be a reference to the theory that an entity of the description given here is in control of the Cosmos. The next sentence throws some light on this; for in b22–28 the issue gradually unfolds and we realize that it is περὶ ὅλου καὶ παντός. For a reasoning from the movement of ψυχή to that of ἔμψυχα, see also 9. 265b32–266a1.

178   *Friedrich Solmsen*

the living being, which at the conclusion of the preceding argument has been shown to move itself "incidentally." Soul has every justification for presenting its claims at this point; for Plato had declared it to be the fountainhead of all cosmic movements, and, as such, capable of maintaining movement in the physical world for ever and ever. The criterion which Aristotle applies as he weighs the claims of Plato's soul principle against those of his own Unmoved Mover is in accord with this situation: which of them is able to maintain a συνεχὴς κίνησις (b20 ff.; see esp. 22 and 23)? Proofs for the eternity of movement in the world have been given in the first chapter of this Book. In our passage Aristotle thinks it sufficient to remind us – briefly but impressively – of what is involved in deciding for the right ἀρχή: εἰ μέλλει...ἔσεσθαι ἐν τοῖς οὖσιν ἄπαυστός τις καὶ ἀθάνατος κίνησις, καὶ μένειν τὸ ὂν αὐτὸ ἐν αὑτῷ καὶ ἐν τῷ αὐτῷ.[23] This, we are given to understand, is what the Unmoved Mover safeguards, whereas ψυχή lacks the essential qualifications for it. It is evidently of no small importance that ψυχή comes to this test and confrontation not in its Platonic definition as αὐτὴ ἑαυτὴν κινοῦσα or ἀεὶ κινουμένη but in the very different character which has just been established for it: it is in the class of ἀκίνητα μὲν κινούντων δὲ καὶ αὐτὰ κατὰ συμβεβηκός (b21 f.). To consider it as some kind of ἀκίνητον, albeit a very imperfect one, clearly facilitates the comparison with the other and better ἀκίνητον. As originator of all cosmic motion Aristotle needs an ἀκίνητον without qualifications (as he himself puts it, an ἀκίνητον καὶ κατὰ συμβεβηκός [b24],[24] something that is not even accidentally moved).

We cannot help wondering what right Aristotle has to put soul at all in the class of unmoved entities. In the disquisition of 259b1–20, it was the ἔμψυχα which were described as ἀκίνητά ποτε (!) and ἠρεμοῦντα, but even the latter word relates to a temporary condition and indicates the absence of locomotion,

[23] 259b24 ff.; cf. the first sentence of the Book (250b11–15) as well as that from the last paragraph of the Book 267a21, b24. Passages in other treatises that are critical of the Platonic World Soul De Caelo B1.284a27–34, Metaph. Λ 6. 1071b37–1072a3, De An. A3. 406b26–407b11) are too remote to call upon for a comparison.

[24] For the text, see Ross' apparatus and commentary ad loc., where the explanation of the intrusive μή is simpler than that given by Jaeger, op. cit., pp. 390 f. (Eng. translation, p. 365).

not of all movement.[25] Still by the end of 259b1–20 we are probably under the impression that soul, when not in locomotion κατὰ συμβεβηκός (i.e., when it does not by moving the body incidentally move itself), is at rest.[26] We may even be meant to regard this as its normal or basic condition. While these inferences are not spelled out and would, if spelled out, not be easy to accept, they must be implied, if the soul is now considered basically an ἀκίνητον – surely a large step from the description of living beings as ἀκίνητά.ποτε (259b5). We have come a long way from the Platonic position.

So far we have in this study tried to understand why Aristotle in *Physics* VIII finds it necessary to pay attention to ἔμψυχα and what he has to say about their alleged character as self-movers. However, in the argument of this Book, the αὐτὸ ἑαυτὸ κινοῦν has also another and quite different place. As we know, ch. 4 arrives at the important proposition: everything that is in motion is moved by something. This being established, Aristotle in ch. 5 feels free to push ahead to the ultimate mover. It is here that his inquiry and reasoning first lead him to the concept of the ἑαυτὸ κινοῦν, and he is, or seems, for a while quite ready to accept it.[27] We need not go here into the very subtle disquisitions through which the "unmoved" as truly ultimate mover [28] emerges from a closer analysis of the self-moved. In ch. 6 this concept is regarded as established. In other words, the self-mover is an intermediate position or stepping stone on the way toward the Unmoved Mover. Nothing in ch. 5 suggests that Aristotle, when referring to an ἑαυτὸ κινοῦν has living beings in mind. Throughout the sections in question the argument remains in a very abstract or conceptual medium so that the question where in the physical world self-movers might be found need not arise at all. At 259a33, immediately before the last discussion of ἔμψυχα begins, Aristotle seems still to be close to his argument of ch. 5; he summarizes his

[25] b5, 10; cf. also in the previous accounts of ἔμψυχα 252b18 f., 23 f., 253a9 f.

[26] b16–20.

[27] See esp. 256a13–21, a33–b3, 257a27–33.

[28] To my mind it is not entirely clear what 256b3–13, 27–257a14 are meant to establish. If we accept Cornford's view of 256b13–27 (see his note in the Loeb edition), 257b26–258a5 gives us Aristotle's first definite commitment to the unmoved ἀρχή. See also my comments in *Aristotle's System of the Physical World* (Ithaca, N. Y.,1960), p. 234 and n. 40.

findings to this point by stating "that the origin (ἀρχή) of movement is, among things in motion, the self-mover, but that of all things (is) the unmoved." [29] This, however, cannot be his final word but must again be a stepping stone; for in 259b32–260a10 we are introduced to a different "first among things in motion" or origin of movement within the realm of things moved. This is the ἀεὶ κινούμενον,[30] i.e., the outermost Heaven or sphere of the fixed stars which owes its movement directly to the Unmoved First Mover. Aristotle finally shows his hand, coming forward with what we know to be his doctrine. Obviously, Plato's concept of the First Mover has in Aristotle's mind become, as it were, split up into two components; treating each of them in isolation from the other, in the end he discards both. On the conceptual level the self-mover, if considered as ultimate principle, does not survive rigorous philosophical analysis and must, even as "first among things moved," or, as penultimate principle, yield place to another entity. In another context where Aristotle begins with what we ὁρῶμεν...φανερῶς (259b1) and proceeds to use empirical or even biological evidence, he arrives at the conclusion that ἔμψυχα and therefore also ζῷα are not truly, and in the full sense of the word, self-movers, that with reference to movement, soul must be defined quite differently, and that when redefined as "unmoved" with qualifications, it cannot compete with the genuine First Mover to whose definition as "unmoved" no qualifications attach.

After all that has been said about the competitive situation at the apex of the hierarchy of movements, the juncture at which we find the definitive discussion of ἔμψυχα and their movement must seem to be entirely appropriate. At 259b1 Aristotle could be confident of having built up a case for an unmoved entity as First Mover and could, therefore, turn to an examination of rival claims. And yet we may doubt whether 259b1–28 was conceived and worked out as an organic part of the argument to which the preceding (259a20–b1) and the following section (259b32–260a19) belong. This argument, concentrating as is announced in

---

[29] The sentence with which translators have struggled appears to mean that as long as we look only to objects in movement for the first principle, a self-moving entity is the answer, whereas if everything is taken into account, it is the Unmoved. See also 7. 261a23 ff.

[30] See 259b33 ff., 260a14 f.

a22, on the ἀρχαὶ τῶν κινούντων,[31] leads us first, by way of recapitulation, to the First Mover (259b1; see also 32 f.), then deduces the eternal First Moved (b32 f.), and finally shows how these two principles in combination are able to account for all forms of movement and rest in the physical world. It is in any case rewarding to read 259b32–260a19 as the immediate sequel to 259a20–b1 (τὸ ἀκίνητον), leaving out our section. The train of thought that emerges is not only unified and compact, but also stylistically homogeneous in its tone of vigorous affirmation and in the sovereign energy with which the sentences move onward, bearing witness to their author's confidence that the system of cosmic movements has yielded its last secrets. Our section 259b1–28 interrupts the triumphant progress of the thought, forcing us to turn aside and give our attention to ἔμψυχα (itself a come-down) and to concentrate, in the midst of a sublime vision, on inferior matters such as food, digestion, sleep, the operation of a lever, accidental locomotion *et alia*. The first words ὁρῶμεν δὲ καὶ φανερῶς.... are a particularly abrupt beginning and cause a jolt (it does not help, but on the contrary, makes the change of direction more disturbing if the sentences beginning with these words are even syntactically connected with the preceding long but well organized sentence [32] which, summarizing what has been achieved, moves ahead and upward). To be sure, the impressions here recorded have a subjective element; they do not amount to a rigorous proof, nor should I deny that at b25 where we read of an

---

[31] The justification for keeping (the unanimously attested) τῶν κινούντων in the text is, I hope, implicit in my opinion about the coherence of the argument. There are doubtless innumerable movents in the physical world; what Aristotle is about to discuss is the "principles" or first of them. In 259b32–260a19 he in effect distinguishes three (for the entity "moved by the Unmoved" is surely also a principle) but concentrates on two, that responsible for eternal motions and that for alterations between rest and movement. Ross removes τῶν κινούντων from his text because he finds it unsatisfactory to refer them (as Simplicius did) to the souls of animals. If 259b1–28 is understood as a digression which interrupts the main line of the argument, this reference is no longer indicated. G. A. Seeck's difficulties with 259a20–b1 disappear likewise if 259b32 ff. is recognized as the organic sequel of that section (see his essay "Nachträge im achten Buch der Physik des Arist.," *Abhdlgg. d. Akad. d. Wiss. in Mainz* [1965] 3, p. 132).

[32] This is done by Ross as well as by the Loeb editors, although the latter recognize the beginning of a new thought in their translation. There are better reasons for beginning a new paragraph at b1 than at b20 (where the Loeb editors actually continue without a break).

ἄπαυστός τις καὶ ἀθάνατος κίνησις and of μένειν τὸ ὂν ἐν αὐτῷ ... κτλ. We find ourselves once more in the realm of sublime subjects and correspondingly sublime thoughts set forth in elevated language.[33] Still it may not be fanciful to think of Aristotle as working out, on a day when the spirit moved him, the arguments designed to dispose of Soul as claimant to the place of his own First Mover. I should not venture to decide whether this was before or after the argument whose beginning is now severed from its continuation was composed. On the hypothesis offered here, it may well have been Aristotle himself,[34] rather than an editor, who, when wishing to incorporate the refutation of ψυχή, inserted it at 259b1, where, as we know, it has a satisfactory relation to the context and yet does damage to the argument as originally conceived.[35]

Institute for Research in the Humanities,
University of Wisconsin

[33] Are the echoes of Parmenides in Diels, *Vorsokr.*[9] B 8 29 ff. intentional? It is tempting to think that Aristotle indicates here how and how far an important thought of Parmenides is implemented in the new system. The ἀκίνητον (*ibid.* 26) must, however, now be attached to the ἀρχή, to say nothing at all of ἄπαυστον (*ibid.* 27) which now belongs to movement.

[34] That Aristotle had planned to work out an argument of this kind *may* be gathered from the "promise" given at 253a20 f., but that passage, even if held to be a part of the original draft, hardly allows further inferences.

[35] The verdict about b28–31 would have to be somewhat different inasmuch as on Jaeger's and Ross' showing (see above, note 3) these sentences should be attributed to a later revision (presumably made after *Metaph.*Λ 8). For sections definitely not in their right places, see Cornford's note on 256b13 ff. (see above, note 19) and my paper in *AJPh* 82 (1961), pp. 270 ff. Yet other sections, too, pose problems and I am by no means convinced that the entire argument of Book VIII was worked out συνεχῶς and that there are no afterthoughts, second thoughts, etc. Whatever may be thought of the specific theses advanced by Seeck (see note 31), his essay has the merits of warning us against considering everything throughout the Book in the best of order. The present paper is indebted to Seeck; for it was the difficulties brought to light by him in 259a20–b1 (sc. the promise in a21 f. of a new argument for the ἀκίνητον not implemented in this section) which caused me to examine the organization of 259a20–260a19.

It has now become important to take account of Hans Wagner's comments on 259b28–31 (*Aristoteles Physikvorlesung*, Aristoteles Werke in deutscher Uebersetzung, XI [Berlin, 1967], p. 685). Succinctly put, connections between this passage and 259b1–28, pointed out by Wagner, make it seem possible that one and the same hypothesis may in both cases explain the later addition.

SOME FEATURES OF THE TEXTUAL HISTORY
OF MARCUS AURELIUS' *MEDITATIONS*[1]

D. A. REES

The materials for the text of the *Meditations* of Marcus Aurelius Antoninus are scanty, and for this reason any investigation which may throw light on them is the more to be welcomed. Even where little or no further light is shed on the text itself, moreover, such an enquiry may have an interest of its own. In the following survey I shall omit many points which are familiar from the editions of Schenkl and Farquharson.

In brief, the materials for the text are as follows:

(1) The *editio princeps*, edited by Xylander and published at Zürich by Andreas Gesner filius in 1558–1559. The manuscript on which this was based (Schenkl's T, Farquharson's P cod.) came, we are told, from the Palatine Library at Heidelberg through the mediation of Michael Toxites (Schütz); apparently it disappeared, and it was not even available to Xylander when he brought out his second edition (Basel, 1568).

(2) Vaticanus Gr. 1950 (A), the only complete ms. extant. The late Paul Maas showed that Darmstadtinus 2773 (D) derives from this.[2]

(3) The C extracts. These, taken from the first four Books, are found among various items of additional matter in seven mss. of the *Eclogae* of Stobaeus.

(4) The X extracts. These are taken from Books 4–12, and are found in 21 mss. known to editors hitherto. A closely related series of extracts is to be found in Monacensis Gr. 529 (Schenkl's B, Farquharson's Mo 2).

---

[1] I should like in particular to thank Professor Aubrey Diller, of Indiana University, for his invaluable help and encouragement.

[2] *JRS* 35 (1945), pp. 144–146 (review of Farquharson).

(5) There are passages, especially from Book 1, quoted in Suidas (the *Suda*).

(6) There are short quotations which go back to Arethas.[3]

There are in fact numerous quotations to be found, with no reference to the source from which they are taken, in various works of the early XV. cent. Byzantine theologian Joseph Bryennius, but as textual evidence they are far from easy to handle.[4] I hope to publish a study of them at a future date.

Farquharson (p. xxxi) lists 21 mss. of the X extracts, 7 in the Vatican (including one in the Barberini collection), 6 in Paris, 4 in Florence, 2 in Venice, one on Mount Athos and one at Wolfenbüttel. Of these, V 6 had been unknown to Schenkl, but was described by W. Weyland.[5] It is a XIV. cent. paper ms. which was formerly ms. 70 in the Colonna collection purchased for the Vatican in 1821; in the middle of the XVI. cent. it belonged to Cardinal Salviati (d. 1553).

There are, however, still other mss. of the X extracts, two of them in the Vatican. One is Vat. Gr. 1404 (ff. 221^r–237^r), of the XIV. cent., which also contains the extracts from Aelian so often found in the X group. It is from the collection of Fulvio Orsini (1529–1600) acquired by the Vatican Library in 1602.[7] Another is Vat. Gr. 1823 (ff. 231 ff.).[8] Yet a third is a ms., probably of the XVI. cent., in the Burney collection in the British Museum (Britannicus Burneianus 80), which I have myself been able to

---

[3] A few passages are quoted in Monacensis Gr. 323 (Farquharson's Mo 1). These appear to add nothing, and there is every reason to believe (with Maas, *loc. cit.*) that they derive from P cod. They are taken from Books 2, 3, 4 and 7.

[4] P. Meyer, "Des Joseph Bryennios Schriften, Leben und Bildung," *Byz. Zeitschrift* 5 (1896), pp. 74–111, esp. pp. 99–100 and 110. It was Professor Aubrey Diller who drew my attention to this article. But there is considerably more of Marcus in Bryennius than Meyer recognized.

[5] W. Weyland, "Zu Schenkls Marc Aurel," *B. phil. Woch.* 34 (1914), coll. 1179–1184.

[6] E. L. de Stefani, "Gli Excerpta della 'Historia Animalium' di Eliano," *Stud. Ital.* 12 (1904), pp. 145–180, esp. p. 152.

[7] P. de Nolhac, *La bibliothèque de Fulvio Orsini*, Bibliothèque de l'école des hautes études, fasc. 74 (Paris, 1887), esp. p. 339.

[8] G. Mercati, "Di due o tre rari codici greci del Cardinale Giovanni da Ragusa," in *Miscellanea bibliografica in memoria di Don Tommaso Accurti*, ed. L. Donati (Rome, 1947), p. 23, n. 46, which mentions also Vat. Gr. 1404.

inspect.[9] It has the usual excerpts from Aelian's *Historia Animalium*, and is mentioned in A. F. Scholfield's Loeb edition of Aelian, Vol. I (1958), pp. xxv–xxvi. The Burney mss. were acquired by the British Museum in 1818 from the library of the Rev. Dr. Charles Burney (1757–1817); no. 80 had belonged previously to Dr. Antony Askew (1722–1772).[10]

Yet a fourth ms. of the X extracts appears to be in a collection of which M. Richard writes: "La location actuelle de cette collection est officiellement un mystère." [11] This is the library of the house at Istanbul belonging to the Patriarchate of Jerusalem (Μετόχιον Παναγίου Τάφου). A. Papadopoulos-Kerameus, in the posthumous Vol. V of his Ἱεροσολυμιτικὴ Βιβλιοθήκη (Petrograd, 1915), gives a catalogue of this collection, of which no. 512 (old no. 424) is, according to him, a XIV. cent. ms. of which item 6 (ff. 83–103) is described as Μάρκου 'Αντωνίνου ἐκ τῶν καθ' ἑαυτόν (with scholia), beginning at "Ἴδιον ἀνθρώπου φιλεῖν καὶ τοὺς πταίοντας (7.22).[12] The ms. is reported as containing other works, such as the *Imagines* of Philostratus, and Paul the Silentiary, which are found elsewhere with the X extracts, but no Aelian is mentioned.

This ms. had in fact been examined earlier.[13] The *Archiv der Gesellschaft für ältere deutsche Geschichtskunde*, ed. G. H. Pertz, 9 (Hanover, 1847), pp. 645–656, prints a list of "Handschriften des Patriarchats von Jerusalem in Konstantinopel" compiled by a Dr. Bethmann who had visited that city in 1845. No. 22 on Dr. Bethmann's list, assigned by him to the XV. cent., is the ms. in question; it is described as Μάρκου 'Αντωνίνου καθ' ἑαυτόν. "Ἴδιον ἂν u.s.w. mit Glossen und Scholien." Papado-

---

[9] *Catalogue of the Manuscripts in the British Museum*, New Series, Vol. I, Part II, The Burney Manuscripts, pp. 35–36. It should, however, be stated that the detailed list of contents is clearly copied from A. M. Bandini, *Catalogus Manuscriptorum Bibliothecae Mediceae Laurentianae* (Florence, 1768), vol. II, coll. 256–258 (on Laur. lv. 7 = L 1).

[10] It is item 574 ("Heraclides & Epictetus, Graecé, corio russico, 4to") in Leigh and Sotheby's sale catalogue of the "Bibliotheca Askeviana" (1784–1785).

[11] *Répertoire des Bibliothèques et des Catalogues de Manuscrits grecs*[2] (Paris, 1958), p. 114.

[12] *Loc. cit.*, p. 72.

[13] Papadopoulos-Kerameus, *op. cit.*, Vol. IV (St. Petersburg, 1899), esp. p. 458.

poulos-Kerameus (*op. cit.*, Vol. IV, pp. 421 ff.) reproduces an earlier catalogue of 1731; our ms. is perhaps no. 209 of this (P.-K., p. 431), but it is difficult to be sure (no. 209 might be Bethmann's no. 46).

The Florentine ms. Marucellianus Gr. A. 148, which contains the X extracts, is of no importance for the text, since it is a copy, made by Anton Maria Salvini (1653–1729), of Laur. lv. 7.[14]

So much for existing manuscripts of the X extracts. But a puzzle is presented by Abraham Gronovius' edition of Aelian's *Historia Animalium* (London, 1744). Among the evidence Gronovius used for Book I was a Codex Bardonii (the property, it seems, of Petrus Bardonius or Bardo, a Doctor of Medicine), which appears to have contained the "Laurentian extracts" (as de Stefani calls them) from Aelian. The evidence for this lies in its reading the nonsensical ἵππος σήπεται for ὑποσήπεται at *H.A.* 1. 28. If so, it may be presumed to have contained, in addition to the Aelian, the X extracts from Marcus. But I have not been able to identify it.

An entry (to which Professor Diller drew my attention) in M. A. Reiser, *Index Manuscriptorum Bibliothecae Augustanae* (1675) is also of interest. Here, under the heading *In armario priori inferioris Bibliothecae* (p. 66), no. 75 is a manuscript containing a considerable variety of works, including the following:

> Marini Neopolitani (sic) Proclus, sive de Beatitudine
> Gorgiae Encomium Helenae
> Excerpta ex Epicteti Enchiridio, et ex M. Antonino
>   Imper.

I know of no traces of this ms. But it is of special interest that here alone, apart from the two parts of Xylander's ms. (Schenkl's T, Farquharson's P cod.), do we find Antoninus and Marinus together. (Marinus' *Life of Proclus* is followed by Gorgias, *Encomium Helenae* in Vat. Pal. Gr. 404, which Schenkl mistakenly thought to be Xylander's ms. of Marinus; but, whereas Xylander's ms. broke off at the opening of ch. 22, Vat. Pal. Gr. 404 contains the whole work, and moreover was written in Madrid by Andreas Darmarius in 1579 [see Farquharson, Vol. I,

---

[14] G. Vitelli, "Indice dei codici greci Riccardiani, Magliabecchiani e Marucelliani," *Stud. Ital.* 2 (1894), pp. 558–562, esp. p. 561.

p. xxvii].) Reiser's no. 75 is probably the Augsburg ms., other than Mo 2 (Mon. Gr. 529), which Meric Casaubon says that Hoeschel examined; if so, it contained part of the X extracts, ending at 9. 40.

One may add that at p. 119 Reiser lists *M. Antonini Imper. de Vitâ suâ libri Duodecim* among those works whose publication was due to Augsburg; this is presumably because it was Xylander's native city.

Of the C extracts, found appended to the *Florilegium* of Stobaeus, six mss. are known, two in the Vatican Library, two (one imperfect) in Oxford, one in Venice, one in Florence and one in Paris. In addition, there may be traces of a lost ms. of these extracts in a Florentine ms., Magliabecchianus Gr. 24 (xxi. 114), of the XV.-XVI. cent., which contains an index to a ms. of Stobaeus' *Florilegium*, including ἔτι καὶ ἄλλα τινὰ κάθως εἰσὶ γεγραμμένα ἐν τῷ τελ τοῦ βιβλίου[15].

But interesting problems are posed by a letter, found in a ms. in Hanover (xlii. 1845), of the Papal scribe Jacob von Questenberg (1486–1527?), written from Rome at some date between 1493 and 1503 to Johann von Dalberg, Bishop of Worms (d. 1503). This letter was the subject of a detailed and careful study by O. von Gebhardt in *Beiträge zur Bücherkunde und Philologie August Wilmanns zum 25. Marz 1903 gewidmet* (Leipzig, 1903), pp. 243–264, in an article entitled "Eine verlorene und eine wiedergefundene Stobaeus-Handschrift." Questenberg, in his letter, offered to translate a manuscript of Stobaeus into Latin for Dalberg, and gave a list of chapter-headings which show the ms., which he described as *liber antiquissimus in biblioth. Pont.*, and as in poor condition, to have been of the Trincavellian group of mss. of Stobaeus to which our C mss. belong. Questenberg writes (f. 124ʳ): *In eodem volumine insunt plurimae quaestiones aliorum philosophorum et sapientum in graeco*; these include extracts from M. Ant. 1. 8, 15, 16 and 3. 3 (possibly there were more). Gebhardt shows that Questenberg's ms. cannot be identified with either Vat. Gr. 954 or Vat. Gr. 955.[16]

It has long been known that Arethas, about A.D. 900, pos-

[15] *Ibid.*, pp. 471–570, esp. pp. 556–557.
[16] See also G. Mercati, "Questenbergiana," in *Opere minori* 4 (1937), pp. 437–459.

sessed a ms. of the *Meditations* which appears to be the source of our textual tradition.[17] Scholia going back to Arethas which quote, or allude to, the *Meditations* are to be found in mss. of Dio Chrysostom (cod. Urb. 124, of the XI. cent.) and of Lucian (see Schenkl and Farquharson). In addition, however, there is extant a letter of Arethas to the Emperor Leo the Wise which quotes two phrases from *Med.* 1. 7: πῶς γάρ, ὅς γε Μάρκῳ πειθόμενος τῷ σοφῷ, φερούσης τάχα πρὸς τοῦτο καὶ φύσεως δεξιότητος, "τὸ ἀκριβῶς ἀναγινώκειν" ποιοῦμαι περὶ πολλοῦ; ἀλλ' ὥσπερ ἐκεῖνο τίθεμαι περισπούδαστον, οὕτω καὶ τὸ λοιπὸν τῆς σοφῆς ἐξηγήσεως, τὸ "τοῖς περιλαλοῦσι μὴ ταχέως συγκατατίθεσθαι". A scholium added at the end of the letter says: τὸν αὐτοκράτορα ʿΡωμαίων λέγει· αὐτὸν γὰρ ἐν τῷ πρώτῳ τῶν ἠθικῶν αὐτοῦ μὴ ταχέως ἀναγινώσκειν φησί. This letter was published by A. Papadopoulos-Kerameus in his *Varia Graeca Sacra* (St. Petersburg, 1909), pp. 267–268, from a manuscript then in the library of the monastery of Cosinitsa which had been written apparently at Constantinople in 1686 (*op. cit.*, pref., pp. xxxi–xxxiv). It has since been republished (with the same scholion) by R. J. H. Jenkins and Basil Laourdas from a Venetian ms. (Marc. Graec. 524) of the second half of the XIII. cent.[18]

So far as I am aware, the first printed quotations from the *Meditations* occur in Book 2 of Reuchlin's *De arte Cabalistica* (Hagenau, 1517). In each case Reuchlin provides both the Greek text and a Latin translation.

(1) At f. xxxv^v–xxxvi^r there is a quotation of ὅτι οὐδὲν ... τοῦ ἐξ αὐτοῦ ἐσομένου, followed immediately by ἡ τῶν ὅλων φύσις ... εἰς ἄλλο τι. The former passage, assigned by Reuchlin (presumably by a slip) to Book 3, is in fact from 4. 36, the latter, which he assigns correctly to Book 7, is from 7. 23. At 7. 23 the 1572 edition of Reuchlin reads αὐτῆς for αὐτοῦ after τῇ ὕλῃ. If not a mere slip, this must refer back to οὐσίας (or φύσις); but it is not found elsewhere. At the end of the quotation, εἰς is Xylander's

---

[17] See esp. A. Sonny, "Zu Ueberlieferungsgeschichte von M. Aurelius ΕΙΣ ΕΑΥΤΟΝ," *Philologus* 54 (1895), pp. 181–183, quoting from the Moscow ms. Cod. Mosc. 315, f. 115^r.

[18] R. J. H. Jenkins, B. Laourdas, "Eight Letters of Arethas on the Fourth Marriage of Leo the Wise," *Ἑλληνικά* 14 (1955), pp. 293–372, esp. pp. 329–330.

reading, whereas A reads ὡς; this may be a point of considerable significance.

(2) At f. xlviiiᵛ, we find ἅπλωσον σεαυτόν from M. Ant. 4. 26. We have not, I think, a quotation from Marcus when at f. xxxixʳ we find *Eam Pythagoras affirmat esse* παγὰν ἀεννάου φύσεως: *Fontem perpetuae naturae.* Though at 8. 51 Marcus writes πῶς οὖν πηγὴν ἀένναον ἕξεις, Reuchlin does not refer to him and his wording is different. However, it is perhaps worth noting that the text of Marcus at this point is not in a good state.

If we are to assess the value of Reuchlin's readings for the text, it is necessary to enquire into their source. Much work has been done which is relevant, but in the end it is not easy to give a perfectly confident answer. A treatment which is of assistance in summing up the position is that of André Vernet in his essay "Les manuscrits grecs de Jean de Raguse (†1443),"[19] while among earlier contributions one may mention particularly articles by P. Thomsen[20] and Cardinal G. Mercati.[21] One remarkable piece of evidence is found in an anonymous treatise *De martyrio sanctorum*, published in Basel (or possibly Strasbourg) in 1492, and identified by Cardinal Mercati as having been written in 1435–1437 by Thomas Aretinus, a Dominican friar who had gone to Constantinople to learn Greek. The most relevant passage runs (ch. xvii):

Hi principes M. Antonius (sic) Verus et L. Aurelius Comodus (sic) doctissimi fuerunt, maxime Antoninus grecis literis clarus. Cuius duodecim pulcherrimas orationes eloquentissime greco sermone εἰς ἑαυτόν *descriptas et longo tempore perditas in lucem ego redegi*

and

Et sic librum illum [sc. Athenagoras, πρεσβεία περὶ τῶν Χριστιανῶν] *et Opera Justini Martyris et Orationes M. Antonini concessi cla. viro magistro Iohanni de Ragusio.*[22]

---

[19] *Basler Zeitschrift für Geschichte und Altertumskunde* 61 (1961), pp. pp. 75–108, esp. pp. 79–80, and p. 97 n. (Mr. Nigel Wilson, of Lincoln College, Oxford, drew my attention to this article).

[20] P. Thomsen, "Verlorene Handschriften von Justins Werken und Marc Aurels Selbstbetrachtungen," *Philologische Wochenschrift* 52 (1932), coll. 1055–1056.

[21] G. Mercati, "Di due o tre rari codici greci del Cardinale Giovanni da Ragusa (†1443)," in *Miscellanea Bibliografica in Memoria di Don Tommaso Accurti. A Cura di Lamberto Donati* (Rome, 1947), pp. 3–26.

[22] The passage was first noticed, and part of it quoted, in 1893 by A. Harnack in *Die Überlieferung und der Bestand der altchristlichen*

John of Ragusa bequeathed his library to the Dominican house in Basel. From there the ms. of Marcus passed into the hands of Reuchlin, who at his death (1522) bequeathed his library to his native town of Pforzheim. A catalogue (now ms. Vat. Pal. Lat. 1925) written about 1623, probably in Pforzheim, gives the following as item 40:

(a) *Maximus Tyrius in membranis elegantissime scriptus mutilus*

(b) *Marcus Imperator de se 12 libri*

(c) 'Ἀλκινόου διδασκαλικὸς τῶν Πλάτωνος δογμάτων.

(d) Xenophontis ἀπομνημονεύματα.[23]

The contents here listed are strikingly similar to, though by no means identical with, those of A (Vat. Gr. 1950).

Reuchlin had apparently intended to leave his library to his nephew, the celebrated Reformer Philip Melanchthon, but changed his mind because of the latter's adherence to Luther.[24] Thirty years later (1552), in his *Oratio continens Historiam Joannis Capnionis Phorcensis*, Melanchthon stated of the collection:

Sunt autem ibi et scripta nondum edita in officinis typographicis, videlicet Marci Antonini Imperatoris liber, cuius vetustas mentionem fecit, orationes Maximi Tirii, et alia quaedam.[25]

Litteratur bis Eusebius, I, 114. More is to be found in G. Golubovich, O. F. M., *Biblioteca bio-bibliografica della Terra Santa e dell'Oriente Francescano*, Tom. V (Florence, 1927), pp. 290–297. Cf. also B. Altaner, "Zur Geschichte der Handschriftensammlung des Kardinals Johannes von Ragusa," *Historisches Jahrbuch* 47 (1927), pp. 730–732.

[23] K. Christ, *Die Bibliothek Reuchlins in Pforzheim* (52 Beiheft zum *Zentralblatt für Bibliothekswesen* [Leipzig, 1924]). See also K. Preisendanz, "Die Bibliothek Johannes Reuchlins," in *Johannes Reuchlin. 1455–1522. Festgabe seiner Vaterstadt Pforzheim, zur 500. Wiederkehr seines Geburtstages*, ed. M. Krebs (Pforzheim, 1955), pp. 35–82.

[24] See Melanchthon's letter (1523) to Georgius Spalatinus (a letter with a distinct flavor of "sour grapes"), printed in *Corpus Reformatorum*, Vol. I (Halle, 1834), coll. 645–646.

[25] *Selectarum Declamationum Philippi Melanchthonis*, Tom. III (Strasbourg, 1562), pp. 280–299, esp. p. 296 (reprinted in *Corpus Reformatorum*, Vol. XI, ed. C. G. Bretschneider [1843]), col. 1009. Henricus Pantaleon, in his *Prosopographia Heroum atque Illustrium Virorum Totius Germaniae*, Vol. III (Basel, 1566), writes of Reuchlin: *Cum etiam anno 1565 Pforzheimii essem, eius biblioca. (sic) in templo custodita iussu principis fuit, in qua etiamnum multa exemplaria Reuchlini manu scripta supersunt* (p. 23).

Since the compilation of the catalogue quoted above, however, our ms. has been completely lost to view, and the most likely explanation is that it was destroyed in the Thirty Years' War. J. H. Majus, in his *Vita Jo. Reuchlini Phorcensis* (1687), tells us that

Bibliothecae Capnionis pars maxima in funesto superiori bello Germanico, a Capuccinis Weilerstadium (vel ut alii existimant, Coloniam) [sc. est] delata. ibique in expugnatione flammis consumta [i.e. in 1648] (p. 528),

and of the Marcus he says, *Nec vola nec vestigium nobis suppetit.*

The question arises whether, as Thomsen and Vernet have thought, this manuscript is in fact that from which Xylander made his edition. If so, Xylander's account of its origin must be seriously inaccurate; but he may have been misled by Toxites, from (or, rather, through) whom he says that he obtained it. But Schenkl, who knew nothing of Reuchlin's connection with the history of the text, suggested many years ago that Xylander's account was unreliable. Nothing, perhaps, can be definitely proved, but it seems not very likely that two fugitive mss. of (apparently) the complete text should be in question, and we have noted above one passage where Reuchlin's text agrees with Xylander's against Vat. Gr. 1950. There are, however, small pieces of indirect evidence to be culled from Mon. Gr. 323 (Farquharson's Mo l), whose extracts show no signs of independence from P cod. [26] At p. 109b Reuchlin's name is found inserted for no apparent reason – a fact which Stich[27] not unnaturally found puzzling. Further, Mo l has extracts from Maximus Tyrius and Alcinous, authors who were also to be found in Reuchlin's ms.

One may reflect that the fate of Reuchlin's manuscript was for centuries, as it appears, bound up with the religious convulsions of Europe – the Turkish pressure on Constantinople (Thomas Aretinus met the death of a martyr, preaching Christianity to the Turks), the Council of Basel (in which John of Ragusa took part), which brought about its transference to a monastic library, Reuchlin, and hence (because

[26] P. Maas, in *JRS* 35 (1945), pp. 144–146.
[27] J. Stich, *Adnotationes criticae ad Marcum Antoninum* (Zweibrücken, 1881), p. 12.

Melanchthon espoused the cause of the Reformation) its home in the library of Pforzheim, and finally destruction, as it appears, in the Thirty Years' War. One reflection more: Theiler, in his edition (1951), published (like Xylander's first) at Zürich, comments (p. 297): "In der Neuzeit ist die erste Kenntnis in eigenartiger Weise mit der Schweiz verknüpft." This was truer than he seems to have realized.

The remainder of this paper will consist of a few brief addenda.

Among the contents of ms. Egerton 602 of the British Museum, which was obtained by that library in 1835, there are numerous Spanish items, among them a "Memorial de los libros griegos de mano de la libreria del señor Don Diego Hurtado de Mendoza" (ff. 289–296). Mendoza (1503–1575) was a Spanish diplomat who spent many years in Italy. Attached to this list, but not intrinsically a part of it (f. 295ᵛ), is a *"Catalogus nonnullorum librorum qui adhuc grece estant"* – i.e., a list of Greek works which at the time of its compilation were still unprinted but were known to exist in manuscript – and among these is *"M. Aurelij imperatoris de vita sua lib. 12."* This second list was published in 1880 by Charles Graux, but remains obscure and is not easy to date with any precision.[28]

Lilius Giraldus, in Dialogue V of his *Historiae Poetarum tam Graecorum quam Latinorum Dialogi* (Basel, 1545), tells us: *Eius certe librum graece scriptum legi, cuius titulus* μάρκου ἀντωνίνου ἐκ τῶν καθ' αὑτόν (p. 603); an earlier passage, *de piscibus non-nihil scripsit* (*Dial.* 4, p. 553), like the wording of the title, suggests, as Farquharson observed, an acquaintance and a confusion arising from the intermingling of extracts from Aelian in some mss. of the X extracts from Marcus.[29]

There is also a reference to be found in Conrad Gesner's *Bibliotheca Universalis* (Zürich, 1545), which lists (f. 53ᵛ)

ANTONINI Augusti itinerarium ex Aldi officina prodiuit.
Eiusdem liber ἐκ τῶν καθ' αὑτόν, *Romae servatur Graece.*
Antoninus Aug. in fragmentis Gregoriani codicis allegatur.

---

[28] C. Graux, *Essai sur les origines du fonds grec de l'Escurial. Épisode de l'histoire de la renaissance des lettres en Espagne*, Bibliothèque de l'école des hautes études, fasc. 46 (Paris, 1880), Appendix 2, pp. 359–386.

[29] *Op. cit.*, Vol. I, p. xxii.

The first reference, to the Itinerary of Antoninus, is not our concern. The second, as was remarked by Mercati,[30] would accord with ms. Vat. Gr. 953 (V 1), which contains the X extracts. This ms. seems to be listed, under the heading Μάρκου Ἀντωνίου ἐκ τῶν καθ᾽ αὑτόν. Ἀνεντίου Μαλίου [sc. Boethius] ..., in a catalogue published by Haase in 1851, from the time of Pope Paul III.[31] The third reference is obscure.

I add a final footnote on a reference in antiquity to Marcus as a philosopher which has escaped editors. A scholium on Plato's *Republic* 5. 473c – the famous passage in which Plato speaks of the possibility of a philosopher born in a kingly position – remarks ση<μείωσαι> τί λέγει, ὅπερ ἐπὶ Μάρκου τοῦ φιλοσόφου, βασιλέως Ῥωμαίων, συνέβη. The note appears to come from a *commentarius recens*; W. C. Greene surmises that it may be of any century from the second to the ninth.[32]

Jesus College,
Oxford, England

[30] G. Mercati, "Di due o tre rari codici greci del Cardinale Giovanni da Ragusa," in *Miscellanea Bibliografica in Memoria di Don Tommaso Accurti* (Rome, 1947), p. 23, n. 46.

[31] *Serapeum* 12 (1851), p. 263.

[32] W. C. Greene, *Scholia Platonica* (Haverford, 1938), p. 233. Cf. T. Mettauer, *De Platonis Scholiorum Fontibus* (Zürich, 1880), p. 37.

LES CRITIQUES DE PLOTIN CONTRE L'ENTÉLÉCHISME D'ARISTOTE: ESSAI D'INTERPRÉTATION DE L'*ENN.* 4. 7. 8⁵

G. VERBEKE

Aristote s'est écarté progressivement du dualisme psychologique de Platon pour élaborer sa propre conception de l'homme: il ne considère plus l'âme comme une substance autonome, originaire d'un monde supérieur et temporairement enfermée dans un corps, mais comme la forme substantielle ou l'entéléchie première d'un corps naturel qui possède la vie en puissance.[1] Le corps et l'âme, loin d'être des réalités étrangères l'une à l'autre, s'appellent réciproquement: le corps est orienté vers un achèvement qu'il ne peut pas se donner à lui-même et l'âme est de par sa nature l'acte premier d'un corps, elle lui apporte la perfection vis-à-vis de laquelle l'organisme corporel était en puissance. L'union de l'âme et du corps, loin d'être violente et contre nature, n'est que la coexistence de deux principes qui sont naturellement unis l'un à l'autre.[2]

Il n'est pas dans notre intention de retracer ici, en ses différentes étapes, l'évolution de la pensée aristotélicienne: le travail a été fait par d'autres, et bien que les conclusions n'en soient pas définitives, on peut en accepter les lignes générales.[3] Il importe cependant de s'interroger sur le sens philosophique profond de

[1] *De An.* 2. 1. 412a27.
[2] *De An.* 2. 1. 412b6–9: Aristote estime qu'il ne faut même pas se poser la question de savoir si l'âme et le corps ne font qu'un; la chose lui paraît évidente: on ne se demande pas non plus si la cire et l'empreinte ne font qu'un ou d'une façon générale si la matière singulière et ce dont elle est la matière forment une unité. A ses yeux, l'entéléchie ou l'acte est au sens propre principe d'être et d'unité, en d'autres termes, toute la perfection et l'unité d'un être proviennent de l'entéléchie qui le constitue.
[3] F. Nuyens, *L'Évolution de la Psychologie d'Aristote*, Aristote, Traductions et Études (Louvain-La Haye-Paris, 1948). Cf. notre étude critique: "L'Évolution de la Psychologie d'Aristote," *Revue philosophique de Louvain* 46 (1948), pp. 335–351.

cette évolution, du moins dans le domaine de la psychologie. Pourquoi la conception platonicienne de l'homme a-t-elle été abandonnée? Quel est le facteur déterminant qui semble avoir amené Aristote à revoir les conceptions psychologiques de Platon? S'est-il détourné de la métaphysique, comme le prétend W. Jaeger, pour s'adonner plutôt à des recherches d'ordre empirique?[4] Nous ne le croyons pas. Si on se base sur l'évolution de la pensée aristotélicienne en matière d'éthique et de psychologie, on peut dire que le maître grec a de plus en plus accentué la *valeur propre de* l'homme, considéré comme étant un principe original qui porte vraiment le poids de ses actes.

Où se situe la différence essentielle entre la morale de Platon et celle d'Aristote? Aux yeux de Platon l'idéal moral ne doit pas être constitué ou inventé par l'homme, il lui est donné comme un modèle immuable et transcendant, il existe de toute éternité et la tâche de l'homme est simplement de le découvrir et de l'imiter autant que possible.[5] La morale de Platon est une morale d'imitation: l'homme véritable, c'est-à-dire l'âme, est originaire du monde des Idées; en vivant une existence terrestre, l'âme essaiera, dans la mesure de ses forces, de réaliser ici-bas la perfection qui existe de façon permanente et sans défaillance dans les réalités transcendantes.[6] Dans l'optique d'Aristote, la

[4] Sur ce point la théorie de W. Jaeger a reçu une correction importante de la part de A. Mansion, surtout en ce qui concerne la date du livre XII de la *Métaphysique*. Cf. "La genèse de l'oeuvre d'Aristote d'après les travaux récents," *Revue Néoscolastique de Philosophie* 29 (1927), pp. 307–341; 423–466.

[5] Aristote s'oppose avec violence à cette morale de Platon qui présente à l'homme des normes transcendantes: prétendre qu'il y a une Idée du Bien ou de n'importe quoi, c'est là, d'après le Stagirite, une affirmation abstraite et vide (λέγεται λογικῶς καὶ κενῶς) (*Eth. Eud.* I. 8. 1217b21). Que veut dire le Stagirite? L'Idée du Bien n'est, à ses yeux, d'aucune utilité pour la conduite de la vie morale: elle ne nous aide en rien à résoudre les problèmes concrets de la vie de tous les jours. Ce n'est pas en contemplant l'Idée du Bien que l'homme pourra découvrir ce qu'il doit faire dans une situation donnée: le Bien transcendant, précisément parce qu'il est transcendant, est au-dessus de notre vie; ce qui nous intéresse, c'est le bien qui peut être réalisé par notre action (πρακτόν).

[6] Qu'on se rappelle le passage bien connu du *Tht.* 176b: ὁμοίωσις θεῷ κατὰ τὸ δυνατόν. L'homme est capable de connaître le monde des Idées: qu'en résulte-t-il sinon que l'âme humaine, du moins dans sa partie supérieure, est apparentée aux réalités intelligibles? L'âme sera en quelque façon simple et immuable comme elles, elle ne périra pas lors de la dissolution du corps, elle est immortelle (*Phd.* 79d). La tâche de l'homme est de devenir davantage ce qu'il est, image du monde transcendant.

tâche éthique de l'homme est sensiblement plus vaste: l'idéal moral n'est pas donné d'avance, il n'est pas réalisé à la perfection dans un monde transcendant, il doit être inventé par l'homme grâce à la réflexion philosophique, la pratique morale individuelle et les traditions de la communauté humaine. On ne peut contempler nulle part l'idéal de la vie humaine, il ne s'offre pas à nous comme un objet d'intuition ni de contemplation; c'est à l'homme lui-même qu'il appartient de découvrir la meilleure manière d'être homme, la physionomie originale de la perfection humaine, le véritable bien de l'homme. Seul le *phronimos*, l'homme prudent, en est capable, parce qu'il a l'expérience de la vie morale et que son regard n'est pas obnubilé par les passions. C'est pourquoi Aristote dira dès le *Protreptique*, que le *phronimos* est la règle de la vie morale:[7] ce n'est pas là une règle donnée une fois pour toutes; c'est une norme qui sans cesse s'invente dans les situations changeantes de la vie. La morale d'Aristote est une éthique élaborée par l'homme et pour l'homme: si l'homme est au centre de cette morale c'est qu'il ne doit pas seulement réaliser l'idéal de sa perfection, mais il doit l'inventer. Les *Éthiques* d'Aristote sont des essais qui se situent dans cette perspective. Indubitablement, le rôle de l'homme est plus important dans la morale d'Aristote que dans celle de Platon.

La même ligne de développement peut se découvrir aussi dans la doctrine psychologique d'Aristote. Pour Platon toute connaissance est présente dans l'âme humaine depuis le début de l'existence: l'homme ne reçoit de son passage en ce monde aucun enrichissement.[8] Sans doute, grâce à ses contacts avec d'autres personnes et à la perception du monde sensible, il pourra réveiller en lui-même un savoir latent qu'il possède depuis toujours. Mais l'homme n'invente rien, l'activité humaine n'apporte rien de

---

[7] I. Düring, *Aristotle's Protrepticus: An Attempt at Reconstruction*, Studia Graeca et Latina Gothoburgensia XII (Göteborg, 1961) B 39: ἔτι δὲ τίς ἡμῖν κανὼν ἢ τίς ὅρος ἀκριβέστερος τῶν ἀγαθῶν πλὴν ὁ φρόνιμος; Il est certain que ce passage peut s'interpréter de deux façons différentes suivant qu'on admet ou non que l'auteur du *Protreptique* accepte la théorie des Idées: si la doctrine des Idées est toujours présente dans cet ouvrage, il n'en reste pas moins vrai que la norme de la vie morale est incarnée dans la personne de l'homme prudent, du *phronimos*. Si on croit que l'auteur du *Protreptique* n'adhère pas à la théorie des Idées, dans ce cas, la différence par rapport à la morale de Platon n'en est que plus accentuée.

[8] *Phd.* 72e: ἡ μάθησις οὐκ ἄλλο τι ἢ ἀνάμνησις.

vraiment original; on pourrait dire que l'homme ne peut découvrir que ce qu'il savait déjà.[9] Si on s'en réfère au mythe d'Er
le Pamphylien, il faut dire que les grandes options ne se prennent
pas ici-bas, le destin de l'homme se joue dans un monde transcendant par un choix englobant qui est fait une fois pour toutes.[10]

Telle n'est pas la conception d'Aristote et on peut s'en rendre
compte en analysant sa théorie de la connaissance: le Stagirite
n'admet pas la préexistence de l'âme. Notre savoir vient-il d'une
existence antérieure à la vie terrestre? Nullement, au moment
de la naissance, les facultés cognitives de l'homme, y compris
l'intellect, sont en puissance.[11] Que signifie cette expression,
sinon que tout est à réaliser par l'homme lui-même? Celui-ci
porte en soi des possibilités exceptionnelles, mais ce sont des
possibilités seulement: il ne s'agit en aucune façon d'un patri-
moine de connaissances déjà présent dont il suffirait de prendre
conscience. Dans l'optique d'Aristote, l'homme est vraiment
l'auteur de son savoir, il est le principe actif de ses connaissances;
le savoir est une "acquisition", parfois difficile, qui pour se
réaliser doit toujours s'appuyer sur l'expérience.[12] Le processus

---

[9] Qu'on ne s'y méprenne pas cependant: aux yeux de Platon, l'effort
de la recherche n'est pas du tout exclu; ce n'est pas une tâche facile de
découvrir les réalités intelligibles, celles-ci ne sont pas l'objet d'une
intuition passive; dans le *Phd.* (79a), Platon affirme que le monde invisible
se découvre τῷ τῆς διανοίας λογισμῷ. C'est là une entreprise bien délicate:
dans son entretien avec Théétète, Socrate ne manque pas de relever
que tout jugement proféré doit être examiné pour voir si c'est du vent
ou de la vie (*Tht.* 157d). On le constate d'ailleurs dans l'entretien de
Socrate avec l'esclave de Ménon: la vérité n'est pas découverte du premier
coup (*Ménon* 81e). Le mythe du *Phdr.* ne montre-t-il pas dans une
description admirable combien difficile il est d'arriver à la "Plaine de
la Vérité", τὸ ἀληθείας ἰδεῖν πεδίον (*Phdr.* 248b)?

[10] Pl. *Resp.* 10. 15. 617d. La proclamation de Lachésis est très significative: chaque homme est responsable de son δαίμων, il ne lui est pas
donné par des puissances supérieures, surtout pas par un Destin aveugle,
c'est l'homme lui-même qui le choisit. L'eudémonie n'est donc pas un don
qui nous est accordé par un hasard bienveillant, tout homme est l'auteur
de son eudémonie. Dieu n'est pas en cause (θεὸς ἀναίτιος). Il est certain que
cette conception de Platon constitue un progrès considérable vis-à-vis des
croyances populaires grecques à cette époque. Il n'en reste pas moins
vrai que, selon le langage mythique, le choix est fait par une âme désin-
carnée dans un monde transcendant.

[11] *De An.* 3. 4. 429b31–430a2.

[12] *De An.* 3. 4. 429a27: Aristote se demande si l'on peut concevoir
l'âme comme le τόπος εἰδῶν et il se déclare d'accord avec cette expression,
tout en y apportant deux restrictions: c'est l'âme intellective seulement

cognitif consiste essentiellement en ce que les données sensibles sont rendues intelligibles par l'intervention de l'intellect actif; même si l'on considère celui-ci comme transcendant et unique, il n'en reste pas moins vrai qu'il est d'une certaine façon présent dans l'âme, puisqu'il y exerce son activité: c'est grâce à lui que l'intellection devient possible.[13] Quelle est la signification profonde de cette théorie de la connaissance? Si on la compare à la doctrine de Platon sur le même sujet, elle est avant tout une mise en valeur de l'homme: aux yeux d'Aristote, le savoir n'est pas un simple don gratuit, il n'appartient pas non plus à l'équipement naturel de l'homme; toute connaissance et toute science sont pleinement des réalisations humaines.

Aristote a progressivement pris conscience de la valeur de l'homme. Qu'en résulte-t-il au point de vue de la conception du composé humain? L'âme ne se conçoit plus comme une substance transcendante qui existe dans le monde des Idées avant d'être enfermée dans un corps et qui n'aspire qu'à se libérer le plus tôt possible de son enveloppe corporelle. La destinée humaine ne se joue pas dans un monde transcendant, mais dans la vie terrestre, au milieu des autres hommes: l'homme est fait pour ce monde-ci, et c'est dans l'existence d'ici-bas qu'il réalisera ou non sa perfection ultime. L'âme n'est donc pas une substance transcendante, elle est l'acte premier d'un corps: ne se trouve-t-on pas devant une sorte de "révolution copernicienne"? La destinée naturelle de l'âme n'est pas de vivre dans un monde supérieur, sa destinée est terrestre seulement; sa définition est en même temps l'indication de sa vocation: être l'acte premier d'un corps.

Plotin n'ignore pas l'importance de la question et l'opposition radicale qu'elle suscite entre Platon et Aristote. C'est pourquoi il s'oppose catégoriquement à la doctrine psychologique du Stagirite et formule une série d'objections pour la combattre. Le but de la présente étude est de découvrir le sens exact de ces objections, de les interpréter et de les juger: ces critiques rencontrent-elles la pensée authentique du Stagirite?[14]

qui est le lieu des intelligibles et en outre elle ne les possède pas en acte, mais en puissance seulement.

[13] *De An.* 3. 5. 430a13: ἐν τῇ ψυχῇ.

[14] On pourrait se demander s'il est justifié de poser la question de cette manière: pourquoi s'interroger uniquement sur le rapport entre les critiques de Plotin et la doctrine d'Aristote, en négligeant le péripatétisme

Comment Plotin conçoit-il l'entéléchisme d'Aristote? Dans son traité *De l'immortalité de l'âme (Enn.* 4. 7) l'auteur donne de cette doctrine un résumé dont on ne peut certes pas dire qu'il soit très précis. Dans le composé humain, l'âme tient le rôle de la forme vis-à-vis d'une matière qui est le corps animé; Aristote, nous dit Plotin, ne veut pas dire que l'âme est la forme de n'importe quel corps, ni du corps en tant que tel, mais d'un corps naturel et organisé qui possède la vie en puissance.[15]

postérieur? Notons tout d'abord que Plotin lui-même place au début de ses critiques la définition aristotélicienne de l'âme telle qu'elle se rencontre dans le *De An.* 2. 1. Pour le reste, on ne manquera pas de tenir compte à l'occasion de certaines interprétations proposées par des représentants de l'École péripatéticienne et il est très possible que Plotin ait été influencé par ces épigones dans sa manière de comprendre la doctrine du Stagirite. En examinant la théorie authentique du maître, il nous sera donc possible de porter un jugement non seulement sur les objections de Plotin, mais aussi sur la doctrine des péripatéticiens postérieurs.

[15] *Enn.* 4. 7. 8[5]. On sait que ce texte ne figure pas dans les manuscrits de Plotin: il nous a été conservé par la *Praep. Evang.* d'Eusèbe. Il est à noter cependant que dans tous les manuscrits de Plotin on a gardé la dernière ligne du passage en question: σωζόμενον καθ' ὅσον ἂν αὐτοῦ μεταλαμβάνῃ, ce qui montre clairement que cette péricope appartenait au texte original et qu'elle doit être insérée à cet endroit, c'est-à-dire avant le début du chapitre 9, du moins en ce qui concerne la dernière partie, lignes 43–50. Pour ce qui est des lignes 1–43, P. Henry estime qu'il n'est pas impossible que ce texte ait été inséré plus tard soit par Plotin lui-même, soit par Eustochius. Ce fragment ne nous est donc pas conservé dans l'édition de Porphyre, mais dans celle d'Eustochius. Cf. P. Henry, *Études Plotiniennes*, I, *Les États du texte de Plotin* (Paris-Bruxelles, 1938), p. 71. Le texte a été repris dans *Plotini opera*, T. II, *Enn.* IV–V, ed. P. Henry et H.-R. Schwyzer (Paris-Bruxelles, 1959) avec, en parallèle, la traduction anglaise de la partie correspondante de la *Theologia Aristotelis*. Nous ne voulons pas insister sur une variante du texte qui, d'après P. Henry, est si bien attestée par la tradition manuscrite qu'elle remonte probablement à Plotin lui-même (*Les États du texte*, p. 120): au lieu de dire comme Aristote que l'âme est la forme d'un corps naturel, notre auteur aurait parlé d'un σῶμα ψυχικόν. D'après P. Henry, il s'agirait d'une des multiples inexactitudes dans la façon de parler et d'écrire de Plotin. V. Cilento estime, par contre, qu'on se trouve devant une faute de la tradition manuscrite et que Estienne et Creuzer ont eu raison de corriger le terme ψυχικοῦ en φυσικοῦ (*Plotino, Enneadi*, Prima versione integra e commentario critico di V. Cilento, Vol. II [Bari, 1948], p. 569). Dans l'édition de P. Henry et H.-R. Schwyzer on a également corrigé la leçon ψυχικοῦ en φυσικοῦ. On note cependant dans l'apparat à côté de ψυχικοῦ: *fortasse ipsius Plotini mendum* et on renvoie à la *Vita Plotini*, 13. 2–5. Si l'erreur remonte à Plotin, elle démontre une grave incompréhension de la définition aristotélicienne: comment peut-on dire d'un corps animé qu'il possède la vie en puissance?

Aristote, on le sait, distingue acte premier et acte second, science et exercice actuel de la science, sommeil et veille. L'âme n'est pas absente du corps durant le sommeil, bien que la plupart de ses activités ne s'exercent pas.[16] Et quant à l'exercice actuel de la science, il faut être en possession de la science pour en être capable : dans l'ordre du devenir et pour le même sujet, l'antériorité revient à la science.[17] L'âme sera donc l'entéléchie première, source et origine des différentes fonctions vitales, qui, elles, ne s'exercent pas de façon ininterrompue. Plotin a négligé cette précision importante et parle simplement d'entéléchie ou de forme.

Pourtant il n'est pas sans importance de préciser la signification de ce terme, car la première critique de Plotin se base sur le sens du mot "forme"; notre auteur en donne une interprétation assez peu philosophique.[18] L'âme serait comme la forme d'une statue d'airain; qu'en résulte-t-il sinon que l'âme se diviserait avec le corps dont elle est la forme? Enlever une partie du corps, ce serait par le fait même retrancher une parcelle de l'âme. La critique peut se résumer comme suit : si on considère l'âme comme la forme du corps, on doit admettre nécessairement qu'elle est divisible.[19] Parlant de la relation entre l'âme et le corps dans un autre traité, Plotin affirme encore une fois que l'âme ne peut être dans le corps à la manière d'une forme présente dans une matière: car en ce cas, l'âme serait inséparable du corps et lui serait postérieure;[20] d'après notre auteur, c'est le contraire qui

---

[16] De An. 2. 1. 412a21.

[17] De An. 2. 1. 412a26.

[18] J. Zabarella, dans son commentaire sur le De An. (In tres Aristotelis libros de Anima commentarii [1606]), se demande pourquoi Aristote emploie le terme ἐντελέχεια (acte) plutôt que εἶδος (forme); voici sa réponse: *Ideo significare volens Aristoteles eam formam, quae non est secundum se ens completum in specie, sed est perfectio et complementum alterius, et est in ipsa re, cuius est perfectio, non extra, ut ponebat Plato, mutavit nomen formae in nomen actus primi, quia nomen* ἐντελέχεια *significat complementum alterius, et est valde accommodatum intentioni Aristotelis, quia non significat semper se subsistentem* (Ed. de Francfort, 1606, col. 115).

[19] Cette interprétation peut s'inspirer d'une comparaison d'Aristote: parlant de l'unité de l'âme et du corps, le Stagirite la compare à celle de la cire et l'empreinte, ou de façon générale à l'unité constituée par une matière singulière et ce dont elle est la matière. Dans l'opinion d'Aristote, il s'agit là simplement de comparaisons qui n'ont d'autre but que de faire comprendre sa doctrine philosophique (De An. 2. 1. 412b6–9).

[20] Enn. 4. 3. 20. 36: Ἀλλ' οὐδὲ ὡς εἶδος ἐν ὕλῃ· ἀχώριστον γὰρ τὸ ἐν

se produit: l'âme ne peut coïncider avec la forme, car c'est elle qui introduit la forme dans la matière.[21] Parler d'une forme séparée n'a pas de sens non plus, car on ne voit pas comment cette forme pourrait être dans le corps. L'âme n'est pas dans le corps comme dans un lieu, sa présence dans l'organisme n'est pas spatiale, car elle est présente tout entière à chaque endroit de la dimension corporelle. Si elle était dans le corps de façon spatiale, dans chaque partie du corps résiderait une partie de l'âme. C'est admettre encore une fois que l'âme est divisible; c'est pourquoi Plotin admet plutôt que le corps est dans l'âme, c'est donc plutôt l'âme qui est le contenant et le corps ce qui est contenu.[22] Et quand il s'agit de savoir si l'âme est divisible ou indivisible, l'auteur se fonde sur le texte bien connu du *Timée* (34a–35a) pour dire qu'elle est en même temps divisible et indivisible: elle est divisible parce qu'elle est présente dans les différentes parties de l'organisme qu'elle anime, mais elle est indivisible aussi parce qu'elle est présente tout entière dans toutes les parties de l'organisme réunies et dans chacune d'elles.[23] Plotin se base d'ailleurs sur la simplicité de l'âme pour prouver qu'elle est immortelle: il se demande si elle pourrait périr par division ou fragmentation; la réponse est négative car l'âme n'est ni une masse ni une quantité.[24] Elle ne peut pas périr non plus par un changement qualitatif, parce que pareille transformation ne peut se faire que dans un être composé de matière et de forme.[25]

ὕλη εἶδος, καὶ ἤδη ὕλης οὔσης ὕστερον τὸ εἶδος. Voici le passage correspondant de la *Theologia Aristotelis* (ed. Henry et Schwyzer): "Nor is the soul like a form in matter, for the form does not depart from matter save by corruption, and the soul is not like that: rather does she depart from the body without corruption."

[21] *Enn.* 4. 3. 20. 38: ἡ δὲ ψυχὴ τὸ εἶδος ποιεῖ ἐν τῇ ὕλῃ ἄλλη τοῦ εἴδους οὖσα. Dans la *Theologia Aristotelis* on lit à cet endroit: "Further, matter is prior to form but body is not prior to soul, for it is soul that puts the form in matter, i.e., it is she that informs matter and that embodies matter."

[22] *Enn.* 4. 3. 20. 14: ἡ δὲ ψυχὴ οὐ σῶμα, καὶ οὐ περιεχόμενον μᾶλλον ἢ περιέχον.

[23] *Enn.* 4. 2. 1. Dans son *Traité de l'immortalité de l'âme* Plotin se demande comment l'âme indivisible peut devenir l'entéléchie divisible d'un corps; l'objection reste la même: *l'âme ne peut devenir l'entéléchie du corps sans devenir divisible comme lui.*

[24] *Enn.* 4. 7. 12, 15: ᾿Αλλ᾽ ἄρα μερισθεῖσα κερματιζομένη ἀπόλοιτο ἄν. ᾿Αλλ᾽ οὐκ ὄγκος τις οὐδὲ ποσόν, ὡς ἐδείχθη, ἡ ψυχή.

[25] *Enn.* 4. 7. 12. 17: ᾿Αλλ᾽ ἀλλοιωθεῖσα ἥξει εἰς φθοράν. ᾿Αλλ᾽ ἡ ἀλλοίωσις φθείρουσα τὸ εἶδος ἀφαιρεῖ, τὴν δὲ ὕλην ἐᾷ· τοῦτο δὲ συνθέτου πάθος. On

Notons en passant que cette critique de Plotin a été reprise par certains auteurs chrétiens, tels Némésius d'Émèse et Claudien Mamert. Tous deux affirment que l'âme ne peut être l'entéléchie du corps parce que, dans ce cas, elle serait une qualité de la matière, nécessairement liée à un corps déterminé.[26] Némésius s'oppose d'ailleurs à une autre partie de la définition aristotélicienne: d'après lui, le corps ne peut posséder la vie en puissance car il n'est un corps que grâce à la forme spécifique; on ne peut donc pas dire de l'âme qu'elle est l'entéléchie d'un corps qui possède la vie en puissance.[27] D'après Némésius l'âme est une substance parfaite et incorporelle (οὐσία αὐτοτελής), elle ne se rattache donc pas nécessairement à un corps. Claudien Mamert la considère aussi comme une *res substantiva*, capable d'exercer certaines activités indépendamment du corps.[28]

Cette critique de Plotin est-elle justifiée? Certainement pas pour autant qu'il s'agit de la doctrine d'Aristote lui-même;[29]

reconnaît dans ce texte l'objection avancée par Cébès contre le troisième argument de Socrate dans le *Phédon*: Cébès concède à Socrate que l'âme ne périra point par dissolution, mais il se demande si elle ne perdra pas progressivement son intensité de façon à s'éteindre totalement (86e–88b). Socrate essaiera de répondre en développant son quatrième argument: l'essence de l'âme c'est d'être principe de vie, elle ne peut donc mourir.

[26] Némésius, *De natura hominis*, c. 2 (Nous citerons le texte de Némésius suivant la traduction médiévale de Burgundio de Pise, dont nous préparons une édition critique): *Aristoteles autem animam entelechiam dicens, nullo minus concordat cum his qui qualitatem eam dicunt.*

[27] Némésius, *De natura hominis*, c. 2: *Oportet autem corpus quod potestate vitam habet, prius actu esse corpus. Non potest autem actu esse corpus, antequam suscipiat speciem.*

[28] E. L. Fortin, *Christianisme et Culture philosophique au cinquième siècle. La querelle de l'âme humaine en Occident* (Paris, 1959), p. 83.

[29] Il est indispensable d'introduire la restriction mentionnée à cause de l'évolution de la doctrine aristotélicienne chez les représentants de l'École péripatéticienne: on connaît le matérialisme de Straton de Lampsaque, de Dicéarque et d'Aristoxène. Voici ce que F. Wehrli écrit à leur sujet: "Es entspricht dem Positivismus Stratons, die ganze Seele als körperlich gebunden und damit sterblich anzusehen; eine Konsequenz ist der Verzicht auf apriorische Einsicht (*frg.* 74). Auf anderem Wege gelangten zur Preisgabe der Unsterblichkeit Dikaiarch (*frg.* 5–12) und Aristoxenos (*frg.* 118–121)." (*Die Schule des Aristoteles: Texte und Kommentar*, Heft V, *Straton von Lampsachos* [Bâle, 1950], p. 71). On sait, d'autre part, qu'Alexandre d'Aphrodise a donné de l'entéléchisme d'Aristote une interprétation totalement matérialiste. D'après lui, l'âme naît du mélange des éléments, elle est le résultat d'une κρᾶσις: ceci ne veut pas dire qu'elle soit simplement la proportion ou l'harmonie du mélange. Elle est la force, la δύναμις, issue d'un mélange qui a été fait dans des

l'entéléchisme du Stagirite n'est en rien entamé par l'objection qu'on vient d'exposer, tout d'abord parce que le terme ἐντελέχεια ne signifie pas, dans la définition aristotélicienne de l'âme, une forme accidentelle et spatiale, comme la forme d'une statue d'airain. Ce terme présente une dimension philosophique beaucoup plus riche: quand il s'agit de l'entéléchie première, l'expression désigne la perfection spécifique d'un être déterminé. D'après Aristote, l'âme confère au corps naturel qui possède la vie en puissance, sa perfection propre, c'est-à-dire la vie dans toute la richesse de ses manifestations, depuis la vie végétative jusqu'à la pensée. Ce que le maître grec désire exprimer en disant que l'âme est l'entéléchie première du corps, c'est que le corps et l'âme ne sont pas des réalités autonomes, accidentellement réunies l'une à l'autre: l'âme apporte au corps organisé la perfection vis-à-vis de laquelle celui-ci est en puissance. Il ne s'agit donc pas d'une forme accidentelle et spatiale, mais d'une perfection spécifique.[30] Tout en affirmant que l'âme est l'entéléchie première du corps, Aristote admet que le principe de la pensée, qui réside dans l'âme humaine, est immatériel. Il ne voit pas d'objection à ce que le corps collabore d'une certaine façon à une activité qui de soi est immatérielle: ne dit-il pas dans son *De anima* que tout exercice de la pensée est dépendant de l'expérience sensible?[31]

proportions déterminées. Dans cette optique, le vivant provient entièrement du non-vivant, la matière se donne à elle-même un principe vital, elle s'actualise elle-même (*De An.*, ed. I. Bruns, p. 24, 3–4; 24, 21). Si l'âme naît du mélange des éléments, peut-on encore dire qu'elle est la cause formelle du corps? Aux yeux d'Alexandre, l'âme est vraiment forme du corps, parce qu'elle lui donne son être et sa définition: elle est cause de l'organisation du corps vivant et principe des différentes activités du composé (*Aporiae*, 2. 24, p. 75, 26–32. Cf. P. Moraux, *Alexandre d'Aphrodise, exégète de la noétique d'Aristote* [Liège-Paris, 1942], p. 48). On comprend que Plotin donne une interprétation matérialiste de la doctrine psychologique d'Aristote, quand on constate que plusieurs représentants de l'École péripatéticienne adoptent le même point de vue. Il est à noter par ailleurs que l'essentiel de la critique de Plotin contre l'entéléchisme d'Aristote se retrouve déjà dans les fragments d'Ammonius Saccas. Cf. G. Bruni, "Note di polemica neoplatonica contro l'uso e il significato del termine ἐντελέχεια," *Giornale critico della filosofia italiana* 39 (1960), pp. 205–236.

[30] *De An.* 2. 1. 412b9: καθόλου μὲν οὖν εἴρηται τί ἐστιν ἡ ψυχή· οὐσία γὰρ ἡ κατὰ τὸν λόγον.

[31] La réserve est très nettement formulée par Aristote: dans certaines

On peut donc conclure que la critique de Plotin passe à côté de la véritable doctrine d'Aristote.

La deuxième critique se rapporte au sommeil: si on accepte l'entéléchisme d'Aristote, Plotin estime que le sommeil ne peut plus s'expliquer, car celui-ci doit se concevoir comme une retraite de l'âme vis-à-vis du corps (ἀναχώρησις); l'âme se retire de l'organisme corporel, puisque la plupart des activités vitales ne s'exercent pas durant le sommeil. Comment l'âme pourrait-elle s'éloigner du corps et s'en isoler, si elle en est une simple qualité? Dire que l'âme est l'entéléchie du corps n'est-ce pas affirmer que notre principe vital est indissolublement lié à l'organisme corporel? [32]

Pour comprendre cette doctrine, il est nécessaire de tenir compte de la conception plotinienne du "moi" ou du "nous." Telle qu'elle est exposée dans l'*Enn.* I. I, on peut distinguer deux niveaux dans la signification de ce terme: il peut désigner le composé d'âme et de corps; car de ce qui affecte le corps, nous n'hésitons pas à dire que cela *nous* affecte.[33] Pourtant le corps ne fait pas partie du moi au sens strict: ce corps animé, appelé par

de ses parties, l'âme n'est certainement pas séparable du corps, tandis que pour d'autres rien ne s'oppose à la séparation, parce qu'elles ne sont l'entéléchie d'aucun organe corporel: οὐ μὴν ἀλλ' ἔνιά γε οὐθὲν κωλύει, διὰ τὸ μηθενὸς εἶναι σώματος ἐντελεχείας (*De An.* 2. I. 413a6). Dans l'optique d'Aristote on ne peut admettre que l'âme soit séparable du corps que si elle a une activité qui soit entièrement (subjectivement et objectivement) indépendante de l'organisme corporel: *Quare dicendum omnino est, operationem hic ab Aristotele vocari propriam animae, si neutro modo pendeat a corpore neque organice neque obiective* (J. Zabarella, *op. cit.,* col. 75). D'après G. Soleri (*L'immortalità dell'anima in Aristotele* [Torino, 1952], p. 151) il importe de distinguer entre les déclarations explicites d'Aristote et ce qui est logiquement et implicitement contenu dans sa doctrine: "Espressamente letteralmente e testualmente, il solo intelletto attivo è detto immortale; tutto il resto è mortale. Implicitamente e logicamente, l'anima intellettiva dell'uomo contenente potenzialmente le funzioni vegetali ed animali è necessariamente immortale." Aristote n'admet certainement pas que la pensée, comme la sensation, se fait à l'aide d'un organe corporel; même s'il n'arrive pas à justifier la survie de l'âme après la mort, on ne peut qualifier sa conception de l'homme comme matérialiste.

[32] *Enn.* 4. 7. 8⁵. Voici le texte correspondant de la *Theologia Aristotelis*: "We say: if the soul is a form, adhering and not separating, like the natural form, then how does she withdraw in sleep, and separate from the body without quitting it?"

[33] *Enn.* I. I. 10.

Plotin "la bête," ne fait partie du moi que pour autant qu'il est atteint par le rayonnement immédiat de l'âme. Le moi au sens strict, c'est l'âme seulement: celle-ci constitue l'homme véritable, celui qui possède les vertus intellectuelles, ayant leur siège dans l'âme séparée.[34] Pareille séparation peut se réaliser même durant cette vie: l'âme peut se retirer du corps de telle façon que la vie, qui n'est que le rayonnement de l'âme, s'éloigne de l'organisme corporel.[35] Parlant des six années qu'il a passées en compagnie de son maître, Porphyre écrit que, durant cette période, Plotin a connu quatre extases, qui étaient des moments d'union intime avec le Dieu qui est au-dessus de toutes choses.[36] Toute la métaphysique de Plotin est d'ailleurs avant tout un effort d'intériorisation: l'homme doit se retirer en lui-même en vue de prendre conscience des principes supérieurs, dont il émane.[37] Porphyre note au sujet de son maître qu'il restait en lui-même tout en étant aux autres.[38] Il était donc tout indiqué pour Plotin d'expliquer le sommeil comme la retraite de l'âme, puisque le véritable moi n'est pas constitué par le composé, mais par l'âme seulement.

La conception du sommeil comme étant une retraite de l'âme, était d'ailleurs assez répandue dans le monde grec: ne lit-on pas dans le *Timée* de Platon que durant le sommeil, en l'absence de toute activité rationnelle, l'homme est capable de divination?[39] Le philosophe est persuadé que le pouvoir de divination n'appar-

---

[34] *Enn.* I. I. 10, 7: ὁ δ' ἀληθὴς ἄνθρωπος ἄλλος ὁ καθαρὸς τούτων τὰς ἀρετὰς ἔχων τὰς ἐν νοήσει. Notons que ce point de vue est nettement différent de celui d'Aristote qui affirme que l'homme semble être principalement la partie rationnelle de son âme; les expressions du Stagirite sur ce point sont particulièrement prudentes et nuancées. Cf. *Protrepticus* (ed. Düring) B 62; *Eth. Nic.* 9. 4. 1166a16–17; 9. 4. 1166a22–23; 9. 8. 1168b30–31; 9. 8. 1168b34–1169a3; 10. 7. 1178a2.

[35] *Enn.* I. I. 10.

[36] Porph. *Plot.* 23: Τέλος γὰρ αὐτῷ καὶ σκοπὸς ἦν τὸ ἑνωθῆναι καὶ πελάσαι τῷ ἐπὶ πᾶσι θεῷ.

[37] *Enn.* 5. I: Ce traité est particulièrement significatif en ce qui concerne la réflexion métaphysique de Plotin: le chemin qui conduit au Principe Suprême ne passe pas par le monde extérieur; c'est en faisant retour sur elle-même que l'âme découvre son origine divine. La première phrase de ce traité indique tout le sens de la recherche: Plotin s'étonne de ce que les âmes aient oublié que Dieu est leur père; elles trouvent entièrement leur origine en Dieu et pourtant elles vivent dans l'ignorance de ce qu'elles sont et de ce que Dieu est (*Enn.* 5. I. I).

[38] Porph. *Plot.* 8: Συνῆν οὖν καὶ ἑαυτῷ ἅμα καὶ τοῖς ἄλλοις.

[39] Pl. *Ti.* 71d.

tient pas à la raison, mais qu'il a été donné à la partie irrationnelle de l'âme : c'est pourquoi il ne s'exerce qu'en l'absence de la
réflexion rationnelle, que celle-ci ait été supprimée par le sommeil, la maladie ou "l'enthousiasme." Platon admet pourtant
qu'il appartient aux prophètes, et donc au travail de la raison,
d'interpréter les données de la divination.[40]

La conception d'Aristote sur la divination dans le sommeil
est assez différente de celle de Platon : le Stagirite estime que le
pouvoir intellectif, loin d'être suspendu, s'accroît durant le sommeil, parce que l'âme devient davantage ce qu'elle est en s'éloig-
nant du corps. En se retirant de l'organisme corporel, elle devient
plus puissante et capable de prévoir l'avenir : le même phénomène
se produit au moment de la mort.[41] On retrouve la même
doctrine dans le *De divinatione* de Cicéron qui, sur ce point,
semble s'inspirer de Posidonius.[42]

Quelle est maintenant la valeur de la critique plotinienne ?
La réponse ne peut être douteuse : cette critique n'entame en
rien l'explication aristotélicienne du sommeil. Dans la partie
plus ancienne de son *De somno et Vigilia*, l'interprétation que
donne Aristote est plutôt d'ordre physiologique :[43] le sommeil
est considéré comme une sorte de concentration de la chaleur
intérieure dans la région du coeur et dans la partie inférieure
de l'organisme, alors que la partie supérieure du corps et les
organes extérieurs se refroidissent.[44] Cette concentration de la
chaleur intérieure est mise en rapport avec la nutrition qui

---

[40] Pl. *Ti.* 71e.

[41] Sextus Empiricus, *Math.* 3 (*frg.* 12, ed. Walzer). Cf. Aristotele, *Della
Filosofia*, Introduzione, Testo, Traduzione e commento esegetico di M.
Untersteiner (Rome, 1963), pp. 22 et 166.

[42] G. Verbeke, *L'Évolution de la doctrine du pneuma du Stoïcisme à
saint Augustin* (Paris-Louvain, 1945), pp. 121–122.

[43] *Aristotelis De insomniis et De divinatione per somnum*, A new edition
of the Greek text with the Latin translations by H. J. Drossaart Lulofs,
Part I, Preface and Greek Text (Leiden, 1947). Le premier chapitre de
l'introduction traite des problèmes d'ordre chronologique : la partie la
plus ancienne du *De Somno* commence p. 455b13 et s'étend jusqu'à la fin
du traité. Cette partie constitue un exposé bien achevé : le passage le plus
caractéristique se rencontre p. 456a5 en ce sens qu'il est en opposition
nette avec l'entéléchisme du *De An.* La partie la plus récente du traité
(depuis le début jusqu'à la p. 455b13) se situe dans le prolongement du
De An. et n'est pas achevée.

[44] *De Somno*, 3. 457a33.

produit tout naturellement une évaporation abondante:[45] cette évaporation remonte au cerveau, s'y refroidit, se condense et se transforme en humeur flegmatique; celle-ci redescend, chasse la chaleur, de telle façon que, d'abord, le cerveau s'alourdit et qu'ensuite, l'animal s'endort.[46] Dans la partie plus récente du même traité, Aristote considère le sommeil du point de vue psychologique: le sommeil y est conçu comme une sorte d'enchaî- nement ou d'immobilité de la partie sensitive de l'âme.[47] Ce qui frappe le Stagirite dans ce phénomène, c'est que toutes les facultés sensitives sont immobilisées en même temps. C'est pourquoi il attribue le sommeil à une fatigue toute naturelle du premier principe de la vie sensitive, le sens commun.[48]

Pour ce qui est de la valeur des rêves, dans son *De divinatione per somnum*, le maître grec se montre plutôt sceptique: peut-on grâce aux rêves prévoir l'avenir? Aristote répond que dans la plupart des cas, il s'agit de simples coïncidences.[49] Il admet cependant qu'on puisse percevoir durant le sommeil des excita- tions trop faibles pour être perçues pendant la veille et que des phantasmes survenant dans le sommeil puissent amorcer cer- taines actions.[50] Dans toute cette interprétation il n'est donc pas question d'une retraite de l'âme: Aristote répondrait à la critique de Plotin qu'il n'accepte pas son explication du sommeil.

Plotin estime en outre que dans l'optique d'Aristote tout conflit entre la raison et le désir est exclu: l'âme ne sera jamais en désaccord avec elle-même et elle n'éprouvera tout entière qu'un seul et même désir. Ici encore Plotin part de la même idée que, selon Aristote, l'âme est une simple qualité de l'organisme cor- porel et qu'elle ne peut être que matérielle.[51] Plus loin dans sa critique d'Aristote, Plotin fera remarquer que les désirs de l'homme s'étendent bien au delà des réalités matérielles, telles la

---

[45] *De Somno*, 3. 456b18: οὐκ ἔστιν ὁ ὕπνος ἀδυναμία πᾶσα τοῦ αἰσθητικοῦ, ἀλλ' ἐκ τῆς περὶ τὴν τροφὴν ἀναθυμιάσεως γίγνεται τὸ πάθος τοῦτο.

[46] *De Somno*, 3. 458a1–5.

[47] *De Somno*, 1. 454b9: ὁ γὰρ ὕπνος πάθος τι τοῦ αἰσθητικοῦ μορίου ἐστίν, οἷον δεσμὸς καὶ ἀκινησία τις, ὥστ' ἀνάγκη πᾶν τὸ καθεῦδον ἔχειν τὸ αἰσθητικὸν μόριον.

[48] *De Somno*, 2. 455a32–455b2; 455b10.

[49] *De Divinatione*, 1. 463a31: τὰ δὲ πολλὰ συμπτώμασιν ἔοικε.

[50] *De Divinatione*, 1. 463a20 ssq.

[51] *Enn.* 4. 7. 8[5].

nourriture et la boisson et il en conclut que le principe de ces
désirs ne peut être matériel.[52]

Disons dès l'abord que la difficulté est sérieuse et que Platon
avait essayé de la résoudre en distinguant dans l'âme humaine
trois parties, dont seule la partie supérieure est rationnelle:
l'homme porte en lui une possibilité de conflit intérieur et une
possibilité d'équilibre qui se réalisera surtout grâce à la vertu de
justice. Plotin a été confronté avec la même difficulté en voulant
expliquer la descente de l'âme: comment l'âme qui appartient au
monde intelligible, peut-elle descendre dans un corps et s'unir
à lui? Du point de vue de l'intellect seul, de la pensée pure, cette
descente est inexplicable: car le νοῦς reste fixé dans le monde
intelligible de façon immuable et éternelle. S'il s'en éloigne, c'est
qu'il y a intervention d'un autre facteur qui s'ajoute à l'intellect,
à savoir le désir (ὄρεξις).[53] L'âme est donc un intellect auquel s'est
uni le désir de réaliser ce qu'il a contemplé dans le νοῦς: c'est
pourquoi elle s'oriente vers le monde sensible; integrée d'abord
dans l'âme universelle elle régit tout l'univers matériel; ensuite
elle désire s'isoler de cette âme universelle et administrer pour
elle-même une partie de l'univers. C'est ce qui l'amène à s'unir à
un corps déterminé qu'elle régira comme son domaine propre:
ceci ne veut pas dire toutefois qu'elle s'y engage totalement,
elle reste au moins partiellement en dehors du corps et indépendante de lui.[54]

En effet, s'il y a dans l'âme un désir qui l'oriente vers le monde
sensible et vers son union au corps, il y en a un aussi qui est
capable de l'élever vers les réalités supérieures, vers le monde
intelligible. Car l'âme n'est pas seulement susceptible de descente ou d'*exitus*, mais aussi d'ascension ou de *reditus*, Plotin
n'hésitera pas à écrire que toute âme tend vers le véritable Bien.[55]
Ceci ne signifie pas toutefois que tout le monde l'atteint: car

[52] *Enn.* 4. 7. 8[5]. 23: καὶ μὴν οὐδὲ τὸ ἐπιθυμοῦν, μὴ σιτίων μηδὲ ποτῶν ἀλλ'
ἄλλων παρὰ τὰ τοῦ σώματος, οὐδὲ αὐτὸ ἀχώριστος ἐντελέχεια.

[53] *Enn.* 4. 7. 13. 4: δ δ' ἂν ὄρεξιν προσλάβῃ ἐφεξῆς ἐκείνῳ τῷ νῷ ὄν, τῇ
προσθήκῃ τῆς ὀρέξεως οἷον πρόεισιν ἤδη ἐπὶ πλέον καὶ κοσμεῖν ὀρεγόμενον καθ' ἃ
ἐν νῷ εἶδεν. Voici le texte correspondant de la *Theologia Aristotelis*: "When
the mind acquires a desire, it proceeds because of that desire in a certain
direction and does not abide in its original place, for it desires greatly
to act and to adorn the things which it has seen in the mind."

[54] *Enn.* 4. 7. 13.

[55] *Enn.* 1. 6. 7.1: ἀναβατέον οὖν πάλιν ἐπὶ τὸ ἀγαθόν, οὗ ὀρέγεται πᾶσα ψυχή.

pour pouvoir l'atteindre les âmes doivent se purifier, elles doivent déposer les vêtements dont elles se sont revêtues dans leur descente.[56] On n'atteint pas le Bien suprême en entreprenant une marche ordinaire ni en se servant d'un attelage ou d'un navire, il faut cesser de s'attacher aux réalités sensibles et tourner le regard vers le monde intérieur: tout le monde possède cette faculté, mais peu d'hommes en font usage.[57] C'est que, pour contempler un objet, l'oeil doit lui devenir semblable: seule l'âme qui est devenue semblable au Bien, est capable de le contempler.[58] Le conflit dont parle Plotin entre la raison et les désirs n'est donc pas inévitable: par un processus de purification intérieure, l'homme peut se détacher du sensible et remonter vers la réalité intelligible.

Que dire maintenant de la critique plotinienne contre Aristote? Il est vrai que pour le Stagirite le conflit entre la raison et l'irrationnel joue un rôle important, surtout dans l'*Éthique* et pourtant on ne peut dire que chez lui l'irrationnel présente la même signification que chez Plotin. Aux yeux de ce dernier l'irrationnel est radicalement et irrémédiablement ce qu'il est, c'est-à-dire désir du monde sensible et des réalités corporelles. C'est pourquoi l'âme doit se purifier, c'est-à-dire se libérer, se débarrasser de tout ce qui la porte vers le sensible et l'y attache. C'est que la véritable destinée de l'homme ne se situe pas ici-bas, la patrie de l'âme est le monde intelligible. Telle n'est pas l'optique d'Aristote: ce qui compte pour lui, c'est la vie sur terre au milieu des autres hommes; la destinée de l'homme se situe dans le monde présent. L'homme doit-il se débarrasser de ses tendances irrationnelles? Nullement, car l'irrationnel n'est pas entièrement dépourvu de raison, il est capable de suivre

---

[56] *Enn.* I. 6. 7.

[57] *Enn.* I. 6. 8.

[58] *Enn.* I. 6. 9; I. 2. 4: En quoi consiste le bien de l'âme: τὸ ἀγαθὸν αὐτῆς τὸ συνεῖναι τῷ συγγενεῖ. Cf. J. Trouillard, *La Purification Plotinienne* (Paris, 1955), pp. 186 ssq.: l'auteur fait remarquer à juste titre que dans l'optique de Plotin, la purification n'est pas avant tout la libération du mal; l'essentiel de la vertu n'est pas l'opposition aux passions ou la domination du psychisme déréglé; il s'agit principalement pour l'âme de s'assimiler aux réalités supérieures: "La purification n'est possible et efficace que par l'extase déjà ébauchée à la racine de l'âme" (p. 188).

les directives de la partie rationnelle;[59] dans le cas de l'homme vertueux, cet équilibre se réalise grâce à la tempérance, au courage et à la modération. On en trouve la preuve dans le fait des admonestations, des reproches et des exhortations: tout cela n'aurait pas de sens, si la partie irrationnelle n'était pas capable d'obéir à la raison.[60] Il y aura donc deux niveaux dans le rationnel: il y a la partie qui possède proprement la raison ou ce qui de soi est rationnel et, en second lieu, la partie qui ne fait qu'obéir à la raison, comme les enfants obéissent à leur père.[61] La tâche de l'homme n'est donc pas de se dépouiller de ses tendances irrationnelles, mais de les "rationaliser."

En admettant que l'âme est l'entéléchie du corps, c'est-à-dire en rejetant un dualisme radical et irrémédiable, Aristote est en état d'expliquer aussi bien le conflit entre le rationnel et l'irrationnel que leur équilibre. La critique de Plotin prend son origine dans une conception foncièrement différente de celle d'Aristote au sujet du conflit entre la raison et le désir du sensible.

Passons maintenant aux critiques qui se fondent sur les fonctions cognitives et végétatives de l'âme: Plotin estime que, dans l'optique d'Aristote, on pourrait encore à la rigueur trouver une explication à la connaissance sensible, mais le savoir intellectuel devient inconcevable. C'est pourquoi, dit Plotin, ceux qui admettent l'entéléchisme ont fait de l'intellect une âme distincte et immortelle. Qu'en résulte-t-il sinon que l'âme intellective est l'entéléchie du corps dans un sens bien différent que l'âme végétative ou sensitive? [62] Le terme "entéléchie" prend donc un

---

[59] *Eth. Nic.* I. 13. 1102b13: ἔοικε δὲ καὶ ἄλλη τις φύσις τῆς ψυχῆς ἄλογος εἶναι, μετέχουσα μέντοι πῃ λόγου; 1102b25.

[60] *Eth. Nic.* I. 13. 1102b33.

[61] *Eth. Nic.* I. 13. 1103a1–3. L'interprétation que nous donnons ici, ne signifie pas que l'opposition entre la raison et la partie irrationnelle de l'âme, telle qu'elle est présentée dans les traités d'éthique, ne pose pas de problèmes dans le cadre de la doctrine psychologique d'Aristote. Si l'opposition en question est plus accentuée dans les ouvrages de morale que dans les autres traités, c'est probablement parce que le Stagirite en a besoin pour l'élaboration de son éthique: au centre de cette discipline se trouve la notion du λόγος, dont la signification ne correspond pas exactement à notre vocable moderne "raison," parce que le logos d'Aristote n'est pas une fonction purement cognitive.

[62] *Enn.* 4. 7. 8[5]. 16: τὴν οὖν λογιζομένην ψυχὴν ἄλλως ἐντελέχειαν ἢ τοῦτον τὸν τρόπον ἀνάγκη εἶναι, εἰ δεῖ τῷ ὀνόματι τούτῳ χρῆσθαι. Voici le

sens différent suivant qu'il s'agit de l'âme comme principe de la vie sensitive ou de l'âme comme principe de la pensée. Aux yeux de Plotin, la connaissance sensible non plus ne peut être conçue comme simplement matérielle. N'est-il pas vrai que les représentations des objets connus sont conservées dans l'âme? Comment le sont-elles? Certainement pas comme des images matérielles, car, dans ce cas, l'âme ne pourrait pas recevoir d'autres images. Ni l'âme intellective ni l'âme sensitive ne peuvent donc être conçues comme des entéléchies inséparables.[63] Qu'en est-il de l'âme végétative? Ici encore, notre auteur arrive à la même conclusion: l'origine de la plante se trouve dans la racine; l'âme végétative est donc d'abord dans un tout petit volume, par exemple, dans une semence, pour s'étendre ensuite à la plante dans toute sa dimension. Il y a aussi le mouvement inverse: quand les autres parties de la plante se dessèchent et rejettent le principe vital, celui-ci se retire dans la racine et n'occupe plus qu'un volume infime. C'est pourquoi Plotin prétend que l'âme végétative non plus ne peut être considérée comme une entéléchie inséparable du corps.[64]

Parmi toutes les critiques présentées par Plotin, celles-ci sont les plus graves: elles touchent incontestablement un des points les plus délicats de la doctrine psychologique d'Aristote, surtout en ce qui concerne le statut de l'intellect.

Plotin s'est penché plus d'une fois sur le problème de la connaissance sensible, parce qu'il a été confronté sur ce point avec la doctrine matérialiste des Stoïciens: d'après ces philosophes, la sensation n'est rien d'autre que la formation d'une représentation de l'objet à l'intérieur de l'âme; quant à la mémoire, elle s'expliquerait par la conservation des images qui ont été im-

texte correspondant de la *Theologia Aristotelis*: "The Materialists recognised that, and consequently they are compelled to acknowledge a second soul and a second mind that does not die. Now we say that there is no second soul other than this rational soul which is in the body at the moment, and she it is of whom the philosophers say that she is the entelechy of the body, though they speak of her as entelechy and a form of perfection in a way different from that in which the Materialists speak."

[63] *Enn.* 4. 7. 8[5].

[64] *Enn.* 4. 7. 8[5]. 33: εἰ οὖν καὶ εἰς ὀλίγον ἔρχεται ἐκ μείζονος φυτοῦ καὶ ἐξ ὀλίγου ἐπὶ πᾶν, τί κωλύει καὶ ὅλως χωρίζεσθαι; Dans l'opinion de Plotin, l'âme végétative n'est pas liée indissolublement à un corps.

primées dans l'âme.[65] Tout s'expliquerait par des processus purement matériels. Plotin s'oppose avec énergie à cette doctrine : d'après lui, la connaissance sensible n'est pas la reproduction matérielle d'une copie de l'objet à l'intérieur de l'âme, puisque le sujet saisit les choses comme existant en dehors de lui;[66] si l'interprétation stoïcienne était exacte, une fois l'image formée dans l'âme, le sujet n'aurait plus à se tourner vers les choses pour les connaître.[67] Non seulement le sujet perçoit les choses comme étant en dehors de lui, mais il peut même se rendre compte de la distance qui le sépare de l'objet connu et calculer les dimensions des choses perçues.[68] Ainsi l'homme essaiera de calculer les dimensions de la voûte du ciel, ce qu'il ne pourrait certainement pas faire si son regard se portait sur une représentation intérieure. D'ailleurs, dans ce cas, on ne connaîtrait jamais les réalités elles-mêmes, on vivrait dans un monde d'images ou de projections.[69] Si on applique un objet directement contre la pupille de l'oeil, on ne le perçoit plus : comment l'âme pourrait-elle percevoir une image imprimée en elle?[70] Enfin, si toute sensation se réduit à l'impression d'une image dans l'âme, comment pourrait-on distinguer l'objet de la vue de celui de l'ouïe?[71] D'après Plotin, la sensation ne se réduit donc pas à la réception passive d'une impression; elle implique toujours une certaine activité vis-à-vis d'un objet vers lequel la faculté psychique est orientée.

Plotin se demande ensuite comment l'âme peut connaître un objet sans qu'elle l'ait assimilé et introduit en elle-même.[72] Pour

---

[65] *Enn.* 4. 6. 1 : il n'y a pas de doute que dans ce texte Plotin s'oppose à la doctrine stoïcienne de la perception sensible : le terme τύπωσις est caractéristique de cette théorie. Nous croyons qu'il est utile d'examiner la critique de Plotin sur cette question, parce qu'elle nous aidera à comprendre son opposition à l'entéléchisme d'Aristote.

[66] *Enn.* 4. 6. 1. 15 : ὡς αἴσθησιν ὁτουοῦν λαμβάνοντες δι' ὁράσεως ἐκεῖ ὁρῶμεν καὶ τῇ ὄψει προσβάλλομεν, οὗ τὸ ὁρατόν ἐστιν ἐπ' εὐθείας κείμενον.

[67] *Enn.* 4. 6. 1. 21 : οὐδὲν γὰρ ἂν ἐδεήθη τοῦ ἔξω βλέπειν.

[68] *Enn.* 4. 6. 1.

[69] *Enn.* 4. 6. 1. 29 : οὐκ ἔσται βλέπειν αὐτὰ ἃ ὁρῶμεν, ἰνδάλματα δὲ ὁραμάτων καὶ σκιάς, ὥστε ἄλλα μὲν εἶναι αὐτὰ τὰ πράγματα, ἄλλα δὲ τὰ ἡμῖν ὁρώμενα.

[70] *Enn.* 4. 6. 1.

[71] *Enn.* 4. 6. 2.

[72] *Enn.* 4. 6. 3. 4 : la question de Plotin est formulée comme suit : εἰ μηδὲν λαβοῦσα εἰς αὐτὴν ἀντίληψιν ὧν οὐκ ἔσχε, ποιεῖται.

lui, la réponse à cette question se trouve dans la nature de l'âme humaine, qui se situe à la frontière de l'intelligible et du sensible. L'âme humaine est le logos ou la raison de toutes choses: elle connaît l'intelligible, en éveillant et en précisant les souvenirs vagues qu'elle porte en elle;[73] elle saisit le sensible en l'éclairant d'un rayonnement qui trouve son origine en elle-même et qui le fait apparaître devant elle.[74] Comment, dans ce cas, peut-on expliquer le souvenir? Quand l'âme s'est efforcée de porter son attention sur un objet, cette disposition ne disparaît pas avec la perception, elle demeure pendant tout un temps dans l'âme comme si l'objet était encore présent; plus l'effort a été considérable et plus la disposition de l'âme reste constante.[75] C'est pourquoi les enfants ont une bonne mémoire: les objets sur lesquels leur attention se porte ne sont pas nombreux.[76] D'ailleurs, fait remarquer Plotin, si les impressions sensibles se conservaient dans l'âme, il ne serait pas nécessaire de réfléchir pour se les rappeler et on ne devrait pas les oublier d'abord, afin de pouvoir s'en souvenir.[77] La mémoire ne peut être la conservation passive d'impressions réçues, car on ne comprendrait pas, dans ce cas, qu'il est possible de l'améliorer grâce à des exercices: comment se fait-il, en effet, qu'on ne retient pas ce qu'on n'a entendu qu'une ou deux fois, alors qu'on le retient après l'avoir entendu plusieurs fois? Comment se fait-il qu'on ne se souvient pas de ce qu'on vient d'entendre et qu'on se le rappelle plus tard?

En outre une mémoire bien exercée ne retient pas seulement les données sur lesquelles elle s'est exercée, mais aussi d'autres connaissances, ce qui signifie qu'elle s'est améliorée de façon générale.[78] C'est que la mémoire, pas plus que les puissances sensitives, n'est une réception passive, elle est une activité, une

---

[73] *Enn.* 4. 6. 3. 14: il est intéressant de noter comment Plotin exprime cette doctrine platonicienne de l'anamnèse, en se servant de la terminologie aristotélicienne de puissance et d'acte: καὶ γίνεσθαι ἐκ τοῦ ἀμυδροῦ τῷ οἷον ἐγείρεσθαι ἐναργεστέρα καὶ ἐκ δυνάμεως εἰς ἐνέργειαν ἰέναι.

[74] *Enn.* 4. 6. 3. 17: καὶ ταῦτα παρ' αὑτῆς οἷον ἐκλάμπειν ποιεῖ.

[75] *Enn.* 4. 6. 3. 19: ὅταν τοίνυν ῥωσθῇ πρὸς ὁτιοῦν τῶν φανέντων ὥσπερ πρὸς παρὸν διάκειται ἐπὶ πολὺν χρόνον καὶ ὅσῳ μᾶλλον τόσῳ ἀεί.

[76] *Enn.* 4. 6. 3.

[77] *Enn.* 4. 6. 3.

[78] *Enn.* 4. 6. 3. 38: ταῦτα γὰρ μαρτυρεῖ πρόκλησιν τῆς δυνάμεως καθ' ἣν μνημονεύομεν τῆς ψυχῆς, ὡς ῥωσθείσης ἢ ἁπλῶς ἢ πρὸς τοῦτο.

certaine force (ἰσχύς).⁷⁹ Pourquoi les souvenirs ne nous viennent-
ils pas immédiatement après la première connaissance mais
seulement plus tard ? Plotin répond : l'âme doit d'abord s'exercer
et se préparer pour que la disposition qui l'oriente vers un objet,
devienne stable.⁸⁰ Il arrive souvent qu'il n'y a pas de parallélisme
entre la mémoire et l'intelligence, ce qui n'est guère compré-
hensible si on conçoit la connaissance comme la formation matérielle d'images qui se conservent dans l'âme. Aux yeux de Plotin,
il n'y a là aucune difficulté, puisque la mémoire et l'intelligence ne
sont pas la même puissance active (δύναμις), elles présentent
chacune leur physionomie particulière.⁸¹

Dans l'opinion de Plotin, la perception sensible constitue
toujours une unité, même dans le cas où l'objet connu présente
une certaine diversité : il faut donc que le principe actif de la
perception soit un.⁸² Comment pourrait-on connaître la différence entre une couleur et un son, si le principe de la perception
ne constituait pas une unité ? Car si le sujet était étendu comme
une ligne, chaque point de la ligne pourrait avoir une sensation
différente ; les différents points seraient étrangers les uns aux
autres et aucun d'eux ne se rendrait compte de ce que l'autre
perçoit. Qu'en résulte-t-il sinon que le sujet de la perception
doit être inétendu ?⁸³

Que dire alors de la perception d'un objet complexe, présentant
une diversité d'aspects ? Le même raisonnement s'y applique :
si le sujet percevant est étendu et que ses différentes parties
saisissent des aspects distincts de l'objet, on ne connaîtra pas
l'objet dans son unité variée. Si, par contre, chaque partie du
sujet perçoit l'objet dans sa totalité, chaque sensation se réduira
à un nombre indéfini de perceptions et de représéntations.⁸⁴

Plotin arrive à la même conclusion en étudiant la perception
de la douleur, où il s'oppose encore une fois au matérialisme
stoïcien : les Stoïciens disent qu'une douleur peut être ressentie

---

⁷⁹ *Enn.* 4. 6. 3. 55 : ἰσχὺς ἄρα τις καὶ ἡ αἴσθησις καὶ ἡ μνήμη.
⁸⁰ *Enn.* 4. 6. 3. 60 : τὴν δύναμιν δεῖ οἷον ἐπιστῆσαι καὶ ἑτοιμάσασθαι.
⁸¹ *Enn.* 4. 6. 3.
⁸² *Enn.* 4. 7. 6 : εἴ τι μέλλει αἰσθάνεσθαί τινος, ἓν αὐτὸ δεῖ εἶναι καὶ τῷ
αὐτῷ παντὸς ἀντιλαμβάνεσθαι.
⁸³ *Enn.* 4. 7. 6 : le principe de la perception doit être comme un centre
(κέντρον), où toutes les lignes venant de la circonférence aboutissent : ἓν
ὄντως.
⁸⁴ *Enn.* 4. 7. 6.

dans le doigt, mais que la sensation est le fait de l'*hégémonikon* établi dans le coeur: il y aurait donc une distinction entre la partie qui souffre et le principe qui perçoit; la douleur serait transmise (διάδοσις) progressivement de la partie souffrante à l'*hégémonikon*.[85]

Plotin rejette catégoriquement cette doctrine: l'homme est capable de situer la douleur qu'il endure et d'autre part la douleur est perçue par l'âme tout entière: ceci veut dire que l'âme est présente toute entière à tous les endroits de l'organisme.[86] En effet, la souffrance ne peut être attribuée ni à l'âme ni au corps, mais au composé des deux:[87] quand l'union de ces deux éléments qui appartiennent à des niveaux différents est menacée, on souffre; par contre si leur union s'affermit, on éprouve du plaisir. Prenons le cas d'une blessure: ce qui souffre, c'est le corps animé; quant à l'âme elle perçoit cette douleur par sa contiguïté avec le corps. Plotin fait une distinction entre la douleur elle-même et la sensation qu'on en éprouve:[88] l'âme ne souffre pas, mais elle perçoit la douleur et comme c'est l'âme tout entière qui la sent, elle est capable de la situer. Si l'âme souffrait elle-même, elle ne pourrait situer la douleur: car étant tout entière dans chaque partie du corps, elle situerait la douleur dans l'organisme tout entier.[89]

Il résulte de tout cela que l'âme doit être une substance immatérielle, elle ne peut se concevoir comme l'entéléchie d'un

---

[85] *Enn.* 4. 7. 7.

[86] *Enn.* 4. 7. 7: Notons que d'après P. Henry (*Les États du texte*, p. 102) les lignes 14–15 devraient se traduire de la façon suivante: "Et il faut que le sensation produite par un seul excitant douloureux, se résolve en une infinité de sensations, *s'il est vrai* que le principe doit éprouver toutes ces sensations et en outre celle qu'il a de lui-même." Cette traduction est inacceptable, parce qu'elle ne s'accorde pas avec l'argumentation de Plotin; il suffit de regarder la phrase suivante pour s'en rendre compte: le *hégémonikon* ne perçoit pas la douleur dans le doigt, mais celle de l'organe qui lui est immédiatement voisin (τοῦ πρὸς αὐτῷ). Pareille interprétation est d'ailleurs en contradiction avec le principe général admis par Plotin que dans le domaine du corporel une partie ne peut avoir connaissance de l'affection d'une autre partie. Qu'en résulte-t-il sinon que le principe de la perception doit "πανταχοῦ αὐτὸ ἑαυτῷ τὸ αὐτὸ εἶναι" (4. 7. 7. 26)?

[87] *Enn.* 4. 4. 18.

[88] *Enn.* 4. 19. 26: ἀλλ' οὖν τὴν αἴσθησιν αὐτὴν οὐκ ὀδύνην λεκτέον, ἀλλὰ γνῶσιν ὀδύνης.

[89] *Enn.* 4. 4. 19.

corps: et cela vaut non seulement pour l'âme intellective, mais aussi pour le principe de la sensation et de la vie végétative. Qu'on songe à la variété de mouvements dont l'âme est le principe! On sait que chaque corps ne possède qu'un seul mouvement; si l'âme était corporelle, elle serait dans le même cas.[90] Qu'on considère la croissance de l'organisme corporel, qui se fait par l'assimilation d'un autre corps: si l'âme est corporelle, son développement devra s'expliquer de la même manière, ce qui comporte de nombreuses difficultés: car si cette addition est d'ordre psychique, il faut se demander d'où elle provient et si elle n'est pas d'ordre psychique, il faut expliquer comment elle est integrée dans l'âme.[91]

Quelle est maintenant la valeur de la critique de Plotin vis-à-vis de l'entéléchisme d'Aristote? Y a-t-il dans la doctrine psychologique du Stagirite une réponse aux objections qu'on vient d'exposer?

D'une façon générale Aristote aurait reproché certainement à Plotin son *spiritualisme exagéré*. Qu'on ne s'y méprenne pas: le Stagirite lui non plus n'admet pas que l'âme soit une grandeur spatiale,[92] elle n'est pas non plus l'harmonie réalisée par le concours d'éléments corporels,[93] car le Stagirite rejette formellement que l'âme soit composée d'éléments.[94] Le maître grec s'oppose catégoriquement à la théorie d'Empédocle qui essaie d'expliquer la croissance des plantes en faisant appel à deux éléments, la terre et le feu. Sa critique est bien significative: il se demande ce qui assurera l'union des divers éléments, si la terre se porte vers le bas et le feu vers le haut. Il leur faut un principe d'union et celui-ci n'est autre que l'âme.[95] Il n'admet pas non plus que le feu puisse être la cause de la nutrition et de la croissance: s'il en était ainsi il n'y aurait pas de limite à la croissance des vivants, car l'accroissement du feu se poursuit indéfiniment, aussi longtemps qu'il y a du combustible, alors que

[90] *Enn.* 4. 7. 5.
[91] *Enn.* 4. 7. 5.
[92] *De An.* 1. 3. 407a2.
[93] *De An.* 1. 4. 407b32.
[94] *De An.* 1. 5. 409b18 ssq.
[95] *De An.* 2. 4. 415b28 ssq.

les êtres vivants se développent jusqu'à une certaine limite, et cette détermination relève de l'âme.[96]

Et pourtant Aristote ne dit pas comme Plotin que toute âme est simplement immatérielle: le principe vital des plantes et des animaux s'insère dans le processus de génération et de corruption: dans ce cas, l'âme réside en puissance dans la semence; aucun vivant ne s'engendre lui-même, il y a toujours un agent extérieur qui fait passer la puissance à l'acte. Il n'en reste pas moins vrai que tout ce processus s'inscrit dans le devenir du monde matériel: les penseurs médiévaux diront que l'âme est produite à partir de la puissance de la matière.[97] L'âme des plantes et des animaux n'est donc pas simplement matérielle comme les quatre éléments et cependant elle ne peut exister indépendamment de la matière.

En est-il de même de l'âme intellective? Il est certain qu'Aristote considère l'intellect comme immatériel: celui-ci ne s'insère plus dans le processus de génération, il est introduit du dehors.[98] Et malgré cela Aristote hésite à lui attribuer une existence indépendante du corps, parce que même la connaissance intellectuelle ne peut se passer de l'expérience sensible. Reste cependant le principe actif de l'intellection: celui-ci est immatériel, éternel et séparé.

Résumons: Aristote n'aurait pas été d'accord avec le spiritualisme de Plotin, au moins sur deux points: il n'admet pas que toute âme est purement immatérielle et il n'admet pas non plus que la pensée soit aussi indépendante du corps que Plotin

---

[96] *De An.* 2. 4. 416a9 ssq.

[97] *Gen. An.* 2. 1. 735a8: Aristote se demande si la semence possède une âme; il répond: δῆλον οὖν ὅτι καὶ ἔχει καὶ ἔστι δυνάμει Cf. 2. 3. 737a17.

[98] *Gen. An.* 2. 3. 736b27: λείπεται δὴ τὸν νοῦν μόνον θύραθεν ἐπεισιέναι καὶ θεῖον εἶναι μόνον· οὐθὲν γὰρ αὐτοῦ τῇ ἐνεργείᾳ κοινωνεῖ σωματικὴ ἐνέργεια. La formule est elliptique et énigmatique: que signifie cette introduction du dehors dans une métaphysique où la liberté créatrice est absente? Tout ce qu'on peut dire avec certitude c'est que l'intellect n'est pas produit par génération, car l'activité intellectuelle ne se fait pas à l'aide d'un organe corporel. D'où vient-il? Aristote ne le dit pas. On ne peut se ranger du côté de M. M. De Corte, qui croit que la faculté noétique "peut venir intégralement *du* dehors (θύραθεν) par le véhicule du sperme éjaculé par le mâle" (*La Doctrine de l'Intelligence chez Aristote* [Paris, 1934], p. 108). On ne voit vraiment pas en quoi cette interprétation pourrait expliquer la position privilégiée de l'intellect comme faculté immatérielle.

ne l'estime. Il faut avouer cependant que dans le cadre de son entéléchisme, il n'est pas arrivé à déterminer la place de l'intellect humain.

Passons maintenant à la dernière objection; elle se rapporte à la transmigration des âmes. Plotin prétend que la même âme passe d'un être vivant dans un autre: il en trouve la preuve dans le fait que des animaux changent d'espèce et se transforment en d'autres animaux. S'il en est ainsi, l'âme ne peut être l'entéléchie d'un corps, car, dans ce cas, elle ne pourrait jamais s'en détacher.[99]

On sait que la doctrine de la transmigration des âmes se retrouve chez plusieurs penseurs du monde hellénique. Peut-on dire qu'elle est d'origine grecque? E. R. Dodds estime que non et il rattache cette croyance populaire au Shamanisme, qui était répandu sur une zone extrêmement vaste, depuis la Scandinavie en passant par le nord de la Russie et de l'Asie jusqu'en Indonésie. Le Shaman était un personnage religieux qui grâce à la solitude et au jeûne, était capable de performances extraordinaires, telles la prédiction de l'avenir, la bilocation ou le dédoublement spirituel et le changement psychologique de sexe. D'après M. Dodds, c'est par le Shamanisme que le dualisme psychologique s'est introduit dans la culture hellénique.[100]

Parmi les philosophes néoplatoniciens, Plotin n'est pas seul à enseigner la transmigration des âmes. Elle est admise aussi par Jamblique qui introduit cependant une précision importante: une âme humaine ne passe jamais dans le corps d'un animal. C'est avec cette restriction que Némésius, évêque d'Émèse, semble adhérer à cette doctrine dans son *De natura hominis*.[101]

[99] *Enn.* 4. 7. 8[5].

[100] *The Greeks and the Irrational* (Berkeley-Los Angeles, 1951), pp. 140 ssq.

[101] D'après B. Domanski (*Die Psychologie des Nemesius* [Münster, 1900], p. 54) Némésius n'aurait pas admis la transmigration des âmes: "Es scheint uns deshalb Ritter mit Unrecht dem Philosophen eine mildere Form der Seelenwanderung in den Mund gelegt zu haben. Nemesius steht dieser Lehre fremd und ablehnend gegenüber" (p. 55). W. Jaeger par contre (*Nemesios von Emesa* [Berlin, 1914], p. 7) est d'avis que Némésius est partisan aussi bien de la préexistence de l'âme que de la métempsycose: "Nemesius glaubt an die Präexistenz und die Wanderung der Seele und scheut sich nicht es zu bekennen, wenn er auch die ἀναβαθμοί des Origenes als 'unschriftgemäss' verwirft." Après avoir exposé le point de

La même restriction se rencontre aussi chez Porphyre, d'après le témoignage de saint Augustin dans son *De Civitate Dei*.[102]

Quant à Plotin, il n'exclut pas le fait qu'une âme humaine passe dans le corps d'un animal; tout dépend de la vie que les hommes mènent durant leur existence sur terre. Ceux qui conservent leur dignité humaine ne seront pas dégradés, mais redeviennent des hommes; ainsi celui qui pratique les vertus civiles, ne perdra pas la valeur qui lui est propre, il restera un homme. Par contre, ceux qui ont vécu selon les sens et qui se sont ravalés au rang des animaux, deviennent des bêtes; Plotin passe en revue différentes catégories d'hommes qui ne se laissent pas guider par la raison et indique chaque fois le genre de bêtes dans lesquelles ils se réincarnent: les amis de la musique, qui se transforment en oiseaux chanteurs; les rois qui n'ont pas suivi les directives de la raison se réincarnent dans des aigles, les astronomes sont changés en oiseaux qui volent très haut; il y a des hommes qui sont transformés en animaux lascifs et gloutons, d'autres en bêtes féroces, il y en a même dont la sensibilité est tellement émoussée, qu'ils deviennent des plantes.[103] Dans l'opinion de Plotin, ces réincarnations successives se présentent comme des rêves qui se suivent ou comme des nuits passées dans des lits différents.[104] Plotin se demande où va l'âme quand elle sort du corps; sa réponse est nette: la loi divine ne peut être évitée; l'âme coupable est transportée là où elle doit subir sa peine, elle aboutit toujours

vue de Jamblique, Némésius ajoute (*De natura hominis*, c. 2): *Et mihi videtur magis hic propter hoc bene coniecturasse non solum Platonis mentem sed et veritatem ipsam, ut est quidem ex multis aliis demonstrare, maxime autem ex his.* Cf. H. Dörrie, *Porphyrios "Symmikta Zetemata"* (Zetemata. Monographien zur klassischen Altertumswissenschaft, 20 [München, 1959]). L'auteur analyse longuement le chap. 2 du *De natura hominis* de Némésius en vue d'y découvrir des éléments empruntés à Porphyre (pp. 111–152); il arrive à la conclusion que ces emprunts ne sont que peu nombreux, et que l'exposé de Némésius se base principalement sur une source du moyen Platonisme.

[102] *De Civitate Dei*, 10. 30. Cf. J. Bidez, *Vie de Porphyre, le philosophe néo-platonicien, avec les fragments des traités* Περὶ ἀγαλμάτων *et De regressu animae* (Gand-Leipzig, 1913), Appendix II, p. 38: *Nam Platonem animas hominum post mortem revolvi usque ad corpora bestiarum scripsisse certissimum est. Hanc sententiam Porphyrii doctor tenuit et Plotinus; Porphyrio tamen iure displicuit. In hominum sane non sua quae dimiserant, sed alia nova corpora redire humanas animas arbitratus est.*

[103] *Enn.* 3. 4. 2.

[104] *Enn.* 3. 6. 6.

au lieu qui lui convient. Si elle se réincarne dans un autre corps, elle le suit là où ce corps prend naissance et subsiste. Le lieu vers lequel l'âme se dirige, dépend donc de ses dispositions intérieures.[105]

Quelle est maintenant la portée de cette objection? Il est certain que si l'âme est l'entéléchie première d'un corps, elle ne peut passer d'un organisme corporel à un autre. Toute la question est de savoir s'il faut admettre la transmigration des âmes: Aristote répond par un "non" catégorique. Étudiant les théories de ses prédécesseurs, le Stagirite leur fait un reproche capital: on parle de l'union de l'âme et du corps sans donner la cause de cette union et on ne définit pas non plus l'état du corps en question.[106] Pourtant cette union ne peut s'établir entre des éléments pris au hasard: si le corps et l'âme sont unis, c'est qu'il y a entre eux quelque chose de commun, comme entre ce qui agit et ce qui pâtit, entre ce qui meut et ce qui est mû. Si on veut expliquer le composé humain, il ne suffit donc pas de dire ce qu'est l'âme, encore faut-il déterminer quel genre de corps est capable de la recevoir. Aristote parle avec dédain des "mythes pythagoriciens" qui supposent que n'importe quelle âme peut pénétrer dans n'importe quel corps.[107] C'est que le corps doit être pour l'âme un instrument approprié: que pourrait faire un charpentier s'il n'avait à sa disposition que des flûtes?[108] Ce passage des âmes d'un corps à l'autre est, aux yeux d'Aristote, simplement absurde: pour ce qui est de l'âme des plantes et des animaux, elle s'insère entièrement dans le processus de la génération et de la corruption, ce qui veut dire qu'elle périt avec le corps. Quant à l'âme humaine, elle ne préexiste pas à son union avec le corps: peut-elle jamais se séparer de lui? Si on fait abstraction de l'intellect actif, il semble bien que d'après Aristote l'âme humaine ne puisse survivre à son union avec le corps,

---

[105] *Enn.* 4. 3. 24. Cf. W. R. Inge, *The Philosophy of Plotinus*, Vol. II (London, 1918), pp. 29 ssq. L'auteur estime que Plotin n'a pas pris très au sérieux la doctrine de la réincarnation: à ses yeux, le philosophe n'est pas consistant sur ce point. Toujours est-il que Plotin ne critique pas cette conception: mais il n'en parle pas souvent: on ne peut certainement pas dire qu'elle occupe une place importante dans sa doctrine psychologique.

[106] *De An.* I. 3. 407b12.

[107] *De An.* I. 3. 407b22: κατὰ τοὺς Πυθαγορικοὺς μύθους.

[108] *De An.* I. 3. 407b25: δεῖ γὰρ τὴν μὲν τέχνην χρῆσθαι τοῖς ὀργάνοις, τὴν δὲ ψυχὴν τῷ σώματι.

puisqu'elle n'a aucune activité qui est totalement indépendante de la matière.

Quelle conclusion peut-on tirer de cette analyse? Nous croyons pouvoir dire comme résultat général de notre étude que la critique de l'entéléchie, telle qu'elle est exposée dans le traité *De l'immortalité de l'âme* (*Enn.* 4. 7) est sommaire et superficielle: Plotin ne semble pas avoir compris la véritable doctrine psychologique d'Aristote et il ne fait pas d'effort spécial pour y pénétrer. A ses yeux, la théorie du Stagirite signifierait que l'âme ne serait qu'une qualité accidentelle de certaines réalités corporelles. On a l'impression que Plotin n'a jamais lu le *De anima* d'Aristote et qu'il s'appuie simplement sur quelques vagues renseignements doxographiques ou sur la doctrine matérialiste de certains représentants de l'École péripatéticienne.[109]

En outre, notre étude a révélé une fois de plus la différence profonde qu'il y a entre ces deux conceptions de l'homme, celle de Plotin et celle d'Aristote. Où se situe exactement cette différence? Toute la question se réduit à savoir où est la véritable patrie de l'homme, quel est le lieu où l'homme peut se développer pleinement, quelle est en somme la destinée à laquelle l'homme est appelé: les réponses de Plotin et d'Aristote suivent des directions nettement opposées; pour Plotin, la patrie de l'âme humaine, qui est l'homme véritable, se situe au delà de ce monde, elle est appelée à vivre avec les réalités intelligibles et son passage à travers la vie terrestre, en union avec le corps, est une "chute" dont elle doit se purifier le plus vite possible. Pour Aristote par contre, la destinée de l'homme se situe ici-bas, dans le monde, et au milieu des autres hommes: même l'idéal de la contemplation n'est pas à ses yeux un abandon du monde ni un mépris des

---

[109] Cf. F. P. Hager, "Die Aristotelesinterpretation des Alexander von Aphrodisias und die Aristoteleskritik Plotins bezüglich der Lehre vom Geist," *Archiv für Geschichte der Philosophie* 46 (1964), pp. 174–187: l'auteur montre que la critique de Plotin (*Enn.* 6. 7. 37–42) contre la conception aristotélicienne de la Divinité est dépendante de l'interprétation d'Alexandre d'Aphrodise concernant la noétique du Stagirite. On sait d'ailleurs par la *Vita Plotini* (14) de Porphyre que les écrits d'Alexandre, comme ceux d'autres péripatéticiens, tels Aspasius et Adraste, étaient utilisés par Plotin comme base de ses entretiens. Cf. P. Henry, "Une comparaison chez Aristote, Alexandre et Plotin," dans *Les Sources de Plotin*, Entretiens sur L'Antiquité Classique, Vol. V (Paris, 1960), pp. 429 ssq.

valeurs terrestres; elle est l'exercice parfait de ce qu'il y a de plus élevé dans l'homme, à savoir l'activité intellectuelle dans ce qu'elle a de plus noble et de plus profond, la réflexion métaphysique. S'il n'y a pas de préexistence et pas de survie après la mort, il s'ensuit que tout l'enjeu de la vie humaine se situe en ce monde et au cours de la vie terrestre.

Louvain

ON CONSOLATION[1] AND ON CONSOLATIONS

P. M. SCHUHL

I must first apologize because I shall speak about an unfashion-able subject. There is something obsolete (is there not?) in the fact that someone from the continent of Europe should speak about consolation – a subject which is quite out of fashion there. People on the continent speak about desolation, not consolation; about anxiety, sorrow, and – as the Germans say – "vom Wesen des Nichts." Europeans teach us that "das Nichts nichtet," that "the nothing" has a "nothingmaking" action. These are the beauties of existentialism; here is the depth of the philosophy of depth! By comparison, is it not merely trivial to speak about consolation?

People become addicted to anxiety by a kind of morbid enjoyment, by what the French call a "délectation morose"; but anxiety (like mourning) should not be a permanent state; that would not be health, but sickness, disease: a pathological state. Anxiety may last long, but it should have an end: it should not become an inveterate evil. As Seneca writes to Marcia (I. 7): *Tertius jam praeteriit annus, cum interim nihil ex primo illo impetu cecidit; renovat se et corroborat, cotidie luctus ... Putet turpe desinere.* But one must leave this state eventually.

This is what the Ancients taught – and not only the Ancients. Everywhere, until, let us say, the earthquake of Lisbon, the bringing of comfort and consolation was considered to be one of the first duties of philosophy. This can be illustrated not only by the works of Greek and Latin authors but by Job, the Psalms (almost all of the Bible, for that matter), and by the Buddha in his Discourse from Benares. Boethius' *Consolatio Philosophiae*

[1] A lecture given at Leicester University, May 11, 1968.

was one of the most translated books in the XIth to the XIVth
century. King Alfred tried his hand at a translation, as did
Arnaud Greban, and others.[2] Or listen to Malherbe's *Ode to his
friend Du Périer, on the death of his daughter Rose*, a poem which
all French school boys and girls know by heart:

> Ta douleur, Du Périer, sera donc éternelle ...
> Et rose elle a vécu ce que vivent les roses,
> L'espace d'un matin.

Or read La Boetie's (Montaigne's friend) *Consolation et misères du
temps*. Man may be defined as an animal who needs consolation.
The child, after bumping against something, suffers, howls, and
screams ... and runs to his mother. I have heard a little boy
saying among his sobs – as if there were a right to compensation
against the strokes of fate: "Please, mother, give me a pear – I
want to be consoled," and man remains always a child.

When you take away from a dog or a cat his little ones, he
does not complain very long. Only the storks complain, they
say (and that would be an interesting study in animal psychology).
For some ancient stoics, this was an argument – but not a good
one, because man is not an animal quite like the others.

Scholars once believed that the word *consolatio* was related to
the word *solus*, "alone"; but now they think that the true
relation is with ὅλος, *solidus*, that is, the integrity of an organism
which shall not be dislocated, nor taken to pieces, but remain
as a strong unity; *consolare* is *consolidare*, "to consolidate,"
"to strengthen." To console is to comfort; the opposite is
to desolate, to leave disconsolate. It is not forgetful insensibility.

In spite of all the emphasis placed on it in previous centuries,
the literary "genre" of the *consolatio* almost disappeared during
the nineteenth century, even though Carducci, Longfellow and
Musset used the theme in some excellent poems. The consolations
of the classical era seemed obsolete. Scipio's astral immortality
could only be accepted as a bizarre, somewhat occult cosmolo-
gical ideal.

As a substitute the Baconian, Faustian, Saint-Simonian Ideal

[2] Cf. Pierre Courcelle, *La consolation de Philosophie dans la tradition
littéraire, Antécédents et postérité de Boece* (Paris, 1967).

flourished – preached in England by d'Eichtal, and heard by Carlisle (in "Jocelyn de Bracelande") and others. Heine in Germany sang of "ein neues Lied, ein besseres Lied."

More recently, scientists have discovered certain medical and psychological techniques and devices which had seemed unrealizable in the past. The results, however, have been disappointing. Nervous depression and anxiety remain prevalent in spite of the tranquilizers and pyschoanaleptic drugs used to attempt to cure them.

"Build yourself a completely watertight grave, where rain cannot fall in, so that you will be safe and quiet after your death"; so ran an advertisement in a recent American magazine. *Animamque sepulcro/condimus* Virgil wrote in *Aeneid* 3. 67–68.

And so it happens that some people feel at present a need to look back to the Ancients; and it is surely true that much of what they said may still be useful to us, for material progress does not necessarily bring with it moral progress. So we must resume their work. I shall list only a few examples here.

Our chemical and pharmaceutical forms of consolation were not unknown to the Ancients. Homer provides the best illustration in *Odyssey* 1. 100 ff.;[3] and Antiphon wrote of τέχνην ἀλυπίας, a technique of insensibility, of "not-grieving," as it were.[4] "Gorgias discovered that drugs (φάρμακα) are to the body what words (λόγοι) are to the soul": "the best drug against grieving is the word."[5] Thus the dominant trend became quite the opposite of the deep pessimism which was revealed to King Midas by Silene; and the Okeanides taught Prometheus the same wise truth that Achilles taught to old King Priam: man must bear what comes from fate. Hence the Stoic *Amor fati*. As Plato said in the *Republic* (10. 603e): "a gentleman (ἐπιεικὴς ἀνήρ) is moderate in his grief." That is the kind of consolation provided by the stelai from the graves of the Kerameikos.

Death, said Socrates (Pl. *Apol.* 40c–41) "is either a sleep, linked with insensibility – or an opportunity to question wise

[3] See P. M. Schuhl, "Les débuts de la psycholopharmacologie dans l'Antiquité grecque," *Annales Moreau de Tours* 1 (1962), p. 5.

[4] Ps. Plut. *Vitae decem oratorum* 1883c; Diels, *Vorsokr.*[9] 80 A 6. See K. Ch. Grollios, *Technē alypias* (Thessalonika, 1956).

[5] Κράτιστον δὴ πρὸς ἀλυπίαν φάρμακοι ὁ λόγος (Plut. *Consolatio ad Apoll.*).

men from olden times." The first alternative became the Epicurean solution.

But the first true παρηγορικός – or παραμυθητικὸς λόγος – was probably written by the Platonist philosopher Crantor of Soloi, a pupil of Xenocrates and Polemon, and friend of Arcesilaus. It was called περὶ πένθους (On Mourning) and was dedicated to Hippocles.[6]

Crantor died young (ca. 270) and on his tomb appeared an epigraph which asserted that he was resting in serenity (ἐν εὐθυμίη).[7]

After the death of his beloved daughter Tullia, Cicero undertook to console himself.[8]

Later, "Consolations" were written by Seneca,[9] by Plutarch, and by Boethius – all of whom used many of the arguments already discussed. Such arguments should be carefully studied, for they can still bring us relief in times of anxiety or grief.

Université de Paris

---

[6] Cf. Cicero, *Acad.* 2. 44. 135: *Legimus omnes Crantoris, veteris Academici de luctu. Est enim non magnus, verum aureolus et, ut Tuberoni Panaetius praecipit, ad verbum ediscendus libellus.* See also Ps. Plato's *Axiochos.*

[7] Cf. P. Boyancé, *"Funus acerbum,"* *Rev. Ét. Anc.* 54 (1952), pp. 275–279; ——, "L'apothéose de Tullia," *ibid.,* 46 (1944), pp. 179–184.

[8] Cf. Cic. *Att.* 12. 14. 3: *etiam feci quod profecto ante me nemo, ut ipse me per litteras consolarer.*

[9] *Ep.* 7. 2. 8: *Animi remedia inventa sunt ab antiquis, quomodo autem admoveantur aut quando, nostri operis est quaerere.* For further work on consolation, see F. Kayser, *De Crantore Academico* (Heidelberg, 1841); C. Buresch, *Consolationum a Graecis Romanisque scriptarum historica critica,* Leipziger Studien zur classischen Philologie 9. 1 (Leipzig, 1886); A. Gercke, *De consolationibus* (Bonn, 1883); C. Martha, *Études morales sur l'antiquité*[4] (Paris, 1905); K. Ch. Grollios, *op. cit.*

ABAMON, PSEUDONYME DE JAMBLIQUE

H. D. SAFFREY

Pour honorer la mémoire du professeur Philip Merlan, qui a si bien montré[1] l'importance du traité trop négligé de Jamblique, *De communi mathematica scientia*, on nous permettre de proposer ici quelques réflexions, encore mêlées d'hypothèses, sur une énigme de l'histoire de la philosophie: l'auteur du traité *De mysteriis*.

Presque tous les savants s'accordent aujourd'hui pour attribuer à Jamblique cet ouvrage. Comme on le sait, la formule *De mysteriis* n'est qu'un abrégé du titre complet, *De mysteriis Aegyptiorum Chaldaeorum Assyriorum*, donné par Marsile Ficin à sa paraphrase latine de ce livre grec, apparemment anonyme.[2] Pourtant l'intitulé véritable se trouve dans la première phrase du texte, attestée, sauf erreur, par tous les manuscrits: Ἀβάμωνος διδασκάλου πρὸς τὴν Πορφυρίου πρὸς Ἀνεβὼ ἐπιστολὴν ἀπόκρισις καὶ τῶν ἐν αὐτῇ ἀπορημάτων λύσεις, "réponse d'Abamon, son professeur, à la lettre adressée par Porphyre à Anébon et solutions des questions qu'elle soulève." Le *De mysteriis* se présente donc comme une lettre écrite par un certain Abamon à Porphyre. Un traité philosophique sous forme de lettre n'a rien pour nous surprendre depuis les lettres philosophiques d'Épicure et de Sénèque.[3] Porphyre et Jamblique sont eux-mêmes coutu-

---

[1] Dans *From Platonism to Neoplatonism*[2] (The Hague, 1960).

[2] Cette traduction paraphrasée a été publiée pour la première fois à Venise, chez Alde, au mois de septembre 1497. Dans l'épître-dédicace au cardinal Jean de Médicis, le futur Léon X, du 9 mars 1489, Ficin décrivait l'ouvrage par ces mots: *quid Aegyptii et Assyrii sacerdotes de religione rebusque divinis senserint.*

[3] Les Allemands appellent ce genre littéraire: *Lehrbrief*; cf. J. Sykutris, dans *RE*, Suppl. Bd. V, col. 202, 47–204, 62, s.v. "Epistolographie," et J. Schneider, dans *RACh*, Bd. II, col. 571, s.v. "Brief."

miers du fait.[4] Dans le cas présent, c'est d'autant plus naturel
que cette lettre d'Abamon est une réponse à une autre de Porphyre. Mais comme personne n'a jamais entendu parler d'un
contemporain de Porphyre portant ce nom, comme aussi, je
crois bien, aucune autre attestation de ce nom d'Abamon n'est
connue,[5] on a été conduit très tôt à suspecter ce nom comme
devant être un pseudonyme. Cette manière de faire est assez
fréquente dans l'antiquité[6] et une importante scholie, qui figure
dans les deux manuscrits principaux du *De mysteriis* et remonte
donc à l'archétype perdu, nous livre la clef du mystère. Le Prof.
M. Sicherl[7] a établi que cette scholie avait Psellus pour auteur et
que l'opinion de Proclus, qu'elle rapporte, a toutes les garanties
d'authenticité: ἰστέον ὅτι ὁ φιλόσοφος Πρόκλος, ὑπομνηματίζων τὰς
τοῦ μεγάλου Πλωτίνου Ἐννεάδας, λέγει ὅτι ὁ ἀντιγράφων πρὸς τὴν
προκειμένην τοῦ Πορφυρίου ἐπιστολὴν ὁ θεσπέσιός ἐστιν Ἰάμβλιχος,
καὶ διὰ τὸ τῆς ὑποθέσεως οἰκεῖον καὶ ἀκόλουθον ὑποκρίνεται
πρόσωπον αἰγυπτίου τινὸς Ἀβάμωνος (Ἀβάμονος codd.),

il faut savoir que le professeur de philosophie Proclus, commentant les
Ennéades du grand Plotin, dit que celui qui répond à la lettre citée ci-
dessus de Porphyre, est le divin Jamblique, et que, parce que cela convient
au sujet et lui est cohérent, il joue le personnage d'un certain égyptien
Abamon.

Autrement dit, Proclus savait ou avait conjecturé que l'auteur
de la réponse à Porphyre était Jamblique sous le pseudonyme

[4] Pour Porphyre, la *Lettre à Marcella*; pour Jamblique, nombreux
extraits dans l'*Anthologie* de Stobée, voir la table de l'ed. Hense, s.v.
"Iamblichus," p. 1185.
[5] Dans l'article "Abammon" dans *RE*, Suppl. Bd. IV, col. 1, 7 ss., par
T. Hopfner, aucun cas parallèle n'est présenté; rien non plus dans l'article
de P. Derchain, "Pseudo-Jamblique ou Abammôn?," dans *Chronique
d'Egypte* 38 (1963), pp. 220–226; et dans une note de son article, "Les noms
théophores en -ammon," *ibid.*, p. 137, n. 1, F. Dunand cite le nom
d'Abammôn pour expliquer qu'elle ne le retiendra pas, et ne renvoie qu'à
l'auteur du *De mysteriis*. Malgré mes recherches, je n'ai pu trouver aucun
autre emploi de ce nom.
[6] Cf. J. A. Sint, *Pseudonymität im Altertum*, Commentationes Aeni-
pontanae XV (Innsbruck, 1960). Le cas du *De mysteriis* n'est pas étudié
dans cet ouvrage.
[7] "Michael Psellos und Iamblichos *De mysteriis*," dans *Byz. Zeitschr.* 53
(1960), pp. 8–19. Sur cette scholie, voir aussi M. Sicherl, *Die Handschriften, Ausgaben und Übersetzungen von Iamblichos De mysteriis*,
Texte und Untersuchungen, Vol. 62 (Berlin, 1957), pp. 20–21, 166.

d'Abamon. Pour le dire en passant, cette scholie nous apprend encore que, au temps de Psellus, la lettre de Porphyre à Anébon figurait en tête de la réponse de Jamblique à Porphyre.

Proclus savait depuis sa jeunesse que l'auteur du *De mysteriis* était Jamblique. Dans son *Commentaire sur le Timée*, qu'il avait achevé à l'âge de vingt-sept ans,[8] donc en 439,[9] un peu plus d'un siècle après la composition du *De mysteriis*, il cite à travers Jamblique l'opinion d'Hermès Trismégiste sur l'origine de la matière. Le *De mysteriis* avait posé la question: "Les Égyptiens connaissent-ils une matière première inengendrée ou une matière première engendrée?" (8. 1, p. 260, 9). A cette question, il est répondu un peu plus loin (p. 265, 6–10):[10]

Quant à la matière, Dieu l'a tirée de la substantialité, de la matérialité en ayant été retranchée par en dessous (παρήγαγεν ὁ θεὸς ἀπὸ τῆς οὐσιότητος ὑποσχισθείσης ὑλότητος). Cette matière donc, qui est vivifiante, le Démiurge l'a prise en mains, il en a façonné les sphères simples et incorruptibles, et avec le résidu extrême qui en restait, il a fabriqué les corps engendrés et corruptibles.

Dans ce texte, nous trouvons l'opinion des Égyptiens sur l'origine de la matière et une application de cette doctrine au démiurge du *Timée*. Écoutons maintenant Proclus dans l'*In Ti.* 1, p. 386, 10–13:[11] "Le divin Jamblique a rapporté que, selon Hermès, la matérialité est dérivée de la substantialité (ἐκ τῆς οὐσιότητος τὴν ὑλότητα παράγεσθαι); et il y a même apparence que Platon tienne d'Hermès cette sorte d'opinion sur la matière." On le voit, Proclus cite en la rapportant à Hermès l'opinion des Égyptiens du *De mysteriis*, et il tire de la suite du texte, relative à l'action du démiurge sur cette matière, la réflexion que Platon devait donc tenir la même opinion qu'Hermès sur ce sujet. Autrement dit, ce que Proclus lisait dans le *De mysteriis*, il le tenait pour l'oeuvre de Jamblique.

---

[8] Cf. Marinus, *V. Procli* 13.

[9] Pour cette date, cf. H. D. Saffrey et L. G. Westerink, *Proclus, Théologie platonicienne*, I (Paris, 1968), pp. XVI–XVII.

[10] Traduction de A. J. Festugière, dans *Révélation d'Hermès Trismégiste*, IV (Paris, 1954), p. 39.

[11] Trad. par A. J. Festugière, *Proclus, Commentaire sur le Timée*, II (Paris, 1967), p. 250 (légèrement modifiée). Le rapprochement de ces deux textes a été fait pour la première fois par J. Bidez, "Un extrait du commentaire de Proclus sur les 'Ennéades' de Plotin," dans *Mélanges Desrousseaux* (Paris, 1937), p. 12.

Si donc l'on admet l'interprétation de Proclus et si l'on considère Abamon comme le pseudonyme de Jamblique, l'historien de la philosophie en vient nécessairement à se poser deux questions: pourquoi Jamblique a-t-il cru bon de répondre à Porphyre sous un pseudonyme et que signifie ce pseudonyme d'Abamon?

Sans être tout à fait contemporains, Porphyre et Jamblique n'avaient au plus qu'une différence d'âge de quinze années, puisque Porphyre naquit en 234[12] et Jamblique entre 245 et 250.[13] D'autre part, ils ne firent connaissance qu'à un moment de leurs vies où cette différence ne représentait plus grand chose, dans la décade 275–285. Nous savons que Porphyre était à Lilybée en Sicile, lorsque Plotin mourut en 270 dans la villa de Zéthos en Campanie.[14] Il n'est pas revenu aussitôt à Rome puisqu'il était en Sicile lorsqu'il composa l'*Isagogè* et le traité *Contre les Chrétiens*.[15] Il eut Jamblique pour élève et ce ne peut avoir été qu'après son retour à Rome. Jamblique devait avoir alors plus de trente ans, un âge relativement élevé pour se mettre à nouvelle école. Cette démarche suppose déjà chez Jamblique une profonde estime pour le successeur du grand Plotin. C'est sans doute à cet enseignement de Porphyre à Rome, que Jamblique fait allusion dans son *De anima*,[16] lorsqu'il écrit: "... d'après ce que j'ai entendu dire (ἀκήκοα) à certains Platoniciens, par exemple Porphyre ...." Les sentiments de Porphyre pour son disciple devaient répondre à ceux de ce dernier puisque Porphyre avait dédié à Jamblique l'un de ces ouvrages, le Περὶ τοῦ Γνῶθι σαυτόν,[17] et que dans la *Vita Plotini*, écrite vers 300, il mentionne le mariage du fils de Jamblique, Ariston, avec Amphiclée qui avait été l'auditrice de Plotin[18] et que Jamblique

[12] Pour cette date, cf. R. Beutler, dans *RE*, Bd. XXII. 1, col. 276, 24, s.v. "Porphyrios 21."

[13] Cf. A. Cameron, "The Date of Iamblichus' Birth," *Hermes* 96 (1968), pp. 374–376.

[14] Cf. Porphyre, *Plot.* 2.

[15] Cf. J. Bidez, *Vie de Porphyre* (Gand-Leipzig, 1913), pp. 58 et 67.

[16] *Apud* Stobée 1. 49. 37, p. 375, 24 Wachsmuth et cf. A. J. Festugière, *Révélation d'Hermès Trismégiste*, III (Paris, 1953), p. 211.

[17] Cf. Stobée 3. 21. 26, p. 579, 6 Hense.

[18] Le Prof. Merlan a appelé l'attention sur ce point dans *Monopsychism, Mysticism, Metaconsciousness* (The Hague, 1963), p. 67, n. 4: il s'agit de Porph. *Plot.* 9, 4.

et son fils durent connaître par l'intermédiaire de Porphyre. Que conclure de l'ensemble de ces renseignements sinon qu'il y eut tout un temps des relations suivies et très amicales de maître à disciple entre Porphyre et Jamblique.

A un moment que nous ignorons, Jamblique quitta Rome et l'école de Porphyre pour rentrer chez lui à Apamée de Syrie où il se mit lui-même à enseigner. Le premier des disciples de Plotin à Rome, Amélius, s'était autrefois retiré à Apamée[19] que Numénius avait déjà rendu célèbre comme centre d'études philosophiques,[20] et peut-être la mort d'Amélius laissait-elle à Jamblique une place à prendre pour assurer la tradition néo-platonicienne. Libanius appelle Apamée "la cité aimée de Jamblique"[21] et il parle "du chœur des philosophes d'Apamée, dont le coryphée était semblable aux dieux,"[22] manière hyperbolique de désigner Jamblique. Vers la fin de sa vie, Jamblique trans-porta son école à Daphné, le célèbre faubourg d'Antioche.[23] Tant à Apamée qu'à Daphné, nous savons que Jamblique eut une grande quantité de disciples, venant naturellement de tous les horizons.[24] Rien d'étonnant si parmi eux se trouvaient des Égyptiens. Nous avons même la certitude qu'à un moment il y eut dans le cercle des familiers de Jamblique un Égyptien piqué de théurgie, mais un peu novice, et que le maître se vit dans l'obli-gation de reprendre au cours d'une évocation. L'histoire est

[19] Cf. Porphyre, *Plot.* 2, 32–33 et 3, 40–41.

[20] Cf. H. C. Puech, "Numénius d'Apamée et les théologies orientales au second siècle," dans *Mélanges Bidez*, II (Bruxelles, 1934), pp. 749–754. On a retrouvé à Apamée une mosaïque représentant Socrate au milieu de six personnages. Elle décorait la maison d'un platonicien, et l'on date cet ouvrage entre 350 et 400; cf. G. M. A. Hanfmann, "Socrates and Christ," *Harv. Stud.* 60 (1951), pp. 205–233; C. Picard, "La mosaïque de Socrate à Apamée-sur-l'Oronte," dans *Rev. Arch.* 61 (1953), pp. 100–102; et L. Jalabert et R. Mouterde, *Inscriptions grecques et latines de la Syrie*, IV (Paris, 1955), n. 1341.

[21] Libanius, *Ep.* 1389, t. XI, p. 431, 13 Förster.

[22] Libanius, *Or.* 52. 21, t. IV, p. 35, 12 ss. Förster.

[23] Cf. Malalas, *Chronographia* XII, p. 312, 11–12 éd. de Bonn et A. Schenk von Stauffenberg, *Die römische Kaisergeschichte bei Malalas* (Stuttgart, 1931), p. 407.

[24] Cf. Eunape, *VS* (Iamblichus), p. 458 Boissonade = p. 11, 10 ss. Giangrande, et voir J. Bidez, "Le philosophe Jamblique et son école," *Rev. Ét. Grec.* 32 (1919), pp. 33–35, où les disciples du philosophe sont énumérés.

contée par Eunape:[25] "Alors qu'un certain Égyptien avait
évoqué Apollon, qu'il était apparu et que tous les assistants
étaient terrifiés de cette vision, Jamblique leur déclara: 'Cessez,
mes amis, de vous émerveiller. C'est là le spectre d'un gladiateur.'
Si grande est la différence entre voir par l'esprit et voir par les
yeux trompeurs du corps!" Sans vouloir identifier purement et
simplement cet Égyptien au correspondant de Porphyre, ce
récit toutefois permet de considérer comme une chose tout à
fait vraisemblable que Jamblique ait eu dans son école un
égyptien du nom d'Anébon, auquel Porphyre a écrit sa lettre
sur la théurgie. En tout cas, dans sa réponse,[26] l'auteur du
De mysteriis déclare explicitement qu'il va répondre à Porphyre
au lieu et place de son disciple Anébon: ... ἐγώ τε εἰκότως τὴν πρὸς
᾽Ανεβὼ τὸν ἐμὸν μαθητὴν πεμφθεῖσαν ἐπιστολὴν ἐμαυτῷ γεγράφθαι
νομίσας ἀποκρινοῦμαί σοι αὐτὰ τἀληθῆ ὑπὲρ ὧν πυνθάνῃ," ... et de
mon côté, considérant naturellement que la lettre envoyée à
Anébon, mon disciple, a été écrite à moi-même, je te répondrai,
sur les questions qu'elle soulève, ce qui est la vérité même."
Ensuite, après avoir comparé Porphyre à Pythagore, Platon,
Démocrite et Eudoxe, qui eux aussi, en leur temps, ont reçu
leur sagesse des Égyptiens, il souligne de nouveau la fiction par
laquelle il prend la place d'Anébon, et même propose à Porphyre
de dépasser l'occasion de cette réponse pour ne plus écouter à
travers lui que n'importe quel "prophète" égyptien anonyme
(ἢ τινα ἄλλον προφήτην Αἰγυπτίων), plus encore, il lui demande
d'oublier celui qui écrit et s'il est meilleur ou pire (que lui,
Porphyre), pour ne plus considérer que la vérité du discours
lui-même. Voilà ce que l'on appelle prendre des précautions
oratoires et manifester la plus extrême délicatesse vis à vis d'un
correspondant infiniment respectable.

Pour résumer toutes ces observations, il semble que l'on puisse
imaginer Anébon comme l'un de ces jeunes étudiants, fils de
riches familles, qui font le tour des professeurs fameux. Il passe
d'abord à Rome chez Porphyre qu'il considère sans aucun doute
à cette époque comme le patriarche des professeurs de philosophie.
Après un séjour plus ou moins long, peut-être à l'instigation de

[25] Eunape, *VS* (Sosipatra), p. 473 Boissonade = p. 40, 8–17 Giangrande.
[26] Cf. *Myst.* I. I, p. 2, 7–14. Je cite d'après l'édition des Places (Paris,
1966).

Porphyre lui-même, il fait voile vers Antioche pour goûter à l'enseignement de Jamblique, l'étoile montante dans le ciel de la philosophie. Les exemples de ces périples sont innombrables dans l'antiquité. Jamblique le séduit ou l'inquiète, et tout naturellement il se retourne vers son premier maître. Il envoie à Rome un compte rendu enthousiaste ou critique, qui sait?, dans lequel il rapporte ce qu'il voit et entend à l'école du maître ἔνθεος. Porphyre prend ombrage de l'influence exercée sur son disciple, ou bien il veut le renforcer dans sa résistance, et c'est la *Lettre à Anébon*. Si, comme les hypothèses précédentes conduisent à le penser, c'est au moment où Porphyre élaborait l'édition des *Ennéades* de Plotin, qu'il composa cette *Lettre à Anébon*, on ne s'étonne plus de la sentir toute remplie du rationalisme plotinien.[27] En soulignant pour Anébon les contradictions internes de la théurgie, il le met vigoureusement en garde contre ces fausses pratiques qui égarent l'esprit en le détournant de la philosophie proprement dite, seule voie vers la vraie connaissance de dieu, et qui asservissent le libre arbitre en le soumettant à l'empire de l'*Heimarnéné*.[28] Retenons ces formules rapportées par Eusèbe de Césarée:[29] "Je suis profondément troublé en pensant que les dieux que nous invoquons comme des supérieurs, reçoivent des injonctions comme des inférieurs"; et comment un simple mortel peut-il se vanter de "terroriser le roi Hélios lui-même, ou Séléné ou quelque autre dieu du ciel"! On voit bien que c'est aux rites de la théurgie et aux doctrines pseudo-philosophiques qui les soutiennent que s'en prend Porphyre. "Peut-on amener les dieux à dire la vérité par des mensonges?" (ψευδόμενον ἵν' ἐκεῖνοι ἀληθεύσωσι.[30] C'est donc cette fausseté que Porphyre, dans sa *Lettre* dénonce à Anébon. Et naturellement par dessus le disciple, la *Lettre* s'adresse aussi au maître, et peut-être à l'école tout entière. Jamblique n'est pas dupe du procédé. C'est pourquoi il décide de répondre lui-même, mais pour ne pas heurter de face le

---

[27] Voir le bel éloge du rationalisme plotinien dans E. R. Dodds, "Tradition and Personal Achievement in the Philosophy of Plotinus," dans *JRS* 50 (1960), pp. 1–7.

[28] Cf. l'analyse de la *Lettre à Anébon* par J. Bidez, *Vie de Porphyre*, pp. 80–87. Je me sépare de Bidez quant à la date de cet écrit qu'il veut placer avant le *De regressu*.

[29] Eusèbe, *Praep. Evang.* 5. 10, p. 242, 15 s. et 243, 2s. Mras.

[30] *Ibid.*, p. 243, 4.

plus vénérable et le plus grand des Platoniciens de son temps, qui fut son professeur et qui reste son ami, il usera d'un subterfuge pour pouvoir rendre publique cette réponse qui prend l'allure d'un manifeste, celui du néoplatonisme syrien face au néoplatonisme romain. C'est pourquoi Jamblique écrit à Porphyre sous le pseudonyme d'Abamon, en inventant une fiction de telle nature que Porphyre lui-même ne pouvait s'y tromper.

Je voudrais en effet suggérer que le pseudonyme d'Abamon a une signification et que cette signification devait être claire pour Porphyre. Le caractère égyptien de ce nom vient du fait qu'il contient celui de la divinité de la ville de Thèbes, transcrit en grec sous les formes *Ammôn*, *Amoun* ou *Amôn*. Ce très ancien dieu local fut, par un procédé assez commun, sous la douzième dynastie égyptienne, identifié avec *Ra*, le dieu soleil, et *Amôn-Ra* devint ainsi le dieu suprême du panthéon égyptien. Il fut ensuite assimilé par les Grecs à Zeus, et bientôt Zeus-Ammôn commença à proférer des oracles dans le désert de Lybie.[31] Ces oracles devaient devenir aussi célèbres que ceux d'Olympie et de Dodone. Mais toujours *Amoun* ou *Amôn* restait le dieu national égyptien. De cette permanence, Jamblique lui-même est un bon témoin, qui écrit dans le *Myst.*:[32] ὁ γὰρ δημιουργικὸς νοῦς καὶ τῆς ἀληθείας προστάτης καὶ σοφίας ... Ἀμοῦν κατὰ τὴν τῶν Αἰγυπτίων γλῶσσαν λέγεται. Au contraire, dans le même temps, Origène[33] défendait aux Chrétiens d'appeler "dieu" le Zeus des Égyptiens: κἂν Αἰγύπτιοι δὲ τὸν Ἀμοῦν ἡμῖν προτείνωσιν κόλασιν ἀπειλοῦντες, τεθνηξόμεθα μᾶλλον ἢ τὸν Ἀμοῦν ἀναγορεύσομεν θεόν. La raison de cette résolution héroïque: plutôt le martyre que d'acclamer publiquement *Amoun* comme dieu, est justement l'opinion universellement répandue, comme le dit Plutarque,[34] qui confond Amoun et Zeus: τῶν πολλῶν νομιζόντων ἴδιον παρ' Αἰγυπτίοις ὄνομα τοῦ Διὸς εἶναι τὸν Ἀμοῦν ὃ παράγοντες ἡμεῖς Ἄμμωνα λέγομεν. Ainsi donc, à l'époque de Porphyre et de Jamblique, *Amoun* ou *Amôn* est bien connu pour être le Zeus des Égyptiens, c'est-à-dire

---

[31] Cf. H. W. Parke, *The Oracles of Zeus; Dodona, Olympia, Ammon* (Oxford, 1967), pp. 194 ss.
[32] *Myst.* 8. 3, p. 263, 7–12.
[33] Origène, *c. Cels.* 5. 46, p. 50, 20–51, 1 Koetschau.
[34] Plutarque, *De Is. et Os.* 9 (*Mor.* 354 C).

le dieu par excellence. Abamôn est donc un nom théophore qui contient *Amôn*, le nom de dieu.

Cela étant, nous devons donc considérer le nom Abamôn comme composé de *Ab* et de *Amôn*, et il nous reste à expliquer *Ab*. Th. Hopfner[35] a proposé d'y reconnaître *'b-'mn*, qui voudrait dire "Coeur d'Amôn." N'étant pas égyptologue, je ne peux me prononcer sur cette étymologie, mais elle ne semble pas rallier tous les savants, puisque Madame Dunand[36] laisse planer un doute dans son article déjà cité. Je voudrais pour ma part chercher dans une toute autre direction. On peut en effet reconnaître dans *ab* l'état construit du mot *aba*, qui veut dire "père" en hébreu, en chaldéen et en syriaque. Ces langues étaient celles que l'on parlait dans les patries de Porphyre, qui était de Tyr en Phénicie, et de Jamblique qui était de Syrie. La construction d'un mot hébraïque ou syriaque avec le nom du dieu égyptien ne semble pas offrir d'impossibilité, surtout pour un nom théophore. Dans ce cas, Abamon signifie "Père d'Amôn," c'est-à-dire "Père de dieu," et le mot Abamôn n'est que la transcription en langage populaire du grec πατὴρ θεοῦ ou θεόπατωρ. Or, nous allons voir que cette expression désigne le théurge.

On sait que le premier néoplatonicien qui ait élaboré une théorie systématique des vertus est Porphyre.[37] Il les classe en quatre degrés: les vertus politiques, cathartiques, théorétiques et paradigmatiques; de plus il désigne le possesseur des vertus théorétiques du nom de "dieu," et celui qui possède les vertus paradigmatiques du nom de "père des dieux." Mais traduisons tout entier ce texte important:[38]

Les vertus ont des buts différents selon leur espèce. Ainsi les vertus politiques ont pour but d'imposer une mesure aux passions relativement

[35] T. Hopfner, dans *RE*, Suppl. Bd. IV, col. 3, 1, s.v. "Abammon."
[36] F. Dunand, "Les noms théophores en -ammon," dans *Chronique d'Egypte* 38 (1963), p. 137, n. 1, qui écrit: Abammon est un cas intéressant, si son étymologie est bien *ib–imn*, "coeur d'Ammon." Il semble donc que pour cet auteur, cette étymologie ne soit pas sûre.
[37] Sur cette théorie, voir en dernier lieu, H. Lewy, *Chaldean Oracles and Theurgy*, Recherches d'Archéologie, de Philologie et d'Histoire, XIII (Le Caire, 1956), pp. 465–466, avec la bibliographie du sujet, n. 27.
[38] Porphyre, *Sent.* 32, 7, p. 22, 3 ss. Mommert.

aux actes accomplis dans le domaine de la nature, les vertus cathartiques ont pour but de nous séparer radicalement des passions, qui jusqu'alors n'avaient reçu qu'une mesure; quant aux vertus théorétiques, elles ont pour but de nous faire agir intellectuellement sans que nous arrivions à cette penseé seulement de nous séparer de nos passions; quant aux vertus paradigmatiques, elles ont pour but celui d'âmes qui n'agissent plus seulement intellectuellement, mais qui en sont venues à se confondre avec la substance de l'intellect. C'est pourquoi, celui qui agit selon les vertus pratiques (= politiques) a été appelé "homme vertueux," celui qui agit selon les vertus cathartiques, "homme merveilleux" ou même "bon démon," celui qui agit selon les seules vertus intellectuelles, "dieu," celui qui agit selon les vertus paradigmatiques, "père des dieux" (ὁ δὲ κατὰ τὰς παραδειγματικὰς θεῶν πατήρ).

W. Theiler[39] a justement fait remarquer que cette appellation de "vertus paradigmatiques" n'est pas très heureuse. En effet, nous sommes avec ce texte de Porphyre devant un développement de la doctrine plotinienne des vertus, tel qu'il est exposé en *Enn.* 1. 2 (19). Pour Plotin, l'âme seule possède des vertus que l'on peut classer en deux degrés: vertus politiques et vertus cathartiques. Le premier développement introduit par Porphyre consiste à subdiviser le degré des vertus cathartiques en cathartiques proprement dites (qui purifient l'âme) et théorétiques (vertus de l'âme purifiée et désormais contemplative). Quand on a atteint ce sommet, celui des vertus cathartiques pour Plotin, celui des vertus théorétiques pour Porphyre, on est, "dieu": εἰ δὲ μηδέν (scil. ἀπροαίρετον), θεὸς μόνον· θεὸς δὲ τῶν ἑπομένων τῷ Πρώτῳ. (Plotin 1. 2. 6. 6–7). En effet, depuis Platon, *Tht.* 176b1, "être assimilé à dieu" est le but visé par la vertu: θεῷ ὁμοιωθῆναι (Plotin, *ibid.*, 1. 3–4). En bon platonicien, Plotin convenait que ces vertus ont des modèles en dieu, mais ils ne sauraient en aucun cas être des vertus: ἐκεῖ δὲ οἷον ἀρχέτυπον ὂν οὐκ ἀρετή (Plotin, *ibid.*, 2. 3–4). Mais ici Porphyre de nouveau prolonge en la gauchissant la doctrine de Plotin: l'âme "qui est parvenue à se confondre avec la substance de l'intellect" introduit en lui aussi des vertus que naturellement on appellera "paradigmatiques." En raisonnant ainsi, Porphyre faisait le premier pas vers cette théorie d'une continuité substantielle entre les divers degrés de l'être, que l'on retrouvera comme une pierre angulaire de la métaphysique de Proclus et du Pseudo-Denys.[40] Pour Plotin,

[39] Dans *Gnomon* 5 (1929), p. 312.
[40] Cf. H. D. Saffrey et L. G. Westerink, *Proclus, Théologie platonicienne*, I (Paris, 1968), p. 67, 2–5 et la note *ad loc.*

l'âme est dans l'intellect comme dans sa cause, pour Porphyre l'âme peut devenir substantiellement intellect. Les raisons de ce raisonnement chez Porphyre ne nous apparaissent pas clairement. Quoi qu'il en soit, on comprendra aisément que si, avec Plotin et Porphyre, on appelle "dieu" celui qui est parvenu au sommet des vertus politiques, cathartiques et théorétiques, il reste évidemment à nommer "père des dieux" celui qui, rempli des vertus paradigmatiques, possède en lui les modèles selon lesquels on fait des dieux.

Sur cette lancée, Jamblique devait ajouter encore un degré à cette classification, et l'on comprend bien pourquoi. Si non seulement l'âme peut devenir substantiellement l'intellect, mais si l'intellect lui-même peut aussi devenir l'Un, il faut au dessus des "vertus paradigmatiques" d'autres vertus que Jamblique, si nous en croyons Damascius,[41] appelait "hiératiques." ὅτι παραδειγματικαὶ ἀρεταὶ αἱ μηκέτι θεωρούσης τὸν νοῦν τῆς ψυχῆς... ἀλλ', ἤδη στάσης ἐν τῷ νοῦν εἶναι κατὰ μέθεξιν... ταύτας δὲ προστίθησιν ὁ Ἰάμβλιχος ἐν τοῖς Περὶ ἀρετῶν, ὅτι εἰσὶ καὶ αἱ ἱερατικαὶ ἀρεταί, κατὰ τὸ θεοειδὲς ὑφιστάμεναι τῆς ψυχῆς, ἀντιπαρήκουσαι πάσαις ταῖς εἰρημέναις οὐσιώδεσιν οὔσαις ἑνιαῖαί γε ὑπάρχουσαι. καὶ ταύτας δὲ ὁ Ἰάμβλιχος ἐνδείκνυται. Si ce degré suprême des vertus s'appelle "hiératique," c'est parce qu'on y atteint par les rites de "l'art hiératique," c'est-à-dire de la théurgie. C'est pourquoi en d'autres textes ce même degré est appelé "théurgique." En particulier dans un texte important de Psellus,[42] qui (peut-être), à travers Proclus, doit remonter jusqu'à Jamblique lui-même.

Celui qui possède la vertu théurgique, on le dénomme *théopatôr* (θεοπάτωρ), car puisqu'il rend les hommes dieux, c'est pour cela qu'il est appelé *théopatôr*. Celui qui possède la vertu théorétique est nommé "divin," celui qui possède la vertu cathartique, "merveilleux," celui qui possède la vertu politique, "vertueux." On appelle aussi le théurge *theopatôr*, parce qu'il est le père de l'âme que nous appelons "dieu" à cause de la vertu théorétique. Il faut donc que celui qui parvient à la complète ressemblance

41 Damascius (*apud* Olympiodorus), *In Phaed.*, p. 114, 16–25. Pour l'attribution à Damascius de ce traité sur le *Phédon*, voir L. G. Westerink, *Damascius, Lectures on the Philebus* (Amsterdam, 1959), pp. XVIII–XX.

42 Psellus, *De omnifaria doctrina*, éd. L. G. Westerink (Utrecht, 1948), § 74, p. 47, 1–13. Il n'est pas impossible que toute la dissertation de Psellus (§§ 66–81) vienne du Περὶ ἀρετῶν de Jamblique, cité par Damascius, *In Phaed.*, p. 114, 21.

avec dieu, soit d'abord "vertueux," ensuite "merveilleux," ensuite
"divin," et enfin *théopatôr*. L'homme merveilleux et le vertueux peuvent
changer et tomber dans le vice, peut-être même aussi l'homme divin,
c'est-a-dire théorétique; quant au théurge ou *théopatôr*, qui est dans un
état de totale possession divine, il ne saurait jamais passer à l'espèce
contraire de la vertu, étant donné qu'il est hors de lui et qu'il est devenu
dieu purement et simplement.

Ainsi le théurge, parce qu'il est définitivement fixé en dieu
et "devenu dieu purement et simplement," est père en l'âme de
tout ce qu'il y a en elle de divin. Il mérite pleinement ce nom de
théopatôr.

Notons en passant l'affection de Jamblique pour ce genre de
composé. Dans le *Myst.* 8. 2. ,nous trouvons deux fois αὐτοπάτωρ,
pp. 261, 13 et 262, 3, une fois μονοπάτωρ, p. 261, 13–14, et une
fois οὐσιοπάτωρ, p. 262, 6. Que le mot θεοπάτωρ soit aussi son
oeuvre, n'aurait donc rien pour nous surprendre. Toutefois il faut
reconnaître que, malgré de longues recherches, nous n'avons
retrouvé ce mot ni dans les fragments de Jamblique, ni dans les
traités de Proclus. Il est pourtant bien certain que ce n'est pas
une invention de Psellus.

La conclusion de cette recherche se tire d'elle-même. Le *De
mysteriis* est-il autre chose qu'une apologie de la théurgie contre
le plaidoyer rationaliste de Porphyre? Pour s'en convaincre,
voudrait-on une déclaration plus formelle que celle-ci:[43]

C'est n'est pas la pensée rationelle, dit Jamblique, qui unit aux dieux les
théurges; qu'est-ce qui empêcherait alors ceux qui font de la philosophie
au degré théorétique de posséder cette union théurgique avec les dieux?
Non, la vérité n'est pas là. Mais l'union théurgique n'est atteinte que
d'une part par l'efficacité rituelle d'actions ineffables et qui dépassent
toute compréhension, à condition de les accomplir de la manière qui
convient, et d'autre part par la puissance de symboles indescriptibles qui
sont compris seulement des dieux.

Ou bien trouverait-on une description plus impressionnante du
théurge que celle-ci:[44]

Le théurge, par la force des symboles ineffables, ne commande aux
puissances cosmiques ni comme un homme ni comme faisant usage d'une
âme humaine, mais c'est comme préétabli au rang des dieux qu'il lance
des menaces qui transcendent sa propre essence (humaine).

[43] *Myst.* 2. 11, p. 96, 13–97, 2.
[44] *Myst.* 6. 6, p. 246, 16–247, 2.

Dès lors n'était-il pas naturel à l'auteur d'un traité qui prétend rassembler la sagesse des Égyptiens, des Chaldéens et des Assyriens, puisqu'il ne voulait pas signer de son nom, de se désigner du nom de θεοπάτωρ, c'est-à-dire Abamôn, nom qui combine aussi en lui-même la langue des Égyptiens, des Chaldéens et des Assyriens.

Paris, CNRS.

DISPLACEMENT IN HIPPOLYTUS' *ELENCHOS*

MIROSLAV MARCOVICH

Some 35 years ago Hermann Fränkel, in a letter to Walther Kranz, pointed out that the (Stoic) comments on Heraclitus' *frgg.* 64 and 66 DK, preserved in Hippolytus' *Elenchos* 9. 10. 7 (pp. 243, 22–244, 1 Wendland), obviously do not correspond with the quotations from Heraclitus and that probably we have to do with a double displacement in the transmitted text of the *Elenchos*, namely:

<table>
<tr><td align="center">Transmitted Text</td><td align="center">Emended Text</td></tr>
<tr><td>

λέγει δὲ (sc. Heraclitus) καὶ τοῦ κόσμου κρίσιν καὶ πάντων τῶν ἐν αὐτῶι διὰ πυρὸς γίνεσθαι λέγων οὕτως· "τὰ δὲ πάντα οἰακίζει κεραυνός" (= *frg.* 64), τουτέστι κατευθύνει, κεραυνὸν τὸ πῦρ λέγων τὸ αἰώνιον. λέγει δὲ καὶ φρόνιμον τοῦτο εἶναι τὸ πῦρ καὶ τῆς διοικήσεως τῶν ὅλων αἴτιον· καλεῖ δὲ αὐτὸ "χρησμοσύνην καὶ κόρον" (= *frg.* 65)· χρησμοσύνη δέ ἐστιν ἡ διακόσμησις κατ' αὐτόν, ἡ δὲ ἐκπύρωσις κόρος· "πάντα γάρ", φησί, "τὸ πῦρ ἐπελθὸν κρινεῖ καὶ καταλήψεται" (= *frg.* 66).

</td><td>

λέγει δὲ καὶ ⟨τὴν⟩ τοῦ κόσμου κρίσιν καὶ πάντων τῶν ἐν αὐτῶι διὰ πυρὸς γίνεσθαι· "πάντα" γάρ, φησί, "τὸ πῦρ ἐπελθὸν κρινεῖ καὶ καταλήψεται" (= *frg.* 66). λέγει δὲ καὶ φρόνιμον τοῦτο εἶναι τὸ πῦρ καὶ τῆς διοικήσεως τῶν ὅλων αἴτιον, λέγων οὕτως· "τὰ δὲ (τάδε H. Sauppe) πάντα οἰακίζει κεραυνός" (= *frg.* 64), τουτέστι κατευθύνει, κεραυνὸν τὸ πῦρ λέγων τὸ αἰώνιον. καλεῖ δὲ αὐτὸ "χρησμοσύνην καὶ κόρον" (= *frg.* 65)· χρησμοσύνη δέ ἐστιν ἡ διακόσμησις κατ' αὐτόν, ἡ δὲ ἐκπύρωσις κόρος.

</td></tr>
</table>

Kranz (Diels, *Vorsokr.*[5–6], I, p. 165 app.) gave Fränkel's suggestion the compliment "mit grosser Wahrscheinlichkeit" but kept to the transmitted text. In like manner, G. S. Kirk (in

1954)[1] and R. Mondolfo (in 1966)[2] called the suggestion "ingenious" but considered it unlikely or unnecessary. In his turn, Karl Reinhardt (in 1942)[3] first ascribed to Fränkel a false restoration of the text, and then gave his verdict: "Zu zeigen, aus was für Gründen das unmöglich ist, wäre z.B. eine Aufgabe für eine Seminarübung." I defended Fränkel's emendation on several occasions (in 1959, 1965, 1966, 1967)[4], but it is evident that the scholars are still afraid of the size of Fränkel's intervention in the transmitted text.

I shall therefore present here four fresh cases (and this number can be easily increased) of tricky displacement in the transmitted text of Hippolytus' *Elenchos* which require similar radical transpositions, thus showing that Fränkel's emendation is both necessary and not unusual as far as the badly damaged, highly corrupt and unsatisfactorily edited text of the *Elenchos* is concerned.

(1) *Elenchos* 5. 7. 34 (p. 87, 7–15 We).

Transmitted Text	*Emended Text*
καὶ ὅτι, φησίν (sc. *Naassenus quidam*) αὐτῶι "πάντα ὑποτέτακται" (I Cor. 15: 27), καὶ τοῦτ' ἔστι τὸ εἰρημένον· "εἰς πᾶσαν τὴν γῆν ἐξῆλθεν ὁ φθόγγος αὐτῶν" (Rom. 10: 18). ὡς τὸ (*cod. edd.*: ὡς δὲ R. Reitzenstein: ὥστε coniec. We.) τὴν ῥάβδον <ἄγει ex Homero add. ed. Gott.> κινήσας ὁ Ἑρμῆς, αἱ δὲ τρίζουσαι ἔπονται (*Odyssey* 24. 5) αἱ ψυχαὶ συνεχῶς οὕτως, ὡς διὰ τῆς εἰκόνος ὁ ποιητὴς ἐπιδέδειχε λέγων·	καὶ ὅτι, φησίν, αὐτῶι "πάντα ὑποτέτακται", ὥς τε "τῆι ῥάβδωι (*scripsi ex Homero*) <ἄγει> κινήσας" ὁ Ἑρμῆς, "αἱ δὲ τρίζουσαι ἔπονται", αἱ ψυχαὶ συνεχῶς, οὕτως [ὡς a dittography] διὰ [τῆς *del.* Reitz.] εἰκόνος ὁ ποιητὴς ἐπιδέδειχε λέγων·

---

[1] G. S. Kirk, *Heraclitus, the Cosmic Fragments* (Cambridge, 1954; reprint 1962), p. 351.

[2] R. Mondolfo, *Heráclito: textos y problemas de su interpretación* (México, Siglo XXI Editores, 1966), pp. 237 f.

[3] K. Reinhardt, *Hermes* 77 (1942), p, 22, n. 1 = *Vermächtnis der Antike* (ed. by C.Becker, Göttingen, 1960), p. 65, n. 33.

[4] M. Marcovich, "On Heraclitus' fr. 66 DK," *Paper to the Third*

"ὡς δ' ὅτε νυκτερίδες μυχῶι ἄντρου θεσπεσίοιο
τρίζουσ<α>ι ποτέονται, ἐπεί κέ τις ἀποπέσησιν
ὁρμαθοῦ ἐκ πέτρης, ἀνά τ' ἀλλήλῃσιν ἔχονται".

(Od. 24. 6–8). πέτρης, φησί, τοῦ   καὶ τοῦτ' ἔστι, <φησί>, τὸ εἰρη-
'Αδάμαντος λέγει.   μένον· "εἰς πᾶσαν τὴν γῆν ἐξῆλθεν
ὁ φθόγγος αὐτῶν."
πέτρης <δέ>, φησί, τοῦ 'Αδάμαντος λέγει.[5]

The text as transmitted and edited simply does not make sense. St Paul's words ἐξῆλθεν ὁ φθόγγος αὐτῶν (Rom. 10:18) are meant by the anonymous Naassene as a commentary on Homer's τρίζουσαι ποτέονται, thus they must follow, not precede, the Homeric quotation.

(2) 5. 12. 2 (p. 104, 16–21 We.)

Transmitted Text   *Emended Text*

ἔστι δὲ τῆς τριχῆι διαιρέσεως   ἔστι δὲ τῆς τριχῆι διαιρέσεως
παρ' αὐτοῖς (sc. *apud Peratas*) τὸ   παρ' αὐτοῖς οἷον <εἰ> μία τις ἀρχή,
μὲν ἓν μέρος οἷον μία τις ἀρχή,   καθάπερ πηγὴ μεγάλη, εἰς ἀπεί-
καθάπερ πηγὴ μεγάλη εἰς ἀπεί-   ρους τῶι λόγωι τμηθῆναι τομὰς
ρους τῶι λόγωι τμηθῆναι τομὰς   δυναμένη. ἡ δὲ πρώτη τομὴ καὶ
δυναμένη· ἡ δὲ πρώτη τομὴ καὶ   προσεχεστέρα κατ' αὐτούς ἐστι <ν
προσεχεστέρα κατ' αὐτούς ἐστι   ἡ> τριάς· καὶ τὸ μὲν ἓν μέρος
τριὰς καὶ καλεῖται ἀγαθὸν τέλειον,   καλεῖται ἀγαθὸν τέλειον, μέγεθος
μέγεθος πατρικόν. τὸ δὲ δεύ-   πατρικόν· τὸ δὲ δεύτερον τῆς
τερον τῆς τριάδος αὐτῶν μέρος   τριάδος αὐτῶν μέρος οἱονεὶ δυνά-
οἱονεὶ δυνάμεων ἄπειρόν τι πλῆθος   μεων ἄπειρόν τι πλῆθος, ἐξ
ἐξ αὐτῶν γεγενημένων (J. Ber-   αὐτῶν γεγενημένων· τὸ <δὲ>
nays: αὐτῶν γεγενημένον *cod.*)·   τρίτον ἰδικόν.
τὸ τρίτον ἰδικόν.

Internat. Congress of Class. Studies (Merida, 1959), pp. 1 ff.; M. Marcovich, *RE* Sup. Vol. X (1965), col. 263, s.v. "Herakleitos"; M. Marcovich, "Hippolytus and Heraclitus," *Studia Patristica* VII (ed. by F. L. Cross, *TU* 92, Berlin, 1966), pp. 255–264, esp. pp. 262 f.; M. Marcovich, *Heraclitus: Greek Text with a Short Commentary*. Editio Maior (The Los Andes University Press, Merida, Venezuela, 1967), pp. 422 and 424.

[5] See M. Marcovich, "Textual Criticism on Hippolytus' *Refutatio*," *Journal of Theological Studies*, N. S. 19 (1968), pp. 83–92.

It is obvious that the words τὸ μὲν ἓν μέρος are displaced in the transmitted text, as already F. G. Schneidewin had pointed out. Now, since we find the same word order in Hippolytus' *Summary* (10. 10) and in Theodoretus' *Haereticarum fabularum compendium* I: 17 as well, it is highly probable that the mistake goes back to Hippolytus himself, who carelessly took it over from his Peratic source.

(3) 5. 26. 36–37 (p. 132, 16–23 We.)

Transmitted Text	*Emended Text*
ὅταν οὖν προφῆται λέγωσιν· "ἄκουε οὐρανὲ καὶ ἐνωτίζου ἡ γῆ, κύριος ἐλάλησεν" (Isaiah I: 2), οὐρανὸν λέγει (cod.: λέγουσι We.), φησί (sc. *Iustinus*), τὸ πνεῦμα τὸ ἐν τῶι ἀνθρώπωι τὸ τοῦ 'Ελωείμ, γῆν δὲ τὴν ψυχὴν τὴν ἐν τῶι ἀνθρώπωι σὺν τῶι πνεύματι, κύριον δὲ τὸν Βαρούχ, 'Ισραὴλ δὲ τὴν 'Εδέμ· 'Εδὲμ γὰρ λέγεται καὶ 'Ισραὴλ ἡ σύζυγος τοῦ 'Ελωείμ. "οὐκ ἔγνω με (*ed. Gott.*: ἐγνώκει *cod.*)", φησίν, "'Ισραήλ" (Is. I: 3)· εἰ γὰρ ἐγνώκει, ὅτι πρὸς τῶι ἀγαθῶι εἰμι, οὐκ ἂν ἐκόλαζε τὸ πνεῦμα τὸ ἐν τοῖς ἀνθρώποις διὰ τὴν πατρικὴν ἄγνοιαν ἐντεῦθεν * * *	ὅταν οὖν <ὁ> προφήτης λέγηι· "ἄκουε, οὐρανέ, καὶ ἐνωτίζου, ἡ γῆ, κύριος ἐλάλησεν", οὐρανὸν λέγει, φησί, τὸ πνεῦμα τὸ ἐν τῶι ἀνθρώπωι, <ἀ>πὸ τοῦ 'Ελωείμ, γῆν δὲ τὴν ψυχήν, τὴν <ἀπὸ τῆς 'Εδὲμ> ἐν τῶι ἀνθρώπωι σὺν τῶι πνεύματι, κύριον δὲ τὸν Βαρούχ. "οὐκ ἔγνω με", φησίν, "'Ισρα ήλ"·'Ισραὴλδὲτὴν'Εδὲμ <λέγει>. ('Εδὲμ γὰρ λέγεται καὶ 'Ισραήλ, ἡ σύζυγος τοῦ 'Ελωείμ.) εἰ γὰρ ἐγνώκει, <φησίν,> ὅτι πρὸς τῶι ἀγαθῶι εἰμι, οὐκ ἂν ἐκόλαζε τὸ πνεῦμα, τὸ ἐν τοῖς ἀνθρώποις διὰ τὴν πατρικὴν ἄγνοιαν ἐνδεθέν.

First, the words 'Ισραὴλ δὲ τὴν 'Εδέμ are meant as a commentary on the quotation from the Old Testament οὐκ ἔγνω με 'Ισραήλ, thus they must be transposed after this quotation. Second, the parenthesized words are no more than a Hippolytean gloss. And third, the last word of the passage should read ἐνδεθέν (in lieu of the transmitted ἐντεῦθεν plus lacuna): cf. 5. 26. 17 (p. 129, 16 We.: Justin) τὸ πνεῦμα γάρ μου ἐνδέδεται εἰς τοὺς ἀνθρώπους and Plato *Phd.* 92a πρὶν ἐν τῶι σώματι ἐνδεθῆναι (sc. τὴν ψυχήν); 81e.

(4) 6. 32. 6 (pp. 160, 27–161, 2 We.)

Transmitted Text	Emended Text

... καὶ ἐποίησεν (sc. Καρπὸς sec. Valentinianos) αὐτὰ (sc. τὰ πάθη τῆς Σοφίας) ὑποστατὰς οὐσίας, καὶ τὸν μὲν φόβον ψυχικὴν ἐποίησεν οὐσίαν (Bernays: ἐπιθυμίαν cod.), τὴν δὲ λύπην ὑλικήν, τὴν δὲ ἀπορίαν δαιμόνων, τὴν δὲ ἐπιστροφὴν καὶ δέησιν καὶ ἱκετείαν <ἄν>οδον (ed. Gott.: ὁδὸν cod.: ὁδὸν ἐπὶ μετάνοιαν C. Bunsen) καὶ μετάνοιαν καὶ δύναμιν ψυχικῆς οὐσίας, ἥτις καλεῖται δεξιά.

... καὶ ἐποίησεν αὐτὰ ὑποστατὰς οὐσίας·καὶ τὸν μὲν φόβον ψυχικὴν ἐποίησεν [ἐπιθυμίαν], τὴν δὲ λύπην ὑλικήν, τὴν δὲ ἀπορίαν δαιμόνων· τὴν δὲ ἐπιστροφῆς <ἐπιθυμίαν> καὶ δέησιν καὶ ἱκετείαν <καὶ> <ἐπάν>οδον καὶ μετάνοιαν, [καὶ] δύναμιν ψυχικῆς οὐσίας, ἥτις καλεῖται δεξιά.

Bernays's emendation of cod. ἐπιθυμίαν into οὐσίαν, accepted by all editors, is not convincing. The corruption of the text is due to the displacement of the word ἐπιθυμίαν. As for my emendation ἐπιστροφῆς ἐπιθυμίαν, cf. Theodoretus, *Haer. fab. comp.* I. 7 (*PG* 83, p. 357 A) λύπην καὶ φόβον καὶ ἀπορίαν εἰσδέξασθαι (sc. τὴν Σοφίαν)· ἔπειτα προσγενέσθαι αὐτῆι καὶ ἐπιστροφῆς ἐπιθυμίαν. As for the reading ἐπάνοδον, cf. Siracides 17, 24 μετανοοῦσιν ἔδωκεν ἐπάνοδον and Nilus, *Epist.* 3. 171 (*PG* 79, p. 464 C) ἔστι γὰρ ἐπάνοδος πρὸς τὸ καλὸν διὰ τῆς μετανοίας.[6]

University of Illinois

---

[6] *Ibid.*, p. 90.

PHILON D'ALEXANDRIE
ET LE PRÉCEPTE DELPHIQUE

PIERRE COURCELLE

Philon d'Alexandrie mentionne expressément le précepte delphique et l'interprétation selon laquelle la science de soi-même
engendre le bonheur.[1] Il rapproche ce précepte de celui de
l'Exode: "Veille sur toi-même," et entend que l'homme doit
s'éloigner du terrestre qui le cerne comme une prison.[2] Se reconnaître soi-même consiste d'abord à repousser de soi le sensible.[3]
Le Sage n'est pas celui qui croit avoir assisté à la création du
monde, comme s'il était le conseiller du Créateur; il ne doit pas
dire de billevesées sur le soleil, la lune et les autres êtres célestes,
tant qu'il n'a pas enquêté sur soi-même: âme, corps, sensation,
raisonnement.[4] Ainsi, dans l'Écriture, Tharé quitta la Chaldée,

---

[1] Philon *Legatio ad Gaium* 69, éd. Cohn-Wendland (Berlin, 1915), VI,
p. 168, 15: Ἐπὶ δὲ Μάκρωνι· "πλέον ἐφυσήθη τοῦ μετρίου· τὸ Δελφικὸν
γράμμα οὐ διανέγνω, τὸ *Γνῶθι σαυτόν·* φασὶ δὲ τὴν μὲν ἐπιστήμην εὐδαιμονίας,
τὴν δὲ ἄγνοιαν κακοδαιμονίας αἰτίαν εἶναι.
[2] Philon *De migratione Abrahami* 8, éd. J. Cazeaux (Paris, 1956), p. 98:
Πάντα τὸν αἰῶνα *γίνωσκε σεαυτόν,* ὡς καὶ Μωυσῆς πολλαχοῦ διδάσκει λέγων
"πρόσεχε σεαυτῷ" (Exod. 34: 12; Deut. 4: 9; 6: 12; 8: 11)· οὕτως γὰρ ὧν τε
ὑπακούειν καὶ οἷς ἐπιτάττειν προσῆκεν αἴσθησιν. Ἄπελθε οὖν ἐκ τοῦ περὶ
σεαυτὸν γεώδους, τὸ παμμίαρον, ὦ οὗτος, ἐκφυγὼν δεσμωτήριον, τὸ σῶμα,
καὶ τὰς ὥσπερ εἰρκτοφύλακας ἡδονὰς καὶ ἐπιθυμίας αὐτοῦ.
[3] *Ibid.*, 13, p. 100: Ἐπειδὰν γοῦν ὁ νοῦς ἄρξηται *γνωρίζειν ἑαυτὸν* καὶ
τοῖς νοητοῖς ἐνομιλεῖν θεωρήμασιν, ἅπαντα τὸ κλινόμενον τῆς ψυχῆς πρὸς τὸ
αἰσθητὸν εἶδος ἀπώσεται, ὃ κέκληται παρ' Ἑβραίοις Λώτ.
[4] *Ibid.*, 136–138, pp. 178–180: Πάριτε νῦν οἱ τύφου καὶ ἀπαιδευσίας καὶ
πολλῆς ἀλαζονείας γέμοντες, οἱ δοκησίσοφοι καὶ μὴ μόνον ὅ ἐστιν ἕκαστον
εἰδέναι σαφῶς ἐπιφάσκοντες, ἀλλὰ καὶ τὰς αἰτίας προσαποδιδόναι διὰ θρασύτητα
τολμῶντες, ὥσπερ ἢ τῇ τοῦ κόσμου γενέσει παρατυχόντες καὶ ὡς ἕκαστα καὶ ἐξ
ὧν ἀπετελεῖτο κατιδόντες ἢ σύμβουλοι περὶ τῶν κατασκευαζομένων τῷ δημιουργῷ γενόμενοι. Εἶτα τῶν ἄλλων ἅπαξ ἁπάντων μεθέμενοι *γνωρίσατε ἑαυτοὺς*
καὶ οἵτινές ἐστε σαφῶς εἴπατε, κατὰ τὸ σῶμα, κατὰ τὴν ψυχήν, κατὰ τὴν
αἴσθησιν, κατὰ τὸν λόγον, καθ' ἕν τι κἂν τὸ βραχύτατον τῶν εἰδῶν ... Μὴ
γάρ μοι περὶ σελήνης καὶ ἡλίου καὶ τῶν ἄλλων ὅσα κατ' οὐρανὸν καὶ κόσμον

pays des astrologues, pour Haran, qui désigne les profondeurs de notre demeure.[5]

Il faut délaisser non seulement l'étude du ciel, mais l'observation du monde physique d'ici-bas: terre, mer, fleuves, végétaux et animaux, et nous consacrer à l'examen de nous-mêmes, qui sommes notre propre demeure;[6] cet examen fait découvrir

οὕτως μακρὰν διῳκισμένων καὶ τὰς φύσεις διαφερόντων ἀερομυθεῖτε, ὦ κενοὶ φρενῶν, πρὶν ἑαυτοὺς ἐρευνῆσαι καὶ γνῶναι.
De fuga et inventione 46, éd. Cohn-Wendland (Berlin, 1898), III, p. 120 (à propos de Gen. 27: 44): "Οἴκησον" οὖν, φησίν, "ὦ τέκνον, μετ' αὐτοῦ" μὴ τὸν ἅπαντα αἰῶνα, ἀλλ' "ἡμέρας τίνας," τοῦτο δ' ἐστι τὴν τῶν αἰσθήσεων χώραν κατάμαθε, γνῶθι σαυτὸν καὶ τὰ σαυτοῦ μέρη, τί τε ἕκαστον καὶ πρὸς τί γέγονε καὶ πῶς ἐνεργεῖν πέφυκε καὶ τίς ὁ τὰ θαύματα κινῶν καὶ νευροσπαστῶν ἀόρατος ἀοράτως, εἴτε ὁ ἐν σοὶ νοῦς εἴτε ὁ τῶν συμπάντων. Ἐπειδὰν δὲ σαυτὸν ἐξετάσῃς, καὶ τὰ ἴδια τοῦ Λάβαν ἀκρίβωσον, τὰς τῆς κενῆς δόξης λαμπρὰς νομιζομένας εὐπραγίας. Cf. Ambroise De fuga saeculi 4. 20, CSEL XXXII. 2, pp. 180–181: *Unde et dicit Rebecca habitandum paucos dies cum illo, non multo tempore, ne corporeis coloretur voluptatibus et saeculi capiatur inlecebris, persuadet autem habitare, ut discat studiosus disciplinae virtutes sensuum et velut situs quosdam carnis atque regiones, ut se cognoscat et noverit vehementiam carnis, quid et qua causa creatum sit, quemadmodum unusquisque sensus operetur.*
⁵ Philon De somniis 1. 54–58, éd. P. Savinel (Paris, 1962), pp. 46–48: Μὴ τὰ ὑπὲρ σὲ καὶ ἄνω, ὦ οὗτος, ἀλλὰ τὰ ἐγγὺς σαυτοῦ κατανόησον, μᾶλλον δὲ σαυτὸν ἀκολακεύτως ἐρεύνησον ... Πρὶν δὲ τὸν ἴδιον οἶκον καλῶς ἐπεσκέφθαι, τὸν τοῦ παντὸς ἐξετάζειν οὐχ ὑπερβολὴ μανίας; καὶ οὔπω σοι μεῖζον ἐπίταγμα ἐπιτάττω, τὴν σαυτοῦ ψυχὴν ἰδεῖν καὶ τὸν νοῦν, ἐφ' ᾧ μέγα φρονεῖς· καταλαβεῖν γὰρ αὐτὸν οὔποτε δυνήσῃ. Ἀνάβαινε νῦν εἰς οὐρανὸν καὶ καταλαζονεύου περὶ τῶν ἐκεῖ, μήπω δεδυνημένος γνῶναι κατὰ τὸ ποιητικὸν γράμμα

ὅττι τοι ἐν μεγάροισι κακόν τ' ἀγαθόν τε τέτυκται (Hom. Od. 4. 392),

καταγαγὼν δ' ἀπ' οὐρανοῦ τὸν κατάσκοπον καὶ 'ἀντισπάσας ἀπὸ τῆς ἐκεῖ ζητήσεως γνῶθι σαυτόν, εἶτα καὶ τοῦτ' ἐπιμελῶς ἐκπόνησον, ἵνα τῆς ἀνθρωπίνης εὐδαιμονίας ἐπιλάχῃς· Τὸν τρόπον τοῦτον Θάρρα μὲν Ἑβραῖοι, Σωκράτην δὲ Ἕλληνες ὀνομάζουσι· καὶ γὰρ ἐκεῖνον ἐγγηράσαι φασὶν τῇ περὶ τοῦ γνῶθι σαυτὸν ἀκριβεστάτη σκέψει, μηδὲν ἔξω τῶν καθ' ἑαυτὸν φιλοσοφοῦντα. Ἀλλ' ὁ μὲν ἄνθρωπος ἦν, Θάρρα δ' αὐτὸς ὁ λόγος ὁ περὶ τοῦ γνῶναί τινα ἑαυτὸν προκείμενος οἷα δένδρον εὐερνέστατον. ἵν' ἔχοιεν εὐμαρῶς οἱ φιλάρετοι τὸν περὶ ἠθοποιίαν δρεπόμενοι καρπὸν σωτηρίου καὶ ἡδίστης ἐμπίπλασθαι τροφῆς. Le même vers de l'*Odyssée* (4. 392) est cité aussi par Philon, *De migratione Abrahami* 195, p. 220, texte cité ci-dessous, n. 11. Selon Diogène Laërce, *Vitae* 2. 21. 1, éd. H. S. Long (Oxford, 1964), I, p. 66, Socrate lui-même l'appliquait à ses propres recherches morales par opposition aux recherches physiques: Γνόντα δὲ τὴν φυσικὴν θεωρίαν εἶναι πρὸς ἡμᾶς, τὰ ἠθικὰ φιλοσοφεῖν ἐπί τε τῶν ἐργαστηρίων καὶ ἐν τῇ ἀγορᾷ· κἀκεῖνα δὲ φάσκειν ζητεῖν·

Ὅττί τοι ἐν μεγάροισι κακόν τ' ἀγαθόν τε τέτυκται.

⁶ Philon De migratione Abrahami 184–186, pp. 212–214 (discours aux "chaldaïsants"): Τί, φησίν, ὦ θαυμάσιοι, τοσοῦτον αἰφνίδιον ἀρθέντες ἀπὸ γῆς εἰς ὕψος ἐπινήχεσθε καὶ τὸν ἀέρα ὑπερκύψαντες αἰθεροβατεῖτε;... Κατάβητε οὖν ἀπ' οὐρανοῦ καὶ καταβάντες μὴ πάλιν γῆν καὶ θάλατταν καὶ ποταμοὺς καὶ

la place de l'intellect qui commande en nous comme il commande dans l'univers.[7] L'attitude de Philon rappelle celle de Socrate qui, dans le *Phèdre* (229d–e), luttait contre les explications physiques des mythes et jugeait plus urgent de se connaître soi-même;[8] elle reparaîtra plus tard, en termes analogues, chez Grégoire de Nysse[9] et dans les *Confessions* de saint Augustin.[10]

Le Sage renonce donc à faire du monde le dieu suprême, et spécialement à pratiquer l'art des horoscopes, selon lequel la révolution des astres cause le bonheur ou le malheur de l'homme; en s'examinent, il se fraie une route qui, à partir de lui-même, lui ouvre l'espérance de découvrir le Père de l'univers.[11]

Sans doute, l'homme ne peut se connaître, c'est à dire saisir pleinement quelle est la substance de son propre intellect; il ne peut dire si l'âme est souffle, sang, feu, air, ni même si elle est corporelle ou non; aussi Adam, symbole de l'intellect, donne-t-il des noms aux autres êtres, mais non à lui-même, parce qu'il ignore sa propre nature; il connaît encore moins l'âme de l'univers et

φυτῶν καὶ ζῴων ἰδέας ἐξετάζετε, μόνους δὲ ἑαυτοὺς καὶ τὴν ἑαυτῶν φύσιν ἐρευνᾶτε, μὴ ἑτέρωθι μᾶλλον οἰκήσαντες ἢ παρ' ἑαυτοῖς· διαθεώμενοι γὰρ τὰ κατὰ τὸν ἴδιον οἶκον, τὸ δεσπόζον ἐν αὐτῷ, τὸ ὑπήκοον, τὸ ἔμψυχον, τὸ ἄψυχον, τὸ λογικόν, τὸ ἄλογον, τὸ ἀθάνατον, τὸ θνητόν, τὸ ἄμεινον, τὸ χεῖρον, εὐθὺς ἐπιστήμην θεοῦ καὶ τῶν ἔργων αὐτοῦ σαφῆ λήψεσθε. Λογιεῖσθε γὰρ ὅτι, ὡς ἐν ὑμῖν ἐστι νοῦς, καὶ τῷ παντί ἐστι.

[7] Philon *De opificio mundi* 69, éd. R. Arnaldez (Paris, 1961), p. 186: Ὃν γὰρ ἔχει λόγον ὁ μέγας ἡγεμὼν ἐν ἅπαντι τῷ κόσμῳ, τοῦτον ὡς ἔοικε καὶ ὁ ἀνθρώπινος νοῦς ἐν ἀνθρώπῳ.

[8] Platon *Phdr.* 229e.

[9] Grégoire de Nysse *In Cant. Hom.* 2. 2 (sur le verset, *Nisi cognoscas te* ...), éd. H. Langerbeck, p. 69: Οὐ θαυμάσεις πλάτη γῆς οὐδὲ πελάγη πρὸς ἄπειρον ἐκτεινόμενα.

[10] Augustin, *Conf.* 10. 8. 15. 10, éd. Labriolle, II, p. 251: *Et eunt homines mirari alta montium et ingentes fluctus maris et latissimos lapsus fluminum et Oceani ambitum et gyros siderum, et relinquunt se ipsos.*

[11] Philon, *De migratione Abrahami* 194–195, pp. 218–220: ... γενεθλιαλογικῆς ἀποστὰς τὸ πρῶτον, ἥτις παρέπεισεν αὐτὸν ὑπολαβεῖν τὸν κόσμον θεὸν τὸν πρῶτον εἶναι, ἀλλὰ μὴ τοῦ πρώτου θεοῦ δημιούργημα, καὶ τὰς τῶν ἀστέρων φοράς τε καὶ κινήσεις αἰτίας ἀνθρώποις κακοπραγίας καὶ τοὐναντίον εὐδαιμονίας. Ἔπειτ' εἰς τὴν ἐπίσκεψιν ἐλθὼν τὴν αὐτὸς ἑαυτοῦ, φιλοσοφήσας τὰ κατὰ τὸν ἴδιον οἶκον, τὰ περὶ σώματος, τὰ περὶ αἰσθήσεως, τὰ περὶ λόγου, καὶ γνοὺς κατὰ τὸ ποιητικὸν γράμμα·

ὅττι τοι ἐν μεγάροισι κακόν τ' ἀγαθόν τε τέτυκται, ἔπειτ' ἀνατεμὼν ὁδὸν τὴν ἀφ' αὑτοῦ καὶ διὰ ταύτης ἐλπίσας τὸν δυστόπαστον καὶ δυστέκμαρτον πατέρα τῶν ὅλων κατανοῆσαι, μαθὼν ἀκριβῶς ἑαυτὸν εἴσεται τάχα που καὶ θεόν, οὐκέτι μένων ἐν Χαρράν, τοῖς αἰσθήσεως ὀργάνοις, ἀλλ' εἰς ἑαυτὸν ἐπιστραφείς.

l'intellect divin.[12] Lorsque Dieu dit à Moïse de se connaître lui-même, il lui signifie seulement de reconnaître sa faiblesse d'homme, incapable ainsi que toute autre créature de saisir l'essence divine.[13] Mais si le Père suprême dépasse l'entendement, le spectacle du monde révèle du moins l'existence de son auteur divin, que l'homme ne doit pas renoncer à chercher.[14] Nous sommes donc fort loin, malgré les apparences, du scepticisme.[15]

L'effort d'introspection constitue un échelon vers la découverte de l'existence d'un Intellect qui dirige le monde: Abraham tombe sur sa face lorsqu'il reconnaît le néant de la race mortelle, nulle part solidement établie, et conçoit du même coup la transcendance de Dieu, immobile dans l'identique et qui fait mouvoir toutes choses.[16] En se reconnaissant comme cendre, l'homme se

---

[12] Philon *Legum allegoriae* 1. 91–92, éd. C. Mondésert (Paris, 1962), p. 93: Ὁ νοῦς ὁ ἐν ἑκάστῳ ἡμῶν τὰ μὲν ἄλλα δύναται καταλαβεῖν, ἑαυτὸν δὲ γνωρίσαι ἀδυνάτως ἔχει· ὥσπερ γὰρ ὁ ὀφθαλμὸς τὰ μὲν ἄλλα ὁρᾷ, ἑαυτὸν δὲ οὐχ ὁρᾷ. οὕτως καὶ ὁ νοῦς τὰ μὲν ἄλλα νοεῖ, ἑαυτὸν δὲ οὐ καταλαμβάνει. Εἰπάτω γάρ, τίς τέ ἐστι καὶ ποταπός, πνεῦμα ἢ αἷμα ἢ πῦρ ἢ ἀὴρ ἢ ἕτερόν τι [σῶμα], ἢ τοσοῦτόν γε ὅτι σῶμά ἐστιν ἢ πάλιν ἀσώματον. Εἶτ' οὐκ εὐήθεις οἱ περὶ θεοῦ σκεπτόμενοι οὐσίας; Οἱ γὰρ τῆς ἰδίας ψυχῆς τὴν οὐσίαν οὐκ ἴσασι, πῶς ἂν περὶ τῆς τῶν ὅλων ψυχῆς ἀκριβώσαιεν; Ἡ γὰρ τῶν ὅλων ψυχὴ ὁ θεός ἐστι κατὰ ἔννοιαν. Εἰκότως οὖν ὁ Ἀδάμ, τουτέστιν ὁ νοῦς, τὰ ἄλλα ὀνομάζων καὶ καταλαμβάνων, ἑαυτῷ ὄνομα οὐκ ἐπιτίθησιν, ὅτι ἑαυτὸν ἀγνοεῖ καὶ τὴν ἰδίαν φύσιν.
Philon *De mutatione nominum* 10, éd. H. Arnaldez (Paris, 1964), p. 36: Καὶ τί θαυμαστόν, εἰ τὸ ὂν ἀνθρώποις ἀκατάληπτον, ὁπότε καὶ ὁ ἐν ἑκάστῳ νοῦς ἄγνωστος ἡμῖν; Τίς γὰρ ψυχῆς οὐσίαν εἶδεν;
Philon *De posteritate Caini* 66, éd. Cohn-Wendland (Berlin, 1897), II, p. 14: (νῷ) τῷ μηδὲ τὴν αὐτοῦ φύσιν ἥτις ἐστὶ καταλαβεῖν δυναμένῳ.
Philon *De Abrahamo* 74, éd. J. Gorez (Paris, 1966), p. 54: Εἰ δ' ἀόρατος ὁ βασιλεύς, μὴ θαυμάσῃς· οὐδὲ γὰρ ὁ ἐν σοὶ νοῦς ὁρατός.
[13] Philon *De specialibus legibus* 1. 44, éd. Cohn-Wendland (Berlin, 1906), V, p. 11 (à propos d'Exode 33: 13 ff): Τὴν δ' ἐμὴν κατάληψιν οὐχ οἷον ἀνθρώπου φύσις ἀλλ' οὐδ' ὁ σύμπας οὐρανός τε καὶ κόσμος δυνήσεται χωρῆσαι. *Γνῶθι δὴ σαυτὸν* καὶ μὴ συνεκφέρου ταῖς ὑπὲρ δύναμιν ὁρμαῖς καὶ ἐπιθυμίαις, μηδέ σε τῶν ἀνεφίκτων ἔρως αἱρέτω καὶ μετεωριζέτω· τῶν γὰρ ἐφικτῶν οὐδενὸς ἀμοιρήσεις.
[14] *Ibid.*, 1. 32, p. 8: Δυστόπαστος μὲν οὖν καὶ δυσκατάληπτος ὁ πατὴρ καὶ ἡγεμὼν τῶν συμπάντων ἐστίν, ἀλλ' οὐ διὰ τοῦτ' ἀποκνητέον τὴν ζήτησιν αὐτοῦ.
[15] Contrairement à ce qu'écrit J. Dupont, *Gnosis* (Louvain-Paris, 1949), pp. 516–518; cf. p. 354. Sur la doctrine philonienne du γνῶθι σαυτόν, cf. A.-J. Festugière, *Le dieu cosmique*[3] (Paris, 1940), pp. 579–581; H. Jonas, *Gnosis und spätantiker Geist* (Göttingen, 1954), II, p. 42.
[16] Philon *De mutatione nominum* 54, p. 56: Λέγεται δ' ἑξῆς· '"Επεσεν Ἀβραὰμ ἐπὶ πρόσωπον" (Gen. 17: 3). Ἆρ' οὐκ ἔμελλεν ὑποσχέσεσι θείαις γνῶναί τε ἑαυτὸν καὶ τὴν τοῦ θνητοῦ γένους οὐδένειαν καὶ πεσεῖν παρὰ τὸν ἑστῶτα εἰς ἔνδειξιν τῆς ὑπολήψεως, ἣν περὶ ἑαυτοῦ τε ἔσχε καὶ θεοῦ, ὅτι ὁ μὲν κατὰ τὰ αὐτὰ ἑστὼς κινεῖ τὴν σύμπασαν στάσιν, οὐ διὰ τῶν σκελῶν – οὐ γὰρ ἀνθρωπό-

purifie et se détourne de son arrogance naturelle; il en vient à se rendre compte que la puissance divine dépasse tout.[17] La pratique de la circoncision signifie non seulement la suppression des plaisirs qui envoûtent la raison, mais le précepte de se connaître soi-même, c'est à dire de préserver l'âme de la présomption, mal grave qui nous fait nous prendre pour des dieux et oublier Dieu.[18]

La connaissance de soi n'est donc pas sa propre fin, mais nous invite à nous fuir nous-mêmes en vue de connaître l'Un.[19] Le vrai saint, parce qu'il se connaît, voit avec lucidité son néant d'être créé, renonce à soi-même et acquiert de ce fait la connaissance de Celui qui est.[20] Au lieu d'oublier par arrogance son propre néant, il se souvient de soi-même comme néant et

μορφος — ἀλλὰ τὴν ἄτρεπτον καὶ ἀμετάβλητον ἐμφαίνουσαν, ὁ δ' οὐδέποτε ἐν ταὐτῷ βεβαίως ἱδρυμένος ἄλλοτε ἀλλοίας δέχεται μεταβολὰς καὶ ὑποσκελιζόμενος, ὁ δυστυχής — ὄλισθος γὰρ σύμπας ὁ βίος ἐστιν αὐτῷ — μέγα πτῶμα πίπτει; ἀλλ' ὁ μὲν ἄκων ἀμαθής, ὁ δ'ἑκὼν εὐάγωγος.

Philon *Quod deus sit immutabilis* 161, éd. Cohn-Wendland (Berlin, 1897), II, p. 90: Καὶ γὰρ Ἀβραὰμ ἐγγίσας τῷ θεῷ ἑαυτὸν εὐθὺς ἔγνω γῆν καὶ τέφραν ὄντα (Gen. 17: 27).

De somniis I. 220, p. 116: ἑαυτὸν ἂν ἔγνω τέφρας καὶ ὕδατος συμφόρημα.

[17] Philon *De specialibus legibus* I. 263, p. 64: Αἰτία δ' οὐχ ἀπὸ σκοποῦ λέγοιτ' ἂν ἥδε· βούλεται τοὺς ἐπὶ τὴν τοῦ ὄντος θεραπείαν ἰόντας γνῶναι πρότερον ἑαυτοὺς καὶ τὴν ἰδίαν οὐσίαν· ὁ γὰρ ἀνεπιστήμων ἑαυτοῦ πῶς ἂν δυνηθείη καταλαβεῖν τὴν ἀνωτάτω καὶ πάνθ' ὑπερβάλλουσαν θεοῦ δύναμιν; Ἔστιν οὖν ἡμῶν ἡ κατὰ τὸ σῶμα οὐσία, γῆ καὶ ὕδωρ, ἧς ὑπομιμνήσκει διὰ τῆς καθάρσεως, αὐτὸ τοῦθ' ὑπολαμβάνων εἶναι τὴν ὠφελιμωτάτην κάθαρσιν, τὸ γνῶναι τινα ἑαυτὸν καὶ ἐξ οἵων ὡς οὐδεμιᾶς σπουδῆς ἀξίων, τέφρας καὶ ὕδατος, συνεκράθη. Τοῦτο γὰρ ἐπιγνοὺς τὴν ἐπίβουλον οἴησιν εὐθὺς ἀποστραφήσεται.

[18] *Ibid.*, I. 10, p. 3: Ἑτέρου δὲ τοῦ γνῶναί τινα ἑαυτὸν καὶ τὴν βαρεῖαν νόσον, οἴησιν, ψυχῆς ἀπώσασθαι· ἔνιοι γὰρ ὡς ἀγαθοὶ ζωοπλάσται ζῴων τὸ κάλλιστον, ἄνθρωπον, ηὔχησαν δύνασθαι δημιουργεῖν καὶ φυσηθέντες ὑπ' ἀλαζονείας ἐξεθείωσαν, τὸν ὡς ἀληθῶς αἴτιον γενέσεως ὄντα θεὸν παρακαλυψάμενοι, καίτοι γε ἐκ τῶν συνήθων ἐπανορθώσασθαι τὴν ἀπάτην δυνάμενοι.

[19] Philon *Legum allegoriae* 3. 48, p. 196: Ὁ δὲ σπουδαῖος ἔμπαλιν ἑαυτὸν ἀποδιδράσκων ἀναστρέφει πρὸς τὴν τοῦ ἑνὸς ἐπίγνωσιν, καλὸν δρόμον καὶ πάντων ἄριστον ἀγώνισμα τοῦτο νικῶν.

[20] Philon *De somniis* I. 59–60, p. 48: Τοιοῦτοι μὲν ἡμῖν οἱ φρονήσεως κατάσκοποι, τῶν δὲ ἀθλητῶν καὶ ἀγωνιστῶν αὐτῆς αἱ φύσεις τελειότεραι· δικαιοῦσι γὰρ οὗτοι τὸν περὶ τῶν αἰσθήσεων σύμπαντα λόγον ἀκριβῶς καταμαθόντες ἐπί τι μεῖζον ἕτερον χωρεῖν θεώρημα, καταλιπόντες τὰς αἰσθήσεις ὁπάς, αἱ Χαρρὰν ὀνομάζονται. Τούτων ἐστὶν ὁ ἐπιδόσεις καὶ βελτιώσεις πρὸς ἐπιστήμης ἄκρας ἀνάληψιν ἐσχηκὼς Ἀβραάμ· ὅτε γὰρ μάλιστα ἔγνω, τότε μάλιστα ἀπέγνω ἑαυτόν, ἵνα τοῦ πρὸς ἀλήθειαν ὄντος εἰς ἀκριβῆ γνῶσιν ἔλθῃ. Καὶ πέφυκεν οὕτως ἔχειν· ὁ λίαν καταλαβὼν ἑαυτὸν λίαν ἀπέγνωκε τὴν ἐν πᾶσι τοῦ γενητοῦ σαφῶς προλαβὼν οὐδένειαν, ὁ δ' ἀπογνοὺς ἑαυτὸν γινώσκει τὸν ὄντα.

aperçoit la transcendance divine.[21] Ce souvenir est en réalité oubli de son moi antérieur, renoncement, recueillement extatique, loin du spectacle du monde, par amour de l'essence de Dieu.[22]

Ainsi, la confrontation entre les vues platonisantes sur le Γνῶθι σεαυτόν et les Écritures conduit Philon à repousser les études physiques et à découvrir un rapport entre l'intellect humain et l'Intellect qui régit le monde. Mais ce repli sur soi, loin d'être complaisance à soi-même ou empiètement sur l'au-delà, s'achève en aveu du néant humain et respect religieux de la transcendance divine.

Paris

---

[21] Philon *De sacrificiis Abelis et Caini* 55, éd. A. Méasson (Paris, 1966), p. 120: Πότε οὖν οὐκ ἐπιλήσῃ θεοῦ; Ὅταν μὴ ἐπιλάθῃ σεαυτοῦ· μεμνημένος γὰρ τῆς ἰδίου περὶ πάντα οὐδενείας μεμνήσῃ καὶ τῆς τοῦ θεοῦ περὶ πάντα ὑπερβολῆς.

De somniis I. 212, p. 112: Διὰ τοῦτο καὶ τοὺς μέλλοντας ἱερουργεῖν περιρραίνεσθαι τοῖς λεχθεῖσιν ἐδικαίωσεν, οὐδένα θυσιῶν ἄξιον νομίσας, ὃς μὴ πρότερον ἑαυτὸν ἔγνωκε καὶ τὴν ἀνθρωπίνην οὐδένειαν κατείληφεν, ἐξ ὧν συνεκρίθη στοιχείων τὸ μηδενὸς ἄξιος εἶναι τεκμηράμενος.

Philon *Quis rerum divinarum heres* 29–30, éd. M. Harl (Paris, 1966), p. 180: Τὴν γὰρ οὐδένειαν τὴν ἐμαυτοῦ μετρεῖν ἔμαθον καὶ τὰς ἐν ὑπερβολαῖς ἀκρότητας τῶν σῶν εὐεργεσιῶν περιβλέπεσθαι· καὶ ἐπειδὰν "γῆν καὶ τέφραν" καὶ εἴ τι ἐκβλητότερον ἐμαυτὸν αἴσθωμαι, τηνικαῦτα ἐντυγχάνειν σοι θαρρῶ, ταπεινὸς γεγονώς, καταβεβλημένος εἰς χοῦν, ὅσα εἴς γε τὸ μηδ' ὑφεστάναι δοκεῖν ἀνεστοιχειωμένος. Καὶ τοῦτό μου τὸ πάθος τῆς ψυχῆς ἐστηλογράφησεν ἐν τῷ ἐμῷ μνημείῳ ὁ ἐπίσκοπος Μωυσῆς. "Ἐγγίσας" γάρ φησιν "Ἀβραὰμ εἶπε· νῦν ἠρξάμην λαλῆσαι πρὸς τὸν κύριον, ἐγὼ δέ εἰμι γῆ καὶ σποδός" (Gen. 18:27), ἐπειδὴ τότε καιρὸς ἐντυγχάνειν γένεσιν τῷ πεποιηκότι, ὅτε τὴν ἑαυτῆς οὐδένειαν ἔγνωκεν.

[22] Philon *De somniis* 2. 232, p. 216: Ὅταν μὲν ἐξ ἔρωτος θείου κατασχεθεὶς ὁ νοῦς, συντείνας ἑαυτὸν ἄχρι τῶν ἀδύτων, ὁρμῇ καὶ σπουδῇ πάσῃ χρώμενος προέρχηται, θεοφορούμενος ἐπιλέληστα μὲν τῶν ἄλλων, ἐπιλέληστα δὲ καὶ ἑαυτοῦ, μόνου <δὲ> μέμνηται καὶ ἐξήρτηται τοῦ δορυφορουμένου καὶ θεραπευομένου, ᾧ τὰς ἱερὰς καὶ ἀναφεῖς καθαγιάζων ἀρετὰς ἐκθυμιᾷ. Cf. *Quis rerum divinarum heres* 69–70 et 265 (éd. M. Harl), pp. 198 et 299.

L. CAELIUS FIRMIANUS LACTANTIUS ÜBER DIE GESCHICHTE DES WAHREN GOTTESGLAUBENS

FRITZ WEHRLI

Der Kirchenschriftsteller Laktanz zählt mit Recht nicht unter die grossen Denker der christlichen Antike und wird darum auch von der Forschung im allgemeinen vernachlässigt. Gerade seine theologische Farblosigkeit macht ihn jedoch für den Historiker zum wertvollen Zeugen der bildungsmässigen Voraussetzungen, unter welchen die Christen sich in konstantinischer Zeit auf breiter Front durchzusetzen hatten. Welche Macht damals ausser der Philosophie auch mythologische Spekulationen synkretistischer Art ausübten, soll im Folgenden an einem ausgewählten Beispiel vorgeführt werden.

Dass Laktanz seine Verteidigung des Christentums, die *Divinae Institutiones*, nicht wie seine Vorgänger als knappe Apologie, sondern als umfassendes Lehrbuch gestaltet hat, entspricht einer neuen, systematisierenden Auffassung des Gegenstandes. Der christliche Glaube ist für ihn ein theologisches Wissen, ohne welches das richtige Tun nicht möglich ist, und welches darum wie die Rechtswissenschaft (Lactant. *Div. Inst.* I. I. 12) oder andere Lehrgebiete einer theoretischen Ausbildung, einer *Institutio*, bedarf. Im Gegensatz zu allen Einzeldisziplinen geht es in seiner christlichen Lehre jedoch um die gesamte Lebensführung, und darum tritt er mit derselben auch den Ansprüchen der Philosophie entgegen, welche auf ihre Weise um die Erkenntnis der Wahrheit, um Weisheit und Tugend bemüht ist (Lactant. *Div. Inst.* I. I. I ff. und *passim*). Dabei lässt Laktanz jedoch keinen Zweifel daran aufkommen, dass menschliches Denken aus eigener Kraft zu keiner Einsicht gelangt und Gott als der einzige echte

Lehrmeister die Wahrheit nur in der jüdisch-christlichen Glaubensüberlieferung offenbart hat.[1]

Die *Divinae Institutiones* verdanken ihren Namen indessen nicht allein ihrem Offenbarungscharakter, sondern auch ihrem Inhalt, nämlich Gott als dem vornehmsten Gegenstand aller Erkenntnis. Dass der Mensch zur andächtigen Betrachtung seines Schöpfers, dessen Majestät alle Dinge umfasst und lenkt,[2] bestimmt sei, erkennt Laktanz an seinem aufrechten Gang und dem in die Höhe gerichteten Blick.[3] Den Griechen ist nach seiner Überzeugung diese Erhebung zu Gott versagt, und dem gemäss billigt er ihnen bloss eine irdische Philosophie zu, welche den vornehmsten Gegenstand der Erkenntnis verfehlt und überhaupt keinerlei Gewissheit vermittelt.[4]

Am tiefsten in Unwissenheit befangen sieht er die Epikureer. Ohne dieselben beim Namen zu nennen, macht er sie für die Irrlehre verantwortlich, wonach es keine göttliche Obhut über die Menschen und kein Weiterleben nach dem Tode gebe; die Folge dieser Anschauung sei, dass jene sich der Herrschaft ihrer Triebe überlassen und danach dem ewigen Tode verfallen.[5]

Wie nahe sich dagegen der Platonismus mit christlicher Lehre berührt, gesteht Laktanz nur andeutungsweise ein. Auf die Propheten als Zeugen des wahren Glaubens lässt er wohl in langer

---

[1] Lactant. *Div. Inst.* 1. 1. 5–6: *veritas id est arcanum summi Dei ... ingenio ac propriis sensibus non potest conprehendi ... non est passus hominem Deus lumen sapientiae requirentem diutius errare ac sine ullo laboris effectu vagari per tenebras inextricabiles: aperuit oculos eius aliquando et notionem veritatis munus suum fecit, ut et humanam sapientiam nullam esse monstraret et erranti ac vago viam consequendae immortalitatis ostenderet.*

[2] Lactant. *Div. Inst.* 2. 1. 5: *maiestatem Dei singularis, quae continet regitque omnia.* Diese Formel geht auf Poseidonios zurück, der sie in einer Würdigung der mosaischen Gotteslehre braucht: *FGrH* 87 F 70, 35 und dazu K. Reinhardt, *Poseidonios über Ursprung und Entartung*, Orient und Antike VI (Heidelberg, 1928), p. 9. Über Laktanz und Poseidonios, vgl. unten, pp. 254 ff.

[3] Lactant. *Div. Inst.* 2. 1. 15: *parens enim noster ille unus et solus cum fingeret hominem id est animal intellegens et rationis capax, eum vero ex humo sublevatum ad contemplationem sui artificis erexit.* Folgt Berufung auf Ovid *Met.* 1. 84 ff. Über die Herkunft des Gedankens, vgl. unten.

[4] Lactant. *Div. Inst.* 1. 1. 17: *omissis ergo terrenae huiusce philosophiae auctoribus nihil certi adferentibus adgrediamur viam rectam.*

[5] Lactant. *Div. Inst.* 2. 1. 3: *... dum existimant nulli deo esse nos curae aut post mortem nihil futuros, totos se libidinibus addicunt et dum licere sibi putant, hauriendis voluptatibus sitienter incumbunt, per quas inprudentes in laqueos mortis incurrant.*

doxographischer Aufreihung die philosophischen Vertreter des Monotheismus und darunter Platon folgen (1. 5. 1–28), doch macht er diesem den Vorwurf, er sei bei der blossen Einsicht stehen geblieben, ohne einen Gottesdienst zu begründen.[6] Darin sieht Laktanz aber einen gemeinsamen Irrtum aller Griechen, nämlich dass sie Weisheit und Frömmigkeit von einander trennen und damit beides seiner eigentlichen Erfüllung berauben.[7] Deren Einheit glaubt er nur in der christlichen Offenbarungsweisheit verwirklicht, welche den einen Gott, den Schöpfer und Herrn aller Dinge, als Vater erleben lässt und dadurch seine fromme Verehrung lehrt.[8]

Dass Laktanz seinen ganzen Kampf mit den Waffen der Gegner führt, lässt sich unschwer erkennen und entspricht der *interpretatio Graeca* des christlichen Glaubens durch seine Vorgänger unter den Apologeten.[9] Am nächsten kommt ihm mit derselben Justin, bei welchem wir auch den Gedanken antreffen

---

[6] Lactant. *Div. Inst.* 4. 4. 6: *Deum vero esse patrem eundemque dominum utrique ignoraverunt, tam cultores deorum quam ipsi sapientiae professores, quia aut nihil omnino colendum putaverunt aut religiones falsas adprobaverunt, aut etiamsi vim potestatemque summi Dei intellexerunt, ut Plato, qui ait unum esse fabricatorem mundi Deum, et Marcus Tullius, qui fatetur hominem praeclara quadam condicione a supremo Deo esse generatum, tamen ei debitum cultum tamquam summo patri non reddiderunt, quod erat consequens ac necessarium.* Vgl. *ibid.* 2. 3. 1.

[7] Lactant. *Div. Inst.* 4. 3. 4: *quoniam igitur, ut dixi, philosophia et religio deorum diiuncta sunt longeque discreta, siquidem alii sunt professores sapientiae, per quos utique ad deos non aditur, alii religionis antistites, per quos sapere non discitur, apparet nec illam esse veram sapientiam nec hanc religionem*; vgl. *ibid.* 4. 3. 6 u. 10.

[8] Lactant. *Div. Inst.* 4. 4. 2: *Deus autem, qui unus est, quoniam utramque personam sustinet et patris et domini, et amare eum debemus, quia filii sumus, et timere, quia servi. non potest igitur nec religio a sapientia separari nec sapientia a religione secerni, quia idem Deus est qui intellegi debet, quod est sapientiae, et honorari, quod est religionis.*

[9] Von Einzelheiten sei als Beispiel bloss die symbolische Auslegung angeführt, welche Laktanz dem aufrechten Gang des Menschen gibt (vgl. oben, Anm. 3). Sie stammt aus der hellenistischen Kosmosandacht und ist für diese nicht allein durch die Ovidverse belegt, welche Laktanz zitiert, sondern vor allem auch durch Cicero (*Nat. D.* 2. 56. 140 und *Leg.* 1. 9. 26). Die massgebende Formulierung scheint von Poseidonios zu stammen, vgl. K. Reinhardt, *RE* XXII, col. 714, s.v. "Poseidonios." Die Übernahme vorgeprägten Gedankengutes lässt sich bei Laktanz daran erkennen, dass die fromme Betrachtung sich nicht mehr auf den gestirnten Himmel in seiner Erhabenheit, sondern auf dessen unsichtbaren Schöpfer richtet.

werden, dass der jüdisch-christliche Monotheismus allein schon durch seinen Inspirationscharakter aller griechischen Weisheit überlegen sei. Es wird sich ausserdem zeigen, dass beide Autoren sogar für diese Grundlegung ihres christlichen Selbstverständnisses letzten Endes einem griechischen Theorem verpflichtet sind.

Griechisch ist die Unterscheidung zwischen göttlicher und menschlicher Weisheit, durch welche zunächst lediglich die Demut einer höheren Welt gegenüber Ausdruck erhalten soll. Sie bestimmt jene spätarchaische Novelle vom Becher oder Dreifuss, welcher für den Weisesten bestimmt ist und schliesslich Apollon geweiht wird, weil keiner der Sieben Weisen sich seiner würdig glaubt (Diog. Laert. 1. 27–29). In ähnlichem Sinne legt sich in der platonischen Apologie Sokrates das delphische Orakel, er sei der Weiseste, zurecht, nämlich der Gott meine vielleicht bloss, er allein habe eingesehen, dass alle menschliche Weisheit angesichts derjenigen des Gottes nichts wert sei.[10] Platon zielt mit dieser Anekdote auf seinen Agnostizismus, welcher nur eine unablässige Bemühung um Erkenntnis, φιλοσοφεῖν, gelten lässt, aber keine als dauernden Besitz. Im übrigen kennt er wohl eine höchste, dem Menschen in der Intuition aufleuchtende Einsicht, welche sich als Offenbarung verstehen lässt. Erst Poseidonios hat diese aber der rationalen Erkenntnis gegenübergestellt und damit das Gegensatzpaar geschaffen, welches Laktanz und seinen christlichen Vorgängern als Mittel diente, ihre Offenbarungswahrheit von allem bloss menschlichen Wissen, der *humana sapientia*, abzusetzen.

Unser Hauptzeuge dafür ist Strabo, welcher in enger Anlehnung an Poseidonios Moses als Begründer der jüdischen Theokratie neben andere priesterliche Weise der Frühzeit stellt. Die Ordnung, deren das politische Zusammenleben bedürfe, beruhe auf göttlicher oder menschlicher Autorität; in der Frühzeit hätten aber von den Göttern ausgehende Befehle das höhere Ansehen genossen. Dies zeige die einstige Bedeutung von Dodona und Delphi, die Wahl von Priestern zu Königen sowie die Befragung von Göttern durch Gesetzgeber wie Minos und Lykurg. Unter den Beispielen der nichtgriechischen Welt führt Strabo

[10] Pl. *Ap.* 23a.

ausser Moses die indischen Gymnosophisten, die Magier, Chaldäer, das etruskische Priestertum und andere auf.[11] Dass er mit seiner Beschränkung auf den politischen Gesichtspunkt den Gedanken des Poseidonios nicht in seiner vollen Tragweite gerecht wird, lässt sich seiner Reihe von barbarischen Weisen ablesen, deren Wissen weit über den Bereich des Staatlichen hinausreichte. Was Poseidonios meinte, waren gotterleuchtete Männer im umfassendsten Sinne, jene Vertreter der aussergriechischen Welt, bei welchen Diogenes Laertius (I Proömium) die Anfänge aller Philosophie suchte. Zusammen mit den inspirierten Königen und Orakelinhabern in Hellas vertraten diese für Poseidonios also eine frühe Kulturstufe, auf welcher die Menschheit durch Offenbarung des göttlichen Willens gelenkt wurde, und auf welcher darum Frömmigkeit und sittliches Verhalten ebenso eins waren, wie es sich nach Laktanz beim christlichen Glauben verhält.[12]

Das hier entworfene, übrigens schon in der älteren Ethnographie vorbereitete Idealbild einer barbarischen Urweisheit, in welches auch die Juden einbezogen waren, haben diese in hellenistischer Zeit für ihre Selbstinterpretation aufgegriffen. Dass sie sich dabei aus dem Kreis der übrigen Völker des Ostens herausnahmen und das Hauptgewicht auf den monotheistischen Gedanken legten, ergab sich von selbst. Damit war aber ein Modell der biblischen Offenbarungswahrheit umrissen, welches die

[11] Strabo 16. 2. 38 = *FGrH* 87 F 70 (Poseidonios): τὸ δὲ πρόσταγμα διττόν· ἢ γὰρ παρὰ θεῶν ἢ παρὰ ἀνθρώπων. καὶ οἵ γε ἀρχαῖοι τὸ παρὰ τῶν θεῶν ἐπρέσβευον μᾶλλον, καὶ ἐσέμνυνον· κτλ. dazu, ausser dem Kommentar von Jacoby, E. Norden, "Jahve in hellenistischer Theologie," *Festgabe für A. v. Harnack* (Tübingen, 1921), pp. 292–301; K. Reinhardt, *Poseidonios über Ursprung und Entartung* (Heidelberg, 1928).
Nach dem Ergebnis der hier niedergelegten Quellenuntersuchungen waren Strabos unmittelbare Vorlage die Historien des Poseidonios. Dass dieser in denselben aber von den religionsgeschichtlichen Gedanken seiner Schrift über die Mantik Gebrauch machte, ist mit Recht aus der Übereinstimmung zwischen dem Strabotext und Cicero *De Divinatione* 1. 40. 87 bis 41. 92 geschlossen worden. Bei Cicero ist die Reihe von Belegen vor allem an Namen von Priesterkönigen reicher als bei Strabo, was durch seine unmittelbare Benützung des gemeinsamen Quellenwerkes zu erklären ist (Reinhardt, *ibid.*, p. 24).
[12] Oben, Anm. 7; vgl. *FGrH* 87 F 70, 37 Strabo nach Poseidonios über die Juden der Frühzeit als δικαιοπραγοῦντες καὶ θεοσεβεῖς ὡς ἀληθῶς ὄντες. Nach Diogenes Laertius 1. 6 gehört zur Lehre der Magier θεραπεία θεῶν und δικαιοσύνη. Als Tugenden der Römer preist Poseidonios F 59 εὐσέβεια und δικαιοσύνη, vgl. K. Reinhardt, *ibid.*, p. 23.

christlichen Apologeten und in ihrem Gefolge Laktanz der griechischen Philosophie entgegenhalten konnten. Wir finden dasselbe z.B. in der einleitenden Bekehrungsgeschichte von Justins *Dialogus*. Nach einer kritischen Unterhaltung vor allem über die platonische Gottes- und Seelenlehre werden hier die alttestamentlichen Propheten als die Wahrheitskünder einer frühen Vorzeit gefeiert, welche von heiligem Geist erfüllt ohne das Mittel dialektischer Beweisführung alles einem Philosophen anstehende Wissen gelehrt hätten.[13]

Dass diese Offenbarungstradition bis in seine eigene Gegenwart reiche, wird zum leitenden Gesichtspunkt für Laktanz, dessen Darstellung von seiner zeitgenössischen Auseinandersetzung mit dem griechischen Polytheismus bestimmt ist. Um diesen als Verblendung, ja als Folge schuldhafter Preisgabe ursprünglicher Einheit erscheinen zu lassen, bedient er sich dabei eines eigentümlichen Mythologems synkretistischen Ursprungs, für welches allem Anschein nach schon von den religionsgeschichtlichen Theorien des Poseidonios Gebrauch gemacht war. Dieser muss die ausserhalb der griechischen Welt erhaltene Autorität inspirierter Weisheit als Nachwirken einer Urzeit verstanden haben, in welcher die Menschen dem göttlichen Willen noch vollkommener nachlebten und die er mit dem Goldenen Zeitalter Hesiods gleichsetzte. Wenn er nach dem Bericht Senecas meinte, damals hätten die Weisen geherrscht,[14] und damit das bekannte idealstaatliche Postulat Platons erfüllt sein liess, so dachte er sich wohl auch die Machtausübung seiner Regenten ähnlich derjenigen

---

[13] Iustinus *Dialogus cum Tryphone* 7: ἐγένοντό τινες πρὸ πολλοῦ χρόνου πάντων τούτων τῶν νομιζομένων φιλοσόφων παλαιότεροι, μακάριοι καὶ δίκαιοι καὶ θεοφιλεῖς, θείῳ πνεύματι λαλήσαντες.... προφήτας δὲ αὐτοὺς καλοῦσιν. οὗτοι μόνοι τὸ ἀληθὲς καὶ εἶδον καὶ ἐξεῖπον ἀνθρώποις, ... συγγράμματα δὲ αὐτῶν ἔτι καὶ νῦν διαμένει, καὶ ἔστιν ἐντυχόντα τούτοις πλεῖστον ὠφεληθῆναι καὶ περὶ ἀρχῶν καὶ περὶ τέλους καὶ ὧν χρὴ εἰδέναι τὸν φιλόσοφον, πιστεύσαντα ἐκείνοις. οὐ γὰρ μετὰ ἀποδείξεως πεποίηνται τότε τοὺς λόγους, ἅτε ἀνωτέρω πάσης ἀποδείξεως ὄντες ἀξιόπιστοι μάρτυρες τῆς ἀληθείας. Den gleichen Gedanken wie Justin, dass die Offenbarungswahrheit keiner dialektischen Beweisführung bedürfe und dadurch ihre Überlegenheit gegenüber der Philosophie an den Tag lege, spricht Laktanz *Div. Inst.* 3. 1. 11 aus: *nec enim decebat ut cum Deus ad hominem loqueretur argumentis assereret suas voces, tamquam aliter fides ei non haberetur, sed ut oportuit locutus est tamquam rerum omnium maximus iudex, cuius est non argumentari, sed pronuntiare.*

[14] Sen. *Ep.* 90. 5: *penes sapientes fuisse regnum Posidonius iudicat.*

in Platons *Politeia*. Auf ein vergleichbares Verhältnis des willigen Gehorsams, bei welchem den Regierten die letzten Einsichten vorenthalten blieben, deutet jedenfalls Senecas Referat, jene Weisen seien mit blossen Ratschlägen und dem Aufweisen des Nützlichen oder Schädlichen ausgekommen;[15] auf eine theoretische Begründung ihrer Anweisungen konnten sie offenbar verzichten. Dass sie selbst sich durch ein Ideenwissen im platonischen Sinne hätten leiten lassen, ist für Poseidonios ausgeschlossen, seinen religionsgeschichtlichen Anschauungen wäre dagegen eine durch Offenbarung gewonnene Erfahrung gemäss, welche sich mit jenem immerhin vergleichen liesse. Ausserdem ist für die von den Göttern ausgehenden Befehle, welche Poseidonios denjenigen menschlichen Ursprungs gegenüberstellt (oben, p. 255, Anm. 11) und welche keiner Zeit angemessener sind als dem Goldenen Weltalter mit seiner Gottnähe, nur die Form der Inspiration denkbar.

Was sich nun bei Laktanz findet, ist nichts anderes als die monotheistische Weiterbildung solcher Auslegungen von Hesiods Weltaltermythos. Gemäss seinem Axiom, dass sittliche Vollkommenheit untrennbar an den wahren Gottesglauben gebunden sei, lehrt er, unter der Herrschaft des Kronos hätten auch die Griechen in jenem gelebt, der darauf folgende Glaubensverlust habe dann jedoch Zwietracht und Gewalt nach sich gezogen und dadurch das Goldene Zeitalter beendet.[16]

---

[15] Seneca a.O.: *hi* (sc. *sapientes*) *continebant manus et infirmiorem a validioribus tuebantur, suadebant dissuadebantque et utilia atque inutilia monstrabant.* Diese Beschreibung ist auf den Gegensatz zur philosophischen Argumentierung angelegt, durch welchen Justin und Laktanz alle Offenbarung charakterisieren (oben, Anm. 13).

[16] Lactant. *Div. Inst.* 4. 1. 1: *unius saeculi stultitia religiones varias suscipientis deosque multos esse credentis in tantam subito ignorationem sui ventum est, ut ablata ex oculis veritate neque religio Dei veri neque humanitatis ratio teneretur, hominibus non in caelo summum bonum quarentibus, sed in terra, quam ob causam profecto saeculorum veterum mutata felicitas est.*
5. 5. 2: *a Saturni temporibus, quae illi vocant aurea, repetunt exempla iustitiae narrantque in quo statu fuerit humana vita, dum illa in terra moraretur. quod quidem non pro poetica fictione, sed pro vero habendum est. Saturno enim regnante, nondum deorum cultibus institutis nec adhuc illa gente ad divinitatis opinionem consecrata, Deus utique colebatur. et ideo non erant neque dissensiones neque inimicitiae neque bella,* etc.
Die geschlossenste Darstellung enthält die *Epitome* 20: *merito igitur poetae commutatum esse aureum saeculum memorant, quod fuerit regnante Saturno. nulli enim tunc dii colebantur, sed unum et solum Deum noverant.*

Wo Laktanz die unmittelbaren Vorlagen für dieses Mythologem fand, lehrt seine wiederholte Berufung auf sibyllinische und hermetische Texte. Von diesen ist zunächst seine eigentümliche Vorstellung bestimmt, der Bilderkult, zu welchem die Griechen vom wahren Gottesglauben abfielen, habe nicht beliebigen Heidengöttern, sondern dem verstorbenen Kronos (Saturnus) und dessen Vater Uranos gegolten. Dass diese und ihre Nachkommen, vor allem Zeus (Juppiter) in Wahrheit gewöhnliche Könige der Urzeit gewesen seien, nicht wie Hesiod lehre unsterbliche Götter, legt Laktanz zunächst unter Berufung auf die ʽΙερὰ ἀναγραφή des Euhemeros in ihrer ennianischen Übersetzung umständlich dar.[17] Zur Bekräftigung zieht er auch Ciceros *De Natura Deorum* heran;[18] das jedoch, woran ihm allein lag, nämlich die monotheistische Weiterbildung von Euhemeros' Göttertheorie, fand er in den *Sibyllinen* und *Hermetica*. Den Hauptbeleg dafür bilden die von ihm zitierten Verse, in welchen eine Sibylle den Hellenen zum Vorwurf macht, den Abbildern toter Könige Opfer darzubringen und sich vom Antlitz des einen grossen Gottes abzuwenden.[19] Dass mit den toten Königen hier tatsächlich Uranos und seine Nachkommen bis auf Zeus herab gemeint sind, gibt ein anderes, ebenfalls von Laktanz angeführtes sibyllinisches Verspaar durch die Erwähnung des berühmten Zeusgrabes in Kreta zu erkennen,[20] denn dieses bildete für

postquam se terrenis ac fragilibus subiugaverunt colentes ligna et aera et lapides, commutatio saeculi facta est usque ad ferrum. amissa enim Dei notitia et uno illo vinculo humanae societatis abrupto vastare se invicem, praedari ac debellare coeperunt.

[17] Die Hauptstelle ist Lactant. *Div. Inst.* 1. 11. 33 ff.; ein grosses Stück des lateinischen Quellenwerkes wird im Wortlaut 1. 14. 2 ff. wiedergegeben. Aus der *Epitome* is damit *cap.* 13 zu vergleichen.

[18] Lactant. *Div. Inst.* 1. 15. 5; 1. 17. 2 u.a.

[19] *Oracula Sibyllina* 3. 545 ff. bei Lactant. *Div. Inst.* 1. 15. 14: *Graeci ... admirati eos* (sc. *reges*) *et susceperunt primi sacra illorum et universis gentibus tradiderunt. ob hanc vanitatem Sibylla sic eos increpat*
ʽΕλλὰς δὴ, τί πέποιθας ἐπ' ἀνδράσιν ἡγεμόνεσσιν
θνητοῖς, οἷς οὐκ ἔστι φυγεῖν θανάτοιο τελευτήν;
πρὸς τί τε δῶρα μάταια καταφθιμένοισι πορίζεις
θύεις τ' εἰδώλοις; τίς τοι πλάνον ἐν φρεσὶ θῆκεν
ταῦτα τελεῖν προλιποῦσα θεοῦ μεγάλοιο πρόσωπον;

[20] *Oracula Sibyllina* 8. 47 ff. bei Lactant. *Div. Inst.* 1. 11. 46: *et sepulchrum eius* (sc. *Iovis*) *est in Creta in oppido Gnosso ... inque sepulchro eius est inscriptum antiquis litteris Graecis ZAN KPONOY id est latine Iuppiter Saturni. hoc certe non poetae tradunt, sed antiquarum rerum scriptores.*

Euhemeros das wichtigste Beweisstück seiner Theorie. Bei ihrer monotheistischen Auslegung konnte man von der immerhin nicht ganz abwegigen Frage ausgehen, welcher Glaube denn vor Einführung des Bilderkultes bei den Griechen geherrscht habe. Vor allem jedoch liess sich die von altersher geläufige Verknüpfung des Kronos mit dem Goldenen Weltalter auswerten, denn dass damals die Menschheit nach Meinung des Poseidonios im Geiste der Weisheit gelenkt wurde, bedeutete nach christlicher Interpretation die Herrschaft des wahren Gottesglaubens. Unter den Bezugnahmen auf die hermetische Literatur ist bei Laktanz besonders das Zitat aus einer Offenbarung des Trismegistos aufschlussreich, wonach dieser Uranos und Kronos als Männer von hervorragendem Wissen, mit welchem er selber verwandt sei, bezeichnet haben soll.[21] Für die hier behauptete Verwandtschaft liesse sich die homerische Genealogie von Hermes-Trismegistos heranziehen, und mit dem Wissen des Uranos und Kronos muss die dem Goldenen Zeitalter verliehene Gotteserkenntnis gemeint sein. Es sieht also aus, als ob die beiden Götter für den Verfasser des Traktates zu jenen Weisen geworden wären, von welchen Poseidonios die Menschen der seligen Urzeit geleitet sein liess. Damit wäre aber der Beweis erbracht, dass dessen Auslegung des hesiodischen Weltaltermythos auch von Autoren der *Hermetica* in euhemeristische Konstruktionen einbezogen wurde, Laktanz bei solchen also das gleiche Mythologem wie in den *Sibyllinen* wenigstens in den allgemeinen Umrissen vorfand. Für seine christliche Deutung des Goldenen Zeitalters benützte er die beiden Schriftengruppen denn auch in ziemlich gleichem Masse, während ihm die Dokumente des echten Euhemerismus (oben, p. 258) nur als Ergänzung dienten.

Wie erklärten sich nun aber Laktanz und seine Gewährsleute die Möglichkeit eines monotheistischen Glaubens in der griechi-

---

quae adeo vera sunt, ut ea Sibyllinis versibus confirmentur, qui sunt tales:
δαίμονας ἀψύχους, νεκύων εἴδωλα καμόντων,
ὧν Κρήτη καύχημα τάφους ἡ δύσμορος ἕξει,
θρησκεύουσα θρόνωσιν ἀναισθήτοις νεκύεσσιν.
21 Lactant. *Div. Inst.* I. II. 61: *apparet ergo non ex caelo esse natum* (sc. *Saturnum), quod fieri non potest, sed ex eo homine cui nomen Urano fuit. quod esse verum Trismegistus auctor est, qui cum diceret admodum paucos extitisse in quibus esset perfecta doctrina, in his Uranum Saturnum Mercurium nominavit cognatos suos.*

schen Frühzeit? In den *Institutiones* 2. 13. 9 ff. erzählt er nach
einem kurzen Bericht über die Sintflut und Noahs Trunkenheit,
welche zur Segnung Sems und Verstossung Chams, des Ahnherrn
der von Gott abgefallenen Kanaaniter, führte, die Geschichte
eines zweiten, der Bibel unbekannten Glaubensverlustes. Über-
völkerung und Mangel hätten einen Teil der Nachkommen
Japhets zur Auswanderung getrieben, und in die weite Welt verstreut seien diese zu den verschiedenen Formen der Götterver-
ehrung übergegangen, welche von den Heiden geübt würden.
Nach einer skizzenhaften Aufzählung derselben, welche sich wie
der flüchtige Auszug einer religionsgeschichtlichen Darstellung
ausnimmt und an letzter Stelle auch der Apotheosen von Königen
gedenkt,[22] bricht Laktanz 2. 13. 13 mit der Bemerkung *nunc ad
principium mundi revertamur* ab, um eine noch genauere Erklärung für die Enstehung des heidnischen Irrglaubens nachzuholen.
Was 2. 14. 1 folgt, ist die Erzählung, Gott habe einst Engel auf
Erden geschickt, um die Menschen vor dem Versucher, *Diabolus*,
zu schützen. Dieser habe sie aber zu Fall gebracht, so dass sie
sich mit sterblichen Frauen versündigten. Darauf seien sie mit
den unreinen Geistern, welche aus dieser Verbindung hervorgegangen, als Dämonen zum Gefolge des Versuchers geworden,
welcher darum von Trismegistos *Daemoniarches* genannt werde.[23]
Was folgt, ist eine Schilderung des bis zur Gegenwart des Autors
dauernden Treibens dieser Dämonen. Sie massen sich nach derselben kultische Verehrung an, suchen die Menschen mit Krank-
heit und Irrsinn heim, sie haben sie aber auch in die magischen
Künste, Beschwörungen und Weissagungen aller Art eingeführt,
ja auf ihre Anweisung geht zurück, dass Abbilder verstorbener
Könige hergestellt und diesen göttliche Ehren dargebracht werden.[24]

---

[22] Lactant. *Div. Inst.* 2. 13. 12: ... *donec processu temporum potentissimis
regibus templa et simulacra fecerunt eaque victimis et odoribus colere insti-
tuerunt. sic aberrantes a notitia Dei gentes esse coeperunt.*
[23] Lactant. *Div. Inst.* 2. 14. 5: *ita duo genera daemonum facta sunt,
unum caeleste, alterum terrenum. hi sunt immundi spiritus, malorum quae
geruntur auctores, quorum idem diabolus est princeps. unde illum Trismegistus daemoniarchen vocat.*
[24] Lactant. *Div. Inst.* 2. 16. 3: *hi sunt qui fingere imagines et simulacra
docuerunt, qui ut hominum mentes a cultu veri Dei averterent, effictos
mortuorum regum vultus et ornatos exquisita pulchritudine statui consecrari-
que fecerunt et illorum sibi nomina quasi personas aliquas induerunt.*

Dieses Mythologem hat eine reiche Vorgeschichte, an welche hier nur in aller Knappheit erinnert werden soll. Sie beginnt im 1. Buch Moses 6: 1–4 mit jener rätselhaften, thematisch beziehungslos in ihrer Umgebung stehenden Erzählung von den Söhnen Gottes, welche zur Zeit Noahs, als die Menschen sich auf Erden zu mehren begannen, deren Töchter zu Weibern nahmen und mit ihnen die Nephilim, von altersher berühmte Riesen zeugten. Näher an den Bericht des Laktanz führen die Apokryphen heran, da sie wie dieser statt von den Söhnen Gottes von seinen Engeln sprechen sowie über ihr und ihrer Söhne Tun auf Erden berichten.[25] Was uns von diesem interessiert, ist die Anleitung der Frauen, heilkräftige Pflanzen und Zaubermittel zu gebrauchen, denn daraus wird offensichtlich das magische Blendwerk, mit welchem die Dämonen bei Laktanz die Menschen in Verwirrung setzen.

Anderseits unterscheidet sich die Darstellung bei Laktanz sowie seinen hermetischen Vorlagen von den Apokryphen durch die Ausrichtung auf die eigene Gegenwart. Seine Dämonen sind nicht irgendwelche Mächte der mythologischen Überlieferung, sondern die Götter des von ihm bekämpften heidnischen Glaubens. Was er von ihrem Wirken sagt, deckt sich zum guten Teil mit der griechisch-römischen Dämonenlehre, nur dass diese sie als göttliche Wesen niederer Art von den grossen, durch die Dichtung berühmten Gottheiten unterscheidet. Laktanz setzt sich mit jener Theorie[26] denn auch unter Erwähnung Hesiods und Platons (*Div. Inst.* 2. 14. 7–8) auseinander; die von derselben gelehrte Funktion der Dämonen, zwischen Göttern und Menschen zu vermitteln, fällt für ihn natürlich weg, und überdies hält er sie für ausnahmslos schlecht.

Verwirrend ist an seiner Darstellung des Abfalls vom wahren Glauben vor allem, dass die Dämonen nicht nur selbst zu Kultinhabern werden, sondern überdies die Verehrung der toten Könige einführen. Der damit hereingezogene Euhemerismus ist mit der Anerkennung von göttlichen Wesen noch so zweifelhafter

---

[25] Henoch 1: 6–36 und Buch der Jubiläen 4: 22 ff. bei E. Kautzsch, *Die Apokryphen und Pseudepigraphen des Alten Testaments* II (Tübingen, 1900).
[26] Als ihre Hauptzeugnisse seien genannt: Pl. *Symp.* 202e ff.; Plut. *De def. or.*; Porph. *Abst.* 2. 36.

Natur seinem Wesen nach unvereinbar, weil durch ihn der Götter-
glaube schlechthin aufgehoben wird. Laktanz hat den inneren
Widerspruch seiner Erzählung denn auch selber empfunden und
ihn durch den Kunstgriff zu überwinden versucht, die Dämonen
hätten sich die Namen der Könige, deren Kult sie veranlasst, selbst
angeeignet.[27] Dies schliesst natürlich die Übernahme ihrer Verehrung in sich, hebt dadurch aber auch die ganze euhemeristische Kritik am Bilderkult aus den Angeln.

Durch den Versuch, widerstrebende Motivreihen zusammenzu-
zwingen, lässt sich nun auch der schon erwähnte Bruch in der
Erzählung *Institutiones* 2. 13. 13 verstehen. Ihre erste Hälfte,
welche von der Auswanderung der Nachkommen Japhets handelt, fände einen sinnvollen Abschluss, wenn der Glaubensverlust
einfach durch menschliche Einsichtslosigkeit und ohne dämoni-
sche Verführung erfolgen würde. Der sich anschliessende, weit
zurückgreifende Bericht über die Entstehung der Dämonen und
ihr verderbliches Wirken schafft ausser den dargelegten Wider-
sprüchen auch chronologische Ungereimtheiten. Obwohl die Dämonen schon in der Urzeit (*Div. Inst.* 2. 13. 13) zum Gefolge des
Verführers werden, finden sie ihre Opfer doch erst viele Genera-
tionen nach Japhet, bleiben sie also entsprechend lang beschäfti-
gungslos, und infolge der Beschränkung auf die heidnische Welt
gelangt dann ihr Wirken nicht zu jener Universalität, die es für
den Glauben hat. Die Dämonologie vermag wohl, alle Anfech-
tungen der Gegenwart zu deuten, wie sie von den Apologeten und
zahlreichen anderen Autoren gebraucht wird, aber nicht, die Entstehung des heidnischen Kultes als Glied einer langen Abfolge
von Geschehnissen plausibel zu machen; ganz unvereinbar ist sie
vollends mit euhemeristischen Erklärungen.

Dass Laktanz für die dargelegte Klitterung allein verantwortlich sei, ist damit nicht erwiesen. Er zitiert zwar gewöhnlich
für die euhemeristische Erklärung des Bilderkultes die *Sibyllinen*
und für seine Dämonologie hermetische Schriften, aber vollständig ist diese Trennung bei ihm nicht. Wie wir sahen, beruft
er sich auf Trismegistos auch für die Behauptung, Uranos und
Kronos seien Männer von hoher Einsicht gewesen (oben, p.
259), und in *Div. Inst.* 2. 16. 1 führt er in dämonologischem

---

[27] Lactant. *Div. Inst.* 2. 16. 3, vgl. oben, p. 260, Anm. 24.

Zusammenhang eine Verurteilung magischer Kunst durch die erythreische Sibylle an. Es wäre auch seltsam, wenn zwischen den beiden Schriftengruppen, welche eine wie die andere den Kampf gegen das Heidentum durch Berufung auf inspirierte Vertreter des Feindes führten, kein Austausch statt gefunden hätte. Jedenfals lässt sich die von Laktanz vorgetragene Geschichte der frühen Menschheit in eine gemeinsame Tradition verschiedener Literaturgattungen einordnen, welche nicht nur das Geben und Nehmen mythologisch-spekulativer Motive, sondern auch ihre sorglos lockere Kombination zuliess.

In direkter Beziehung steht die alttestamentliches und griechisches Sagengut zusammenschliessende Darstellung des Laktanz zu jenen *Sibyllinen*, welche ebenfalls Noah und Kronos als Glieder einer einheitlichen Generationenabfolge behandeln. Die vollständigste von ihnen, Buch 1. 1–324 führt von der Weltschöpfung über Adam und Eva bis zum Erscheinen des Gottessohnes auf Erden und lässt das sechste, goldene Weltalter mit der Herrschaft des Kronos unmittelbar auf die grosse Flut folgen (283 ff.). Das Bruchstück einer Variante dieser Aufreihung findet sich in Buch 3. 97–217, wo die Zeit des Kronos als zehnte Epoche seit der Flut an diejenige des babylonischen Turmbaus angeschlossen ist. Wir haben für die *Sibyllinen* mit einer grossen Anzahl solch kunstlos gefügter Schöpfungen zu rechnen, welche Gottes strafendes und erlösendes Walten in der Geschichte der Menschheit vor Augen führen. Laktanz war von der gleichen eschatologischen Gesamtvorstellung bestimmt wie die anonymen Vertreter dieser Literatur, er griff aus ihrer Thematik aber nur die Teile heraus, welche er für sein Vorhaben brauchte, nämlich aus dem einstigen Abfall der Heiden vom wahren Glauben die Bedrängnisse seiner eigenen Zeit zu deuten.

Zürich

PTOLEMY'S
VITA ARISTOTELIS REDISCOVERED

INGEMAR DÜRING

In a discussion at the Fondation Hardt[1] Professor Richard Walzer reminded classical scholars and historians of philosophy that they largely ignore the fact that Arabic translations of hitherto unknown Greek texts are becoming known in steadily increasing numbers, either through editions of the Arabic texts or, more often, because more detailed information about existing manuscripts is now available. The following example well illustrates his point.

Some twelve years ago I attempted to collect a number of facts transmitted to us in nine late epitomes of a *Vita Aristotelis*, two Greek, one Latin, two Syriac, and four Arabic *Vitae*. I concluded that these epitomes were extracts from a *Vita* written by a certain Ptolemy. Having examined the evidence and the solutions reached by other scholars I came to the result which I summarize here.[2] The author is possibly identical with the Neo-Platonic Ptolemy mentioned by Iamblichus, Proclus, and Priscianus.[3] The book was dedicated to Gallus, presumably a Roman of high standing and a contemporary phil-Aristotelian. Ptolemy's book contained a biography, numerous aphorisms and anecdotes referring to Aristotle, the text of Aristotle's Will, and a catalogue of Aristotle's writings. The biography has a clear tendency: it is a glorification of Aristotle,[4] based on some typical Neo-Platonic

---

[1] *Porphyre*, Entretiens Fondation Hardt XII, 1965 (Geneva, 1966), p. 275.

[2] For further details, see my *Aristotle in the Ancient Biographical Tradition*, Studia Graeca et Latina Gothoburgensia V (Göteborg, 1957), pp. 208–246, abbreviated hereafter as *Biogr. Trad.*

[3] The references in V. Rose, *De Aristotelis librorum ordine et auctoritate commentatio* (Berlin, 1854), p. 45.

[4] I quote here *Biogr. Trad.*, pp. 470 f.

conceptions. Aristotle is called δῖος Ἀριστοτέλης. He was entrusted to Plato in compliance with an oracle of the god in Delphi. He made an extraordinary impression on Plato, and when Plato went to Sicily Aristotle was deputized as head of the Academy. He was held in great honor by Philip and Alexander and was very influential in political affairs, "using philosphy as an instrument." [5] He dissuaded Alexander from attacking Persia, telling him that the omens were unfavorable. He was great as a benefactor both of individuals and cities. The inhabitants of Stagira honored him in many ways after his death. They believed that "their coming to the place where Aristotle's remains were buried would purify their minds." We are told that a swarm of bees was found around the urn containing Aristotle's ashes.

Although Ptolemy's biography contains much fictitious material of a clearly Neo-Platonic character, it cannot be denied [6] that it is a scholarly work, based on extensive investigations and a thorough knowledge of the Hellenistic biographical tradition. Of particular interest is the Arabic text of Aristotle's Will, [7] since we can compare the Greek and the Arabic text paragraph by paragraph. As a matter of fact, the Arabic text of the Will is in certain respects superior to that given by Diogenes. According to my opinion this shows that Ptolemy copied Andronicus' version of the Will. [8] Another important fact is that Ptolemy in his catalogue of Aristotle's writings gives a list of the treatises included in Andronicus' edition which we can check with the arrangement of these treatises in our best mediaeval manuscripts. [9] In sum, I concluded that Ptolemy used Andronicus' book for his account of the Will and for his catalogue of Aristotle's writings, and that he thoroughly searched the Hellenistic biographical tradition in order to find material for achieving his purpose: a glorification of Aristotle.

At the *Fourth Symposium Aristotelicum* held at Göteborg in August 1966, Professor J. Owens gave me a letter from Professor Muhsin Mahdi of the Department of Oriental Studies in the

[5] Cf. *Vita Marciana* 15, *Biogr. Trad.*, p. 99.
[6] See further my remarks, *Biogr. Trad.*, p. 471.
[7] I quote *Biogr. Trad.*, p. 470.
[8] *Biogr. Trad.*, p. 470; cf. my *Aristoteles* (Heidelberg, 1966), p. 14.
[9] *Biogr. Trad.*, p. 242.

University of Chicago. Professor Mahdi had found an Arabic manuscript of the *Vita* in codex Ayasofya, Istanbul, No. 4833, folios 10a–18a.[10] It has been possible to acquire a microfilm of this manuscript. My colleague Bernhard Lewin has read the microfilm and has given me the following information about its contents:

The title of the *Vita* is "This is the treatise of Ptolemy, containing the Will of Aristotle, the catalogue of his writings, and part of his biography, dedicated to Gallus."

In the late Arabic tradition the author is called Ptolemy-al-garīb, i.e., "the unknown Ptolemy, or the Stranger."[11] The surname occurs for the first time in the *Fihrist* (= Bibliography) of Ibn an-Nadīm,[12] completed in the year 938. A reasonable explanation is that Ibn an-Nadim wished to distinguish this Ptolemy from the famous author of the *Almagest* and that he did not know anything about him.[13]

Ptolemy introduces his work with a dedicatory letter to Gallus which shows that this friend or patron of his was an amateur:

Remembering what you have said to me, namely that you have need of a book containing [the titles of] the books of Aristotle, I should like immediately to point out to you what has been written about that [subject] by Andronicus from the city of Rhodes. You have asked me to write a book as concise and explanatory as possible about [this subject]. I have therefore thought [it useful] to write this book for you and to concentrate upon the purpose of [describing] Aristotle and what he has said. I have tried to avoid causing bewilderment, because, in doing so, I thought it to be a merit [i.e., the best way to meet your wish], since you are a man different from those who have a thorough knowledge of the writings of Aristotle. I also wish to stress the facts he [tells us] in his books.[14]

In the subsequent section some words are, according to Professor Lewin, almost illegible. The author proceeds to say as follows:

As to your opinion that the disposition (?) of this book is something that you yourself wish to judge (?) [I should like to point out] that the

[10] Mahdi has described the manuscript in his edition of al-Farabi's *Philosophy of Aristotle* (Beirut, 1961), pp. 25 ff.
[11] *Biogr. Trad.*, p. 209.
[12] *Biogr. Trad.*, pp. 193–196.
[13] *Biogr. Trad.*, pp. 209–211.
[14] Cf. *Diog. Laert.* 3. 47 and 10. 29.

order of the books of Aristotle is given in the books [themselves]. This is quite evident, and the reader need not accept my word about it without realizing [the fact] for himself. For the order of the sciences forming the subjects of the books is obvious [even] to an ignoramus, to say nothing of those who have [real] knowledge and insight into how [the sciences] follow one upon another. Quite contrary to what some people maintain, the sciences are separate branches of knowledge and do not follow upon one another [haphazardly]. If this [method] is suitable for the study of Plato, as many people of a [certain] body of philosophers maintain [fol. 11a], it is even more appropriate with regard to the writings of Aristotle.

It is a reasonable guess that Ptolemy refers to the proper order of Aristotle's writings in Andronicus' book Περὶ πίνακος τῶν 'Αριστοτέλους συγγραμμάτων.[15] It is less probable that he refers to the prolegomena used in the Neo-Platonic schools as introductions to the study of Aristotle's writings since the prolegomena that we possess,[16] are of much later date than our Ptolemy, who presumably wrote his book in the middle of the third century.

So far the dedicatory letter to Gallus poses no serious problems. The author begins by acknowledging his indebtedness to Andronicus, clearly stating that Andronicus has written a book containing a catalogue of the books of Aristotle. What follows now is, however, baffling.

You will realize the truth of what I say about the order of the books and know that this book is written by me with complete care, [further] that it is a unique book and that I have not asked anybody for help [or consulted any other book] in order to [arrange] the order. That is to say that the book of Andronicus has not been at my disposal.

In my opinion this cannot be true. It cannot be disputed[17] that the text of Aristotle's Will transmitted to us in the Arabic tradition and now found in codex Ayasofya 4833 differs from the text transmitted from Hermippus by Diogenes Laertios. In introducing the text of the Will, Ibn-abi-Usaibi'a expressly states: "Ptolemy says in his book to Gallus on the life of Aris-

---

[15] *Biogr. Trad.*, pp. 420–425. Theoretically it is possible that Ptolemy knew a book by Adrastos of Aphrodisias, Alexander's teacher, with the title Περὶ τῆς τάξεως τῶν 'Αριστοτέλους συγγραμμάτων or τῆς 'Αριστοτέλους φιλοσοφίας. But, apart from the title, we know absolutely nothing of this book; cf. *Biogr. Trad.*, pp. 242–243.

[16] *Biogr. Trad.*, pp. 444–450.

[17] See my discussion, *Biogr. Trad.*, pp. 219–221, 238–241.

totle: When Aristotle was about to die, he wrote his Will which we now communicate." There can be no doubt that Ptolemy got the text of the Will from Andronicus, not from Hermippus. Professor Lewin suggests a possible solution, namely, that the Arabic translator made certain additions to Ptolemy's dedicatory letter. Mr. Lewin says that it is not uncommon in Arabic literature for an author to claim that he has used no books or authorities as sources even in cases where we can check that he presents a literal translation of an existing Greek original.

Ptolemy proceeds:

> Therefore, if you now possess this book written by me, you must not give up trying to get that one [i.e., the book written by Andronicus]. You must not wonder that in the book of Andronicus about one thousand (sic!) sayings are recorded, whereas I record less [than that].

It seems to me extremely improbable that Andronicus' book contained a collection of aphorisms and anecdotes. Ibn-abi-Usaibi'a, however, transmits from al-Mubaššir [18] a large collection which is now found also in Ayasofya 4833.

Ptolemy continues:

> The reason is that I prefer to record the treatises ascribed to Aristotle and those ascribed to Theophrastus, the number of which is not small.[19] To begin with I shall give a brief account of the biography and history of Aristotle. Then I shall recount his Will which he made at the moment of his death, as it has been related to us, because you have asked for it. Then I shall record the catalogue of his books except those which are to be considered as derived from others, since [enumerating them] would be wearisome to you.[20] If you want [me to enumerate them], I shall not fail to undertake it for you, even if you are absent from me,[21] and to write to you and then teach you [about them] when we meet again.

---

[18] See *Biogr. Trad.*, p. 221.

[19] In this sentence I see an indication that Ptolemy regarded the Catalogue as the most important part of his book. The excellent *Index generalis* of Andronicus, contained in his *Vita*, in my opinion, definitely proves that Ptolemy knew and reproduced Andronicus' Πίναξ. Cf. *Biogr. Trad.*, pp. 244–245.

[20] It is certain that Andronicus discussed some writings ascribed to Aristotle which he considered inauthentic, *Biogr. Trad.*, p. 91. It is possible that his book contained a list of pseudo-Aristotelian writings. In the texts preserved to us a list of pseudepigrapha is found in the *Vita Hesychii* Nos. 188–197, *Biogr. Trad.*, pp. 88–89.

[21] I surmise that Ptolemy collected his material in the libraries of Alexandria and that his friend Gallus resided in Rome.

After this dedicatory letter follows the text of the biography, the Will, the aphorisms, and the catalogue of Aristotle's writings, fol. 11a–18a. The text is word for word almost identical with that reproduced by Ibn-abi-Usaibi'a and translated into English (except the aphorisms), *Biogr. Trad.*, pp. 213–231. In my comments on Usaibi'a's version of Ptolemy's *Vita* I have repeatedly stressed the fact that Ptolemy must have had a thorough knowledge of the Hellenistic tradition about Aristotle.[22]

It appears from my survey of the Arabic tradition[23] that we have three main sources: al-Mubaššir, al-Qifti, and Ibn-abi-Usaibi'a. Their common source is probably a translation or summary of Ptolemy's book.[24] Whether this translation was made by the famous Ishāq ibn Hunayn is an open question.[25] But, thanks to the rediscovery of the Arabic original of Ptolemy's *Vita*, it will now be possible to find out whether the language of this *Vita* agrees with the language in translations which can with certainty be ascribed to Hunayn. It is possible that Professor Lewin will undertake such an investigation and provide an edition of the text of the *Vita* in Ayasofya 4833. But it would, of course, be of great help if a search could be made for other manuscripts of this *Vita*.

University of Göteborg

---

[22] See especially *Biogr. Trad.*, pp. 232–237.
[23] *Biogr. Trad.*, pp. 189–246.
[24] *Biogr. Trad.*, p. 209.
[25] *Biogr. Trad.*, p. 190.

DE NOVO PINDARI FRAGMENTO ARABICO

MARIANUS PLEZIA

Qui ephemerides orientalibus litteris illustrandis destinatas diligenter evolvunt, noverunt ii quidem novum Pindari fragmentum
recens in lucem prolatum esse.[1] Quo de fragmento ego cum iam
in consessu Academiae Cracoviensis breviter verba fecissem,[2]
nunc uberius disputare mihi proposui; neque enim ignoro eius
modi munus gratum futurum fuisse viro eximio, cuius memoriae
hoc volumen dicatum est.

Servatum est illud fragmentum Arabica lingua expressum atque libello qui inscribitur "Epistula Aristotelis ad Alexandrum
de administratione civitatum" inclusum. Cuius libelli textus in-
teger typis adhuc vulgatus non est,[3] exstat tamen in codicibus
Constantinopolitanis aliquot, quorum nos adhibuimus tres: Aya
Sophya 2890, Fatih 5323, Kőprűlű 1608. Nos autem cum dico,
intellegi praeter me velim virum doctissimum litterarumque
orientalium peritissimum Iosephum Bielawski Varsoviensem, qui
mecum illius epistulae editionem paravit atque propediem in
vulgus editurus est. Cuius beneficio amicitiaeque debeo Pindari
verborum contextum Arabicum eorumque versionem Latinam,
quae talia sunt:

Arabice (Aya Sophya f. 125, Fatih f. 74, Köprülü f. 120ᵛ):
Wa-ḫalikun 'an jakūna ḳawlu Findārūs 'ajdan šabīhan bi-haḏā
ḥajtu jaḳūlu:
'Inna's-sunnata ta'ūlu bi'l-'umūri kullihā ilā'l-'adli wa-hijā allatī
tuḥaḳḳiḳu al-ḥaḳḳa wa-lahā ḳuwwatun ka-ḳuwwatihi.

---

[1] J. Bielawski in *Annalibus Orientalibus* (*Rocznik Orientalistyczny*)
28. 1 (1964), p. 17; M. Grignaschi in *Museo* (*Le Muséon*) 80 (1967), p. 226.

[2] M. Plezia, "Pindar i prawo," *Sprawozdania z posiedzeń Komisji
Oddziału PAN w Krakowie* (1966), II, p. 425 s.

[3] E mutilo codice Vaticano Arab. 408 primum editus est a J. Lippert,
De epistula pseudaristotelica περὶ βασιλείας *commentatio* (Halis Saxonum
diss., Berolini, 1891).

Latine:

"Item recte se habet Pindari sententia, praecedentibus haud dissimilis, cum dicit:

Verum enimvero Lex cum omnibus quae sua sunt ad Iustitiam accedit; eadem (Lex) est, quae veritatem ad effectum adducit et vim possidet (parem) atque eius (veritatis) est."

Mitto quaestionem, quemnam epistula illa verum habuerit auctorem, cum e Graeca lingua eam conversam esse nemo neget. Id tantum addo nobis eandem atque Mario Grignaschi opinionem probari, qui dixit hanc epistulam Arabice redditam esse a Sālim quodam, cognomine Abū-l-Alā', qui chalifo Hišam (724–743) a secretis fuisse traditur.[4]

Non magno certe acumine opus est in agnoscendis vocabulis quibusdam Pindaricis, quae ad huius fragmenti sensum conformandum maximam vim habent, cum talia sint, ut etiam ex Arabica Latinaque translatione pelluceant. Est nempe Lex – Νόμος, Iustitia – Δίκα, veritas – ἀλάθεια. Legem pari modo atque iustitiam in personas constitutas esse quisque videt; offenditur autem eius modi νόμος apud Pindarum in *frg.* 169, Δίκα etiam multo saepius: *Ol.* 13. 7; *Pyth.* 8. 1 et 74, cf. *Ol.* 7. 17. Veritas animans–ne sit an notio abstracta iure ambegeris, cum modo "ad effectum adducatur," modo "vim possidcat," sed neque talia apud Pindarum desunt, qui discrimen inter personificationes atque abstracta consulto non numquam confudisse videtur.[5] "Vis" illa fortasse κράτος fuit, quod vocabulum Pindaro praeter "vim" etiam "victoriam" significare solet,[6] nisi tota locutio "vim possidet parem atque ..." e Graeco τόσσον κρατεῖ ... ὅσσον translata sit.

Minus perspicua sunt cetera, inter quae imprimis illud "accedit" curiositatem legentis movet. Erit enim, si verbo verbum reddideris, προσέρχεται, quod quidem apud Pindarum uno solo loco consensu codicum traditum legitur: *Pyth.* 6. 51 τίν τ', Ἐλέλιχθον... μάλα ἁδόντι νόῳ, Ποσειδάν, προσέρχεται, sed ab omnibus editoribus in tritum προσέχεται mutatur. At legitur tamen προσέρχεσθαι verbum a Graecis scriptoribus aliquando usurpatum sensu "accedendi ad aliquem eius consulendi gratia" vel "adeundi

---

[4] M. Grignaschi in *Bulletin d'études orientales* 19 (1965–66), pp. 12 ss.
[5] F. Dornseiff, *Pindars Stil* (Berlin, 1921), p. 52.
[6] Io. Rumpel, *Lexicon Pindaricum* (Lipsiae, 1883), p. 260.

reverenter," ut apud Xen. *Mem.* I. 2. 47 (bis) atque apud Thuc. 4. 121.[7] Quam significationem cum nostro fragmento tum illi Pythionicorum loco maxime accommodatam esse nemo est quin videat. His dictis iam quasi in transitu moneo illud "ad effectum adducere" translatum mihi videri e Graeco τελεῖν, quod et poetis epicis et Pindaro notissimum fuisse constat.[8]

Sed missis iam meris vocabulis ad vim eorum sensumque aestimandum accedere placet. Δίκας apud Pindarum notio sane maximi est momenti, quippe quae "firmissimum civitatum fundamentum" sit (*Ol.* 13. 6) et una cum sororibus suis Εὐνομία atque Εἰρήνα "aureis filiis consultae Themidis," divitias viris largiri dicatur (*ibid.*). Filiam eius Ἡσυχίαν urbes maximas efficere dicit poeta (*Pyth.* 8. 1). Damagetus denique, in Rhodiorum re publica summis honoribus functus, Δίκα ἁδών vocatur (*Ol.* 7. 17). Quodsi in fragmento nostro Lex eam "reverenter adit," imago haec idem significare putanda est, quod Plutarchus prosa oratione expressit, cum dixit (*Ad princ. inerud.* 780e): δίκη μὲν οὖν νόμου τέλος ἐστί. Ipse ceterum Pindarus, ut vidimus, legem cum iustitia cognatione quadam coniunctam esse declaravit, cum Δίκαν Εὐνομίας sororem finxit (*Ol.* 13. 6–8).

Lex igitur, quae Iustitiam "reverenter adeat," cum eadem "veritatem ad effectum adducat," videndum nobis est, quidnam apud Pindarum ἀλάθεια valeat. Valet autem plurimum,[9] id quod vel inde perspici potest, quod in *Ol.* 10. 4 Iovis filia vocatur, quodque eam in *frg.* 205 ita alloquitur poeta

> Ἀρχὰ μεγάλας ἀρετᾶς, ὤνασσ' Ἀλάθεια, μὴ πταίσῃς ἐμὰν
> σύνθεσιν τραχεῖ ποτὶ ψεύδει.

Νόμος denique et ipse summis celebratur laudibus in notissimo illo *frg.* 169, ubi " rex omnium, mortalium atque immortalium" appellatur, qua de re paulo infra pluribus agendum nobis erit.

Sed tamen ipsa necessitudo, quae inter tres has: legem, iustitiam, veritatem in fragmento Arabice tradito intercedat, digna est, quae accuratius examinetur, praesertim cum ea sit, quam alibi in litteris Graecis antiquioris aetatis facile non inveneris.

---

[7] Cf. etiam *Thesaurum Linguae Graecae* VI, 1912.
[8] Rumpel, *op. cit.*, p. 436.
[9] C. M. Bowra, *Pindar* (Oxford, 1964), pp. 31 ss.

Νόμος enim atque δίκη licet non infrequenter iuxta se nominentur, minime tamen easdem res significare solent. In memoriam revoces, si libet, vel celeberrimos illos Hesiodi versus (*Op.* 276 ss.), ubi Iuppiter diversam legem (νόμον) hominibus, diversam vero piscibus, bestiis volucribusque alatis dedisse narratur, quae invicem se devorent, cum nullam noverint iustitiam (δίκην), qua nihil sit melius. E quo loco luce clarius apparet δίκην nihil esse nisi νόμου speciem quandam, quae hominum propria sit.[10] Theognis vero Megaris temporibus suis ad summos honores accedere queritur homines novos (v. 54) οἱ πρόσθ'οὔτε δίκας ἤδεσαν οὔτε νόμους. Herodotus denique in Scythiae descriptione commemorat Androphagos (4. 106), qui ἀγριώτατα πάντων ἀνθρώπων ἔχουσι ἤθεα, οὔτε δίκην νομίζοντες οὔτε νόμῳ οὐδενὶ χρεώμενοι. Ex his ceterisque exemplis, quibus utriusque vocis usus usque ad medium saec. V illustratur, manifestum fit νόμον illo tempore consuetudinem vel morem potissimum significavisse,[11] δίκην vero iustitiam et fas, sed eo quidem pacto, ut alterum ex altero numquam penderet neutrumque alteri subiectum esset. Dixit sane Solo (*frg.* 24. 18 ss. Diehl[3])

Θεσμοὺς δ'ὁμοίως τῷ κακῷ τε κἀγαθῷ
εὐθεῖαν εἰς ἕκαστον ἁρμόσας δίκην
ἔγραφα,

qua re leges suas ad iustitiae normam institutas esse ostendit [12] sed in ipso hoc loco examinando id animadversione vel dignissimum est, quod leges illas θεσμούς non νόμους vocavit. Nondum quippe νόμος legis publicae significationem obtinuit, id quod Athenis demum centum annos post Solonem factum esse constat, cum in titulis hoc vocabulum ante a. 500 a.Chr.n. non appareat.[13] At contra δίκη atque νόμος ut synonyma usurpari coeperunt posteriore parte saec. V inde a Gorgia [14] atque ab Anonymo Iamblichi,[15] donec saec. IV in locum δίκης, quae vox iam prisca et

---

[10] F. Heinimann, *Nomos und Physis* (Basel, 1945), p. 62.
[11] Heinimann, *ibid.*, pp. 62 et 74 ss.
[12] R. Hirzel, *Themis, Dike und Verwandtes* (Leipzig, 1907), p. 133.
[13] Heinimann, *op. cit.*, p. 72; M. Ostwald, "Pindar, *Nomos* and Heracles," *Harvard Studies in Classical Philology* 69 (1965), p. 135, adn. 63.
[14] Diels, *Vorsokr.*[9] II, p. 298. 21.
[15] Diels, *Vorsokr*[9]. II, p. 403. 10 et p. 404. 23.

obsoleta visa erat, νόμος solus successit unica iustitiae appellatio.[16]

In illo tamen Pindari fragmento noviter reperto existimando id quam maxime admirationem movet, quod notiones νόμου atque ἀληθείας adeo arte sibi coniunctae sint. Cum enim δίκη atque ἀλήθεια a Graecis inde ab antiquissimis temporibus secum componebantur sibique erant significatione proximae,[17] νόμος et ἀλήθεια (vel quod aliud vocabulum ipsam rei veritatem designabat) pro contrariis potius habebantur.[18] Vide Herodotum 4. 39: λήγει δὲ αὕτη (ἡ ἄκτη), οὐ λήγουσα εἰ μὴ νόμῳ, ἐς τὸν κόλπον τὸν Ἀράβιον. Empedocles autem dixit (Diels, *Vorsokr.*[9] 31 B 9,5) ἥ θέμις οὐ καλέουσι, νόμῳ δ' ἐπίφημι καὶ αὐτός. Tum Sophocles minime obscure veritatem atque opinionem communem (τὸ νομισθέν) sibi in vicem opposuit (*frg.* 83 Nauck: τό τοι νομισθὲν τῆς ἀληθείας κρατεῖ). Non est denique quod moneam sophistis contentionem νόμου atque φύσεως sollemnem factam esse.[19] Quae cum ita fuerint, Pindari sententia, qua affirmavit a lege veritatem ad effectum adduci, iure notabilis videri potest, praesertim cum perpenderis, quanti poeta ille veritatem aestimaverit.

Non tamen omnino defuerunt auctores, qui Pindaro illam legis iustitiaeque cum veritate coniunctionem commendare possent. Nemo est quin intellegat quantum in Orphicorum religionibus Δίκη dea valuerit, cuius cognitionem illi-ne Hesiodo (*Op.* 256–260), an utrique antiquioribus etiam fabulis debuerint,[20] aliis diiudicandum relinquo. Plato certe (*Leg.* 715e) τὸν παλαιὸν λόγον commemorat (quem Orphicorum traditionem fuisse scholiasta affirmat), secundum quem τῷ θεῷ ἀεὶ συνέπεται Δίκη τῶν ἀπολειπομένων τοῦ θείου νόμου τιμωρός.[21] Is etiam, cuius est oratio *Contra Aristogitonem I*, quae Demosthenis fuisee ferebatur, nominat (25. 11) τὴν ἀπαραίτητον καὶ σεμνὴν Δίκην, ἥν ὁ τὰς ἁγιωτάτας ἡμῖν τελετὰς καταδείξας Ὀρφεὺς παρὰ τὸν τοῦ Διὸς θρόνον φησὶ καθημένην πάντα τὰ τῶν ἀνθρώπων ἐφορᾶν.[22] Item Anaxarchus

---

[16] Hirzel, *op. cit.*, pp. 384 ss.
[17] Hirzel, *op. cit.*, pp. 108 ss.
[18] Heinimann, *op. cit.*, pp. 85 ss.
[19] Heinimann, *op. cit.*, pp. 110 ss.
[20] Heinimann, *op. cit.*, p. 70.
[21] Diels, *Vorsokr*[9]. 1 B 6 = O. Kern, ed., *Orphicorum fragmenta* (Berlin, 1922), frg. 21.
[22] Diels, *Vorsokr.*[9] 1 B 14 = Kern, *op. cit.*, *frg.* 23.

sophista, Alexandri M. comes, "antiquos sapientes" testes invocavit οἱ τὴν Δίκην πάρεδρον τῷ Διὶ ἐποίησαν (Arr. *Anab*. 4. 9. 7; cf. Plut. *Alex*. 52. 4). Non aliter sensit auctor *Oraculorum*, quae sub Epicharmi nomine circumferebantur, cum ἐν Δικταίου Διὸς τῷ ἄντρῳ κείμενος ὕπνῳ βαθεῖ ἔτη συχνὰ ὄναρ ἔφη ἐντυχεῖν αὐτὸς θεοῖς καὶ θεῶν λόγοις καὶ 'Αληθείᾳ καὶ Δίκῃ (Diels, *Vorsokr*.⁹ I, p. 32. 19 ss.). Prona inde coniectura est tres illas Iustitiam, Veritatem, Legem in antiquissimis Orphei sectatorum fabulis magnas partes egisse. De lege (νόμος) quidem dubium id videri possit, etsi apud Platonem (*Leg*. 716a) Δίκη divinae legis custos eademque vindex est; cum tamen hymnus, quo Orphici Νόμον deum venerati erant,[23] posteriori (Christianae certe) aetati tribuendus esse videretur, erant qui νόμον a priscis Orphicorum religionibus alienum fuisse putabant.[24] Nobis tamen id minoris momenti est, utrum Pindarus, quem Orphicorum fabulis fuisse imbutum satis constat,[25]νόμον in personam constitutum ab eis conformatum acceperit, an ipse finxerit, ut id de Platone quoque suspicandum esset, si hic legis divinae mentionem non in antiqua illa traditione (ὁ παλαιὸς λόγος) invenisset. Haec tamen utcumque fuerunt, is qui pari modo atque Orphici Δίκην deam ea quae ab hominibus agerentur diligenter inspicere crederet, atque idem bene maleque actorum rationem post mortem nobis reddendam esse censeret, non procul certe afuit a cognitione legis cuiusdam divinae, cuius Δίκη custos esset. Itaque veri simillimum videtur Pindarum Orphicorum vestigia secutum legis cum iustitia veritateque coniunctionem ita animo effinxisse, ut id in Arabico illo fragmento factum esse deprehendimus.

Illustrato explanatoque, quantum fieri potuit, hoc fragmento, quod tam insperato tamque singulari casu ad nos delatum est, considerare iuvat, qua ratione id cum reliquis nobilissimi poetae carminibus, quae vel integra vel lacerata nobis tradita sunt, cohaereat. Neque longa circumspectione opus est, ut affinitas eius cum celeberrimo illo fragmento 169, quod verbis νόμος ὁ πάντων βασιλεύς incipit, cuique his novissimis annis complures accesserunt versus in papyro Oxyrrhynchia servati, ipsa paene

---

[23] Hymnus 64 atque *fragmenta* 105, 159, 160 Kern.
[24] Heinimann, *op. cit.*, p. 69, qui etiam Gundert auctorem affert (*Gnomon* 13 [1937], p. 340).
[25] J. M. Lagrange, *Les mystères: L'orphisme* (Paris, 1937), pp. 149 ss.

per se eluceat. Nullibi enim ceterum, quantum nobis quidem cognitum est, ita accurate de νόμῳ egit poeta, qui item in posteriore eius carminis parte, nobis deperdita, enodavisse tandem putandus est, quo pacto id fieri posset, ut νόμος summam etiam vim (τὸ βιαιότατον) iustam redderet.[26] Quae cum ita sint, satis probabile videtur fragmentum Arabice traditum ad idem atque *frg.* 169 carmen pertinere; pro certo id tamen afirmare non ausim, cum neque omnia Pindari scripta ad nos pervenerint, neque verba prosa oratione Arabice translata de metro, quo Graece composita erant, quippiam iudicare sinunt nedum statuere idem id fuisse metrorum genus atque illud quo *frg.* 169 conscriptum est. Utrumque tamen fragmentum ad eandem rem spectare manifestum est, unde etiam spes nobis exoritur fieri posse, ut aliquantum lucis afferatur intricatissimae quaestioni, tot hominum doctorum contentionibus vexatae, cuius nempe naturae νόμος ille fuisse putandus sit.[27]

Sed tamen inde capiat interpretatio nostra exordium, ut primum *frg.* 169 atque id forma illa pleniore, qua nunc e papyro Oxyrrhynchia recuperatum prostat, cum *frg.* 81 comparetur. Laudat ibi poeta Geryonem, de quo etiam *frg.* 169. 6–8 agit, sed ipse sibi silentium imponit, cum dicit τὸ δὲ μὴ Διὶ φίλτερον σιγῶμι πάμπαν. Simili ratione *frg.* 169. 14–17 honorifica mentione prosequitur Diomedem

> Διὸς ὑποστάντα μέγαν
> παῖδ᾽ οὐ κόρῳ ἀλλ᾽ἀρετᾷ,
> κρέσσον γὰρ ἁρπαζομένων τεθνάμεν
> πρὸ χρημάτων ἢ κακὸν ἔμμεναι.

Cum autem secundum *frg.* 169 νόμος vim Geryoni Diomedique a Hercule allatam iustam reddat, existimemus necesse est νόμον illum idem esse atque τὸ Διὶ φίλτερον. Ipse quidem νόμος in *frg.* 169. 1–2 apposito ὁ πάντων βασιλεύς, θνατῶν τε καὶ ἀθανάτων ornatur, qua re procul dubio in eodem loco ponitur atque Iuppiter πατὴρ

---

[26] Ita recte Ostwald, *op. cit.*, pp. 126 et 130.
[27] Singulorum opiniones nominatim laudant Ostwald, *op. cit.*, pp. 121 ss. atque E. Thummer in *Anzeiger für die Altertumswissenschaft* 19 (1966), pp. 320–322. His addas novissimum C. Pavese, "The New Heracles Poem of Pindar," *Harvard Studies in Classical Philology* 72 (1967), pp. 47–88, cuius disputationem ego iam absoluta hac commentatiuncula nactus sum, serius quam ut observationibus eius uti possem.

ἀνδρῶν τε θεῶν τε idemque πάντων κύριος (*Isthm.* 5. 59). Item non multum a Iove distat νόμος in fragmento nostro Arabico, quippe qui reverenter adeat Δίκην, quam Iovi assidere factaque mortalium inspicere cognovimus, idemque veritatem "Iovis filiam" (*Ol.* 10. 4) "ad effectum adducat" paremque ei vim possideat.

Unde facile perspici potest νόμον in utroque fragmento nominatum eundem esse atque, si nostris vocabulis procul a poetica sublimitate positis uti licet, ordinem quendam a Iove ipso constitutum significare. Ex illo tamen fragmento, quod Arabice traditum ad nos nunc quidem pervenit, certiores fimus ordinem illum non ex mero summi dei arbitrio pendere neque formula "sic volo sic iubeo, stat pro ratione voluntas" circumscribi posse, sed in ipsa rerum natura summaque iustitia positum esse. Haud disimili ratione νόμου notionem animo effinxisse videtur Pindarus in postremis carminis *Nemei* I versibus, ubi Tiresiam ad Herculis nascentis ortum inducit vaticinantem ποίαις ὁμιλήσει τύχαις (*Nem.* 1. 61) addentemque deinde (*ibid.* 69–72)

> αὐτὸν μὰν ἐν εἰρήνᾳ τὸν ἄπαντα χρόνον
> ἐνσχερῶ,
> ἡσυχίαν καμάτων μεγάλων ποινὰν λαχόντ᾽ ἐξαίρετον
> ὀλβίοις ἐν δώμασι, δεξάμενον θαλερὰν Ἥβαν
>   ἄκοιτιν, καὶ γάμον
> δαίσαντα, πὰρ-Δὶ Κρονίδᾳ, σεμνὸν αἰνήσειν νόμον.

Νόμος igitur ille, qui σεμνός nuncupatur, vocabulo a Pindaro ad res divinas designandas potissimum usurpato,[28] procul dubio nihil differt a Iovis voluntate, qui filio suo multas molestias adversaque perpesso maxima tandem praemia paraturus est. Hercules vero legem illam patrisque voluntatem in fine demum rerum suarum laudabit, postquam ipse eam servaverit eaque in ipso expleta erit. Quae cum ita sint, eorum virorum doctorum opinio recte se habuisse apparet, qui iam pridem νόμον in *frg.* 169 nihil nisi Iovis voluntatem esse arbitrati sunt, eos autem a vero aberravisse necesse est, qui νόμον illum nuper etiam ita interpretati sunt, ut eum consuetudinem quandam omnibus probatam esse dicerent.

Hunc ad modum si recte Pindari sententiam explicavimus, νόμος eius non multum distat ab eo, de quo Heraclitus dixit

---

[28] Rumpel, *op. cit.*, p. 409.

278   *Marianus Plezia*

(Diels, *Vorsokr.*⁹ 22 B 114): τρέφονται γὰρ πάντες οἱ ἀνθρώπειοι νόμοι ὑπὸ ἑνὸς τοῦ θείου· κρατεῖ γὰρ τοσοῦτον ὁκόσον ἐθέλει καὶ ἐξαρκεῖ πᾶσι καὶ περιγίνεται. Quorum similitudo ea in re consistit, quod tam philosophus quam poeta unam eamque divinam legem esse affirmat, quae ubique dominetur. Pindarus eius originem ad Iovis voluntatem refert, Heraclitus autem id considerat, quae ratio inter divinam unam legem multasque leges humanas intercedat. Nihilne tamen Pindari etiam interfuit, quem ad modum νόμος ὁ πάντων βασιλεύς ad ius civile se habeat? Ad quam quaestionem si responderimus, solvemus fortasse et alteram, qua re id factum sit, ut νόμος summam etiam vim iustam reddat.

Illud ἄγει δικαιῶν τὸ βιαιότατον admirabile sane contraque communem hominum opinionem dictum esse nemo infitias ibit, praesertim cum βία atque δίκη inde ab antiquissimis temporibus pro contrariis haberentur.²⁹ Audi, quaeso, Hesiodum ita dicentem (*Op.* 274 s.):

Ὦ Πέρση, σὺ δὲ ταῦτα μετὰ φρεσὶ βάλλεο σῇσι
καὶ νυ δίκης ἐπάκουε, βίης δ'ἐπιλήθεο πάμπαν

Solo autem si praedicat (*frg.* 24. 16 Diehl³):

ταῦτα μὲν κράτει
ὁμοῦ βίην τε καὶ δίκην συναρμόσας
ἔρεξα

et ipse admirationem auditorum venatur et minime affirmat legibus suis vim iustitiam et vice versa factas esse. Quae quidem maxime sibi opponuntur in iure civili, cum id vel maximum sit meritum civitatis bene ordinatae, ut in ea quae sua esse quis dixerit vi repetere minime liceat, sed iure tantum vindicare. Eandem rem Pindarus quoque respexisse videtur, cum dixit (*frg.* 169. 8) Herculem Geryoni boves abegisse ἀπράτας τε καὶ ἀπριάτας ³⁰ cumque addidit (*ibid.* 16 s.): κρέσσον γὰρ ἁρπαζομένων τεθνάμεν πρὸ χρημάτων ἢ κακὸν ἔμμεναι. Hoc quidem mirum non immerito dixeris; quid enim? magnus ille Achilles, summae virtutis

²⁹ Hirzel, *op. cit.*, p. 130.
³⁰ Utor coniectura Ostwaldi, *op. cit.*, pp. 113 s. Quaecumque tamen ipsa poetae verba fuerunt, de sensu eorum ambigi minime licet, utpote quem explanationes Platonis atque Aelii Aristidis extra omne dubium ponant: Herculem Geryonis boves abegisse, quamvis possessionem eorum nulle iure nactus esset.

exemplar atque effigies, nonne Briseida sibi abduci toleranter passus est et Minerva auctore vim vi minime reppulit (*Il.* 1. 188 ss.)? Nonne in ea re munus virtutis ergo ab exercitu acceptum sibi adimi magis doluit quam proprietatem ademptam, nedum dicam quam puellam amatam? At Pindaro κακός esse videtur, qui proprietatem suam non viriliter defendit.

Nova haec est veteris fabulae existimatio,[31] sed ea quidem poetae subicit cogitationem inesse illi fabulae aliquid, quod a suis suique temporis opinionibus discrepet. Suo enim tempore res alicuius proprias non tam possessoris ἀρετή quam leges tutabantur. Itaque Pindarus, qui quantum antiquis fabulis addictus fuerit non est quod commemorem, animadvertit secumque reputat necesse esse, si fabula de Hercule Geryoneque auctoritatem suam atque pondus conservatura sit, ut alius quidam existat νόμος a iure civili diversus, attamen utpote τὸ Δὶ φίλτερον summa vi praeditus. Talis νόμος qui ἄγει ὑπερτάτᾳ χειρί aliquando vim etiam iustam reddit, quae coram civili νόμῳ nullo modo excusari possit. Ita fit, ut Pindarus duas iuris species esse intellegat, quae multo post ius civile atque ius naturae appellatae sunt. Neque est in ea re aliquid quod vehementer miremur, cum eo ipso tempore, medio fere saeculo V a.Chr.n., altioris ingenii homines eius modi differentiam in iure etsi nondum forte perceperint, at certe senserint, qua re factum est, ut leges in civitatibus constitutae reprehendi coepissent ab eis, qui modo antiquiorem quandam, divinam potissimum legem, modo non violanda singuli hominis iura propugnarent.[32] Apud Pindarum nullus adhuc reprehensioni locus est, sed sentit et ipse latius quam leges civitatis legem divinam valere neque hanc cum illis usquequaque congruere. Neque id aliter quam religione pro tempore explicare potest poeta, sed persuasum habet legem divinam Iovis voluntate niti, quae etsi ἀνυπεύθυνος sit, certe tamen ne hilum quidem a summa iustitia discedat.

Reliquum est, ut explanemus, quare ii qui Pindaro aetate proximi fuerunt scriptores [33]: Herodotus (3. 38) et Plato (*Grg.* 484b, cf. *Leg.* 889e) non ea ferme ratione qua nos priores *frg.* 169 versus

---

[31] Ostwald, *op. cit.*, pp. 130 s.

[32] V. Ehrenberg, "Anfänge des griechischen Naturrechts," nunc in sylloge cui est titulus *Polis und imperium* (Zürich-Stuttgart, 1965), pp. 359–379.

interpretati sint. Herodotus nimirum Pindari sententiam de lege omnium rege eo consilio laudat, ut confirmet opiniones iudiciaque hominum nullibi paria esse, sed locis moribusque obnoxia. Apud Platonem vero Callicles Pindarum testem affert eorum quae ipse dicit de iure potentioris, quod idem esse contendit atque naturae legem.[34] Posteriores demum auctores: Chrysippus (SVF III. 314) atque Plutarchus (*Ad princ. inerud.* 780 c) ita illorum versuum sensum explicaverunt, ut a nobis id propositum est. Haec autem propterea ita accidisse opinor, quod ardua illa sententia de lege, quae summam etiam vim iustam reddat, mox in proverbium atque, ut nos dicere solemus, in verbum alatum abiit, quod iis quoque notum fuit, qui – ut Callicles Platonicus aperte profitetur – reliqua carminis, e quo id sumptum erat, omnino ignorarent. Cum autem illa aetate, quae Pindarum proxime secuta est, notio τοῦ νόμου magis magisque comparatam minimeque simplicem vim obtineret atque diversa prorsus significaret, memorabilis summi poetae locus multorum in ore fuit, qui id tantum considerabant legis iustitiam illic in dubium esse vocatam minimeque curabant, quid alibi idem vates de summae legis origine dixisset.

Cracoviae

---

[33] Cuncta de illo fragmento antiquorum testimonia collegit Al. Turyn in apparatu editionis suae (*Pindari carmina cum fragmentis* [Cracoviae, 1948 = Oxonii, 1952], pp. 352 s.).

[34] E. R. Dodds, ed., *Plato, Gorgias* (Oxford, 1959), pp. 270–272.

LA RÉFUTATION DE LA MÉTENSOMATOSE
D'APRÈS
LE THÉOLOGIEN KARAÏTE YŪSUF AL-BAṢĪR

GEORGES VAJDA

Dans l'idéologie de l'antiquité finissante, à la connaissance de laquelle notre jubilaire a apporté des contributions capitales, les spéculations sur la migration des âmes jouent un rôle non négligeable. Nous avons donc pensé que la présentation d'une pièce fort peu connue, empruntée au dossier concernant le même problème dans la pensée judéo-arabe, ne serait pas déplacée dans le volume d'hommage offert à Philip Merlan.

Sans revenir sur la question de la métensomatose dans la pensée juive, magistralement traitée naguère par G. Scholem,[1] nous voulons simplement soumettre au lecteur la traduction annotée d'un chapitre, le vingt-quatrième, emprunté au manuel de théologie écrit en arabe (*Kitāb-al-Muḥtawī*; titre de la version hébraïque: *Séfer Neʿīmōt*) du Karaïte Yūsuf al-Baṣīr, auteur de la première moitié du *XIe* siècle;[2] la place nous étant mesurée, nous ne relèverons que très succinctement les textes antérieurs et contemporains qui illustrent la même problématique. Notons, une fois pour toutes, que pour le fond, le texte que

---

[1] *Gilgul*; *Seelenwanderung und Sympathie der Seelen*, cinquième chapitre (pp. 193–247, 297–306) du recueil d'études *Von der mystischen Gestalt der Gottheit* (Zürich, 1962); rédaction antérieure: *Eranos Jahrbuch* 24 (1956), pp. 55–118.

[2] Il suffit de référer ici aux indications bibliographiques chez Zvi Ankori, *Karaites in Byzantium* (New York, 1959), p. 81, n. 65; quant aux textes, original arabe et version hébraïque de Tobie b. Moïse, disciple de l'auteur, actuellement disponibles, nous nous permettons de renvoyer à notre article "La démonstration de l'Unité divine d'après Yūsuf al-Baṣīr," dans le volume d'hommage à G. Scholem (Jérusalem, 1968). Le texte que nous traduisons se trouve aux fol. 90r–91v du ms. D. Kaufmann 280; la version hébraïque se lit dans le ms. de Leyde, Or. 4779 (ancien Warner Hebr. 41) aux fol. 40v–41r. Deux brefs extraits, en arabe et en hébreu, ont été publiés, d'après ces manuscrits, dès 1906, à Budapest, dans une dissertation doctorale d'Andor Goldberger, pp. xiv–xv.

nous faisons connaître n'offre rien d'original; son intérêt réside dans le choix et l'arrangement des arguments et la façon dont il insère le problème dans le système général de la théodicée mu'-tazilite.

En effet, la réincarnation de l'âme qui aurait déjà traversé une existence terrestre dans un autre corps est envisagée uniquement ici comme une solution – non retenue – au problème de la souffrance en apparence gratuite des animaux dépourvus de raison ou des enfants qui n'en jouissent pas encore, donc moralement irresponsables, les uns et les autres. Or Dieu étant juste et soumis, si l'on peut dire, aux mêmes normes éthiques que celles dont la raison humaine et d'ailleurs le consentement universel reconnaissent la validité et le caractère contraignant,[3] la nécessité s'impose de découvrir une issue au problème ainsi posé, sous peine de se trouver en face d'un Dieu unique, mais en quelque sorte amoral, contradiction interne pour la pensée mu 'tazilite, ou, conséquence encore plus grave, de reconnaître, à côté du Dieu principe du bien, un second principe souverain, celui du mal.[4]

La réponse donnée par notre auteur tient en deux points: d'une part, l'hypothèse de la métensomatose est psychologiquement et logiquement indéfendable; d'autre part, elle est inutile, car toute souffrance à première vue gratuite peut s'expliquer rationnellement comme infligée en vue d'un avantage ultérieur, du moins dans un au-delà de la vie terrestre; c'est la solution que nous fournit la thèse mu'tazilite de la compensation (*'iwaḍ*) octroyée par Dieu à tout être vivant, homme ou animal, ayant souffert ici bas sans péché antécédent.[5]

Réfutation des partisans de la métensomatose [6]

[3] Ces problèmes sont discutés dans les chapitres XIX à XXII du *Kitāb al-Muḥtawī*.

[4] Théorie réfutée dans les chapitres XIII et XIV.

[5] Thèmes du chapitre XXIII, alors que les chapitres XXV et XXVI ont pour objet la critique des théories qui cherchent à aplanir la contradiction entre la justice divine et la souffrance gratuite sans recourir ni à la compensation ni à la métensomatose.

[6] L'original emploie le terme *tanāsuḥ*, usuel dans cette signification en arabe: voir l'article *Tanāsukh*, dans *Encyclopédie de l'Islam*, 1ère édition, t. IV (1934), pp. 681–682 (B. Carra de Vaux). La version hébraïque offre, au lieu d'un terme précis, une paraphrase assez lâche: "Réfutation des propos de celui qui dit que l'âme (*ruaḥ*) sort de l'homme et entre dans la bête."

Les partisans de la métensomatose pensent que les douleurs physiques n'étant [moralement] justifiées que si elles sont méritées, les souffrances de la bête doivent être dues à ce qu'un homme ayant péché dans une vie antérieure, expie maintenant dans un corps de bête.[7]

Cette thèse est insoutenable pour les raisons que voici:

(1) Elle n'aurait de valeur que si le sujet[8] qui souffre actuellement se souvenait d'avoir résidé jadis en un autre corps et se remémorait le temps et la nature de ses crimes. On ne peut pas plus oublier ces choses que l'on ne peut oublier d'avoir été jadis chef militaire [et] administrateur politique[9] dans un pays étranger.

(2) La soumission du sujet aux obligations a dû commencer à un certain moment puisque la série des réincarnations ne peut etre infinie *a parte ante*.[10]

Nous dirons dès lors [aux partisans de la métensomatose]: [à raisonner comme vous,] nous sommes devant un dilemme. Ou bien [l'âme réincarnée] passe d'un corps en un autre corps ou bien elle passe en un corps, à partir d'un non-corps. S'ils optent pour la première solution, ils s'engagent dans une régression à l'infini, ce qui est absurde. Si l'on adopte l'autre solution [il faudra bien reconnaître qu'il y eut] un premier corps où l'âme avait été transférée de son lieu propre et là commença son existence [terrestre] et son assujettissement au précepte pénible. Mais alors, leur dira-t-on, elle n'a pas péché auparavant; de quel droit Dieu la ferait-il souffrir alors qu'elle n'est point coupable? Vous admettez vous-mêmes que Dieu n'inflige la souffrance qu'à partir du moment où il impose ses commandements.[11] Et puis, s'il est moralement bon que Dieu soumette l'homme au précepte pénible, qu'est-ce qui empêche qu'il lui inflige la souffrance

---

[7] "Les souffrances …"; nous avons resserré la phrase arabe dont voici le mot à mot: "cela les a conduits à la thèse que l'âme de la bête se trouvait [antérieurement] dans un corps autre [que celui où] elle [réside présentement] et elle a péché dans ce corps-là; elle a donc mérité le mal qui l'a frappée une fois qu'elle a été transportée dans le corps de la bête."

[8] L'hébreu construit cette phrase de manière à la rapporter à "la bête," ce qui est, en un sens, logique, car dans l'énoncé de la thèse critiquée l'auteur ne fait état que de la métensomatose en un corps de bête; sa critique n'a cependant de sens que si elle vise la réincarnation successive d'une même âme en divers corps humains.

[9] En arabe: *amīran wamusayyiran lil-'asākir mudabbiran lil-umūr*; le traducteur, Karaïte byzantin, glose en grec: *stratēgos eite kritēs*.

[10] Car cela impliquerait l'éternité du monde *a parte ante*, conception déjà réfutée dans la première partie du traité (chapitres III et IV).

[11] Dans le texte arabe, ce développement est non seulement formulé avec une concision extrême, mais défiguré par un *homoïteoleuton*. La version hébraïque permet de rétablir le sens général, mais elle a, à son tour, le défaut de paraphraser et gloser excessivement l'original trop laconique. La dernière phrase de la traduction proposée ci-dessus est précisément l'une de ces gloses dont on peut d'ailleurs douter qu'elle interprète fidèlement la pensée de l'auteur.

sans faute antécédente? En effet, l'épreuve pénible en question est bonne parce qu'elle procure la récompense, de même que, selon notre doctrine, la souffrance est parfois bonne, et lorsqu'elle est méritée, et en tant qu'elle procure un avantage. Dans l'ordre visible, la culpabilité [antécédente] et l'avantage [présent ou futur] font à titre égal que la souffrance ne soit pas mauvaise; par conséquent, dans l'ordre invisible, nier ceci de l'un est le nier de l'autre. Si donc nos adversaires sont fondés à soutenir que seule la culpabilité légitime la souffrance,[12] d'autres pourront dire que seul l'avantage[13] la justifie, ce qui revient à nier la légitimité du châtiment dans l'autre monde encore plus qu'ici bas.[14]

En outre, la souffrance est comme les autres actes qui peuvent être bons ou mauvais.[15] C'est donc la même chose de soutenir que la souffrance n'est jamais bonne et que manger n'est pas bon. Et il revient au même

[12] La souffrance doit avoir un motif qui lui est antérieur.

[13] C'est-à-dire un motif ultérieur.

[14] Pour comprendre cette conclusion, il faut accorder que châtiment = souffrance. Ceci admis, le châtiment (éternel) dans l'au-delà n'est pas moralement justifié, car aucun bien ultérieur ne peut en résulter; mais il ne se justifie pas davantage dans ce monde-ci, car s'il est vrai que la souffrance n'est légitime qu'en vue d'un bien futur, le châtiment, qui, par définition, est infligé pour une faute antérieure, ne répond pas à cette exigence. Il est cependant clair que sans cette concession, le raisonnement est vicié par une pétition de principe: la souffrance est, si l'on veut, le mode de réalisation du châtiment; elle a cependant une plus grande extension logique que ce dernier: tout châtiment est souffrance, mais toute souffrance n'est pas châtiment, à moins qu'on n'ait démontré, ce qui n'est pas le cas, que les deux notions sont coextensives. Dans son ensemble, l'argument (adressé, ne l'oublions pas, à des adversaires qui veulent résoudre le problème de la souffrance, à la fois par la métensomatose et dans une perspective monothéiste) pourrait se formuler comme suit: Du moment que l'on admet que la dure discipline à laquelle l'homme responsable est soumis ici-bas afin de gagner son salut ("la récompense") dans l'au-delà est moralement justifiée, pourquoi la raison répugnerait-elle à accorder cette justification à la souffrance apparemment gratuite, pourvu qu'elle vaille au patient une *compensation*, c'est-à-dire un avantage, dans l'au-delà. Or, nous venons de le rappeler, la régression à l'infini étant absurde, l'assujettissement au précepte a, comme toutes choses hormis Dieu, un commencement absolu. Parallèlement, rien n'empêche d'admettre, dans le cas de la souffrance gratuite, un tel commencement, c'est-à-dire de reconnaître que, même sans faute antécédente, il puisse y avoir souffrance, qui sera moralement bonne si elle est assortie de compensation ultérieure. Bref, si l'on tient compte que le monde n'est pas éternel et que Dieu ne fait que le bien – or ces deux points sont déjà acquis –, la justification morale de la souffrance par la métensomatose n'a plus de raison d'être; la vraie solution est apportée par la théorie de la compensation qui procède ainsi des deux grands principes de la théologie mu'tazilite: Unité (*tawḥīd*) dont relève la doctrine de la non éternité du monde, et Justice ('*adl*) qui exclut toute iniquité et tout acte moralement répréhensible de la part de Dieu.

[15] Susceptibles d'être qualifiés ainsi soit du point de vue moral, soit du point de vue pratique (utilitaire).

de dire qu'elle n'est pas bonne et qu'elle n'est pas bonne [quoique] méritée.[16]

Ce sont les Dualistes qui soutiennent que la souffrance n'est bonne à aucun égard. Cette thèse est fausse et nous le prouvons par la même méthode que celle qui nous a convaincus de la fausseté de la métensomatose.

En effet, de même que nous savons qu'il est bon que le malfaiteur soit blâmé parce qu'il mérite de l'être, de même reconnaissons-nous qu'il est bon de supporter les incommodités des voyages en raison de l'avantage qui en résulte.

Ce qui a conduit à leurs thèses les partisans de la métensomatose et les Dualistes, est la répugnance que l'on éprouve à faire souffrir autrui et la délicatesse du coeur que nous trouvons principalement chez les personnes d'un bon naturel, à cause de laquelle on a de la peine à faire du mal aux bêtes, encore que l'on soit convaincu que c'est moralement bon. Notons pourtant que les partisans de la métensomatose conviennent que la souffrance puisse être moralement bonne pour une partie des raisons pour lesquelles nous l'admettons nous-mêmes.

La thèse des Dualistes est suffisamment réfutée par le fait que, nous l'avons montré, il est de science nécessaire qu'il est bon que nous corrigions nos enfants et que nous supportions les incommodités durant les voyages, en vue du profit qui en résulte, et aussi qu'il est moralement bon de blâmer le malfaiteur.

Ce même argument vaut contre les partisans de la métensomatose et les accule même à une contradiction à laquelle échappent les Dualistes.

On leur dira en effet : qu'est-ce qui vous engage à soutenir que Dieu fait passer l'âme d'un être vivant d'un corps en un autre ? S'ils répondent :[17] la souffrance de l'enfant dépourvu de raison ne peut être moralement bonne que si son âme est châtiée dans le corps actuel pour des péchés commis dans un corps antérieur, on leur répliquera : pourquoi dites-vous alors qu'il est bon d'infliger la souffrance lorsqu'elle est méritée ? Nous savons que, dans l'ordre visible, cette façon d'agir est justifiée, car [notoirement, dans les relations entre humains] on considère comme moralement bon[18] de blâmer le malfaiteur, de recouvrer ses créances avec dureté, de s'adresser mutuellement des reproches, d'avoir des discussions d'intérêt. Ceci n'implique-t-il pas qu'il est moralement bon de la part de Dieu d'infliger la souffrance en vue de l'avantage du patient comme il est bon de notre part, de faire souffrir nos enfants en vue du leur, du moment que le châtiment infligé aux rebelles est légitimé par la bonté morale du blâme

[16] Ce paragraphe forme transition entre la discussion de l'opinion des monothéistes que le spectacle de la souffrance gratuite a conduits à la théorie de la métensomatose, et la critique de la doctrine dualiste qui fait dépendre toute souffrance d'une puissance autonome du mal.

[17] A la place de *famin qawlihim* du manuscrit, la suite des idées exige de lire *fa' in qālū*.

[18] En vérité, il s'agit ici d'attitudes fort diverses, mais qui ont en commun d'être approuvées par ce que l'on croyait être le consentement universel. Les qualifier indistinctement de "bon" est un sophisme qui amalgame les authentiques valeurs éthiques (même au sentiment de notre auteur et des penseurs de la même tendance) avec ce qui n'est irréprochable que formellement.

adressé au malfaiteur et de la réclamation énergique soulevée à l'endroit du débiteur. Si les choses sont ainsi, les partisans de la métensomatose font une distinction [indue] entre deux choses que l'on ne saurait séparer[19] et ils portent sur [une situation dans] l'invisible un jugement contraire à celui qui vaut de son homologue dans le visible, ce qui, sans aucun doute, est une bévue.

La vérité est que l'avantage qui compense la souffrance lui ôte son caractère de souffrance et la rend moralement bonne, de même que la compensation accordée par Dieu à l'enfant fait que la souffrance de celui-ci ne soit pas l'effet d'une injustice. Cette considération met en évidence la fausseté de leur opinion qui explique la souffrance de l'enfant comme le châtiment de péchés commis par son âme dans un corps d'où elle a été transportée dans le corps où elle réside actuellement.

Les arguments opposés par Yūsuf al-Baṣīr aux partisans de la métensomatose se détachent fort nettement de son exposé.

(1) La métensomatose comme sanction infligée pour des péchés commis lors du séjour antérieur de l'âme dans un autre corps n'aurait de sens que si le sujet souffrant dans la vie actuelle conservait le souvenir de sa vie antérieure. L'expérience enseigne que ce n'est absolument pas le cas.

(2) Le châtiment présuppose l'assujettissement de l'homme responsable au précepte divin. Or même en concédant une série de migrations de l'âme, il demeure que ce processus a eu un commencement, une première incarnation de l'âme dans un corps, état pour lequel l'explication de la souffrance comme suite d'une faute antécédente ne vaut pas; par conséquent, cette explication n'est pas convaincante puisqu'elle ne peut être étendue à la totalité des cas qu'elle concerne.[20]

[19] L'erreur consiste à séparer la souffrance infligée aux enfants par Dieu, ce qui ne saurait se justifier, selon les partisans de la métensomatose, que comme le châtiment de péchés antécédents, et celle que nous leur faisons subir de notre côté, ce qui est moralement bon, à condition d'être justifié par un avantage ultérieur. Mais, dirons-nous à nos adversaires, du moment que la souffrance en apparence gratuite reçoit sa justification, dans l'ordre visible, par un avantage ultérieur, pourquoi n'en serait-il pas de même dans l'ordre invisible? Autrement dit, si nous admettons la théorie de la compensation, le problème de la souffrance gratuite trouvera une solution satisfaisante, sans qu'il soit besoin de recourir à la métensomatose avec son cortège de difficultés que nous connaissons.

[20] Nous avons ici une application de la méthode de réfutation par raisonnement hypothétique, extension de la cause aux effets, procédé couramment utilisé par la dialectique des *Mutakallimūn*; voir sur ce point le texte de Qirqisānī traduit et expliqué par l'auteur de ces lignes, *REJ* 122 (1963), pp. 14–15.

A ces deux arguments qui constituent la critique négative de la réfutation se joint un troisième, critique constructive, qui démontre l'admissibilité rationnelle d'une "souffrance" infligée non en raison d'une faute antécédente, mais en vue d'un avantage ultérieur; il ouvre ainsi la voie à la solution du problème par la "compensation" dans la vie éternelle.

L'appareil spéculatif ainsi constitué ne se retrouve dans sa totalité[21] que chez les théologiens musulmans d'obédience muʿtazilite comme on peut le voir le plus commodément en se reportant au *Šarḥ al-uṣūl al-ḥamsa*[22] issu de l'enseignement du grand cadi ʿAbd al-Ǧabbār (mort en 415/1023–4) dont l'oeuvre immense rassemble toute la spéculation du siècle d'or (IVe/Xe) du muʿtazilisme.[23] S'il est évident que le théologien Karaïte a construit sa doctrine à force d'emprunts, il ne s'est pas contenté de copier ses sources ni de les résumer servilement: l'agencement des

[21] C'est pourquoi nous écartons tout de suite du débat les deux auteurs judéo-arabes qui ont pris position à l'égard du problème antérieurement à Yūsuf al-Baṣīr: Saadia, *Amānāt* VI, 8, éd. S. Landauer, pp. 207–211 (pp. 259–263 de la traduction de S. Rosenblatt, Saadia Gaon, *The Book of Beliefs and Opinions* [New Haven, 1948]), qui ne fait pas état du premier argument, bien qu'il évoque rapidement le second (mais en le développant en un autre sens) et qu'il admette, lui aussi, la solution de la "compensation" pour le problème de la souffrance gratuite, et Qirqisānī, *K. al-Anwār wal-marāqib* III, 17, éd. L. Nemoy, pp. 307–314, qui développe le premier argument, dans un style fort différent de celui de notre auteur, mais ignore le second. Samuel Poznański qui a édité jadis, le premier, ce morceau de Qirqisānī ("Aus Qiriqisâni's Kitâb al-'anwâr w'al-marâqib," *Semitic Studies in Memory of Alexander Kohut* [Berlin, 1897], pp. 435–456), sans la traduire (très bref résumé, p. 437 sq.) en fait à tort la source de Yūsuf al-Baṣīr qu'il ne connaissait alors que par l'analyse de P. F. Frankl, *Ein muʿtazilischer Kalâm*, pp. 38–41.

[22] Edité par ʿAbd al-Karīm ʿUtmān (le Caire, 1384/1965). La page de titre en anglais porte: *Sharh al-Ossoul al-Khamsah ... edited by Dr. Abd el-Karim Ousman.*

[23] Indications bibliographiques dans la première note à notre article "La connaissance naturelle de Dieu selon al-Ǧāḥiz critiquée par les Muʿtazilites," *Studia Islamica*, fascicule 24 (1966), p. 19.

Dans le *Muġnī*, la discussion se situe au t. XIII, publié au Caire en 1960, p. 410 et suivv., texte incomplet, cf. p. 411, n. 2; la question de la souffrance légitime y est traitée aux pages 318–330 et 369–380, cf. aussi p. 416. Yūsuf a certainement connu ces textes, mais il n'est guère possible d'établir des rapprochements précis entre son exposé concis et les développements diffus de la grande encyclopédie de ʿAbd al-Ǧabbār. Il est inutile de faire état ici des textes d'hérésiographes sunnites comme ceux de ʿAbd al-Qāhir al-Baġdādī, *Uṣūl al-dīn* (Istanbul, 1346/1928), p. 235 sq. ou d'Ibn Ḥazm, *al-Fiṣal* (le Caire, 1321/1903), I, 90–94.

matériaux, leur réduction quantitative dans le cadre équilibré de son livre, la mise en ordre des arguments doivent être considérés jusqu'à preuve du contraire comme son apport personnel. C'est ce dont nous pouvons aisément nous convaincre en prenant connaissance des passages du *Šarḥ al-uṣūl al- ḫamsa* qui se recoupent avec les deux arguments négatifs opposés dans le *Kitāb al muḥtawī* à la thèse de la métensomatose.

Le *Šarḥ* (édition citée, p. 483, lignes 3 et suiv.) explique que l'incapacité de distinguer entre les souffrances moralement justifiées et celles qui ne le sont pas, a engendré plusieurs erreurs doctrinales.

Ceux qui considèrent toute souffrance sans exception comme mauvaise et tout plaisir comme bon, ne peuvent les assigner au même auteur: ce sont les Dualistes.

Ne reconnaître comme moralement bonne que la souffrance méritée (par une faute antécédente) est une erreur qui a acculé les uns à la croyance en la métensomatose, les autres à une absurdité évidente, la contestation de la réalité des souffrances des animaux et des jeunes enfants.

La thèse des partisans de la métensomatose est formulée ainsi (483, 11–13):

Les [sujets soumis à des souffrances en apparence gratuites] ont [jadis] résidé dans un corps (litt. "moule," *qālab*) dans lequel ils désobéirent à Dieu. Dieu les a transférés dans le corps (*qālab*) actuel où il leur inflige ces châtiments [qui nous paraissent injustifiées]. Les tenants de cette opinion sont les partisans de la métempsycose (*aṣḥāb al-tanāsuḫ*); ils nient que l'être vivant et sensitif soit l'ensemble que voici (*hāḏihi l-ǧumla al-mušār ilayhā*) et ils affirment [qu'il y en a] un autre.[24]

Quant à ceux que l'auteur muʿtazilite appelle *ǧabriyya*, tenants du serf arbitre, c'est-à-dire la majorité des Musulmans sunnites, ils résolvent le problème en soustrayant la souveraineté divine à la loi morale que la raison humaine tient pour être de validité universelle.

---

[24] Si je ne me méprends pas tout à fait, l'auteur veut dire ceci: les partisans de la métensomatose ne pensent pas que la personne humaine soit réellement l'ensemble psycho-somatique (qui peut d'ailleurs être un animal) donné à l'expérience comme le sujet individuel dont l'existence terrestre connaît un commencement absolu par la naissance physique et une fin non moins absolue par la mort physique: la personne est quelque chose de différent qui peut prendre résidence successivement en différents complexes psychosomatiques.

L'auteur s'attache d'abord à montrer que la souffrance sans faute antécédente peut se justifier soit en vue de la compensation, soit à titre d'exemple instructif (*i'tibār*). La place nous manque pour traduire intégralement ces développements.

Quant à la métensomatose, le *Šarḥ* la réfute ainsi (487, 12–488, 3):

Les tenants de la métensomatose [25] professent que les âmes humaines [26] sont transférées d'une résidence en une autre [27] lorsqu'un homme désobéit à Dieu dans un corps (qālab), Dieu le transfère [28] dans un autre corps où il le châtie. Ce qui prouve clairement la fausseté de cette opinion c'est que s'il en était ainsi le sujet [29] aurait nécessairement souvenir des événements importants, comme la perte de ses parents, la confiscation de ses biens précieux, les fonctions de commandement, de judicature, d'enseignement, etc., [événements] qui s'étaient produits dans sa vie alors qu'il se trouvait dans un corps antérieur, [30] puisque [garder souvenir de telles choses] est le fait d'un sujet jouissant de la plénitude de ses facultés. [31] Or c'est chose connue qu'aucun homme actuellement vivant [32] ne possède de tels souvenirs. L'opinion qu'ils professent ne repose dès lors sur rien.

S'ils objectent: il arrive qu'on perde de tels souvenirs par suite de troubles mentaux qui suspendent le fonctionnement de la raison, [33] [nous répliquons que] les choses ne se passent pas comme ils le prétendent. En effet, si un juge de village ou un chef de quartier était momentanément frappé de démence et qu'il reprît ensuite sa raison et revînt à son bon

[25] Litt.: "du transfert" (*naql*).

[26] Litt.: "ces âmes-ci" (*hāḏihi l-arwāḥ*).

[27] Litt.: "subissent transfert dans ces résidences-ci" (*tuntaqal bihāḏihi l-hayākil*). Le terme *haykal* comme *qālab* que nous retrouverons immédiatement, désigne le corps matériel.

[28] C'est-à-dire transfère son âme.

[29] Litt.: "l'un d'entre nous."

[30] Litt.: "dans ce corps (qālab)-là."

[31] Litt.: "est de l'intégrité de la raison" (*kamāl al-'aql*). En d'autres mots: si le prétendu sujet de la migration est privé de mémoire, il n'est pas un être raisonnable; partant, il est irresponsable, et le châtiment qu'il subirait selon la thèse critiquée sera dépourvu de sens et de justification.

[32] Litt.: "dans ce corps-ci."

[33] Litt.: "l'intervention de la cessation de la raison met obstacle à cela" (*inna taḥallula zawāli l-'aqli yamna'u min ḏālika*, cf. pour l'expression et le fond, *Muġnī* XIII, 413, 8–9: *taḥallala bayna ḥālatay kamāli l-'aqli wazawāli l-'aql*.

L'objection revient à dire, semble-t-il: dans certains troubles psychiques, des cas d'amnésie interviennent au cours d'une seule et même existence; il est concevable dès lors que le choc causé par la mort physique à la fin d'une vie antérieure et le transfert de l'âme en un autre corps puissent avoir le même effet.

sens, il retrouverait le souvenir des fonctions qu'il avait exercées. On leur fera la même réponse s'ils mettent l'oubli au compte du temps long [écoulé entre la vie antérieure et la vie présente], car lorsqu'il s'agit d'affaires de cette importance, la longueur du temps n'a pas d'influence [sur la vivacité du souvenir]; elle n'en a que sur ce qui est insignifiant.

Voilà donc réfutée l'opinion des tenants de la métempsycose (*tanāsuḫ*).

Ecole Pratique des Hautes Etudes, Paris

II. PHILOSOPHIA MODERNA

DREIERLEI PHILOSOPHIEGESCHICHTE

VICTOR KRAFT

Die Geschichte der Philosophie wird und wurde auf verschiedene
Weise geschrieben. Man braucht nur auf einige bekannte Darstellungen der allgemeinen Philosophiegeschichte zu verweisen.
Die umfassendste Geschichte der Philosophie, die von Überweg,
hat sich die Aufgabe gestellt, die philosophischen Lehren, fast
ausschliesslich die europäischen, in chronologischer Reihenfolge
zu referieren und die zugehörige Literatur anzuführen, ein Kom-
pendium. Hingegen hat Theodor Gomperz in seiner ausführlichen Geschichte der antiken Philosophie *Griechische Denker*[1]
ihre Lehren auf eine breit ausgeführte kulturhistorische Basis
gestellt und sie aus dieser verständlich zu machen gesucht und
jeweils ihre Eigenart mit Lehren anderer Zeiten kontrastiert.
Diese Art der Philosophiegeschichtsschreibung hat B. Russell
schon auf dem Titelblatt seiner Philosophiegeschichte "History
of Western Philosophy" programmatisch zum Ausdruck gebracht: "Philosophie des Abendlandes."[2] Ihr Zusammenhang mit
der politischen und sozialen Entwicklung, der historische Rahmen, nimmt einen ebenso grossen Raum ein wie der Bericht
über die philosophischen Lehren. In seinem *Lehrbuch der Geschichte der Philosophie* hat W. Windelband die Philosophie
verschiedener Perioden in einen systematischen Zusammenhang
gemäss den zu seiner Zeit vorherrschenden Problemen gebracht.[3]

In den geschichtlichen Darstellungen der Philosophie finden
sich vielfach auch Wertungen. Die Originalität, die Tragweite, die
zusammenfassende Systematisierung wird bei einzelnen Philo-

---

[1] T. Gomperz, *Griechische Denker*[3,4] (3 Bde.; Berlin, 1922–1931).
[2] B. Russell, *History of Western Philosophy* (London, 1946).
[3] W. Windelband, *Lehrbuch der Geschichte der Philosophie*[15] (Tübingen,
1957).

sophen hervorgehoben, bei anderen die blosse Fortführung einer Schultradition angemerkt. W. Stegmüller hat in seinen *Hauptströmungen der Gegenwartsphilosophie* der Darstellung eines jeden Philosophen eine "Würdigung," also eine Wertung folgen lassen.[4] Auch Kritik wird in historischen Darstellungen geübt, stellenweise oder durchgehends, z.B. in Russells Philosophiegeschichte. In extremer Weise ist sie in R. Wahles Philosophiegeschichte *Die Tragikomödie der Weisheit* aufgetreten, "... wie alle die schillernden Seifenblasen spekulierenden Hochmuts platzten, wird unsere Geschichte der Philosophie in deutlicher Kürze darstellen."[5]

Die Geschichtsschreibung der Philosophie zeigt also mehrfache, sehr verschiedene Aspekte.'[6] Sie deutlich zu erfassen und in iher Eigenart gesondert auseinanderzulegen, ist unerlässlich, damit man sich klar darüber ist, welches Ziel philosophiegeschichtlicher Arbeit man vor Augen hat und welche Anforderungen dafür zu erfüllen sind.

I

Für die Geschichte der Philosophie ist es charakteristisch, dass sie in der Geschichte der Lehren einzelner Philosophen besteht, ähnlich wie die Geschichte der Kunst die *Oeuvres* der einzelnen Künstler behandelt. Sie stellt nicht das Wachstum eines bestimmten Wissensgebietes dar wie die Geschichte einer Spezialwissenschaft, wenigstens gegenwärtig.

1. Die erste Aufgabe für eine Geschichte der Philosophie muss es natürlich sein, die philosophischen Lehren, die im Laufe der Zeit aufgetreten sind, ihrem Inhalt nach darzustellen. Das ist die einer *Doxographie.* Dazu muss zuerst das Material an philosophischen Doktrinen gesammelt und zeitlich bestimmt werden.

---

[4] W. Stegmüller, *Hauptströmungen der Gegenwartsphilosophie* (Wien, 1952).

[5] R. Wahle, *Die Tragikomödie der Weisheit* (Wien, Leipzig, 1915), p. 3.

[6] So Theodor Gomperz, *Griechische Denker*, Vorwort: "Die Darstellung soll sich von einem nicht allzu dürftigen kulturhistorischen Hintergrund abheben und ein subjektives Gepräge nur in so weit tragen, als die Hervorhebung des Wesentlichen eine möglichst scharfe, die Scheidung des Bleibenden und Bedeutsamen von dem Gleichgiltigen und Vergänglichen eine möglichst durchgreifende sein soll."

Wenn die Schriften nicht, wie in den Druckwerken der Neuzeit, allgemein zugänglich vorliegen, sondern in Handschriften überliefert sind, müssen diese ediert werden. Damit setzt die Quellenkritik ein, die Prüfung der Quellen auf ihre Verlässlichkeit, besonders wenn die Schriften aus zweiter Hand überliefert sind. Diese Aufgabe erfüllen Arbeiten wie *Die Fragmente der Vorsokratiker* von Diels[7] oder *Die Upanishads* von Deussen.[8]

2. Die Quellenschriften müssen ev. übersetzt werden und damit treten neue Anforderungen auf. Den ursprünglichen Sinn von Ausdrücken in Schriften, die aus einem fremden Kulturkreis stammen oder auch nicht der Gegenwart oder jüngsten Vergangenheit des eigenen Kulturkreises angehören, getreu wiederzugeben, darf nicht leicht genommen werden. Es erfordert kulturhistorische Kenntnisse, die ausserhalb der Philosophie liegen. So kann z.B. "eudaimonia" nicht einfach mit "Wohlergehen" oder "Glückseligkeit" übersetzt werden, sondern man darf nicht übersehen, dass darin auch die Vorstellung, einen guten Dämon zu haben, mit eingeschlossen ist. Der Sinn einer philosophischen Lehre kann durch die Überlieferung undeutlich geworden sein, er kann auch in der Originalschrift nicht deutlich zum Ausdruck gebracht sein; dann muss der Sinn erst durch eingehende Analyse zur Klarheit gebracht werden. So hat Professor Merlan die Stellung der Neu-pythagoräer und Neu-Platoniker zu Monismus und Dualismus klarzustellen unternommen.[9]

3. Zum Unterschied von der Sammlung und Edition und Überzetzung der philosophischen Quellenschriften werden diese in einer Geschichte der Philosophie nicht *in extenso* vorgelegt, sondern sie werden ihrem wesentlichen Inhalt nach referiert; gewöhnlich werden die Lehren eines Philosophen aber nur im Ganzen zusammengefasst. Dabei ergeben sich mancherlei Möglichkeiten der Verfehlung. Was als das Wesentliche einer Lehre vorgeführt wird, kann aus der subjektiven Sicht des Geschichtsschreibers als solches erscheinen. Es kann durch das bestimmt

[7] H. Diels, W. Kranz, *Die Fragmente der Vorsokratiker*[9] (Berlin, 1960).
[8] *Sechsig Upanishad's des Veda aus dem Sanskrit übersetzt und mit Einleitungen und Anmerkungen versehen von Paul Deussen*[2] (Leipzig, 1905).
[9] P. Merlan, "Monismus und Dualismus bei einigen Platonikern," *Parusia*. Festgabe für J. Hirschberger (Frankfurt/Main, 1965), pp. 143–154.

werden, was zur Zeit des Historikers im Vordergrund des philosophischen Interesses steht, oder es kann durch den persönlichen Standpunkt des Historikers bestimmt werden. Auch wenn dieser den Inhalt einer philosophischen Schrift, einer Lehre nur verdeutlichen, nur interpretieren will, kann er etwas in sie hineinlegen, was ihr fremd ist. Er kann sie auch in einer Richtung ausdeuten, die nur ansatzweise in ihr enthalten ist. Das geht über ein getreues Referat hinaus, damit wird eine Lehre weitergebildet. Das geschieht umso eher, je geistvoller und selbstständiger ein Historiker der Philosophie ist. Historische Lehren aus der Gegenwart heraus verstehen wollen oder sie von seinem persönlichen Standpunkt aus interpretieren, heisst sie missverstehen und missdeuten. Ein krasses Beispiel dafür hat Professor Merlan in seiner Vorrede zu Heinrich Gomperz' "Philosophical Studies" angeführt: die Auslegung Platons im neukantischen Sinn durch Natorp.[10] Für eine getreue Wiedergabe der historischen Doktrinen muss die verschiedene Geisteshaltung, in der sie wurzeln, zugrundegelegt werden.[11]

4. Die Sammlung, die Edition und die Interpretation der philosophischen Lehren, die im Laufe der Zeit aufgetreten sind, gibt erst das Material für die Geschichte der Philosophie, aber noch nicht ihre Geschichte. Dieses Material wird im Einzelnen unter verschiedenen Gesichtspunkten monographisch bearbeitet. Die erste Aufgabe einer Geschichte der Philosophie ist es, das überlieferte Material chronologisch zu ordnen. Das stellt mitunter eine besondere Aufgabe, wie z.B. bei den platonischen Dialogen. Ferner müssen die historischen Beziehungen zwischen den Lehren auch in der Hinsicht ermittelt werden, inwiefern spätere von früheren abhängig sind, indem sie deren Inhalt übernehmen oder weiterführen oder ob sie ein neues Problem oder eine neue Lösung bringen. So hat Professor Merlan mit der Akribie eines Philologen die Beziehung untersucht, welche

[10] P. Merlan, Foreword to H. Gomperz, *Philosophical Studies* (Boston, 1953), p. 7.
[11] Vgl. H. Gomperz, *Die Lebensauffassung der griechischen Philosophen und das Ideal der inneren Freiheit*[3] (Jena, 1927), pp. 2 f.: "... auszugehen nicht von jenen Punkten ihres Denkens und Fühlens, die uns Heutigen die bedeutendsten scheinen, sondern vielmehr von jenen, die diesen Rang für sie selbst eingenommen haben."

zwischen der Zahlenlehre des Neu-Platonismus und dem Sefer Yezira besteht.[12]

Eine Geschichte der Philosophie gibt den Monographien gegenüber eine zusammenhängende Darstellung, mindestens der Abfolge der historischen Doktrinen. Diese können darin nicht jede einzeln *in extenso* vorgeführt werden, sondern sie können nur in ihrem wesentlichen Inhalt referiert werden; und auch nicht alle, sondern nur die wichtigeren oder die wichtigsten. Auch nicht alle einzelnen Philosophen, die bekannt sind, werden behandelt, sondern nur die bedeutenderen. Es wird das ausgewählt, was an Lehren und Philosophen für wesentlich gehalten wird. Diese Auswahl bringt eine Gefahr mit sich. Was einem Historiker als wichtig und was ihm als unwichtig erscheint, hängt von seinen Gesichtspunkten und Wertungen ab. So hat z.B. Russell, wie er im Vorwort seiner "Philosophie des Abendlandes" erklärt, bei der Philosophie des frühen Mittelalters "unerbittlich alles ausgelassen, was mir von geringer oder gar keiner Bedeutung für die zeitgenössische oder nachfolgende Philosophie zu sein schien."[13] Welche philosophischen Lehren der Vergangenheit im historischen Sinn wichtig sind, muss aus den geistigen Verhältnissen ihrer Zeit heraus beurteilt werden. Deshalb setzt die Auswahl der Lehren und der Philosophen in einer Geschichte der Philosophie, so wie schon das richtige Verständnis der Texte, geistesgeschichtliche Kenntnisse voraus, die ausserhalb der Philosophie liegen, die der allgemeinen Kulturgeschichte entnommen werden müssen. Wenn die Auswahl vom Standpunkt der jeweiligen Gegenwart aus erfolgt, dann hat das zur Folge, dass auch die Geschichte der Philosophie zu verschiedenen Zeiten immer neu geschrieben werden muss, weil sie immer wieder anders aufgefasst wird. Nur wenn die überlieferten Lehren und Philosophen aus dem geistigen Verhältnissen ihrer Zeit verstanden und beurteilt und darnach ausgewählt werden, enthält die Geschichte der Philosophie einen bleibenden, unveränderlichen Bestand.

---

[12] P. Merlan, "Zur Zahlenlehre im Platonismus (Neuplatonismus) und im Sefer Yezira," *Journal of the History of Philosophy* 3 (1965), pp. 167–181.

[13] Russell, *op. cit.*, p. ix.

II

1. Damit stehen wir vor der eigentlich historischen Aufgabe einer Geschichte der Philosophie: die philosophischen Lehren werden als historische Erscheinungen erfasst, die unter bestimmten Bedingungen entstanden sind, unter denen einer bestimmten geistigen und materiellen Kultur. Die philosophischen Lehren gehören nicht nur verschiedenen Zeiten an, sondern auch verschiedenen Kulturkreisen, nicht nur dem europäischen, auch dem indischen, dem chinesischen, dem islamischen. Dadurch sind verschiedene Bedingungen für sie gegeben, ein verschiedener Gesichtkreis, verschiedene Interessen, eine verschiedene Geistesart. Die chinesische Philosophie wurzelt in anderen Voraussetzungen als die europäische. Sie ist aus einem patriarchalischen Geist hervorgegangen. "Die chinesische Weltweisheit ist sehr viel einfacher und primitiver als unsere Philosophie. ... Daher erscheinen uns viele Aussprüche der chinesischen Weisen als Selbstverständlichkeiten, aber sie waren es zu ihrer Zeit noch nicht. ..." [14] Die chinesische Philosophie war vor allem auf die Leitung des praktischen Lebens eingestellt. Das soziale Verhalten, die Sitte, in Fortführung der Tradition, und die Staatsführung stehen im Vordergrund des Interesses. In der taoistischen Lehre vom Nicht-handeln, d.i. keine eigenwilligen Ziele anzustreben, die ihre originale ist, kommt eine Haltung zum Ausdruck, die der abendländischen Aktivität gegensätzlich gegenübersteht. Die chinesische Lebensphilosophie ist noch sehr von den religiösen Vorstellungen vom Himmel als dirigierender göttlicher Macht beherrscht. Die Spekulationen über das Tao als Weltprinzip stellen kein philosophisches System in unserem Sinn dar. Sie nach der Art eines solchen darzustellen, etwa unter der Kategorie "agnostischer Pantheismus," wäre durchaus verfehlt: es würde ihrer Eigenart nicht gerecht werden. Noch viel stärker ist die *indische* Philosophie in der Religion verwurzelt. Sie hat die in ihr gegebene Grundposition festgehalten (Verneinung des Lebensdranges zur Vermeidung des Leidens und der Wiedergeburt), und die Voraussetzungen dafür in verschiedener Weise ausgebaut.

---

[14] A. Forke, *Geschichte der alten chinesischen Philosophie* (Hamburg, 1927), p. ix.

Das Erkennen bildet den Weg zur Erlösung, es wird nicht rein um der Erkenntnis willen gesucht. Anders gerichtete Lehren, materialistische und hedonistische, sind aus dem Widerspruch gegen die religiöse Tradition hervorgegangen. Noch einseitiger war die islamische Philosophie an die Religion gebunden; sie diente zur Begründung des Glaubens durch die Vernunft, wie auch im europäischen Mittelalter. Das leisteten beide mit Hilfe der aus der Spätantike überlieferten Lehren, neuplatonischer und aristotelischer, ohne selbständige Grundkonzeptionen. Eine Philosophie aus rein theoretischem Interesse, als Erkenntnis um der Erkenntnis willen, ist nur im Abendland bei den Griechen entstanden und in der Neuzeit gepflegt worden.

So sind es sehr verschiedene geistige Situationen, aus denen philosophische Lehren hervorgegangen sind. Aus ihnen müssen diese begriffen werden, als Ausdruck der geistigen Interessen und Wünsche für die Lebensgestaltung, die in einem Kulturkreis zu einer Zeit vorhanden waren. Die historischen Bedingungen, unter denen sie entstanden sind, müssen aufgewiesen werden und wie die Lehren mit diesen zusammenhängen, muss im Einzelnen aufgedeckt werden. Es genügt nicht, eine allgemeine kulturgeschichtliche Einleitung einem jeden Abschnitt der Philosophie-Geschichte vorauszuschicken. Eine wirklich historische Darstellung erfordert, dass die philosophischen Lehren als geistesgeschichtliche Erscheinungen in ihrer Bedingtheit durch die jeweiligen Verhältnisse verständlich gemacht werden; und zwar nicht nur durch die allgemeinen Verhältnisse einer Kultur zu einer Zeit, sondern auch durch die besondere Situation der Philosophen, die sie aufgestellt haben. Dass die geistige Arbeit im europäischen Mittelalter ausschliesslich von Angehörigen der Kirche geleistet wurde, ist der Grund dafür, dass die Philosophie an den religiösen Glauben gebunden war und sich nur im Zug seiner rationalen Begründung entwickeln konnte. Erst als sie in der Neuzeit wieder von Laien aufgenommen wurde, konnte sie sich selbständig entfalten.

Der Bedingtheit durch die allgemeinen Verhältnisse steht die individuelle Originalität und Schöpferkraft einzelner Philosophen gegenüber. Durch sie wird eine neue Entwicklung eingeleitet, es werden neue Gesichtspunkte eingeführt, bisherige umgebildet oder aufgehoben. Die Eigenart des schöpferischen

Individuums steht selbständig neben der allgemeinen Geistes-
verfassung. Sie bildet einen wesentlichen Faktor gerade in der
Philosophiegeschichte. So sehr die individuelle Eigenart auch
an der allgemeinen Geisteshaltung teilhat, kann sie doch nicht
aus ihr allein abgeleitet werden; für sie können nur individuelle
Bedingungen aufgewiesen werden, biographische.

Die Philosophie hat einerseits aus den Kenntnissen und den
Bedürfnissen einer Gesellschaft ihre Probleme und das Material
zu ihrer Lösung erhalten, andererseits aus der individuellen
Begabung und Initiative. Aber nur aus beiden Komponenten
zusammen wird sie historisch erklärbar, nicht aus einer Komponente allein; auch nicht aus den grossen Individuen, was gerade
für die Philosophie naheliegt. Aber Platon ist genauso durch das
geistige Milieu Griechenlands im 5. und 4. Jahrhundert bedingt,
durch die Sophisten und die Eleaten und Pythagoräer und
Sparta, wie Konfuzius und Laotze durch die chinesische Geisteshaltung oder Buddha durch die indische. So steht eine Geschichte der Philosophie, wirklich als Geschichte geschrieben, als
ein Zweig der Kulturgeschichte neben den anderen, neben der
Literaturgeschichte, der Kunstgeschichte, der Sozial- und der
Wirtschaftsgeschichte u.a.

2. Damit haben wir aber in dem, was uns die Philosophiegeschichte bietet, nur immer Produkte eines Kulturkreises zu
einer Zeit vor uns, die bedingt sind durch dessen spezielle Verhältnisse und die je nach diesen verschieden sind. Sie gehören
infolge dessen immer einer bestimmten historischen Situation zu.
Durch diese Relativität sind die philosophischen Lehren verschiedener Kulturkreise, ja sogar solche weit auseinanderliegen-
der Zeiten desselben Kulturkreises, innerlich voneinander getrennt. Jede hat ihre selbständige Eigenart. Diese Sonderung hat
Spengler ins Extreme übertrieben; die Kulturen stehen heterogen
nebeneinander, jede für sich und ohne innere Gemeinsamkeit mit
den anderen und darum ohne Verständnis für einander. Das
gälte auch für ihre Philosophien. Das ist unhaltbar.

Rein historisch betrachtet stellt sich die Philosophie als eine
Mannigfaltigkeit von Doktrinen dar, die sich im Laufe der Zeit
gewandelt haben. Sie gibt im Ganzen eine blosse Abfolge, aber
keine fortschreitende Entwicklung. Denn eine solche setzt eine
innere Gemeinsamkeit, einen sachlichen Zusammenhang voraus,

wodurch die historischen Lehren untereinander verbunden werden; und sie setzt voraus, dass die Wandlungen in ihnen in einer
bestimmten Richtung gehen. Der zufolge können die überlieferten Lehren als reifer oder als überholt gewertet werden. Sie
können auch in der Hinsicht gewertet werden, dass eine Lehre
durch ihre Originalität hervorragt oder dadurch, dass sie ton-
angebend geworden ist und weithin fortgewirkt hat oder dadurch,
dass sie die bisherigen Ansätze systematisch zusammenfasst.
Diese rein sachliche Feststellung kann in Form einer Wertung
ausgesprochen werden. Es ist der Wert unter dem historischen
Gesichtspunkt. Er betrifft nur die Bedeutsamkeit einer Lehre
innerhalb einer Epoche. Aber eine Entwicklung kann höchstens
innerhalb eines Kulturkreises festgestellt werden, weil nur innerhalb eines solchen die erforderliche Gemeinsamkeit besteht. Für
die Gesamtheit der Philosophie fehlt hingegen ein ineinander-
greifender Zusammenhang und darum auch eine gemeinsame
Basis für eine solche Wertung. Denn die grossen Kulturen, die
europäische, die indische, die chinesische, stehen selbständig
nebeneinander und damit auch ihre Philosophien.

III

1. Damit stellt sich nun die grosse Frage: Haben wir in der
Geschichte der Philosophie nur eine Vielfalt von gedanklichen
Schöpfungen vor uns? Stehen sie da wie die Werke der Kunst,
bedeutende neben geringeren, im Sinn historischer Wirksamkeit
oder zeigt sich in ihrer Abfolge eine Entwicklung, eine zunehmen-
de Klärung und Lösung und Überwindung, wie in der Geschichte
einer Fachwissenschaft? Lässt sich in der Geschichte der Philosophie ein Fortschreiten zu bleibenden Ergebnissen erkennen?
Diese Frage führt über eine rein historische Betrachtung der
Philosophie hinaus, denn sie bringt an das historisch Vorliegende
einen *kritischen* Gesichtspunkt heran. Damit stehen wir vor dem
3. Gesichtspunkt, der für eine Geschichte der Philosophie in
Betracht kommt.

Die Voraussetzung für eine Entwicklung ist (1) ein gemeinsames Gebiet, in dem die Entwicklung vor sich geht, und (2) ein
gemeinsames Mass, durch das der Fortschritt bestimmt wird.
Ein gemeinsames Mass, an dem *alle* philosophischen Lehren

gemessen werden können, ist in der Logik gegeben. Darnach kann
an den philosophischen Lehren eine Kritik geübt werden. Es
können Widersprüche in ihnen und andere Verstösse gegen die
Logik aufgedeckt werden, und es kann auch ein Fortschritt durch
systematischen Aufbau festgestellt werden. Aber es ist eine bloss
formale Kritik. Die Frage geht jedoch nach einem Fortschritt in
sachlicher Hinsicht in der Philosophie. Diese Frage kann durch
eine logische Kritik nicht entschieden werden. Dafür kommt es
auf eine sachliche Kritik an. Wenn diese von einem subjektiven
Standpunkt aus geübt wird, ist es erst die Frage, ob dieser
richtig, ob er allgemeingültig ist. Wenn eine Kritik mehr als eine
blosse, subjektive Stellungnahme sein soll, muss sie von einer
allgemeingültigen Grundlage aus erfolgen. Wie steht es damit in
Bezug auf die Gesamtheit der Philosophie?

2. Was die Geschichte der Philosophie vor uns hinstellt, sind
in erster Linie die grossen philosophischen Systeme. Sie sind
miteinander unverträglich. Darum können nicht alle insgesamt
wahr sein. Ist nun eines von ihnen allein das wahre? Das lässt
sich nicht entscheiden. Auf der Linie der grossen philosophischen
Systeme gibt es keine Entwicklung auf ein endgültiges hin. Auch
Hegels System kann nicht als das einzig mögliche gelten. Aus
dieser Sicht ist es verständlich, dass ein Fortschritt in der
Philosophie überhaupt verneint wird. "Es gibt keinen Fortschritt wie in den einzelnen Wissenschaften, der darin besteht,
dass das Alte überholt und überwunden wird, sondern es gibt
nur ein Fortschreiten zu neuen Fragen und neuen Sichten."[15]
Die Geschichte der Philosophie bietet nur eine Mannigfaltigkeit
von Denkmöglichkeiten, die unentscheidbar nebeneinander stehen, ebenbürtig wie die Werke der Kunst. Man kann nur Typen
der Weltanschauung aufstellen, wie es Dilthey getan hat. Aber
damit verliert die Philosophie einen wissenschaftlichen Charakter.
Das ist dann unvermeidlich.

3. Aber die Philosophie wollte doch immer Erkenntnis sein,
Erkenntnis der Welt und der Lebenswerte. In ihrem Beginn in
der griechischen Antike war sie mit Erkenntnis überhaupt
gleichbedeutend und lange darüber hinaus bis noch in Newtons
"*Philosophia naturalis*" war mit "Philosophie" Wissenschaft ge-

---

[15] A. Diemer, I. Frenzel, edd., *Philosophie*, Das Fischer-Lexikon XI
(Frankfurt/Main, Hamburg, 1958), p. 107.

meint. Auch die indische Philosophie wollte Erkenntnis geben, durch welche Erlösung erlangt wird. Und auch die chinesische Philosophie betrachtete ihre Lehren als gültige Einsichten, also als Erkenntnis. Wenn die Philosophie Erkenntnis zu sein beansprucht, dann besteht eine Gemeinsamkeit für alle überlieferten Lehren; sie sind insofern kommensurabel. In dem Anspruch auf Erkenntnis ist die Grundlage für eine Kritik gegeben, die objektiv und allgemeingültig ist, und der alle überlieferten Lehren unterworfen sind. Die Erkenntnis ergibt das Kriterium für eine Sichtung der Lehren, ob sie ein dauerndes Ergebnis bilden oder überholt und bloss historisch sind. Damit wird es möglich, festzustellen, ob in der Philosophie ein Fortschritt stattgefunden hat, ob es in ihr eine Entwicklung gibt.

Dazu ist eine klare Bestimmung erforderlich, worin Erkenntnis besteht. Erkenntnis wird gewöhnlich als wahres Urteil definiert. Worin Wahrheit besteht, darüber herrscht keine Einigkeit und keine hinreichende Klarheit. Auch hinsichtlich der Erkenntnis bestehen verschiedene Richtungen: Phänomenalismus, Existenzialismus, Neu-Hegelianismus, Neo-Positivismus. Jede begründet die Erkenntnis in anderer Weise und demgemäss fällt eine Kritik der überlieferten Lehren verschieden aus. Vor allem in Bezug auf die Metaphysik widerstreiten sie einander. Es gibt keinen allgemein anerkannten Standpunkt für die Kritik. So erscheint es wieder problematisch, ob sich in der Philosophie allgemeingültige Erkenntnis erweisen lässt oder ob sie nur Denkmöglichkeiten vorführt.

4. Aber dieser Zustand muss nicht als endgültig betrachtet werden. Erkenntnis liegt zweifellos in den Fachwissenschaften vor und dieser Erkenntnisbegriff muss auch für die Philosophie geltend gemacht werden, wenn sie eine ebenbürtige Erkenntnis enthalten soll. Wenn der Begriff der Erkenntnis so gefasst wird, wie er in den Fachwissenschaften massgebend ist, dann besteht Erkenntnis in Urteilen, die stichhaltig begründet sind, einerseits durch die Logik, andererseits, wenn es sich um Aussagen über Wirklichkeit handelt, durch Erfahrung, das heisst in letzter Linie durch Wahrnehmung.[16]

Unter diesem Gesichtspunkt ergibt sich eine Kritik der his-

---

[16] Vgl. V. Kraft, *Erkenntnislehre* (Wien, 1960) u. *Die Grundlagen der Erkenntnis und der Moral* (Wien, 1968).

torischen Philosophie, dass die grossen philosophischen Systeme diesen Anforderungen an Erkenntnis nicht gerecht werden. In ihnen sind über Erfahrungserkenntnissen spekulative Konstruktionen errichtet, die nicht zu begründen sind, weil sie über das erkenntnismässig Begründbare weit hinausgehen. Sie können darum nicht als Erkenntnisse angesehen werden. Gerade für die hervorragendsten Schöpfungen der Philosophie lässt sich daher auch kein Fortschritt feststellen. Auch hinsichtlich der Ethik zeigt es sich, dass ihre verschiedenen Richtungen dogmatisch aufgestellt sind, dass ihnen eine erkenntnismässige Begründung mangelt. Schliesslich ist Erkenntnis auf diesem Gebiet überhaupt verneint worden.

Aber andererseits ist es offensichtlich, dass mindestens in der europäischen Philosophie eine Entwicklung auf dem Gebiet der Logik und der Erkenntnislehre stattgefunden hat, in der Antike und auch im Mittelalter und besonders in der Neuzeit. In der Auseinandersetzung der Lehren untereinander und im Streben nach Beweis, auch für den religiösen Glauben, ist die Logik ausgebildet worden und sind die Bedingungen für die Gültigkeit als Erkenntnis immer deutlicher erfasst worden; die Fragen sind geklärt und die Antworten präziser formuliert worden und die Grenzen des Erkennbaren sind aufgewiesen worden. Der Fortschritt in der Philosophie erfolgt so auf der Linie der Erkenntnislehre.

Aber das Interesse der Philosophie war im Lauf ihrer Geschichte in erster Linie auf ein Weltbild gerichtet. Wenn auch die bisherigen Systeme einer Kritik nicht standgehalten haben, so muss die Philosophie auf ihr Hauptanliegen doch nicht verzichten. Bei einem Weltbild handelt es sich um Wirklichkeitserkenntnis und diese muss auf Erfahrung gegründet sein. Die Erfahrungserkenntnis wird in den Fachwissenschaften erarbeitet, und deshalb ist ein Weltbild von den Erkenntnissen der Fachwissenschaften abhängig. Es ist die Aufgabe, ein einheitliches Gesamtsystem der erfahrungswissenschaftlichen Erkenntnis aufzustellen. Dafür lassen aber die Fachwissenschaften trotz ihres grossen Fortschrittes gegenwärtig noch zu viele entscheidende Fragen offen. Ihre Ergebnisse sind noch zu fragmentarisch, um den Aufbau eines solchen Systems hinreichend zu bestimmen. Aber man darf erwarten, dass mit dem weiteren Fortschreiten der fachwissenschaftlichen Erkenntnis auch ein Weltsystem eine immer deutlichere Gestalt annehmen wird.

Damit sind die Bedingungen für eine *kritische* Geschichte der Philosophie nicht nur klargestellt, sondern es ist auch gezeigt, dass diese möglich ist – und das durch sie der fundamental wichtige Nachweis geführt werden kann, dass die Geschichte der Philosophie eine, wenigstens teilweise, Entwicklung aufweist. Die kritische Analyse der überlieferten Lehren bildet eine nicht zu vernachlässigende Aufgabe der Philosophiegeschichte. In ihr wird diese erst für eine Philosophie, die mehr sein soll als ihre eigene Geschichte, fruchtbar. Sie ist aber bisher nicht programmatisch aufgenommen worden, sondern Kritik wird in historische Darstellungen nur gelegentlich eingestreut.

Wien

SOCRATES IN HAMANN'S
SOCRATIC MEMORABILIA AND NIETZSCHE'S
BIRTH OF TRAGEDY: A COMPARISON

JAMES C. O'FLAHERTY

In the year 1759 the twenty-nine year old Johann Georg Hamann (1730–1788), later to acquire the sobriquet *Magus im Norden,* launched his formal career as a writer with a brief essay bearing the curious title, *Socratic Memorabilia, Compiled for the Boredom of the Public by a Lover of Boredom.*[1] One hundred and thirteen years later, in 1872, the twenty-seven year old Friedrich Nietzsche published his first major work under the singular, but more sober title, *The Birth of Tragedy from the Spirit of Music.*[2] It is an interesting and significant fact that both writers commenced their careers with works in which Socrates appears as the central figure. It happens, however, that the accounts of the Greek philosopher appearing in the two works are so different that one might well wonder whether the authors were writing about the same historical personage. This fact strikes us as all the more surprising when we remember that, despite the deep religious gulf which separates them, the two thinkers have much in common.

Since I am chiefly concerned in the present study with the major differences between the Hamannian and Nietzschean interpretations of Socrates in the essays mentioned, it may be well to call attention at this point to the similarities of the two treatises. First of all, it should be noted that both thinkers are in sharp opposition to the spirit of their age: Hamann levels his attack against the contemporary Enlightenment and Nietzsche

---

[1] J. G. Hamann, *Sokratische Denkwürdigkeiten für die lange Weile des Publicums zusammengetragen von einem Liebhaber der langen Weile. Mit einer doppelten Zuschrift an Niemand und an Zween* (Amsterdam, 1759). The actual place of publication was Königsberg.

[2] F. Nietzsche, *Die Geburt der Tragödie aus dem Geiste der Musik* (Leipzig, 1872). Later the title was changed to: *Die Geburt der Tragödie oder: Griechentum und Pessimismus.*

against the prevailing materialism and philistinism of the nineteenth century; both advocate irrationalism as an antidote for excessive rationalism; each essay is a confession of faith, Hamann's in Christianity, Nietzsche's in pagan Greek religion with Dionysus as the supreme deity and Richard Wagner as his contemporary high priest; in each Socrates appears as the forerunner and ally of Christ.[3] Both writers subvert the Winckelmannian interpretation of Greek culture as characterized by "noble simplicity and tranquil grandeur"; both writers are at odds with the rationalistic philologists and historians of their day; and, finally, the two essays are couched in a prose which is metaphorical and often poetic, in every case the opposite of the learned jargon employed in the schools.

Having noted the important similarities which we find in the *Socratic Memorabilia* and *The Birth of Tragedy*, we must now turn to the even more important differences. Both works are, however, so many-faceted that it would not be possible to compare them in any great detail. (Hamann's essay, despite its relative brevity, bristles with references and allusions which need elucidation). I shall therefore confine myself to those points of difference which allow the radically diverging conceptions of Socrates to come into clear focus. My method will be to quote the exact words of the two authors freely whenever possible. Both Hamann and Nietzsche are acknowledged masters of language, and, even though I have cited all quotations and titles in English translation, I trust that the advantage of reaching a wider audience will outweigh the loss which translation entails.

In *The Birth of Tragedy* Nietzsche develops the thesis that Attic tragedy grew out of Dionysian music, and that its greatness is a result of the felicitous union of the irrational and rational aspects of human nature. These aspects he called the "Dionysian" and the "Apollonian" elements of the human psyche.[4] In

[3] Nietzsche avoids mentioning Christ or Christianity by name in the work itself, but his intent is clear; further, we have his own word in this connection. See "Versuch einer Selbstkritik," in F. Nietzsche, *Gesammelte Werke* (Munich, 1920), Musarionausgabe, Vol. III, pp. 10–12.

[4] M. L. Baeumer traces the use of the conceptual opposites, "Apollonian-Dionysian," before (and after) Nietzsche's employment of them. See "Die Dionysische-Entwicklung eines literarischen Klischees," *Colloquia Germanica* 3 (1967), pp. 253–262.

the course of time, however, Socrates, the arch-rationalist and unflagging optimist, appeared on the scene to destroy the fusion which had made the tragedy of Aeschylus and Sophocles possible. "Socrates," Nietzsche writes, "might be designated as the specific *non-mystic*, in whom the logical nature is developed, through a superfoetation, to the same excess as instinctive wisdom is developed in the mystic."[5] But where Nietzsche sees the archetypal man of reason, who succeeds in destroying the highest form of culture, Hamann sees the archetypal man of faith, who is himself destroyed by a hostile world because of his faith. In Nietzsche's view the Socratic influence in the fields of art and religion is negative; in Hamann's view it is positive. Which of these conflicting opinions is closer to the historical facts is a question which lies outside the scope of the present study. It is my purpose simply to call attention to the striking contrast afforded by these two important thinkers who have, in many ways, so much in common.

In the *Memorabilia* Hamann's primary purpose was to answer the attempt of two of his rationalistic friends to reconvert him to the tenets of the Enlightenment. In 1758 Hamann had undergone a radical religious experience in London, which led him to adopt the standpoint of evangelical Christianity, a standpoint which he was to defend militantly throughout his life. This sudden defection from his earlier rationalism so offended one of his friends, Johann Christoph Berens (1729–1792), that he enlisted the aid of the young university professor, Immanuel Kant, in persuading Hamann to abandon his newly-won faith. Hamann's formal answer to his friendly critics was his little work on Socrates. Instead of merely defending his position, he opens an attack on that of Berens and Kant and of the Enlightenment in general. By appealing to Socrates, the most revered philosopher of the eighteenth century, and by attempting to show that the Enlighteners were really anti-Socratic, Hamann hoped to create a sort of philosophic Trojan horse with which he would penetrate the citadel of the Enlightenment. That the

---

[5] *The Birth of Tragedy*. Trans. W. A. Haussmann in *The Complete Works of Friedrich Nietzsche*, O. Levy, ed. (London, 1923), Vol. I, p. 105. Hereafter references to this volume will be made in the text only with the letter "N" followed by the page number.

work did constitute a telling blow against the prevailing rationalism is a well-known fact of German cultural history.

Hamann makes a claim for his essay on Socrates which Nietzsche does not, and one which is important for an understanding of his concept of the Greek philosopher. In the dedication of the work, "To the Two," he writes: "I have written about Socrates in a Socratic manner" (61: 10).[6] In other words the very *form* of the essay is supposed to reflect something about the true nature of Socrates. Since this is so, it is necessary to say a word about the literary form which he has created.

As previously indicated, the essay is relatively brief. In the original edition of 1759 it consisted only of sixty-four pages in small octavo. It was, nevertheless, divided into seven parts as follows: two dedications, "To the Public, or Nobody, the Well-known," and "To the Two"; an "Introduction"; three "Sections" (*Abschnitte*); and, finally, the "Peroration" (*Schlussrede*).

Thus the *Socratic Memorabilia* exhibits to a marked degree the most striking characteristic of all Hamann's formal writings, namely, concentration. It was his procedure to pack as much meaning as possible into a word or phrase, and all too often he attempted to pour too much new wine into the old wineskins of language. This is not the place to enter upon a disquisition on Hamann's much-discussed and baffling style, but it should be said that the *Memorabilia* appears upon initial reading to a great extent unintelligible, especially if one approaches it without the aid of a commentary. This obscurity does not obtain with regard to the general drift or meaning of the whole. I do not think that any reader, whether of the eighteenth or the twentieth century, could fail to grasp the author's main intention. Further, most of the obscurities can be cleared up, if one is willing to go to the trouble of doing so.

In order to veil his meaning Hamann employs a variety of technical literary devices, e.g., antonomasia, metonymy, periphrasis, epithets, obscure Biblical, classical, and contemporary

[6] References to the text of the *Socratic Memorabilia* are to my translation of that work, *Hamann's Socratic Memorabilia: A Translation and Commentary* (Baltimore, 1967). This translation is accompanied by a reproduction of the Nadler text (Vienna, 1950), to which the parenthetical notes in the text refer.

allusions.[7] All this can be explained on the basis of his main principle, namely, that the appearance must not exhaust the reality for which it stands or, to be more specific, language must not reveal all of its meaning at first or even second glance. This relationship of appearance and reality involves a kind of irony, and irony is, of course, central to the Socratic teaching: "Analogy constituted the soul of his [Socrates'] reasoning, and he gave it irony for a body" (61: 10–12).

When Hamann says that he has written on Socrates in a Socratic manner, what he means is that he presents his treasure in an earthen vessel, for such was the manner, he maintained, in which Socrates himself actually spoke:

The critics were not satisfied with his allusions, and censured the similes of his oral discourse at one time as being too farfetched and at another time as vulgar. Alcibiades, however, compared his parables to certain sacred images of the gods and goddesses, which were carried, according to the custom of that time, in a small case, on the outside of which only the form of a goat-footed satyr was visible (80: 4–9).

If we are to take Hamann at his word, we must accept the often eccentric and involuted form of his prose as an emblem of a higher meaning. It is obvious that he believed such a literary form more faithfully represents the Socratic spirit than a more conventional and pleasing form could possibly do.

Nietzsche makes no similar claim concerning *The Birth of Tragedy*, that is, he does not maintain that the reader can infer from the style of his work anything about the nature of Socrates or Socratic thought. In the first place, Nietzsche's avowed purpose in the work is to show how tragedy developed from Dionysian music, which, he maintained, is the true expression of the tragic sense. Socrates does become the central figure of the work, but we do not find his name mentioned until halfway through the treatise where he is rather abruptly revealed as the real destroyer of the Apollonian-Dionysian harmony. The way had been prepared for this disclosure, however, by the earlier discussion of the corrosive influence of Euripides, Socrates' putative disciple in the art of play-writing. But from now on the stage is dominated by the overwhelming figure of Socrates:

[7] See *Hamann's Socratic Memorabilia, ibid.*, pp. 61–85.

Dionysus had already been scared from the tragic stage, and in fact by a demonic power which spoke through Euripides. Even Euripides was, in a certain sense, only a mask: the deity that spoke through him was neither Dionysus nor Apollo, but an altogether new-born demon, called *Socrates*. This is the new antithesis: the Dionysian and the Socratic, and the artwork of Greek tragedy was wrecked on it (N, 95).

Even if Socrates had been the announced subject of *The Birth of Tragedy*, Nietzsche could not have claimed that he was writing about Socrates in a Socratic manner, for it was precisely the Socratic manner, as he conceived it, which was to be reprobated. What we actually have in this work is an account of the rationalistic Socrates presented in an impassioned and artistic prose which, though uneven in style, at the same time expresses very keen metaphysical and psychological insights.

Sixteen years after the publication of *The Birth of Tragedy* Nietzsche was hypercritical of it, describing it as "doubtful" and "disagreeable":

I say again, today it is an impossible book to me, – I call it badly written, heavy, painful, image-angling and image-entangling, maudlin, sugared at times even to feminism, uneven in tempo, void of all will to logical cleanliness, very convinced and therefore rising above the necessity of demonstration, distrustful even of the *propriety* of demonstration, as being a book for initiates, as "music" for those who are baptised with the name of Music .... It should have *sung* ... and not spoken! What a pity, that I did not dare to say what I then had to say, as a poet: I could have done so perhaps! Or at least as a philologist: – for even at the present day wellnigh everything in this domain remains to be discovered and disinterred by the philologist! (N, 5–6).

What this amounts to when we extract the main ideas from Nietzsche's dithyrambic prose is that years later, in his Zarathustra period, Nietzsche finds his earlier work badly written, a work which is neither fish nor fowl, neither poetry nor philology. There can be no doubt that his judgement is too severe. For our present purpose, however, it is sufficient to point out that he does not approve of the logic of the work, a point to which we shall return below. *The Birth of Tragedy* is actually an account of Socrates in a manner inimical to the rationalistic, non-musical Socrates portrayed in it, not because of its inconsistencies or lack of logical cleanliness, but because, with all its faults, it has considerable aesthetic appeal. We must conclude that the form of Hamann's work harmonizes with his conception of Socrates, whereas Nietzsche's is at odds with his conception. This is not to say that Hamann's essay possessed the greater literary merit, for the two works are scarcely comparable in this regard. But it does point up an important difference between them.

Having given some consideration to the origin of the two essays at hand and to the significance of the forms in which they are cast, we may now turn our attention to their contents. Before doing so, however, it should be noted that Hamann's treatise contains three levels of meaning. First, it is ostensibly an account of the life of the historical Socrates; secondly, it is at the same time a "metaschematized"[8] account of Hamann's relation to his friends, Kant and Berens; and, thirdly, it refers at crucial points to the life and death of Christ. Since it is characterized by the presence of these three levels, one should not be surprised to find Hamann shifting abruptly from one level to another.

In comparing the contents of the Hamannian and Nietzschean works it is best to start with their respective treatments of the Socratic ignorance, for it clearly forms the center around which Hamann's thought revolves, and serves to throw into sharp relief the Nietzschean counter-emphasis. The centrality of the Socratic ignorance for Hamann is attested by such statements as:

The opinion of Socrates can be summarized in these blunt words, when he said to the Sophists, the learned men of his time, "I know nothing." Therefore these words were a thorn in their eyes and a scourge on their backs. All of Socrates' ideas, which were nothing more than expectorations and secretions of his ignorance, seemed as frightful to them as the hair of Medusa's head, the knob of the Aegis (73: 2–9).

Or again:

From this Socratic ignorance readily flow the peculiarities of his manner of teaching and thinking. What is more natural than that he always felt himself compelled to ask and to become wiser ... (75: 32–34).

The Socratic ignorance appeared like the "hair of Medusa's head" to the rationalistic Athenians since it amounted to a denial of their theoretical knowledge. Socrates did not admit to ignorance

---

[8] The Hamannian "metaschematism" means, in this case, the identification of himself with Socrates, but Kant, Berens, and the Enlighteners in general with the Sophists who were Socrates' opponents.

of their kind of knowledge. Rather the contrary. He could have beaten the rationalists (whom Hamann indiscriminately calls "Sophists") at their own game. Hamann then employs an anecdote about card players to emphasize his point. Socrates is compared to an honorable card player who also happens to be a very skilful sleight-of-hand artist. When invited by cardsharps to a game of cards, he responds:

> I don't play, that is, with people such as you, who break the rules of the game, and rob it of its pleasure.... If you had proposed to me that we hold a contest to determine which one of us was the best sleight-of-hand artist at cards, then I would have wanted to answer differently, and perhaps to join in a game in order to show you that you have learned to fix cards as poorly as you understand how to play those that are dealt to you according to the rules of the game (72: 38–73: 3).

The cardsharps represent, of course, the opponents of Socrates, who will not admit that their kind of knowledge involves deceit – a kind of intellectual legerdemain.

The rationalists are deceivers in Hamann's opinion because they cause men to believe in the autonomy of reason. Truth is not attained simply through reason, but its acquisition involves also an irrational process. Therefore, to confess one's ignorance is not to say that one lacks the proper theoretical knowledge, but to acknowledge the impotence of mere theory. Socrates did not say in effect: I don't have the theoretical knowledge I should have, and therefore must confess my ignorance. What he did say was: I know theoretical knowledge is not enough, and I know this because I *feel* it. Hamann (73: 10) sums up the matter by saying: "The ignorance of Socrates was sensibility (*Empfindung*)." Philip Merlan has suggested that the term *Empfindung* might well be translated "live attitude." [9] In any event, it is true that Hamann saw Socrates as rejecting the dry bones of abstract knowledge, which bespeak death rather than life: "... between sensibility and a theoretical proposition there is a greater difference than between a living animal and its anatomical skeleton" (73: 10–12).

If Socrates' awareness of his own ignorance arose from feeling or sensibility, what sort of knowledge is that? Does feeling have

[9] P. Merlan, "From Hume to Hamann," *The Personalist* 22. 1 (January, 1951), p. 12.

a legitimate role to play in cognition? Hamann answers such questions by pointing to the role of faith, which is largely to be equated with feeling, in all human cognition. In so doing he was influenced considerably by the English philosopher Hume,[10] even though he arrived at quite different results from Hume. "Our own existence," Hamann wrote, "and the existence of all things outside us must be believed, and cannot be determined in any other way" (73: 21–22).

Hamann's formulation raises important epistemological questions, which cannot be discussed here. But it should be pointed out that his idea results in establishing not only the outer, objective world of phenomena on the basis of faith, but also the inner, subjective world of one's own individual existence. Whereas Kant found it necessary to eliminate faith to make room for philosophy, Hamann makes it the basis of his world-view, which he imputes to Socrates. Faith is, in his judgment, not only the pillar upon which subjectivity ("our own existence") and objectivity ("all things outside us") both rest, but it is also the overarching reality which holds them together so that the dualism inherent in the subject-object epistemology is overcome.

If the positive side of this epistemology is represented by a stress on faith, the negative side is represented by an attack on the alleged certainty of both empirical and logical reasoning.

With regard to empirical certainty Hamann writes:

What is more certain than the end of man, and of what truth is there a more general and better attested knowledge? Nevertheless, no one is wise enough to believe it except the one who, as Moses makes clear, is taught by God himself to number his days. What one believes does not, therefore, have to be proved, and a proposition can be ever so incontrovertibly proven without on that account being believed" (73: 22–28).

On the other hand, neither does logical reasoning provide certainty. Only faith is able to do that: "Faith is not the work of reason, and therefore cannot succumb to its attack, because faith arises just as little from reason as tasting and seeing do" (74: 2–5). This epistemology is characteristic of Hamann, to be sure. It is not characteristic of the historical Socrates. But in the Hamannian view Socrates was preeminently the man of faith and

[10] See P. Merlan, "From Hume to Hamann"; also E. Metzke, *J. G. Hamanns Stellung in der Philosophie des 18. Jahrhunderts* (Halle-Saale, 1934), esp. pp. 75–78.

the enemy of speculative reason. In the introduction to the *Socratic Memorabilia* the Magus states very bluntly what he considered to be the insolence of reason: "To dissect a body and an event into its primary elements means attempting to detect God's invisible being, His eternal power and Godhead" (64: 13–15). Reason is thus no source of genuine certainty, and its excessive use becomes an affront to deity.

The maieutic approach to knowledge is further evidence of Socrates' anti-speculative tendency. For the one who does not present his interlocutor with a truth at which he has arrived with the aid of his autonomous reason alone, but who seeks to draw the truth out of his partner by skilful questioning is no arrogant theorist: "Socrates was, therefore, modest enough to compare his theoretical wisdom with the skill of an old woman who merely comes to the aid of the mother's labor and her timely birth, and renders assistance to both" (66: 16–19).

To Hamann's interpretation of Socrates as a man of faith there can be no sharper contrast than the interpretation of Nietzsche. For, according to Nietzsche, the Socratic confession of ignorance was in actuality a confession of the importance of theoretical knowledge:

The most decisive word, however, for this new and unprecedented esteem of knowledge and insight was spoken by Socrates when he found that he was the only one who acknowledged to himself that he *knew* nothing; while in his critical pilgrimage through Athens, and calling on the greatest statesmen, orators, poets, and artists, he discovered everywhere the conceit of knowledge. He perceived, to his astonishment, that all these celebrities were without a proper and accurate insight, even with regard to their own callings, and practised them only by instinct (N, 103).

In such a way Nietzsche inverts the Hamannian conception. Whereas Hamann's Socrates is characterized by feeling and faith, the Socrates of Nietzsche is a proponent of a "new and unprecedented esteem of knowledge." Again Nietzsche writes: "Socrates might be designated as the specific *non-mystic*, in whom the logical nature is developed, through a superfoetation, to the same excess as instinctive wisdom is developed in the mystic" (N, 105). And further: "He who has experienced even a breath of the divine naiveté and security of the Socratic course of life in the Platonic writings, will also feel that the enormous driving-wheel of logical Socratism is in motion, as it were, *behind* Socrates, and that it must be viewed through Socrates as through a shadow" (N, 105–106). Socrates' confession constitutes, then, an indirect confession of faith in reason. Under his aegis great art was destroyed, for "optimistic dialectics drives *music* out of tragedy with the scourge of its syllogisms: that is, it destroys the essence of tragedy, which can be explained only as a manifestation and illustration of Dionysian states, as the visible symbolisation of music, as the dream-world of Dionysian ecstasy" (N, 111). For Nietzsche, Socrates was "that despotic logician" who had doubts only too late and too little about his logical universe. (N, 112–113).

It is illuminating that Nietzsche almost entirely ignores the Socratic maieutics, mentioning it only once and then quite incidentally in connection with his training of the elite youth of Athens. (Sec. 15) Upon reflection, however this fact is hardly surprising, for after all Socrates' maieutic activity does not fit readily into the conception of that philosopher as the obsessive exponent of theoretical knowledge. Yet this neglect must seem strange, for as Hamann says: "His [Socrates'] teaching has always been compared to the art of midwifery." (66: 2–3) By skillful questioning Socrates believed he could demonstrate to his interlocutor that he was really in possession of a wisdom more valuable than the speculations of the Sophists or the clichés of priest and politician who would manipulate him. (77: 5–9)

Whereas Hamann sets Socrates in sharp opposition to the Sophists, Nietzsche identifies Socrates with them in *The Birth of Tragedy*. Thus:

It is in this tone, half indignantly and half contemptuously, that Aristophanic comedy is wont to speak of both of them [Socrates and Euripides] – to the consternation of modern men, who would indeed be willing enough to give up Euripides, but cannot suppress their amazement that Socrates should appear in Aristophanes as the first and head *sophist*, as the mirror and epitome of all sophistical tendencies. (N, 102).

Nietzsche then proceeds to speak of the "profound instincts of Aristophanes" in relegating Socrates to the Sophists. In Hamann's scheme, however, it is the Sophists who take the blame for the devolution of Greek culture which Nietzsche ascribes to Socrates. Nowhere is the difference between the two versions of Socrates more apparent than in their interpretations of the Socratic *daimon*. One may imagine Hamann's Socrates saying something like this: "I know that I am not in possession of rational knowledge, but I am in possession of something far better than such knowledge, namely, a *daimon* which instructs me in both what I should do and refrain from doing." It is instructive that Hamann suddenly shifts, when he introduces his discussion of the *daimon*, from a religious context to an aesthetic one. Here he is influenced by the obsession of the literary critics of the eighteenth century with the quest for clearly formulated rules of procedure whereby one might create great works of art. In this context Hamann writes: "What for a Homer replaces the ignorance of the rules of art which an Aristotle devised after him, and what for a Shakespeare replaces the ignorance or transgression of those critical laws? Genius is the unanimous answer" (75: 3–5). He then makes it clear that such a genius or tutelary spirit is to be equated with the Socratic *daimon*, for he adds immediately: "Indeed, Socrates could very well afford to be ignorant; he had a tutelary genius, on whose science he could rely, which he loved and feared as his God, whose peace was more important to him than all the reason of the Egyptians and Greeks, whose voice he believed ..." (75: 6–10).

It should be noticed first of all that the Magus interprets the Socratic *daimon* as positive.[11] It appears in a negative role, however, on the ethical plane: "Reverence for the voice in his heart, to whose sound he was always attentive, excused him from attending political meetings" (78: 11–13). On the religious plane the Socratic *daimon* became for Hamann a prototype of the Holy Spirit. For instance, he compares the "empty understanding of a Socrates" to the "womb of a pure virgin" (75: 11–13). Hence, Socrates' dependence on his tutelary spirit or *daimon* has a profound religious meaning. The attempts which the devotees

[11] E. M. Butler writes of Hamann's influence on Goethe: "The daimon of Socrates, rediscovered and reinterpreted by Hamann, the intuitive all-knowing, all powerful genius, found its way straight to the one spirit alive which could harbour it, and forthwith began dictating terms." *The Tyranny of Greece over Germany* (Boston, 1958), p. 94. Cf. A. Henkel, *Wandrers Sturmlied. Versuch, das dunkle Gedicht des jungen Goethe zu verstehen* (Frankfurt a.M., 1962) for a fascinating study of Hamann's influence in a particular instance.

of reason have always made to explain the *daimon* in rational terms must for this reason always fail. (Cf. 75: 14–31) In this connection Hamann's irony comes to the fore: "So much has been written about this by so many sophists with such conclusiveness that one must be astonished that Socrates, in spite of his celebrated self-knowledge, could also be so ignorant in this matter that he would not answer Simias about it" (75: 25–19). Hamann then adds, continuing in his vein of irony, that the reader can readily obtain facile explanations of the Socratic *daimon* among the intelligentsia. "No cultivated reader of our day lacks talented friends who will spare me the effort of going into more detail about Socrates' tutelary spirit" (75: 29–31).

In order to contrast Nietzsche's conception of the Socratic *daimon* most vividly with that of Hamann, one may imagine Socrates saying something like this: "I know that I do not know, but others are content to act out of sheer instinct, and mistakenly call it knowledge. I am quite aware of this, but they are not." The following statement of Nietzsche's touches the heart of the matter:

> As key to the character of Socrates is presented to us by the surprising phenomenon designated as the "daimonion" of Socrates. In special circumstances, when his gigantic intellect began to stagger, he got a secure support in the utterances of a divine voice which then spake to him. This voice, whenever it comes, always *dissuades*. In this totally abnormal nature instinctive wisdom only appears in order to hinder the progress of conscious perception here and there (N, 105).

Nietzsche then continues with a statement which is directly contradictory to Hamann's idea of the *daimon* as the fountainhead of instinctive creativity: "While in all productive men it is instinct which is the creatively affirmative force, consciousness only comporting itself critically and dissuasively; with Socrates *it is instinct which becomes critic, it is consciousness which becomes creator* – a perfect monstrosity ..." (My italics; N, 105). Doubtlessly Hamann would also consider this a monstrosity, but he would see in it a monstrous misunderstanding of the meaning of the Socratic *daimon*.

Whereas Hamann had related the *daimon* to sensibility or *Empfindung*, it becomes for Nietzsche a powerful logical impulse, which annihilated everything in its path originating in feeling or instinct. It was, he maintained, the logical drive of Socrates which had, in making itself felt through Euripides, done away with the older and superior form of Greek tragedy.

Who is it that ventures single-handed to disown the Greek character, which, as Homer, Pindar, and Aeschylus, as Phidias, as Pericles, as Pythia and Dionysus, as the deepest abyss and the highest height, is sure of our wondering admiration? What demoniac power is it which would presume to spill this magic draught in the dust? What demigod is it to whom the chorus of spirits of the noblest of mankind must call out: "Woe! Woe! Thou hast it destroyed, the beautiful world; with powerful fist; in ruin 'tis hurled!" (N, 104).

However, Nietzsche is not entirely consistent in his representation of the *daimon* as negative, for it also issued in a creative impulse albeit one of which Nietzsche does not entirely approve. Although Socrates, as Nietzsche assures us, had, by virtue of his influence on Euripides, destroyed the older drama, he succeeded, by virtue of his influence on the young Plato, in channeling that writer's creative impulse into a more rational form:

In very truth, Plato has given to all posterity the prototype of a new form of art, the prototype of the *novel*: which must be designated as the infinitely evolved Aesopian fable, in which poetry holds the same rank with reference to dialectic philosophy as this same philosophy held for many centuries with reference to theology: namely, the rank of *ancilla*. This was the new position of poetry into which Plato forced it under the pressure of the demon-inspired Socrates (N, 109).

Nietzsche continues along this line, becoming more explicit as to the nature of the change wrought by the new emphasis on reason:

Here *philosophic thought* overgrows art and compels it to cling close to the trunk of dialectics. The *Apollonian* tendency has chrysalised in the logical schematism; just as something analogous in the case of Euripides (and moreover a translation of the *Dionysian* into the naturalistic emotion) was forced upon our attention (N, 109–110).

From the philosophical standpoint the preceding passage is a crucial one, since in it Nietzsche translates the historical process which he has been discussing into philosophical terms. But I shall say more about this below.

It should be observed that Nietzsche actually uses the terms relating to the *daimon* in two different ways: first, it refers to the tutelary spirit or warning voice to which both Plato and Xenophon refer; second, it refers to the overwhelming logical power which characterized Socrates. Nietzsche does not seem to be conscious of this semantic shift in each case, although a dim awareness of it seems to emerge when, in referring specifically to the tutelary spirit, he uses the form closer to the Greek, "Daimonion." At least at this point one must agree with Nietzsche's later judgment on *The Birth of Tragedy* that it is void of "logical cleanliness." Hamann recognized the tendency of those who interpret Socrates as primarily a man of theory to associate the *daimon* with his rational powers – and Nietzsche agrees with the eighteenth century Enlighteners in making Socrates a man of theory – and consequently speaks of their "anti-Socratic *daimon*" (76: 15).

When we raise the question as to how the idea of beauty is conceived in the two treatises, we are again faced with diametrically opposed views. In order to understand Hamann's conception it is necessary to distinguish between the Socratic actuality, that is, the person of Socrates and his natural mode of speaking, on the one hand, and his doctrines on the other. As far as his doctrines are concerned, Hamann appears to ascribe to Socrates the typical Greek view that beauty always requires symmetry, balance, harmony, grace, and all the qualities which we normally associate with the "classical" ideal of beauty. Socrates' ugliness must have caused him much pain: "Thus Socrates doubtless had to suffer and strive inwardly with himself as a result of his delight in a harmony of external and internal beauty" (68: 5–7). That Socrates accepted the notion prevailing among the Greeks "that a good soul by its virtue renders the body the best that is possible"[12] is attested by his reaction to the criticism of Zopyrus that the ugly facial features of Socrates bespoke a wicked soul behind them: "He [Socrates] did not deny that his hidden inclinations corresponded with the discoveries of the physiognomist ..." (67: 34–36) but, Hamann adds, Socrates strongly resisted those natural inclinations to vice reflected in his appearance.

The actuality of Socrates' person and discourse is, however, quite another matter. The real root of the Magus' ideas in this connection is not to be found in his classical studies but in the

[12] Plato, *The Republic*. Trans. P. Shorey, Loeb Classical Library (Cambridge, Mass., 1963), Vol. I (3. 13), p. 265.

Bible. From his intense study of both the Old and New Testaments he developed the so-called doctrine of *Knechtsgestalt*, which means that God reveals Himself most fully in lowly form, in the form of a servant.[13] Here the temporal appearance does not exhaust the divine reality for which it stands, but in its incompleteness and inadequacy it becomes a fitting surrogate for that which it represents. If the God of the Old Testament revealed Himself in the often trivial or contemptible details of the life of the Jews, and if Christ, "the fairest of the sons of men," appeared as "a man of sorrows, full of wounds and stripes" (68: 17–19) or as "the teacher of mankind, gentle and lowly in heart" (79: 31–32), it is not surprising that a Socrates, the prototype and the prophet of Christ, should appear in a form scandalous to the beauty-loving Greeks. This form was for Hamann further evidence of the divine presence in Socrates: "He who would not suffer Socrates among the prophets must be asked who the Father of Prophets is and whether our God has not called himself and shown himself to be a God of the Gentiles" (77: 12–15).

But not only was the physical appearance of Socrates an affront to the normal sensibilities of the Greeks, his very speech seemed to reflect a baffling togetherness of noble and ignoble elements:

The critics were not satisfied with his allusions, and censured the similes of his oral discourse at one time as being too farfetched and at another time as vulgar. Alcibiades, however, compared his parables to certain sacred images of the gods and goddesses, which were carried, according to the custom of that time, in a small case, on the outside of which only the form of a goat-footed satyr was visible (80: 4–9).

The Athenians, who were destined to recognize Socrates' great nobility of soul only after his death (81: 20–22), were thus confronted with the paradox of one who showed them beauty in an unlikely form.

---

[13] The German word *Knechtsgestalt* is derived from the passage in Philippians 2: 6–11, where Christ is described as appearing among men in the "form of a servant." See *Hamann's Socratic Memorabilia*, pp. 13, 79–80, 126, 129. See also H. Schreiner, *Die Menschwerdung Gottes in der Theologie J. G. Hamanns*[2] (Tübingen, 1950), pp. 44–68; cf. K. Gründer, *Figur und Geschichte. J. G. Hamanns "Biblische Betrachtungen" als Ansatz einer Geschichtsphilosophie* (Freiburg and Munich, 1958), pp. 21–92.

A discussion of Hamann's treatment of the idea of beauty in the *Memorabilia* must necessarily touch upon the form of the essay itself.[14] I have already called attention to the fact that Hamann identified the form of his work with what he conceived to be the Socratic actuality. This means that the content of the work is supposed to be of more worth than the vessel which contains it. Hence the author's comparison of it to "mold", which, upon close and sympathetic scrutiny, is seen to be "a microscopically tiny forest" (61: 6–9) or, again, as "newly clothed Graces" (67: 12). Such a close identification of the form of a literary work with the Socratic idea is peculiar to Hamann's treatment; Nietzsche, as already observed, makes no similar claim for his essay.

It is clear that for Hamann Socratic beauty involves a paradox, hence is essentially irrational. Nietzsche, on the other hand, inverts this idea. For him the essence of "aesthetic Socratism" is reasonableness: "to be beautiful everything must be intelligible"; this is "the parallel to the Socratic proposition 'only the knowing one is virtuous'" (N, 98). The nature of aesthetic Socratism is best seen according to Nietzsche in the work of Euripides, who carried out the implications of the Socratic principle in his drama:

> With this canon in his hands Euripides measured all the separate elements of the drama, and rectified them according to his principle: the language, the characters, the dramaturgic structure, and the choric music .... Thus Euripides as a poet echoes above all his own conscious knowledge .... With reference to his critico-productive activity, he must often have felt that he ought to actualise in the drama the words at the beginning of the essay of Anaxagoras: "In the beginning all things were mixed together; then came the understanding and created order" (N, 98, 100).

Nietzsche stresses that Euripides eliminated myth and miracle from the drama, since they are not amenable to reason. In so doing he subverted the older drama of Aeschylus and Sophocles under the aegis of Socrates:

> He who wishes to test himself rigorously as to how he is related to the true aesthetic hearer, or whether he belongs rather to the community

---

[14] I have treated this subject extensively in the monograph, "The Concept of Form in the *Socratic Memorabilia*," contained in *Hamann's Socratic Memorabilia*, pp. 3–131.

of the Socrato-critical man, has only to enquire sincerely concerning the sentiment with which he accepts the *wonder* represented on the stage: whether he feels his historical sense, which insists on strict psychological causality, insulted by it, whether with benevolent concession he as it were admits the wonder as a phenomenon intelligible to childhood, but relinquished by him, or whether he experiences anything else thereby. For he will thus be enabled to determine how far he is on the whole capable of understanding *myth*, that is to say, the concentrated picture of the world, which, as abbreviature of phenomena, cannot dispense with wonder (N, 173–174).

In other words Socratic man insists on an aesthetic appearance which is greater than the reality for which it stands; for Euripides' dramas purport to be tragedies, but in actuality they are something less. It is characteristic of the Socratic-Euripidean drama that it leaves no residue or mystery of of the ineffable; therefore, we can conclude that the Socratic notion of beauty, as interpreted by Nietzsche, leaves no room for strangeness or for the truly awe-inspiring, and is consequently lacking in real depth. (Even the "notorious" *deus ex machina* of Euripides fails to add the missing dimension to his dramas, for it is merely a device to guarantee "the future of his heroes" [N, 100]).

Hamann would no doubt agree with Nietzsche's brilliant analysis and defense of myth and miracle. In fact, he expressly deplores the destruction of myth, but instead of charging Socrates for the demise of myth and miracle, he blames the Sophists (68: 20–24). "Through the cleverly devised myths of their poets, the heathen were accustomed to such contradictions [i.e., that the gods should appear in lowly forms] until their Sophists, like ours, condemned such things as a parricide which one commits against the first principles of human knowledge" (68: 20–24). Thus the heirs of ancient Sophistry are, even in the eighteenth century, at work destroying myth. How reprehensible this activity is in Hamann's eyes is clear from his use of such a term as "parricide" to describe it.

It should be reiterated that it is the Socratic actuality and Hamann's interpretation of it which stand in contradiction to Nietzsche's thesis, not the aesthetic doctrines of the Hamannian Socrates. For Nietzsche, however, the actuality of Socrates, his homeliness and the satyrical form of his discourse, plays no part in *The Birth of Tragedy*. It is aesthetic Socratism which is the villain of the piece. In the case of Hamann, Socrates' aesthetic *principles* fade into the background.

We have now considered the major points of difference between the Hamannian and Nietzschean versions of Socrates as they emerge from the two works under consideration. A word should be said about the manner in which the two authors relate Socrates to the idea of tragedy. Nietzsche's position is, of course, quite clear and explicit: Socrates or rather Socratism is the deadly enemy of tragedy. It was inevitable that this would be so, since his thoroughgoing rationalism issued quite naturally in an optimism which is incompatible with the pessimistic view of life expressed in tragedy.

For who [asks Nietzsche] could mistake the *optimistic* element in the essence of dialectics, which celebrates a jubilee in every conclusion, and can breathe only in cool clearness and consciousness: the optimistic element, which, having once forced its way into tragedy, must gradually overgrow its Dionysian regions, and necessarily impel it to self-destruction? ... (N. 110).

It is true that Nietzsche seems to recognize the tragic element in the death of Socrates as, for example, in his almost lyrical description of the philosopher's last days: "He met his death with the calmness with which, according to the description of Plato, he leaves the symposium at break of day, as the last of the revellers, to begin a new day. ... The *dying Socrates* became the new ideal of the noble Greek youths ..." (N, 106). But even so, this does not alter Nietzsche's picture of Socrates as the "despotic logician" who destroyed Attic tragedy. Movingly tragic though his death was, Socrates remains nevertheless the subverter of the tragic art.

Hamann was not, of course, directly concerned with the aesthetic problem of the nature of tragedy. His problem was primarily a religious and philosophical one. Yet his essay contains, as I have undertaken to show elsewhere, a "proto-drama," depicting the life and death of Socrates. The Magus' account is necessarily dramatic, because unlike Nietzsche, he is concerned with the life of Socrates rather than with his doctrines. But we can in all justice say that Hamann's account contains the elements of tragedy? This is a legitimate question, inasmuch as Hamann clearly portrays Socrates as a sort of pre-Christian saint. If, however, we accept the idea that there are two types of tragic heroes, namely, those who finally accept the moral order by which they are judged (as, for example, Richard III in Shakespeare's play of the same name, or the Karl Moor of the fifth act of *Die Räuber*) and those, on the other hand, who never acknowledge the legitimacy of the moral order by which they are judged (as, for example, Götz von Berlichingen in Goethe's play of the same name, or Maria Stuart in Schiller's play), we may clearly place Hamann's Socrates in the latter category. Thus, Socrates, on trial for his life, answered the accusations against him "with such seriousness and courage, with such a pride and indifference, that, judging by his facial expression, one would have held him to be a commanding officer of his judges rather than an accused person" (81: 1–4). In his impassioned and moving "Peroration" Hamann makes it quite clear that the world will always destroy a Socrates and a Christ.

It is true that Hamann places the life and death of Socrates within a Christian frame of reference, and to the extent that this is the case, one hesitates to speak of tragedy in the traditional sense. But it is necessary to remember that the *Socratic Memorabilia* is actually written on three levels, and on the level dealing with the historical Socrates the reader is presented with genuine tragedy. Eternal evidence of the tragic quality inhering in Hamann's account of Socrates is the impact it had on the young Goethe. Under its influence he conceived the plan – which he never carried out – of writing a tragedy based on the life of Socrates. Further, it is ironical that Nietzsche himself manifested a susceptibility to Hamann's "heroic" portrayal of Socrates, thus singling out precisely that quality in Hamann's treatment of Socrates which is lacking in *The Birth of Tragedy*. Thus, he writes in *Philosophy in the Tragic Age of the Greeks* (1873): "Mankind so rarely produces a good book in which the battle-hymn of truth, the song of philosophical heroism is sounded – and these books often perish quickly. Yet let us not complain, rather let us heed Hamann's message of reproach and comfort which he directs to the scholars who complain about lost works."[15] Nietzsche then cites an anecdote from the *Socratic Memorabilia*.

[15] *Die Philosophie im Tragischen Zeitalter der Griechen* in *Gesammelte Werke* (Munich, 1921), Musarionausgabe, Vol. IV, p. 161.

It is significant also that the phrase "philosophical heroism" which Nietzsche has employed stems from Hamann's essay (63: 33). Here we have the interesting spectacle of the portrayer of the *untragic* Socrates responding positively to a work which portrays the *tragic* Socrates.

The present discussion would be incomplete without a reference to still another significant difference between the two versions of Socrates, namely, the fact that Hamann's portrayal is shot through with humor, whereas that of Nietzsche is completely humorless. Both accounts are characterized by a keen sense of irony, but the matter is quite different with regard to humor. Despite Hamann's sense of the tragic element in the life of Socrates, he manages to maintain the perspective of humor throughout, often crude, sometimes scurrilous, sometimes even bordering on the blasphemous. For example, the *Socratic Memorabilia* is supposed to act as a cathartic on his friends, Kant and Berens. In a *reductio ad absurdum* of the so-called medical theory of catharsis he likens his treatise to laxative pills which will purge the emotions of his friends (59: 24–27). Thus, in Hamann's scheme even tragedy cannot be separated from humor.

But even on the sublimest religious level the Magus cannot refrain from humor.[16] In referring to the Virgin Birth of Christ he mentions the absurd theory of a notorious English quacksalver to the effect that it is possible for a virgin to conceive a child simply through the action of wind (75: 10–13). Or again his facetiousness erupts in a trivial context as when he refers to Xanthippe's venting her wrath on Socrates by means of her chamber-pot (79: 19–22). Kierkegaard has called Hamann "the greatest humorist in Christendom,"[17] and whether that be true or not, it is certainly true that the *Memorabilia* is generously interlarded with the author's peculiar brand of humor. *The Birth of Tragedy*, although presenting Socrates as the fountainhead of

[16] O. Mann sees Hamann's humor as stemming directly from his Christian faith. Thus, he says that Hamann's Christian existence "machte ihn über die sokratische Ironie hinaus zum Humoristen. Denn der Humor ist begründet in der Erfahrung entschiedener und unversöhnlicher Gegensätze, und der humoristische Stil in dem Bestreben, solche Spannung als eine Seinslage unmittelbar darzustellen." *Hamann: Hauptschriften* (Leipzig, 1937), p. xlii.

[17] Quoted by W. Lowrie, *Kiergegaard* (London, 1938), p. 165.

rationalistic optimism, possesses, as I have already indicated, no humor whatsoever.

Although this study is not concerned with the question of the historical validity of either account of Socrates, I shall nevertheless venture the opinion that Hamann's interpretation does more justice to the historical figure which emerges from the pages of Plato – and, in a limited sense, of Xenophon – than Nietzsche's interpretation. The basic flaw in Nietzsche's representation of Socratic thought lies, in my opinion, in the ambiguity of his idea of reason. If Socratic thought is essentially syllogistic, and if it is to be equated with Apollonian reason (as it clearly is at times), how can Nietzsche speak of a "fraternal union of the two deities" in which "Dionysus speaks the language of Apollo" and "Apollo ... finally speaks the language of Dionysus"? (N, 167). This formulation would logically call for a Dionysus speaking in syllogisms, which is precisely what that god may not do. Another serious question must be raised about Nietzsche's linking of the *irrational daimon* to the *rational* side of Socrates' thought. Whether or not one accepts Philip Merlan's statement that "only the interpretation of Hamann and Kierkegaard ... does full justice to the demonic element in the Platonic ... Socrates,"[18] it is true that Nietzsche's account of the *daimon* in *The Birth of Tragedy* is characterized by a basic inconsistency.

Nietzsche's ambivalent attitude toward Socrates remains one of the great riddles of his thought, and deserves a word here. The figure of Socrates continued to evoke such strong feelings for him throughout his life that one wonders what the depth-psychological roots of his attitude were. While the answer to this riddle will probably never be found, the most plausible explanation is that Socrates is the great counterfigure to the superman, an ideal which, though not formulated when *The Birth of Tragedy* was written, is nevertheless implicit in Nietzsche's idealization of Wagner in that work. We have seen how Nietzsche presents Socrates as a demigod, thus as superhuman. Moreover, we have seen how Nietzsche presents Socrates as a destroyer on a colossal scale, an Attila or Genghis Khan, as it were, in the realm of

[18] P. Merlan, "Form and Content in Plato's Philosophy," *Journal of the History of Ideas* 8. 4 (October, 1947), pp. 416 f., n. 33.

culture; but unlike the vanished empires of those military conquerors, Socrates' rationalistic rule has lasted over two thousand years. Thus against his will Nietzsche has depicted a superman, beside whom even the ideal figure sketched in Zarathustra fades into paler colors. One might say that the Nietzschean image of Socrates is the *superman reversed*, and was for that very reason so disconcerting to its creator. Hamann remained fascinated throughout his life with Socrates, because he identified with the Athenian. Nietzsche, on the other hand, remained fascinated with Socrates, because, longing to identify with so heroic a figure, he could *not* do so, since that hero was dedicated to the service of the arch-enemy.

Hamann's version of the life and thought of Socrates, though obviously not justified on all scores, nevertheless generally escapes the internal inconsistencies which beset Nietzsche's work. Thus Hamann represents Socrates as consistently rejecting what Nietzsche calls the "superfoetation" of logic. Whereas the Nietzschean Socrates has the "imperturbable belief that, by means of the clue of causality, thinking reaches to the deepest abysses of being, and that thinking is able not only to perceive being but even to *correct* it" (N, 116), Hamann places Socrates in a context in which the precept holds that "to dissect a body and an event into its primary elements means attempting to detect God's invisible being, His eternal power and Godhead" (64: 13–15). Nietzsche's depiction of Socrates in *The Birth of Tragedy* is without doubt a caricature, and there is evidence to believe that he was, in certain moods and at certain stages, conscious of that fact.[19] Nevertheless, *The Birth of Tragedy* is a work of

---

[19] K. Hildebrandt offers a fairly complete survey of the conception of Socrates which emerges in other works of Nietzsche. See *Nietzsches Wettkampf mit Sokrates und Plato* (Dresden, 1922). W. Kaufmann has undertaken to show that even in *The Birth of Tragedy* Nietzsche's basic admiration for Socrates shines through, and in so doing he has illuminated further the ambivalence in Nietzsche's conception of Socrates; however, this fact cannot change the nature of the principal antithesis set forth in *The Birth of Tragedy*: that of Socrates and Dionysos. See W. Kaufmann, *Nietzsche: Philosopher, Psychologist, Antichrist* (Princeton, 1950), pp. 342–360. E. Bertram maintains that in hating the rationalistic Socrates, Nietzsche was really hating the rationalist within himself, but that he could identify with the "music-making" Socrates. See E. Bertram, *Nietzsche: Versuch einer Mythologie* (Berlin, 1929), pp. 341 ff.

genius, which will continue to be a document of primary importance for Western civilization, and this in spite of its major flaw, the perverse portrait of Socrates. As for the future of the *Socratic Memorabilia*, there are signs that it, along with Hamann's other writings, is giving fresh stimulus to Hellenic studies.[20]

Wake Forest University
Winston-Salem, North Carolina

---

[20] For example, see U. Mann, *Vorspiel des Heils. Die Uroffenbarung in Hellas* (Stuttgart, 1962), esp. pp. 15, 132, 333, 397. Although Mann approaches his task from the standpoint of theology, his book is devoted chiefly to a study of Greek culture. In the recent article, "Die pythagoreischen Symbole," *Antaios* 9. 3 (September, 1967), p. 285 F. Vonessen assigns Hamann first place as a guide in interpreting Greek culture.

J. G. HAMANN AND THE PRINCESS GALLITZIN
AN ECUMENICAL ENCOUNTER[1]

RONALD GREGOR SMITH†

I want to talk about two Germans, who lived in the latter half of the eighteenth century, in a very different world from ours – two extraordinary people, who can be recognized for what they are only if I succeed in describing their circumstances to you. But in trying to do this, I want at the same time to present them to you as very relevant people for us. There is a twofold assumption here, which I want to exemplify rather than to argue. It is this: first, these two people are not like us; but second, because they are real people, working out their destiny with immense self-consciousness, they can affect us in a quite definite way, if we let them. The first part of this assumption, that they are not like us, is connected with a view of history which sees people wrestling with their own circumstances, which are always unique and unrepeatable. So I consider it naive and misleading to suppose

---

[1] This paper was originally written for a conference of the Religious Broadcasting Department of the British Broadcasting Corporation, at which I was invited to speak on something that "had nothing to do with the immediate problems of the radio." I have retained the rather colloquial form, but have added a few bibliographical footnotes. My own study of Hamann, *J. G. Hamann: A study in Christian Existence* (London and New York, 1960), contains a bibliography which is full enough to lead the interested reader further. I am happy to think that in this contribution I am able to pay a fairly direct compliment to our honored colleague, Dr. Philip Merlan, for in a number of essays he had indicated that he shared my love of the eccentric, enigmatic, and lovable figure of Johann Georg Hamann. I list Dr. Merlan's contributions to Hamanniana, so far as I know them: "Parva Hamanniana I. Hamann as a Spokesman of the Middle Class," *Journal of the History of Ideas* 9 (1948), pp. 330–334; "Parva Hamanniana II. Hamann and Schmohl," *ibid.* 10 (1949), pp. 567–574; "Parva Hamanniana III. Hamann and Galiani," *ibid.* 11 (1950), pp. 486–489; "Hamann et les *Dialogues* de Hume," *Revue de Métaphysique et de Morale* 59 (1954), pp. 285–289; "Johann Georg Hamann," *Claremont Quarterly* 3 (1954), pp. 33–42.

that people are always fundamentally the same, confronting the same kinds of choices, and making the same kinds of decisions, and failing or succeeding in precisely the same way. This part of my assumption I hope to illustrate by the lives of these two. And the other part of the assumption, that such people are nevertheless of immense relevance to us, is connected with a view of history which may be stated quite briefly: history is what happens to people. More precisely, it is what goes on in people now. More precisely still, it is what we are and do.

With these assumptions I want to try to bring these two alive before you.

Johann Georg Hamann (1730–1788) was called in his lifetime the *Magus* in the north. This does not mean the wizard of the north, but the wise man, who like the wise men of the gospel had seen the star of Bethlehem. Hamann lived for the most part of his life in Königsberg, at that time a busy international sea-port and a lively intellectual centre. Immanuel Kant lived and taught there all his life, and he and Hamann knew and respected one another, after their fashion. But Hamann was a poor and struggling employee in the service of the government. He worked first as a translator, mostly between French and German, for his superiors in the civil service were all Frenchmen, put there by the Solomon of the north, Frederick the Great. Later he was the overseer of the Customs warehouse. All his life was spent in a struggle with material difficulties. He came of a respectable family, of the growing middle classes.

These circumstances of Hamann's life were not merely fate, but they were destiny. For Hamann chose them. He chose to be of no account. He refused to make himself into a serviceable member of society. This was a decision which arose from his specific Christian experience. And with this remark I am in the thick of as yet unexamined assumptions. These assumptions may be summarized in two assertions, which hold good not only for Hamann but also, I think, with due modifications, for everyone. The first assertion is that there is something which we may call a recognisably Christian experience; and the second is that this experience is expressed in the infinitely various contexts of human existence.

In Hamann's life the specific Christian experience came in the form of an assault upon him by the actuality of the Bible. I cannot here go into the extraordinarily moving story of what is conventionally described as his conversion. He was in London when it happened, as the emissary of a commercial house in Riga. In loneliness and poverty he made what he called the descent to hell of self-knowledge, and out of this he rose into Christian life. This experience cannot be identified with pietism. Pietism in that time had quite definite forms and a definite history. Today it is less easy to detect, especially as there is a temptation among religiously-minded people to identify pietism with a proper faith. For Hamann this specific experience led him away from all conventional expressions of Christianity. It led him to make a sharp renunciation of the commercial career which was opening up for him. Kant himself paid him a visit, when he got back to Königsberg, to persuade him to give up his bigoted orthodoxy (for so Kant understood the change which had come over Hamann). But Hamann was clear that he could not conform to the expectations of his time. The kingdom of "total reason" which Kant stood for, and the world of usefulness and conformity to the norms of harmony in individual life which his business friend Berens stood for, were abjured by Hamann when the life of the Christian God pierced his soul.

The consequence was that he chose, as he said, "to serve from below." He was making here a strict allusion to Christ whose life was humiliation, and in whose life Hamann had found God's speech to himself.

This choice ran counter to the whole spirit of the age. It meant the recognition of himself as an exception; and the witness that all Christian experience points in the same direction: through self-knowledge to going against the stream of the world.

But this movement inwards, then outwards in opposition, is concluded by a remarkable turning or *bouleversement*, which is much misunderstood, both in the church and in the world. For simultaneously with what is described in the words of the gospel as losing your life there is a movement of regaining, even of re-assimilation. You are taken out of the world, and in the same movement you are put back into the world. Are you the same person? Is the world the same world? For Hamann the answer to these questions was clear. You are certainly the same person in the same world; but you are at the same time utterly different, because now you know yourself to be in God's world.

Does this difference show itself? Is the Christian visibly and specifically different from the non-Christian? Perhaps these questions are framed in a way which does not permit of a proper answer. For the humility which is perhaps the chief mark of the Christian for Hamann is an attitude, indeed an action, of such a kind that it is at its purest quite concealed. But if there is complete concealment, where is the witness? Are we not called to proclaim the gospel? I think that Hamann's answer to this is that every movement towards the completest incognito is a reflection of God's movement towards men in Christ, that is, a movement of intolerable love concealed within the utmost humility. It is only apparent in the form of faith, which is raised to the highest pitch precisely in the movement towards concealment. There is an obvious rejoinder to this kind of analysis – that the church is a visible structure with real people in it, whose task as obedient believers is to witness to their faith. As I understand Hamann, he certainly did not abandon the form and structure of the church – indeed, he went further than most of us, at any rate in Scotland, normally go, when he made no effort to hear popular preachers, but said once that he would rather hear truth from a Pharisee than from an angel of light. But Hamann also saw, in a quite shattering way, that it was not the specific effort or form of the witness which really counted in the end, but, simply, the Spirit of God, the grace of God, which accomplished everything, even the response of faith. In this he was very Lutheran, and, I should add, very Pauline – and that, in turn, means as Christian as you can be.

But at the same time, because his Christian faith was lived out in the world, it cannot be called purely and simply Christian; but it is Christian in the circumstances of his time. For Hamann this means that he was resolutely opposed to mere ratiocination, and to abstractions of every kind. Whether rightly or wrongly, he saw in Kant's philosophy a different presupposition about truth and virtue. For him everything depended upon the individual and his place in the moment, and this meant that man by himself is unfinished. This negative attitude to the assumptions of the

Enlightenment opened the way for a positive assessment of life in terms of the Romantic movement. This is at any rate how Hamann's contemporaries and successors saw his protest. I think it was in fact more than this: the Romantic movement in life and letters did not succeed in containing the whole story either of Hamann's life or of the possibilities of Christianity. For if we define the Romantic movement as a concern with history, especially remote history, as being of a single continuous piece with the present, evoking the mystery and wonder of the past as a possibility which can simply be expressed now, then we must say that Hamann did not see Christian existence in this way. Instead, he saw it, though certainly as a mystery and a wonder, yet as something taking place in a *coincidentia oppositorum*, in a life which recognises human heterogeneity, its irrevocable dialectic, a life which is a unity of opposites, a life sustained only by the perpetual miracle of God's speech, his Word to man, in and through the life of nature and history.

But all the same, Hamann's protest did make possible the Romantic attitude to life within a Christian view; and in this sense alone, he is the door through which his heirs and successors passed into the splendid realm of the early nineteenth century, a time full of movement and hope.

This, then, is the first of our two figures: the north German Protestant, bourgeois, eccentric, living in uncertainty, with many friends, yet having nothing; a writer, yet one who hardly ever wrote anything that could be called a proper book. He might have got away with a few talks on the Third Programme; but for TV or the Light Programme he would just have seemed a clown, and an incomprehensible clown at that.

The other figure of the story, Amalie von Gallitzin (1748–1806), is very different. The daughter of a Prussian general, she was early married to the Russian ambassador to the Hague, Prince Gallitzin. Two children were born of the marriage. The beginning was not unpropitious. The Russian diplomat, perceiving in the lady of his choice an intense intelligence and interest in letters, produced, in order to win her sympathy, two letters from Diderot and Voltaire. Some years later Diderot describes her as

a very lively, gay and witty woman, and of a pleasant appearance; quite young, well educated and talented ... very good, of extreme sensibility, having perhaps too much for her happiness ... she can argue like a little lion. I love her madly ....

Diderot could not have foreseen the course her life was to take. The life of the court, and the superficial deism in which she had hitherto rested, appeared more and more empty to her. Her husband was – I do not say merely superficial, but, as the Dutch philosopher Hemsterhuis said of him – "extremely feeble." She was bored by him. By 1774, six years after her marriage, when she was just 26, she changed her mode of life completely. In 1779 she moved to Münster in Westphalia, with her two children. The course of her life, both inwardly and outwardly, I can give here only in hasty outline. The first major influence upon her life was that of the Greek philosophers, especially Socrates, as mediated to her by the eclectic philosopher, Hemsterhuis. Hemsterhuis is not much known today; but in his time he was a much valued writer. It was the union in him of extreme simplicity with an active share in the world which attracted Amalie von Gallitzin. For her decision to renounce the world she lived in was by no means a simple monastic intention. Primarily she wanted to devote herself to the instruction of her children, and at the same time, for this very reason, to her own self-instruction. So she went to Münster, for a short visit, and stayed for the remainder of her life.

It is not my intention to describe the life that ensued in Münster. It is a story for itself, and includes some the of most interesting figures in the Roman Catholic revival in Germany.[2] In Münster the Princess Gallitzin returned to the Catholic faith in which she had been brought up. But, like Hamann, she too did not change her nature so much as her direction. In a letter to her friend Hemsterhuis she wrote:

[2] The story is told in *Le Cercle de Münster*, by Pierre Brachin, Bibliothèque de la Société des Études Germaniques V (1952), and in Ewald Reinhard's *Die Münsterische "Familia Sacra"* (Münster, 1953). But a great deal of material still awaits publication and assessment, in particular the Gallitzin Archives in Münster and the Fürstenberg Archives in Darfeld. Dr. Siegfried Sudhof speaks of some 2,000 to 3,000 letters from Fürstenberg to the Princess Gallitzin.

I am more and more convinced that a sensibility as monstrous as mine
does infinite harm to the harmony of the whole, and I have long resolved
to work daily to make myself master of it. I have even made more progress
in this regard than I could have dared to flatter myself, I mean in regard
to details; but it is also true that my sensibility in being concentrated has
become stronger and more forceful than before, in fact, more like a
volcano.

This, I think, remained true all her life. She was a woman of
almost unique powers of introspection, and she used them for the
training, in almost excruciating fashion, of her intellectual
talents and her emotional attitudes. The saving grace was that
these talents were also directed outwards. She had at least one
simple conviction which she derived from her Christian intentions: she did not simply retreat into herself. Her friends in
Münster were much involved in plans for reform and improvement.[3] So, too, the Princess, who diligently educated not only
her own two children but those of her friends.

But though the air was full of change, and the friends in
Münster had every chance to carry out their plans in a spirit of
freedom and exhilaration, which is, I think, not very easy to
equal today, there was one important respect in which the
movement of revival was in danger of running into a cul-de-sac.
That was precisely in the will for harmony. This desire runs
through all the writings of the friends. They all, but especially
the Princess, were obsessed with the desire for self-realisation,
conceived as a means for knowing the will of God, and so realising
union with God. She was always "passionately striving to reach
specific goals" (Jacobi). And Goethe, who visited her in 1792,
later describes the feeling of gentleness and mildness which
filled him there. He said:

The princess could not be described as other than loving. She early
reached the feeling that the world gives us nothing, that one must withdraw into oneself, and be concerned with time and eternity in an inner and
restricted circle. She had grasped both these truths. She found the highest
temporal in the natural, and here one thinks of Rousseau's maxims about
bourgeois life and the education of children. So she wanted to return to

---

[3] One thinks especially of the vicar general of the diocese and prime
minister, Franz Freiherr von Fürstenberg, who worked tirelessly for
reform and improvement in the schools and monasteries (he even institu-
ted courses of study and reading with examinations in the latter) and had
plans for the founding of the university.

what was simple and true in everything, no corsets or high heels, no powder, and hair falling down in natural curls. Her children learned swimming and running, perhaps wrestling as well. So it was for their temporal and present life; the eternal and future life they had found in a religion which promises with holy assurances that which others leave to hope. A beneficence, the mildest effect of a serious asceticism, was the beautiful mediating factor between the two worlds. Their life was filled with religious exercises and well-doing ....[4]

In a letter to Jacobi, Goethe adds the significant words: "I wished I seemed as harmonious to myself as that beautiful soul. ..."

Harmony, self-perfection, this was Goethe's ideal. It was also the ideal of the Enlightenment. In another sense it was the goal of the Romantics, too.

Is it a Christian goal? The encounter between Hamann and Princess Gallitzin suggests that it is not. The attraction which she had long felt for Hamann arose, I think, mainly from the common ground of a love of Socrates. Hamann's first publication was a kind of essay about Socrates in a Socratic vein; and the Princess Gallitzin even reached such a pitch of enthusiasm as to write *"O Sancte Socrate, ora pro nobis."* But Hamann had moved far during the hard years of his life; and when he finally arrived in Münster, in 1787, for what were to prove to be the last months of his life, he came to what seems to me to be the last stage possible in Christian understanding.

Here is how he seemed to Amalie von Gallitzin, as she wrote, after he was dead, in her diary:

Hamann says, *"Ma seule règle, c'est de n'en point avoir."* All the good we human beings are capable of is merely negative; whether in relation to ourselves or others. We can only strive to remove what prevents us from seeing more clearly and presenting the influence of the Godhead – a striving for systemlessness, for no system, and for the Socratic, simple and lofty consciousness of our ignorance, frailty and weakness. He who attains this will be, without any great strain, humble, long -suffering,and, therefore, loving with his whole heart, and will possess the peace which passes understanding.[5]

Is this mere nothingness? Entire negation? Rather, it is the basic patience and receptivity of Christian faith, which knows

[4] From the *Campagne in Frankreich*, 1792.
[5] *Briefwechsel und Tagebücher der Fürstin Amalie von Gallitzin*, Neue Folge (Münster, 1876), III, p. 351.

that it is absolutely dependent on God, and loves, or tries to love, in the way Christ did, "without striving for love and enjoyment from others in return."

This humility to the utmost was a mortal blow at the whole course of the Princess Gallitzin's piety. It meant that every effort at self-realisation and self-perfection was a denial of the reality of the Christian situation. This the devout Catholic spirit of Princess Gallitzin both perceived, and acted upon.

Something important of Hamann's spirit and teaching has remained in my soul, the conviction, namely, that the effort to attain to a good conscience, ... was a very dangerous ferment in me; and that the chief thing in faith must be the enduring of my nothingness and complete confidence in God's mercy. I had a living impression at that time – but only after a long struggle with Hamann – that my pleasure in the bitter dislike of my own imperfections and weakness was actually the most secret and perilous hiding-place of my pride.[6]

This simple but catastrophic re-adjustment of the proportions of life has still one more result upon what we may do. In Hamann's words,

If I sow a seed in the earth, I do not stand around and listen and watch to see if it grows, but I sow and go away and sow somewhere else, and I leave to God the growth and the increase.[7]

At another point in her diary, she speaks of him as a "Christian clothed in rags," and ends the passage with the words:

What truth do I know, can I know, as truth? Only one, believe in the Lord, love him, and hope for his day.[8]

We may now ask what this story says to us. These people, as I said, are not like us. They have their own conflicts, which are not ours, their own society and its problems, which are not ours. There has been nothing like that breeze of the Spirit in Europe since then. There was not then that hardening of doctrines and confessional attitudes which drives us all, willy-nilly, into static positions, in which we see the positions of others so clearly, but with such hopelessness. Yet these people can reach out to us, precisely in the strength of that same Spirit, and help to make our history with us.

[6] *Ibid.*, p. 349.
[7] *Ibid.*, p. 101.
[8] *Ibid.*, p. 331.

They can do this, I suggest, in three specific ways. And this you may take as the three-pronged moral of my tale.

First, the pietism which was the background of Hamann's early life, and which was the form that Princess Gallitzin's religious effort took till she met Hamann, is not the ultimate form of Christian faith. The spring of faith is dependence, a sense of our nothingness and of God's mercy. The form of faith flows from this sense, as a relation or being bound up in a community. But this community is not a state of affairs. It is a happening, something that takes place, an event. The spirit is where the spirit blows. The forms and practices of the church, its various forms and practices, are there, stuck in our history, and we cannot avoid them, even if we try. But the community does not live by the forms, it lives only by faith in the Spirit, and the community is people only, people with God.

Second, there is only one way to turn in order to catch this wind of the spirit, and that is, against the stream. Certainly,

> In a world of fugitives
> One who moves in the opposite direction
> Will appear to run away,

but it is the only way, and it is narrow as well. In other words, self-knowledge, solitude, recognition of yourself as the exception – these are absolutely essential for faith. We are able to classify such attitudes nowadays, and so write them off, as introspection, or individualism, or even as narcissism. It is increasingly difficult to find the real person, the Thou, in a world where the collective and the mass are increasingly dominant. I have always thought that the power of radio lies not in the immense numbers that can be reached, but in the fact that one can speak to one. I am reminded of a remark of Harman Grisewood's when he was asked why the management had taken off a very witty revue called, I think, "Vulgar Fractions," and he said it was because it had discovered that there were too many people listening.

But, lastly, if neither the forms nor the practices are the ultimate, and if the ultimate way is through each single person, one by one, knowing himself, but knowing also that he cannot by any possible means make himself what he wants to be, then, under these conditions, we may conclude that we are quite literally without precept or prescription. Nothing could be worse for any of our planning than to do it too well. We simply cannot plan the ways and the forms of the Spirit. I am personally so disposed to anarchism that I can well understand it if you think that I am acting like the devil's advocate. But I must insist on this: if we really mean what we say about our dependence upon God, and about his guiding power upon us, from the beginning to the end of our days, and upon the course of all human events, likewise from the beginning to the end of days, then I must ask again for openness, for confidence in the Spirit, for reliance upon no forms or practices or plans, and for a trained and expectant readiness for the unpredictable – to be ready for the unready. If you ask whether this is a burden that can be carried, especially by people whose fate it is to be planners and producers within settled forms of society, then I can only ask in return: are the forms so settled? Do you want them to be so settled? Is there not a destiny bigger than the fates we all endure, which might even make our expectations for our society richer than they are at present? God knows where the change from our present calamities is to come if not from God, and from those who wait upon him.

University of Glasgow

THE LOST PORTRAIT OF EDMUND HUSSERL BY FRANZ AND IDA BRENTANO

HERBERT SPIEGELBERG

The Portrait and Brentano's Early Perspective on Husserl

We owe to Philip Merlan some intriguing information about Franz Brentano's relations with Sigmund Freud.[1] So I venture to hope that he might also have been interested in an iconographic item about the personal relations between Franz Brentano and Edmund Husserl which until recently was believed to be totally lost. Its partial reconstruction may at the same time throw new light on their early philosophical connections.

In his "Erinnerungen an Franz Brentano"[2] Husserl inserted the following sentences about Brentano's versatility:

In St. Gilgen beteiligte er sich gerne an den Porträtbildern seiner Frau, die eine tüchtige Malerin war, hineinbessernd, oder ihre Bilder im Werden ganz übernehmend: aber freilich musste sie dann wieder nachhelfen und manches wieder gut machen. So hat er mich im Jahre 1886 gemeinsam mit seiner Frau gemalt: "ein liebenswürdiges Bild," wie Robert Vischer,[3] der feinsinnige Kunsthistoriker, urteilte.

Subsequently Brentano gave this portrait to the young Husserls as an engagement present. On December 29, 1876, Husserl referred to it in a letter as follows:

Sie haben meiner Braut durch das grosse Geschenk, welches Sie ihr mit meinem Portrait gemacht haben, eine unbeschreibliche Freude bereitet! Jeder ihrer letzten Briefe brachte mir hiervon erneute Kunde. Sie findet das Bild prächtig, trefflich, lebensvoll, von der gehörigen Stellung und Beleuchtung, geradezu zum Sprechen ähnlich. Ja sie gesteht mir, dass sie mit dem Wechsel und der Auswahl der Stellungen und Beleuchtungen

---

[1] "Brentano and Freud," *Journal of the History of Ideas* 6 (1945), pp. 375–377; *ibid.*, 10 (1949), p. 451.

[2] Appendix II to Oskar Kraus, *Franz Brentano* (München: C. H. Beck, 1919), p. 162.

[3] Husserl erroneously put in the name of Robert's father Theodor, as Mrs. Elly Husserl Rosenberg informed me.

schier die ganze freie Zeit verspiele und verträume. Kurz sie ist sowohl von dem Werke als auch von dem Künstler, der die Sendung überdies mit so liebenswürdigen Zeilen begleitet, ganz begeistert. So sind meine Erwartungen noch übertroffen worden.

After their wedding the Husserls displayed the portrait prominently in their home. For some time before her marriage Husserl's daughter Elly kept it on a wall in her room in Freiburg. When in 1939, after Edmund Husserl's death, his papers and books were transferred to Louvain, the portrait was put into a van with Mrs. Husserl's personal belongings, which were to be shipped to the United States. On September 16, 1940, this van with the portrait was destroyed by fire in the harbor of Antwerp as a result of an allied air raid.[4]

When in April, 1966 I had occasion to ask Mrs. Rosenberg about this portrait, she was kind enough to send me a little snapshot of hers, showing her room in the Freiburg apartment with the portrait at an angle on one of the walls (Plate I). I took this snapshot to Mr. Herbert Weitmann of the Photographic Services of Washington University, St. Louis, who turned it over to two of his assistants, Messrs. Bayard Fitzgerald and John Oytman. They managed to enlarge the picture on the wall in the snapshot sufficiently to yield an expressive face and also to spread out the picture in a way which neutralized the perspective distortion. Even so, the reproduction was blurred by many distracting reflections and left many areas ambiguous (Plate II). Miss Marilyn Roth, an art student at Webster College, toned down these reflections by retouching. At this stage Mrs. Rosenberg also sent me from her collection copies of two contemporary photos of young Husserl as a student. (See Plate III for the later one.) On this basis and in an attempt to take account of written comments by Mrs. Rosenberg, Miss Roth also tried to resolve some of the remaining ambiguities (Plate IV).

Obviously the result is at best an approximation. The only qualified judge, Mrs. Rosenberg, points out that the reproduction does not show the blond, curly hair and the blue eyes

---

[4] See H. L. Van Breda, "Le Sauvetage de l'héritage husserlien et la fondation des Archives Husserl," *Husserl et la pensée moderne*, Phaenomenologica II (The Hague: Martinus Nijhoff, 1959), p. 39. The reference to *two* such portraits in the text seems to be based on a misunderstanding.

Plate I
Snapshot of the Original

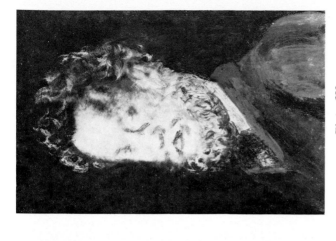

Plate IV
The Projection Retouched

Plate III
A Contemporary Photo

The Lost Portrait of Edmund Husserl by
Franz and Ida Brentano

Plate II
Photographic Enlargement
and Projection

of the original. She also feels that the narrow steep head of the final version has something deadly serious about it compared with the friendliness and naturalness of the original as she remembers it.

Thus the final photo is at best a doubtful copy of a copy of a painting that represented an original through the eyes of two gifted amateurs. The only hope is that this reconstruction is still better than the nothing of total destruction left by the Antwerp bomb.

However, the real value of this reconstruction seems to me neither iconographic nor aesthetic. Subsequent tradition and the comments of the editors of Brentano's works have often given the impression that Brentano had a very dubious opinion of his erstwhile student Husserl. Much of this can be discredited by a study of their extant correspondence. The portrait, however, unique not only as a portrait painted by a philosopher but as that of a pupil by his teacher, tells an additional part of the story. Brentano had singled out this particular student as worthy of a special portrait. With all its imperfections, the reconstruction can show that in 1886 Brentano had seen in Husserl's eyes a spark, if, not yet, the spark of genius. As Mrs. Rosenberg, to whom I am so deeply indebted for her help in this iconographic venture, put it to me, the portrait throws a certain light on the relation between the two philosophers, and it is a bright and warm light.

Brentano's Later Perspective on Husserl

It is often believed that in his later years Brentano took a rather dim view of Husserl's philosophical achievements and in particular of his phenomenology. And it is certainly true that at least in two letters to Hugo Bergmann of September 6, 1907 and March 27, 1908 [5] Brentano expressed himself not only in puzzled but rather unfavorable terms about Husserl's philosophizing, even after Husserl had visited him in Florence in an attempt to explain his new views to his former teacher.

The entire relation between the always revered master and the

---

[5] "Briefe Franz Brentanos," *Philosophy and Phenomenological Research* VII (1946), pp. 86 f., 93 f.

344 Herbert Spiegelberg

emancipated pupil would require a full-scale study, in which their voluminous correspondence between 1891 and 1915 would have to be a center piece. It certainly deserves full publication.[6]

But it is perhaps even more important to inquire into the basis for Brentano's low opinion of Husserl's work. In the Bergmann letters Brentano himself mentioned specifically Emil Utitz as the source of his information. Indications are that almost all his evidence about Husserl was based on similar oral reports.

But there is even more conclusive proof for the fact that Brentano never made a study of any of Husserl's publications. Even when he recommended Husserl to Carl Stumpf for possible "Habilitation" in Halle (October 18, 1886) Brentano pointed out that he had not seen any of his written work.

Husserl had sent Brentano copies of his *Philosophie der Arithmetik* (1891) with its printed dedication and of the first volume of his *Logische Untersuchungen* (1900) and other reprints with handwritten inscriptions. According to Professor Chisholm, to whom I am indebted for this and other pertinent information, none of these shows any markings in the text.

The most telling case is actually the one of the *Philosophie der Arithmetik*. Some time in 1891 (the letter has no specific date) Brentano wrote Husserl a brief but warm acknowledgment, but added that he would have to postpone reading the book. Then in 1904, as shown in a letter of October 7, Brentano rediscovered the volume, and, in the belief that he had not yet acknowledged the dedication, sent him his apologies and renewed thanks. But even then he did not take a look inside. For the pages of the book, now in the Brentano Archives at Brown University under Professor Chisholm's direction, are still uncut. However, this fact must be seen in the light of Brentano's inability to read such a work after his unsuccessful operation for cataract in 1903.

As for the *Logische Untersuchungen* there is Brentano's own testimony in a letter to Oskar Kraus of September 28, 1904 that

---

[6] Thus far only two of Brentano's letters to Husserl, without the corresponding letters by Husserl or any information about them, have been published by Oskar Kraus in *Wahrheit und Evidenz* (Leipzig, 1930), pp. 153–161; English translation in the edition by Roderick M. Chisholm (London, 1966), 135 ff. For other samples see my *The Phenomenological Movement*[2] (The Hague, 1965), pp. 89 f.

he had "not seen the two fat volumes of his (Husserl's) *Logische Untersuchungen*," which had impressed so many of his own friends, especially in Munich.

Under these circumstances it seems safe to assert that Brentano's later verdict on Husserl as a philosopher was not based on direct acquaintance with the texts of his writings. There is also a good deal of evidence that his secondary sources of information were not always unbiased.[7]

Washington University, St. Louis

---

[7] See especially Oskar Kraus in *Wahrheit und Evidenz*, pp. XXIX–XXIII ("Psychologism and Phenomenologism") and the headline of p. 153 ("... on the Basic Mistakes in a so-called 'Phenomenology'"). Kraus's animosity also appears in his note about Husserl in the original of Brentano's manuscript; see *The Phenomenological Movement*, Illustration, opposite p. 27.

EPICUREANISM AND SCEPTICISM IN THE EARLY 17th CENTURY

RICHARD H. POPKIN

By the early 17th century there was a good deal of interest and concern with Epicurean physics, especially among chemists and medical doctors, and some interest and concern with Epicurean moral theory and theology. People who were sceptical of traditional morality and theology were being accused by fanatics like le père Garasse of being Epicureans, even if their professed views were fideistic (like those of Pierre Charron).[1] In this paper I will not attempt to survey the various writers of Epicurean tendencies of the period, their affinities to scepticism, and the accusations made against them. Instead I shall treat just two figures, Pierre Gassendi and Uriel Da Costa, and shall try to show that each of them tried to combine an aspect of Epicureanism with a type of scepticism – Gassendi joining an epistemological scepticism with Epicurean physics, and Da Costa joining a religious scepticism with portions of Epicurean theology. The later fusion of these two views produced, I believe, the modern scientific unbeliever.

Pierre Gassendi (1592–1635), apparently began his intellectual career as a philosophical sceptic, a follower of Sextus Empiricus, Montaigne and Charron.[2] His first work, the *Exercitationes*, presents a strenuous critique of Aristotelianism as well as a formulation of a mitigated Pyrrhonian scepticism. By the time he had finished the two books of this work, he had become serious-

---

[1] François Garasse said of Charron that he "étouffe et étrangle doucement et comme avec un cordon de soie le sentiment de la religion et mène son lecteur à une philosophie épicurienne," *Apologie du Pere Francois Garesse, de la Compagnie de Jesus, pour son livre contre les Atheistes & Libertins de nostre siècle* (Paris, 1624), p. 135.

[2] Cf. Gassendi's letter to Henri Du Faur de Pibrac, April, 1621, in Pierre Gassendi, *Opera Omnia* (Lyon, 1658), Vol. VI, pp. 1–2.

ly interested in Epicureanism. In his final statement of his views, the *Syntagma Philosophicum*, he set forth his fusion of scepticism and atomism, as a *via media* between a complete scepticism about the possibility of gaining knowledge, and a dogmatic contention that men could know the real nature of things.

For Gassendi some knowledge is possible. We can know through our senses how things appear to us, and we can know,by means of the interpretations of our reason, some matters about objects that are not immediately evident to us. But none of this really enables us to overcome a fundamental scepticism about the possibility of attaining genuine knowledge about reality. We are unable, for the various reasons put forth by the sceptics, to find out what things are like in themselves, why they have the nature they do, etc. Nonetheless, we have some means for discovering something about objects, through our experience, through careful reasoning and interpretation of our experience and through experimental verification of our reasonings and interpretations.

In a serious sense Gassendi remained a philosophical or epistemological sceptic all of his life. But he saw no reason to draw the negative conclusion from this scepticism that nothing at all could be known. A limited amount could be known with the resources available to us, but this would never amount to what the dogmatic metaphysicians were seeking, knowledge of the real nature of things. We would know a "shadow of truth," but not truth itself.[3]

In terms of this mitigated scepticism which was much like the epistemological position of his friend, le père Mersenne,[4] Gassendi

[3] For Gassendi's scepticism see his *Exercitationes Paradoxicae Adversus Aristoteleos*, esp. Book II, and *Syntagma Philosophicum*, Book I. See also R. H. Popkin, *History of Scepticism from Erasmus to Descartes* (Assen, 1964), pp. 102–108 and 143–148, and "Gassendi, Pierre," in *Encyclopedia of Philosophy* (New York, 1967), Vol. III, pp. 269–273; B. Rochot, *Les Travaux de Gassendi sur Épicure et sur l'atomisme* (Paris, 1944), and "Gassendi et le Syntagma philosophicum," *Revue de Synthèse* 47 (1950), pp. 67–79; and G. Sortais, *La Philosophie Moderne depuis Bacon jusqu'à Leibniz* (Paris, 1922), Vol. II.

[4] Marin Mersenne's position appears in his *La Verité des sciences contre les sceptiques ou pyrrhoniens* (Paris, 1625). See also R. Lenoble, *Mersenne ou la naissance du mécanisme* (Paris, 1943); and Popkin, *History of Scepticism*, pp. 132–143; "Father Mersenne's War against Pyrrhonism," *Modern Schoolman* 34 (1956–1957), pp. 61–78; and "Mersenne," *Encyclopedia of Philosophy*, V, pp. 282–283.

then went on to develop his Epicurean atomism, not as a metaphysical theory about what went on in the *real* world, but as an explanation of what went on in the world that we do in fact know, the world of appearances. Epicurus' atomic theory was for Gassendi a model for accounting for our experiences, for relating one experience to another, but it was not a description of ultimate reality. Atomism, in present day terms, was a scientific hypothesis. Its constituent elements were constructed from experienced data. By reflection and reasoning from the data, the atomic hypothesis was developed, and then the various items of our experienced world were interpreted in terms of the theory. As Rochot has pointed out, the end result of Gassendi's method was to find an order in the phenomena we are acquainted with, an "ensemble de rapports qui les unissent." [5] And, in applying this method, Gassendi remained on the sceptic's side maintaining that our knowledge actually extends only as far as these relationships and the appearances, not to a real world beyond. However, he also contended that the relationships discovered by his method and by his atomism constituted valuable and useful knowledge of the world in which we live.

Gassendi's sceptical Epicureanism is probably the first major formulation of the modern scientific outlook. It already separates science from metaphysics, and is based on a method much like that of the pragmatists and the positivists. Gassendi revived Epicurus' atomism to transform the ancient metaphysical theory into a hypothetical model for explanation, for relating phenomena to one another. By encasing the Epicurean theory within a sceptical view of the possibility of attaining genuine knowledge, Gassendi managed to make Epicurean materialism a systematic model for modern mechanism without offering it as the metaphysics of the "new philosophy." Science could be the way of proceeding even though in some fundamental sense all was in doubt with regard to knowledge of reality.

Gassendi's fusion of scepticism and Epicureanism did not incorporate Epicurus' theology with its denial of the immortality of the soul and of Divine Providence. Gassendi rejected the Epicurean contention that the atomic world was uncreated. For Gassendi, Epicureanism was compatible with Christianity, as

[5] Rochot, "Gassendi et le Syntagma," p. 77.

long as the atomic theory dealt only with the created world which was created and run by God. Gassendi accepted the doctrines of Christianity on faith, and found that they did not conflict with his scientific views, since these did not deal with the *real* world. He rejected the atomic explanation of the human soul, and accepted the doctrine of the immortality of the soul on faith.

There are those who have contended that Gassendi was really a "libertin" and an unbeliever, but his stated version of sceptical Epicureanism was also that of a Christian Epicureanism. He provided a view that could be a satisfactory formulation of the achievements of the new science, without involving any tenets of his church. His hypothetical Epicureanism, limited by his scepticism, shorn of its irreligious metaphysics, could provide a way for modern science without rejecting the values or beliefs of the Judeo-Christian tradition.

For a long time it was assumed that because Gassendi was an Epicurean materialist he must have been, or should have been a secret atheist. Gassendi was a priest, and was not seriously challenged on religious matters during his lifetime. The way he stated his position makes it possible to combine his scientific theories with a religion accepted on faith. And, as a result his viewpoint was often found more acceptable by religious thinkers in the 17th century than that of the other new philosophers.[6]

In contrast to Gassendi's joining of an epistemological scepticism and Epicurus' atomism into an acceptable religious view, another kind of fusion of scepticism and Epicureanism was offered at about the same time by Uriel Da Costa to create a challenge to the whole Judeo-Christian tradition. Da Costa (1585–1640), was a Portuguese New Christian, who had studied canon law at the University of Coimbra. He and his family reverted to Judaism. He then fled to Amsterdam to avoid persecution by the Inquisition.[7] As soon as he arrived in Holland

[6] For instance, the very anti-Cartesian Jesuits, René Rapin and Gabriel Daniel, had a very high opinion of Gassendi. On this, see R. H. Popkin, "The Traditionalism, Modernism and Scepticism of René Rapin," *Filosofia* 15 (1964), p. 8 and n. 31.

[7] The most accurate account of the development of Da Costa's religious views in Portugal, based on Portuguese Inquisition records, appears in I. S. Révah, "La Religion d'Ureil da Costa, Marrane de Porto," *Revue de l'Histoire des Religions* 161 (1962), pp. 45–76.

he found that his version of Judaism, apparently based on Marrano practices in Portugal and his Biblical studies, was not that of the Jewish community. He then seems to have written a series of theses against the rabbinical tradition and practices.[8] These were followed by a work, all copies of which were confiscated, arguing against belief in the immortality of the soul, and insisting that Biblical Judaism did not include such a view. This led to Da Costa's excommunication and his briefly being jailed. Several years later, after having suffered from being a lonely outcast, he rejoined the Synagogue and apologized for his heresies and misbehavior. As he said, he resolved "to be an ape among apes."[9] However, his own convictions and behavior led him into conflict with the Jewish community, and to a second excommunication. After seven years of being treated as a pariah, he again submitted, was made to recant publicly, was scourged in the Synagogue with thirty-nine lashes and was trod over by the whole congregation as he lay prostrate in the doorway. After this humiliation, he then wrote his autobiography, describing some of his trials and tribulations, and setting forth his views about religion (especially his contention that all extant religions are man-made), and finally ended his stormy career by shooting himself.[10]

Da Costa's autobiography was first published in 1687, at least 40 years after his death, as an appendix to Philip van Limborch's dispute with the Jewish philosopher, Isaac Orobio da Castro, over the truth of the Christian religion.[11] There is some doubt that the document is really his autobiography or is the full original text. Limborch printed it from a Latin manuscript (now at the University of Amsterdam library) he had received

---

[8] These appear in C. Gebhardt, *Die Schriften des Uriel Da Costa*, Bibliotheca Spinozana, Tom. II (Amsterdam, 1922), pp. 3–10 (in Hebrew), followed by German and Portuguese translations. They come from Rabbi Leon da Modena's answer.

[9] Uriel da Costa, *Exemplar Humanae Vitae*, in Gebhardt, p. 110.

[10] Most of the biographical information comes from Da Costa's autobiography, the rest from Philip van Limborch's preface to the original publication of it.

[11] Cf. Philip van Limborch, *De Veritate Religionis Christianae amica collatio cum Erudito Judaeo* (Amsterdam, 1687). This work was also published in Dutch at the same time. The original Latin was republished in Basel in 1740, and an English translation of the Da Costa appendix, entitled *The Remarkable Life of Uriel Acosta, an eminent Freethinker, with his Reasons for rejecting all Revealed Religion* appeared in London in 1740.

from his uncle, the Arminian leader, Simon Episcopius. It omits much of Da Costa's career. But, whether genuine, complete or whatever, the work caused a sensation. Pierre Bayle devoted an interesting article (Acosta) to him, based entirely on the auto-biography. The work was translated into English and German, and since then he has been seen as a martyr of religious bigotry, the spiritual father of Spinoza (there is a 19th century painting showing the young Spinoza sitting on Da Costa's lap), and the father of modern unbelief. Bayle concludes his article by saying "c'etoit un personnage digne d'horreur, un esprit si mal tourné, qu'il se perdit miserablement par les travers de sa fausse Philosophie."[12]

When Da Costa first started enunciating his "fausse Philo-sophie," he was immediately denounced by the famous rabbi, Leon da Modena, as an Epicurean and a denier of God, for opposing the views of the rabbis.[13] In the Talmudic tradition an "Epikoros" (derived from the name of the philosopher) is an Epicurean, a sceptic, and a non-believer. The rabbis felt that the worst kind of Epikoros was a Jewish one, because he would be more lawless, and more deliberate in his negation.[14] The term denotes both, or alternately, a follower of Epicurean philosophy, and a religious sceptic. In Maimonides' *Guide for the Perplexed*, a summary of Epicureanism is presented, which includes the denial of Providence, the claim that all happens by chance, that there is no governance of anything, that the atoms mingle by chance, and that all is generated by chance. Then Maimonides says that there were those in Israel who were unbelievers who also professed these opinions.[15]

Da Costa seems to have progressed from being a partial Epicurean to a full-blooded Epikoros. In 1623, just before his book on the mortality of the soul appeared, he was denounced

[12] Limborch, in his preface, just says he got the manuscript from his uncle, who received it from "a very eminent citizen." For the Bayle citation, see article "Acosta," end of Rem H., in the *Dictionnaire Historique et Critique*.

[13] Cf. Gebhardt, *op. cit.*, pp. 150–151, where the text is given in Hebrew and German.

[14] Cf. *The Babylonian Talmud* (Socino, ed.) *Seder Nezikin*, Vol. V (London, 1935), p. 244.

[15] Cf. Moses Maimonides, *The Guide of the Perplexed*, Pines translation (Chicago, 1963), III, 17, p. 464.

by a Samuel da Silva as one who defended Epicurus' principles, and who by his denial of the immortality of the soul, disputed the being of God by inference.[16] Da Costa had argued that the soul was only part of the human organism, and died with it. Though Da Costa's arguments are mainly Aristotelian and Biblical (we have them only from Da Silva's answer to him), the denial of human immortality was immediately taken to be an Epicurean view. In the autobiography, Da Costa insisted that at the time he had not read Epicurus, and had a bad opinion of his views. Later on, "having heard the sentiments of some impartial lovers of truth, concerning him and his doctrine, I have found reason to change mine, and to be sorry for the injustice I did him then, in pronouncing so great a man to be both absurd and mad."[17]

Da Costa, at the end of his life, insisted that he still had not read any of Epicurus' works (and did not seem to know that they were lost except for the letters). But by then he had developed some Epicurean themes into a genuine scepticism about Judeo-Christianity. From denying the religious tradition and the immortality of the soul, he went on to insist that Judaism, and then all religions, were human inventions, and to deny any Providence. (The great rabbi of Amsterdam, Menasseh ben Israel, denounced him as an Epicurean for this last heresy.)[18] Da Costa appears to have ended his intellectual journey as a kind of Stoic Deist, contending that right reason and the law of nature take precedence over the Law of Moses and the Gospel, and that an adequate morality can be based on reason and nature "if men would follow the dictates of right reason, and live according to the laws which nature dictates to them, they would all mutually love and help one another."[19]

By the end of his life, Da Costa was almost a genuine Epikoros,

[16] Samuel da Silva, *Tratado da Immortalidade* (Amsterdam, 1623), part of which is published in Gebhardt, *op. cit.* On this point, see Gebhardt, pp. 161–163, and pp. 108–109 where Da Costa mentions the charge.
[17] Da Costa, in Gebhardt, p. 109. The translated quotation is from Uriel Acosta, *A Specimen of Human Life* (New York, 1967), pp. 16–17.
[18] In Manasseh ben Israel's *De Resurrectione Mortuorum* (1636), cited in Gebhardt, pp. 188–189.
[19] Da Costa, *A Specimen of Human Life*, p. 40; in Gebhardt, p. 122. A somewhat similar view was offered a few years later by Juan de Prado, who was excommunicated along with Spinoza. Cf. I. S. Révah, *Spinoza et le Dr. Juan de Prado* (Paris, The Hague, 1959).

a sceptic about the truth or importance of the Judeo-Christian tradition. Though not an Epicurean in the strict sense, since he did not knowingly build upon theories of Epicurus, he did in fact use Epicurean elements as stepping stones to his religious scepticism. His denial of the immortality of the soul and of Divine Providence, his assertion that religions were human inventions based on fear, led him gradually to a complete doubt of Judeo-Christianity. For Da Costa, Epicureanism was coupled with scepticism in a quite different way from that of Gassendi's philosophy. Epicurus' theology, rather than his physics, was joined to a genuine scepticism about the merits of the revealed religious tradition and therein he was able to reject the whole fabric of the past. Da Costa was perhaps the first modern man to step outside the Judeo-Christian tradition, and to proclaim himself a *man* rather than a Jew or a Christian. "These are the men who are continually vaunting, I am a *Jew* , or I am a *Christian*, ... He who pretends to be neither of these and only calls himself a man, is far preferable." [20] It has been claimed that Don Quixote is the first modern man when he proclaims," I am a man without any lineage." [21] However, when one examines this passage in context, it can be seen that it is said in answer to Sancho Panza's claim that he is an Old Christian. Don Quixote says *he* is not, and so, by inference, he is a New Christian (that is, a Jew). Then he is still part of the Judeo-Christian tradition. Da Costa, on the other hand, tried to set himself apart from Jews and Christians, and tried to be simply a man, a man resting on his right reason and the laws of nature alone. His personal tragedy was that in his day, even in Holland, it was not yet possible to be both an Epikoros in spirit and an Epikoros in fact. To exist, he had to be in a religious community. To be himself, he could not so live.

A generation later, Spinoza was able to live as both a non-believer and as an individual attached to no religious group. Da Costa's sceptical, irreligious Epicureanism could lead him to proclaim defiantly what it would be like to be the new man, the man free from the Judeo-Christian tradition, but the world was

[20] Da Costa, *Specimen*, p. 43, Gebhardt, p. 122.
[21] See the discussion towards the end of chap. XXI, Book I of *Don Quixote*.

not quite ready for such an individual. Da Costa's union of Epicurean theology and religious scepticism gave him a vision of what man might become, but it took another generation to produce a true modern Epikoros, and to produce him through the fusion of the type of sceptical Epicureanism of Gassendi (that is, modern science) and of Da Costa (that is, modern unbelief).

Da Costa's combination of elements of Epicurean theology and religious scepticism lacked both a theory of what the world was actually like, and a thoroughgoing basis for a critique and rejection of Judaism and Christianity. The latter was provided by one of Gassendi's friends, Isaac La Peyrère, (1594–1676), apparently also a descendant of Portuguese New Christians from Bordeaux.[22] He was raised as a Calvinist, and became a courtier, working for the Prince of Condé. Though he is usually portrayed as a "libertin" and an unbeliever (Bayle reported that one of his religious associates said of him, "La Peyrère was the best man in the world, the sweetest, who tranquilly believed very few things"[23]), he actually does not seem to have been an Epikoros. From the time of his first work, *Rappel des Juifs*,[24] (1643), he seems to have believed in a mystical theology, which he was still working on at the end of his life. He believed that the coming of the second Messiah, that of the Jews, was about to appear. His scandalous reputation comes from his other major work, the *Prae-Adamitae*, (1655) (though written much earlier). In this work he denied that Biblical history was world history. His critique of the Bible, and his radical reinterpretation and reevaluation of it, provided the seeds for the rejection of Scripture as a serious picture of the nature and destiny of man. La Peyrère applied the latest scientific evidence of the day to the stories in the Bible, and found that there must have been people before Adam, that most of mankind must have had an origin independent of Noah, and that the Bible could at best only portray the origins and devel-

---

[22] On La Peyrère, see my article on him in the *Encyclopedia of Philosophy*, IV, p. 391.

[23] Cf. Bayle's article "Peyrère, Isaac la," Rem. G, in the *Dictionnaire*.

[24] (Isaac La Peyrère) *Du Rappel des Juifs* (n.p. 1643). A later version of this work exists in manuscript at Chantilly. The book apparently circulated among religious thinkers of the period. Mersenne read it, as did some of the Papal advisers.

opment of the Jews. He challenged the accuracy of the texts, the accuracy of the copies that have come down to us, and the accuracy of the prevailing interpretations of the Message.

Shortly after the *Prae-Adamitae* appeared, La Peyrère was arrested, and his book was condemned. He survived, as an adroit courtier, by turning Catholic, and apologizing in person to the Pope. He abjured his opinions, and blamed them on his unfortunate Calvinist upbringing. His *Apologie* reeks of insincerity and hypocrisy.[25] Then he retired to the pious Oratory, where he continued working on his heretical theories.[26]

While La Peyrère was having his troubles, a young reader of his opus, Baruch de Spinoza, went on to develop his scientific criticism of the Bible, and to develop a theory of the nature of the cosmos that thoroughly excluded the Judeo-Christian picture of the world. Spinoza's "higher criticism" led him to a complete rejection of the Biblical conception of man's history, and to a reinterpretation of Judeo-Christianity in terms of psychology, and sociology, as the effects of superstition and fear. Spinoza's metaphysics finally provided a world view in which modern science, not religion, could explain everything. Although Spinoza's physics and metaphysics were definitely not Epicurean, his theology, as Bayle pointed out, was in agreement with that of Epicurus.[27] Spinoza denied any Providence, any divine governance, and any personal immortality. Much of the brilliant appendix to Book I of the *Ethics* could have been written by Epicurus or his followers. And, Spinoza had provided both a philosophy and a non-Biblical perspective for a modern Epikoros. After Spinoza, one could have strong reasons for believing Da Costa's claim that Biblical religion was just a human invention. One could conceive of a world operating only by physical laws, and one could see, from the aspect of eternity, a universe to be

[25] Cf. Isaac La Peyrère, *Apologie de la Peyrère* (Paris, 1633). See esp. p. 50.

[26] He there became a good friend of the sceptical Bible critic, Father Richard Simon, who seems to have preserved his last works. La Peyrère did a French edition of the Bible, with notes, that was suppressed. Bayle reports that at the Oratory, La Peyrère was writing books that would be burned as soon as the author died. See Bayle's article "Peyrère," Rem. G.

[27] Cf. Bayle's article "Spinoza," in the text, almost at the end: "Il est d'accord avec Epicure en ce qui regarde la rejection de la Providence, mais dans tout le reste leurs Systêmes sont comme le feu et l'eau."

understood by scientific reasoning and not by religious faith. Modern science and religious scepticism had been combined to supply the ideology of the new Epikoros.

In the generation after Spinoza, many cried out against his "atheism." Bayle, who was so sensitive to the tensions in the intellectual world, saw Spinoza as a most major figure, "a systematic atheist," and Bayle devoted his longest article to discussing and trying to refute him. Bayle, though himself more likely a tepid believer than an Epikoros, was fascinated by Spinoza, by the Epicureans and atomists (he devoted an inordinate number of lengthy articles to the major, the minor, and to the practically unknown ones), and by the religious sceptic and the Bible critics. He explored their theories, played with their ideas, and revealed the harrowing possibilities of the world they were pointing to. He also advanced the shocking theory that a society of atheists could be moral, and that Epicurus and Spinoza were more moral than most Christians. Bayle's ruminations were to provide a good deal of the ammunition for the new Epikoroses.

By the time of David Hume, "the great infidel," as he was known to his contemporaries, the sceptic could openly ally himself with Epicurus to attack all forms of religion, and all attempts to reconcile religion and science. Although Hume rejected what he called "the hideous hypothesis of Epicurus" because of its contention that everything happens by chance, when Hume first presented his sceptical reasons for rejecting religious claims, in his essay "Of a Particular Providence and of a Future State," he made Epicurus his spokesman. Epicurus offered the sceptical arguments that were to demolish natural religion, and to show that modern science cannot provide any basis for religion.

In the course of a little over a hundred years the intermingling of scepticism, Epicureanism, and modern science had helped to shape the character of modern unbelief, and to provide the ideology for a world apart from Judeo-Christianity. Gassendi's modest sceptical Epicureanism might have provided a way of keeping the old religious and new scientific worlds together, accepting the former on faith, and the latter only as a probable hypothesis restricted to the world of appearance. However, it was

Da Costa's forceful, sceptical Epicureanism, joined to the fruits of the new science, and applied to religion that was to have the greater impact. Once modern science was joined to this kind of religious scepticism, the modern Epikoros was able to take the stage and play his major role in modern intellectual history. Those who would try in the present to overcome the hollow world of the modern Epikoros will have to do so in the full light of the force and the effect of the tradition started by Da Costa, La Peyrère, Spinoza, Bayle, and Hume. If the world of Judeo-Christianity can, in some sense, be made meaningful in the world of modern science, it can only happen when the power of the Biblical critics and the irreligious sceptics has been fully appreciated.

University of California, San Diego

PETRAŻYCKI'S CONCEPT OF ADEQUATE THEOREM IN THE LIGHT OF EARLIER RELATED DOCTRINES

TADEUSZ KOTARBIŃSKI

In his *Introduction to the Science of Law and Morals*,[1] Leon Petrażycki (1867–1931) analyzed the concept of adequate theorem, obviously without realizing the fact that similar ideas had been expounded several times before in the history of logic and methodology. My intention is to compare below the texts of his predecessors with his own. I have already done that twice: for the first time very briefly in my paper "On the History of the Concept of Adequate Theory" (in Polish, published in *Przeglad Filozoficzny*, 1936, in the issue dedicated to the Third Congress of Polish Philosophers), and for the second, much more comprehensively, in a paper bearing the same title and published in *Przeglad Filozoficzny*, 1937, No. 3. Both papers are included in my collected papers, *Reflections on Thinking* (in Polish Scientific Publishers: Warsaw, 1958). On this occasion I would like to complete my earlier writings on the subject by quoting the sources.

What does Petrażycki himself state concerning this matter? Here are his words:

By a class concept ... is meant the idea of those objects which have certain properties, that is, the idea of all that which can be conceived as having certain properties. By a class ... is meant the objects corresponding to such an idea, that is, all those objects (things, phenomena, etc.) that have, or can be conceived as having, given properties. For instance, the idea of all those objects which are of white colour is a class concept, namely the concept of the class of white objects. That class consists of all those objects

---

[1] *Wstęp do nauki prawa i moralności* (*Introduction to the Science of Law and Morals*), authorized translation into Polish by Jerzy Lande, from the third edition (1908) of the Russian original entitled *Vvedeňe v izučeňe prava i nravstvennosti* (1st Polish edition, 1930; 2nd ed., 1959). All quotes will be taken from the 2nd edition.

which are of that colour or can be conceived as having that colour (*Introduction to the Science of Law and Morals*, p. 74).

The function of forming concepts ... has to perform the extremely important task of creating and defining such classes of objects which could be the subject matter of scientific theorems and systematic mutual relationships between such theorems (*ibid.*, p. 94).

Not all class concepts and classes, blameless from a general logical standpoint, are valuable in science. Such class concepts and classes as "the cigars which cost 50 cents each" do not violate logic, but their scientific value would be more than doubtful (*ibid.*, p. 121).

Those class concepts and classes are to be considered as satisfying the task of comprehending and scientifically explaining the various phenomena, with respect to which adequate scientific theories exist or can be formulated (*ibid.*, p. 122).

By a theory is meant ... the stating ... of truths concerning classes of objects, regardless of whether such statements are single or ... form sets ... (*ibid.*, p. 122).

Scientific theories are theories justified in a consciously methodical (and systematic) manner ... (*ibid.*, 122).

By "adequate" scientific theories we mean theories in which that which is stated ... is true exactly about that class of objects about which it is stated .... Hence if about a species belonging to a genus ... something is stated which ... is true about the entire genus ... then we do not have to do with adequate theories ... (*ibid.*, p. 124).

For instance ... it can be stated about "cigars which weigh 10 grammes each" that ... they are subject to gravitation, that they expand when heated ... (*ibid.*, p. 125).

The non-scientific character of such theories, their scientific lameness, consists in their inadequacy, that is, in their being stated only about cigars which weigh 10 grammes each, while in fact they apply to all physical bodies ... (*ibid.*, p. 126).

Those theories ... in which statements refer to too narrowly defined groups of objects shall be termed lame (since they are associated ... with images of objects ... based on insufficient ... foundations) (*ibid.*, p. 128).

Those theories which have the defect that their statements are not restricted to the limits within which they are true, but go beyond those limits, may be termed jumping, as contrasted with the lame theories (since their statements jump beyond their natural limits into alien fields) (*ibid.*, 139).

... some sociologists claim that ... the conditions of production of material goods ... are the factor that determines all other phenomena, ... others reduce everything to the imitation by members of society of eminent individuals ... still others see the source of everything in the properties of the race ... etc., etc., ... sociology offers ... a large collection of jumping theories (*ibid.*, p. 140).

Should anyone have naive confidence in such culinary terms as "spices" and "game" and write a treatise on "The Anatomy of Spices" or "The Physiology of Game," he would probably produce many examples of theories that would be both jumping and lame (*ibid.*, p. 149).

... the principle of adequacy of theories ... includes the basic recommendation ... of an ordering of theoretical knowledge (*ibid.*, p. 154).

... the task of constructing proper class concepts ... consists ... in defining classes of objects such that when appropriate theorems are referred to them ... then adequate ... theories are formed (*ibid.*, p. 155).

An overwhelming majority ... of classes which ... we can form ... has no distinct names for its members ... (*ibid.*, p. 159).

When we want ... to justify ... a theory ... we have to establish the existence of necessary logical or causal nexus (tendency) between the *differentia specifica* ... of a class of objects (as the theoretical subject) and something else (that which is stated about a given class, that is, the theoretical prodicate)*ibid.*, pp. 185).

Theories in which predicates are associated ... with specific ... properties, with the *differentiae specificae* of the theoretical subjects ... are free from lameness (*ibid.*, p.189).

The specific properties of the classes under investigation ought to serve as the scientific foundation for all ... theoretical theses; they are the true *fundamenta theoriae*. The content of a theory should be the exposition of that which is logically or causally linked with the specific property of the class under investigation, as well as explanations and proofs of such relations (*ibid.*, p. 192).

Complying with these assumptions, Petrażycki constructed his theory of law, which is shown, for instance, by the following declaration:

Conscious scientific construction of classes and class concepts ought to comply not with the recommendations of this or that language, that is with terminological habits developed unconsciously by historical processes but with the task of comprehending and explaining the various phenomena, in particular with the task of constructing correct scientific theories, that is, such sciences of classes of phenomena in which that which is stated and explained has a logical or causal nexus with the specific nature (*differentia specifica*) of the classes so constructed.

Complying with that recommendation, we have constructed a higher, generic class termed ethical phenomena, and we have divided that class, in accordance with the nature of the ethical emotions involved, into two subclasses, two species: (1) those ethical phenomena which are imperative-attributive in nature, which we have termed "law," and (2) those ethical phenomena which are purely imperative, which we have termed "morals."[2]

If the various characteristic properties of the classes so constructed are in connection with the properties suggested as a basis of classification, or can be explained by them (or can be deductively predicted and discovered by means of them), or if they help to establish certain laws (tendencies) that are specifically proper to the adopted classes (are adequate with respect to them), then the classification is scientifically justified, and the more phenomena it can explain the greater its scientific value.

As can be seen from the preceding paragraphs, the differences in the intellectual composition of legal and moral experiences and their respective

---

[2] *Teoria prawa i państwa w związku z teoria moralności* (*The Theory of Law and State as Related to the Theory of Morals*), Jerzy Lande, ed. (Warsaw, 1959), I, p. 192. The Russian original appeared in St. Petersburg in 1909.

projections are connected with, and explained by, the attributive nature of the legal emotions, on the one hand, and the purely imperative nature of the moral emotions, on the other (*The Theory of Law and State*, p. 196).

Since the characteristic properties of the intellectual composition and the projections of legal mentality, indicated above, which distinguish it from moral mentality, are connected with the attributive nature of the corresponding emotions of duty, then the class of ethical experiences with imperative-attributive emotions, and not any other class, is the adequate class, proper from the scientific standpoint, and the appropriate general theorems and their further (future) expansions ought to be referred to that class exactly. Referring them to any other class would be tantamount, from the scientific standpoint, to constructing defective theories, lame, jumping, or totally false (*ibid.*, p. 198).

These excerpts from Petrażycki's works do not require any summing up as they give a clear picture of his opinion about the essence of adequate theorems and their rôle in science, as he interpreted those problems. But the appeal for the adequacy of general scientific theses has had a history of more than 2000 years.

In Aristotle's *Posterior Analytics* we read as follows:

I say that something is about everything, if it is not so that it applies to this or that but does not apply to another one; ... for instance, if creature can be predicated about every man, then whatever can truly be termed man, can also truly be termed creature. ... For we raise objections in this way: when we are asked whether something applies to everything we say that it does not apply to something .... And I say that something is an attribute of something as that something, if it is its attribute on the strength of what that something is .... But if by it, then also on the strength of it; for instance, if a creature struck with an edge dies, and dies on the strength of having been struck, then it dies by having been struck, and it does not happen only by chance that it dies. Thus that which is predicated ... as being inherent in something because of that something, ... is predicated by it and of necessity (Arist. *An. Post.* 1. 4. 73a28–74b19).[3]
... In this way let that: about everything, and that: on the strength of that something, be defined, and by generality, as I say, that which is an attribute of everything and on the strength of itself, and as such, is an attribute. ... And: because of itself and as such, is the same, ... for instance

---

[3] Arist. *An. Post.* 1. 4. 73a28–74b19: Κατὰ παντὸς μὲν οὖν τοῦτο λέγω ὃ ἂν ᾖ μὴ ἐπὶ τινὸς μὲν τινὸς δὲ μή ... οἷον εἰ κατὰ παντὸς ἀνθρώπου ζῷον, εἰ ἀληθὲς τόνδ' εἰπεῖν ἄνθρωπον, ἀληθὲς καὶ ζῷον ... καὶ γὰρ τὰς ἐνστάσεις οὕτω φέρομεν ὡς κατὰ παντὸς ἐρωτώμενοι ... ἐπί τινι μή ... Καθ' αὑτὰ δ' ὅσα ὑπάρχει τε ἐν τῷ τί ἐστιν ... εἰ δὲ δι' αὑτό, καθ' αὑτό, οἷον εἴ τι σφαττόμενον ἀπέθανε, καὶ κατὰ τὴν σφαγήν ,ὅτι διὰ τὸ σφάττεσθαι, ἀλλ' οὐ συνέβη σφαττόμενον ἀποθανεῖν. τὰ ἄρα λεγόμενα... καθ' αὑτὰ οὕτως ὡς ἐνυπάρχειν τοῖς κατηγορουμένοις ... δι' αὑτά τέ ἐστι καὶ ἐξ ἀνάγκης.

two right angles are an attribute of a triangle as a triangle.[4] For a triangle is equal to two right angles because it is a triangle. And by generality, something occurs whenever it is shown with reference to anything and by priority. For instance, to have two right angles is not a property of a figure by generality, because it can be shown with reference to a figure that it has two right angles, but not with reference to just any figure, and he who shows that does not use just any figure, because a quadrangle is a figure and does not have angles that are equal to two right angles,[5] while just any isosceles [6] has angles equal to two right angles, but not by priority, because triangle is prior (*An. Post.* I. 4. 73b25–39).[7]

And it should not be forgotten that it often happens that a mistake is made, and that which a person shows to be an attribute by generality and by priority is not such an attribute, although it seems that it can be shown that it is an attribute by generality and by priority. We make such a mistake whenever either it is not possible to find anything superior to something singular or a number of singulars, or it is possible to find only something that has no common name .... And I say that a proof is a proof of something as such by priority whenever it is a proof by priority and by generality. ... And that a ratio is interchangeable crosswise [8] with

---

[4] Aristotle refers here – and also below, in a formulation which may be misleading because of its brevity – to the theorem that the sum of the inner angles of a triangle equals two right angles.

[5] The statement that the sum of the inner angles of a quadrangle equals two right angles would not be true.

[6] Aristotle takes as his example the sequence of three terms, in the order of increasing generality: "isosceles triangle," "triangle," "geometrical figure." Whoever would state that an isosceles triangle as such has the sum of its inner angles equal to two right angles, would make a true statement, but that statement would not be true by priority, since the predicate would not refer to the first of those three terms to which it might refer: the first term which covers all the objects endowed with the property specified by the predicate, namely the property "having the sum of its inner angles equal to two right angles," and all such objects, is the term "triangle," second in the above sequence. The third term in the sequence, "geometrical figure," would not satisfy that condition, since it covers quadrangles as well, and these do not have the sum of all inner angles equal to two right angles.

[7] *An. Post.* I. 4. 73b25–39: Τὸ μὲν οὖν κατὰ παντὸς καὶ καθ' αὑτὸ διωρίσθω τὸν τρόπον τοῦτον. καθόλου δὲ λέγω ὃ ἄν κατὰ παντός τε ὑπάρχῃ καὶ καθ' αὑτὸ καὶ ᾗ αὑτό .... τὸ καθ' αὑτὸ δὲ καὶ ᾗ αὑτὸ ταὐτόν, οἷον ... καὶ τῷ τριγώνῳ ᾗ τρίγωνον δύο ὀρθαί (καὶ γὰρ καθ' αὑτὸ τὸ τρίγωνον δύο ὀρθαῖς ἴσον). τὸ καθόλου δὲ ὑπάρχει τότε, ὅταν ἐπὶ τοῦ τυχόντος καὶ πρώτου δεικνύηται. οἷον τὸ δύο ὀρθὰς ἔχειν οὔτε τῷ σχήματί ἐστι καθόλου (καίτοι ἔστι δεῖξαι κατὰ σχήματος ὅτι δύο ὀρθὰς ἔχει, ἀλλ' οὐ τοῦ τυχόντος σχήματος, οὐδὲ χρῆται τῷ τυχόντι σχήματι δεικνύς. τὸ γὰρ τετράγωνον σχῆμα μέν, οὐκ ἔχει δὲ δύο ὀρθαῖς ἴσας) – τὸ δ' ἰσοσκελὲς ἔχει μὲν τὸ τυχὸν δύο ὀρθαῖς ἴσας, ἀλλ' οὐ πρῶτον, ἀλλὰ τὸ τρίγωνον πρότερον.

[8] If a : b = c : d, then a : c = b : d, and this, according to Aristotle, is true regardless of whether the letters stand for numbers, lengths, solids, or time periods.

respect to numbers, lines, solids, and periods of time alike, ... that can be demonstrated by one proof holding for all. But that was assumed separately, because all these do not have a common name – a number, length, solid, period of time – and differ from one another generically. ... Should therefore anyone demonstrate by a proof about every triangle that it has two right angles, but do it separately about an isosceles and a scalene and an equilateral triangle, then he would still not know that a triangle has two right angles (unless it were in a sophistical way); he would not know whether this applies to the triangle by generality and whether there not may be any other triangle than those. For he would not know that this holds for the triangle as triangle, nor that it holds for every triangle, for he would know only by enumeration. And he would not know about every one by genus, and whether there is not a triangle that he does not know.[9] ... And a proof is by generality if a property by priority remains if another property is removed, for instance, if two right angles are a property of an isosceles triangle, then they will nevertheless remain its property if the property of being an isosceles is removed. But not if the figure is removed. ... To what then does it apply by priority? Now to the triangle, and because of that it also is a property of the remaining ones, and this is a proof by generality (*An. Post.* I. 5. 74a4–74b4).[10]

For instance, the subjective complement "geometrical figure that has the sum of its inner angles equal to two right angles" is reversible with respect to the subject "triangle," because every triangle is such a figure, and every such figure is a triangle, and therefore it may be said that that subjective complement refers

[9] The person in question would not know whether, in addition to the various kinds of triangles, previously analyzed in turn, there is no exceptional kind of triangle to which the statement about the sum of the inner angles of a triangle equal to two right angles would not apply.

[10] *An. Post.* I. 5. 74a4–74b4: Δεῖ δὲ μὴ λανθάνειν ὅτι πολλάκις συμβαίνει διαμαρτάνειν καὶ μὴ ὑπάρχειν τὸ δεικνύμενον πρῶτον καθόλου, ᾗ δοκεῖ δείκνυσθαι καθόλου πρῶτον. ἀπατώμεθα δὲ ταύτην τὴν ἀπάτην, ὅταν ἢ μηδὲν ᾖ λαβεῖν ἀνώτερον παρὰ τὸ καθ᾽ ἕκαστον ἢ τὰ καθ᾽ ἕκαστα, ἢ ᾖ μέν, ἀλλ᾽ ἀνώνυμον ... λέγω δὲ τούτου πρώτου, ᾗ τοῦτο, ἀπόδειξιν, ὅταν ᾖ πρώτου καθόλου ... καὶ τὸ ἀνάλογον ὅτι καὶ ἐναλλάξ, ᾗ ἀριθμοὶ καὶ ᾗ γραμμαὶ καὶ ᾗ στερεὰ καὶ ᾗ χρόνοι ... ἐνδεχόμενόν γε κατὰ πάντων μιᾷ ἀποδείξει δειχθῆναι, ἀλλὰ διὰ τὸ μὴ εἶναι ὠνομασμένον τι ταῦτα πάντα ἕν, ἀριθμοὶ μήκη χρόνοι στερεά, καὶ εἴδει διαφέρειν ἀλλήλων, χωρὶς ἐλαμβάνετο ... οὐδ᾽ ἄν τις δείξῃ καθ᾽ ἕκαστον, τὸ τρίγωνον ἀποδείξει ἢ μιᾷ ἢ ἑτέρᾳ ὅτι δύο ὀρθὰς ἔχει ἕκαστον, τὸ ἰσόπλευρον χωρὶς καὶ τὸ σκαληνὲς καὶ τὸ ἰσοσκελές, οὔπω οἶδε τὸ τρίγωνον ὅτι δύο ὀρθαῖς, εἰ μὴ τὸν σοφιστικὸν τρόπον, οὐδὲ καθ᾽ ὅλου τριγώνου, οὐδ᾽ εἰ μηδὲν ἔστι παρὰ ταῦτα τρίγωνον ἕτερον. οὐ γὰρ ᾗ τρίγωνον οἶδεν, οὐδὲ πᾶν τρίγωνον, ἀλλ᾽ ἢ κατ᾽ ἀριθμόν ... καθόλου τίνος ἡ ἀπόδειξις; δῆλον ὅτι ὅταν ἀφαιρουμένων ὑπάρχῃ πρώτῳ. οἷον τῷ ἰσοσκελεῖ χαλκῷ τριγώνῳ ὑπάρξουσι δύο ὀρθαί, ἀλλὰ καὶ τοῦ χαλκοῦν εἶναι ἀφαιρεθέντος καὶ τοῦ ἰσοσκελές. ἀλλ᾽ οὐ τοῦ σχήματος ... τίνος οὖν πρώτου; εἰ δὴ τριγώνου, κατὰ τοῦτο ὑπάρχει καὶ τοῖς ἄλλοις, καὶ τούτου καθόλου ἐστίν ἡ ἀπόδειξις.

to that subject by generality and by priority. But, although every isosceles triangle is a geometrical figure that has the sum of its inner angles equal to two right angles, it is nevertheless not true that every such figure is an isosceles triangle, and hence that subjective complement refers to the isosceles triangle by generality, but not by priority.

In another place the same *Posterior Analytics* reads:

I say that it is by generality about that which is not reversible, and that it is by priority and by generality about that with which the details are not reversible, but the whole is reversible and does not reach any further (2. 17. 99a34–36).[11]

The texts quoted above hold the nucleus of the entire doctrine of the essence of adequate theorems and their position in science. Thus, adequate theorems are not only general in this sense that the subjective complement applies to every object covered by the extension of the subject of a given sentence, but also such that the subjective complement applies to those objects only and does not reach beyond the extension of the subject. Thus the subject and the subjective complement are mutually reversible. But this does not suffice to make a theorem scientific. It is also required that the coincidence between the extensions of the subject and the subjective complement be not incidental, but that there should be a nexus between them, and examples of such a nexus are given by Aristotle. Not only is it true that every triangle and only every triangle has the sum of its inner angles equal to two right angles, but it is also true that it has such a sum as such, as triangle, because of what a triangle is in general. Thus we have to do here with a kind of logical nexus. But in the example which refers to this – that every creature dies when struck by an edge – the nexus is of some other kind, i.e., causal. We would like to have better examples of such a nexus, because the example in question shows a causal nexus by pointing to the possibility of a causal interpretation of the phrases "by itself" or "on the strength," but nevertheless we have here to do with an obviously inadequate thesis, since it is common knowledge that the various creatures die not because of having been struck

---

[11] *An. Post.* 2. 17. 99a34–36: τοῦτο γὰρ λέγω καθόλου ᾧ μὴ ἀντιστρέφει, πρῶτον δὲ καθόλου ᾧ ἕκαστον μὲν μὴ ἀντιστρέφει, ἄπαντα δὲ ἀντιστρέφει καὶ παρεκτείνει.

with an edge. Aristotle's example of the botanical thesis which states that leaves fall away from plants because the sap condenses at their bases, would be to the point here.[12] I may add that, as in the case of Petrażycki's theory, one of the causes of the frequent inadequacies of scientific statements is the lack of a common term that would linguistically single out the totality of those objects about which a given subjective complement could be predicated adequately.

In Greek antiquity, but much later, special terms were coined to stand for adequacy and its component requirements concerning the relation between the extensions of the subject and the subjective complement. Alexander of Aphrodisias (ca. 200 A.D.), a commentator on Aristotle's works, wrote as follows:

... it is said that a definition is an analytic formulation that states adequately (where analysis names a concise exposition of that which is defined, and adequately means for them without excess and without shortage) (Alex. Aphr. *Ad Topica Comm.* 1. 5, p. 42. 27–43. 4 Wallies).[13]

The Greek term translated as "adequately" is "apartizontos" (which is an adverb formed from the verb "apartizein" = "to adjust"), and the phrases "without excess" and "without shortage" are used here to replace the term "aperittos," which corresponds to the negation of Petrażycki's "lameness," and the term "anellipos," which corresponds to the negation of the "jumping manner" in his terminology.

The present author knows nothing about the fortunes of the idea discussed in this paper in the Middle Ages. The sources seem to be silent. It is only in France in the period of the Renaissance that the problem of the adequacy of general statements reappears

[12] *An. Post.* B. 17. 99a23–29: τὸ φυλλορροεῖν ἅμα ἀκολουθεῖ τῇ ἀμπέλῳ καὶ ὑπερέχει, καὶ συκῇ, καὶ ὑπερέχει, ἀλλ' οὐ πάντων, ἀλλ' ἴσον. εἰ δὴ λάβοις τὸ πρῶτον μέσον, λόγος τοῦ φυλλορροεῖν ἐστιν. ἔσται γὰρ πρῶτον μὲν ἐπὶ θάτερα μέσον, ὅτι τοιαδὶ ἅπαντα, εἶτα τούτου μέσον, ὅτι ὀπὸς πήγνυται ἤ τι ἄλλο τοιοῦτον. τί δ' ἐστὶ τὸ φυλλορροεῖν; τὸ πήγνυσθαι τὸν ἐν τῇ συνάψει τοῦ σπέρματος ὀπόν.

[13] Alex. Aphr. *Ad Topica Comm.* 1. 5, p. 42, 27–43, 4 Wallies: οἱ δὲ λέγοντες ὅρον εἶναι λόγον κατὰ ἀνάλυσιν ἀπαρτιζόντως ἐκφερόμενον, ἀνάλυσιν μὲν λέγοντες τὴν ἐξάπλωσιν τοῦ ὁριστοῦ καὶ κεφαλαιωδῶς, ἀπαρτιζόντως δὲ τὸ μήτε ὑπερβάλλειν μήτε ἐνδεῖν, οὐδὲν ἂν λέγοιεν τὸν ὅρον διαφέρειν τῆς τοῦ ἰδίου ἀποδόσεως. λόγος γὰρ καὶ τὸ "ζῷον γελαστικόν", καὶ ἀπερίττως τε καὶ ἀνελλιπῶς σημαίνει τὸν ἄνθρωπον· οὔτε γὰρ ἐπὶ πλέον οὔτε ἐπ' ἔλαττόν ἐστι τοῦ ἀνθρώπου.

in Petrus Ramus' studies on logic and methodology (second half of the 16th cent.). There are many references to the fragment of *Posterior Analytics* quoted above in excerpts, which say that a general scientific statement ought to hold true with reference to all the things covered by the extension of the subject; that that about which a statement is made ought by itself, as such, to have the properties ascribed to it in the subjective complement; and that those properties ought to be its attributes not only by generality, but also by priority. Ramus and his commentators bore the reader by repeating in the Latin texts the original Greek terms κατὰ παντός, καθ' αὐτό, καθόλου πρῶτον.[14]

To distinguish and to emphasize the principle associated with those terms (principles which he ranks high, blaming Aristotle for having made little use of them,[15] and even for having often violated them) Ramus introduced special terms. He writes:

> Here are three rules of reliable instructions of the art: the first, κατὰ παντός, the rule of truth; the second, καθ' αὐτό, the rule of justice; the third, καθόλου πρῶτον, the rule of wisdom. May they have these names.[16]

And the commentator (was he Guilielmus Rodingus Hassus?) adds in his note:

> The third rule ... recommends that every learned thesis be not only of necessity true and specific, but also general by priority, and hence, if it is a generic thesis, let it be stated with reference to a genus, and if it is specific, let it be stated with reference to a species. ... The reason is not to be sought long. That which is specific is not an attribute of the entire genus, and if that which is generic is stated with reference to a species, then the same thing will have to be often repeated and restated. ... This

---

14 Cf. the commentaries to Aristotle's *Physics*. For instance, *P. Rami scholarum physicarum libri octo, in totidem acroamaticos libros Aristotelis.* Recens emendati per Joannem Piscatorem Argent. Francofurti 1583, *passim.*

15 For instance on p. 125, *ibid.*, the objection is formulated generally, and specifically concerning Aristotle's physics, that it discusses motion as if it were specific to physics, whereas in fact it belongs to the fields covered by all disciplines; cf. p. 85.

16 *Tres hae sunt leges documentorum artis propriorum: prima*, κατὰ παντός, *lex veritatis: secunda*, καθ' αὐτό, *lex justitiae: tertia*, καθόλου πρῶτον, *lex sapientiae dicatur.* (Petri Rami veromandui, regii professoris, *Dialecticae libri duo:* ex variis ipsius disputationibus, et multis Audomari Talaei commentariis denuo breviter explicati, a Guilielmo Rodingo Hasso, editio quinta, Francofurti MDXCI, p. 90).

third rule is termed by Ramus the rule of wisdom. ... Grammarians state ... that some names are primitive, and others are derivative, and also that the form of some is simple, and of others, complex. In this way they state with reference to a species that which is generic, and consequently they have to repeat the same thing about pronouns, verb, adverb, etc., and fall into tautologies. Should they have made these statements generic, saying that some words are primitive and others are derivative, that some are simple and others are complex, they would have complied with the rule καθόλου πρῶτον.[17]

We notice here new arguments in favor of the adequacy of general scientific statements, as compared with those used by Aristotle. Ramus, like Petrażycki, was mainly concerned with this, that the subjective complement ought to be linked with the subject as such, and that it ought to be specifically necessary to it. We can also notice here an appeal for economy of words: why should we repeat over and over again and separatcly about the various subclasses what can be said about the entire class of objects, and only about it, in one formulation? Likewise, new elements can be seen in the justification of the "rule of justice" (καθ' αὑτό): if the subjective complement is to be an attribute of the subject as such, then the exposition of a given discipline ought to be defended against interference of the subject matter and conceptual apparatus of any other discipline; for instance, logical, etc., problems ought not to be smuggled into the teaching of physics.[18]

---

[17] *Tertia lex est* καθόλου πρῶτον, *haec sancit, ut omnia axiomata artium non solum necessario vera et propria sint, verum etiam universaliter prima, i. si generalia sint, generaliter doceantur, si specialia, specialiter .... Caussa in promptu est. Quod enim speciale est, non omni generi convenit: et si, quod generale est, specialiter doceatur, idem tibi saepius iterandum ac docendum fuerit, unde tautologia nascetur. Haec tertia lex a P. Ramo dicitur lex sapientiae. ... Grammatici ... docent aliud nomen esse primum, aliud derivatum: item esse aliud figurae simplicis, aliud compositae: et sic, quod generale est, specialiter docent: et propterea idem illis in Pronomine, Verbo, Adverbio, et in caeteris repetendum, et tautologia committenda. Quod si generaliter dixissent, vox alia est primitiva, alia derivativa, item alia simplex, alia composita, legem* καθόλου πρῶτον *servassent* (ibid., pp. 91–92).

[18] *At, inquam, in Physicis lex* καθ' αὑτό, *nihil nisi physicum esse patietur* (p. 48) ... *cum tamen lex* καθ' ὅλου *generaliter et semel imperet, ne decretum ullum fiat in arte per accidens, sed per se tantum* (p. 49) ... *non tamen artium reliquarum praeceptis logica praecepta protinus includenda sint. Lex justitiae* καθ' αὑτό, *fines artium longe secus regendos imperat* (p. 57, quoted from a commentary to Aristotle's *Physics* A; see above). *Secunda lex praecipit, ut quodlibet artis axioma sit* καθ' αὑτό, *per se et homogeneum, id est artis, in*

Francis Bacon, who was almost half a century younger than Ramus, took over from the latter the principle of the adequacy of general scientific statements to apply it in an original manner. As is known, he was dedicated to the pursuit of science because he believed that the relationships discovered by science could help produce useful inventions and advance technology. Accordingly he reflected on the structure of the best rules of useful action. To Bacon every rule of useful action is a precept for obtaining in a given substance the desired property (b) by imparting to it the substance of another property (a), which entails the former. But if a given precept recommends obtaining the property b through a certain modification of the property a (for instance, by obtaining in the substance the property d, which is a synthesis of the properties a and c), then such a precept is somewhat cumbersome and too tight, as is also another analogous precept which recommends obtaining the property b by another modification of the property a (for instance, by obtaining in the substance the property f, which is a synthesis of the properties a and e). The former precept states that d ($= a$ and c) entails b; the latter, that f ($= a$ and e) entails b. Since, however, only a is essential here, the best precept would be one stating simply that a entails b. It would be a precept that least restricts the freedom of action: the agent is instructed that he can obtain in a given substance the desired property through the intermediary of the property a, without being restricted by the instruction of looking for a synthesis of that property with any other property. Such a precept would be reversible, which means that it would not only be true that a entails b, but it would also be true that b can be obtained only through the intermediary of a.

The thesis stating the reversible dependence of b on a would thus be an adequate theorem. Bacon uses neither that term, nor Aristotle's καθόλου πρῶτον, nor Alexander's ἀπαρτιζόντως, and speaks only about a free and reversible precept, but in so doing he unmistakably refers to Ramus' "rule of wisdom." Thus that rule stood at the cradle of Bacon's universal methodological

qua docetur, proprium, et tanquam ejusdem corporis membrum. ... Appellatur P. Ramo lex justitiae, quia suum cuique arti tribuit. Omnes enim artes suis terminis distinctae, usu vero conjunctae esse debent (p. 91, quoted from Dialectics, as above).

reform,[19] which he later formulated in his *Novum Organum*. It turns out in this way that Bacon's *Novum Organum* was not only an antithesis, but also a positive continuation of Aristotle's *Organon*.

I quote a significant fragment of Bacon's *Valerius Terminus*. That work was first published in print only in 1734, but its Chapter II, in which we are interested here, must have been born in Bacon's mind probably in the early 17th century. Here is the text:

The fulness of direction to work and produce any effect consisteth in two conditions, certainty and liberty. Certainty is when the direction is not only true for the most part, but infallible. ... If therefore your direction be certain, it must refer you and point you to somewhat which, if it be present, the effect you seek will of necessity follow, else may you perform and not obtain. If it be free, then must it refer you to somewhat which if it be absent the effect you seek will of necessity withdraw, else you may have power and not attempt. This notion Aristotle had in light, though not in use. For the two commended rules by him set down, whereby the axioms of sciences are precepted to be made convertible, and which the latter men have not without elegancy surnamed the one the rule of truth because it preventeth deceit, the other the rule of prudence because it freeth election, are the same thing in speculation and affirmation which we now observe. ... Let the effect to be produced be *Whiteness*; let the first direction be that if air and water be intermingled or broken in small portions together, whiteness will ensue, as in snow, in the breaking of the waves of the sea and rivers and the like .... This direction is certain, but very particular and restrained, being tied but to air and water. Let the second direction be, that if air be mingled as before with any transparent body, such nevertheless as is uncoloured ... that ... being beaten to fine powder ... becometh white; the white of an egg ... by concoction becometh white; here you are freed from water. ... Let the third direction exclude ... the restraint of an uncoloured body ... in wine and beer, which brought to froth become white. Let the fourth direction exclude the restraint of a body more grossly transparent than air .... In all these four directions air still beareth a part. Let the fifth direction then be, that if any bodies, both transparent but in an unequal degree, be mingled as before, whiteness will follow; as oil and water beaten to an ointment .... Now are you freed from air, but still you are tied to transparent bodies. To ascend further by scale I forbear, partly because it would draw on the example to an over-great length ,but chiefly because it would open that which in this work I determine to reserve. ... But ... we admit the sixth direction to be that all bodies or parts of bodies which are unequal equally, that is, in a simple proportion, do represent whiteness. ... This sixth direction, which I have thus explained, is of good and competent liberty. ...[20]

[19] Cf. Ellis's preface to *Valerius Terminus*, in *The Works of Francis Bacon*, Spedding, Ellis, and Heath, edd., Vol. III (London, 1887), pp. 201–205.
[20] *Valerius Terminus*, *ibid.*, pp. 235–237.

Here the track breaks. The present author is not aware of any methodologist after Bacon reverting to the idea of adequate theses. It was only Petrażcyki, who offered it to the readers without referring to anyone, as a product of his own independent mind. In all probability he had not heard of his predecessors in that field.

Warsaw

VALUE AND EXISTENCE

MARVIN FARBER

I. THE LOCATION OF VALUE

The question of the place of values in the world of existence requires the determination of the place of man in the natural world. This question has received conflicting answers in the philosophical literature. The term "value" has been defined narrowly and broadly; and the nature of man has been accepted in traditional forms or on the basis of scientific knowledge and explanation. The overextension of the concept of value, to make it apply to all existence as a general ontological principle, has been prominent.

If one understands the concept of value to apply to organic and cultural beings, no good purpose is served in making it into a general ontological concept. The only way to speak of value in relationship to existence would then be by way of the needs and interests of living beings. Thus understood, value is a limited concept, and is, strictly speaking, inapplicable to the general process of natural existence.

Whether anything would be really accomplished by seeking to determine broad ontological characteristics that are common to value and existence should be considered. To be sure, there must be some common features, for one does not leave the process of existence in dealing with values. The question is, whether the determination of broad, invariant features accomplishes anything positively, apart from the doubtful aim to treat value as fundamental in ontology. For such usage might be misleading by tending to obscure the limited range of the concept of human or organic value. The one advantage of such usage might be the assimilation of value to real existence. But that can be assured without resorting to overextended concepts.

Whitehead construed the concept of value in a very wide

sense.[1] His recognition of limitation as a condition of value
has its region of justification, but it does not lead very far. It is
also true that the absence of inhibiting circumstances may be of
positive value. That depends upon the total situation, and the
various sets of interests that may be involved. A quantitative
criterion is implied, when one speaks of inhibiting more value
than is realized. This requires the full consideration of actual
cases.

Valuation as a cognitive activity, and the realizaton of value as
an existential process, are decidedly within the natural world.
The concept of value is founded upon existential materials
without which it could not be realized. As such, it has ontological
characteristics that mark it off from other types of being. Thus
there is continuity with the basic process of existence; and there
are special conditions with distinctive features of organization
when value is realized.

It is possible to argue plausibly in favor of the view that
value is being realized when the leaves of a plant are turned to
the sun, or when rain falls on the trees. Plant values are then
being realized, and that belongs to a chapter in the descriptive
account of existence.

Values are not simple objects, like the old-fashioned atoms.
They must be realized. They involve temporal events, with
interests or needs on the one hand, and the means to fulfill the
interests or needs on the other. A nontemporal conception of
value would consign values to the honorific realm of ideal forms,
where nothing happens. The special conditions attaching to
values in connection with human needs, or animal needs, or
organic interests, are all temporalistic.

Obviously, everything depends upon the meaning assigned
to "value." If it is left as an undefined term, or if it is declared
to be indefinable, its ontological destiny will certainly be as
insecure as it will be indefinite. "Indefinable" might mean
merely that we are incapable of defining the term, which would

[1] Cf. A. N. Whitehead, *Adventures of Ideas* (New York: Macmillan Co.,
1933), pp. 324, 341, 345. Cf. also *Modes of Thought* (New York: Macmillan
Co., 1938), p. 151, where Whitehead refers to the value-experience as
"the very essence of the universe," and of existence as being "in its own
nature ... the upholding of value-intensity."

leave matters indefinite. If more than that is meant, a breach in the unity of existence will have been suggested. That would amount to a proposed avenue of escape from nature. The best answer is provided by the accomplished fact of a workable definition of value.

If value were conceived to be a general condition of reality, there would be no point in seeking to get outside nature. Nature (or any part of reality) as value-conditioned might be a suitable place of abode for spiritual beings; that is to say, if the approved kind of value is instated as the condition. The important question is whether any method of justification of such a view other than simple declaration is possible.

Both the general, ontological conception of value and the conception of value as realization are reactions to the fact of human finitude and the temporality of existence. Protesting would be as futile as supplication. Simple faith in a supertemporal realm of values would not satisfy everyone. The many-sided line of attack on the most stubborn facts of human existence had its philosophical representatives, with the understanding and location of value one of the main concerns. If value is incapable of definition in natural terms, or from any point of view, then there is presumably (or hopefully) an aspect of man that lifts him above the natural order. Further steps in the argument are conveniently at hand, culminating in a philosophy of man, a "philosophical anthropology," connecting him with a supertemporal realm.

The view that value conditions reality is an ontological thesis resting upon nothing in fact. It may be established with the help of appropriate definitions and assumptions; or it may be made attractive as a form of thinking in accordance with "the heart's desires." What could make such a view plausible, from the human perspective? Man's brief, precarious existence would leave much to be explained on the basis of a value-conditioning theory. While seeming to confer an optimistic view, it merely serves to call renewed attention to man's unsatisfactory status. For a value-conditioned reality ought to improve man's position greatly, if he is not to raise just as weighty objections against the value-conditioning process on the grounds motivating him to reject a self-sufficient natural world.

The portrayal of man as a friendless creature in an indifferent cosmos stands or falls on grounds of fact. The facts are not to be altered by epistemological, logical, or ethical arguments. It must not be forgotten that man is a product of a long evolutionary process, and is therewith indebted to the sun's rays rather than to any beneficent beings or value-determining ontological principles. The progressive amelioration of his position through the growth of understanding and technology goes along with the recognition of his place in the natural world.

If one now asks how value can be introduced into a "value-free" process of existence, the question is assumptive. Something is read into the concept of value that would make it an intrusion into nature, rather than a process as natural as breathing and eating. The definition of value in terms of the fulfillment of human needs or interests (that is to say, in natural and cultural terms) locates value entirely within the world-order. That definition may be rejected in favor of another type of definition. But it can be defended as the concept of need-value, or interest-value. Pleasure-value is another possibility. Each type of definition has its merits and its limitations. If anything is left out, that can only be decided upon after an examination of actual or possible needs and interests.

Even if this were granted, it might still be objected that there is no basis for obligation in the process of natural existence. The "is" of existence is taken to be "oughtless"; and the "ought" to be "is-less." How then can an "ought" be derived from the "is"? Verbally at least, the case is closed, and there appears to be an impasse to reason, another victory apparently for those who seek to "transcend" the world.

Obligation, the "ought," should be capable of definition in intramundane terms, just as value has been found to be so definable, in more than one way. An assumptive conception of value could be rendered untouchable in terms of the natural world-order. If there is a need-value, or an interest-value, however, there can also be a hypothetical type of obligation, in the "if, then" form.

Thus it may be said that if one is to lead a successful and contented life, he must provide for future needs. In that case, the decision to lead a successful and contented life commits one to providing for future needs. This is not an absolute obligation, in the sense in which a formalist or intuitionist, or an authoritarian moralist, recognizes obligation. It is hypothetical, and the relevant facts must be consulted, to determine whether the reasoning is sound. The obligation is relative to a person's positive acceptance of the goal to be achieved, or, considered "in the third person," relative to his interests no matter how he views them. Hence the obligation is relative, and not absolute. In this way, one can see that it is no reproach to nature to point out that there is no absolute obligation rooted in existence in general, or in human existence. The concept of obligation is to be traced to the frame of hypothetical reasoning, in which a choice is expressed by an individual, or by a group, or in which there is objective reference to their needs and interests.

Hence it is not necessary to leave nature for a meaningful conception of obligation, any more than it is necessary to do so for a meaningful conception of value. The present conceptions of value and obligation accord with the facts of human behavior. If they are not absolute, that is simply an advantage to all except assumptive reasoners. The conceptions of value and obligation here set forth may be used in incomplete, modifiable, experimentally conceived systems of values and value decisions, with the requirement that they be factually based. The factual basis comprises the following: the nature of human needs as normal organic functions and their derivative forms of expression; variable individual needs and interests; socially conditioned needs and interests, at different times and places. The value-decisions are twofold, and include (*a*) types of choice and decision actually made by individuals and groups, and (*b*) types of decision that may be made logically, by way of an act of choice resolving a hypothetical form of reasoning. There is a further distinction, already noted, under (*b*), for decisions may represent (1) conscious choices of individuals or groups; or they may be expressed (2) "in the third person," and proceed from the objectively determined needs and interests of individuals or groups – in the last analysis, from the needs and interests of humanity in general. The two cases, (1) and (2), may be congruent, but, as often happens, they may diverge widely; and there may be numerous gradations of divergence.

The theme of value and obligation does not take us away from the field of existence. The basic concept of value is defined in terms of existing organic and cultural events, that is to say, the realities of human history show how needs are satisfied as a matter of fact, through social, economic, scientific, aesthetic and other activities. Conceptions of obligation vary widely in history. In other words, social-historical existence illustrates a great variety of ways in which needs are satisfied, and in which choices enter into the determination of obligation. The choices are not always those of the individuals concerned. They are often mandated choices, imposed by a dominant group or class upon the existing society.

When one speaks of the existing world, he should not think of physical nature alone, or merely add organic nature. The process of human history, the different forms of social organization, occasioning vast changes in individual behavior, needs, and interests – all of this must be highlighted in an account of the nature of existence. The knower is an individual member of a social-historical group. He is also an organism, and a complex physical event with spatiotemporal properties. This total view of the scope of existence renders baseless all talk of the extrusion of value and obligation from the field of natural existence. The latter should not be portrayed as devoid of the experiences and activities of human beings. It includes not only thunder and rainfall, but also industrial conflicts, the cerebral activities of scientists, and the creative achievements of composers. All phases of human experience belong to the real world, even though many "intentional" objects of experience may have to be assigned to artificial domains or universes of discourse. Such domains, including real numbers, points of space, centaurs, etc., are not separate types of "being," but are, rather, of the order of fictions, or of imaginary objects. Just as natural existence is not to be oversimplified, the realm of being is not to be cut up into a variety of "irreducible" types of being. The impoverishment of nature as well as the enlargement of ontology are two types of error arising from devices that have been prominently utilized for the purpose of going beyond the field of natural existence. They express cardinal misrepresentations of the nature of existence, and must be regarded as major sources of confusion.

II. THE REALIZATION OF VALUE

Value as realized in human experience is defined entirely in terms of elements of existence. One can call attention to its processional character by speaking of the realization of value. It is realized when the conditions for its occurrence are sufficient and favorable. In addition to the physical and organic factors, there are social-historical conditions underlying the possibility of the realization.

Care must be taken, however, that the location of value in existence does not turn out to be a springboard for the total spiritualization of the natural world, if not its subordination to a higher order of being. In that case, the usage would be in effect a kind of Trojan horse, much as was the case with "ideas" in the history of idealism – this time in the service of a value-idealism. It is not merely a question of usage, if there is a will to etherealize and conquer. For the usage becomes a means of concealment instead of clarification. Although the result would be still a kind of unification, it would now be an unfounded, dogmatic unity, instated by illicit procedures,[2] and with unwarranted claims concerning the nature of man and alleged higher levels of reality. In short, one should sell his acquiescence to usage dearly, and make it always subject to reconsideration, lest he fall prey to fallacious processes. It does not matter how sincerely such devices may be revered by partisans of the cause being served.

Realization, or "becoming real," involves a process of change. In its wider sense, the formation of the Niagara river gorge and of the Great Lakes illustrates "realization." This is also true of a hen laying eggs, the appearance of freckles, and malignant processes in an organism. To regard value as realization is not to grant the converse, and to designate every case of realization as value. For that would mean the equating of value with existence. If they are coextensive, then why are they not identical? That would lead to a value ontology, and would have its appeal if the discussion were to remain on the level of generalities. Just as much could be accomplished without mentioning the term

[2] Cf. M. Farber, *Naturalism and Subjectivism* (Springfield: Charles C. Thomas, 1959), and *Phenomenology and Existence* (New York: Harper & Row, 1967).

"value." There is, then, no defensible purpose to be served in generalizing the scope of value. The scientific language in use to name the manifold events of the natural and cultural world offers the best available means of designation. Terms that are ethically or valuationally "neutral" may then be used in the construction of a value theory.

The conception of value as realization has much to speak for it. In addition to expressing the temporal character of value as an event, it calls attention to the fact that there is a realization of a potentiality, a fulfillment of an interest. If value is to be realized by parts of the existent world – namely, by living beings in relationship to the world – then the process of existence must be so constituted that such realization is possible. Everything that occurs in the realization of value must be interlocked with and have its place in the total process of existence, so that one can speak of a kinship of "being." The basis for the realization of value is found in the more general pattern of potentiality and actuality. As we view the nature of things, there are always potentialities that are being actualized. In perceptual experience there is an actualization of the potentialities inherent in the percipient being and in the event-stimulus along with the intervening medium. This pattern is present in conceptual thinking, in aesthetic appreciation, and in the fulfillment of needs generally.

The same may be said of events in physical nature, so that there is a uniformity of structure in this general respect. Only it is not very significant to point this out in the context of natural science. The chief point in doing so is to indicate the inclusion of the domain of value in the domain of nature, and the basic truth that value-realization can be assimilated to the potentiality-actuality pattern of natural existence. For the definition of value is descriptively founded, and every item in value-realization has its place in natural existence.

All values, whether organic or cultural, are resultants of processes of realization, and are modes of natural existence. Their peculiar nature involves features not present in natural existence except in relationship to living beings. What R. B. Perry has called the "bias" of living beings includes two types of value-realization: the satisfaction of the needs of organisms without conscious purpose; and the fulfillment of needs, desires, or interests of organisms capable of acting with conscious purpose. The latter demarcation brings us to human values. The location of man in the cosmos, the determination of his relationship to the rest of physical nature and of the animal kingdom, the nature of man as a natural event, as the maker as well as product of cultural development – all of these lines of factual inquiry constitute a set of prolegomena to any philosophy of values that can be said to have the rigor of science and to conform to the facts of experience.

This is to view values as dynamic occurrences, as fulfillments of the needs of organic beings in a changing world. In its direct concern with what actually occurs when values are being realized, this view differs from the conception of values as a species of static objects, or strata of objects.

It is misleading to state that value is "attached" to an object, as, say, beauty is to an attractive person. That is to regard value as static, as a kind of essentially determinate quality of a "higher" order that is ontologically "founded" upon something "lower." Relations of dependence and independence can be clarified as possible arrangements or structures; and the practical, aesthetic, and ethical attitudes or types of experience of the knowing subject can be distinguished descriptively. The results would amount to a set of essential determinations, supposedly lifted out of their natural setting and valid independently of natural events. In short, such determinations belong to what may be called a "geometry" of experience. They are intended to outline the molds of relational patterns for experience, into which the desires and fulfillments of real beings will fit. Such a mode of treatment of values, in terms of the essential structures that can be found in experience, is not to be dismissed as unsound. The point is that it is a partial, selective, and ancillary approach to the understanding of values; just as a geometry is partial, selective, and ancillary in its use in physical science. The "geometry" of values, or the essential-structural approach to values, can aid in describing modes of the realization of value, including relations of intention and fulfillment, with their various degrees of consummation. The degrees of consummation range all the way from the "one" case of complete fulfillment to the "null" case of complete disappointment.

If the "geometry" or essential theory of values is led by an analogy to the geometry of space, it will be recalled that alternative definitions of fundamental ideas are possible – "point," for example. But certain "essential" conditions must be recognized in all such definitions. That is seen when the Euclidean definition of a point is compared with its definition in terms of "sphere" and "inclusion." There is by no means an unlimited freedom of variation. Alternative definitions must be capable of use in the system of geometrical knowledge. Although different modes of presentation of that system are possible, they must all be equivalent, so that there may be a key of translation from one mode of presentation to another. In other words, the one Euclidean system S may be represented by MP_1, MP_2 ... MP_n, all of the modes of presentation being equivalent, and inter-translatable.

Greater variability is possible in the case of non-Euclidean geometries, the alternative systems being judged with respect to their possible application to physical reality, or their use for physical theory. There is the greatest possible freedom for formal construction, with the nature of reality as the final test, if one is to speak of "material" truth or of usefulness.

The comparison of value philosophy with geometry is instructive. Alternative modes of presentation of a value philosophy are also possible. But there is less freedom of construction in the concrete system and less freedom in the choice of basic concepts, defined or undefined. The ideal fictions in use in geometry are nothings so far as physical reality is concerned. There is room for considerable choice without affecting the formal "facts" of geometry. Whether one begins with undefined points, or undefined spheres, makes no real difference. Again, what one does with the parallel axiom is a matter of freedom of construction. The time of reckoning comes when application to the real world is considered.

In the case of the philosophy of human values, one is restricted initially as well as finally by the nature of the facts concerned. There are alternatives nevertheless, depending upon the definitions and premises, as illustrated by the definition of value in terms of the satisfaction of needs, or in terms of pleasure. With a set of premises, including a principle of quantity, a value system can be constructed which can then be tested by its degree of application to human beings and social groups. Unlike a purely formal system, however, there is far less deductive determination, and far more openness and incompleteness. One must consider the facts concerning human beings and society on the one hand; and the conscious preference of value principles on the part of individuals and groups, on the other. Although both of these factors overlap, they present separate and additional complications that must be considered. They amount to two avenues of inquiry, which must, however, be viewed at all times in their mutual relationships. The one avenue is by way of knowledge of the actual interests of human beings in relationship to their social system, and of the potentialities of social systems for the realization of value. The other avenue is by way of the conscious decisions or choices of values, ideals, and goals, made by individuals or groups.

Terms in use in the sciences and in ordinary experience may be used to describe the needs, desires, or interests of individuals and groups. Thus, "normal" functioning, "health," "pleasure" as a motive, or "avoidance of unpleasantness" as a motive, the satisfaction of organic needs or of social and cultural needs, etc., can be treated factually. It may be ascertained descriptively how human beings may be said to prosper, or to be satisfied, in one respect or another. No "obligation" is read into such an account from another source. There is no law that there should be law, in the Kantian sense. The simpler the economy, the easier it is to understand the conduct of individuals and groups in terms of causal and motivating factors. From the actual decisions and choices made historically, an additional factual indication can be obtained concerning the arrangements for the realization of values that are really approved, as distinguished from arrangements that are forced upon people by persons in power. The arrangements for the values of the dominant class in a slave-holding society, and the much hated practices of feudal society, are illustrative cases in point.

Although actual preferences in the realm of values are matters of fact, and can be accounted for as facts, the factor of choice should be considered separately. The avoidance of danger may well be the choice of most people. But individuals are free to incur dangers if they so desire, for the sake of other values. Unless one is prepared to nail down a watertight, confining "essential" view of man, a plurality of choices must be allowed for. Whether they are compossible choices can only be determined by an examination of the consequences. For conflicts in interests are encountered in the normal course of the experience of an individual, and still more in the experience of groups and classes.

The field of existence comprises natural events and cultural activities, individual aspirations and social conflicts, scientific inquiry and pure reflective analysis, ethical insight and moral striving. Existence is thus the alpha and the omega of the philosophy of values. Whether human choices are viewed factually or considered formally, the ultimate test is provided by the facts of existence. Man and society being what they are, there can be no unlimited freedom of preference. There is always dependence upon natural resources and upon the technological level of society. Mere survival imposes restrictions, and much more is required for the maximum realization of value under given historical conditions.

It may be tempting to ascribe the lower level of fulfillment that has been the lot of man historically to unenlightened choices. But slavery was not "chosen" by the slaves; and neither do workers in an industrial society "choose" their place in the social system. In dealing with the element of choice one must therefore be careful not to confine his discussion to disengaged abstractions. Man and society are not to be reduced to stereotyped abstractions, but are to be taken as they actually exist, as natural and cultural events. Hence only a science-oriented philosophy can be equipped to consider the ideal of informed rational choice. The basis for that ideal must be found in the needs and interests of man as he has existed historically, as a member of a social system.

State University of New York at Buffalo

PHENOMENOLOGY, TYPIFICATION, AND THE WORLD AS TAKEN FOR GRANTED

MAURICE NATANSON

I

Husserl distinguishes between phenomenological psychology and transcendental phenomenology. The former has alliances with and owes allegiance to the natural attitude, the naive horizon through which *we* as common-sense men live our lives together in *our* world. Although phenomenological psychology transcends the natural attitude in certain respects, it remains oriented toward naive experience. There are as well different levels of analysis possible to phenomenological psychology, starting from the empirical domain and moving to a reflexive examination of intentional consciousness. The levels mirror each other in varying degrees of purity and depth. Transcendental phenomenology, on the contrary, is possible only in virtue of a declaration of independence from the presuppositions of the natural attitude. The reflecting ego is no longer one among others in the world of fellow-men but rather a ground of intentional consciousness out of which the *alter ego* as a transcendental correlate is constituted. In different terms, an eidetic analysis which would justify claims made at the level of phenomenological psychology is both possible and ultimately necessary, whereas transcendental phenomenology already presupposes the eidetic reduction and could not, in principle, be pursued within the mundane sphere. The methodological connection between phenomenological psychology and transcendental phenomenology involves an isomorphism of levels: everything discovered at the psychological level has its transcendental analogue. That the converse is also possible says something of critical importance about the meaning of mundane existence and the General Thesis of the natural attitude underlying that existence: mundanity is a constituted reality whose sedimented structure may be explored through phenomenological reduction.

According to Alfred Schutz's reading of Husserl, "in essence all analyses carried out in phenomenological reduction must retain their validation in the correlates of the phenomena investigated within the natural sphere."[1] Thus, one may move from the reduced sphere to mundane correlates, and one may turn from a phenomenological psychology of the mundane order to questions of their transcendental constitution. We shall be concerned here with an examination of Schutz's conception of a phenomenology of the natural attitude, and, in particular, with his claim that "phenomenological methods can ... be applied with the greatest success within the empirical sphere. ..."[2] The distinction between phenomenological psychology and transcendental phenomenology involves a difference in stance with respect to the natural attitude. A phenomenology *of* the natural attitude is possible within the horizon of phenomenological psychology. Indeed, Schutz considered his own work to fall directly in this category. Its province is the intersubjective social world which the social sciences seek to comprehend. Transcendental phenomenology remains a valid and ultimately necessary correlate in accounting for the genesis of meaning leading to the constitution of the social world, but a fully integral and rich domain of analysis exists in its own right at the psychological level.[3]

Within the mundane sphere there is possible a descriptive

---

[1] A. Schutz, *Collected Papers*, Vol. I (The Hague, 1962), p. 139.

[2] *Ibid.*, p. 113.

[3] Schutz writes (*ibid.*, p. 132): "For Husserl there is ... no doubt that all the hitherto existing cultural and social sciences are related in principle to phenomena of mundane intersubjectivity. Hence, the transcendental constitutive phenomena, which only become visible in the phenomenologically reduced sphere, scarcely come within the view of the cultural sciences. However, a psychology from which a solution of the problems of the cultural sciences might be expected must become aware of the fact that it is not a science which deals with empirical facts. It has to be a science of essences, investigating the correlates of those transcendental constitutional phenomena which are related to the natural attitude. Consequently, it has to examine the invariant, peculiar, and essential structures of the mind; but that is to say it examines their *a priori* structure. The concrete description of the spheres of consciousness as it has to be undertaken by a true descriptive psychology within the natural attitude

account of essential features of man's life within the social world. The task of a constitutive phenomenology of such a descriptive account is to make evident the intentional history and dynamic of mundanity. All of this can be achieved within the horizon of phenomenological psychology and without invoking or engaging in transcendental phenomenology. The strategic advantage of such a restricted endeavor was recognized by Husserl himself. In his *Encyclopaedia Britannica* article he gives priority to phenomenological psychology,

> partly because it forms a convenient stepping-stone to the philosophy and partly because it is nearer to the common attitude than is the transcendental. Psychology, both in its eidetic and empirical disciplines, is a "positive" science, promoted in the "natural attitude" with the world before it for the ground of all its themes, while transcendental experience is difficult to realize because it is "supreme"and entirely "unworldly." Phenomenological psychology, although comparatively new, and completely new as far as it uses intentional analysis, can be approached from the gates of any of the positive sciences: and, being once reached, demands only a re-employment, in a more stringent mode, of its formal mechanism of reduction and analysis, to disclose the transcendental phenomena.[4]

The central gain that Schutz sees in the development of a phenomenology of the natural attitude, set apart from transcendental considerations, is two-fold: first, it emphasizes a continuity between what might be called "general sociology"[5] and a philosophy of social structure. Thus, Max Weber's analysis of types may be viewed as continuous with a phenomenology of typification.[6] Second, it emphasizes a continuity between naive, unreflective action in the social world by men living within the natural attitude and the development of a critical awareness of

---

remains, however, the description of a closed sphere of the intentionalities. That is to say, it requires not only a concrete description of the experiences of consciousness, as in the Lockean tradition, but also necessarily the description of the conscious (intentional) "objects in their objective sense" found in active inner experiences. But such a true *psychology of intentionality* is, according to Husserl's words, nothing other than a *constitutive phenomenology of the natural attitude.*"

   [4] (14th edition, 1929), Vol. 17, p. 701.

   [5] Schutz, *op. cit.*, p. 137.

   [6] See A. Schutz, *Der sinnhafte Aufbau der sozialen Welt* (2nd. unrevised edition, Vienna, 1960), available in English as *The Phenomenology of the Social World*, translated by G. Walsh and F. Lehnert (Evanston, Illinois, 1967).

the presuppositions and implications of philosophical naiveté.[7]

Very simply, Schutz maintains that not only apart from transcendental phenomenological reduction but even within the horizon of the natural attitude, within the field of empirical social science, it is possible to pursue a phenomenological psychology of the social world, radical enough to merit the name of phenomenological philosophy yet accessible to investigators within the mundane attitude of daily life. We are now prepared to see such a phenomenological psychology at work.

II

For men in the midst of daily life, the philosophical and conceptual problems underlying ordinary, common-sense existence are, without reflection or design, simply set aside. What we may call the theoretical architecture of existence is acknowledged, when it is at all, only in fugitive and tenuous form. The most solid and evident fact about mundane life – the life of working and acting and pursuing ordinary ends through typical means – is its very on-going givenness: awakening after sleeping, arising to attend to the day's affairs, meeting and speaking with fellow-men, sharing with them a common arena of action, coming to terms

---

[7] Schutz writes (*Collected Papers*, Vol. I, pp. 136–137): "... a special motivation is needed in order to induce the naive person even to pose the question concerning the meaningful structure of his life-world, even within the *general thesis*. This motivation can be very heterogeneous; for example, a newly appearing phenomenon of meaning resists being organized within the store of experience, or a special condition of interest demands a transition from a naive attitude to a reflection of a higher order. So-called rational action can be given as an example of the latter. Rational action is given when all the ends of action and all the means which will lead to it are clearly and distinctly presented, as, for example, in the case of economic action. If such a motivation for leaving the natural attitude is given, then by a process of reflection the question concerning the structure of meaning can always be raised. One can always reactivate the process which has built up the sediments of meaning, and one can explain the intentionalities of the perspectives of relevance and the horizons of interest. Then all these phenomena of meaning, which obtain quite simply for the naive person, might be in principle exactly described and analyzed even *within the general thesis*. To accomplish this on the level of mundane intersubjectivity is the task of the mundane cultural sciences, and to clarify their specific methods is precisely a part of that constitutive phenomenology of the natural attitude of which we have been speaking."

with the manifold issues and obstacles which constitute much of the business of work and creation, enjoying the available pleasures of play and love, planning for that which is deemed desirable, devising and pursuing and entreating real and imaginary schemes and ideals, resting and sleeping again, dreaming and regaining the world abandoned for a time. The philosophical underpinnings of this daily world, familiar to its inhabitants in eminently typified fashion, are, in Schutz's language, simply and cardinally "taken for granted." He writes:

The term "taken for granted" ... means to accept until further notice our knowledge of certain states of affairs as unquestionably plausible. Of course, at any time that which seemed to be hitherto unquestionable might be put into question. Common-sense thinking simply takes for granted, until counterevidence appears, not only the world of physical objects but also the sociocultural world into which we are born and in which we grow up. This world of everyday life is indeed the unquestioned but always questionable matrix within which all our inquiries start and end.[8]

What is taken for granted, in this sense, may be broadly listed under the headings of metaphysical and situational constants. Metaphysically, it is taken for granted that we are born into the world, born of parents, born into a world which already has an historical past, born into a world which has already been interpreted by others, born into a social reality which includes and involves fellow-men with whom we may communicate, born into a sociocultural milieu sustained by the agency of language, born into a world as sexed beings, and, finally, born into a world in which we are destined to die, transcended by others and the history they will generate.[9] Situationally, each of us occupies a

[8] *Ibid.*, pp. 326–327.

[9] Despite the fact that each of us has no direct experiential access to our birth or our death, there is an inherent *social* dimension to these transcendent events, a reference to fellow-men. As Philip Merlan writes ("Time Consciousness in Husserl and Heidegger," *Philosophy and Phenomenological Research*, Vol. VIII [1947], p. 35), "To be sure, we know that we were born; to be sure, we know that we shall die; to be sure, we know that we are finite. But in what way do we know all of this? Not in the way of our personal experience; on the contrary, my birth is something that I have forgotten already; my death something still impending, still expected. But obviously what is always already forgottten, and what is always still expected can never become an object of my personal experience. Birth and death are events perceived as events by which the life of others is limited, and only in so far as I identify myself with others, do I know that I must have been born and shall certainly die."

"zero" or "null" point at the center of socio-spatial coordinates. At any moment, each of us is "here" as distinguished from the "there" occupied by the *alter ego*. Movement from "here" to "there" is immanently held to be possible. And not only may I occupy the "there" now taken by the Other, but when I do so I will then, it is assumed, see things as he does, that is, as anyone would normally see things from that vantage point. It is also the case that I assume that my place can be taken by a fellow-man in essentially the same fashion with essentially the same possibilities and consequences. Moreover, such exchanges, along with a vast range of other activities, are held to be repeatable: I can do again and again, as Husserl suggested, the typically same act, and I assume that the Other can as well.

The world of fellow-men encountered in daily life is organized in a typology of spatio-temporal proximity and distance. Schutz refers to those fellow-men who died before we were born as predecessors; to those who are living during our life-time as contemporaries; to those contemporaries with whom we share a face-to-face relationship as consociates; and to those who will be born after we die as successors. The physical presence of the *alter ego* in face-to-face relationships tends to dominate and render subordinate the connections we have with fellow-men whose power and importance in social structure are a product of their very absence. Altogether, the metaphysical and situational constants (only some of which have been presented here) form the foundational features of the world as taken for granted by men in daily life. That each individual meets the world in his own way and comes to terms with its constants in his own fashion is a function of what Schutz terms the "biographical situation" unique to each person. But even the biographical situation has its *a prioris*, its own essential features. The massive consequence of a social reality founded on and informed by trans-temporal elements eidetic to common-sense experience is a typified and typifying conception of daily life.[10] Schutz's exploration of the

[10] Schutz writes (*Collected Papers*, Vol. I, pp. 59–60): "The world ... is from the outset experienced in the pre-scientific thinking of everyday life in the mode of typicality. The unique objects and events given to us in a unique aspect are unique within a horizon of typical familiarity and pre-acquaintanceship. There are mountains, trees, animals, dogs – in particular Irish setters and among them my Irish setter, Rover. Now I may look

world as taken for granted is by way of a phenomenology of typification, and it is in the common-sense thinking of everyday life that he locates "the origin of ... constructive or ideal types."[11]

It is now possible to say that to take the world for granted is to typify its presentations and states of affairs, whether they be objects in the world of nature or events in social reality. Before turning to some of the modes of typification, it might be helpful to take a more careful look at one example of typification at work in everyday life. Earlier, we spoke about the exchangeability of the "here" and "there" of *ego* and *alter ego* within the space of the social world. In the analysis of that transposition, Schutz refers to their relationship as the "reciprocity of perspectives," and holds that the concrete differences between the placement of man and fellow-man can be overcome within common-sense thinking by two idealizations: the "interchangeability of stand-points" and the "congruency of the system of relevances." In the first idealization, I take it for granted and assume my *alter ego* does the same that were an exchange effected, we would both

at Rover either as this unique individual, my irreplaceable friend and comrade, or just as a typical example of 'Irish setter,' 'dog,' 'mammal,' 'animal,' 'organism,' or 'object of the outer world.' Starting from here, it can be shown that whether I do one or the other, and also which traits or qualities of a given object or event I consider as individually unique and which as typical, depends upon my actual interest and the system of relevances involved – briefly, upon my practical or theoretical 'problem at hand.' This 'problem at hand,' in turn, originates in the circumstances within which I find myself at any moment of my daily life and which I propose to call my biographically determined situation. Thus, typification depends upon my problem at hand for the definition and solution of which the type has been formed. ... But the world of everyday life is from the outset also a social cultural world in which I am interrelated in manifold ways of interaction with fellow-men known to me in varying degrees of intimacy and anonymity. To a certain extent, sufficient for many practical purposes, I understand their behavior, if I understand their motives, goals, choices, and plans originating in *their* biographically determined circumstances. Yet only in particular situations, and then only fragmentarily, can I experience the Others' motives, goals, etc. – briefly, the subjective meanings they bestow upon their actions, in their uniqueness. I can, however, experience them in their typicality. In order to do so I construct typical patterns of the actors' motives and ends, even of their attitudes and personalities, of which their actual conduct is just an instance or example. These typified patterns of the Others' behavior become in turn motives of my own actions, and this leads to the phenomenon of self-typification well known to social scientists under various names."

[11] *Ibid.*, p. 61.

be at the same distance from objects and in essentially the same relationship to them which pertained in each case before the transposition. In the second idealization, I take it for granted along with my *alter ego* that considerations unique to my and his biographical situation may be set aside in the perception and even, within certain limits, the interpretation of common objects. The two idealizations constitute the "reciprocity of perspectives"; working together, they also provide the constitutive basis for the establishment of the "we" relationship. Thus my awareness of an object or event as well as the Other's awareness is suppressed in its idiosyncratic specificity and replaced by a construct which, by extension, becomes common to anyone who typically shares the perspective in question. Schutz writes:

> By the operation of these constructs of common-sense thinking it is assumed that the sector of the world taken for granted by me is also taken for granted by you, my individual fellow-man, even more, that it is taken for granted by "Us." But this "We" does not merely include you and me but "everyone who is one of us," i.e., everyone whose system of relevances is substantially (sufficiently) in conformity with yours and mine. Thus, the general thesis of reciprocal perspectives leads to the apprehension of objects and their aspects actually known by me and potentially known by you as everyone's knowledge. Such knowledge is conceived to be objective and anonymous, i.e., detached from and independent of my and my fellow-man's definition of the situation, our unique biographical circumstances and the actual and potential purposes at hand involved therein.[12]

The reciprocity of perspectives as a major illustration of typification in everyday life leads back to the larger question of the modes through which typification operates. Consciousness, what might be termed social awareness, and language are paradigmatic instruments of typification. Taken together, they provide a phenomenological base for the appraisal of Schutz's conception of typification. It is necessary to obtain a sketch of man in daily life as a typifying creature. The outlines are available: my awareness of a fellow-man is typified from the outset, for I see him not simply as a thing, a physical entity in space, but as a being like myself, a person present to the world and sharing with me a coherent *schema* of its activities and significations. Seeing the Other is then locating him as a being who locates me.

[12] *Ibid.*, p. 12.

Our awareness of each other involves an interlocking system of conceptions and evaluations through which common elements of purpose and response are constituted. Schutz's urgent point is that the constructions through which we typify our social world are naively realized and are immanent to the flow of common-sense existence. In my relationship with the *alter ego*, degrees of intimacy and anonymity are the means through which already operative typifications are varied and refined in multiple ways. Nor is communication with the Other restricted to verbal or written forms. Prior to, apart from, as well as along with language there is a rich and complex domain of proto-linguistic response to fellow-men through gesture, common elements of occasion, the interpretation of stance, silence, and suggestion. Communication has its failures as well as its successes, and this means that within the context of the world as taken for granted men experience linguistic fragmentation as well as coherence and good results. In the course of mundane life, language is presupposed as the agency through which the constructs of social order are built and sustained. Schutz writes, "the typifying medium *par excellence* by which socially derived knowledge is transmitted is the vocabulary and the syntax of everyday language." [13] In art as well as in life there are examples of purposeful and uncontrived failures or distortions of the typifying instrument: experiments in style which sever syntactical continuity, the object or event described made stranded and stark; the groping, halting mode of speech common enough even in or especially in academic scenes to identify a student generation. "I'm studying like Chaucer," one assassin of language told me not long ago. But deviations have their own typified character and point back to their origin in the world as taken for granted. They are elements along with more pedestrian phenomena of the social world which Schutz's "general sociology" has tried to describe. A critical glance toward his procedure is now possible.

III

The dominant character of the natural attitude within which common-sense life is lived is its intersubjective nature. *Ego* and

[13] *Ibid.*, p. 14.

alter ego animate the world in their mutual taking for granted their reciprocity of perspectives. Within daily life, then, there is no philosophical problem of intersubjectivity to puzzle men in action in common-sense pursuits. The major advantage of a phenomenological psychology of mundane existence is that it can proceed *within* the horizon of intersubjectivity, whereas transcendental phenomenology confronts the problem of the constitution of the *alter ego* from the outset. The advantage, though, has its limits. The givenness of mundane existence within the natural attitude is both acknowledged and transcended in phenomenological attitude, whether psychological or transcendental. In one sense, the naive, taken for granted world is simply *there*, indubitable in the plausibility of its manifestness to all of us. But expressing that givenness, pointing out its shape and content, is a philosophic act, one that is not on a par with mundane acts. Turning to questions about the possibility of there being mundane life with its natural attitude, inquiring into the possibility of intersubjectivity, moves the inquirer out of the horizon of the life-world onto the terrain of transcendental phenomenology. The movement is allowed for, of course, in Schutz's analysis, but it is not clear as to how the transition is effected. The ambiguity lies not so much in the relationship between psychology and the transcendental as it does in the uncovering of the mundane *as* mundane within the natural attitude. There are three operative levels which Schutz exploits: first, the taken-for-granted world as simply and naively given; second, the proper concern of the social sciences in describing and accounting for social action within the taken-for-granted world; third, the province of phenomenological psychology, which interests itself in the philosophical presuppositions and methodology involved in the social scientist's labors. At the first level, common-sense men go about their business in naive fashion as far as philosophical problems are concerned; at the second level, social scientists, who are also philosophically naive in the sense of not confronting the conceptual presuppositions of their science, go about their business of describing social structure; at the third level, the phenomenologist emerges as the one responsible for a reflexive examination of the other two domains. How does he get started? We come back in this way to what was posed

earlier as the problem of the relationship between phenomenological psychology and transcendental phenomenology.

Within the horizon or orientation of the natural attitude, a
problem arises over and against a backdrop of the unproblematic,
ongoing world. A problem, in this sense, is always an emergent
from a secure and taken-for-granted matrix. Now Schutz holds
that even within the general thesis of the natural attitude, a
problem not only emerges but may be seen in continuing degrees
of philosophic depth. Seen by whom? In principle, the phenomenologist alone, on Schutz's account, can achieve the vantage
point necessary to uncover the thematic character of the mundane,
but the possibility for doing so rests on a transcendental condition: it must be possible to thematize the mundane within the
mundane. Although one is not required to raise this question as a
phenomenological psychologist, I think it can only be answered
in terms of transcendental phenomenology. If, however, we
accept the phenomenological principle that all analyses carried
through in the transcendentally reduced sphere hold good as well
for a psychology of the mundane order,[14] then the emergence of
the world no longer as taken for granted but as genuinely and
pervasively problematic in root-philosophic fashion is a transcendental theme which Schutz's analysis cannot avoid. His
strategy is not avoidance but separation of functions. The
transcendental is relegated to the domain of the constitution of
meaning, the analysis of the genetic history of the sedimentation
of meaning involved in all objects of consciousness. This leads,
however, to a severance between the status of the social world in
its substantive aspect and the constitution of meaning underlying its presentational character, that is, its interpreted aspect.
For Schutz,

only such an ontology of the life-world, not a transcendental constitutional analysis, can clarify that essential relationship of intersubjectivity which is the basis of all social science – even though, as a rule, it is
there taken for granted and accepted without question as a simple datum.[15]

The separation of the transcendental has its implications for
Schutz's treatment of the major theme of typification.

[14] *Ibid.*, p. 132.
[15] *Collected Papers*, Vol. III (The Hague, 1966), p. 82.

That there is typification at all is, in a preliminary way, accepted by Schutz as the starting point for his analysis. Of course, a phenomenology of typification follows swiftly upon the acceptance of the fact of men in mundane life taking their world for granted. But to begin with, the naive world of the natural attitude is already a typified one, built up out of the manifold constructs through which men interpret their fellow-man's as well as their own action in the social world. It must be remembered that, for Schutz,

> our relationship with the social world is based upon the assumption that in spite of all individual variations the same objects are experienced by our fellow-men in substantially the same way as by ourselves and vice versa, and also that our and their schemes of interpretation show the same typical structure of relevances. If this belief in the substantial identity of the intersubjective experience of the world breaks down, then the very possibility of establishing communication with our fellow-men is destroyed.[16]

If typification is a pervasively essential feature of the social world as initially given to men in daily life, then the taken-for-grantedness of the natural attitude is an anonymous creation, whatever the causal grounds for acceptance may be. And, in fact, such anonymity is the emblem of mundanity. My relation to Others and even, in part, to myself is articulated through constructs which are essentially the same as those constructed by fellow-men in their response to me. The self manifests itself to Others and to itself as well in adumbrated form, for only a fragmentary aspect of the individual is presented in the social scene. The interlocking of constructs and types which is the framework of social reality for Schutz succeeds in establishing a world within whose typified forms common-sense existence unfolds. It has been suggested that "it would be of interest to compare Schutz's analysis of conduct in everyday life ... with Heidegger's interpretation of the anonymity of *'das Man.'*"[17] Without going into Heidegger, it might be said that for Schutz the anonymity of types and the entire dynamic of typification has an ontological ground fundamentally different from Heidegger's placement of the inauthentic *"Man."* Schutz assigns no value

---

[16] *Collected Papers*, Vol. II (The Hague, 1964), p. 143.
[17] A. Gurwitsch, Introduction to Schutz's *Collected Papers*, Vol. III, p. xvii, n. 8.

predicate to typification; rather, he accepts it as the very condition for there being a social world. In this sense, typification serves the entirely valid, let alone necessary, function of enabling *ego* and *alter ego* to confront each other, to go about the affairs of life, and to come to terms with the primordial fact that knowledge, interpretation, and evaluation are themselves features of the social world they endeavor to comprehend. The anonymity of the typified world is then both inescapable and liberating. It provides the ground for individuation and existential identity.

The status of typification as a given may also be approached in terms of the natural standpoint. Although the concept of typification and the instrument of phenomenology may be strange to common sense, appeals to some of their by-products strike a resonant chord. "On the whole," daily life exhibits an orderly pattern of typical relationships which, "for the most part," arc easily recognizable and which, "in the main," can be catalogued by sociologists and social psychologists whose disciplines, "in the long run," depend on the data of the everyday world. Whatever the status of daily life may be and whether or not men in daily life agree with what has just been said, the phrases "on the whole," "for the most part," "in the main," and "in the long run" are, "by and large," comprehensible in a way which goes beyond their familiarity in ordinary usage. Their status in ordinary parlance presupposes a history of encounter with the most varied and peculiar situations. Such phrases are themselves examples of linguistic typifications which, in turn, help to organize the common fund of experience. The claim that "more often than not" dogs have tails turns less on a sampling of dogs than on the typifying force of the "more often than not." Being wrong in some cases of such typification may prove as instructive as being right because they reveal the typifier as well as the typified. Such generalizing typifications reflect the fundamental style of typification itself, for the objects and events referred to by the phrases are problematic only in contrast to the taken-for-granted character of the language. A common-sense world bereft of these broadly gauged qualifiers would be strange indeed. Some rather remarkable substitutes would have to be found. Schutz told the story of the Rabbi who confided to his students, "Is it not a wonder that two plus two equals four and two times two equals four?" The next day one of the students blurted, "Rabbi, last night I had an insight! Not only is two plus two four and two times two four but eight divided by two is also four!" The Rabbi swayed over that a minute and replied, "Yes, that's true. But this is highly sophisticated!"

Within the natural attitude, then, there may be a sensitivity to the force of typification, but that there is typification seems to transcend the very situation of the mundane world with which the phenomenological psychologist begins. How then does the transcendental find its analogue in the taken-for-granted world? In Schutz's view the answer lies in the very limits of the faith that is placed in the system of constructs and types in virtue of which common-sense life is lived. Though typification itself is taken for granted, our commitment to its plausibility involves a continuing act of faith. There must be a willingness to believe not only in the integrity and survival of the system of inter-locking typifications but also in its efficacy in a world disclosed to us in fragmentary and oblique ways. Schutz writes:

> The intrusion of the transcendental into this world of everyday life is either denied or dissimulated by common reason. But it shows its in-vincible force in the experience of all of us that the world of everyday life with its things and occurrences, its causal connections of natural laws, its social facts and institutions is just imposed upon us, that we can understand and master it only to a very limited extent, that the future remains open, undisclosed and unascertainable, and that our only hope and guidance is the belief that we will come to terms with this world for all good and practical purposes if we behave as others behave, if we take for grant-ed what others believe beyond question. All this presupposes our faith that things will continue to be what they have been so far and that what our experience of them has taught us will also stand the test in the future.[18]

The irruption of the transcendental comes within the system of typifications at whose center lies the individual who supports and sustains them. The danger of breakdown, then, comes from within the self and not from the world. The profound though artificial suspicion the phenomenologist raises about the taken-for-granted world may be understood, perhaps, as the transcen-dental illumination of the challenge inherently given to the faith of the individual within the natural attitude. If this inter-pretation is permissible, then the rejoining of the separated

[18] *Collected Papers.* Vol. II, p. 157.

realms of the psychological and the transcendental is possible, not only as the genetic counterpart to an ontology of the social world but as the initial source of the creation as well as constitution of mundanity. Phenomenology may then be understood as the discipline which attends to the taken-for-granted world both in its mundane exemplification and in its transcendental aspect. From either standpoint, social life is seen as part of what an older tradition called "the inverted world." Taken together, phenomenological psychology as practiced by Schutz and transcendental phenomenology as inaugurated by Husserl provide a unity which clarifies and enlarges the philosophical enterprise common to both.

University of California, Santa Cruz

AUSGANGSPROBLEME ZUR BETRACHTUNG DER KAUSALEN STRUKTUR DER WELT[1]

ROMAN INGARDEN

I. DER ZUSAMMENHANG ZWISCHEN DEM KAUSALPROBLEM UND DEM PROBLEM DER FORM EINER WELT

Wollen wir entscheiden, ob die uns in der Erfahrung gegebene Welt wirklich eine "Welt" in unserem Sinne ist,[2] dann müssen wir zuerst die ontologisch betrachtete Form einer Welt überhaupt etwas genauer ausarbeiten als dies im Band II dieses Werkes geschah. Denn es muss möglich sein, auf Grund einer weiter geklärten Form der realen Welt gewisse Fragen zu formulieren, welche sich auf Grund der empirischen Wissenschaft von der Welt entscheiden liessen. Bei einer tiefer gehenden Betrachtung der Form einer Welt überhaupt bildet aber das Kausalproblem ein Thema, das unsere volle Aufmerksamkeit erheischt. Und zwar aus zwei Gründen. Erstens ist die kausale Beziehung, oder genauer gesagt, der unmittelbare kausale Seinszusammenhang für die Form einer realen Welt charakteristisch:

[1] Die hier gegebenen Betrachtungen bilden die ersten beiden Paragraphen der Einleitung zu dem Buche *Über die kausale Struktur der realen Welt*, das in den Jahren 1950–1954 niedergeschrieben aber nicht veröffentlicht wurde. Es wird jetzt als Band III meines Werkes *Der Streit um die Existenz der Welt* zum Druck vorbereitet. Es bildet zuerst eine genauere Ausarbeitung der Auffassung des kausalen Seinszusammenhanges, die zum ersten Mal im III. Band der *Studia Philosophica, Commentarii Societatis Philosophorum Polonorum* und dann am Internationalen Kongress für Philosophie in Rom, 1946, unter dem Titel ''Quelques remarques sur la relation de causalité'' veröffentlicht wurde und später im ersten Band des Buches *Der Streit um die Existenz der Welt* – zuerst in polnischer (1947–1948), dann auch in deutscher Fassung (Tübingen, 1964), erschien. Das Buch *Über die kausale Struktur der Welt* entwickelt dann die Anwendung dieser Auffassung auf die formale Ontologie der realen Welt.

[2] Vgl. *Der Streit um die Existenz der Welt*, Band II/2 (Tübingen, 1965), Kap. XV, pp. 95–258.

er tritt, sofern man ihn in einem hinlänglich strengen Sinne fasst,[3] in einer und nur in einer realen Welt (genauer: in einer Welt vom Typus der realen Welt) auf, zweitens aber übt er im Aufbau der realen Welt eine wichtige strukturelle Rolle aus: einerseits bildet er eine, obwohl nicht die einzige Hauptgrundlage der *Einheit* der realen Welt; andererseits aber ergibt eben der kausale Seinszusammenhang – falls er sich durch gewisse formale Eigentümlichkeiten auszeichnet, auf die ich später eingehen werde – den Grund dafür, dass die Welt nicht ein einziger, schlichter individueller Gegenstand ist, sondern ein ganzes gegenständliches Seinsgebiet bildet, das eine Mannigfaltigkeit seinsselbständiger, obwohl zugleich wesensmässig von einander partiell abhängiger und in anderer Hinsicht partiell unabhängiger, individueller Gegenstände in sich enthält. Die kausale Beziehung – in ihrer Rolle, die sie in dem Gesamtaufbau der realen Welt spielt – steht auch mit der Zeitstruktur der realen Welt, und damit mit dem Problem ihrer Seinsweise, im engen Zusammenhang, und insbesondere mit der Frage, ob die reale Welt ihrem Wesen nach seinsursprünglich oder seinsabgeleitet ist. Es kann auch das Problem aufgeworfen werden, ob die Raumstruktur der Welt mit der kausalen Struktur der Geschehnisse in der realen Welt irgendwie zusammenhängt. Damit würde die Raumstruktur nicht bloss mit der materialen Qualifikation der physischen Natur, sondern auch mit der Art, in der sich etwas in der Welt ereignet, verbunden sein. Natürlichspreche ich hier von dem realen

---

[3] In Band I (§ 12, pp. 90–110) suchte ich zu zeigen, dass der Kausalzusammenhang eine innerweltliche Beziehung ist, d.h. eine Beziehung, deren Glieder Elemente einer und derselben Welt sind. Infolgedessen ist die kausale Beziehung nicht mit der Beziehung zwischen dem seinsursprünglichen und dem seinsabgeleiteten Sein – also etwa zwischen dem etwaigen Weltschöpfer und der Welt – nicht zu identifizieren. Andererseits kann sie nur zwischen zwei realen Gegenständlichkeiten bestehen. Sie darf also nicht auf den Fall angewendet werden, in welchem ein Bewusstseinssubjekt, etwa ein Dichter, eine seinsheteronome Gegenständlichkeit, etwa in einer Dichtung, bildet. Auch das Verhältnis zwischen einer Idee (in unserem Sinne) und einem unter sie fallenden individuellen Gegenstand hat mit der kausalen Beziehung nichts zu tun. Erst wenn man den Kausalbegriff auf eine bestimmte Art des Seinszusammenhanges zwischen zwei Realitäten, die zu einer und derselben Welt gehören, einengt, ist es möglich, einige wesentliche und charakteristische Züge der ursächlichen Beziehung aufzuweisen und sie in ihrer Rolle für die Form der realen Welt zu erfassen.

Raum der Welt und nicht von dem idealen Raum der reinen
Geometrie.

Dies sind die weiten Perspektiven, die uns das Problem der
ursächlichen Beziehung eröffnet und die sich erst viel später
konkreter gestalten lassen werden. Wenn ich sie bereits hier
erwähne, so liegt es daran, dass gerade ihr Zusammenhang mit
der Streitfrage um die Weise der Existenz der realen Welt uns
aufs neue zur Beschäftigung mit der ursächlichen Beziehung
zwingt. In diesem Zusammenhang liegt auch der Grund, dass
das Kausalproblem auf eine andere Weise gefasst werden muss,
als dies gewöhnlich geschieht. Die kausale Beziehung wurde von
der realen Welt, in der sie ja stattfinden soll, fast ausnahmsweise
abstrahiert und gewissermassen nur im Einzelfall behandelt.[4]
Man interessierte sich für ihr Wesen und nahm sich zu diesem
Zwecke ein Paar von Gegenständen, insbesondere von Ereignissen vor, von denen das eine die sog. "Ursache," das andere die
sog. "Wirkung" sein sollte. An diesem einzelnen Paar suchte man
dann die näheren Eigentümlichkeiten dieser Beziehung zu klären.
Man war z.B. bestrebt, die Fragen zu beantworten, was die
Glieder dieser Beziehung bilde, ob sie notwendig oder zufällig
sei, ob sie einen Zeitunterschied zwischen ihren Gliedern fordere
oder ob im Gegenteil die Wirkung mit der Ursache gleichzeitig
sein müsse u. drgl. m. Dies alles – und verschiedenes Andere –
muss natürlich untersucht und so oder anders entschieden werden. Diese Isolierung der Betrachtung der Kausalprobleme von
anderen Fragen nach der Struktur der realen Welt hat die Bedeutung des Kausalproblems nicht bloss stark herabgesetzt,
sondern auch zu einer schiefen Auffassung seines Sinnes geführt, was sich dann in der Gestaltung des Determinismus-
problems ungünstig ausgewirkt hat. Vielleicht sind es erst die
Ergebnisse der modernen Physik, die das Problem der kausalen
Beziehung mit den konkreten Fragen des physikalischen Geschehens in der materiellen Welt, und genauer in der Mikrowelt,
in einen näheren Zusammenhang gebracht haben. Indem man
aber in der Physik der Gegenwart sofort vor das Entweder-Oder
(Kausalgesetze oder blosse statistische Gesetze) gestellt wurde,

---

[4] So ist es z.B. bei Hume, dessen Betrachtung der kausalen Beziehung
für ihre spätere Behandlung in der modernen Philosophie ausschlag-
gebend geworden ist.

ist die Art der Behandlung des Kausalproblems trotz allem nicht anders geworden. Es bleibt dabei, dass man diese Beziehung an einem isolierten, aus dem konkreten Geschehen herausgerissenen Einzelfall untersucht. Indessen, erst wenn man die kausalen Beziehungen nicht als isolierte Fälle betrachtet, sondern als Glieder in einem ganzen System von Fällen, in einer umfassenden Situation, wie sie doch in der realen Welt stattfinden müssen, ist es möglich, gewisse Aspekte dieser Beziehung ans Licht zu bringen, die sonst nicht beachtet werden.

Man wird mir vielleicht vorwerfen, dass ich da zwei Namen vergessen habe, d.h. Laplace und Kant. Denn Laplace spricht ja von einer kausalen Ordnung der ganzen Welt, indem er einen unbedingten Determinismus im Weltgeschehen vertritt, und Kant betrachtet auch ganze Kausalketten in der Welt und bringt sie mit dem Problem der endlichen oder unendlichen Weltgeschichte in Zusammenhang.

Ich habe die beiden Männer, die in der Geschichte des Kausalproblems eine entscheidende Rolle gespielt haben, nicht vergessen. Aber dies ändert an der Sachlage, um die es sich bei mir handelt, nicht das mindeste. Denn auch Laplace betrachtet die kausale Beziehung als ein Ereignispaar für sich, ohne weiter nach den Bedingungen seines Eintretens zu fragen. Er iteriert dann sozusagen einfach dieselbe, schematisch gefasste Struktur und setzt aus einer Mannigfaltigkeit überall gleicher Beziehungen die ganze Welt in *ein* System zusammen, das in seiner konstanten Form sich vom Moment zum Moment wiederholt. Gerade die überall gleiche Form der kausalen Beziehung ermöglicht dann dem hellsichtigen Geist die ganze Welt zu überschauen und von einem momentanen Querschnitt der Welt alle anderen Querschnitte sowohl in die Zukunft als auch in die Vergangenheit hin zu berechnen. In ihrer kausalen Struktur ändert sich die Welt im Laufe der Zeit nicht, alles is eindeutig bestimmt und berechenbar von irgendeinem beliebig gewählten Querschnitt der Welt aus. Das ist der ausnahmslose Determinismus der Laplaceschen Weltauffassung, der nur eine Folge seiner Betrachtungsart der kausalen Beziehung ist.

Ähnlich verfährt im Grunde auch Kant in der *Kritik der reinen Vernunft*, wenn er die Ketten ursächlicher Beziehungen ins Auge fasst. Er ist dabei nur an dem Problem der zeitlichen bzw.

räumlichen Endlichkeit oder Unendlichkeit der Welt interessiert
und sucht auf diesem Wege gewisse metaphysische bzw. erkenntnistheoretische Fragen zu lösen. So beschäftigt er sich bekanntlich mit dem Problem des Anfangs und der eventuellen endlichen
bzw. unendlichen Fortsetzung der Kette der ursächlichen Beziehungen in der Zeit und im Raume. Er bringt sich aber nicht
zum Bewusstsein, dass die kausalen Beziehungen sich in der
Welt nach allen Richtungen fortpflanzen und auch in der Zeit
fortsetzen, ohne dabei an jeder Weltstelle bzw. in jedem Zeitmoment auf dieselbe Situation treffen zu müssen. Er fasst die
kausale Beziehung als eine für sich selbst genügende Form eines
Ereignispaares, das sich in ihrer immer gleichen Form überall
und jederzeit wiederholen kann. Die kausale Struktur der Welt
ist überall homogen und bleibt auch völlig unwandelbar in jedem
Zeitmoment. Dies steht mit der Auffassung der Ursache bzw. der
ursächlichen Beziehung als einer apriorischen Kategorie, als
einer subjektiven Verstandesform zusammen, die eben wegen
ihrer Apriorität stets und überall auf identische Weise angewendet werden muss. Diese Auffassung hat es Kant unmöglich gemacht, die kausale Beziehung als einen Tatbestand zu betrachten, der in einer konkreten Situation auftritt, die nicht überall
und nicht in jedem Moment die gleiche sein muss. Die Welt im
Sinne Kants – freilich nur die Erscheinungswelt – hat eine in der
Zeit und im Raum homogene kausale Struktur, die erst ermöglicht, nach der Endlichkeit oder Unendlichkeit der Welt im Raum
und in der Zeit zu fragen. So hat auch der Indeterminismus des
freien Willens bei Kant sofort die Gestalt des gegenseitigen
Sichausschliessens zweier Grundtypen des Geschehens und damit
auch zweier ''Welten'' – der Erscheinungswelt und der Welt der
Dinge an sich – angenommen. Deswegen konnte einerseits die
''freie'' Willensentscheidung nur als ein ursachloses Ereignis gefasst werden, andererseits war es nicht möglich, den Versuch zu
unternehmen, die ''freien'' Willensentscheidungen als einen
besonderen Fall der Kausalität zu fassen und sie gerade aus der
kausalen Struktur der Welt verständlich zu machen. Das ganze
Kausalproblem nahm von vornherein die Gestalt einer merkwürdigen, in ihrem letzten Grunde unverständlichen subjektivistischen Umdeutung der realen Welt an, so dass weder die
kausale Struktur der Welt genauer untersucht noch das echte

erkenntnistheoretische Problem der Rechtmässigkeit des Erkennens der Welt in dieser kausalen Struktur richtig gefasst und vorurteilslos in allen seinen Einzelheiten erwogen werden konnte. Dieses erkenntnistheoretische Grundproblem wurde ohne eine nähere Erwägung sofort im *negativen* Sinne entschieden [5] und

---

[5] Kant würde vielleicht dagegen Protest erheben, dass ich hier seine transzendentale Theorie der Kategorien als eine negative Lösung des erkenntnistheoretischen Problems der Erfassung der realen Welt gekennzeichnet habe. Er hätte auch darin zum Teil recht, indem nur die *eine* Seite seiner Entscheidung – dass wir nämlich die reale Welt an sich vermittels und durch die Kategorien und die Anschauungsformen nicht erkennen können – negativ ist, während die Auffassung der Kategorien als "notwendiger" und damit auch als "allgemeingültiger" Verstandesformen der Erkenntnis der Welt, sowie die Auffassung des Raumes und der Zeit als notwendiger Anschauungsformen den positiven Schritt zur Begründung der Möglichkeit der Erfahrung und damit doch zu einer eigentümlichen und uns nach Kant einzig zugänglichen Art der Erkenntnis der Welt bildet. Aber dieses Positivität liegt nur in der *Absicht*, in welcher die *Kritik der reinen Vernunft* unternommen wurde, nicht aber in deren *Ergebnis*. Und dies gilt bei *beiden* Deutungen der Auffassung, die Kategorien und die Anschauungsformen seien apriorische notwendige Formen der Erkenntnis, die sich auf Grund der Kantischen Ausführungen in der *Kritik* aufdrängen und tatsächlich in der Geschichte der Philosophie vorgeschlagen wurden. Bei der ersten Deutung sind die Kategorien und die Anschauungsformen der Erkenntnis als solche wesensnotwendig, unabhängig davon wessen Erkenntnis sie ist. Ein Erkennen, das sich der Kategorien und der Anschauungsformen entzieht – wenn dies überhaupt möglich sein sollte (was im Sinne dieser Deutung bestritten wird) – wäre *kein* Erkennen. Nach der zweiten – durch viele Stellen der *Kritik* nahegelegten – Deutung, sind die Kategorien und die Anschauungsformen nur der unsrigen, menschlichen Erkenntnisweise wesensnotwendig, wobei es dann ein Geheimnis bildet, warum wir, Menschen, gerade durch eine solche Erkenntnisweise ausgezeichnet sind. Andere, nicht-menschliche Erkenntnissubjekte (Gott, Engel, Tiere, Bewohner anderer Weltkörper u. drgl. m.) könnten im Prinzip entweder über andere Erkenntnisweisen verfügen, die ganz andere Kategoriensysteme und Anschauungsformen mit sich führen würden, oder überhaupt gar keine Kategorien und Anschauungsformen verwenden, so dass sie die Welt, wie sie an sich ist, ohne diese Formen zu erkennen vermöchten.

Das Ergebnis ist aber, wie gesagt, in *beiden* Fällen negativ. Denn bei der ersten Deutung würde es entweder zum Wesen der "Erkenntnis" (bzw. des "Erkennens") gehören, dass sie das Ansichseiende unter dem ihm wesensfremden und damit es verfälschenden Aspekt der Kategorien und der raum-zeitlichen Formung fassen müsste, und eben deswegen es nur *verkennen* bzw. es auf eigentümliche Weise *verdecken* würde. Hält man aber daran fest, dass es zum Wesen der Erkenntnis gehört, alles Seiende (und insbesondere auch das vom Erkennen unabhängig und an sich Seiende) unverfälscht und durch nichts verdeckt in seinem eigenen Sosein

dann wurde nur die Notwendigkeit dieser Entscheidung durch
die Paralogismen- und Antinomien-Theorie "begründet." [6]

An diesem erkenntnistheoretischen und subjektivistischen
Aspekt des Kausalproblems können wir hier vorbeigehen, da es
sich uns hier lediglich um das Wesen und die Form der kausalen
Beziehung selbst handelt. Beides muss geklärt werden, bevor
man zu erkenntnistheoretischen Fragen übergeht und bevor man
entscheidet, ob die Welt, in welcher Kausalzusammenhänge bestehen, eine blosse, wie Kant sagt, "Erscheinungswelt," also
in phänomenologischer Sprache bloss eine reine intentionale
Welt sei, die von dem Erkenntnissubjekt kategorial geformt
oder ob sie *mit* bzw. *in* ihrer kausalen Ordnung und Struktur
"an sich" besteht. Dass aber die kausale Beziehung so oder so mit
der Form einer möglichen realen Welt aufs engste verbunden ist,
das ist es, was zuvor gezeigt werden muss. Und dies eben erfordert, dass diese Beziehung als etwas zu betrachten ist, was
in bestimmt gearteten und doch in individuellen Fällen ver-

zu enthüllen, dann muss das – nach Kant – sich der Kategorien bedienende
Erkennen zu der echten Realität führen und die von den Kategorien und
der raumzeitlichen Formung freie, "an sich seiende" Welt muss dann als
überhaupt nicht vorhanden gefasst sein. Die Welt der "Erscheinungen"
bleibt dann als die einzig bestehende Welt übrig. Wird die letztere aber,
im Sinne Kants als "blosse Erscheinung," als unsere "Vorstellung" gefasst, dann wird die Realität im Sinne des transzendentalen Idealismus
für ein bloss intentionales Gebilde gehalten und damit des echten Reali-
tätscharakters beraubt sein. Hält man dagegen daran fest, dass jedes
ohne die Kategorien und die Anschauungsformen bestehende Seiende im
strengen Sinne unerkennbar sei und infolgedessen nicht angenommen
werden darf, dann muss dessen Bestehen einfach geleugnet werden. Geht
man aber zu der zweiten Deutung der Kantischen Auffassung über, so ist
die für alle Menschen notwendige, sich der Kategorien bedienende
"Erkenntnis" nur eine auf die menschlichen Subjekte beschränkte
Illusion, deren Illusionsnatur nicht das Mindeste dadurch geschwächt
wird, dass wir alle in sie gebannt sind und uns von ihr nicht befreien
können. Könnten wir aufhören, Menschen zu sein, ohne zugleich aufzu-
hören zu existieren, dann erst könnten wir eine echte Erkenntnis der
Welt, wie sie an sich ist, erlangen. Aber auch die transzendentale Einsicht, dass wir bei unserem Erkennen einer merkwürdigen Illusion unter-
liegen, könnte an ihrer Illusionsnatur nichts ändern und erlaubt uns keine
echte, positive Erkenntnis der realen Welt zu erlangen. Wir wissen von
der Welt, wie sie an sich ist, nicht mehr dadurch, dass wir wissen, sie in
ihrem Eigensein und Sosein nicht erkennen zu können. So endet auch bei
dieser Deutung der Kantische Theorie mit einem negativen Ergebnis.

[6] Dieses Anführungszeichen soll meinen Zweifel zum Ausdruck bringen,
dass diese "Begründung" wirklich gelungen ist.

schiedener Situationen in Millionen Fällen beständig in der realen Welt stattfindet und nach allen ihren Richtungen verstreut ist. Dieser Umstand erlaubt uns zwei wichtige Begriffe bezüglich der kausalen Beziehung zu bestimmen, die bis jetzt – so viel ich weiss – nicht gebildet wurden. Es sind dies: (1) der Begriff der *Verteilung* in der realen Welt der zu einem Ereignis gehörenden Ursachen und Wirkungen, und (2) der Begriff des *Bereiches* von Ursachen bzw. Wirkungen, die zu einem Ereignis zugehören. Wir wollen diese Begriffe gleich am Anfang unserer Betrachtungen bestimmen, da sie ihre Richtlinien festlegen.

II. DER BEREICH UND DIE VERTEILUNG DER URSACHEN BZW. DER WIRKUNGEN IN DER WELT

Bezüglich der kausalen Beziehung hat man sich hauptsächlich mit zwei Problemen bzw. Problemgruppen beschäftigt: (1) mit Fragen, welche das Wesen und die Form der kausalen Beziehung betreffen und deren Lösung zu einem Begriff dieser Beziehung führen soll, (2) mit dem sogenannten Kausalprinzip. Dabei ging es vorwiegend um die Formulierung dieses Prinzips, die in der Geschichte der Philosophie auf verschiedene Weise gefasst wurde, und um die Frage, ob dieses Prinzip in der realen Welt vorbehaltlos gilt oder gewisse Ausnahmen zulässt. Diese Frage führt bekanntlich zu zwei entgegengesetzten Weltauffassungen: zu dem sogenannten "Determinismus" und zu dem "Indeterminismus." Die beiden zu bestimmenden Begriffe des Bereiches und der Verteilung der zu einem Ereignis gehörenden Ursachen bzw. Wirkungen stehen, wie sich später zeigen wird, mit dem Problem des Determinismus im Zusammenhang und ihre Klärung wird uns erlauben zu zeigen, dass es noch verschiedene Typen der "deterministisch" verstandenen kausalen Ordnung der realen Welt geben kann. Diese Möglichkeit wurde bis jetzt übersehen. Man ist in den bisherigen Betrachtungen – ohne eine höhere Analyse durchgeführt zu haben – sofort zu einem bestimmten Typus des "Determinismus" gekommen und hat ihn für *den* Determinismus gehalten. Deswegen hat man auch jeden Versuch, die kausale Ordnung der Welt auf eine etwas andere Weise aufzufassen, für den "Indeterminismus" gehalten, vor dem man immer wieder zurückgeschreckt ist.

Ohne unsere Auffassung der ursächlichen Beziehung, die schon vor vielen Jahren von mir veröffentlich wurde, hier vorauszusetzen oder sie genauer zu entwickeln, können wir hier ein Moment dieser Beziehung hervorheben, das übrigens mit Ausnahme ganz weniger Autoren immer anerkannt wird. Es kommt nämlich darauf an, dass jede kausale Beziehung zweigliedrig ist. Das eine Glied ist die Ursache, das andere die Wirkung. Die Spinozistische Rede von der *causa sui* ist also entweder falsch, oder das Wort *"causa"* hat in dieser Wendung einen völlig anderen und zwar einen solchen Sinn, bei welchem jene *"causa"* nicht Glied einer kausalen Beziehung sein kann.[7] Wir sind zugleich geneigt zu behaupten, dass die Glieder der kausalen Beziehung entweder Ereignisse oder Vorgänge sind, obwohl das Wort "Ursache" oft so verwendet wird, dass es dann ein Ding oder einen in der Zeit verharrenden Gegenstand überhaupt bezeichnet.[8] Die in der Zeit verharrenden Gegenstände werden aber auf diese Weise mit der kausalen Beziehung in Verbindung gebracht, dass jeder Vorgang bzw. jedes Ereignis in einem solchen Gegenstand sein Seinsfundament finden muss, d.h. sich an ihm vollzieht oder stattfindet.[9] Endlich muss die Ursache im strengen, von uns festgelegten Sinne von den Umständen, unter denen sie eintritt, unterschieden werden, wobei natürlich der Begriff des "Umstandes" geklärt und bestimmt werden muss. Sie bildet mit der Gesamtheit der Umstände zusammen die hinreichende aktive Bedingung des Eintretens des Ereignisses, das ihre Wirkung ist. Sie allein aber, ohne diese Umstände, kann die Wirkung nicht auslösen. Die Ursache ist m.a.W. ein Faktor, der die Gesamtheit der Umstände als die unentbehrliche aber nicht hinreichende Bedingung der Wirkung zu ihrer hinreichenden Bedingung ergänzt oder umwandelt. Die Ursache kann aus *einem* Ereignis oder

---

[7] Die Zustimmung zu dieser Behauptung wird uns später dazu zwingen, zu zeigen, auf welche Weise die Glieder einer kausalen Beziehung von einander abgegrenzt werden können und wie ihre gegenseitige Verschiedenheit und Abgrenzung erwiesen werden kann.

[8] Die Scheidung zwischen Ereignissen, Vorgängen und den in der Zeit verharrenden Gegenstanden wurde im II. Band des *Streites um die Existenz der Welt* ausführlich begründet. Die Frage, ob Dinge zu Gliedern der kausalen Beziehung gemacht werden können, wurde im § 13 des genannten Werkes negativ beantwortet.

[9] Dies habe ich im Kapitel V und im Kapitel XIV des genannten Buches zu zeigen versucht.

Vorgang bestehen, dann ist sie einfach. Sie kann aber auch aus mehreren zugleich eintretenden Ereignissen oder zugleich sich vollziehenden Vorgängen zusammengesetzt sein. Ob aber auch die Gesamtheit der Umstände ebenfalls einfach oder zusammengesetzt sein kann, ist erst zu erwägen. Das Ereignis, welches nach der Ergänzung der Gesamtheit der Umstände durch die Ursache, oder *mit* dieser Ergänzung zugleich eintritt, ist die *unmittelbare* Wirkung der betreffenden Ursache. Dieses Ereignis kann aber selbst einen Bestand von Umständen zur hinreichenden Bedingung eines anderen Ereignisses ergänzen und damit selbst eine Ursache sein, die ihrerseits eine neue, unmittelbare Wirkung auslöst. So kommen wir zu dem Begriff einer *mittelbaren* Wirkung und auch einer *mittelbaren* Ursache. Wenn man dann nach der Ursache einer mittelbaren Ursache usw. fragt, so kommt man auf die Idee einer ganzen "Kette" von Ursachen und Wirkungen eines bestimmten Ereignisses oder Vorgangs. Wählen wir ein bestimmtes Ereignis E_1 (Vorgang V_1), so nennen wir die Gesamtheit der Ursachen von E_1 (bzw. V_1) den Ursachen*bereich* und die Gesamtheit der Wirkungen von E_1 (V_1) den Wirkungs*bereich* dieses Ereignisses (Vorgangs).

Ist aber die Bildung eines solchen Begriffes nötig und zweckmässig? Wäre es nicht einfacher und richtiger zu sagen, dass die Gesamtheit der Ursachen einfach die Gesamtheit aller in der Welt stattfindenden und von dem Ereignis E_1 (V_1) früheren oder nicht-späteren Ereignisse (Vorgänge) ist?

Ich antworte: Die Notwendigkeit oder die Entbehrlichkeit der Bildung des Begriffes des Ursachenbereiches eines Ereignisses (Vorgangs) – das ist im Grunde das Problem der Geltung des radikalen Determinismus in der realen Welt. Dieses Problem ist aber – der allgemeinen herrschenden Meinung über die Richtigkeit des rakikalen Determinismus entgegen – nicht so leicht zu beantworten und erfordert umfangreiche und schwierige Betrachtungen, die vor allem den Sinn dieses Determinismus zu klären und zu bestimmen haben und die wir auch im Nachfolgenden durchzuführen beabsichtigen. Hier muss aber ein blosser Hinweis ausreichen.

Bei einem vorgegebenen Bestand von Umständen und einem

zu erwirkenden Ereignis E_1 (oder Vorgang V_1) ist der ihn zu einer hinreichenden Bedingung des E_1 (V_1) ergänzende Faktor – also seine "Ursache" – nicht ganz beliebig, sondern muss entweder in seiner generellen Art oder sogar in seiner Individualität[10] *entsprechend* eindeutig bestimmt sein, oder aber zu einer *Auswahl* möglicher, ihrer Art nach verschiedener "Ursachen" gehören, von denen *eine* individuelle eintreten muss, damit es zu dem Ereignis E_1 (V_1) käme. Dass es eben so ist, zeigt sich eben am besten darin, dass es zu bestimmt gearteten Ereignissen, die als Wirkungen von etwas behandelt werden sollen, strenge Kausalgesetze gibt, welche bei der empirischen Erforschung der realen Welt gesucht und auch gefunden werden. Dies weist seinerseits darauf hin, dass in der Gesamtheit der in der Welt im Vergleich zu E_1 früheren oder nicht-späteren Ereignissen immer solche Ereignisse vorhanden sind, die sich nicht dazu eignen, Ursache von E_1 zu sein bzw. zu dem Ursachenbereich von E_1 zu gehören, und dass somit der Ursachenbereich von E_1 nicht mit jener Gesamtheit der Ereignisse in der Welt identisch ist.

Die blosse Berufung auf das empirische Bestehen gewisser Kausalgesetze reicht aber nicht hin, um zu erweisen, dass der Ursachenbereich eines jeden Ereignisses von der Gesamtheit der in der Welt stattfindenden von ihm früheren oder nicht-späteren Ereignisse immer verschieden sein muss. Dies kann nur durch die Aufdeckung der kausalen Struktur der realen Welt gezeigt werden, was eine schwierige und komplizierte Untersuchung erfordert. Zu ihrer Vorbereitung dient eben die Einführung des Begriffes des Ursachenbereiches eines Ereignisses E_1 (oder Vorgangs V_1), das als Wirkung von etwas erfasst werden soll. Um aber hier nichts vorauszusetzen, lassen wir es als eine offene Frage stehen, ob der Ursachenbereich von E_1 (V_1) immer nur eine Auswahl aus der Gesamtheit der von E_1 (V_1) früheren oder nicht-späteren Ereignisse in der Welt bildet oder sich mit ihr einfach deckt.

[10] Dies ist auch ein offenes Problem, ob alle Ursachen bloss ihrer Art nach entsprechend bestimmt werden müssen und somit in gewissem Sinne wiederholbar sein können, oder ob es im Gegenteil Ursachen geben kann, die in sich qualitativ streng individuell und infolgedessen einzig oder – besser gesagt – einmalig sind.

Auf eine analoge Weise wie der Begriff des Ursachenbereiches eines Ereignisses (Vorgangs) können wir den Begriff seines Wirkungsbereiches bilden. Wir verstehen darunter die Gesamtheit der zu E_1 gehörenden Wirkungen des E_1. Wir wollen hier nicht ohne weiteres voraussetzen, dass jedes Ereignis in der Welt eine Ursache bzw. eine Wirkung hat bzw. haben muss – was wiederum mit der Geltung des radikalen Determinismus im Zusammenhang steht. Wir können aber trotzdem sagen, das *wenn* ein Ereignis E_1 unmittelbare und mittelbare Ursachen und andererseits auch entsprechende Wirkungen hat, es sich durch die Bestimmung seiner beiden Bereiche, der Ursachen und der Wirkungen, charakterisieren lässt. Ohne hier die Forderung aufzustellen, dass bei jedem Ereignis genau angegeben werde, aus welchen Ereignissen die beiden Bereiche jeweils bestehen, können wir hier nur auf die möglichen Grenzfälle hinweisen, mit welchen man von vornherein rechnen muss. Entweder kann nämlich der Ursachen- bzw. der Wirkungsbereich *maximal* sein, d.h. mit der Gesamtheit der von E_1 nicht-späteren bzw. nicht-früheren in der Welt überhaupt stattfindenden Ereignisse sich decken, oder eine *Auswahl* der Ereignisse von der Gesamtheit der entsprechenden Ereignisse in der Welt bilden, oder er kann endlich *minimal* sein, d.h. dass *keine* Ursachen bzw. keine Wirkungen des Ereignisses E_1 in der Welt vorhanden sind. Dies letztere soll hier nur als eine prinzipielle Möglichkeit erwähnt werden, die erst in einer entsprechenden Untersuchung bestätigt bzw. ausgeschlossen werden soll.

Wir haben aber gesagt, dass jedes Ereignis (Vorgang) an einem in der Zeit verharrenden Gegenstand (insbesondere an einem Ding) stattfinden muss. Diese Gegenstände befinden sich an verschiedenen Orten im Weltraum, wobei es so sein kann, dass diese durch Dinge eingenommenen Orten die Gesamtheit der Stellen des Weltraumes ausfüllen oder aber in Weltraum so verstreut sind, so dass es in ihm leere durch Dinge nicht besetzte Stellen gibt. In beiden Fällen können wir von einer *Verteilung* der Dinge besonderer Art im Weltraum sprechen. Und da an ihnen Ereignisse (Vorgänge) stattfinden, so können wir von einer Verteilung der Ereignisse in der Welt sprechen. Fassen wir diejenigen Ereignisse, die zu einem Ursachenbereich (oder zu einem Wirkungsbereich) eines Ereignisses E_1 gehören, ins Auge, so

lässt sich der Begriff der Verteilung der Ursachen bzw. der
Verteilung der Wirkungen des E_1 in der Welt bilden. Je nach
dem Fall führt die Verteilung zur Bestimmung einer Punkt-
mannigfaltigkeit (oder Stellenmannigfaltigkeit) im Weltraum,
an denen die Ursachen bzw. die Wirkungen von E_1 stattfinden.
Man kann sagen, dass diese Stellenmannigfaltigkeit ein *Feld*
bildet, in dessen Grenzen sich alle zu einem Ursachen- bzw.
Wirkungsbereich von E_1 durch das Feld seiner Ursachen bzw.
durch das Feld seiner Wirkungen zu charakterisieren. Der Umfang und die Gestalt dieses Feldes kann sehr verschieden sein,
je nach der Art der Ereignisse, die durch ihr Ursachen- oder
Wirkungsfeld charakterisiert werden, wobei noch die Situation,
in welcher sich E_1 in einem Moment befindet, von Bedeutung sein
kann. Wir lassen hier wiederum die Frage ganz offen, ob dieses
Feld endlich oder unendlich sein kann, und insbesondere, ob es
sich gegebenenfalls mit dem All des Weltraums deckt oder
nicht.

Insbesondere wird uns im Folgenden die Frage beschäftigen,
wie sich im Einzelnen das Ursachen- bzw. Wirkungsfeld von E_1
in Bezug auf den Gegenstand gestaltet, an dem E_1 stattfindet.
Es kann nämlich vorkommen, dass dieser Gegenstand selbst
räumlich ist, also einen "Raum" einnimmt. Dann lässt sich der
ganze Weltraum in zwei "Felder" einteilen: in den Raumausschnitt, den dieser Gegenstand selbst einnimmt, also in das
"Innere" des Gegenstandes, und in den Raumausschnitt, der
sich ausserhalb des betreffenden Gegenstandes befindet, also
das "Äussere" von ihm bildet. Das Ursachenfeld von E_1 kann
also entweder ganz im Inneren oder ganz im Äusseren des Gegenstandes sein, oder aber zum Teil im Inneren und zum Teil im
Äusseren desselben liegen. Natürlich lässt sich der Begriff des
"Inneren" und des "Äusseren" auf Gegenstände erweitern, die
nicht räumlich im strengen Sinne sind, wie z.B. eine menschliche
Person, das "Innere" bildet dann der Gesamtbestand der in dem
Gegenstande bestehenden Sachverhalte, das "Äussere" dagegen
umfasst alle Gegenstände und Sachverhalte, welche nicht zu dem
betreffenden Gegenstande gehören. In allen Fällen können wir
fragen, ob ein in oder an einem Gegenstande G stattfindes
Ereignis E_1 bloss "äussere" Ereignisse zu seiner Ursache (bzw.
Wirkung), oder bloss "innere" Ereignisse oder endlich zum

Teil "innere" und zum Teil "äussere" Ereignisse zu seiner Ursache (bzw. Wirkung) hat.

Das Studium dieser verschiedenen möglichen Fälle bei Ereignissen verschiedener Grundart kann uns über die kausale Struktur der Welt belehren. Auf die Gestaltung sowohl der Ursachen- bzw. Wirkungsbereiche als auch der Ursachen- und Wirkungsfelder kann in erster Linie die Natur oder die Gattung der in der Welt sich vollziehenden Vorgänge und der stattfindenden Ereignisse einen Einfluss haben. Eine grosse Rolle spielt aber auch die Form des Gesamtbestandes der Umstände, unter denen die kausalen Beziehungen stattfinden. Es ist möglich, dass die Umstände eine besondere Form haben mussen,[11] damit es zu der besonderen Art der Beziehung zwischen zwei Tatsachen, wie es die kausale Beziehung ist, komme. Und diese besondere Form der Umstände setzt ihrerseits eine Form der in der Zeit verharrenden Gegenstände und ihres Zugleichseins voraus und führt andererseits zu einer sozusagen überkausalen aus der Mannigfaltigkeit der kausalen Beziehungen sich ergebenden Grundstruktur der Welt, welche von der Form, welche der radikale Determinismus der Welt vorschreibt, verschieden ist.

Dies alles ist nur ein Ausblick, der in den folgenden Untersuchungen ausgearbeitet und dessen Ergebnisse begründet werden müssen. Es handelt sich aber in ihnen nicht um blosse, an einzelnen Fällen ursächlicher Beziehungen durchgeführte Untersuchungen, die natürlich auch möglich und notwendig sind, aber zu den Aufgaben der positiven, empirischen Einzelwissenschaften gehören. Es handelt sich um eine Betrachtung, die zur Aufgabe hat, gewisse allgemeine Möglichkeiten, Notwendigkeiten und auch Unmöglichkeiten zu erwägen, um auf diesem Wege zu einer allgemeinen Einsicht in die mögliche kausale Grundstruktur der Welt zu kommen. Um aber derartige Betrachtungen durchführen zu können, muss zuerst die Form der kausalen Beziehung selbst viel genauer und tiefer analysiert werden, als dies in meiner ersten erwähnten Skizze geschah.

Polnische Akademie der Wissenschaften   Kraków

---

[11] Ich habe darauf in meinem ersten Artikel über die kausale Beziehung (1946) hingewiesen, als ich sie mit dem Problem der relativ isolierter Systeme in Zusammenhang gebracht habe. Diese ganze Angelegenheit muss aber im Folgenden wesentlich auseinandergelegt werden.

PHILOSOPHY AS CRITICISM AND PERSPECTIVE

NEAL W. KLAUSNER

A memorial volume is a more personal document than most philosophical essays. It not only pays tribute to one who has left us but also gives each participant the opportunity to review his own thought and relate it to that of the honored person. I am indeed happy to join with others in acknowledging the high quality of Professor Merlan's work and also to say how much our close association many years ago has meant to me. The intervening years, with only occasional meetings, have not dulled my affection but have increased my early esteem as I watched and learned from his scholarly and philosophical achievement. I do not think I could press an "ism" on Professor Merlan, although I know how deep his sympathies were toward phenomenology and existentialism. But his incisive and persistent critical scholarship it seems to me, kept him from being totally annexed by any single point of view. And in that sentence lies the theme of my paper. It will be a personal statement, a kind of assessment, a kind of looking-back and a gathering-in. There may be little or much that my friend would have accepted. But it does not matter. I have never measured my friendships in terms of philosophical agreement. Moreover I am sure that Professor Merlan would not have denied that differences in philosophy are signs of vitality rather than decadence.

I want to begin with a few words about philosophy as criticism and then to say something in greater detail about philosophy as perspective. I shall open and close the essay with a quotation from Plato. In the light of Professor Merlan's scholarship in Greek philosophy this seems appropriate. In the seventh letter (assuming its authenticity) Plato plans to test Dionysius' alleged interest in philosophy. He suspected that the young tyrant was "crammed with borrowed doctrines" and needed to be taught first what the philosopher's task demanded. He writes:

To such persons, one must point out what the subject is as a whole, and what its character, and how many preliminary subjects it entails and how much labour. For on hearing this, if the pupil be truly philosophic, in sympathy with the subject and worthy of it, because divinely gifted, he believes that he has been shown a marvellous pathway and that he must brace himself at once to follow it, and that life will not be worth living if he does otherwise. After this he braces both himself and him who is guiding him on the path, nor does he desist until either he has reached the goal of his studies, or else has gained such power as to be capable of directing his own steps without the aid of the instructor. It is thus, and in this mind that such a student lives, occupied indeed in whatever occupations he may find himself, but always beyond all else cleaving fast to philosophy and to that mode of daily life which will best make him apt to learn and of retentive mind and able to reason within himself soberly ... (Pl. *Epist.* 7. 340b–d).[1]

There are other descriptions of philosophy, the philosopher, and the philosophic way of life in Plato, but this one seems to mark most clearly the life and achievement of Professor Merlan. It also gives me the opportunity to say something about my own views. The philosopher has been pictured in many ways since Plato's day, some complimentary, some uncomplimentary. Only the former interest me now. He has, for example, often been thought of as the wise man or the learned man, or the unperturbed man, or the great systematizer of knowledge. Today most of us feel a bit foolish if we are described in these terms. We know too much about human fallibility to accept such labels. In more recent times the philosopher may be thought of as a critic of language, and this seems for many to cut us down too meanly. We have, it is said, something more noble to do than to construct ideal languages or to reform the ordinary ones. But still the role of critic has been cherished in philosophy ever since the Greeks and we must never relinquish it.

And this, I think, is where I want to begin – not with the loyalties or commitments of the philosopher but with his reluctance to be attached. This is a methodological stance only, for he can hardly be a critic without a point of view. Put somewhat

[1] *Plato*, Vol. VII, translated by R. G. Bury, Loeb Classical Library (London, 1929), pp. 527–529.

crisply, a philosopher is a thinker who is never wholly with anyone; neither with another philosopher, nor a state, nor an institution, nor a god, nor even with himself. He strives to maintain a critical distance from every claim made upon him by science, art, religion, morality and custom. As a thinker he is ceaselessly prodded by an after-thought. He may vigorously defend his beliefs; he may be stubbornly convinced of the errors of an opponent; he may even exhibit a passionate loyalty to "the truth," and a fervent opposition to what he regards as false. But he must endure at all times the persistent, often frustrating inner voice, that says to him in every believing-situation, "You could be wrong. Why not look at it this way?"

Thus, unless restrained by sympathy arising from his belief that all men are in a similar predicament, the philosopher in this role is somewhat uncivil and importunate. He demands the freedom and the right to differ, to dissent, and to criticize – not because he has all the answers, but because he is not sure he or anyone else has all the questions. He "begs to differ" not just to be different but for a nobler end, namely, the triumph of reason over unreason, a victory which Plato suggests is achieved not by force but by persuasion. But one need not be "divinely gifted" to learn to reason soberly within oneself.

The philosopher's criticism, however, is something more than a mere stance or attitude. His insistence upon reasoning is not merely a plea to be reasonable, but to follow the rules of proper reasoning – rules which have been discovered, devised, or invented (which term is correct?) in the long history of his work. He accepts the Socratic demand to follow the argument wherever it leads and the Peircean imperative never to let down the bars of inquiry. This, in part, is what it means to be critical, to be logical, and logic is his only tool. It is reason with a small "r" rather than a capital "R" that guides him. For it is this reason that is capable of asking questions of itself – indeed, must frequently turn a sceptical eye toward its own procedures. Even those who offer a defense for unreason must learn some rules of intelligibility to make their points, for there can be no philosophical conversation unless there is mutual agreement to accept and defend the conditions which allow for disagreement. Philosophy depends largely on argument, but to argue is not to play a game. To see this, consider the differences between being "defeated" in a game and being "defeated" in an argument.

If philosophical criticism is not seeking victory in a game, it also is not a challenge to debate. Perhaps it is more like an appeal for help. Contemporary forms of criticism often begin (or end) with, "it is meaningless" or "muddled" or "nonsense." But they could be more gentle by saying, "here is something that seems inexplicable if what you say is true." Thus the phenomenologist may assert that we experience only essences. And an existentialist may reply: "But have you thought of the possibility that existence precedes essence?" And the positivist puts his case: "Only that which is empirically verifiable or tautologous is meaningful." And the anti-positivist says: "Have you thought of the verification of your first principle?" Galileo and Locke said we should distinguish between two kinds of qualities, those whose existence is dependent on their being perceived, and those whose existence is independent of the observer. "Yes," answered Berkeley, "but haven't you noticed that they are never really found apart from each other?" "All knowledge comes from experience," said the British empiricists. "Of course," replied Kant, "but have you ever thought to ask for the conditions of experience?" "The nature of body is geometrical extension," said Descartes, and Leibniz wondered how, if this were true, anything can happen. "There are eternal immutable forms of all things," said Plato, and then, perhaps shocked by his own assertion, asked, "Of mud too?" and "Of hair?" The analytic-synthetic distinction seemed secure until Quine and others asked, "Have you thought about the problem of synonymy?" And so the dialogue, the dialectic, the argument, or the conversation goes, with little desire to bring it to a close for there is no score to keep, no victory to record, no trophy to be awarded. The result is perhaps only a slight case of understanding. In short, philosophical criticism begins not only with "what do you mean by ...?" but also with "have you thought of this?" An omniscient being would have no need to philosophize and an imbecile no desire to. Somewhere in between are the rest of us who must perpetually question others to find out where they are and where we might be. But there is no hurry. In philosophy there are no emergencies, no deadlines, no rush orders, only persistent inquiry.

In the history of thought, however, criticism has not been the only activity of the philosopher. For many, another more exciting demand has been made upon the imagination; another goal which surpasses the first in dignity and daring has enticed them to find the Scheme, the System, the Whole Plot, into which the entire range of human experience can be fitted, and without which nothing makes sense. In his first role the philosopher is weary of partisan loyalties and the importunate pressures of reformers. He knows how easy it is to be taken in once the bars against criticism have been lowered. But in the second role he is lured by the aesthetic attraction of imaginative creativity and the appeal of rational coherency.

It is fashionable these days to dismiss this aim of the philosopher as futile, or as nonsense, or as the result of something buried deep in the Unconscious. The pendulum may be swinging back for there are signs that philosophers may now confess to metaphysical interests without acute embarrassment. Professor Merlan has defended this speculative activity not only for itself, but for its utility. In an interesting article he wrote of the metaphysicians' right to say to those scientists who reject metaphysics:

I precede you in that I anticipate what later will be a scientific theory, and I precede you in that I provide you with a frame of reference which will make it possible for you to understand what you are doing, although I formed my concepts before you were doing it. My realm is the realm of possibilities, preceding your actualities. I do not deny the right of my more modest colleague to clean up after you. May I, however, claim the privilege of lighting up a multiplicity of paths in front of you, on any of which you may find yourself walking one day? If you ask me what the source of my light is, perhaps it wouldn't be immodest to reply: Never mind, just assume it is illegitimate contraband – but, legitimate or not, it does give light.[2]

Philosophers who are unwilling to relinquish this traditional interest make a thorough-going effort "to tell the whole story." For no one else does it. Nor do they try – not the sciences, not religion, not history and not art. Perhaps some fiction writers make an attempt and often metaphysics has been regarded as nothing more than rather dull fiction. Philosophers, of course,

[2] P. Merlan, "Metaphysics and Science – Some Remarks," *The Journal of Philosophy* 56 (1959), p. 618.

never succeed in telling the whole story, for the will is weak, the time is short, and the plot is enormously detailed. Thus in one sense there can be no successful philosophy. All must fail because of incompleteness and human fallibility. But such a consequence does not deter the philosopher, for he is not a man trying to become a god, but a man trying to find himself, that is, to discover his possibilities and limitations in this kind of a world. He knows that although the first words have been said in philosophy, the last have not. He does not have the privilege of escape into an orthodoxy as a refuge from dialectic, or an excuse for failing to ask the next question. Neither as a critic nor as a metaphysician is he entitled to issue directives or communiqués or periodic reports of progress.

No doubt some philosophers have had enormous confidence in their own constructions. There is a beautiful example in Bradley's *Appearance and Reality*:

We hold that our conclusion is certain, and that to doubt it logically is impossible. There is no other view, there is no other idea beyond the view here put forward. It is impossible rationally even to entertain the question of another possibility. Outside our main result there is nothing except the wholly unmeaning, or else something which on scrutiny is seen really not to fall outside. ... Our result, in brief, cannot be doubted, since it contains all possibilities.[3]

Few philosophers took this seriously enough to abandon their own points of view and become disciples of Bradley. They still had some questions to ask.

It will be best to state my major position immediately and then to develop it in detail. It is quite unoriginal, but I can take some comfort in Peirce's statement that "any philosophical doctrine that should be completely new could hardly fail to prove completely false."[4] The point is simply this: all philosophical systems, points-of-view, and so on, are most illuminating and successful when taken as perspectives. The idea, as I have said, is certainly not new. Its frequent appearance in the writings of major philosophers first drew my attention to it. But it seems to me to deserve a central rather than peripheral place in

[3] F. H. Bradley, *Appearance and Reality* (London, 1925), pp. 518–519.
[4] J. Buchler (ed.), *Philosophical Writings of Peirce* (New York, 1955), p. 269.

philosophy. It maintains that all knowledge is perspectival; that whatever is regarded as the real, objective world, is a world known, experienced and interpreted from the perspective of the human organism. Other alternatives to "perspective" are acceptable; for example, "point-of-view," "context," or "station." My claim is that a perspective is inescapable – which may be trivial, but it is often forgotten, and I think it has important as well as interesting consequences for philosophy. My argument will be largely inductive in character. I want to give a number of instances of the common occurrence of claims to perspectival knowledge in various disciplines. The first is from aesthetics and is reported by Ernst Cassirer:

> The painter Ludwig Richter relates in his memoirs how once when he was in Tivoli as a young man he and three friends set out to paint the same landscape. They were all firmly resolved not to deviate from nature; they wished to reproduce what they had seen as accurately as possible. Nevertheless the result was four totally different pictures, as different from one another as the personalities of the artists. From this experience the narrator concluded that there is no such thing as objective vision, and that form and color are always apprehended according to individual temperament.[5]

And this from a contemporary biologist:

> As a further example consider a rabbit. This is known as a perceptual thing by a cook, a bio-chemist, a physiologist, and an anatomist. But to each one it will be known as more, but the more will be different in each case. The bio-chemist knows the rabbit in terms of chemical composition, the physiologist knows it in terms of parts exhibiting functions and the anatomist knows it as a system of parts in spatial relations of a certain kind. Thus in one sense the object of study is different in the three cases depending on different modes of abstraction, and in another sense it is the same.[6]

Two philosophers make a similar point about history. Collingwood puts it this way:

> The historian (and for that matter the philosopher) is not God, looking at the world from above and outside. He is a man, and a man of his own time and place. He looks at the past from the point of view of the present: he looks at other countries and civilizations from the point of view of his own. This point of view is valid only for him and the people situated like him, but for him it *is* valid. He must stand firm in it, because it is the only one accessible to him, and unless he *has* a point of view he can see nothing at all.[7]

[5] E. Cassirer, *An Essay on Man* (Garden City, New York, 1954), p. 186.
[6] J. H. Woodger, *Biological Principles* (New York, 1929), pp. 139–140.
[7] R. G. Collingwood, *The Idea of History* (Oxford, 1946), p. 108.

And Karl Popper wrote:

It is possible, for example, to interpret "history" as the history of class struggle, or of the struggle of races for supremacy, or as the history of religious ideas, or as the history of the struggle between the "open" and the "closed" society, or as the history of scientific and industrial progress. All these are more or less interesting points of view, and *as such* perfectly unobjectionable. But historicists do not present them as such; they do not see that there is necessarily a plurality of interpretations which are fundamentally on the same level of both, suggestiveness and arbitrariness (even though some of them may be distinguished by their *fertility* − a point of some importance). Instead, they present them as doctrines or theories, asserting that "all history is the history of class struggle," etc. And if they actually find that their point of view is fertile, and that many facts can be ordered and interpreted in its light, then they mistake this for a confirmation, or even for a proof, of their doctrine.

On the other hand, the classical historians who rightly oppose this procedure are liable to fall into a different error. Aiming at objectivity, they feel bound to avoid any selective point of view; but since this is impossible, they usually adopt points of view without being aware of them. This must defeat their efforts to be objective, for one cannot possibly be critical of one's own approach, and conscious of its limitations, without being aware of it.

The way out of this dilemma, of course, is to be clear about the necessity of adopting a point of view; to state this point of view plainly, and always to remain conscious that it is one among many, and that even if it should amount to a theory, it may not be testable.[8]

The substitution of "philosophy" for "history" in this statement would describe my position very well. But there is also some support from a cultural anthropologist:

According to the conceptual framework of my culture, I perceive my own behavior differently from the way in which people of another cultural framework view theirs. And which of these is the true way? When I throw a ball, do I perform an aggressive causal act, as my culture predisposes me to believe? Or does the ball leave my hand, as the Greenland Eskimo puts it, or do I merely actualize the ball's potential to move as the Navaho would have it? These are different ways of perceiving the same situation, but which is the truth? Are they all true, all different facets of the same truth?

I turn to the study of other cultures largely to answer this question. I believe that these are all different codifications of the same reality, and different responses in terms of these codifications. My own culture, with its laws of logic, its principles of cognition, its rigidly defined limits of validation, offers me a strongly bounded and precategorized view of reality. This one way of perceiving; it is a finite way − yet reality, itself, I believe to be infinite.

When I study other cultures, I find a different codification, I get a

[8] K. R. Popper, *The Poverty of Historicism* (London, 1957), pp. 151–152.

different glimpse of reality, from a different starting point. I find other equally self-consistent systems of symbolization, with diametrically opposed principles of validation of experience. Thus I am enabled to some extent to go beyond my own finite view; I am enabled to see my culture as one of many possible systems of relating the self to the universe, and to question tenets and axioms of which I had never been aware (Dorothy Lee).[9]

Again, the substitution of "philosophy" for "culture" will illuminate my point. In his *Ideology and Utopia*, Karl Mannheim expresses the same theme:

One can point out with relative precision the factors which are inevitably forcing more and more persons to reflect not merely about the things of the world, but about thinking itself and even here not so much about truth in itself, as about the alarming fact that the same world can appear differently to different observers.[10]
If we examine the many types of ontological judgments with which different groups confront us, we begin to suspect that each group seems to move in a separate and distinct world of ideas and that these different systems of thought, which are often in conflict with one another, may in the last analysis be reduced to different modes of experiencing the "same" reality.[11]

In his extended study of personal knowledge Michael Polanyi rejects the ideal of scientific detachment and tries to show that into each instance of knowing every person makes a "passionate contribution" to what is being known. "Any attempt rigorously to eliminate our human perspective from our picture of the world must lead to absurdity."[12]

It is time now to terminate this string of evidence with statements from other well-known philosophers. Morris Cohen wrote in *A Preface to Logic*, "Metaphysical propositions are perspectives. They determine the point of view from which all human experience or all our sciences and anticipations can be coordinated."[13]

G. H. Mead is clearly supporting this position when he writes:

... it is only in so far as the individual acts not only in his own perspective but also in the perspective of others, especially in the common perspective of a group, that a society arises and its affairs become the objects of a

[9] D. Lee, *Freedom and Culture* (Englewood Cliffs, N.J., 1959), p. 2.
[10] K. Mannheim, *Ideology and Utopia* (London, 1949), p. 5.
[11] *Ibid.*, p. 89.
[12] M. Polanyi, *Personal Knowledge* (New York, 1958), p. 3.
[13] M. Cohen, *A Preface to Logic* (New York, 1944), pp. 62–63.

scientific inquiry. The limitation of social organization is found in the inability of individuals to place themselves in the perspectives of others, to take their points of view. I do not wish to belabor the point, which is commonplace enough, but to suggest that we find here an actual organization of perspectives, and that the principle of it is fairly evident. The principle is that the individual enters into the perspective of others, in so far as he is able to take their attitudes, or occupy their points of view.[14]

In spite of the astonishing range and depth of Alfred North Whitehead's philosophy he too knew that he could not be released from the boundaries of a perspective.

We can enlighten fragmentary aspects of intelligence. But there is always an understanding beyond our area of comprehension. The reason is that the notion of intelligence in pure abstraction from things understood is a myth. Thus a complete understanding is a perfect grasp of the Universe in its totality. We are finite beings; and such a grasp is denied to us.

This is not to say that there are finite aspects of things which are intrinsically incapable of entering into human knowledge. Whatever exists, is capable of knowledge in respect to the finitude of its connections with the rest of things. In other words, we can know anything in some of its perspectives. But the totality of perspectives involves an infinitude beyond finite knowledge.[15]

Recently a British philosopher, in reviewing English philosophy since 1900, wrote:

We have become familiar enough with the idea that phenomena may be viewed in more than one way, comprehended within more than one theory, interpreted by more than one set of explanatory concepts. It has thus become almost impossible to believe that some *one* way of seeing, some *one* sort of theory, has any exclusive claim to be the *right* way; the notion of "reality" itself, it would commonly be held, must be given its sense in terms of some particular theory or view, so that the claim that any such theory reveals or corresponds to "reality" can be given a circular justification which is also open, in just the same way, to quite other views as well (G. J. Warnock).[16]

George Santayana made the same point, more poetically, when he wrote:

Looking at the moon, one man may call it simply a light in the sky; another, prone to dreaming awake, may call it a virgin goddess; a more observant person, remembering that this luminary is given to waxing and waning, may call it the crescent; and a fourth, a full-fledged astronomer, may say ... that it is an extinct and opaque spheroidal satellite of

14 G. H. Mead, *The Philosophy of the Present* (Chicago, 1932), p. 165.
15 A. N. Whitehead, *Modes of Thought* (New York, 1958), p. 58.
16 G. J. Warnock, *English Philosophy Since 1900* (London, 1958), p. 144.

the earth, reflecting the light of the sun from a part of its surface. All these descriptions envisage the same object – otherwise no relevance, conflict, or progress could obtain among them. What the object is in its complete constitution and history will never be known by man. ...[17]

I will bring this, perhaps tedious and certainly repetitious, part of my argument to a close with a statement from a contemporary philosopher. (The cases, however, could be greatly increased.) Bertrand Russell wrote, in 1958:

I think we can, however imperfectly, mirror the world, like Leibniz's monads; and I think it is the duty of the philosopher to make himself as undistorting a mirror as he can. But it is also his duty to recognize such distortions as are inevitable from our very nature. Of these, the most fundamental is that we view the world from the point of view of the *here and now*, not with that large impartiality which theists attribute to the Deity. To achieve such impartiality is impossible for us, but we can travel a certain distance towards it. To show the road to this end is the supreme duty of the philosopher.[18]

All of these statements suggest that every philosophical system, all forms of religious belief and doctrine, indeed every scientific, ethical and aesthetic claim is an expression from a distinctive perspective. The position must be taken seriously and its consequences explored. Epistemologically this means that anything that is known or experienced in any way is grasped by capacities and within limitations that are strictly human. This would seem to be the starting point of all reflection on experience, a predicament that is utterly unavoidable. Recognition of this should have an immediate effect on our attitudes. We ought to regard with disfavor and distaste any dogmatic claim that there is just one way of looking at things, or one theory which is exclusively the right one. The truths man may reasonably affirm are not the unshakeable foundations of his intellectual world but always provisional formulations that give temporary relief from the fatigue of constant inquiry. Often these claims appear as contradictory because we cannot stand in all perspectives at once. This calls for tolerance as a creative force – not as indifference or resignation. A biographer of John Stuart Mill put the point well when he said about Mill:

[17] G. Santayana, *Scepticism and Animal Faith* (New York, 1929), pp. 176–177.
[18] B. Russell, "My Philosophical Development," *Hibbert Journal* 57 (1958), p. 8.

For him, truth was no single element, but a gem of many faces, each capable of different, even contradictory appearance. It was impossible to grasp the whole from a single point of view; and conversely, every honest point of view achieved an aspect of the truth. That any act of vision depends at least as much upon the situation and the circumstances of the seer as upon the object seen, was Mill's position in philosophy (Michael St. John Packe).[19]

It is here that criticism and perspective come together in philosophy. For anyone who criticizes without understanding is both a fool and a dogmatist. Comprehension, at some level, must always precede the criticism which depends so much upon the differences in linguistic patterns. Of course, not all perspectives can be reconciled. There are genuine conflicts in every important area of intellectual concern and thus to accept one side may necessarily lead to the rejection of another. Still, to acknowledge our perspectival predicament should make us willing to adopt temporarily the adversary's point of view so that we can know it from the inside.

Our perspectives are revealed in our judgments. This means that language has an enormously significant role in representing any perspective and that the minimum requirement for sharing a perspective is to understand the language – a chore not always accepted with equanimity. Thus the language of a Hegel or a Heidegger or a Husserl may be a barrier to getting into their contexts. But it is certainly clear that no single judgment can adequately represent the total perspective any more than one verified proposition makes a science, or one true statement a philosophy, or one cherished belief a religious creed. Our perspectives do not arise atomistically, nor are they constructed unconsciously (though unconscious elements may enter any perspective). They are finite harmonies, or tentative unities. Nothing can be in a perspective unless it stands in relationship to something else. An unrelated object is a perspectival impossibility – it could not be known, recognized, compared, combined, or in any other way become a part of human experience. Any change in relations necessarily changes the perspective. Similarly our judgments must be related or interconnected until a determinate point of view begins to emerge. This perspective, with the

[19] M. St. John Packe, *The Life of John Stuart Mill* (New York, 1954), p. 246.

aid of language, becomes potentially shareable. If this is not the case all hope of knowledge and community must be abandoned.

One cannot have a perspective without having a place to stand. And a serious philosopher has the duty to explore and bring to our attention everything of significance which he sees from his station. It is in such an existential context that inquiry can be free, discoveries can be made and viewpoints can be modified. Unhappily it is also evident that our perspectives may become so fixed and frozen that any modification is accomplished only with reluctance or even with agonizing reassessment. We have invented many ways of fixing perspectives – political legislation, moral codes, ecclesiastical doctrines, and perhaps scientific theory are common in civilization. They often claim finality, but the claims are specious. The fixing of perspectives is the characteristic of all orthodoxies, and fanaticisms. Irrationality may be defined as the unwillingness to share or participate in any way, in other perspectives. A fanatic is one who refuses to allow for alternative perspectives. To be creative in the arts, sciences, and in philosophy one must be able to release oneself from the "fixities" and find new ways of looking, new ways of judging, and new ways of describing what one sees. The perspectivist is rightly suspicious of all absolutes and all absolutists.

There are important consequences here for a theory of truth. If we must accept only those truths which are relative to a chosen or shared perspective then it is within intra-perspectival and inter-perspectival truths that we must work out our philosophies, our sciences, our arts, and our religions. Truth and knowledge are approximations to an ideal. They are partial and fragmentary. But that is not the same thing as to be false. What a philosopher can hope for is a greater articulation of the ideal as it is revealed in his unique perspective. When this is soberly and honestly done, and accepted as a duty, as Russell insisted, the philosopher achieves the mastery of the content of the perspective and is able to call to attention something ignored or missed in another's perspective. In this way philosophy, science, religion and art may each have a perspective of reality in human experience, and by sharing this, contribute to the establishment of a rational community. If these human interests are perspectively determined, then it is an error to regard them as necessarily hostile to each other. What seems incompatible from a narrow perspective may become reconcilable from a wider point of view.

There are at least two serious misconceptions of perspectivism. In the first place the point may be accepted too quickly and easily. It might be thought that since there is some truth wherever you look, it doesn't really matter where you stand. This is mockery, and distortion. To see from a perspective does not lead to a rejection of all standards and, therefore, invalidate all criticism. That there are different perspectives, each with varying glimpses of truth, is not something to be intuitively entertained by a superficially gay and hospitable mind which gives equal welcome to nonsense and wisdom without discrimination. Rather, it is something to be reflectively ascertained by a mind willing to subject itself to the discipline of trying to see from another's perspective and thus perhaps to enlarge and illuminate his own point of view. Our danger is not that there are too many perspectives. The real peril lies in the fact that we may become the victims of those who insist that their perspective alone is the right one. They would force us into a sameness in which the limits of permissible diversity are too narrowly prescribed.

The second misconception regards perspectivism as leading to the absence of all commitment and conviction, to a kind of anarchy in matters of belief. But I do not think this is a necessary consequence though we may have to admit it as a possible one. Scepticism has an historical and honorable place in philosophy. But scepticism is not the same thing as impatient dismissal or a perpetual arched eyebrow. As Santayana has said, it is an exercise – not a life. The perspectivist does not advocate an evasive neutrality or a passionless acquiescence in matters of belief. He can and should defend and attack, for then he may see more clearly the horizons of his own perspective, extend that of another, and together share some illumination. An honestly worked out perspective, which is nevertheless recognized as a perspective, does not mean lack of conviction or vacillation in belief. It simply means that we acknowledge our human fallibility, our humility, and our willingness to grow. There is no such thing as an incorrigible philosophy, or science, or art, or religion. The perspectivist keeps in mind the distinction between a temporarily dazzling scepticism and sober, persistent inquiry, which, because

of our limitations, can never rest in dogmatic certainty. Moreover, this stance permits a splendid independence of thought. One
is not tempted to live up to the intellectual Joneses and dissipate
his mental resources in the struggle to appear well-off, respectable
and up-to-date; or to be annexed too quickly by the fresh
"isms" and the newest style of analysis. There is a detachment
that is available to the perspectivist which keeps him from rejecting ancient problems just because they are no longer modish,
or because they cannot be expressed clearly in preferred linguistic
patterns.

But it would be a mistake to think that the human limitations
we must endure are the kind that can be surmounted. We cannot
make an assault on them or take measures against them. We
cannot free ourselves from them by changing the social order,
voting the right man into political office, getting the proper
amount of exercise, mastering calculus, or modifying the genetic
code. There is no escape from the perspectival predicament,
though one can, of course, shift and share perspectives. That I
have taken a feature of visual experience and extended it to cover
all thought and action, is obvious. It is certainly reminiscent of
Stephen Pepper's root-metaphor method, although I have not
the space to derive and develop the categories that might be
appropriate for explanation if we adopt this position. All philosophical views must start with truisms, or, at the very least, with
something taken as true. Although we are limited, we are not,
therefore, diseased. We cannot be cured of our fallibility, but we
need not be morbid about it either. Rather, it makes the whole
human enterprise somewhat uncertain and exciting.

My argument so far, if it can be dignified with such a name, has
only served to call attention to the pervasive and inescapable
fact of perspectives. But, if I may extend the metaphor, one
cannot have a perspective unless one has a place to stand. This is
as close as I can come to a defense of realism. That there is a
world not of my own making; that it had its own way of existing
before I experienced it and will continue to have it when I am no
longer able to experience; that all thought and action are completely unintelligible without the assumption of an external,
independent, reality – all this seems to me to be the minimum
requirement of a philosophy of perspectives. We cannot ask here

for proof. I do not know what sense of the word "proof" is needed for this task. G. E. Moore insisted that he could prove the existence of an external world by holding up his right hand and saying, "Here is one hand," and then by holding up his left and saying, "And here is another." He regarded this as perfectly rigorous. Contemporary philosophers have questioned its rigor but have failed to supply a much better argument. W. E. Hocking reported a conversation with A. N. Whitehead about "The Real," in which Whitehead remarked: "The simplest notion of The Real ... is History. And what is the prime character of History? Compulsion – symbolized by the traffic cop – No, this is still too intellectual – *being tackled at Rugby, there is the Real.* Nobody who hasn't been knocked down has the slightest notion of what the Real is. ..."[20] Few would accept this as an improvement on Moore, yet it would be silly to deny the experience of "encountering" something. What this something is *per se*, what it is without man, we can never know except from our particular perspective. But whatever is distinguishable in any perspective is real. A philosophy that demands the absolute distinction between appearance and reality is a failure. Appearances are realities in different perspectives. Something is not just real to us – it is always real from a specific point of view. Thus there is possible an infinite number of perspectives of the real, and inexhaustible descriptions of it. The real cannot be inventoried, nor catalogued, for what is an item in one perspective, or true in one context, or meaningful in one system, may receive radical modification in another.

Within the perspectival predicament we can distinguish between the perspectival standpoint, interpretation, and objective. Our standpoint is clearly that of fallible human creatures able to transcend occasionally some of our limitations. We are objects in space and time but we are not things. We are persons with certain dispositions and capacities which make us distinct from other sorts of things but do not separate us from the natural order. We see with human eyes, hear with human ears, touch with human hands. If we had microscopes for eyes, audio-tubes for ears, and radio waves for hands we would not know our

[20] G. L. Kline (ed.), *Alfred North Whitehead, Essays on His Philosophy* (Englewood Cliffs, N.J., 1963), p. 13.

familiar world. There would be a different one in a different perspective, as John Locke pointed out. Upon occasion we may get into these perspectives for a while, but soon must return to our natural station.

The perspectival interpretation is our attempt to describe what we see from the perspectival standpoint. Here belong all the "ists" and "isms": the idealists, materialists, pragmatists, theists, positivists, existentialists, Buddhists, mechanists, vitalists – to mention only a few of a very large company. Certainly the perspectivist does not want to reduce the list nor to make light of their contributions. He knows that serious philosophy can be done only within a perspective and that every philosopher, no matter what his perspective, has the duty, as Russell says, "to make himself as undistorting a mirror as he can." Why defend one interpretation, rather than another? William James thought temperament had a good deal to do with it. And we do know that certain moods or dispositions are suitable in one perspective but not in another. A clashing of moods may distort the perspective and make it difficult if not impossible to understand all that it suggests or embodies. Thus the mood of the laboratory is inappropriate in a worship service, and the mood of a football game is inappropriate in a concert hall. Of course, I do not mean "inappropriate" in the sense of "etiquette." I mean that the mood itself can be an obstacle or an aid to understanding, discovery and enjoyment.

The logical rigor of one perspective or the aesthetic appeal of another may be important reasons for any choice. Or a perspective may be found to be compatible because it makes possible a greater degree of coherence of our reliable information. But I think I would stress fertility, that is, the capacity of a perspective not only to order and interpret a wide range of facts but also its power of suggestiveness. It should permit both control and novelty. Fertility, of course, is not proof or confirmation of a position but it may be a significant aspect in its defense. As there are open and closed societies, so there are open and closed philosophical theories. I prefer an open society and an open philosophical perspective. If philosophies are perspectives and philosophizing is the effort to bring out all the significant features of a perspective, then we need not be dismayed by the charge that there is no progress in philosophy. Its seemingly interminable disputes and differences are ways of bringing now this and now that into the foreground of interest. Perspectives in philosophy will not give final answers to specific philosophical issues because there are no final answers to the fertile questions. To recognize, for example, that all philosophies are perspectives, will not provide us with built-in solutions to such questions as "are there universals?" Or, "is time real?" Or, "does man survive his bodily death?" Or, "is any being absolutely perfect?" Or, "do we really know another's mind?" But it will encourage us to ask what aspects of experience lead us to raise such questions, or what characteristics of experience give rise to these persistent and often value-laden concerns.

The perspectival objective is the reality which is interpreted. It is the "real" of perspective realism, although it has many other names in the history of thought. It is extraordinarily hospitable, permitting but not demanding many alternative interpretations of itself. It is that which in certain arrangements becomes a vast burning gas; in others, a blind impulse toward complexity; and in others, a self-awareness of existence. Some men have said it was created, others that it just is. Some men have said it leads to confrontation with God, others that it leads to nothing beyond itself. Some men have seen in it something that responds to adoration. To others it seems to be sheer indifference. Here are the roots of tragedy. Since no man can have all perspectives, and those he can share are extremely limited, there will always be potentialities unrealized. In part, tragedy emerges in the conflict of values which are equally good but not mutually achievable. But more generally, it lies in the fact that to stand thoroughly committed to one perspective may exclude the possibility of standing in another. Tragedy is a timeless principle of which suffering and evil are temporal phases. Every fulfilled hope and every realized ideal has left behind a landscape of might-have-beens, without which the world is somehow tragically impoverished. The proper response to tragedy is not horror, or resignation or despair. It is, as Dewey has said, reconciliation, which brings together in understanding the differences of our different perspectives. The sense of tragedy is an achievement of enlightened maturity. It is only dimly present in the young who make brief esxcursion out of the security of their samenesses, or their restricted perspectives.

Perspectives may be shared; hence interperspectival communication is possible. Thus a dialectic of perspectives emerges where dialectic is conceived as "talking things through." It need not lead to acquiescence but it should approach understanding. Trans-perspective experiences are often regarded as evidence in support of an hypothesis, or as carrying weight in a court, or as justification for a rule of behavior. It is also characteristic of perspectives that they may overlap. Thus my perspective as a philosopher overlaps my perspective as a member of a college faculty. Some historical and intellectual contexts will permit certain perspectives which others must disallow. There will undoubtedly be a conflict of perspectives on many occasions which cannot be resolved by stubborn reiteration, nor by self-imposed blindness, nor by claims to infallibility. When this occurs the uses of reason come to our aid. To repeat: perspective realism regards philosophy not as a challenge to debate, but as an appeal for help. Its aim is not victory but cooperative inquiry.

I have used the term "perspective realism" a number of times. I thought I had invented it many years ago but in 1956 McGilvary's Carus Lectures were published (they were delivered in 1939) under the title *Toward a Perspective Realism*.[21] I have no recollection of ever seeing the term before 1958, when I found McGilvary's book and read it with some astonishment. He said many of the things I had been thinking about for a long time. The work was incomplete, as is well-known, but full of suggestions. When Arthur Murphy reviewed it for the *Journal of Philosophy*, he thought that "perspectivism" was through as a viable and tenable position. It had gone, he said, about as far as it could. Since his criticisms are those that would occur to most opponents of perspective realism, I think it will be useful to quote extensively from the last part of his review:

It seems to me that "perspectivism" here has gone about as far as it can go. For we are now told not only that everything is whatever it is perceived to be but also whatever it is interpreted as being in the "perspective" or "point of view" of thought. McGilvary observes that "One

21 E. B. McGilvary, *Toward a Perspective Realism*, ed. by A. G. Ramsperger (La Salle, III, 1956).

advantage that can be claimed for this perspectivist view is that it recognizes that other views, even opposing views, are tenable from the respective points of view of those who hold them" (p. 194). Thus epistemological idealism, Lovejoyean dualism, and the doctrines of the fundamentalist who upholds the literal truth of the Biblical doctrine of creation are irrefutable, given the premises from which they proceed. "And how can you disprove that premise except by drawing your conclusion from a fundamentally different premise?" (p. 195). In the perspective of "perspectivism" this is the way that matters stand. But for opposing views it is not. In the perspectives of the fundamentalist and Professor Lovejoy, all views are *not* equally tenable and for them it is not an "advantage" in a theory that it maintains that they are. Between these "apparently" conflicting claims "who's to judge?" There seems to be no place here for a judgment that claims a truth that is not (in another equally tenable perspective) compatible with its own negation (p. 163).

... we now know that if "perspectivism" is correct, it is only in the perspective of McGilvary and others similarly conditioned that such information is evidence for anything at all. In the perspective of Bergson, of early man, or of Professor Lovejoy, the facts tell different stories. These perspectives are no less "natural" as physically conditioned, than that of the perspectivist, and in each the real relational character of things is objectively disclosed. So why should we say "if perspectivism is correct"? Of course it is, and so are the theories that reject it. In such a situation, once more, "who's to judge?" McGilvary does not tell us ... (pp. 163–164).

It will be clear from the foregoing discussion that in the reviewer's judgment McGilvary's "perspective realism" is an untenable philosophical theory and that his own development of it suffices to show that this is the case. For those of us who, thirty years ago, regarded such "perspectivism" as a hopeful and important contribution to epistemology, this is a disappointing conclusion to reach. But it is also an instructive one. It is by the thoroughness and honesty of his inquiry that McGilvary has made plain its self-defeating implications and the work that he has done will not need to be done again (pp. 164–165).[22]

If Murphy is right that this work will not have to be done again, what will we do with the statements previously quoted from many sources? Certainly the philosophers were not being merely coy nor excessively humble or modest. They were, I am sure, acknowledging the inescapable human perspectival predicament. We think and act within an encompassing reality which we can never have as an object of knowledge, but of which we are a part. Any effort to seize the whole as it is beyond the human condition will fail, for it ignores the essential elements of subjectivity in all knowledge.

In the *Timaeus*, Plato wrote:

[22] A. E. Murphy, "McGilvary's Perspective Realism." *The Journal of Philosophy* 56. 4 (1959), pp. 163–165.

Wherefore, Socrates, if in our treatment of a great host of matters regarding the Gods and the generation of the Universe we prove unable to give accounts that are always in all respects self-consistent and perfectly exact, be not Thou surprised; rather we should be content if we can furnish accounts that are inferior to none in likelihood, remembering that both I who speak and you who judge are but human creatures, so that it becomes us to accept the likely account of these matters and forbear to search beyond it (*Ti.* 29c–d).[23]

We are, even as philosophers, but "human creatures." This is our perspective, from which we can only give "likely accounts."

Grinnell College, Grinnell, Iowa

---

[23] *Plato*, Vol. VII, translated by R. G. Bury, *op. cit.*, p. 23.

WAS HEISST AUTORITÄT?

HELMUT KUHN

Mit welcher Erschütterung diese unsere Zeit erfahren wird, wie hochgespannte Hoffnung vergebens gegen die Furcht vor unausdenklichen Katatastrophen kämpft, wie bohrend die Frage nach der Zukunft gestellt wird von Menschen, die ihren Standort auf früher Geschaffenem und Überliefertem verloren haben – diese sich ausbreitende Unseligkeit des aktiven Bewusstseins lässt sich von keinem Symptom deutlicher ablesen als dem Zerfall der Autorität. Gegen diesen Zerfall zu Felde zu ziehen scheint sinnlos. Müsste doch der Verteidiger der Autorität selbst Autorität besitzen oder sich auf Autoritäten berufen dürfen. Was er wiederherstellen will, müsste er als wirksam voraussetzen. Er müsste seine Apologie auf eine in der Geschichte wirksame Tradition gründen können. Aber er wird finden, dass dieser Grund aufgesprengt oder mindestens tief erschüttert ist durch eine Interpretation, welche die Geschichte unter Leitbegriffen wie Seinsverlust, Nihilismus, Entfremdung als die Selbstzerstörung der Vergangenheit versteht. Der so Entwurzelte soll seine Zukunft um den Preis der Vergangenheit erkaufen. Aber welche Zukunft?

In diesem Dilemma mag eine Besinnung auf das Wesen der Autorität am Platz sein, umsomehr, als dieser Essay einen Forscher ehren soll, dem wir tiefe Einblicke in *die* Autorität verdanken, deren Quellen in der philosophisch-literarischen Tradition des Abendlandes fliessen. Als wegweisend stellen wir unserer Analyse einen Abschnitt des "Autorität "betitelten Kapitels aus Goethes *Materialien zur Geschichte der Farbenlehre* (3. Abt.) voran:

Indem wir nun von Überlieferung sprechen, sind wir unmittelbar aufgefordert, zugleich von Autorität zu reden. Denn genau betrachtet, so ist jede Autorität eine Art Überlieferung. Wir lassen die Existenz, die Würde, die Gewalt von irgendeinem Dinge gelten, ohne dass wir seinen Ursprung, sein Herkommen, seinen Wert deutlich einsehen und erkennen. ... Gegen die Autorität verhält sich der Mensch, so wie gegen vieles andere, beständig schwankend. Er fühlt in seiner Dürftigkeit, dass er, ohne sich auf etwas Drittes zu stützen, mit seinen Kräften nicht auslangt. Dann aber, wenn das Gefühl seiner Macht und Herrlichkeit in ihm aufgeht, stösst er das Hülfreiche von sich und glaubt, für sich selbst und andre hinzureichen.

Das Kind bequemt sich meist mit Ergebung unter die Autorität der Eltern; der Knabe sträubt sich dagegen; der Jüngling entflieht ihr, und der Mann lässt sie wieder gelten, weil er sich deren mehr oder weniger selbst verschafft, weil die Erfahrung ihn gelehrt hat, dass er ohne Mitwirkung anderer doch nur wenig ausrichte.

Ebenso schwankt die Menschheit im ganzen. Bald sehen wir um einen vorzüglichen Mann sich Freunde, Schüler, Anhänger, Begleiter, Mitlebende, Mitwohnende, Mitstreitende versammeln. Bald fällt eine solche Gesellschaft, ein solches Reich wieder in vielerlei Einzelnheiten auseinander. Bald werden Monumente älterer Zeiten, Dokumente früherer Gesinnungen, göttlich verehrt, buchstäblich aufgenommen; jedermann gibt seine Sinne, seinen Verstand darunter gefangen; alle Kräfte werden aufgewendet, das Schätzbare solcher Überreste darzutun, sie bekannt zu machen, zu kommentieren, zu erläutern, zu erklären, zu verbreiten und fortzupflanzen. Bald tritt dagegen, wie jene bilderstürmende, so hier eine schriftstürmende Wut ein; es täte not, man vertilgte bis auf die letzte Spur das, was bisher so grossen Wertes geachtet wurde. Kein ehemals ausgesprochenes Wort soll gelten, alles, was weise war, soll als närrisch erkannt werden, was heilsam war, als schädlich, was sich lange Zeit als förderlich zeigte, nunmehr als eigentliches Hindernis.

"Autorität" bezeichnet, wie seine Quelle, das lateinische *auctoritas* andeutet, eine Art von Urheberschaft. Was da unter der Form der Autorität entspringt und sich geltend macht, ist der normative Anspruch, der von einer Person (oder Personen) ausgeht. In diesem allgemeinen Bedeutungsrahmen aber zeigt sich das Wort als mehrdeutig. Es benennt (1) eine eigenschaftliche Wirkung (nur im Singular), (2) das Subjekt dieser Wirkung (die Person selbst oder deren Äusserung, (3) das Amt oder die Funktion als Rechtsgrund der Wirkung. Im Folgenden wird die erste dieser Bedeutungen im Mittelpunkt stehen, während die beiden anderen als Ableitungen behandelt werden. Dabei unterscheiden wir: (I) *Die faktische Autorität*, (II) *Die Rechtfertigung des Anspruchs* (*Autorität und Freiheit*), (III) *Die Wirkungssphären der Autorität*.

I. FAKTISCHE AUTORITÄT

Autorität ist eine soziale Wirklichkeit, d.i. eine Beziehung von

Person (oder Personen) zu Person (oder Personen). Auf der einen
Seite steht die Person (Mensch oder Gott), die als Inhaber von
Autorität den Anspruch erhebt, als Richtmass anerkannt zu
werden, auf der anderen Seite die diesen Anspruch Anerkennenden. Der Anspruch kann unmittelbar durch Befehl oder Anordnung geäussert werden wie im Verhältnis zwischen Herren und
Knecht oder mittelbar, durch Lehren, Verhaltensregeln, Grund-
sätze oder vorbildliche Schöpfungen, und diese Vermittlungs-
formen heissen dann, ebenso wie ihr Urheber, autoritativ. Die
Person in Autorität bestimmt, die Person als Adressat der Bestimmung unterwirft sich. So konstituiert jede Autorität eine
Art von Herrschaftsverhältnis. Aber die Bestimmungskraft des
normativen Anspruchs – und demgemäss die Art des Herr-
schaftsverhältnisses – ist verschieden je nach Umfang des Anspruchs. Er kann (a) *schlechthin total* sein, wie im Verhältnis
Gottes zum Menschen, oder des Vaters zum unmündigen Kind:
er bezieht sich dann auf die personale Existenz als Ganzes; (b)
spezifisch-ganzheitlich wie innerhalb der Berufsordnung: die
Person als solche in ihrer Fähigkeit zur Mitwirkung am gemein-
schaftlichen Leben wird durch eine Norm in Anspruch genommen, die gegründet ist in der zu erfüllenden Aufgabe, vertreten
und geltend gemacht durch eine vorgesetzte Person – die Autorität des Meisters gegenüber den Lehrlingen, des Herrschers gegenüber Untertanen oder Staatsbürgern, des Vorgesetzten gegenüber Untergebenen; oder schliesslich (c) *okkasionell und partiell*
– die Autorität des Fachmanns gegenüber den Fachunkundigen,
des Verkehrspolizisten gegenüber Fahrern und Passanten, des
Arztes gegenüber dem Patienten. In all diesen autoritativen
Über- und Unterordnungsverhältnissen wird von dem durch
Autorität Ermächtigten Macht ausgeübt. Doch ist Autorität
nicht gleichzusetzen mit Macht. Von Autorität wird nur dort gesprochen, wo der massgebende Anspruch besiegelt wird durch den
freien Akt der Hinnahme auf Seiten des Angesprochenen.
Autorität liegt demnach in der Mitte zwischen blossem Ansehen,
das als solches noch keine Ansprüche erhebt, und einer Macht, die
ihre Ansprüche notfalls auch gegen den Willen der Angesprochenen durchsetzt. Da alle menschliche Gemeinschaft im geordneten
Zusammenwirken besteht, da aber Zusammenwirken nur möglich ist auf Grund der Anerkennung gemeinsamer Normen (des

Guten überhaupt, des allgemein oder im besonderen Fall Nützlichen, Förderlichen, Trefflichen usf.) so ergibt sich, dass alle
Gemeinschaftsformen gelenkt, durchdrungen und zusammenge-
halten werden durch ein differenziertes Zuteilungssystem von
Autorität. Dabei ist zu unterscheiden zwischen einer funktionell
zugeteilten und einer erworbenen Autorität, anders gesagt
zwischen einer Amtsautorität, die den Amtsträger zu bestimmten autoritativen Akten rechtlich ermächtigt, und einer persönlichen Autorität. Die Stabilität einer Gemeinschaftsordnung
beruht auf der Autorität der ersten, ihre Lebendigkeit auf der
zweiten Art von Autorität. Im ersten Fall *hat* eine Person Autorität kraft ihrer Stellung, im zweiten *ist* sie Autorität durch sich
selbst.

II. DIE RECHTFERTIGUNG DES ANSPRUCHS
(AUTORITÄT UND FREIHEIT)

Autorität ist zunächst ein bipolares gesellschaftliches Faktum.
Aber dies Faktum muss ständig neu vollzogen und verwirklicht
werden. Der wesentliche Anteil bei diesem Vollzug kommt nicht
dem zu, der Autorität besitzt, sondern dem, der sie anerkennt.
Denn Autorität kann wohl stattfinden, ohne dass die autoritative
Person den Anspruch auf Geltung zum Ausdruck bringt, nicht aber
ohne die gewährte Anerkennung. Die Frage ist also, wie wir dazu
kommen, die für alle Autorität konstitutive Anerkennung zu
gewähren und den darin implizierten Akt der Unterwerfung zu
vollziehen. Widerstrebt das nicht dem natürlichen Hang zur
Selbstbehauptung in Freiheit? In Beantwortung der Frage ist
zunächst auf die Ratlosigkeit und die Gesellschaftlichkeit des
Menschen hinzuweisen. Die fragliche Anerkennung bedeutet für
den Anerkennenden nicht allein und nicht in erster Linie ein
Bezwungenwerden und also eine Einengung freien Tun-wollens,
sondern im Gegenteil eine Befreiung: die Autorität zeigt ihm, der
nicht weiss, wohin er sich wenden und was er tun soll, den Weg
der Nacheiferung. Sie zeigt ihm, was er tun oder werden kann.
Autorität kann blind machen. Nichtsdestoweniger kann und soll
sie ihrem Wesen entsprechend belehren. Im übrigen ist ein
starkes Motiv aller Anerkennung *die* Anerkennung, die bereits
von anderen gewährt wird. Darauf weisen Sprichwörter hin wie:

"Wer hat, dem wird gegeben," oder "Nothing succeeds like success" (Dean Inge). Kraft der "imitativen Akkumulation" – Anerkennung entzündet Anerkennung – erheben sich die für alle sichtbaren autoritativen Figuren über die Fülle derer, die unverächtliche Ansprüche auf Beachtung und Nacheiferung machen könnten. Diese Regel der Kristallisation der Autorität in wenigen ragenden Gestalten ist ein unentbehrliches Moment in jeder Traditionsbildung, wie überhaupt Tradition definiert werden kann als Autorität in geschichtlicher Fortwirkung. Sie unterscheidet sich (wenn nicht immer in fragloser Deutlichkeit) von der Mode, die Bewunderung aber keine oder nur ephemere Autorität erzeugt.

Die Neigung, als Autorität anzuerkennen, was viele oder alle anerkennen und vielleicht von je anerkannt haben, kann Anlass geben zu jenem billigen Zynismus, der die Menschenherde mit dem Hammeln des Panurge vergleicht. In Wirklichkeit ist das bei den Stoikern beliebte Argument *e consensu omnium* (oder: *gentium*) – der Geltungsanspruch dessen, was immer, überall und bei allen gilt (Cic. *Tusc.* 1. 13. 30) – nicht sinnlos, solange wir an dem Begriff einer sich gleichbleibenden menschlichen Natur festhalten. Und Aristoteles konnte mit guten Gründen die Ansicht verteidigen, dass Viele als Gesamtheit in Sitten und Einsicht die Einzelnen übertreffen (Arist. *Pol.* 3. 11). Dennoch kann der Anspruch der Autorität durch keine faktische Übereinstimmung gerechtfertigt werden. Die Gültigkeit des *"Athanasius contra mundum"* kann sich in immer neuen Situationen wiederholen. Und so wesentlich ist die Fähigkeit und das Recht des Einzelnen, jede von menschlicher Zustimmung besiegelte Autorität durch Prüfung herauszufordern und sie, wenn sie die Prüfung nicht besteht, zu verwerfen, dass die Verneinung dieses Rechts die Freiheit des Menschen und damit seine personale Würde verneinen muss.

Gewiss, Autorität ist traditionsbildend. Aber sie trägt auch in sich die Möglichkeit einer Kritik aller gesellschaftlichen Faktizität und ihrer Ansprüche. Diese dialektische Wahrheit spiegelt sich in dem scheinbaren Widerspruch, der die wirkliche Verteilung der Autorität in der Geschichte kennzeichnet. Auf der einen Seite gilt das Alte als ehrwürdig, gerechtfertigt durch Bewährung, Quelle unfraglicher Autorität. Der Skeptiker David

Hume hat auf dieser Überzeugung seine konservative Staats-philosophie aufgebaut. Auf der anderen ist das Alte das Veraltete. Es gilt, das Neuentdeckte zu sehen und sich danach zu richten. Dann wird Originalität oder Fortschrittlichkeit zum Ausweis der Autorität. Doch ist es offensichtlich, dass keine der beiden ein-ander widersprechenden Legitimationsweisen eine echte Recht-fertigung liefern kann. Wir sprechen von einer Prüfung, die der An-erkennung von Autorität vorauszugehen hat. Noch immer bleibt die Frage offen, welchen Masstabs sich diese Prüfung bedient.

Die Entscheidung, so muss die Antwort lauten, liegt bei der Frage, ob der Anspruch der jeweiligen Autorität *auf Wahrheit* beruht. Und wir nehmen an, dass die dem Einzelnen unmittelbar zugängliche Wahrheit jedes weitere Fragen nach Berechtigung abschneidet. Wahrheit ist demnach der eigentliche und letzte Ursprung von Autorität. Aber öffnen wir mit dieser Behauptung nicht Tor und Tür für eine hemmungslose, alle reale Autorität auflösende Kritik? Nun – das Problematische der an sich unum-stösslichen Behauptung liegt in der Redeweise von einer "dem Einzelnen unmittelbar zugänglichen Wahrheit." Dieser Satz, absolut genommen, ist genau so unhaltbar wie der gegenteilige Satz, wonach dem Einzelnen in seiner durchschnittlichen Exis-tenz der Zugang zur Wahrheit überhaupt verwehrt ist. Das Phänomen der Autorität enfaltet sich in einer Wirklichkeit, die zwischen diesen Extremen liegt. Autorität muss sich prüfen lassen; dennoch ist Autorität gerade darum unentbehrlich, weil sie uns im Einzelfall die Wahrheitsprüfung erspart. Ihre Funk-tion und Bedeutung für den Aufbau des menschlichen Daseins beruht auf der Abstufung der Zugänglichkeit der Wahrheit nicht nur nach Personen sondern nach Regionen der Wahrheit, denen verschiedene Wirkungssphären der Autorität zugeordnet sind.

III. WIRKUNGSSPHÄREN DER AUTORITÄT

Die freie Hinnahme der Autorität verlangt nach einer Mög-lichkeit der Prüfung des autoritativen Anspruchs durch den Angesprochenen. Nun ist die Wahrheit als Basis der Autorität, auf welche die Prüfung zielt, Wahrheit bezüglich des jeweils Guten oder Nicht-guten, d.h., die Prüfung ist Sache der prak-tischen Vernunft. Wenn wir nun der auf Rechtfertigung zielenden

Prüfung im einzelnen nachgehen, bedienen wir uns wiederum
– in umgekehrter Reihenfolge – der dreifachen Unterscheidung
nach Wirkungsumfang, und wir beginnen mit: (c) *Die Autorität
okkasionell-partieller Natur.* Der Fahrer folgt blindlings den
Anordnungen der Verkehrspolizei, den Signalen wie auch der
mündlichen Anordnung. Sie sind für ihn Autorität. Er weiss, dass
eine Verkehrsordnung nötig ist und er akzeptiert die im Rahmen
dieser Ordnung erlassenen Vorschriften als sinnvoll. Er braucht
sich an der Strassenkreuzung nicht mit der Überlegung aufzu-
halten, ob die Vorfahrtssignale aufs zweckmässigste angebracht
sind – er braucht und er darf es nicht. Er muss den Akt der für
alle Autorität konstitutiven *Annahme* vollziehen, der nicht
Aufhebung, aber Suspendierung der Prüfungsmöglichkeit impliziert – jenes Sich-anvertrauen, Auf-Treu-und-Glauben Hin-
nehmen, ohne welches ein Mitspielen im alltäglichen Dasein unmöglich wäre, am wenigsten in dem mit komplizierten Apparaten
umstellten Dasein des modernen Zivilisationsmenschen. Die
Güter, um die es hier geht (z.B. Verkehrssicherheit oder Gesund-
heit) sind unproblematisch, ihrem Sinn nach leicht erkennbar,
und die Autorität ist vorwiegend funktionaler, d.h. nicht-perso-
naler Art. Sie haftet an der Rolle des Einzelnen, nicht an seiner
Persönlichkeit.

(b) *Die Autorität spezifisch-ganzheitlicher* Natur, verkörpert in
dem Staatsmann, Heerführer, Schriftsteller, Künstler, Gelehrten,
Forscher, Erfinder. Der normative Anspruch ergeht hier an den
ganzen Menschen, doch nicht an den Menschen als solchen,
sondern an ihn in spezifischer Eingrenzung: an ihn als politisches
Wesen, das Gefolgschaft zu leisten vermag, oder als kunstlieben-
des oder als wissensdurstiges Wesen, das sich bezaubern, hin-
reissen oder belehren lässt. Auch hier bewegen wir uns noch wie
bei Autorität der partiellen Art (c) im Bereich von spezifischen
Diensten und Leistungen. Aber diese Leistungen lassen sich von
der Ganzheit der Person nur unvollständig ablösen, und der von
ihnen hergeleitete normative Anspruch greift tiefer in das
persönliche Dasein hinein – wir sind unterwegs zur Autorität vom
Typus (a). Die Frage nach dem die Autorität begründenden
Guten geht hier zwar nicht unmittelbar auf "das gute Leben,"
aber sie rührt doch an dies entscheidende Problem. Demgemäss
wird Autorität zu einer vorwiegend persönlichen Auszeichnung.

Einmal errungen haftet sie am Namen. Das Aufsteigen zu solcher Autorität wird hier nicht allein, aber doch zuerst und vor allem im Binnenkreis der Sachkenner und Mit-könner erworben, und hier wirkt sie sich schulbildend, traditionssetzend oder bahnbrechend aus; und das Hinauswirken über diesen Kreis auf die breite Öffentlichkeit ist (nicht immer aber oft) Folge jenes ersten Erfolgs. Das rechtfertigende Gute liegt hier im Wesen der spezifischen Tätigkeit selbst – das öffentliche Wohl im Wirken des Staatsmannes, die wortgewaltige Weisheit im Tun des Schriftstellers, die Wahrheitsentdeckung im Forschen, die Schönheit im Schaffen des Künstlers. Das sind Formen des Guten, deren Beurteilung zwar in besondererem Mass dem Urteil der Sachkenner unterliegt, aber nicht im Sinn eines ausschliesslichen Vorrechts: ein viel grösserer Kreis, die ganze "gebildete Öffentlichkeit" steht im Lichtkreis solcher Autorität und wirkt an ihr mit. Wir haben also, soziologisch gesprochen, zwischen einem Innenkreis und einem Aussenkreis der Autorität zu unterscheiden: der erste das Ursprungsfeld, der zweite die Sphäre der Ableitung. Die Art der Ableitung aber differenziert sich auf einer Skala zwischen zwei Extremen. An dem einen Pol steht das künstlerische Werk: der Innenkreis der Mitschaffenden, Nachschaffenden und Kenner geht unmerklich über in den weiten Kreis der Kunstliebenden. Autorität verbindet sich hier mit der Kraft der Menschenbildung und mit dem Glanz des Ruhms. Am anderen Pol gruppieren sich die Leistungen höchst spezialisierter Art wie die Entdeckungen des Naturforschers. Auch der "Mann auf der Strasse" ist bereit, die Autorität eines Einstein oder Heisenberg zu akzeptieren, weil er die Autorität der Wissenschaft akzeptiert. Nicht Ruhm aber Berühmtheit ist hier zu erlangen. Eine besondere, nicht auf dieser Skala lokalisierbare Stellung nimmt der Herrscher, das Staatsoberhaupt und der Staatsmann ein. Er verfügt über kein hochspezialisiertes Wissen oder Können. Das Gemeinwohl, dessen Förderung ihm obliegt, ist verständlich für alle, wenn auch in verschiedenen Graden der Klarheit: so tendieren die beiden Kreise zur Verschmelzung. Wie beim Künstler kann hier Autorität sich mit Ruhm verbinden. Auf der anderen Seite aber liegt die Quelle der Autorität in Funktion und Rang, und erst in zweiter Linie in der Person, die den Rang verkörpert. Dabei ist die persönliche Autorität für den leitenden Staatsmann schlechthin unentbehrlich. Denn er hat Macht. Macht aber ohne Autorität ist politisch unerträglich. Der Mächtige, der keine Autorität besitzt, muss die ihm verweigerte Anerkennung dennoch fordern und notfalls zu erzwingen suchen: statt autoritativ zu sein wird sein Regiment dann autoritär; und das ist ein anderes Wort für despotisch.

Öffentliche Autorität ist eine Frucht der Übereinstimmung, die ihrerseits wieder Übereinstimmung erhält und erzeugt. So kann weder ein Staat noch überhaupt irgend eine menschliche Gemeinschaft ohne Autorität existieren. In anerkannten Autoritäten spiegelt sich der in Begriffen nie adäquat auszudrückende Kanon der gemeinsamen Existenz. So bedeutet Autoritätsverfall Desorientierung und Gemeinschaftszerfall. In das Chaos muss dann gewaltsam eine Art von Ordnung gebracht werden: mit den sog. Führern der auf den totalitären Staat zusteuernden Massenbewegungen unseres Jahrhunderts bietet sich, von Propaganda ausstaffiert, ein Autoritätsersatz an. Wohl kann die Berufung auf Autoritäten ein Symptom der Erstarrung sein – ein Surrogat für eigenes Denken. Doch ihr Missbrauch darf nicht den Sinn für den Nutzen ihres Gebrauchs verdunkeln. Sie liefert die für eine gebildete Verständigung unentbehrlichen Kurzformeln des Denkens und leiht den in der Tradition schlummernd Erkenntnissen lebendige Gegenwart. Mitgegenwärtig in aller öffentlichen Autorität ist eine fundamentale Anerkennung, welche die Lebenswürdigkeit des Daseins der eignen Person, des eignen Volkes, und der Völker überhaupt in der menschlichen Geschichte bejaht. Der Nihilismus, d.i. die Verneinung der Lebenswürdigkeit, löscht auch mit einem Atemzug die Rechtmässigkeit aller Autorität aus. Dennoch ist die Urbejahung, von der alle Autoritätsbejahung abhängt, keine Selbstverständlichkeit. Diese Feststellung führt zu (a) – der Autorität *von totalem Geltungsanspruch.*

Wir beachten einen Sachverhalt, der bisher unbemerkt blieb. Die für alle Autorität konstitutive Annahme des normativen Anspruchs setzt eine grundlegende Bereitschaft bei denen voraus, die diesen Akt vollziehen. Die Autorität von Typus (c) – streng limitiert und okkasionell – verlangt nicht mehr als eine Haltung allgemeiner Fügsamkeit – diese Autorität will *geachtet* werden. Typus (b) greift viel tiefer in die Existenz ein und die Anerkennung gewinnt ein neues Gewicht – die Autorität will *geehrt* werden. Schliesslich Typus (a): der Anspruch ergeht an den ganzen Menschen, die Unterwerfung, die auf alle Einschränkungen verzichtet, wird zur Selbstüberantwortung; und diese Autorität von totalem Umfang muss alles verlangen – sie will *verehrt* werden. Autorität, wir wiederholen es, benennt ein faktisches interpersonales Verhältnis. Die zuletzt genannte, ihrem Range nach erste Form der Autorität aber, total in ihrer Forderung, verwirklicht sich primär nicht in der Beziehung von Mensch zu Mensch sondern im Gott-Mensch-Verhältnis – unter Menschen aber nur dort, wo der sich unterordnende Partner im Stand der noch im Werden begriffenen Person ist (das Verhältnis des Unmündigen zu Vater und Mutter) oder wo die mit Autorität ausgestattete Person göttliche Eigenschaften annimmt oder Gott vertritt wie der Heilige im Verhältnis zu seinen Verehrern. Und schliesslich kann noch an die Autorität des leidenschaftlich Geliebten gedacht werden. Aber damit nähern wir uns schon der Gefahrenzone der Divinisierung der menschlichen Person: die Autorität droht, idolatrische Züge anzunehmen.

Jede in einer Person investierte Autorität bedarf der Rechtfertigung. Nur auf Gott, der, eins mit dem Guten schlechthin, selbst letzter Rechtfertigungsgrund aller Autorität ist, trifft dieser Satz nicht zu, genausowenig, wie sich die Unterscheidung von Autorität und Macht auf Gott anwenden lässt. "Ist das Gottgefällige gut oder ist es vielmehr das Gute, das als solches Gott gefallen muss?" Diese berühmte, von Plato in *Euthyphron* entwickelte Dichotomie vermenschlicht Gott. Die Anerkennung der totalen göttlichen Autorität führt zu der platonischen und christlichen Bestimmung der menschlichen Existenz als des Versuches einer Angleichung an Gott nach dem Mass menschlicher Kräfte (ὁμοίωσις θεῷ κατὰ τὸ δυνατόν, Pl. *Tht.* 176b, *imitatio Dei*). In den "Religionen des Buches," d.h. im Judentum, Christentum und Islam, nimmt die totale Autorität Gottes die Form der Autorität des Wortes Gottes in der Heiligen Schrift an. Auf diese Weise wird die Schriftlichkeit der Autorität zu einem Wesenszug der abendländischen Kultur. Neben die Bibel, Hauptquelle der Autorität der Kirche, treten das *Corpus Juris* als Dokument des römischen Rechts, die Kirchenväter, vor allem Augustin, schliesslich noch die lateinischen und griechischen

Autoren, mit einer Verschiebung des Autoritätsgewichtes von der Spätantike auf die Klassik in der Renaissance. Innerhalb der Kirche gewinnt die Scholastik im 13. Jahrhundert, dank vor allem dem Werke des Thomas von Aquin, autoritative Geltung. Im Ganzen wird Autorität verstanden als abgeleitet von drei obersten Quellen: von der durch die Kirche interpretierten Heiligen Schrift (als der Offenbarung des Willens Gottes), von der Natur (verstanden als Schöpfungsordnung) und von menschlicher Weisheit, dokumentiert in den Schriften und Werken der Alten. *Auctoritas* und *ratio* sind die "beiden Triebräder der mittelalterlichen Tradition" (M. Grabmann, *Gesch. d. scholast. Methode* [Berlin, 1957], I, p. 130), und zum Stil der scholastischen Summen gehört, nach dem Vorbild von Abälards *Sic et non*, die Zusammenstellung von einander widersprechenden *auctoritates*.

Die Neuzeit ist gekennzeichnet durch eine Erschütterung dieser autoritativen Ordnung. Die Autorität der Heiligen Schrift wird problematisiert durch philologische Quellenkritik, und dafür werden das Altertum als solches, die Tradition als solche mit einer Art von Autorität bekleidet. Die Autorität der Natur wird in der Theorie problematisiert durch eine mechanistische Naturinterpretation, und zugleich tritt eine neue Wissenschaftsform als Autorität hervor: die mathematische Naturwissenschaft und die durch sie ermöglichte Technik. Praktisch-politisch wird die Natur problematisiert durch die moderne Verwandlung und darauffolgende Auflösung des Naturrechts. Dafür behauptet sich der Wille des souveränen Volks als revolutionäre Autorität – ihr historisches Symbol das Regicidium. Und schliesslich gerät auch die Autorität der griechisch-römischen Antike in den Strudel der Problematisierung. Mit dem Klassizismus geht nicht nur die normative Geltung der griechisch-römischen Kunst unter – die Kontinuität der künstlerischen Stiltradition und schliesslich der Begriff der Kunst selbst geraten ins Wanken. Ähnlich die Autorität der griechischen Metaphysik: die Kritik erschöpft sich in neuen und immer radikaleren Formen der Verneinung der Möglichkeit von Metaphysik. Wie aber alle begrenzte Autorität auf die absolute hinweist, so hat die Autoritätskrise der modernen Welt ihren zentralen Wirbel in der Leugnung Gottes. Das Wort vom "Tod Gottes" wird Symbol der Negationen, die, nach den Worten Nietzsches, "diese Erde von ihrer Sonne losketteten"

(*Die fröhliche Wissenschaft*, III, 125). Doch geht überall die Auflösung alter zusammen mit der Aufrichtung neuer Autorität, und
keine Geschichtsphilosophie kann angesichts des ungeheuren
Verschleisses die Rechnung über Gewinn und Verlust mit auch
nur annähernder Gewissheit aufstellen. In dem Prozess des
Kommens und Gehens und in der Abfolge und Verkettung von
Fortschritt und Absturz behauptet jedoch die Autorität als
Ordnungsprinzip mit der ihr eigentümlichen Staffelung der
normativen Ansprüche ihren in der menschlichen Natur be-
gründeten Platz.

München

III. LITTERAE

ECLOGA EPICUREA

THOMAS G. ROSENMEYER

> il ne s'agit nullement, ici, d'un monde de la compensation
> et de la justification, ou certaines tendances seraient
> exprimées ou contr-exprimées par certains actes; le roman
> abolit délibérément tout passé et tout profondeur, c'est un
> roman de l'extension, non de la comprehension.
>
> Roland Barthes

Literary origins are a melancholy business. Only in an age when men are certain of their own preferences and intentions do we find a corresponding lack of scruple regarding historical reconstruction. Herder thought he knew where the epic came from; Pope similarly knew where, and how, and by whom the first pastorals were sung. Pope's answer, in his *A Discourse on Pastoral Poetry*,[1] that the pastoral is the oldest literary genre, and that bucolic ditties were first composed by the early herdsmen who were both simple and good, is an answer almost as old as the genre itself. It is one of the answers given by the ancient "anthropologists," from Dicaearchus to Varro and beyond.[2] More commonly, however, the ancient scholars derive the genre from a background of ritual, specifically the worship of Artemis in various avatars.[3] The first eclogues, the scholiasts argue, were rustic hymns and dances offered to he goddess in times of stress. But as long ago as 1821 F. G. Welcker[4] carefully went through the evidence adduced by the scholiasts and found it wanting. Similar ritual reconstructions have come crashing down on our

---

[1] See B. A. Goldgar, *Literary Criticism of Alexander Pope* (Lincoln, Neb., 1965), p. 93.

[2] See especially Lucretius 5. 1379 ff.

[3] C. Wendel, *Scholia in Theocritum Vetera* (Leipzig, 1914), pp. 2–3, 8–9, etc.

[4] F. G. Welcker, "Ueber den Ursprung des Hirtenliedes," *Kleine Schriften* I (Bonn, 1844), pp. 402–411.

heads with increasing velocity.[5] In any case, if the scholiasts were right, it is difficult to understand why we know of no pastoral writings prior to the third century B.C., whereas other forms of poetry, supposedly the fruits of ritual ceremony, came to be secularized, and works of art, much earlier.

Welcker's own view was that the pastoral came into being when Theocritus copied the singing practices of the herdsmen in his native Sicily. On this view Theocritus was a scholar-poet, an Alexandrian Jacob Grimm, who attended the local harvesters' festivals, to obtain material and inspiration for his humble verse. Theocritus, in other words, was a folklorist. The trouble is, as Welcker himself readily admitted, that we know next to nothing about ancient popular singing contests. It would be churlish to deny that the Sicilian countryside (and the Coan, and Arcadian, and Egyptian, for that matter) was alive with song. Some of the singing may have been of a substance resembling details in the Theocritean pastorals. The refrains, and the rhymes and ana-phoras, which are so prominent in Theocritus' major work, may well be called popular. But of singing contests organized by the herdsmen themselves for their own enjoyment, there is not the slightest hint in the early tradition. E. Reisch, in his book *De Musicis Graecorum Certaminibus* (Vienna, 1885) which gives all the evidence available then, has nothing whatever about rustic contests prior to Diodorus, in the first century B.C. Nor are the later parallels helpful. Dimitrios Petropoulos [6] has collected the songs, amoebean and otherwise, of modern Greek herdsmen and rustics, and tried to demonstrate their resemblance to Theocritus' poems. But an analysis of the material assembled by him shows that it consists in the main of boasting, invective, and *versus Fescennini*, with some love poetry, all of them quite remote from the distinctive themes and patterns of the Hel-lenistic pastoral.

That Theocritus had forerunners, that his poetry was in part conditioned by earlier, particularly literary formulations, cannot be doubted. For the amoebean there are analogues in drama,

---

[5] For drama, see G. F. Else, *The Origin and Early Form of Greek Tragedy* (Cambridge, Mass., 1965).

[6] D. Petropoulos, in *Laographia* 18 (1959), pp. 5–93. Cf. also *Laographia* 15 (1954), p. 395, on the awarding of prizes by village committees.

especially comedy.[7] Philosophical dialogue, whatever *its* origins, also served to pave the way for pastoral *controversiae*. Above all, the *skolia* and the symposiac literature of Theognis and his followers[8] give us much that points in the direction, not only of alternate singing but also of the performance of songs within a circle of appreciative listeners. Many incidental parallels are furnished by Homer, Alcman, Anacreon, and others. Love of nature, romantic *eros*, simple humor, parody and self-parody, self-portraits of poets in disguise, and the humanization of the gods, all of them important to the total effect of the pastoral, are features which can be instanced long before Theocritus.

The question then should be, not what were the seeds of the pastoral, or when was the first pastoral performed, but rather: what is there about Theocritus which is sufficiently different to make us think of him as presenting a novel type of poetry, varied yet roughly consistent in its norms, which cannot be said to derive logically or organically from any one earlier source, or even from several of them in combination. The question is not about a genre; as good Socratics, we would first have to define what that genre is, and critics like William Empson, as acquisitive as he is imaginative, have put the genre and its properties in extreme jeopardy.[9] The question is, happily, about a poet and his work. The new thing about Theocritus, if I may put it so crudely, is an attitude, a way of looking at man in his world, and at the artist in that world, a "philosophy" perhaps, whereby Theocritus takes his position alongside certain non-poetic writers of his day. In spite of the notorious hazards involved in such an

---

[7] Cf. the contest between the Just and the Unjust Argument in Aristophanes *Clouds* 889 ff.

[8] R. Reitzenstein, *Epigramm und Skolion* (Giessen, 1893), ch. 2, refers to Theognis 993–6, a stanza which, except for the nature of the prize, has a positively Theocritean ring about it:

Εἰ θείης, ᾽Ακάδημε, ἐφίμερον ὕμνον ἀείδειν,
ἆθλον δ᾽ἐν μέσσωι παῖς καλὸν ἄνθος ἔχων
σοί τ᾽εἴη καὶ ἐμοὶ σοφίης πέρι δηρισάντοιν,
γνοίης χ᾽ὅσσον ὄνων κρέσσονες ἡμίονοι.

[9] W. Empson, *Some Versions of Pastoral* (Norfolk, Conn., 1950). For a saner and more workable appreciation of the genre, see the essays of Renato Poggioli, particularly his "The Oaten Flute," *Harvard Library Bulletin* 11.2 (1957), pp. 147–184; and J. F. Lynen, *The Pastoral Art of Robert Frost* (New Haven, 1960).

attempt,[10] I think it can be shown that some of the suggestions, not to say ideas, implicit in the major *Idylls*, are reminiscent of what is found in the utterances of the moral philosophers whose teachings ushered in the new culture of which Theocritus is a part. Above all, it seems, we might profitably look at Epicurus. There is no need to ask, even if the evidence permitted it, for a direct contact between the poet and the philosopher, though an examination of the philosophical and literary preferences of the Hellenistic rulers should produce interesting results.[11] It is sufficient to observe that on many scores Epicurus and Theocritus appear to be talking the same language, despite the fact that one uses the privileged speech of philosophy, and the other the vernacular of poetry. Ettore Bignone, an expert in both Theocritus and Epicurus, did not choose, except in passing, [12] to

[10] See the warnings of M. Pohlenz, "Die hellenistische Poesie und die Philosophie," *Charites Fr. Leo* (Berlin, 1911), pp. 90, 101. Cf. also the perennial question whether Epicurus had an influence on Menander; negatively: T. B. L. Webster, *Studies in Menander* (Manchester, 1950); positively: P. Harsh in *Gnomon* 25 (1953), p. 44, n. 1. Pohlenz's scepticism is perhaps best controverted by the example of Fontenelle, usually typed a Stoic but equally definable as an Epicurean in the succession of Gassendi. He wrote, not only pastoral poems and an essay on the composition of pastoral poetry, but also a treatise on the plurality of worlds (1686) in which he argues that earth and man are not in the center of the universe; and a *Histoire des Oracles* (1687) which, like his *De l'origine des Fables* (1689) makes gentle fun of revealed religion. The connection between Deism and pastoral poetry in the seventeenth and eighteenth centuries deserves closer study.

[11] See Diog. Laert. 10. 25: he mentions, among the students of Epicurus, "the two Ptolemies from Alexandria, the dark-haired and the blond." See also Plutarch *Adv. Colot.* 1107d–e; *De coh. ira* 9. 458a. The monograph of A. Pridik, *Koenig Ptolemaios I und die Philosophen*, Acta Univ. Tartuensis B, vol. 30, fasc. 1 (Dorpat, 1932), is inadequate.

[12] E. Bignone, *Teocrito* (Bari, 1934), p. 50. Cf. also A. Grilli, *Il problema della vita contemplativa nel mondo greco-romano* (Milan, 1953), p. 180, a cursory reference to Theocritus. In the first chapter of his book Grilli defines the essentials of the Epicurean *vita contemplativa* as follows: (a) an aversion to the demands of prestige; (2) an aversion to politics; (3) *otium*; (4) the elimination of society and family ties. He does not mention Theocritus in this connection. Contrast Poggioli (*supra*, note 9), p. 154: "As a conscious or unconscious philosopher, the shepherd is neither a stoic nor a cynic, but rather an epicurean; and observes with natural spontaneity the ethics of that school. His eudaemonism is not only spiritual but physical as well; and includes the practice of hedonism." Poggioli has in mind the herdsmen of the later European pastoral tradition as well as the ancient; for Theocritus, and probably also for Virgil, we would have to modify his statement because the ancient herdsman is never a conscious philosopher.

comment on what the two might have in common. This should certainly put us on our guard. But in the case of Virgil's *Eclogues* and *Georgics* there is general agreement that the poetry is full of Epicurean elements,[13] and it was largely on this evidence that Tenney Frank called Virgil an outright Epicurean.[14] If it can be shown that it is the tradition of the pastoral, rather than Virgil in particular, that is to be associated with Epicureanism, Frank's biographical thrust would lose much of its sting.

Comparisons are odious, especially when the *comparanda* are poetry and prose. Perhaps I shall be forgiven if I simply try to indicate some of the important features of the pastoral, on the assumption that the Epicurean complements will be readily apparent to Professor Merlan's friends. The goatherd Lycidas, in the seventh *Idyll*, addresses Simichidas as follows:

> Simichidas, where are you going at this noon hour
> When even the lizard sleeps on his rock wall,
> And the larks, the tomb birds, stay put?[15]

Lycidas is surprised that Simichidas is afoot; he may well be, for in the pastoral grove men are ordinarily at rest, standing, more often sitting or reclining. (I distinguish the pastoral landscape from the Hesiodic field, the real country of drudgery and sweat, which Theocritus manipulates as a counterpoint to the pastoral vision in *Idyll* 10, Milon's Song of Lityerses.) The time is the noon hour, when the sun burns too fiercely for comfort, when the whole of nature enters into a state of suspension, when time stands still. The stabilization of the flux is one of the principal ingredients in the pastoral harmony. The mechanics of much of the poetry are

---

[13] See especially Virgil *G.* 2. 458 ff., and the comments by F. Klingner, "Ueber das Lob des Landlebens in Virgils Georgica," *Hermes* 66 (1931), pp. 159–189. For the problem of the cosmogony in *Ecl.* 6, see the discussion prompted by the paper of A. La Penna, "Esiodo nella cultura e nella poesia di Virgilio," *Hésiode et son Influence*, Entretiens Fondation Hardt VII (Geneva, 1962), pp. 213–270. See now also A. Traina, *"Si numquam fallit imago*: Reflessioni sulle Bucoliche e l'epicureismo," *A&R* 10 (1965), pp. 72–78: T. explains *Ecl.* 2. 25 ff. as an echo of the Epicurean theory of mirrors. His conclusion: the *Eclogues* are *not* an Epicurean poem, but are built on an Epicurean substratum.

[14] Tenney Frank, *Virgil* (New York, 1922), pp. 102 ff., esp. p. 109.

[15] 7. 21–23: Σιμιχίδα, πᾶι δὴ τὸ μεσαμέριον πόδας ἕλκεις, / ἁνίκα δὴ καὶ σαῦρος ἐν αἱμασιαῖσι καθεύδει, / οὐδ'ἐπιτυμβίδιοι κορυδαλλίδες ἡλαίνοντι;

put at the disposal of the demands of fixity. The frequency of anaphora is symptomatic; it acts as an operatic elaboration of the sense of ἀρχή; the first impression or response is allowed to order the sequel, and to block the momentum. Refrain may be used for a similar purpose; especially in the second *Idyll* (not strictly a pastoral) it compels us to anchor our sympathies within a single limited area, thus counteracting and in the end defeating the tremendous centrifugal forces openly at work. The pastoral arrests movement; it fixes and transfixes the present, and thereby beautifies and palliates it. The elimination of κίνησις may become radical; then the pastoral turns not on a pseudo-death, the paralysis of the noon hour, but death proper, and is transformed into a dirge. But ordinarily, in Theocritus, the noon peace is not remote or eschatological. On the other hand, its calm is always precarious, because it is recognizably short-lived and artificial. The crude forces swirling beyond it continually threaten to upset the balance which the pastoral bower seems to offer.[16] The disturbances which the herdsmen attempt to shut out are largely those of the city; they are politics, business, hard labor, litigation, all the social and moral oppressions which make men into slaves and worse. During the noon hour men become princes, at peace with themselves and with the world of trees and animals and brooks which share their music with them. It is an intimate world; there are no barriers of language or nationality or club membership, and the guileless way in which Chromis from Libya and the ferryman from Calydna move in and out of the picture, without the need of formal introduction, draws the listener to share in the good fellowship and φιλία.[17]

[16] In the atomic universe, everything is always in motion; the only rest that is possible, beside death (which is, itself, merely rearrangement) is the equilibrium of balanced motions of the *minimae res*. Thus we may speak of an animated calm. Time, in Lucretius, is both *eventum eventi* (1. 449 ff.) and a destroyer. The same abivalence is felt in Theocritus; during the pastoral experience time is in abeyance, but we feel that the pastoral moment is perilously snatched from the flux.

[17] For Epicurean friendship, see the statements collected by A. J. Festugière, *Epicurus and his Gods* (Oxford, 1955; Cambridge, Mass., 1956), p. 37. On intimacy without dependence, see *Rat. Sent.* xl. It is perhaps significant that Epicurus was the first philosopher to present his thought in the form of letters to friends; cf. J. Sykutris in *RE* Sup. Vol. V, col. 185 ff., s.v. "Epistolographie." Compare the epistolary form of Theocritus *Idylls* 11, 13, and 7. 96–127.

The feelings expressed are sometimes coarse, sometimes gentle, but always unaffected, rarely resigned or cold, or pretentious. The amoebean structure is, among other things, a formal documentation of the spirit of equality. Men need one another, and therefore respect one another, even when the chaffing is at its sharpest; they give gifts, not because they want to flaunt their possessions – they do not own anything of commercial value – but rather because the giving of these tokens, the pipe or the cup or the cloak, is the most concrete signalling of what they feel for each other. No effort is wasted, no achievement remains unacknowledged, in this world of trust and companionship.

It is, of course, a world of withdrawal. The "greene cabinet," as Spenser calls it, offers a haven within which man may engage in his favorite zoological pursuit: the study of himself. Nature, in the *Idylls*, is not an object of study or appreciation.[18] True enough, cicadas and sheep and wolves and oaks and rocks and lilies are featured as partners of man; they have their own zest for living, they rejoice and mourn and make music with the herdsmen. Together they constitute a symphonic order which, in effect, sounds the harmony of the universe, though Theocritus is careful to avoid such programmatic words as φύσις, κόσμος, and ἁρμονία. But whereas in the nineteenth century romantics Nature comes to be the spiritual reservoir and the teacher of man, Theocritus' animals and brooks are merely the instrumentalists, responding to the moods set by joys and miseries which are purely human. Man is the singer of the song; the pastoral is not about nature but about man – man in his quintessence as a sentient but also discriminating creature, a being of strong feelings, of simple judgments, and of delicate needs. Above all, the pastoral is a testimony to man's ability to live for pleasure and yet not descend to the level of sheer animal energy, and to express his delights and despairs in a language whose refinement and musical charm confirm the traditional Greek view that men are, at heart, akin to the beings who make their home on Parnassus and Olympus. The gods themselves, in Theocritus, are

18 If she were, she would take on the iridescence of Lucretius' *natura*: strong, healthy, animal, but subject to exhaustion and death (1. 1042; 2. 1131; 5. 235 ff.). The pastoralist – and this distinguishes him from the Petrarchan – can use nature only if he accepts her as alive and energizing.

454 Thomas G. Rosenmeyer

shunted into a purely auxiliary position; they may counsel, or sneer, or serve as warning examples, but they are not worshipped. The focus is on man; and the figures of Daphnis and Comatas absorb the brilliance, the larger-than-life mysteriousness which prior to the Hellenistic age was the preserve of the gods.

I hope that this rapid summary of some of the salient features of Theocritus' art has already pointed in the direction of where we must look for Epicurean correspondences. When Theocritus begins his first poem with an emphatic anaphora of ἁδύ

'Αδύ τι τὸ ψιθύρισμα καὶ ἁ πίτυς, αἰπόλε, τήνα, / ἁ ποτὶ ταῖς παγαῖσι, μελίσδεται, ἁδὺ δὲ καὶ τύ / συρίσδες ....

we are reminded of the similar treatment of *suave* at the beginning of Lucretius' second book, with its openly Epicurean argument. 'Ηδονή is the overriding aim of the Epicurean, and among the various types of pleasure the ἡδονὴ καταστηματική, the pleasure which resides in perfect stillness, is best.[19] But this is not the ἀταραξία of the Cynics and the Stoics; it is not the cold-blooded imperturbability exhibited, for example, by the cruel lover of that very successful *Moritat*, Theocritus' non-pastoral *Idyll* 23. The ἀταραξία of Epicurus is always enlivened by grace and by a modicum of irony.[20] The secret is probably that there is no talk of virtue;[21] ἀταραξία is recommended because it gives pleasure, and ultimately *is* pleasure, not because it satisfies a moral

[19] For nature as a source of pleasure, see Praxilla *frg.* I = 747 PMG: Adonis is asked by the people in the underworld what was the κάλλιστον that he left behind, and he answers:

Κάλλιστον μὲν ἐγὼ λείπω φάος ἠελίοιο,
δεύτερον ἄστρα φαεινὰ σεληναίης τε πρόσωπον
ἠδὲ καὶ ὡραίους σικύους καὶ μῆλα καὶ ὄγχνας·

The naiveté of the inexperienced hedonist puts the utterance within the pastoral realm.

[20] Diog. Laert. 10. 136: ἡ μὲν γὰρ ἀταραξία καὶ ἀπονία καταστηματικαί εἰσιν ἡδοναί· ἡ δὲ χαρὰ καὶ ἡ εὐφροσύνη κατὰ κίνησιν ἐνεργείαι βλέπονται. For this judicious balancing of motion and rest, cf. also *Gnom. Vat.* xi. The irony springs from the Epicurean dilemma masterfully sketched by P. De Lacy, "Process and Value: An Epicurean Dilemma," *TAPA* 88 (1957), pp. 114–126: it is best to be a detached observer of process, but value comes only from being experientially involved. Thus the Epicurean intends a combination of animal sentience and human distance.

[21] There is no absolute justice; *Rat. Sent.* xxxiii: οὐκ ἦν τι καθ'ἑαυτὸ δικαιοσύνη ....

imperative. Nor can the distinctive joy[22] of Epicurus be squared with the life in the city. "We must free ourselves from the prison house of routine tasks and city affairs."[23] And a catalogue listing the characteristics of the Epicurean σοφός, possibly from Diogenes of Tarsus, says, among other things, that he will love the country.[24] Epicurus' protest against the city took the form of action: he bought a garden. The garden may have been, as Wycherly insists on the evidence of Pliny, in the city itself.[25] But the location is less important than its significance to the school, which came to be known by its name, and less important also than the use to which it was put. Hiero II, as Athenaeus tells us,[26] used *his* garden in Syracuse to transact business; Epicurus made his garden into a place of refuge, a meeting place for men and women who recognized no other social ties but the bonds of friendship, who wanted to enjoy an existence uncluttered by all the things which make life into a problem in logistics. Epicurus did not, any more than the pastoral, preach the noble savage: "Simplicity too has a limit, and the man who does not observe it comes to be indistinguisable from one who fails because of his lack of restraint."[27] It is only the excess of culture, what Plato called the feverish city, that has to be avoided. Λάθε βιώσας does not mean: hide your head in the sand, like the ostrich; but: do not live in such a manner that your life enters into a state of friction with other lives. There is no warning here against sharing experiences, against sharing even emotions – only against involvements which might get the better of one's search, along with friends, for the quiet happiness which is the great fulfillment. The simplicity, then, is not gross but stylish, a

[22] For the use of the term "joy" to translate Epicurus' ἡδονή, see P. Merlan, *Studies in Epicurus and Aristotle*, Klassisch-Philologische Studien XXII (Wiesbaden, 1960), p. 15.

[23] *Gnom. Vat.* lviii. The translation of ἐγκύκλια is not certain, since Aristotle uses the word to refer to activities and to opinions.

[24] φιλαγρήσειν: Diog. Laert. 10. 120.

[25] R. E. Wycherly, "The Garden of Epicurus," *Phoenix* 13 (1959), pp. 73–77, on the basis of Pliny, *HN* 19. 51.

[26] Athenaeus 542a.

[27] *Gnom. Vat.* lxiii, with Usener's readings λιτότητι and μεθόριος, in spite of von der Muehll's καθαριότης approved by Diano and Arrighetti. The ms. reading λεπτότητι strikes me as extremely unlikely, in view of the importance of λεπτότης as a technical term in Epicurean physics.

humane primitivism. The style shows also in the writing; the ancient critics felt that Epicurus' prose presented an admirable mixture of clarity, simplicity, and elegance.[28]

There are other interesting parallels, such as Epicurus' demotion of the gods,[29] and his own veneration as a *Gottmensch* by the members of the Garden corporation.[30] Theocritus, admittedly, is not a teacher. He is concerned neither with ethics nor with cosmology. His herdsmen are not exemplars of παιδεία. But they are men and women who voice moods and needs remarkably similar to the premises of the Epicurean canon; they move through, or rather rest in, the same world of beauty and restfulness and ironic detachment which Epicurus also upheld as a last refuge from the terrors of a larger chaos. There are differences. Theocritus is a poet, a lyricist, a singer about love. His subtle manipulation of the ambivalences of love has little in common with Epicurus' hardheaded rejection of the romantic passion,[31] though here too there are intriguing points of contact, under the heading of κίνησις versus στάσις. Epicureanism, as it were, forms the boundary which separates two important strands in the pastoral texture. Where passion and pain are neutralized via parody, as in *Idyll* 3, or via embalmment, as in the sculptured image of the lovers on the cup of *Idyll* 1, Epicurus' caveats are accepted; where they break through the fetters of courtesy and stability,

[28] H. Usener, ed., *Epicurea* (Leipzig, 1887), pp. 88–90.

[29] See W. Schmid, "Goetter und Menschen in der Theologie Epikurs," *Rh. Mus.* 94 (1951), pp. 97–156 for a sane and thorough treatment of Epicurus; further, the same author in *RACh* Vol. V (Stuttgart, 1962), col. 730 ff., s.v. "Epikur." The *locus classicus* for the *otium* of the gods is Lucretius 1. 44–49 = 2. 646 ff. I am inclined to accept the passage in its position in Book 1; I assume, however, that several lines, containing an address to Memmius, have dropped out before it.

[30] Diog. Laert. 10. 18; Plut. *Adv. Colot.* 17. 1117b; Philod. περὶ εὐσεβείας p. 104 Gomperz.

[31] For Epicurus' views about love, see the controversy between A. J. Festugière in *Rev. Ét. Grec.* 65 (1952), p. 259 and R. Flacelière, "Les Épicuriens et l'amour," *Rev. Ét. Grec.* 67 (1954), pp. 69–81. I would side with the latter. Note the parallel between Lucretius 4. 1160–61 and Theocr. 10. 26–27. C. Bailey, *Lucretius* Vol. III (Oxford, 1947), pp. 1310–1311 speculates that the Lucretius lines are more likely to have been influenced by poetry than by a philosophical source such as Epicurus' Περὶ Ἔρωτος. I do not think that we need to come down heavily on one side or the other; certainly Plato *Resp.* 474d ff. is relevant.

as in *Idylls* 1, 2, 7, and (in a different manner) 10, Epicurus is rejected. The parody need not mean a negation of πάθος, but only an amused recognition of its inevitability; then also Epicurus is left behind. Ultimately Theocritus transcends Epicurus more or less as Euripides transcends the Sophists. Euripides conformed to some of the Sophistic perspectives but rebelled against their fond hope that the passions are manageable. Similarly Theocritus, through his passionate lovers, protests against the anemia of ἀταραξία.

Even more important, predictably, they differ on the issue of music. Epicurus appears to have held that music is all right to listen to, as entertainment, but that it has no power to influence the soul for better or for worse. Music is mere sound, it appeals to αἴσθησις which is ἄλογος.³² Thus Epicurus declares war on the traditional authority of music as an educational and ethical influence. The *Idylls*, also, are written to be recited rather than sung; to this extent Theocritus falls in with the Hellenistic abrogation of the power of music. But we can hardly say that Theocritus has no music. Singing, and instrumental music, are pervasive in the bower; without the music which we are asked to conjure up for ourselves as we listen, the pastoral landscape would be poorer, and indeed meaningless. In Theocritus music is nothing less then the affirmation of the dignity and the divinity of man. Epicurus laughs music out of court; Theocritus remakes it, in the image of his poetic landscape. But this is a difference in temper, in creative procedure, rather than in essence. It should not prevent us from recognizing the large elective affinities which prompt Epicurus and Theocritus to take their pleasure in one and the same grove.

³² Cf., most recently, A. Ronconi, "Appunti di estetica epicurea," *Miscellanea Rostagni* (Turin, 1963), pp. 7–24. Also A. J. Neubecker, *Die Bewertung der Musik bei Stoikern und Epikureern*, Akad. Berlin. Inst. f. gr.-roem. Altertumsk., Arbeitsgr. f. hellenist.-roem. Philos. V (Berlin, 1956), p. 41. The example of Lucretius shows that it is possible to be an Epicurean and a poet, in spite of the official condemnation of poetry within the school; see also J. H. Waszink, "Lucretius and Poetry," *Med. nederl. Akad., Letterk.* 17. 8 (1954), p. 1, arguing against W. Schmid in *Gnomon* 20 (1944), p. 13. I am less concerned with the question of how an Epicurean manages to go against the school veto, and write poetry; rather, I am interested in what kind of poetry would best conform to what is intrinsically tolerant of poetry within Epicureanism, if Epicurus had personally been more tolerant.

Finally, some remarks of a more venturesome nature. The words of Roland Barthes prefixed to this essay pertain to the new novel created by Robbe-Grillet. Elsewhere Barthes says that the new novelist insists on facing reality with no other power than that of his eyes; the world, for him, is a chain of optic impulses and visual impressions, and must be registered in this fashion, without recourse to psychology, confession, religious hypostasis or any of the other instruments whereby the older novelists, including both the romantics and the naturalists, managed to establish all manner of ties between objects, and thereby to efface the hard outlines of the objects themselves.[33] Metaphors, especially anthropomorphisms, are to be avoided, because they interfere with the direct appreciation of the surfaces of things.

Other writers, such as Natalie Sarraute and Sartre (in a famous study of Camus)[34] have similarly pleaded for a return to the pleasures of seeing, without interpreting, without systematizing, and without "internalizing." Now whether the poetics underlying the "Voyeur" is compelling or not,[35] there is much that rings familiar. Lucretius emphasizes that we are alive in the present, that past and future do not concern us (3. 830 ff.). He stresses the geometrical nature of things, and singles out sight as the basic sense because it is analogous to touch. Like Robbe-Grillet, Lucretius makes his way of looking at the world a call for freedom; in fact, Robbe-Grillet's battle cry might have been sounded by him: "To reject our so-called "nature" and the vocabulary which perpetuates its myth, to propose objects as purely external and superficial, [Lucretius would have said: insentient and atomic] is not – as has been claimed – to deny man; but it is to reject the "pananthropic" notion contained in traditional humanism, and probably in all humanism. It is no more in the last analysis than to lay claim, quite logically, to my freedom."[36] Lucretius' "wachestehende Woerter" (the term is Richard Heinze's) are our best evidence that the Epicurean stance, with its alertness to the

---

[33] Roland Barthes, *Essais Critiques* (Paris, 1964), p. 39.
[34] J. P. Sartre, *Literary and Philosophical Essays* (New York, 1955).
[35] Robbe-Grillet has written his own poetics in *For a New Novel* (New York, 1965).
[36] Robbe-Grillet, *ibid.*, p. 57.

shapes of things and to the relation between shape and mass, is poetically fruitful, whether Epicurus himself approves of verse or not. Where the distinction between organic and inorganic is minimized, and where the magnet – solid, life-filled, orderly, mysterious but natural, amenable to scientific investigation but also immediately enjoyable – is the paragon of all objects (6. 906 ff.), we are dealing with a world which is best reproduced by means of nouns; verbs, and especially adjectives, take on a secondary role. In Lucretius, characteristically, it is the diseased world of Book 6 which requires to be described with an accumulation of special adjectives; for the rest, the adjectives possess little more force than the *epitheta ornantia* of the conventional epic.

I would argue that in its small way, and without shouting, Theocritus' pastoral was, for his generation, what Robbe-Grillet's novel attempts to be for ours. The open form of the bucolic drama, its serial exploration of the hard objects of its minuscule world, its avoidance of similes and metaphors and significant adjectives (the evidence for this I hope to present on another occasion), its eschewing of all larger commitments – all this betokens a self-discipline analogous to the restrictions of the *nouveau roman*. The "anonymity" of the pastoral lyric of which John Crowe Ransom speaks in his analysis of *Lycidas*[37] is but another index of the pastoralist's fiction that he sketches the world as it suggests itself to the senses, without the pressures of a system or an interpretation. Αἴσθησις rules supreme; experience is corporeal rather than inward; arrangement is haphazard, as the *clinamen* of particles happens to strike the eye.[38] Above all, pain is muted, because the avowal of pain would gainsay the principal insight that all is matter, that the feelings are epiphenomenal, and that the only viable response to the world around us is the contentment (in Robbe-Grillet's case, the trance?) that comes from accepting the setting without anxiety. I am not, of course, suggesting that the poet, any more than the novelist, *or* the

[37] Ransom's essay is reprinted in C. A. Patrides, *Milton's Lycidas* (New York, 1961).

[38] It is because of these qualities of the pastoral that I am sceptical of analyses that emphasize structural symmetries and Aristotelian virtues in Theocritus.

philosopher, is really trying to talk about the world as it is. Rather, he creates his own world, in the image of the larger world whose structure or the lack of it he thinks he has intuited; or again as a refuge from the chaos of his fears. For Epicurus and Theocritus, the Garden and the *locus amoenus* provide the stillness which permits a temporary blocking of the swirl of politics, of passion, and of the *flammantia moenia mundi*; for Robbe-Grillet, the island of the salesman is both universe and refuge, both the storm and the calm, hence an emblem of the modern malaise.[39]

University of California, Berkeley

[39] The occasion referred to on p. 459 has come about more quickly than the publication of this essay. For a more detailed argument, and much overlap, see now my *The Green Cabinet: Theocritus and the European Pastoral Lyric*, University of California Press, 1969.

MENANDRO E IL PERIPATO

MARCELLO GIGANTE

1. In un articolo del 1911 (*Die hellenistische Poesie und die Philosophie*, Χάριτες *Fr. Leo*, pp. 76 ss., ora in *Kleine Schriften* II [Hildesheim, 1965], pp. 1 ss.) M. Pohlenz esaminava, con finezza non disgiunta da cautela, i rapporti tra motivi e concetti, comuni a filosofi e poeti nell'età ellenistica, discriminandone i molteplici fili e riconducendo alla tradizione letteraria l'origine di alcuni motivi poetici, che più facilmente potessero richiamare il contemporaneo fiorire del pensiero. Il senso dell'interiore raccoglimento è, per esempio, comune ai filosofi e ai poeti: esso è storicamente e socialmente condizionato e rinviene diversa espressione nella speculazione dei filosofi e nella fantasia degli artisti. Né vi sono filosofi puri (Cleante) né poeti immuni da esperienze o simpatie filosofiche (Leonida), ma il fatto che Fenice di Colofone abbia attinto ai Cinici la sua dottrina filosofica non significa che tutta la poesia ellenistica debba esser vista come espressione di una fede filosofica: dalla *Konfirmationspoesie* di Fenice " si possono trarre così scarse conclusioni per tutt'intera la poesia, quanto da Telete per il carattere della filosofia contemporanea" (p. 7). Al marcato individualismo nella filosofia fa riscontro – annota il Pohlenz, p. 14 s. – la valutazione dell'individualità nella poesia; ma ciò non significa un "reciproco influsso" di filosofia e poesia, bensì solo che esse hanno le radici nello stesso terreno (p. 15: "Philosophie und Poesie gleich fest im selben Erdreich wurzeln"). Il Pohlenz inoltre può addirittura indicare una legge stilistica ("ein Stilgesetz," p. 19 s.): "Auch wo Philosophie und Poesie in Personalunion vereinigt sind, sucht man die Scheidewand aufrecht zu erhalten." Potrebbe sembrare che in un epigramma (IX 359) Posidippo risenta particolarmente dell'influsso dei Cinici; in realtà si muove nell'orma delle intuizioni di

Sofocle e di Bacchilide "e non si preoccupa affatto di ciò che
dicono i filosofi" (p. 22). Teocrito quando nel *Ierone* svolge il
motivo della φιλοκέρδεια non dipende dalle diatribe della filosofia
popolare, ma da motivi specialmente svolti da Pindaro.

Anche Callimaco svolse una volta un aneddoto dalla vita dei
Sette Sapienti, aborrendo però dal modo diatribico. Teocrito e
Callimaco risolvevano in poesia o in arte ciò che i pensatori risolvevano in filosofia. L'ideale della "vita tranquilla" è rappre-
sentato da Teocrito nelle *Talisie*, così bene come sul piano
teoretico il concetto della vita felice è svolto da Zenone e da
Epicuro (p. 29). Alcuni frammenti di Filita possono rivelare
contatti con la letteratura consolatoria, ma questa si rifà principalmente all'antica poesia, a cui attinge anche Filita. Anche il
motivo filiteo della libertà dal dolore e dal travaglio non ha nulla
a vedere con la dottrina epicurea della κατασττηματικὴ ἡδονή
(p. 36). Insomma, per l'ammissione di un influsso filosofico sui
poeti ellenistici il Pohlenz prescriveva estrema cautela (p. 24),
concludendo che filosofia e poesia, anche nella consonanza di
motivi, rinvengono nella parola scritta un'espressione autonoma
ed originale.

2. L'interpretazione generale del Pohlenz veniva accettata da
W. Kroll (*Studien zum Verständnis der römischen Literatur* [Stutt-
gart, 1924; Darmstadt, 1964], p. 85), il quale rilevava che nella
Commedia non ricorrono frasi stoiche o epicuree, ma addirittura
"luoghi comuni a buon mercato" e che "gli echi di formulazioni
filosofiche" (se l'uomo conosca se stesso, se la felicità dipenda dal
merito, se sia preferibile una vita dedita al godimento o al
guadagno) "si possono ritenere casuali." E, per quel che riguarda
in particolare Menandro, il Kroll scriveva: "Menandro, che fu
vicino ai filosofi del suo tempo, concede, certo, nelle sue commedie, uno spazio abbastanza ampio all'elemento gnomico, ma
con sicuro senso dello stile ("mit sicherem Stilgefühl") egli lascia
che i suoi personaggi dicano solo tanto quanto saprebbero dire
senza educazione filosofica."

3. Anche nella poesia ellenistica la via del sentimento non è la
via del pensiero e la simiglianza o identità del motivo è indicativa
del clima culturale dell'epoca, della sensibilità particolare a

determinati temi, che contraddistinguono una fase storica della civiltà, ma non può indurre a considerare e valutare il poeta *sub specie philosophiae*. Il poeta ellenistico, che programmaticamente persegue la novità nella parola e nel verso, non rinunzia ad attingere motivi alla sua dottrina di lettore e cultore di letteratura, ma non può mai esser equiparato ad un mitologo, ad uno storico, ad un filosofo. E, innanzi tutto, egli ha la consapevolezza storica di venire a situarsi, con la sua opera, in una tradizione culturale e poetica, nei cui confronti egli esercita le sue reazioni di consenso e di dissenso, e, soprattutto, esperisce le sue innovazioni, che, anche se non sono rivoluzionarie – ma neppure mediocri –, gli assicurano un ruolo nella civiltà poetica contemporanea, nel momento stesso in cui la sua opera, divincolandosi tra gli anelli della catena del passato, anticipa e propone lo sviluppo dell'avvenire.

Ogni posizione critica rilevante corrisponde ad una persuasione, convalidata dall'interpretazione dei testi, e, nel contempo, ad una reazione ad indirizzi di diversa impostazione. La liberazione della poesia ellenistica dall'ipoteca di scuole filosofiche, fu, certo, una buona conquista del Pohlenz. L'esemplificazione può naturalmente esser diversa, ma il principio ermeneutico che la ispira e la illustra è corretto. La formulazione del Pohlenz può essere ulteriormente verificata ed anche specificata (le generalizzazioni non possono, in nessun caso, essere del tutto soddisfacenti): in essa è tuttavia implicito che diversi sono i gradi della poesia e diverse le stature dei poeti. Se una particolare filosofia determina in modo prevalente l'ispirazione di un poeta, non è escluso che l'esposizione di una dottrina diventi anche espressione dell'anima del poeta, di tutta la sua personalità umana ed artistica, ma è altresì frequente la possibilità che un pensiero resti pura riflessione, mera constatazione, senza riscattarsi in immagine e ritmo. E, in tal caso, è innegabile che abbia influito sul poeta il tecnicismo del linguaggio di una determinata sètta; ma nel medesimo caso sarebbe assurdo giudicare tutta l'opera di quel poeta dal punto di vista di quella filosofia affiorata nell'adozione di un termine tecnico o di un'espressione apparentemente caratteristica.

La cautela critica, invocata dal Pohlenz, è un invito a considerare soprattutto la poesia (ellenistica) come opera di poeti e non di filosofi, ma non a rinunziare alla filosofia, se essa può essere d'aiuto all'intelligenza della poesia. Il ruolo della filosofia nell'interpretazione della poesia è uguale a quello della cultura e della storia politica e sociale dell'epoca ed è pari a quello della tradizione colta, nella cui storia il poeta naturalmente s'inserisce. In altri termini, l'educazione filosofica è una delle componenti della cultura e della dottrina del poeta, che può agire, se agisce, sulla libertà creatrice del poeta, al pari di altri stimoli interiori e di altre sollecitazioni culturali. Delimitato così, un influsso "filosofico" viene ad esprimere l'interiorità stessa del poeta e non ad indicare una professione di fede in una determinata filosofia.

Ma vale soprattutto il principio che il poeta dev'essere interpretato nella storia della sua formazione poetica, vale a dire nell'ambito delle fonti a lui più congeniali, con le quali arricchisce i contenuti della sua poesia e conquista i suoi mezzi espressivi. Tale processo formativo è insieme sviluppo del suo spirito e creazione del suo mondo poetico: è un fatto, individuale e individualizzante, di una personalità che nulla dei fermenti di pensiero o di poesia, remoti e contemporanei, ritiene estraneo alla formazione, alla conquista e all'espressione di se stesso.

4. Ancora, la finezza analitica del Pohlenz ci può esser di guida. In una nota "Menander und Epikur" pubblicata per la prima volta in *Hermes* 78 (1943), pp. 270 ss. = *Kleine Schriften* II, pp. 38 ss., lo studioso prospettava la possibilità – negata recisamente dal Reitzenstein – che può derivare dall'etica stoica o esserne influenzato il celebre verso menandreo di Terenzio *Heaut.* 77:

homo sum: humani nil a me alienum puto

pur rendendosi conto che nulla sappiamo della cronologia dell'*Heautontimorumenos* di Menandro e che, soprattutto, l'umanità di Menandro che si forma nei circoli ateniesi, fondamentalmente diversa dalla concezione universalistica del semita Zenone, si lascia intendere senza varcare i confini dell'Attica. E, infatti, alla base del verso menandreo c'è un sentimento attico e antico, che rinviene una nuova espressione: la buona *polypragmosyne*, che Teseo nelle *Supplici* di Euripide riconosce come tratto essenziale del suo popolo (v. 577):

τοιγὰρ πονοῦσα πολλὰ πόλλ' εὐδαιμονεῖ.

La *polypragmosyne*, che in Euripide e in Tucidide indica l'attività del cittadino al servizio dello stato, in antitesi all'inutile vita dell'uomo dedito ai propri interessi, in Menandro diventa interesse dell'uomo per l'uomo, partecipazione dell'uomo alle sorti del suo simile: in difformità dall' "isolamento teoretico dell'uomo singolo" proclamato da Epicuro, l'uomo menandreo vive ed agisce nella società umana, che non è più la polis del V secolo, ma una comunità, in cui un individuo non si sente estraneo all'altro. L'uomo non si muove più per la grandezza della polis, ma neppure è chiuso nel suo individualismo: dunque, "lebt in Menander das alte Gemeinschaftsgefühl in neuer Form weiter" (p. 42).

Le radici della formazione spirituale di Menandro sono innanzi tutto da ricercare nella sua educazione letteraria attuata sui testi dei grandi scrittori attici; è utile, ma scarsamente rilevante, richiamare i concetti dell' οἰκεῖον e dell' ἀλλότριον elaborati da Zenone o da Teofrasto, è utile additare l'antitesi fra la concezione umana e sociale di Menandro e l' "egocentrica" *apragmosyne* di Epicuro, ma è evidente che la pur legittima *syncrisis* con le posizioni teoretiche contemporanee non esaurisce il problema della comprensione storica di Menandro. La "nuova forma" che Menandro dà al concetto della buona *polypragmosyne* non può esser sminuita ad accatto di termini da una scuola filosofica: essa è una grande espressione artistica, incisiva, pregnante, raffinata, fatta di parole semplici, che prendono rilievo dalla loro sapiente giacitura e, perciò stesso, una grande espressione dell'umanità e della solidarietà umana del poeta, in cui può riconoscersi, non solo e non tanto, uno stoico come Panezio, ma la buona parte dell'umanità che crede alla validità della concezione umana e sociale, finemente espressa dal poeta. La "nuova forma" non è un fatto esteriore, ma è il poeta stesso che sa dare la nuova dimensione di un antico motivo in un verso originale: così la "lingua" comune diventa "parola" personale, l'arte e il pensiero si immedesimano: unità di forma e contenuto, poesia.

5. Col grosso volume (*La formazione spirituale di Menandro* [Torino, Bottega d'Erasmo, 1965]: Lezioni "Augusto Rostagni" a c. dell'Istituto di Filologia Classica dell'Università di Torino, vol. II, pp. XVII–247) Adelmo Barigazzi si è proposto di raggiun-

gere una nuova interpretazione di Menandro, anzi, come egli dice, la scoperta di "verità nuove" (p. XVII), della "vera" formazione spirituale in Menandro: la verità è quella in cui crede lo studioso, che è scettico nell'oggi, ma fiducioso nel domani. Il lettore che oggi non crede alle sue "verità," crederà domani quando si sarà risolta la crisi attuale di una società, scarsamente dotata di sensibilità morale ed estetica. Ma tralasciamo la delusione dell'autore che nel secolo XX non imperi quel sistema etico-estetico del primo Peripato, di cui, a suo modo di vedere, il giovane Menandro fu interprete fedele e gioioso messaggero, e veniamo al merito, per dirla con un altro comico.

In primo luogo, il *Menandro* del B., il cui impegno e la cui preparazione sono fuori discussione, è un libro mutilo: studia la formazione del poeta, quale preludio o premessa allo studio dell'arte di Menandro (p. XVI), non esaurisce Menandro. Ci sia consentita l'obbiezione: quale può essere la validità di una ricerca "preliminare," se questa non è subito "inverata" nel complesso della personalità del poeta? Non è sufficiente l'ottimistica speranza del B. che il lettore intanto affini la sua sensibilità: il lettore ha il diritto di sapere in che cosa consista l'arte di un poeta, la cui opera è stata da lui setacciata ed epurata, in modo che da essa nulla risulti che non sia stato insegnato da Aristotele o da Teofrasto, e tutto ciò che possa far intravedere o sospettare una presenza epicurea risulti bandito. In qual senso potrà evolversi l'arte di un poeta, severamente arrolato nella filosofia "peripatetica"? Con tale ricerca preliminare, a me pare che manchino addirittura le basi per un'impostazione del problema artistico di Menandro.

Se il B. mostra che Menandro non ha una sua poetica, ma si muove negli schemi formulati e approntati per lui dal Peripato, donde mai potrà nascere e svilupparsi l'arte del poeta? Se arte vi sarà, sarà arte che promana da una formula teorica, non da Menandro. Oppure, l'arte avrà per il B. il senso tecnico-teatrale di espediente spettacolare; ma il suo Menandro, avulso dalla storia del teatro ateniese, "lontanissimo" da Aristofane, allontanato per quanto possibile da Euripide, come potrà evolversi? Sarà possibile l'evoluzione di un poeta, che nell'interpretazione del B., dispiega la sua arte a porre in versi una proposizione di Aristotele, un enunciato di Teofrasto, un programma di Demetrio Falereo?

Un tale Menandro, mortificato e imbalsamato nei trofei della speculazione "peripatetica," difficilmente potrà avere una sua vita di artista e di poeta: i suoi personaggi, buone copie dei tipi descritti da Aristotele o catalogati da Teofrasto, sono il prodotto delle analisi psicologiche eseguite nella scuola; i suoi motivi altro non sono che categorie o concetti elaborati (sembrerebbe, per lui) dagli instancabili filosofi. Nessun filosofo fu così fedele al maestro, quanto questo "artista" alle prediche del Liceo!

6. La tesi, sostenuta dal B., a me pare viziata dal pregiudizio che l'Atene in cui si forma Menandro si debba identificare col Peripato e la società in cui vive debba essere espressa (o deformata) dalle lenti peripatetiche. Depauperato della sua interiorità. castigato finanche nel suo sorriso, soffocato dalle lezioni del Peripato, questo Menandro risulta svilito come personalità umana, incenerito come poeta. Le ricerche del Tierney, del Post, del Webster sono apparse al B. insufficienti, perchè sono moderate e discrete, perchè gli autori non sono immemori che studiano un poeta; il B. non sembra avere sufficientemente considerato che altro è additare il *milieu* culturale e sociale in cui si è formato un poeta, altro è costringere un poeta in una sètta e trasformare uno dei tramiti della sua educazione umana in una trappola, senza evasioni e senza deviazioni.

Dal punto di vista rigidamente positivistico, il libro del B. è impeccabile. Una massiccia ricerca unilaterale di fonti "peripatetiche" si riversa abbondante e soffocante su un verso di Menandro: le fonti spiegate, sviscerate, tradotte, aprono un baratro, in cui il povero verso del povero poeta affonda e naufraga. Che cosa rimane, infatti, dello "spirito" o della "spiritualità" del poeta? Che senso può avere la paternalistica definizione di Menandro "poeta della bontà umana," se quella presunta bontà è un residuo di una lezione "peripatetica," un rigurgito di quella fossa dottrinaria in cui il poeta è stato sepolto vivo?

7. La tesi d'un Menandro, apostolo del Peripato, si è costituita nel B. con l'accumulo delle tracce "peripatetiche" nella sua Commedia, anzi delle tracce del "particolare clima peripatetico nell'Atene fine sec. IV" (p. 34). Ma il B. stesso talvolta è con-

sapevole del rischioso estremismo della sua tesi. A p. 115, a conclusione della lezione su *Menandro, l'Epicureismo e lo Stoicismo*, egli scrive:

In ogni caso, non vorrei che qualcuno si raffigurasse un Menandro fanatico propugnatore e divulgatore delle idee di una scuola filosofica, che si sarebbe servito della scena solo o principalmente a questo scopo: egli è soprattutto un artista, ma il suo modo di vedere e giudicare le cose è conforme ad un'etica determinata, nella quale viene a coincidere anche l'indirizzo estetico, di modo che etica ed arte si sostengono e si chiariscono a vicenda. Questa filosofia è per noi, senza alcun dubbio, la peripatetica.

Ma a pp. 159 s. l'arrolamento di Menandro nelle file "peripatetiche" è asserito, contro il Webster, in modo piuttosto drastico:

Ci troviamo di fronte a idee troppo specifiche, che investono la natura stessa della commedia menandrea, a concetti non sempre facili, che il poeta cerca di chiarire semplificandoli e applicandoli all'atto pratico, cioè trasportandoli dall'astrattezza alla concretezza. ...

E, a pp. 218 s. il rapporto tra commedia menandrea e dottrina "peripatetica" è così stabilito: "illustrare i caratteri della commedia di Menandro è lo stesso che illustrare la dottrina peripatetica sul genere comico e viceversa." E a p. 224: "la commedia di Menandro ... attua e precisa nei particolari la teoria peripatetica." E a pp. 229 s.: "il Peripato, che tanto influì sulla nuova estetica della poesia ellenistica, ebbe subito il suo poeta, che seppe rappresentare fedelmente l'alto ideale umano di quella filosofia"; a p. 108: "Menandro fu il poeta dell'etica del Peripato"; a p. 114: "E Menandro sotto la protezione dell'amico potente potè studiare con tranquillità ed attuare i criteri etico-estetici del Peripato relativi alla commedia scrivendo molti dei suoi drammi." Inoltre, se i personaggi di Menandro (quelli educati) "divulgarono efficacemente e dovunque il pensiero etico della scuola peripatetica" (p. 230), Menandro stesso impersona la figura del magnanimo, delineata nell'*Etica Nicomachea*. Scrive, infatti, il B. a p. 41:

Ed ecco apparire la figura del magnanimo, del μεγαλόψυχος, che è uno degli aspetti più salienti dell'etica del Peripato. Il carattere magnanimo viene descritto molto bene in quelle parti dell'*Etica Nicomachea* in cui il filosofo, dopo aver parlato della natura etica e del suo carattere volontario, descrive le virtù particolari nei libri IV e V. La magnanimità comprende tutte le virtù o segue ogni virtù. Il magnanimo non bada alle piccole cose, mira in alto alle cose degne di sè, non tiene conto degli onori delle persone dappoco e neppure delle ingiurie, si compiace solo degli onori tributatigli dai buoni e dai competenti, ma li considera solo come un riconoscimento alle sue qualità superiori, senza dar loro importanza, chè si sente staccato da ogni cosa esterna, onori, potenza, ricchezze. Perciò non si meraviglia di nulla, giudica con sincerità, vive con semplicità, non cura biasimi e lodi nè le vicende della fortuna, non trasmoda nè nella gioia nè nel dolore quando è fortunato o sfortunato, si muove lentamente, parla con voce grave, chè nè la fretta nè il parlar violento o stridulo conviene a chi non dà importanza che a poche cose. Sembra di vedere il ritratto di Menandro. ...

Dunque, Menandro modellò se stesso sul carattere magnanimo descritto con magnanima antiveggenza da Aristotele e modellò i suoi personaggi sui caratteri, prodigalmente delineati da Aristotele e da Teofrasto.

8. Nel Seicento così poetava Charles Perrault:

Ménandre, j'en conviens, eut un rare génie,
Et pour plaire au théâtre une adresse infinie.
Virgile, j'y consens, mérite des autels.
Ovide est digne encore des honneurs immortels,
Mais ces rares auteurs, qu'aujourd'hui l'on adore,
Étaient-ils adorés quand ils vivaient encore?
Écoutons Martial: Ménandre, esprit charmant,
Fu du théâtre grec applaudi rarement;
Virgile vit les vers d'Ennius le bonhomme,
Lus, chéris, estimés des connaisseurs de Rome,
Pendant qu'avec langueur on écoutait les siens,
Tant on est amoureux des auteurs anciens;
Et malgré la douceur de sa veine divine,
Ovide était connu de sa seule Corinne;
Ce n'est qu'avec le temps que leur nom s'accroissant,
Et toujours plus fameux d'âge en âge passant,
A la fin s'est acquis cette gloire éclatante
Qui de tant de degrés a passé leur attente.

La chiave per intendere le parole di Marziale (5. 10. 9: *rara coronato plausere theatra Menandro*) è dal B. trovata ed additata nella preparazione filosofica ed estetica di stampo "peripatetico" di Menandro: l'insuccesso, cioè, fu dovuto al fatto che "il volgo non è affatto sensibile a certe distinzioni morali e tanto meno ad un'estetica che si eleva insieme al concetto etico, ad un'estetica insomma fondamentalmente concettuale" (p. 160) e quindi alla novità dell'opera di Menandro: "ciò che fa riflettere e non è facile – scrive l'autore a p. 174 – non può essere gradito subito: il trionfo degl'innovatori è sempre lento a venire." E, modestamente, il destino che il B. si prefigura col suo libro è proprio quello stesso di Menandro (p. XVII): "Ma non m'illudo di riuscire a persuadere subito tutti: le verità nuove sono sempre lente a farsi strada."

9. Il capitolo primo è un profilo semplicistico del passaggio dell'uomo greco da "cittadino della polis" a "cittadino del mondo," attraverso notazioni o osservazioni tratte, per lo più da testi oratori e da Plutarco, senza alcuna precisazione di ordine metodologico. "La caratteristica dell'Atene del sec. V è l'attaccamento profondo alla patria" scrive il B. a pp. 1 s., ma a p. 16 afferma che l'assenza dell'ozio, l'attività costante, la πολυ-πραγμοσύνη "era la caratteristica dell'Atene del sec. V." Se dobbiamo credere al B., i Persiani "non sanno perchè combattono e questa loro incoscienza è significata dal sordo e confuso rumore con cui essi affrontano la battaglia di Salamina" (p. 2) e "dopo la caduta di Atene le città greche combattono fra loro per una egemonia che non è ispirata a qualche ideale politico, ma a fini bassi ed egoistici" (p. 3). Poi venne "l'unificazione" ad opera della potenza macedonica (p. 3), nonostante il "nazionalismo" di Demostene (p. 4), nonostante "il partito nazionalista" (pp. 4 s.): "il dramma di Atene era finito: col partito nazionalista era stato sconfitto ciò che di antico c'era ancora nella vita ateniese; con la polis era spenta la città" (*sic*, p. 6). Il B. oltre che di "nazionalismo" demostenico, parla di "riabilitazione" di Licurgo (p. 5), di "quinta colonna" (p. 6), di "epurazione" ad opera di Licurgo (p. 10) e crede di fare opera di critico, se non di storico, affermando che "i nazionalisti non avevano capito il vero significato dei nuovi avvenimenti" (p. 6) e che Licurgo "non ha capito" "la condizione spirituale dell'Atene del suo tempo." Tacciare di stupidità Demostene e Licurgo significa rinunzia ad intendere; tale rinunzia ci appare grave, quando tutti sanno quale sia stato il ruolo di Demostene nella crisi della democrazia ateniese. Il B. adoperando il termine "nazionalismo" è fuori della ricerca

storiografica moderna: se Demostene non è l'ultimo o il penultimo "eroe" della libertà greca, è, certo, qualcosa di più di un fanatico sciovinista, sopravvissuto a se stesso. Sono assenti nel discorso del B. le fonti storiche e storiografiche: il B. si serve di un passo di Isocrate o di Demostene o di Licurgo, senza discernimento critico, ovvero col vecchio pregiudizio di dimostrare *a posteriori* che gli oppositori della politica di Filippo erano dei poveri sprovveduti superstiti, dei classicisti della politica, fuori della realtà effettuale, dominati dagli schemi esteriori della grandezza del passato.

Dopo averci appreso la caratteristica del sec. V, il B. ci insegna che "una caratteristica del sec. IV" è una "generale irrequietudine" (p. 13), di cui "la ricchezza viene considerata come unico rimedio," e che nell'età ellenistica "il traffico commerciale coopera grandemente alla formazione di quel sentimento di universalità, che ricevette impulso particolarmente dalla filosofia" (p. 13). Così il IV secolo, specialmente la seconda metà, è dominato dalla filosofia, al punto che l'uomo "che abita sotto il medesimo sole per quanto in plaghe diverse" è "figlio della filosofia, ha bisogno della filosofia" (p. 14). E "uno dei documenti più importanti" per comprendere questo "secolo irrequieto" (p. 18) è la Commedia Nuova, "pur nella perdita quasi totale di questo genere letterario" (*sic*). Così il B. si apre la via "nuova" per studiare la commedia menandrea come documento filosofico, anzi "degli insegnamenti filosofici," di un rinnovato "ideale umano," del cosmopolitismo: "questo è il frutto incommensurabile (*sic*) del sacrificio della libertà di Atene" (p. 18). E questa frase avrebbe il suo significato, se coloro che lottarono per la libertà di Atene non fossero stati catalogati dal B. come "nazionalisti."

10. Anche il capitolo secondo (*Un peripatetico al governo di Atene*) può considerarsi propedeutico e vuol essere una caratterizzazione di Demetrio Falereo governatore di Atene e della storia dell'ultimo quarto dell' "irrequieto" IV secolo. Comparato al capitolo primo, questo non contiene ingenuità e imprecisioni: abbiamo avuto un sospiro di sollievo, quando finalmente il B. parla di "partito democratico" (p. 19) e non nazionalistico, e siamo indulgenti quando il B. scrive che "la forma di governo era ancora la repubblicana" e che in realtà "Atene divenne un

principato," perchè l'esposizione dei fatti storici è ben concatenata e condotta. Anche l'opinione generale che "la commedia nuova non è politica" (p. 22) e che "gli avvenimenti politici non costituiscono più l'intreccio di una commedia nè stanno nello sfondo di una allegoria" (p. 23) è accettabile, anche se poi Menandro nel *frg.* 238 "accenna alla nuova istituzione dei *gynaiconomoi* sotto Demetrio di Falero" (p. 23) e altrove si adegua "allo spirito della legislazione di Demetrio Falero" (p. 42). Ma già in questo capitolo si avanza la tesi generale di un Menandro, che, in quanto "scolaro di Teofrasto" e amico del Falereo, egualmente scolaro di Teofrasto, porta nelle sue commedie gli insegnamenti etici, estetici e politici del Peripato, anche se il B. continui ad affermare, come si suole, che la commedia viva "della vita quotidiana" (p. 24). Qui c'è una manifesta contraddizione, perchè, come ammette lo stesso B., tra l'insegnamento "peripatetico" e "la vita quotidiana" non c'è proprio nulla di comune. Ma che la tesi generale non regga, si vede già da uno dei particolari, che il B. adduce a suo sostegno. Che Menandro possa aver condiviso "le tendenze politiche della scuola peripatetica" il B. deduce dai *frgg.* 549 e 546. Nel *frg.* 549

> καλόν γε βασιλεὺς τῇ μὲν ἀνδρείᾳ κρατῶν,
> τὰ δὲ τοῦ βίου δίκαια διατηρῶν κρίσει

se una fonte filosofica dev'essere additata, io penserei alla concezione platonica dell' ἀνὴρ βασιλικός e a quella academica del βασιλεύς quale risulta dai dialoghi pseudoplatonici, che segnano l'evoluzione estrema del pensiero politico di Platone. Così anche nel *frg.* 546, se è menandreo, è più probabile un fondo platonico che "peripatetico":

> δεῖ τὸν πολιτῶν προστατεῖν αἱρούμενον
> τὴν τοῦ λόγου μὲν δύναμιν οὐκ ἐπίφθονον,
> ἤθει δὲ χρηστῷ συγκεκραμένην ἔχειν.

Anzitutto si parla di un προστάτης τῶν πολιτῶν (non τῶν ἀνθρώπων), poi della celeberrima δύναμις τῶν λόγων (ο τοῦ λόγου) che, diversamente dai Sofisti, Platone concepiva appunto οὐκ ἐπίφθονος, al servizio della verità, corretta dall' ἦθος χρηστόν, vale a dire dall'animo onesto e probo del reggitore.

Quanto aleatoria sia l'ipotesi "peripatetica" risulta anche da ciò che sùbito dopo afferma il B.: "In ogni caso è da notare come egli ponga l'accento soprattutto sul τρόπος χρηστός, per cui accenni politici del genere acquistano facilmente carattere morale e fanno parte della concezione etica generale del poeta." Qui (e, se non erro, anche altrove) il B. pare confondere ἦθος e τρόπος, due concetti distinti già chiaramente in Platone (p. es. *Leg.* 924) e che non sono affatto monopolio del Peripato.

Per quanto riguarda la tradizione biografica, il B. dà molto peso alla notizia di Panfila (presso Diog. Laert. 5. 36 = *test.* 7), secondo cui Teofrasto fu maestro (διδάσκαλος) di Menandro e all'altra che collega Menandro al Falereo (Diog. Laert. 5. 79 = *test.* 8). Anzi, poichè il Falereo "probabilmente" ascoltò Aristotele, "non è escluso che l'abbia udito anche Menandro"! Poichè il Wilamowitz negò che Menandro fu alunno di Teofrasto (*Der Glaube der Hellenen*, II, p. 285, n. 1: "Ob die Ueberlieferung von persönlichen Beziehungen der beiden Männer auf Tatsachen beruht, ist unsicher. Schüler Theophrasts ist der frühreife Dichter nicht gewesen"), il B. non si limita a dimostrare il contrario, ma aggiunge l'ipotesi di un Menandro, alunno di Aristotele. Tendenziosa è pure la svalutazione della notizia straboniana (14. 638 = *test.* 6) sulla *synefebia* di Menandro e Epicuro: è vero quanto mostra il B., che la notizia non può significare un'amicizia fra i due, ma è cavilloso negare il valore dell'accostamento, del contemporaneo fiorire della filosofia epicurea e della commedia menandrea. È vero che il Falereo "attuò nella pratica la teoria peripatetica" (p. 33), ma, naturalmente, è dubbio che Menandro attinga a Teofrasto "il concetto generale della funzione della donna nella società" (pp. 34 s.).

Poichè il B. pone un diaframma tra μέση e νέα, non è mai sfiorato dal sospetto che anche Menandro talvolta possa porre in caricatura un filosofo. Dal *frg.* 634 che do nella sua traduzione ("Sopporta la sventura e il danno con dignità: questa è la prerogativa dell'uomo fornito di senno, non lamentarsi aggrottando le ciglia"), il B. ricava la deduzione: "Qui si ammette l'importanza di Tyche e ad essa si contrappone l'efficacia delle virtù" (p. 39). Eppure, io credo noto a tutti i lettori che quando un comico scrive la frase "aggrottare le ciglia" vuol porre in ridicolo il filosofo, che con un'aria di sopracciò medita, investiga, ragiona e scopre le grandi verità della sua testa, che non hanno nulla in comune con l'esperienza e la pratica della vita. Naturalmente da un atteggiamento spirituale siffatto non è da inferire nulla di eccezionale e, tanto meno, che Menandro faccia la parodia di un filosofo peripatetico o (orrore!) di Teofrasto, ma semplicemente che Menandro non ignora che i filosofi che aggrottavano le ciglia suscitavano se non la diffidenza (anche dei suoi personaggi bene educati), il sorriso, l'ironia, il compatimento di chi esperiva con reale sofferenza le difficoltà e i casi della vita. O, in altri termini, non si abbia paura di dire che Menandro, almeno in questo, è nella tradizione della μέση e riprende un *topos* gradito alla sensibilità popolare. Menandro, certo, non concepiva o rappresentava le sue commedie nel Liceo.

Che Menandro "derida" i Cinici è invece categoricamente affermato dal B. (p. 39, n. 101), il quale afferma sùbito – a scanso di equivoci – che "la dignità menandrea, spirituale e fisica (!), non aveva molto da condividere con quei filosofi simili a mendicanti." Anche qui la questione è malposta: una volta rivendicata la purezza "peripatetica" di Menandro, docile "alunno" di Teofrasto, i poveri Cinici devono essere banditi dall'orizzonte filosofico del poeta. Ora, non è che Menandro debba amare i Cinici e non "deriderli": è che il poeta non ignora il successo popolare di quella filosofia e allude alle bisacce di Monimo e alle stravaganze di Cratete (*frgg.* 215 e 104), sicuro di far sorridere gli spettatori. Per il B., il poeta "peripatetico" non può che "deridere" i Cinici e considerare con serietà solo i precetti della "sua" scuola e modellare conseguentemente i suoi personaggi: così quel principe da fiaba popolare che è, a mio parere, il Sostrato del *Dyscolos* diventa per il B. un esortatore "al buon uso della ricchezza" (nell' umanissima scena col padre, vv. 797 ss.) in conformità "all'insegnamento del Peripato e allo spirito della legislazione di Demetrio Falereo" (p. 42) e il disgraziato Cnemone, che afferma essere "cosa pia l'incenso e la focaccia," un sacrificio semplice e povero, non è che il portatore delle idee sui sacrifici agli dèi, espresse da Teofrasto nel libro *De pietate* (pp. 42 s.). E anche quel che non sappiamo sia stato trattato da Teofrasto "non sarà mancato in Teofrasto" (pp. 44 s.: "nel passo citato del *Dyscolos* [vv. 806 ss.] c'è in più il concetto della beneficenza, ma non sarà mancato in Teofrasto"). E, dunque, nulla è in Menandro che prima non fosse in Teofrasto!

11. Nel terzo capitolo (*Homo sum: humani nil a me alienum puto*) il B. stringe ancora il legame tra filosofia e società "peripatetica" e la commedia menandrea. "Il *Dyscolos* contiene l'esaltazione della φιλανθρωπία secondo le idee peripatetiche" (p. 48). L'incantevole Sostrato "educato alle nuove idee" e "pieno di ardore nell'applicarle" piega il padre Callippide, cioè la vecchia generazione, alle nuove teorie filosofiche: una sorta di apostolo che trasmette gli umori della linfa "peripatetica" ai vecchi rappresentanti dell'egoismo; analogamente, Gorgia "ricupera alla società" il patrigno misantropo. Naturalmente, "c'è anche una particolarità linguistica che ci riconduce all'insegnamento del Peripato: in bocca a Cnemone, quando parla della solidarietà umana, non compare il termine φιλία, ma εὔνοια, proprio nel senso specifico in cui l'usa Aristotele di ἀντιφίλησις" (p. 52)! Così, anche Cnemone è assorbito negli schemi dottrinari. Ma "tutto il pensiero" di Menandro "relativo alla società" (p. 54) è peripatetico; l'etica del Peripato "è di guida" a Menandro anche nella castigatezza del linguaggio e nella "misura dello scherzo e del ridicolo." Fra i varî echeggiamenti della dottrina "peripatetica" nei personaggi menandrei, merita di esser qui ricordato quello della dottrina teofrastea dell' οἰκείωσις nel discorso di Gorgia a Daos (*Dysc.* 238 ss.). Teofrasto, quale studioso di botanica (p. 65), sarebbe inoltre il suggeritore del paragone dell'albero e dell'insistenza sul concetto di natura nel *frg.* 337:

> ὦ Παρμένων, οὐκ ἔστ' ἀγαθὸν ἐν τῷ βίῳ
> φυόμενον ὥσπερ δένδρον ἐκ ῥίζης μιᾶς,
> ἀλλ' ἐγγὺς ἀγαθοῦ παραπέφυκε καὶ κακόν,
> ἐκ τοῦ κακοῦ τ' ἤνεγκεν ἀγαθὸν ἡ φύσις.

A me pare evidente che le "osservazioni" o le "investigazioni naturalistiche" di Teofrasto non hanno in nulla suggerito il paragone menandreo: il B. ha perso di vista il significato del passo, pur di rintracciare Teofrasto. Il motivo menandreo è questo: il bene e il male sono per natura indissociabili: accanto al bene cresce il male, dal male germoglia il bene: "un bene nella vita non è come un albero che cresce da una sola radice, ma vicino ad un bene cresce anche un male, e dal male la natura porta alla luce un bene." Se bisogna pensare a suggestione filosofica, io penso ad una variazione del pensiero di Socrate, appena liberato dalla catena, sull'origine unica della gioia e del dolore (*Phd.* 60b).

12. Nel capitolo quarto (*Menandro e l'etologia peripatetica*) campeggiano i *Caratteri* di Teofrasto: i punti di contatto con personaggi menandrei non sono nè casuali nè insignificanti, nè Teofrasto ha attinto alla Commedia, ma la Commedia a Teofrasto, nonchè ad Aristotele. "La commedia di Menandro si collega con questa letteratura peripatetica relativa allo studio della psicologia e alla rappresentazione coerente dei caratteri per mezzo di particolari efficaci e di un linguaggio adatto" (p. 71). Se i connotati di un personaggio comico non hanno riscontro in fonti "peripatetiche," il poeta, tuttavia, ha "applicato al tipo tradizionale l'analisi psicologica approfondita dalla scuola peripatetica" (p. 76): solo in questi casi e in tali limiti il B. ammette una "tradizione" della μέση, che è da lui regolarmente svalutata: la μέση non ha caratteri; Menandro li crea, ispirandosi all'ideale etico del Peripato, "plasmando con coerenza figure completamente nuove" (p. 80).

Ma il tentativo più massiccio per difendere l'integralismo "peripatetico" di Menandro è il capitolo quinto (pp. 87–115: *Menandro, l'Epicureismo e lo Stoicismo*). Qui abbiamo il conato di destoricizzare Menandro, di svellerlo dal *milieu* culturale del suo tempo e di mostrarlo un povero nano incantato sulle spalle solide del Falereo e di Teofrasto. Può darsi che il B. abbia ragione quando afferma che la "tendenza di spiegare Menandro attraverso Terenzio e Plauto ha danneggiato la comprensione del poeta greco, come artista," ha però certamente ragione anche quando proclama, di rincalzo, che "abbiamo abbastanza per potere spiegare Menandro con Menandro" (p. 104). Ma se ha questa ragione, lo studioso ha il torto di non aver mai applicato questo sano criterio nel suo libro: infatti, egli spiega continuamente Menandro col Peripato e innalza ad unico canone esegetico la pertica "peripatetica": da questo punto di vista, il capitolo quinto è esemplare.

Si può consentire col B. che dimostra inattestata un'amicizia tra Menandro ed Epicuro, ma non più consentire quando supporrebbe che Menandro "ne mettesse in caricatura la dottrina"

(p. 89), sulle orme di Alessi, che per il resto è tanto diverso da Menandro. Gli indizi, le prove sulla presenza della dottrina epicurea in Menandro – quali furono indicati dal Bignone, dal Büchner e specialmente dal De Witt – possono anche non persuadere tutti, ma certo la dimostrazione in contrario del B. è troppo pregiudizievole per essere persuasiva. Il B. si preoccupa di raffigurare un Menandro immune da qualsiasi altro contatto dottrinario che non sia quello del Peripato, come se Epicuro e Zenone non fossero esistiti e le tracce di un motivo epicureo contaminassero la purezza di Menandro. Che il romanzetto di Alcifrone e la rappresentazione di Menandro o del Falereo come uomini dediti al piacere non siano documenti storici, nessuno dubita; ma la tradizione su cui si sviluppa un'aneddotica, sia pur deformata, ha sempre un'anima di autenticità. È difficile credere che Menandro godesse di beni esterni, perchè Aristotele e Teofrasto avevano dimostrato contro Speusippo che il piacere non è un male, nè d'altra parte dobbiamo scorgere nei frammenti menandrei, in cui s'accenna al piacere, un'eco autentica di dottrina epicurea. Ma che nel *frg.* 620 – dove si distinguono i mali necessari dai mali aggiunti, cioè quelli naturali dai non naturali – sia illegittimo rinvenire un'eco di un particolare dell'etica epicurea, è una mera presunzione del B., il quale riduce esclusivamente il concetto all'etica aristotelica. Che il passo dell'*Andria* terenziana (vv. 959 ss.) abbia "un senso generico" (p. 98) e non contenga un δόγμα 'Επικούρειον come voleva la fonte di Donato e hanno mostrato il Bignone e il De Witt, è un'opinione che fa comodo al B., ma non convince affatto. Se il B. non è alieno dal supporre "un'influenza epicurea nella terminologia" (p. 97), non si vede perchè i termini debbano essere concepiti come espressione priva di concetti. Così pure, che nel monologo di Gnatone dell'*Eunuco* terenziano non vi sia allusione alla *vita beata* come vuole il Büchner, ma "pensieri generici" (p. 102), può credere solo il B. Che tutti i particolari della dimostrazione del De Witt sullo spirito menandreo ed epicureo degli *Adelphoe* non siano rigorosi (è difficile veramente ammettere che *consuefacio* del v. 414 sia una ripresa dell'accezione epicurea di συνεθίζω) non autorizza tuttavia la conclusione del B. che gli *Adelphoe* "riflettono la dottrina etica del Peripato" (pp. 107 s.). Ed è altrettanto azzardato affermare e dimostrare che "per quel che riguarda il pensiero sulla fortuna, Menandro è nettamente fuori dell'influenza stoica ed epicurea" (p. 111).

13. A siffatti eccessi il B. sembra sottrarsi nel capitolo sesto (*Menandro e l'etica della tragedia*), in cui ammette che un ruolo debba assegnarsi alla tradizione tragica specialmente euripidea, anche se questa poi è sempre filtrata e rinnovata dalla formazione aristotelico-teofrastea di Menandro. Il B. ha buon gioco nel contestare al Webster alcune derivazioni menandree da Sofocle o da Euripide, ma riesce sempre poco accettabile "l'elaborazione peripatetica" (p. 120), a cui Menandro sottoporrebbe quel "materiale vecchio." Credo anch'io all' "elaborazione" da parte del poeta di motivi o concetti che gli provenivano dal teatro tragico, ma parlerei di elaborazione personale, non "peripatetica." Anche in un capitolo come questo, bene impostato e condotto, è tuttavia predominante il vizio originario: che il rapporto con Euripide non debba spiegarsi in senso evolutivo, ma come "ritorno" "in seguito alla dottrina etico-estetica del Peripato" (p. 123) è poco plausibile, se non sibillino. Ammetto che la "nuova umanità" dei personaggi menandrei "non è spiegabile col solo riferimento ad Euripide" (p. 125), ma non ammetto che l'umanità dei personaggi sia il risultato delle speculazioni e delle analisi psicologiche del Peripato: essa è creazione di Menandro, non insensibile, come uomo di cultura, a tutte le componenti filosofiche della cultura contemporanea. Il B. ha certamente ragione a mostrare che per una retta interpretazione dell'importante *frg.* 416 non basta ricorrere al pensiero anassagoreo di Euripide, e ad aderire perciò alla dimostrazione del Bignone che additò nel frammento una derivazione dal *Protrettico* di Aristotele, per quel che riguarda "il rapporto tra l'immagine della vita come una fiera e la contemplazione delle cose celesti" (p. 118). Ma il B. stesso avverte onestamente che il paragone della vita con un'adunanza festiva è di origine pitagorica, anche se "Eraclide Pontico ha trasferito nell'episodio di Pitagora i tre βίοι del *Protrettico* aristotelico" (p. 130). Come però non basta la fruizione menandrea di una immagine pitagorica per affermare che Menandro è pitagorico o pitagorizzante, così l'adozione di un motivo o di un carattere riscontrabile nella speculazione "peripatetica" non autorizza a costringere Menandro negli schemi di

quella scuola. Il Bignone, che non aveva lenti "peripatetiche," poteva tranquillamente scoprire pensieri epicurei e pensieri aristotelici nei frammenti di Menandro (come del resto in altri Comici), senza fare del poeta il rappresentante di una sètta. Il confronto tra il *frg.* 416 di Menandro e il *frg.* 219 di Alessi è opportuno: ma non credo che Alessi, riprendendo l'immagine pitagorica della vita come adunanza affollata, abbia solo voluto "illustrate un motivo antichissimo" (p. 132) e Menandro abbia voluto solo opporre ai travagli della vita il rimedio della "contemplazione della natura." L'uno e l'altro sono ridotti dal B. a illustratori o seguaci di un motivo filosofico, senza che egli sospetti che Alessi e Menandro, riprendendo e sviluppando in diversa guisa un'immagine di origine pitagorica, possano esprimere anch'essi una propria visione del mondo.

Nel capitolo settimo (*La dottrina peripatetica della responsabilità e il prologo della "Periciromene"*) il B. si dichiara insoddisfatto dell'impostazione del Webster "che le idee peripatetiche avevano varcato le pareti della scuola ed erano molto diffuse in Atene alla fine del sec. IV e al principio del sec. III" (p. 159) e, come al solito, pone il poeta in un banco della scuola peripatetica, docile pupillo di Aristotele e Teofrasto. Aristotele distingue due generi di offese e quattro specie; nel *frg.* 359 la quadruplice classificazione è ridotta a duplice; tale semplificazione non è neppure di Menandro, ma appartiene "all'ambiente del Peripato." E, quindi, Menandro semplifica e divulga, secondo gli ultimi dettami della scuola. Con più di un esempio, il B. dimostra che la commedia menandrea si fonda su un'offesa, un danno, una colpa involontaria, non deliberatamente commessa; la concezione di Menandro è basata sulla teoria etico-estetica, da lui imparata a scuola. Il prologo della *Periciromene* viene interpretato dal B. come un documento della dottrina peripatetica sulla responsabilità delle azioni umane (pp. 152 ss.): l'Agnoia del prologo adombra la distinzione peripatetica fra errore involontario e colpa deliberatamente commessa (p. 159), applicata da Menandro nel *frg.* 359.

Un altro sostegno alla tesi generale è dato dal B. nel capitolo ottavo (*Una nuova interpretazione della "Samia"*): la commedia è interpretata come "il dramma di due nobili caratteri che si sentono offesi l'uno dall'altro in ciò che hanno di più caro, la dignità morale; un dramma di anime condotto senza un complicato intreccio esterno, ma con una linearità semplice e chiara" (p. 190); i due personaggi, Demea e Moschione, "sono una novità" e "di questa novità il poeta è debitore all'etica del Peripato" (p. 172). Specialmente Moschione rispecchia meglio "l'interesse e l'entusiasmo per le novità delle idee morali del Peripato" (p. 174).

In questo capitolo affiora il problema della "tecnica" di Menandro. Il B. sembra essersi costruito questo schema: Menandro giovine è dominato dallo "spirito etico del Peripato" e tale "pensiero etico, come capita di solito *nei giovani discepoli di qualche dottrina filosofica*" (p. 190) ha il sopravvento sulla tecnica, poi "il poeta progredirà nella tecnica," "ma a quello spirito etico egli non rinuncerà più, nè poteva rinunziare essendo l'anima della sua opera e il suo stesso modo di pensare." Tuttavia a me pare che l'escogitato espediente non si possa considerare un'impostazione del problema: è uno schema autoschediastico. Il B. prima fa pesare gravemente sul poeta la dottrina "peripatetica" e poi se lo immagina nello sforzo – a quanto pare, vano – di liberarsene.

14. Un terzo sostegno alla tesi di Menandro "divulgatore della morale peripatetica" (p. 217) è dato dal B. nel capitolo nono (*La dottrina peripatetica del carattere e la predica di Onesimo*). Qui il B. si dilunga specialmente sulla dottrina del τρόπος χρηστός, del carattere virtuoso, di origine aristotelica. Il Menandro che profila il B. "non può usare un linguaggio esattamente scientifico: deve chiarire i concetti, portarli al livello della mentalità della maggior parte degli spettatori" (p. 210). Talvolta il poeta "sembra parafrasare" un passo di Aristotele, ma sempre, secondo la ricostruzione del B., è nell'orma di Aristotele. Ed effettivamente il B. scrive un perpetuo commento a versi menandrei con citazioni dall'*Ethica Nicomachea* e talvolta piega il testo menandreo a significanze allotrie. Così il *frg.* 545 (καλὸν οἱ νόμοι σφόδρ' εἰσίν· ὁ δ' ὁρῶν τοὺς νόμους | λίαν ἀκριβῶς, συκοφάντης φαίνεται) è inteso dal B. (p. 194): "chi adegua la propria condotta solo alla forma della legge, non alla luce della virtù, non è un buon cittadino." Il testo, invece, non sottintende alcun riferimento alla virtù o contrapposizione tra legge e virtù, significa semplice-

mente: "Gran bella cosa le leggi, ma chi vede le leggi con eccessiva sottigliezza si trova a fare il delatore" ovvero *summum ius, summa iniuria.* Così negli ultimi due versi del *frg.* 568 (καιρός ἐστιν ἡ νόσος | ψυχῆς· ὁ πληγεὶς δ᾽ εἰς ὃ δεῖ τι τρώσκεται) il B. vede una del tutto inesistente allusione al τρόπος, in quanto spiega εἰς ὃ δεῖ = εἰς τὸν τρόπον (p. 196, n. 32). In realtà i versi – se il testo è probante, in quanto δ᾽ εἰς ὃ δεῖ è correzione del Wyttenbach della lez. ms. δ᾽ εἴσω δή – significano: una coincidenza è la malattia dell'anima: chi ne è colpito, è ferito là dove deve essere colpito, cioè nell'anima. La malattia dell'anima è, ovviamente, l'amore.

Centro del capitolo è l'interpretazione in chiave esclusivamente aristotelica della "predica di Onesimo" (*Epit.* 726 ss.), in cui, eliminato qualsiasi riecheggiamento di pensieri epicurei o stoici, il B. sostiene che Menandro ha voluto chiarire "un pensiero filosofico avvicinandolo a concetti tradizionali e servendosi di immagini più facilmente comprensibili" (p. 202) ovvero che Onesimo critica Smicrine in modo ' conforme alla morale peripatetica" (p. 203). E non vorrei accusare il B. di confusione, ma, in ogni caso, nella stessa pagina 207 una volta il τρόπος "è un modo di essere con determinate attitudini, equivalente a ἕξις," un'altra il "modo in cui ognuno ha sviluppato l'ἕξις φυσική." Ma c'è poi qualcosa di veramente incredibile. Onesimo dice (729 ss.) nella traduzione del B.: "Ci sono, per così dire, mille città in tutto; ognuna ha trentamila abitanti. A uno a uno, gli dèi mandano ciascuno di questi in rovina o lo preservano?" Il B. suppone che "Menandro abbia pensato al censimento dell'Attica eseguito da Demetrio Falereo" ovvero "che Menandro, per bocca di Onesimo, prenda lo spunto dal censimento dell'Attica di Demetrio e lo applichi agli altri stati" (p. 211). Non vi è, dunque, scampo: o Aristotele o Teofrasto o Demetrio Falereo.

Così nell'ultimo capitolo (*Menandro e l'estetica del Peripato*) possiamo leggere (p. 218): "Se Aristotele fosse vissuto ancora qualche anno, così da udire alcune commedie di Menandro, egli avrebbe visto in lui il poeta capace di realizzare i suoi principi estetici." E poichè questo non accadde, Menandro portò "a perfezione da una parte il principio teorico di Aristotele" e influì "dall'altra a sua volta sull'evoluzione posteriore di quella teoria. I due aspetti sono indissolubili: illustrare i caratteri della commedia di Menandro è lo stesso che illustrare la dottrina peripatetica del genere comico e viceversa" (pp. 218 ss.). La Commedia Nuova sarebbe impensabile "senza l'estetica del Peripato, la quale mirava a raggiungere il medesimo fine che si proponeva l'etica" (p. 221). Al sistema etico-estetico del Peripato Menandro deve i concetti della compostezza dignitosa e della filantropia, con i quali caratterizza i suoi personaggi educati e soprattutto la sua "serietà" di poeta comico. E così pure la novità della Commedia Nuova "impregnata dei principi etico-estetici del Peripato" (p. 228) assicurò a Menandro il posto accanto ad Omero. Strano a dirsi, non perchè avesse creato delle idee, ma perchè le divulgò (p. 230).

Consummatum est: Menandro "veramente può esser detto il poeta del Peripato."

Ma perchè risulti l'illegittimità del metodo seguito dal B. di spiegare Menandro col Peripato e il Peripato con Menandro, basti pensare quanto invece sia legittimo, coerente e costruttivo spiegare – come è stato fatto, con buoni risultati (v. p. es. I. Lana, *Lucio Anneo Seneca* [Torino, 1955]) – Seneca tragico con Seneca filosofo, le sue tragedie con le sue opere filosofiche: non v'è dubbio, e si può concretamente provare, che alcuni concetti – come l'ira – filosoficamente elaborati dal pensatore risultano dominanti in alcune scene delle sue tragedie.

15. A mio parere, per l'interpretazione di un poeta come Menandro che fiorisce nell'età di Epicuro, di Teofrasto, di Zenone – per limitarci ai filosofi – si pone correttamente il problema del rapporto della sua Commedia con le filosofie contemporanee. Il Comico – dell'ἀρχαία, della μέση e della νέα – non è rimasto mai indifferente allo svolgimento del pensiero contemporaneo, specialmente alla dimensione della reazione popolare alle speculazioni filosofiche. Per Aristofane o per un Alessi si tratta di parodia o di caricatura o di ironia: è una sollecitazione che il comico riceve dal pubblico stesso, il quale, a sua volta, è lieto di rinvenire a teatro l'espressione della sua diffidenza o del suo gusto sulla bocca dei suoi personaggi o di apprendere le novità filosofiche del momento, le teorie cosmogoniche e geometriche o matematiche o razionalistiche o ateistiche oppure di vedere allusi certi tipici rappresentanti delle scuole contempo-

ranee nel loro modo di rovinare la gioventù o di passare la vita di ogni giorno. È indubbio che le speculazioni filosofiche abbiano fornito materia di comicità più o meno schernevole ai poeti nè è però negabile che i poeti al di là della caricatura (raramente, della satira) si nutrissero degli umori sani delle dottrine che rappresentavano giocosamente sulla scena. Per quel che possiamo giudicare, Menandro è alieno dalla parodia o caricatura filosofica: nella sua commedia, che prima di tutto vuole conquistare con la sua novità il pubblico, la filosofia entra con la medesima discrezione, con cui entrano alcuni avvenimenti politici o personali della storia contemporanea. I personaggi, quali ha creato Menandro, rispecchiano le condizioni della civiltà contemporanea, notoriamente basata non sui valori del cittadino, ma su quelli dell'uomo, su un orizzonte di vita aperto all'unione, alla comprensione, alla solidarietà. Non più Ateniesi o Spartani, ma neppure Greci o Barbari: uomini bensì di una sola società, i cui problemi sono comuni a tutti e a ciascuno. L'aria che respira Menandro è quella della sua epoca, nella sua città: non è l'aria dell'Academia, del Liceo, del Giardino, della Stoa, ma l'aria comune a tutti i cittadini, che ormai guardano alla città, come ad una parte del mondo, non roccaforte di una religione o di una filosofia, bensì libero ricettacolo delle idee, che venivano esprimendo particolarmente i filosofi, che andavano sempre più assumendo il ruolo di salvatori di anime.

Accentuandosi la crisi dei valori politici e religiosi tradizionali, Menandro, che non ignora i momenti della storia della cultura greca nella sua varia, diseguale e complessa fioritura, coglie i motivi fondamentali della sua epoca, esprimendoli in un linguaggio aderente alle possibilità del suo pubblico e alla misura del suo gusto educato, del suo temperamento meditativo, della sua forza persuasiva. Che Euripide non sia rimasto immune dall'influsso sofistico della tecnica antilogica (e, del resto, neppure Sofocle) è un fatto ovvio e significativo allo stesso tempo; che in Menandro trovino varia eco termini del linguaggio filosofico contemporaneo o motivi o problemi agitati nelle scuole filosofiche, è un fatto altrettanto ovvio e significante.

Un medesimo problema era comune a più di una scuola filosofica (che, infatti, ne dava soluzione diversa): di qui la difficoltà di un riferimento preciso ad una determinata scuola e di qui la

Menandro e il peripato

deduzione che non è questione di capitale importanza l'individuazione della "fonte." Menandro sente il problema, poniamo, della divinità, della provvidenza, del demone individuale: è un problema filosofico, ma è certo che lo sente come poeta, lettore di Sofocle e di Euripide, non come filosofo formatosi in un'aula del Liceo o sui manuali di filosofia popolare. Che Menandro parlasse degli dèi con Teofrasto è possibile, ma il fatto non sarebbe cosa diversa dai colloqui che Euripide aveva con Protagora sullo stesso argomento.

Come l'eco di Protagora in Euripide non ci autorizza a considerare il poeta un sofista *tout court*, così l'eco di Epicuro o di Zenone o di Teofrasto in Menandro non ci autorizza a considerare il comico un epicureo o uno stoico o un peripatetico. Il significato delle notizie tradizionali sulla *sinefebia* di Epicuro e Menandro o sul "magistero" di Teofrasto non può esser frainteso o detorto a fini pregiudiziali: sono gli uomini rappresentativi di un'epoca, che non vivono in eburnee torri isolate, ma in modo diverso esprimono le esigenze e le contraddizioni dei loro contemporanei. Per quanto riguarda, infatti, la problematica contemporanea nessun fossato li divide, ma per le soluzioni e per il modo che le esprime, ognuno ha la sua inconfondibile, individualissima personalità. Una commedia di Menandro non è un trattato filosofico, ma, poichè non è neppure un mero intreccio di situazioni e di accidenti, è anche espressione di arte, di umanità, di idee, di fermenti, di aspirazioni che non possono essere racchiuse in una formula scolastica.

Una commedia di Menandro è un fatto poetico e teatrale, uno spettacolo, una rappresentazione, non una lezione di filosofia.

Trieste, Italy

GOETHES "HOMMAGE À MOZART" – BEMERKUNGEN ZU "DER ZAUBERFLÖTE ZWEITER THEIL"[1]

ARTHUR HENKEL

Goethe hat mehrfach bezeugt, dass er Mozart – wie adäquat er seine Musik auch verstanden haben mag – als eine prototypische Erscheinung des Genialen ansah. Ein Genie wie Raffael war er ihm: von der Gunst der "Götter" beglänzt, von den "Dämonen" umlauert. Freilich hatte er es nicht ganz leicht, das Neue der mozartschen Tonsprache gleich zu gewahren. Die *Entführung aus dem Serail* missfiel ihm anfangs so, dass er sie garnicht zu Ende anhörte. Als ihm aber dann die Bedeutung gerade dieses Werks aufging, kam es zu dem Ausruf: "Die Entführung schlug alles nieder!" – und das bezog sich auch darauf, dass ihm seine eignen Singspielversuche, in den Kompositionen etwa Kaysers, Reichardts u. anderer nun gründlich überholt erschienen. Wir erinnern uns auch, dass Goethe zu den ersten gehörte, welche die revolutionäre Bedeutung des *Don Giovanni* erkannten. Und an Schiller schreibt er Ende 1797: "Ihre Hoffnung, die Sie von der Oper hatten (denn Schiller hatte im vorhergehenden Brief von der Operngattung geschwärmt, weil sie auf servile Naturnachahmung verzichte und das Ideale auf dem Theater erlaube), würden Sie neulich im Don Juan auf einen hohen Grad erfüllt gesehen haben, dafür steht aber auch dieses Stück ganz isoliert und durch Mozarts Tod ist alle Aussicht auf etwas Ähnliches vereitelt." Dem Sinne nach gleichlautende Äusserungen über die *Zauberflöte* liessen sich hier anreihen. Und fast alle enthalten das Bedauern darüber, dass, nachdem die Dämonen (wie Goethe es später einmal drastisch formulierte) unter anderen Genialen so auch Mozart "ein Bein

---

[1] Den verehrten Jubilar zu erfreuen, nahm ich ein Thema wieder auf, das ich vor einigen Jahren skizziert habe, in der *Zeitschrift für Deutsche Philologie* 71. 1 (1951), pp. 64–69.

gestellt" hatten, es nie mehr dazu kommen werde, dass Mozart Goethes Worte, Libretti – oder, wie er im Alter klagte, gar den *Faust* komponiert hätte. (Und wie ironisch die andere Seite: den Text seines "Veilchen"-Liedes hielt Mozart aufgrund eines Druckfehlers für Verse Gleims!)

Gleichwohl – und damit haben wir unser Thema gewonnen – fasst Goethe vier Jahre nach Mozarts Tod, 1795, den Plan zu einer Fortsetzung der *Zauberflöte*. 1794 hatte er Mozarts Werk auf die Weimarer Bühne gebracht, nach Prag und Frankfurt die dritte Aufführung ausserhalb Wiens. Wir wissen von Goethes Bemühungen, die Originalpartitur der *Zauberflöte* zu erwerben. Sein Gehilfe in der Theaterleitung, Kirms, der die Verhandlungen führte, hatte indessen keinen Erfolg. Jedenfalls wendet sich Goethe an den Wiener Komponisten Wranitzky, bietet ihm ein Libretto der Fortsetzung an: er möge es an die Wiener Hofbühne vermitteln, der Preis sei: 100 Dukaten. ("Nur die Lumpe sind bescheiden" – heisst es ja einmal bei Goethe.) Die Summe muss erheblich gewesen sein, denn Wranitzky antwortet in einer uns heute belustigenden Betretenheit, selbst Iffland und Kotzebue, die Bestsellerdramatiker jener Zeit, bekämen bloss 25 Dukaten. Und als Goethe das Fragment gebliebene Werk dann doch zum Druck bringt, in einem Taschenbuch des Bremer Verlegers Wilmans, 1802, drückt sich der gesunkene Marktwert seines Libretto-Versuchs schon darin aus, dass das Honorar in zwei kleinen Kisten Wein besteht.

Inzwischen aber hatte Goethe, nach dem Scheitern seines Angebots an Wien, etwa 1798 seinen Plan wiederaufgenommen. Seine Begünstigung der Gattung Singspiel auf dem Weimarer Theater, der Erfolg von Mozarts *Zauberflöte* allerorten, ökonomische Gründe: dass man ja für die Fortsetzung keine neuen Dekorationen und Kostüme brauche – und der edlere Grund: dass er mit seiner *Zauberflöte zweiter Theil* Mozart auf seinem Theater ehren könne, das alles lockte ihn, wenngleich Schiller abriet und darauf drängte, die Hauptsache nicht zu vergessen: den *Faust*. 1798 scheint das, was wir heute von dem Fragment kennen, fertig gewesen zu sein. Aber weitere Verhandlungen mit Berliner Komponisten wie Anselm Weber und Zelter blieben ohne Erfolg. Und so scheint, nach Lage der Dinge, darin, dass die theatralische Verwirklichung seines Plans ausblieb, der Grund zu suchen, dass er unvollendet blieb. So lässt sich Goethe auch in diesem Sinne vernehmen, wenn er als Bedingung dafür, das Fragment zu vervollständigen, nennt, "mit dem Komponisten zusammenleben und für ein bestimmtes Theater arbeiten" zu müssen; so schreibt er im Mai 1801 an Zelter.

Daher scheint Goethe um diese Zeit entschieden zu haben, das Ganze, so wie es war, d.h. etwas mehr als den ersten Akt, als Torso stehen zu lassen. Denn wie die Handschrift zeigt, hat der Dichter eigenhändig den Untertitel *Entwurf zu einem dramatischen Mährchen,* unter dem die Exposition (im schon genannten Wilmansschen Taschenbuch) erschienen war, durchgestrichen und durch den neuen Untertitel *Fragment* ersetzt. Dieses an sich auch "technisch" zu motivierende Verfahren gewinnt allerdings einen Akzent, wenn man beachtet, wie und womit Goethe das *Fragment* schliesst. Er bringt eine so pointierte, ja symbolische Endsituation, dass man versucht ist, nicht nur nach äusseren Gründen für den Abbruch der Arbeit zu fragen, sondern nach inneren: warum Goethe gerade hier innehielt, in einem tiefsinnigen Tableau.

Freilich rumort der Plan noch gelegentlich in seiner Phantasie. Wie soll man es anders verstehen, wenn er 1803 den Freund Zelter sehr direkt fragt: "Wie steht es um die Musik des 2. Teils der *Zauberflöte?"* Der aber versteht nicht und bezieht die Frage auf die Musik zu einer anderen Zauberflötenfortsetzung, die gerade in Berlin auf dem Spielplan war; und Goethe insistiert dann auch nicht. Elf Jahre später aber ist es nun Zelter, der den Freund bittet, das Fragment doch zu vollenden. Da aber will Goethe nicht mehr. Denn inzwischen hat *Faust II* manches geerbt, was er an symbolischer Substanz in seine *Zauberflöte* hatte einbringen wollen. Und es kommt auch die lebenslängliche Scheu Goethes hinzu, das was durch den Druck für ihn beseitigt, erledigt, abgetan ist – für ihn in gewisser Weise also tot –, zu einem zweiten Leben zu erwecken. Das hat merkwürdigerweise erst die Literaturforschung versucht.[2] Während die anderen Bemühungen

[2] Ich nenne nur die Monographie von V. Junk, *Goethes Fortsetzung der Mozartschen Zauberflöte* (Berlin, 1900), und die Aufsätze O. Seidlins, *Goethes Zauberflöte, MDU* 35. 2 (1943), pp. 49–61; und H. G. Gadamers, in *Vom geistigen Lauf des Menschen. Studien zu unvollendeten Dichtungen Goethes* (Godesberg, 1949).

Goethes um die musikalische Bühne (vom Theater sind die
ohnedies zu Recht längst vergessen) von der Literaturgeschichte
fein säuberlich im Museum der Literatur eingeordnet wurden,
hat die Forschung den von Goethes Zauberflötenfragment ausgehenden Reiz immer wieder verspürt. Vielleicht war es die Ver-
suchung zu einem historischen Traum: einer Art Geistergespräch
Goethes und Mozarts nachzugehen; vielleicht konkreter die
Neugier, das eigentümlich Goethesche in der Symbolik auch dort
zu entdecken; und nicht zuletzt die poetische Faszination, die
von Goethes überlegenem Spiel und ironisch-ernster Wiederholung der Zauberflötenwelt ausgeht. Und dabei entsteht auch
der Reiz der Frage, wie Goethe es anstellt, die Differenzierung,
welche allein Mozarts Musik dem unschuldig-abgefeimten Flick-
werk Schikaneders verliehen hatte, seinem Text mitzuteilen: den
Tiefsinn der Oberfläche der Zauberoper und die Weisheit im
Gewande der Naivetät.

Liest man Goethes Promemoria an Wranitzky genauer, so wird
sein Bewusstsein vom künstlich zu produzierenden Einfachen
deutlich. "Ich habe gesucht, für den Komponisten das weiteste
Feld zu eröffnen, und von der höchsten Empfindung bis zum
leichtesten Scherz mich durch alle Dichtungsarten durchzu-
winden." Und als künstlerisches Ziel gibt er an: "... man kann
ohne Übertreibung ... die Situationen und Verhältnisse steigern."
Wer sich in Goethes Welt etwas auskennt, denkt der Bedeutsamkeit des Goetheschen Grundbegriffs der "Steigerung"
auch an dieser Stelle nach. Es ist dies ein Kunstgesetz aller
"zweiten Teile" in Goethes Dichtung: *Faust II, der neue Paris,*
die neue Melusine, der neue Pausias und das Blumenmädchen
– um nur einige Beispiele zu nennen. Steigerung heisst dabei
immer: "wiederholte Spiegelung" (so sagt Goethe selbst), d.h.
eine höhere Reflexionsstufe, auf welcher der primäre Mythos
selbst Gegenstand der Deutung wird.

Bevor wir diese Andeutung aber anlässlich unseres Fragments
näher zu erläutern versuchen, scheint es nötig, den Gang der
Handlung, welche Goethe erfindet, darzustellen. Sie setzt dramatisch folgerichtig mit dem Motiv der ungestillten Rache des
Monostatos ein, der die "Sohlenstreich," die ihm Sarastro ver-
ordnet hatte, kaum vergessen haben dürfte. Er war ja schon in
der ersten *Zauberflöte* (ii. Auftritt) auf die Seite der Königin

der Nacht getreten. Und ebenso ist dramatisch tauglich das
Motiv der weiterhin zur Rache entschlossenen Königin. Goethe
hat also die Schwarz-Weiss-Verhältnisse vereinfacht. Gut und
Böse sind klar geschieden. "O höre deinen Freund! höre deinen
künftigen Gatten!" – so redet Monostatos gleich am Beginn die
Königin an. Aber wir müssen der Verlockung widerstehen, in die
Nächtigkeit dieser Liebe hinein zu spekulieren. Die dramatische
Spannung also erwächst aus der missglückten Rache im 30.
Auftritt der der Mozartschen *Zauberflöte*, der nun ein neuer Ver-
such folgen wird. Diesesmal richtet er sich gegen das Kind
Taminos und Paminas, den Sohn, im Augenblick seiner Geburt.
Und so beginnt die "Fortsetzung" mit dem Triumphgesang des
Monostatos und seiner Mohrengesellen. Doch nur halb ist der
infernalische Auftrag der Königin der Nacht ausgeführt. Das wird
im folgenden Bericht vor dieser, die mit Donnerschlag in Fin-
sternis und Wolken erscheint, deutlich. Übrigens hat Goethe die
Königin der Nacht bei ihrem ersten Erscheinen in einem Monolog
neu stilisiert:

> Wer ruft mich an?
> Wer wagt's mit mir zu sprechen?
> Wer diese Stille kühn zu unterbrechen?
> Ich höre nichts – so bin ich denn allein!
> Die Welt verstummt um mich, so soll es sein.

Wir hören weniger die leidende Mutter, der die Tochter ge-
raubt wurde, vielmehr die Steigerung der Rache ins Nachtschwar-
ze, ins Nichts: "Woget ihr Wolken hin, / Decket die Erde, / Dass
es noch düsterer, / Finsterer werde! / Schrecken und Schauer, /
Klagen und Trauer / Leise verhalle bang, / Ende den Nachtge-
sang / Schweigen und Tod." Und wenn sie vom Raub des
Knaben erfährt, werden Blitze und Elmsfeuer und Nordlicht zum
Feuerwerk des Nichts. "Leuchtet der hohen / Befriedigten
Wuth!" Aber der Triumph ist voreilig. Zwar konnten Monostatos und seine Gesellen das Neugeborene rauben und in einem
goldenen Sarg verschliessen, aber es gibt, wie immer im Märchen,
nicht bloss Zauber – es gibt auch Gegenzauber, wenn er auch –
wie hier – den Zauber nicht gänzlich aufheben, nur mildern kann.
Denn den Räubern wurde unter dem Gegenzauber Sarastros der
Sarg schwerer und schwerer und haftete schliesslich ganz an der

Erde. Doch hatte Monostatos dem Sarg schnell das Siegel der Königin der Nacht aufgedrückt, das den Knaben ewig in sein Gefäng-
nis bannensoll. Die Symbolik ist einfach und scheint die der Märchen: böse-dunkel-schwer auf der einen Seite; gut-licht-leicht auf
der anderen. So wird der Sarg nach dem Verschwinden der Räuber
wunderbarerweise federleicht. Man bringt ihn zum "Brüderlichen
Orden" Sarastros, den wir ja auch aus Mozart-Schikaneder
kennen. Aber der Fluch der Königin wirkt: als Bann. Mit
Wahnsinn sind Tamino und Pamina geschlagen, wenn sie einander ansehen; und Tod droht dem Knaben, wenn sie ihn zu
Gesicht bekämen. Und um sein Leben zu erhalten, muss der
Sarg immerfort bewegt werden, getragen von den Frauen, gemäss
einer Verheissung: "Solang ihr wandelt, lebt das Kind." Herrscht
also in der Sphäre der "hohen Menschen" Jammer und Leid,
so in der vogelleichten Papagenowelt Verdruss: die "lieben,
kleinen Kinderlein" bleiben aus (und das ist ja in der Märchen-
welt immer ein Unglück). Und hier hat sich Goethe so an Rhyth-
mus und Struktur der mozartschen Papagenowelt gehalten, dass
die Musik sich nur aus der Wagerechten der Worte zu erheben
brauchte. Als Beispiel stehe diese Szene, mit ihrer reizvollen
"musikalischen" Umkehrung im zweiten Szenenteil:

> (Wald und Fels, im Hintergrund eine Hütte, an der einen
> Seite derselben ein goldner Wasserfall, an der andern
> ein Vogelherd.)
> Papageno, Papagena
> sitzen auf beiden Seiten des Theaters von einander abge-
> wendet.
> Sie (steht auf und geht zu ihm):
> Was hast du denn, mein liebes Männchen?
> Er (sitzend):
> Ich bin verdriesslich, lass mich gehn!
> Sie:
> Bin ich denn nicht dein liebes Hennchen?
> Magst du denn mich nicht länger sehn?
> Er:
> Ich bin verdriesslich! bin verdriesslich!
> Sie:
> Er ist verdriesslich! ist verdriesslich!

Beide:
Die ganze Welt ist nicht mehr schön.
Sie (setzt sich auf ihre Seite).
Er (steht auf und geht zu ihr):
Was hast du denn, mein liebes Weibchen?
Sie:
Ich bin verdriesslich, lass mich gehn!
Er:
Bist du denn nicht mein süsses Täubchen?
Will unsre Liebe schon vergehn?
Sie:
Ich bin verdriesslich! bin verdriesslich!
Er (sich entfernend):
Ich bin verdriesslich! bin verdriesslich!
Beide:
Was ist uns beiden nur geschehn?

Es ist kaum nötig, darauf hinzuweisen, wie Goethe in der symmetrischen Reimanordnung: Männchen / Hennchen – Weibchen / Täubchen auf das Vokabular Schikaneders anspielt, aber zugleich mit den Bestandteilen eines Vogelmenschentums ein heiteres Wortspiel treibt. Und in der Wortchoreographie der Szene dürfen natürlich auch nicht die Staccato-Motive des "Pa, Pa, Pa" fehlen. Ja es kommt zu direkten Zitaten ("Erst einen kleinen Papageno – Dann wieder eine kleine Papagena ..."). Wichtiger aber ist – und das gehört ebenfalls zum Prinzip der "Steigerung," dass die zauberkräftigen Musikinstrumente, Flöte und Glockenspiel, nun in der Hand Papagenos und Papagenas sind. Sie schaffen ihnen ein rechtes Schlaraffenleben, treiben ihnen allerlei Tiere in die Netze. Und das Auswahlprinzip ist die Geniessbarkeit: "Sieh! die Löwen machen schon / Frisch sich auf die Reise. / Gar zu mächtig sind sie mir. / Sie sind zähe Speise." Ebenso die Papageien: "Glänzend farbig sind sie zwar; / Aber schlecht zu speisen." Willkommen sind dagegen Vögel und Hasen, und Goethe vergisst nicht die Regieanweisung, dass all dieses Viehzeug auf der Bühne erscheinen soll, samt Löwen, Bären, Affen. Aber wie gesagt: es herrscht hier gleichwohl Verdruss. Die gewohnte Vergnügtheit stellt sich erst wieder ein, als ihnen ein unsichtbarer Chor rät, auch für ihre

Elternwünsche die Zauberinstrumente zu erproben, und ihnen den ersehnten Kindersegen in der Hütte verheisst. Dass dies in Form von Eiern vor sich geht, versteht sich – aber es sind goldene Eier (wie im Märchen).

Es folgt ein drittes Zauberflötenbild: die Sphäre Sarastros. Gemäss einer Goethe lieben Maurervorstellung, wie sie uns auch im Epenfragment *Die Geheimnisse* begegnet, oder in der "Gesellschaft vom Turm" aus *Wilhelm Meisters Lehrjahren*, verquickt er gern das Ordensmotiv mit dem der Lebenswanderung. So ist es in Sarastros Orden Sitte, immer für ein Jahr einen Bruder auf Wanderschaft zu senden. Denn – so heisst die Begründung – wandernd allein lernt er "die erhabne Sprache der Natur, die Töne der bedürftigen Menschheit" kennen. Hier wäre an die Bedeutsamkeit des Wandermotivs im Bildhaushalt Goethes zu erinnern. Es gehört zu den Grundsymbolen: Wandern symbolisiert Leben, seine Bewegung, Produktivität, Probe, Bewährung, verhindert alle Verfestigung, allen Dogmatismus u.s.w. Hier ist nun ein Motiv, das auch das Märchen kennt, zugeordnet: ein edler Stein wird bei der Rückkehr vorgewiesen. Ist er rein, so hat sich der Pilger bewährt. Und das zeigt sich nun bei der Rückkehr eines solchen Bruders. Das Los aber schickt nun Sarastro auf die Reise. Er hat – so erfahren wir – mittlerweile die Herrschaft des Sonnenreichs an Tamino abgetreten. Gleichwohl scheidet er mit Trauer und mit bösen Ahnungen. Goethe deutet hier offenbar motivierend voraus auf eine drohende Spaltung im Orden, nachdem sein Mittelpunkt Sarastro ihn verliess. Darauf scheint sich das Paralipomenon zu beziehen, das für das Schlussbild des Spiels "die überwundenen Priester" nennt. Im Fragment folgen sodann zwei unausgeführte Szenen. Goethe scheint die erste als Pantomime gedacht zu haben. Pamina weiht das "Kästchen" – so heisst jetzt der Sarg des Pamina-Tamino-Kindes – der Sonne. Unter Gebet auf einen Altar gesetzt, versinkt es mit Donner und Erdbeben. Paminas Verzweiflung ist die letzte in einer – wie die Regieanweisung sagt – "bedeutenden Folge von Leidenschaften," welche die Musik ausdrücken soll. Die andere unausgeführte Szene bringt im Kontrast dazu die Beglückung der Vogelmenschen. Sie haben die verheissenen Eier in der Hütte gefunden. Sarastro kommt hinzu, und mit seiner Zauberhilfe fangen die Eier an zu schwellen, bis zwei Jungen und ein Mädchen herausspringen – ein beliebter Bühnen-Effekt der Zeit. (So sah der junge Clemens Brentano in Frankfurt die Demoiselle Jung aus einem Ei springen – die spätere Marianne v. Willemer.) Und bei dieser Gelegenheit ruft sich der Dichter selbst zu, er müsse "sorgen, dass die bei dieser Gelegenheit vorfallenden Spässe innerhalb der Gränzen der Schicklichkeit bleiben." Sarastro berichtet aber auch von der Trauer bei Hofe und bringt die lustige Vogel-menschenfamilie auf den Weg dorthin: sie sollen die trauernden Eltern erheitern. Dieser Besuch der Naturkinder im Vorsaal des Hofes gibt Gelegenheit zu scherzhafter Gegenüberstellung von naiver prahlerischer Unbefangenheit, wenn Papageno mit einem Riesenvorrat an goldenen Eiern prahlt, und schranzenhafter, begehrlicher Neugier – wobei Goethe auch seinen eigenen Sammeltrieb persifliert ("Ich wollte mir nur ein Paar in mein Naturalien-Kabinett ausbitten"). Mit starken affettuosen Kontrasten soll die folgende Szene wirken: solange die Flöte Papagenos ertönt, ist die Trauer Paminas und Taminos verscheucht, ihr Verstummen lässt sie in Verzweiflung versinken. Und so muss der wackere Papageno, angefeuert von den mitleidigen Damen des Hofes, aus Leibeskräften blasen und darf kaum Atem holen ("Blase, Papageno, blase / Halte nur doch diessmal aus!").

Priester bringen die Nachricht, dass das Kind im Kasten in einem Gewölbe unter der Erde, bewacht durch Feuer, Wasser, Wächter und Löwen, schier verschmachte. Und die Szene verändert sich in ein unterirdisches Gewölbe, das Kästchen auf dem Altar, transparent und Licht sendend. Damit beginnt der zweite Akt der Goetheschen Fortsetzung. Noch einmal nehmen Tamino und Pamina die Feuer-und-Wasser-Probe auf sich: Goethe hat auch dies unter ein Gestaltungsgesetz gestellt, das er einmal "par ricochet" nannte. Dieser ballistische Ausdruck meint, dass eine Kanonenkugel abprallt und einen zweiten Bogen beschreibt. So hat er auch die geharnischten Männer beibehalten, ihnen aber nicht – wie bei Mozart – das Pathos einer frommen Hoffnung beigelegt ("Erleuchtet, wird er dann im Stande sein ..."), sondern das Raunen von der ewigen menschlichen Sinnlosigkeit, von dem Rätsel der Zeit als solcher. So lautet der Wechsel von Chor und Wächtern:

Chor (unsichtbar):

Wir richten und bestrafen:
Der Wächter soll nicht schlafen;
Der Himmel glüht so roth.
Der Löwe soll nicht rasten,
Und öffnet sich der Kasten,
So sei der Knabe todt.

(Die Löwen richten sich auf und gehen an der Kette hin und her.)

Erster Wächter:
(ohne sich zu bewegen),
Bruder, wachst du?

Zweiter:
(ohne sich zu bewegen),
Ich höre.

Erster:
Sind wir allein?

Zweiter:
Wer weiss?

Erster:
Wird es Tag?

Zweiter:
Vielleicht ja.

Erster:
Kommt die Nacht?

Zweiter:
Sie ist da.

Erster:
Die Zeit vergeht.

Zweiter:
Aber wie?

Erster:
Schlägt die Stunde wohl?

Zweiter:
Uns nie.

Zu Zweien:
Vergebens bemühet
Ihr euch da droben so viel.

Es rennt der Mensch, es fliehet
Vor ihm das bewegliche Ziel.
Er zieht und zerrt vergebens
Am Vorhang, der schwer auf des Lebens
Geheimniss, auf Tagen und Nächten ruht.
Vergebens strebt er in die Luft,
Vergebens dringt er in die tiefe Gruft.
Die Luft bleibt ihm finster,
Die Gruft wird ihm helle.
Doch wechselt das Helle
Mit Dunkel so schnelle.
Er steige herunter
Er dringe hinan;
Er irret und irret
Von Wahne zu Wahn.

Während sich Pamina und Tamino dem Kästchen nähern, erscheint in einer Wolke die Königin der Nacht, die Wächter anstachelnd. Da erklingt die Stimme des Kindes im Kästchen, dem Ruf von Vater und Mutter antwortend. Ein Chor spendet Hoffnung: "Ihn halten die Grüfte / Nicht lange mehr auf; / Er dringt durch die Lüfte / Mit geistigem Lauf." Und in dieser Wendung: *mit geistigem Lauf* hat Goethe einen Wink zu Deutung der Symbolik seines Fragments gegeben. Der Deckel des Kästchens springt auf. In heller Glorie erscheint ein Genius. "Hier bin ich, ihr Lieben! / Und bin ich nicht schön? / Wer wird sich betrüben / Sein Söhnchen zu sehn. / In Nächten geboren, / Im herrlichen Haus, / Und wieder verloren / In Nächten und Graus. / Es drohen die Speere, / Die grimmigen Rachen, / Und drohten mir Heere / Und drohten mir Drachen; / Sie haben doch alle / Dem Knaben nichts an." Und mit der Szenenanweisung schliesst Goethe sein Fragment: "In dem Augenblick, als die Wächter nach dem Genius mit den Spiessen stossen, fliegt er davon."

Der Genius entweicht – entweicht nicht auch der Genius dieser Dichtung? – so könnte man pointiert fragen? Um in einem anderen Bezirk weiterzuleben? Hatte damit dieser Entwurf seine Bestimmung erfüllt, die ihm Goethe selbst schon bald zusprach: eine "Stimmung zu was Besserm" vorzubereiten? So schreibt er am 9 Mai 1798 an Schiller. Was Besseres – das konnte nur der

Faust sein. Hat Goethe schon damals an die Euphorionhandlung des zweiten Faust gedacht? Doch ehe wir diese Frage erörtern, ist der Bericht über Goethes Fragment zu vervollständigen. Denn ausser diesem mehr oder weniger ausgeführten Teil gibt es Paralipomena, die verraten, dass der Genius wieder eingefangen werden sollte, wahrscheinlich mit Hilfe der Papageno-Kinder. Er sollte dann wieder entweichen, wohl auch in die Gewalt des Monostatos zurückfallen. Schliesslich aber sollte das Reich des Lichtes in einer gewaltigen Schlacht über Monostatos und seine Scharen siegen, wobei dem Papageno eine neue Variation des *miles gloriosus* zugedacht war ("Die guten Herren siegen / Doch fällt auch mancher Mann / O könnt ich jetzt doch fliegen / Da ich nur hüpfen kann"). Die weiteren Einzelheiten und Winke aus der geplanten Fortsetzung brauchen uns wegen ihrer Undeutlichkeit nicht zu interessieren. Wir fragen nach der Zentralerfindung: mir scheint, es ist die des Knaben im Kästchen. Wie ist sie einzubeziehen in Goethes erklärte Absicht," die Situation und Verhältnisse zu steigern?" Wir haben festzuhalten, dass Goethe zunächst jenes märchenhafte *Ägypten* Schikaneder-Mozarts beibehielt. Und nun kann man vermuten, dass er in dem Bild des Knaben, den er spät und überraschend als Genius bezeichnet, eine Variation jener Mythen geben wollte, in denen frühe Kulturen den Wechsel von Nacht und Tag, Vergehen und Entstehen zu fassen versuchten. Und wenn man im Bereich ägyptischer Mythologie nach einem Primär-Bild sucht, so stösst man auf den Osiris-Mythos, dem auch in der *Zauberflöte*, neben Isis, der Kult des Sarastroschen Sonnenreichs gilt. So berichtet Plutarch im 13. Kapitel seiner Schrift *De Iside et Osiride* von einer Rache an Osiris; eine Stelle, die unsere Aufmerksamkeit verdient. Es heisst da:

Typhon … stellte dem Osiris mit List nach, wobei er Männer zu Mitverschworenen machte, und zur Helferin eine aus Äthiopien anwesende Königin namens Aso hatte. Er nahm heimlich das Mass von des Osiris Körper, verfertigte nach dieser Grösse eine schöne, reichgeschmückte Lade und brachte sie zum Gastmahl. Als aber alle sich über den bewundernswerten Anblick freuten, versprach Typhon, wie im Scherz, die Lade dem zum Geschenke, der darin liegend sie genau ausfüllen würde. Alle nach der Reihe versuchten es, aber keiner wollte passen, bis zuletzt Osiris selbst hineinstieg und sich niederlegte. Da liefen die Verschworenen hinzu, verschlossen von aussen die Lade mit Nägeln, gossen heisses Blei darüber, trugen sie an den Fluss hinaus und entsandten sie … ins Meer.

Die Unterschiede zu Goethes Erfindung sind deutlich. Aber das zentrale Bild: ein göttliches Wesen, durch List in ein verschlossenes Behältnis gebracht und dann dem Element übergeben, lässt eine Beziehung vermuten. Natürlich kannte Goethe den antiken Schriftsteller gut. Und wenn nicht aus eigner Plutarchlektüre, so konnte Goethe gerade *diese* Variante des Osirismythos auch in dem mythologischen Lexikon Benjamin Hederichs finden, das, wie wir wissen, ihm stets zur Hand war und aus dem er auch für den zweiten Faust sich mit mythologischem Wissen anreicherte. Übrigens hat Goethe auch bekannt, dass er für die Erfindung des faustischen Müttermythos sich durch die Müttergottheiten habe anregen lassen, von denen ebenfalls Plutarch erzählt. Goethe liebt esoterische Spiele dieser Art: er liebt die verdeckte Anspielung, welche pedantische Gelehrsamkeit vermeidet und dennoch seinen dichterischen Bildern eine metamythologische Dimension verleiht. So sagt er anlässlich der *Helena* einmal zu Eckermann, für das grosse Publikum sei "die Freude an der Erscheinung" die Hauptsache, "dem Eingeweihten wird zugleich der höhere Sinn nicht entgehen, wie es ja auch bei der *Zauberflöte* und anderen Dingen der Fall ist."

Wir wollen noch einige Daten sammeln, die uns erlauben, Goethes Fragment nicht bloss als eine dramatische Gelegenheitsarbeit anzusehen, sondern ihr einen Sinn abzugewinnen, der aus seinem dichterischen Bildhaushalt stammt. Auch Goethes Stück gehorcht einer "Moral," wie schon der märchenhafte Licht-Nacht-Dualismus der *Zauberflöte* sittlich verstanden wurde. Und Hegel, in seiner *Ästhetik*, meinte: im Sinne "einer mittelmässigen Moral, die in ihrer Allgemeinheit vortrefflich ist." So singt denn auch der Priesterchor bei Goethe: "Recht zu handeln, / Grad zu wandeln, / Sei des edlen Mannes Wahl." Und die mit der freimaurerischen Lehre und einer liberalen Humanität übereinstimmenden Leitbegriffe der Priesterschaft sind denn auch: Weisheit, Reinheit, Prüfung, das Gute, Demut, Gehorsam gegen die Götter. Goethe hat diese Moralität zu einer bewussten sittlichen Selbständigkeit in den "hohen Menschen" (wie Jean Paul sagen würde): Tamino und Pamina, gedeutet. Das ist eine höhere Stufe der Moralität als die der magischen Weltdeutung. Ihnen sollten wohl die in den Paralipomena sich findenden Verse in den Mund gelegt werden: "Nein, durch keine Zaubereyen /

Darf die Liebe sich entweihen / Und der Talisman ist hier" –
wobei eine begleitende Geste sicher auf das eigne Herz hätte
deuten sollen. Und möglicherweise ist in einem weiteren Paralipomenon, das der Pamina zugedacht war, so etwas wie die
sittliche Idee von Goethes Fortsetzung überhaupt zu erblicken:
"Und Menschenlieb und Menschenkräfte / Sind mehr als alle
Zauberey." Das ist ja eine Goethesche Grundüberzeugung.

Eine weitere Beobachtung: Goethe hat die dämonischen Seiten
der Musik (als Zauberflötenmotiv) deutlich gedämpft, verharm-
lost, ja ironisiert. In gewisser Weise gehört ja Mozarts *Zauberflöte*
in eine Geschichte der Orpheus-Opern, deren Gemeinsames ist, dass
darin Musik als Musik in ihrer verwandelnden Kraft thematisiert
wird. Wo noch die zauberische Flöte Taminos die Elemente
Feuer und Wasser bannte und Symbol der tröstenden Anwesen-
heit des Guten war, gelingt ihr in der Hand Papagenos in der
Szene bei Hofe nur eine illusionäre und durch die Komik des
ausgehenden Atems deutlich ironisierte, kurzatmige, ja täusch-
ende Wirkung. Und was Papageno und Papagena mit Flöte und
Glockenspiel zuhause anstellen, denunziert die Musik als rein
kulinarischen Zwecken dienend. So wäre das Ethos des Goethi-
schen Libretto antimagisch, sittlich-human? Und eine weitere
Beobachtung: wenn der Osiris-Mythos in der Tat Pate stand beim
Zentralmotiv vom Knaben im Kästchen, so haben wir nach dem
Genius zu fragen, der schliesslich den Deckel des Kästchens
sprengt. Verdrängt hier eine griechisch-römische mythologische
Vorstellung die orientalisierende Isis-Osiris-Sarastrosphäre der
Zauberflöte? Hat der Dichter das Fallenlassen der ägyptisierenden
Fabel in Gestalt verwandelt? Goethe hat selten sein Missver-
gnügen am ägyptischen Altertum verleugnet. Zu sittlicher und
ästhetischer Bildung – so meint er einmal – fruchte es uns wenig.
In der Klassischen Walpurgisnacht des zweiten Faust sind die
Sphinxe und die tiermenschlichen Bildungen des alten Mythos
wesentlich als Vorstufen der griechischen Gottheiten zu deuten,
die in der Gestalt des schönen menschlichen Leibes erscheinen, als
der Vollendung des Mythos überhaupt. Und man darf sich der
polternden Absage an alles Ägyptische in den *Zahmen Xenien*
erinnern, wo es mit deutlicher Anspielung auf die Zauberflötenwelt heisst: "Nun soll am Nil ich mir gefallen / Hundsköpfige

Götter heissen gross / O, wär ich doch aus meinen Hallen / Auch Isis und Osiris los!"

Waren es also doch vorwiegend innere Gründe, die Goethe veranlassten, das Ganze als Fragment zu belassen? Sah er ein, dass ihm weder die Einschmelzung der barocken Reststruktur des Wiener Volkstheaters noch die Einschmelzung der orientalisierenden Zauberflötenwelt in seine Vorstellung eines heiter-sittlichen Singspiels gelingen werde? Oder sah er ein, dass sich die hier angeschlagenen Motive als von einem spezifischen Gewicht erwiesen, das zu schwer war für dieses "par ricochet"? Musste er Schiller, der auf die Vollendung des *Faust* drängte, nicht recht geben, und klingt es nicht wie Selbstbeschwichtigung, wenn er jenem versicherte, "eine so leichte Composition" könne "zu jeder Zeit und Stunde gearbeitet werden"?

Ich vermute, dass ihm der Gedanke kam, Tamino und Pamina seien vielleicht doch nicht die rechten Eltern für eine symbolische Behandlung des Genius der Poesie. Denn das ist, wenn man ihn in den Symbolismus Goethes einbezieht, zweifellos jener das Kästchen sprengende Genius. Und wir wollen nun versuchen, diese Figur auf die Genius - und die Kästchen-Symbolik Goethes zu beziehen. In diesen Bereichen sind wir ja durch das Buch Wilhelm Emrichs über die *Symbolik von Faust II* belehrt worden.[3]

Es ist auffällig, wie oft in Goethes Dichtungen Gold- und Schmuckkästchen, Kapseln, Büchsen, Truhen zu finden sind, die mehr als Requisiten darstellen. Immer ist ein Geheimnis damit verbunden; sie schützen und bewahren zugleich etwas Zartes, Hohes, Idealisches. Von seiner Schweizer Reise im Jahre 1797 schreibt Goethe an Schiller einmal: "Was noch idealistisch an mir ist, wird in einem Schatullchen, wohlverschlossen, mitgeführt, wie jenes undenische Pygmäenweibchen" – und spielt damit an auf einen poetischen Plan, der dann später in dem Märchen von der *neuen Melusine* ausreifen wird. An einen Schmuckkasten heftet sich in dem Drama *Die natürliche Tochter* das Geschick jener Fürstentochter, die das Geschick des "edlen

---

[3] Zweite Auflage (Bonn, 1957). Cf. auch seinen Aufsatz, "Das Problem der Symbolinterpretation im Hinblick auf Goethes "Wanderjahre,'" *DV* 26 (1952), pp. 331–352; und F. Ohly, "Zum 'Kästchen' in Goethes 'Wanderjahren,'" *Z.f.dt.A.* 91 (1962), pp. 255–262.

Bluts im Exil"[4] zu bestehen hat. In der *Pandora* begegnet das Symbol des verschlossenen Kastens ebenso wie in den *Wanderjahren*, wo der Sohn Wilhelm Meisters, Felix, in einer Felsschlucht ein geheimnisvolles Kästchen findet, an das sich dann das Geheimnis seiner Liebe zu Hersilie knüpft. Vor allem aber ist die Truhe voll wabernden Goldes im Maskenzug des Plutus, im zweiten Faust, ein tiefsinniges Symbol, das Behältnis von Segen und Fluch. Und so können wir vermuten, dass Goethe auch dem Kästchen, in welches der Genius seiner Zauberflötenfortsetzung gebannt ist, diese Symbolqualität zudachte: es ist das Symbol des Geheimnisses überhaupt. Es birgt das Geheimnis des produktiven Geistes, der dort noch ganz "bei sich" ist. Und so spricht auch Goethes Tamino vom "verschlossenen Glück." Der Genius ist das Kind Taminos und Paminas. Der Dichter hat offenbar an der symbolischen Qualität weitergesponnen, die Mozarts *Zauberflöte* meinte. Es ist längst erkannt worden, dass in der Ehe der beiden jene glückliche Synthese von männlichem und weiblichem Prinzip bezeichnet wurde, die in der Sarastrowelt, als der Sphäre von Männerbund, Staatlichkeit, Verschwiegenheit und Licht, und der Welt der Königin der Nacht als der weiblichen Nächtigkeit in hassvoller Feindschaft einander gegenüberstand.[5] Der Genius aber ist der der Poesie, die sich über die Grundantinomie der Menschheit erhebt, sie "überfliegt" und damit zugleich versöhnt. Die Speere der zeitlosen Wächter, die Löwen (als die Symbole der Gewalt) können ihm nichts anhaben. In den Lüften ist sein Reich – und damit deutet er voraus auf das Geschick des Euphorion, des Kindes von Faust und Helena.[6] Wenn wir dies erkennen, dass er ein Genius der Poesie ist, so werden die um ihm geordneten Erfindungen des Dichters verstehbar: er ist gefährdet, die dunklen Mächte der Nachtseite der Welt bedrohen schon seine Geburt, sie versiegeln das Kästchen, seine Waffe ist das Schwerwerden – diesen Zug scheint Goethe aus der Christophoros-Legende übernommen zu haben. Den auf Pflege und Bewahrung des Geistes der Poesie bedachten Frauen wird er federleicht; aber da Goethe der Bewegungslosigkeit, dem Erstarren die Symbolik des Todes zuordnete, muss er getragen

---

[4] M. Kommerell, *Gedanken über Gedichte* (Frankfurt, 1943), p. 401.
[5] Cf. die genannte Arbeit Gadamers.
[6] Cf. die überzeugenden Hinweise Seidlins.

werden, bewegt – ein Symbol der Hoffnung auf das Leben des Geistes und der Phantasie. Und dass der liebenden Anrede dann die Stimme des Genius antwortet, ist eine Allegorie des Dialogs, ohne welchen der Produktive nicht auskommt. Schweben, Fliegen und die Flügel des Genius (so wurde er ja in der Antike dargestellt) sind dann unschwer auf die weltüberhobene Phantasiekraft zu beziehen.

Goethe hat sein Fragment mit diesem Bild des entfliegenden Genius geendet – in einem Symbol, welches vorausdeutet auf den endlichen Sieg der Lichtwelt. Die Vervollständigung seiner Geniusallegorie behielt er der Euphoriongestalt vor. Sie erst ergänzt Goethes Bild vom Geschick der Poesie in der Welt um den tragischen Aspekt. Wenn der Chor im 3. Akt des zweiten Faust noch fasziniert den wilden Sprüngen Euphorions zujubelt: "Heilige Poesie, / Himmelan steige sie, / Glänze, der schönste Stern, / Fern und so weiter fern, / Und sie erreicht uns doch / Immer, man hört sie noch, / Vernimmt sie gern." – weiss er selbst von seiner Bedrohtheit durch den Tod, kennt er die Tragik des meteorischen Flugs, die im Sturz sich erfüllt. "Und der Tod / Ist Gebot." Wie die Welt mit dem tragischen Scheitern der dichterischen Existenz fertig wird, das hat Goethe im Kommentar des Chors gesagt: "Wolltest Herrliches gewinnen, / Aber es gelang dir nicht. / Wem gelingt es? – Trübe Frage, / Der das Schicksal sich vermummt, / Wenn am unglückseligsten Tage / Blutend alles Volk verstummt. / Doch erfrischet neue Lieder, / Steht nicht länger tief gebeugt: / Denn der Boden zeugt sie wieder, / Wie von je er sie gezeugt." Ihm bleibt also der Trost der fortgehenden Geschichte der Poesie. Mephisto aber kommentiert zynischer: "Die Flamme freilich ist verschwunden, / Doch ist mir um die Welt nicht leid. / Hier bleibt genug, Poeten einzuweihen, / Zu stiften Gild- und Handwerksneid; / Und kann ich die Talente nicht verleihen, / Verborg' ich wenigstens das Kleid."

Wir wissen, dass Goethe in seine Euphoriongestalt das Geschick Byrons hineingedeutet hat. "Ein schöner Jüngling – so lautet die Szenenanweisung – stürzt zu der Eltern Füssen, man glaubt in dem Todten eine bekannte Gestalt zu erblicken; doch das Körperliche verschwindet sogleich, die Aureole steigt wie ein Komet zum Himmel auf, Kleid, Mantel und Lyra bleiben liegen." Byron war ihm der Prototyp eines genialen Scheiterns der modernen, der romantischen Poesie. Dem Genius seiner Zauberflötenfortsetzung hat er nicht die auf die Dichtung weisenden Embleme beigelegt, wie dem Euphorion: Leier und Stirnbinde und Schleiergewand. Sondern er hat ihn in allegorischer Allgemeinheit belassen. "Er dringt in die Lüfte / Mit geistigem Lauf" – singt der Chor. Goethe liebte es, die Verewigungen genialer Menschen in den Sakulärisationsformen der Auferstehung und der Versetzung unter die Sterne bildlich zu deuten. Für viele Beispiele nenne ich seine Verklärung Schillers: "Er glänzt uns vor, wie ein Komet entschwindend, / Unendlich Licht mit seinem Licht verbindend," – so heisst es im *Epilog zu Schillers Glocke*. Und so möchte ich schliesslich die Vermutung wagen, dass Goethe, als er erkannte, dass ohne einen Mozart seine *Zauberflöte* Fragment bleiben müsse, in dem Genius, welcher sich der Gefangenschaft im Reiche der Königin der Nacht entwindet, seine Huldigung an den grösseren Genius Mozarts symbolisierte. Wenn er diesen Genius wie Prospero seine Ariel in die Lüfte entweichen lässt, so ist es auch der Abschied von einem unerfüllten dichterischen Traum.

Heidelberg

GORGIAS BEI GOETHE

ALBIN LESKY

Möchte, Philip Merlan gewidmet, dieser kleine Fund über Jahr-
läufte und Kataklysmen hinweg als ein Zeichen der Erinnerung
an jene Stunden gelten, in denen wir im Eranos Vindobonensis
beisammen sassen!

In Goethes Drama *Die natürliche Tochter* findet sich im 5. Auftritt des 2. Aufzuges eine Szene, in der Eugenie das Prunkkleid
und das Geschmeide empfängt, die sie bei ihrem Erscheinen am
Hofe tragen soll. Mit stürmischer Freude bewundert sie Stück
um Stück, da ruft ihr die Hofmeisterin warnend zu (1064 f.):

> Doch deinem Herzen, deinem Geist genügt
> Nur eigner, innrer Werth, und nicht der Schein.

Eugenie erwidert (1066 f.):

> Der Schein, was ist er, dem das Wesen fehlt?
> Das Wesen, wär' es, wenn es nicht erschiene?

Hier ist in epigrammatischer Verdichtung ausgesprochen, was
einen Grundzug hellenischen Wesens bildet. Von der Freude
homerischer Helden an den erhaltenen Geschenken als Grad-
messern ihres Wertes bis zu der Intensität, mit der die euripide-
ische Alkestis von der Bedeutung ihres Opfers spricht oder
Inschriften eine vollbrachte Leistung künden, überall finden wir
jene hohe Bewertung einer Epideixis, die den Neueren mit ihrer
Verpflichtung, Bescheidenheit zumindest zu heucheln, fremd,
ja mitunter anstössig geworden ist. Ich habe Goethes Verse oft
als eines jener Zeugnisse zitiert, die ihn in jener unreflektierten
Nähe zu Griechischem zeigen, wie sie sich sonst nur noch bei
Hölderlin findet. Nun aber erweist sich, dass diese Verse nicht
nur ihrem Gehalt nach griechisch sind, sondern dass sie auch ihre
Form von einem griechischen Autor übernommen haben.

Im Kommentar des Proklos zu Hesiods *Erga* 758[1] (= Diels, *Vorsokr.*[9] 82 B 26) lesen wir eine kleine Abhandlung über die banale Weisheit, dass man seinen Ruf bei den Leuten durchaus nicht als geringe Nebensache betrachten dürfe: οὐ γὰρ ἁπλῶς ἀληθὲς ὃ λέγει Γοργίας:

τὸ μὲν εἶναι ἀφανὲς μὴ τυχὸν τοῦ δοκεῖν,
τὸ δὲ δοκεῖν ἀσθενὲς μὴ τυχὸν τοῦ εἶναι.

Wir haben den Satz in dieser Form ausgeschrieben, um die Übereinstimmung seiner Struktur mit jener von Goethes Versen unmittelbar ins Auge fallen zu lassen; an sich lockt seine echt gorgianische Gestalt mit der chiastischen Stellung von εἶναι und δοκεῖν sowie dem Reim der jeweils in die Mitte gestellten Wörter ἀφανές und ἀσθενές dazu. Man mag mit der Annahme spontaner Parallelen weitherzig sein wie immer, hier kommt man damit nicht durch. Ist die Abfolge der beiden Glieder bei Goethe auch umgekehrt, so ist das Gefüge der Antithese doch nicht unabhängig von dem griechischen Bikolon zu denken, das sich als Vorbild erweist. Die Frage freilich, wo Goethe vor 1803, dem Jahre der Vollendung der *Natürlichen Tochter*, die Proklos-Gorgias-Stelle fand, ist mit Sicherheit nicht zu beantworten. Zwei Vermutungen sind erlaubt. Goethe hat sich wiederholt mit Hesiod beschäftigt. Davon sprechen die Tagebücher des Jahres 1797, aber auch die aus 1803, dem Jahre der *Natürlichen Tochter*.[2] Sollte ihm dabei auch der Kommentar des Proklos in die Hände gekommen sein? Wahrscheinlicher aber ist eine andere Überlegung. "Was Goethe zunächst von griechischer Philosophie entgegentrat, war jene doxographische Vulgata, die Lehrmeinungen und einzelne Aussprüche mit den Namen der einzelnen Philosophen zusammenstellte." So Schadewaldt,[3] der an Goethes Bericht über seinen philosophiegeschichtlichen Mentor im 6. Buche von *Dichtung und Wahrheit* erinnert. Wir müssen für unsere Frage bei recht vagen Vermutungen bleiben, vielleicht gelingt es der Goetheforschung einmal, den Weg der Vermittlung

---

[1] Nach der Zählung bei Rzach handelt es sich um den Vers 760.
[2] E. Grumach, *Goethe und die Antike* (Berlin, 1949), p. 218.
[3] Nachwort, "Goethes Beschäftigung mit der Antike," zu dem in A. 2 genannten Buche, p. 983 = W. Schadewaldt, *Goethe-Studien* (Zürich, 1963), p. 39.

zu klären, auf dem des Proklos Gorgiaszitat zum Vorbild für zwei Verse der *Natürlichen Tochter* wurde.

Mit der Feststellung der Abhängigkeit der einen Stelle von der anderen ist freilich noch lange nicht alles getan. Nun wird erst recht die Frage nach dem geistigen Bereiche dringend, in dem eine jede von ihnen steht. Unser Gorgias-Fragment hat unverdient wenig Beachtung gefunden, wenngleich es an die Interpretation allerlei Anforderungen stellt. Das wird unmittelbar aus der wenig glücklichen Übersetzung deutlich, die sich bei Diels-Kranz findet: "Das Sein ist unkenntlich, weil (wenn?) es ihm nicht gelingt zu scheinen, das Scheinen unkräftig, weil (wenn?) es ihm nicht gelingt zu sein." Da befremdet es zunächst, die kausale Auffassung der Partizipia der konditionalen vorgezogen zu sehen. Ein μή bei kausalem Partizip ist nicht unmöglich, in klassischer Zeit aber eine Ausnahme.[4] Die konditionale Interpretation ergibt sich nicht nur an sich als die nächstliegende, sie wird auch durch den Zusammenhang empfohlen, in dem das Zitat bei Proklos erscheint. Der Schein bei den Menschen, ihre Meinung, ist nicht, wie Gorgias meint, unter Umständen ein ἀσθενές, wirksam nur, wenn damit die Wirklichkeit, das εἶναι erfasst ist. W. Schmid hat in seiner Literaturgeschichte[5] zwar frei, aber dem Sinne nach im wesentlichen richtig paraphrasiert: "Das Sein trete nicht in Erscheinung ausser mit Hilfe des Meinens, das Meinen sei haltlos ausser mit Hilfe des Seins." Wir können das übernehmen, ersetzen jedoch das "Meinen" durch "Scheinen," denn klärlich will Gorgias, "den man in einem weitern Sinne Schüler des Parmenides nennen kann,"[6] hier den Bereich des Seienden zu dem der Doxa in eine bestimmte Beziehung bringen. Der Versuch bei Diels-Kranz, die Partizipia kausal zu fassen, mag von dem Wunsch bestimmt sein, die beiden Bereiche im Sinne des Parmenides zu trennen. In Wahrheit stellt Gorgias hier jedoch eine Verbindung zwischen Sein und Schein her. Schmid (*ibid.*) hat das richtig gesehen: "Hier ist doch ein Sein wenigstens als auslösender Faktor oder Stütze für eine (mit dem Sein natürlich sich nicht

[4] Schwyzer-Debrunner, *Griechische Grammatik*, Vol. II (München, 1950), p. 594.
[5] Schmid-Stählin, Vol. III (München, 1940), p. 71.
[6] So O. Gigon, *Grundprobleme der antiken Philosophie* (Bern, 1959), p. 42.

deckende) δόξα angenommen," Diese ist eben von dem Bereiche des
Seins nicht brückenlos getrennt, sie kann sich vielmehr von dort
her mit echtem Gehalte füllen, wie anderseits das Sein das Scheinen braucht, um zum Er-scheinen zu gelangen. So verstanden
wird unsere Stelle nicht zur Stütze der Lehre des Parmenides,
sondern zum Widerspruch gegen diese. Wir werden uns darüber
ebensowenig wundern, wie wir mit Schmid fragen wollen, ob
unser Gorgiaszitat mit dem völligen Nihilismus vereinbar sei, der
aus den Nachrichten über die Schrift des Gorgias περὶ τοῦ μὴ
ὄντος ἢ περὶ φύσεως spricht. Hat man doch richtig erkannt, dass
Gorgias nicht als Philosoph zu verstehen ist, der ein bestimmtes
System verteidigt und auf dieses festgelegt werden darf. Die von
den Eleaten weit abliegende geistige Situation des Gorgias hat
C. M. J. Sicking, der auch eine gute Doxographie für die eben
genannte Schrift bietet, treffend gezeigt.[7] Ausser Zweifel aber
bleibt es, dass sich auch unser Gorgiaszitat über εἶναι und δοκεῖν
in einem von Parmenides konstituierten Vorstellungsbereich
bewegt.

Goethes Verse sind in einer ersten Schicht einem anderen
Horizonte zugehörig. Eugenie ist, wenngleich illegitim, so doch
von hochadeliger Herkunft und steht vor ihrer Zulassung zum
Hofe. Wesen und Stellung geben ihr nicht allein die Berechtigung,
ihren Wert er-scheinen zu lassen und nicht im Bereiche des ἀφανές
zu verbleiben, sie verpflichten sie auch dazu. In *Wilhelm Meisters
Lehrjahren* lässt Goethe seinen Helden solche Überzeugung in
einem Briefe mit allem Nachdruck aussprechen:[8] "Wenn der
Edelmann durch die Darstellung seiner Person alles gibt, so gibt
der Bürger durch seine Persönlichkeit nichts und soll nichts
geben. Jener darf und soll scheinen; dieser soll nur sein, und was
er scheinen will, ist lächerlich oder abgeschmackt."

Und doch würden wir die Verse Goethes, von denen wir aus-
gingen, missverstehen, wollten wir sie nur auf eine ständisch
begrenzte Epideixis beziehen. Schadewaldt[9] führt sie in einem

[7] C. M. J. Sicking, "Gorgias und die Philosophen," *Mnemos.* Series 4,
17 (1964), pp. 225–247; vgl. auch die Gorgias-Kapitel bei M. Untersteiner, *I sofisti*, Vol. I (Milano, 1967); dort, p. 221, Anm. 4 auch über den
Gegensatz von εἰδέναι und δοξάζειν bei Gorgias.
[8] Fünftes Buch, 3. Kap. *Jub. Ausg.* Vol. XVIII, p. 14, 21–26.
[9] W. Schadewaldt, "Goethes Begriff der Realität ," *Jahrb. d. Goethe
Gesellsch.*, N. F., 18 (1956), p. 69 = *Goethe -Studien* (Zürich, 1963), p. 230.

Zusammenhange an, in dem er davon spricht, wie sich Goethe von der Erscheinung leiten lässt, wie es für ihn die φαινόμενα sind, in denen sich Wahrheit und Wirklichkeit offenbaren. Dass hierin aber auch eine Problematik beschlossen war, die weithin Goethes Naturbetrachtung ebenso bestimmte wie sein Dichten, das hat vor vielen Jahren Oskar Walzel in seiner Vorrede zu Goethes Schriften zur Literatur mit Nachdruck ausgesprochen.[10] Der ungewöhnlichen Kraft sinnlichen Beschauens, dem Erfassen der Gegenstände bis in ihre kleinsten Züge steht früh die Frage nach dem Gesetz dieser äusseren Gestaltung gegenüber. "Sein Künstlerauge konnte die Schönheit der Erscheinung niemals dem ganz aufopfern, das hinter ihr verborgen lag: der Idee." Und: "Diesem organischen Zusammenhang von Idee und Erscheinung ist er nachgegangen, seitdem Shaftesbury ihn auf das Problem hingelenkt hat." Was Goethe seine Eugenie angesichts des Schmuckes sagen lässt, das hat er in seinem Gedicht *Epirrhema*[11] auf die gesamte Betrachtung der Natur bezogen:

<blockquote>Freuet euch des wahren Scheins.</blockquote>

In der Vereinigung von Sein und Schein eröffnet sich das εἶναι der δόξα, die dann als ἀληθὴς δόξα einen höheren Rang beanspruchen darf, als er ihr bei Platon zukommt. So nähern sich die beiden Aussprüche, die uns hier beschäftigten, bei aller Verschiedenheit der Ausgangspositionen letzten Endes doch in einer gewissen begrifflichen Konvergenz. Freilich mit dem einen Unterschiede, dass das, was für Gorgias ein zu pointierter Fassung lockender Gedanke am Wege war, für Goethe eine sein Denken und Schaffen bestimmende Überzeugung gewesen ist.

Wien

---

[10] *Jub. Ausg.* Vol. XXXVI, pp. lxxiv–lxxv.
[11] *Jub. Ausg.* Vol. II, p. 249.

ANTIKE MOTIVE IM EPICEDION DES EOBANUS HESSUS AUF DEN TOD DÜRERS

ÜBER EINE HUMANISTISCHE MOTIVKONTAMINATION U.A. AUS DEM EPITAPHIOS BIONOS

WOLFGANG SCHMID

Das materialreiche Buch von H. Lüdecke und S. Heiland über *Dürer und die Nachwelt* (Berlin, 1955) behandelt in dem den deutschen Humanisten und Reformatoren gewidmeten ersten Kapitel u.a. auch die zahlreichen Elegien, Epitaphien und Epicedien auf den Tod Albrecht Dürers.[1] Unter diesen Trauergedichten nimmt keine geringe Stelle ein das *Epicedion in funere Alberti Dureri* des Helius Eobanus Hessus[2]; es befindet sich in der 1531 in Nürnberg erschienenen und in die *"Operum farragines"* von 1539 aufgenommenen Zusammenstellung von *"Illustrium ac clarorum aliquot virorum memoriae scripta Epicedia,"* war jedoch schon vorher – eben im Todesjahr Dürers (1528) – in einem Büchlein publiziert worden, das zusätzlich ein Gedicht ähnlichen Inhalts von Thomas Venatorius (Gechauf) enthielt.[3] Diese Sonderausgabe liess Eoban u.a. auch an Martin Luther gehen, dessen die Zusendung bestätigender Dankesbrief erhalten ist; der entscheidende Satz in ihm lautet: *De Durero sane pium est optimo viro condolere; tuum vero est gratulari, ut quem Christus tam instructum et beato fine tulit ex his temporibus turbulentissimis et*

---

[1] Vgl. auch E. Panofsky, *Albrecht Dürer*[3] (Princeton, 1948), Bd. I, p. 10 (über Pirkheimers Grabspruch für seinen Freund Dürer).

[2] Hier sei an Dürers-sich im Britischen Museum befindende-Federzeichnung des Eoban erinnert: Angaben darüber bei Panofsky, *ibid.*, Bd. II, Handlist Nr. 1024; die Federzeichnung wurde für einen Holzschnitt benutzt, vgl. *ibid.*, Handlist Nr. 413.

[3] Der lateinische Text von Eobans Epicedion auf Dürer wird im Folgenden nach der Frankfurter Ausgabe von 1564 (*Operum Helii Eobani Hessi farragines duae, ex novissima auctoris recognitione quam fieri potuit emendate editae*), pp. 280–286 zitiert; der Titel des Trauergedichts lautet dort: *In morte consummatissimi pictoris Alberti Dureri Nurenbergensis Epicedion ad Joachimum Camerarium*. Eine leider an verschiedenen Stellen gekürzte Übersetzung ist mitgeteilt bei Lüdecke-Heiland, *op. cit.*, pp. 35–39 (dazu die Einordnung, *ibid.*, pp. 263 f.).

forte adhuc turbulentioribus futuris, ne, qui dignus fuit non nisi optima videre, cogeretur pessima videre.[4]

Das Trauergedicht kann sich mit den wertvollsten unter Eobans Schöpfungen, insbesondere den besten seiner "Christlichen Heroiden,"[5] nicht messen, da es in der Gedankenbewegung manche Härten aufweist. Zwar der Wechsel der Anrede zwischen Camerarius (Joachimus) und Dürer (Albertus) folgt aus der Konzeption als solcher (*In morte ... Dureri ... Epicedion ad ... Camerarium*) und kann sich bekanntlich auf Vorbilder aus der antiken lateinischen Poesie berufen.[6] Aber wenn man dies auch grundsätzlich zugibt, wird man doch die Häufung folgender Anreden nicht eben geschickt finden (p. 284 der Ausgabe von 1564, Vers 112 ff.):

> *Invida cur non hoc* (sc. *reparationem Phoenicis*) *homini*
> * natura dedisti?*
> *Vivere nempe feris*[7] *dignior ille fuit.*
> *Postquam dura semel Dureri fata subisti,*
> * Tu quoque perpetua nocte sepultus eris.*
> *Nec spes ulla tui similem, aut te posse reverti!*
> * Heu ubi Pythagorae vana palingenesis?*

Das mittlere dieser drei Distichen wird mancher beim ersten Lesen auf Camerarius beziehen (*tu quoque* dann in der Bedeutung *sicut Durerus*), aber ein Hin- und Herspringen der Anrede von der Natur über Camerarius zu Dürer wäre denn doch zu unwahrscheinlich. Also ist folgende Deutung unerlässlich, mag sie auch einigermassen künstlich wirken: "Nachdem Du, Dürer, das harte Geschick eines Durerus erlitten hast, wirst auch Du, wie alle

---

[4] *Kritische Gesamtausgabe von Luthers Werken, Briefwechsel*, Bd. IV (Weimar, 1933), pp. 459 f., Nr. 1266 = *Luthers Briefwechsel*, bearbeitet von E. L. Enders (1884 ff.), Bd. VI, pp. 255 ff. Luthers Anspielung auf die von ihm so pessimistisch beurteilten politischen Verhältnisse lässt an Eobans *De tumultibus horum temporum Querela* (Nürnberg, 1528) denken.

[5] Zur Beurteilung der eigenartigen literarischen Form der *Heroides sacrae* vgl. jetzt die Gesichtspunkte bei H. Dörrie, *Der heroische Brief* (Berlin, 1968), pp. 369 ff.

[6] Als Beispiel eines solchen 'legitimen' Wechsels der Anrede sei etwa der Begleitbrief von Catulls Allius-Elegie genannt (68. 1–40; vgl. 68. 2 mit 68. 21).

[7] Kurz zuvor war u.a. von besonders langlebigen *cervi* die Rede gewesen.

Menschen, von ewiger Nacht umfangen sein." Nun, die Frage
nach der formalen Struktur ist ein weites Feld; wir wollen uns
hier auf die inhaltliche Seite beschränken. K. O. Conrady sagt
von dem Gedicht, es enthalte "Zeilen, in denen humanistische
Klänge durchtönen[8]"; das ist bei einem Humanisten sicher nicht
falsch, bedarf aber einer genaueren Differenzierung in der Weise,
dass zu fragen ist, ob der antike Gehalte aneignende Humanist
nur allgemeine, nicht auf bestimmte Dichterstellen festzulegende
Topoi sich zunutzemacht oder aber literarische Allusionen im
eigentlichen Sinne zuwegezubringen bemüht ist. Prüfen wir, wie
es in dieser Hinsicht mit den Verszeilen steht, die Conrady an-
führt und deren Inhalt er mit den Worten umschreibt: "Die
Blüten der Blumen verwelken zwar, aber sie kommen wieder.
Uns Menschen, die wir doch *rerum domini*, Herren der Dinge, und
schönstes Werk der schaffenden Natur sind, uns verweigert das
Schicksal die Wiederkehr."

(102) *Intereunt herbae, flores moriuntur adulti,*
　　　　Sed redeunt vitam restituente Deo:
　　　Nos rerum dominos, naturae opera optima matris,
　　　　Cum semel occidimus, fata redire negant.

Der Hinweis auf den Kontrast zwischen der Einmaligkeit des
Menschenlebens und der ständigen *reparatio* im Leben der Natur
und im Kosmos ist uns nicht nur aus der hellenistischen Philosophie,[9] sondern auch aus der hellenistisch-römischen Dichtung
wohlbekannt – es genügt an die grossartige Formulierung des
Gedankens in der Horazode 4. 7 oder an die schlichteren Hende-
kasyllaben Catulls zu erinnern (5. 4 ff.):

　　soles occidere et redire possunt:
　　nobis, cum semel occidit brevis lux,
　　nox est perpetua una dormienda.

　　[8] K. O. Conrady, *Lateinische Dichtungstradition und Deutsche Lyrik des
17. Jahrhunderts*, Bonner Arbeiten zur deutschen Lit., hrsg. von B. von
Wiese, Bd. IV (1962), p. 287.
　　[9] Hierüber besonders eindringlich E. Hoffmann, in: Cassirer-Hoffmann,
Gesch. der antiken Philos., Band I des *Lehrbuches der Philosophie*, hrsg.
von M. Dessoir (Berlin, 1925), p. 219, neubearbeitet in: *Festschr. für G.
Radbruch* (Heidelberg, 1948), pp. 7 ff. (wieder abgedruckt: E. Hoffmann,
Platonismus und christl. Philos. [Zürich und Stuttgart, 1960], pp. 108 ff.);
vgl. auch die Kommentare zum *Gnomol. Vatic. Epicureum*[14] (γεγόναμεν
ἅπαξ, δὶς δὲ οὐκ ἔστι γενέσθαι κτλ.).

Wirklich charakteristische *loci similes*, die für sichere *imitatio* Horazens oder Catulls sprächen, hat der fragliche Kontext des *Dürer-Epicedion* nicht aufzuweisen.[10] Insbesondere fehlt bei Horaz wie bei Catull jene für den Eoban-Passus so charakteristische Erweiterung des Gedankens durch den Hinweis darauf, wie paradox es ist, wenn der den Dingen (der Natur oder des Kosmos) in mancher Hinsicht überlegene Mensch darin hinter diesen zurückstehen soll, dass ihm im Gegensatz zu ihnen die Wiederkehr versagt bleibt. Müsste nun diese Erweiterung als Zutat des christlichen Humanisten gelten, so hätte der Dichter das pagane Hauptmotiv etwas verchristlicht – *vitam restituente Deo* –, dagegen den biblischen Gedanken vom Primat des Menschen innerhalb der Schöpfung – Genesis 1 : 26; 28 – durch Umstellung vom 'creator' auf die *natura mater* säkularisiert. Eine derartige Beurteilung der Stelle wird man sich aber kaum zu eigen machen wollen, wenn sich herausstellen sollte, dass die Verknüpfung der "Gegenüberstellung: Lebensvorgang in der Natur – Leben des Menschen" (Conrady) mit dem als widersprüchlich hierzu empfundenen Gedanken einer Vorrangstellung des Menschen in der paganen Dichtung – und zwar solcher der die besonderen Studien Eobans gegolten haben – sehr wohl nachweisbar ist. Dies ist in der Tat der Fall: es lässt sich zeigen, dass die herausgehobene Stelle im Epicedion auf Dürer einen sententiösen Passus im *Epitaphios Bionos* voraussetzt – voraussetzt in einem Sinne, der nicht an eine mehr oder minder unbewusst einfliessende Reminiszenz denken lässt, sondern an echte, auf ein Auskosten literarischer Bezüge ausgehende *imitatio*. Da man im Zusammenhang mit der Interpretation des *Dürer-Epicedion* den *Epitaphios Bionos* noch gar nicht herangezogen zu haben scheint,[11] sollen die folgenden Nachweise in einen etwas weiteren Rahmen hineingestellt werden, wobei wir gut tun, auch auf Eobans eigene Theokritübersetzung – in ihr ist der als theokritisch angesehene und als 19. Eidyllion bezeichnete *Epitaphios*

---

[10] Zu ihnen wird man Hor. *Carm.* 4. 7. 21 *cum semel occideris* oder Catull. 5. 5 *cum semel occidit ... lux* (*Dürer-Epiced.*: *cum semel occidimus*) nicht rechnen.

[11] Auch nicht in dem die Wirkungsgeschichte von Moschos (sowie Pseudo-Moschos) behandelnden Aufsatz von L. Raminella Marzo, "Mosco attraverso i secoli," *Maia* 2 (1949), pp. 14 ff.

Bionos enthalten – einzugehen[12].

Wir beginnen (a) mit dem für unsere Zwecke relevanten Kontext des *Epitaphios* und der zwischen ihm und dem *Dürer-Epicedion* bestehenden Motivähnlichkeit, um dann (b) die lateinische Übersetzung des *Epitaphios* heranzuziehen sowie (c) den Nachklang einer weiteren Dichterstelle im *Dürer-Epicedion* zu behandeln; endlich soll (d) noch Eobans *Epicedion auf Mutianus Rufus* in den Kreis der Betrachtung einbezogen werden, was uns dazu verhelfen wird, *interpretatio* (der Theokritübersetzung) und *imitatio* oder gar *aemulatio* (in den Trauergedichten auf Mutian und Dürer) des Humanisten in ihrem zeitlichen Verhältnis zueinander zu bedenken.

(a) Der *Epitaphios Bionos*[13] lässt sich durch die mit dem "Refrain" oder "Schaltvers"[14]

ἄρχετε, Σικελικαί, τῷ πένθεος ἄρχετε, Μοῖσαι

gegebene Möglichkeit der Abgrenzung in 15 Abschnitte einteilen; der dreizehnte dieser Komplexe lautet (99 ff.):

αἰαῖ ταὶ μαλάχαι μέν, ἐπὰν κατὰ κᾶπον ὄλωνται,
ἠδὲ τὰ χλωρὰ σέλινα τό τ' εὐθαλὲς οὖλον ἄνηθον,
ὕστερον αὖ ζώοντι καὶ εἰς ἔτος ἄλλο φύοντι·
ἄμμες δ' οἱ μεγάλοι καὶ καρτεροί, οἱ σοφοὶ ἄνδρες,
ὁππότε πρᾶτα θάνωμες, ἀνάκοοι ἐν χθονὶ κοίλα
εὕδομες εὖ μάλα μακρὸν ἀτέρμονα νήγρετον ὕπνον.
καὶ σὺ μὲν ὧν σιγᾷ πεπυκασμένος ἔσσεαι ἐν γᾷ,
ταῖς Νύμφαισι δ' ἔδοξεν ἀεὶ τὸν βάτραχον ᾄδειν.
ταῖς δ' ἐγὼ οὐ φθρνέοιμι· τὸ γὰρ μέλος οὐ καλὸν ᾄδει.

Wehe!, wenn die Malven im Garten verwelkt sind und der grüne Eppich und der schönsprossende krause Dill, dann erwachen sie später wieder zu neuem Leben und blühen ein weiteres Jahr. Wir aber, die Mächtigen und Gewaltigen, wir, die weisen Menschen, schlafen, sobald wir einmal gestorben sind, taub in der hohlen Erde einen langen, endlosen und tiefen Schlaf. Den Nymphen aber gefiel es, dass der Frosch immerdar singe. Ich jedoch beneide sie nicht; denn er singt kein schönes Lied.

Man erkennt auf den ersten Blick, wie nahe sich die Wendung ἄμμες δ' οἱ μεγάλοι καὶ καρτεροὶ κτλ. im *Epitaph. Bion.* (102) und die Formulierung *nos rerum dominos* eqs. (*Epiced. in funere Dureri*, p. 284, Vers 104) stehen: eben diese Berührung ist es, die

---

[12] Allerdings wird in einer zusätzlichen Bemerkung festgestellt: *Sunt qui hoc carmen Moscho tribuant. Nam Theocriti non esse argumento est ipsius Theocriti in eo facta mentio.*

[13] Vgl. zu ihm jetzt die Berner Dissertation von Vroni Mumprecht, *Epitaphios Bionos* (Zürich, 1964).

[14] Den letzteren Ausdruck braucht z.B. Wilamowitz, *Die Textgeschichte der griechischen Bukoliker* (Berlin, 1906), p. 68.

fast stärker als die Gemeinsamkeit dessen, was man das "Hauptmotiv" der beiden Stellen nennen könnte, für deutliche Anspielung auf den *Epitaphios* spricht. Will man nicht bei einer blossen
Vermutung stehen bleiben, so muss man freilich hier etwas
weiter ausholen. Zunächst sind einige Bemerkungen zur Erklärung der griechischen Textstelle vonnöten.[15]

Waren im Anfang des *Epitaphios* (Vers 5 f.) Rosen, Anemonen
und Hyazinthen aufgefordert, sich an der Trauer um den toten
Sänger zu beteiligen, so ergeben die hier genannten einfachen
Pflanzensorten – darunter auch relativ geringwertige Nutz-
pflanzen – den wirkungsvollsten, schärfer nicht zu denkenden
Gegensatz zu den μεγάλοι καὶ καρτεροί und σοφοὶ ἄνδρες (102) und
lassen damit den Widersinn einer Ordnung, die dem personalen
Sein die Möglichkeit natürlicher Palingenesie vorenthält, nur
umso wirkungsvoller hervortreten. Die den Menschen als solchen
charakterisierende σοφία erlaubt an sich den Gedanken an ganz
mannigfache Qualitäten in sehr verschiedenen Bereichen (vgl.
die ganz allgemein gehaltene Formulierung in Sophokles' *Anti-
gone* 365 σοφόν τι τὸ μαχανόεν), lässt sich aber eben auch speziell
von der Begabung der musischen Existenz verstehen – bei
Theokrit *Id.* 17. 6 werden die Sänger σοφοί genannt –; damit ist
die Möglichkeit einer Beziehung der Sentenz auf Bion gegeben.
Dass der Frosch nach dem traurigen Ereignis weiterquakt, führt
im Schlussvers des Abschnitts (107) zu der Bemerkung, die
seinem unschönen Gesang zuhörenden Nymphen seien nicht zu
beneiden: ταῖς δ' ἐγὼ οὐ φθονέοιμι κτλ. (ταῖς aus dem τοῖς der
Handschriften bereits von Meineke hergestellt). Wenn die Calliergiana[16] hier ein τῷ aufweist, in dem man vielleicht eher eine
verwehte Überlieferungsspur[17] als eine Konjektur etwa des
Musurus erblicken darf, so lässt sich dieser – z.B. von Ph. E.
Legrand[18] in den Text gesetzten, aber wohl schwerlich richtigen –

---

[15] Vgl. den verdienstlichen Kommentar von V. Mumprecht (*op. cit.*,
pp. 110 ff.) z.St., dem ich in einem Einzelpunkt folge.

[16] Callierges, Zacharias, Θεοκρίτου εἰδύλλια ἒξ καὶ τριάκοντα ... κτλ.
(Rom, 1516); vgl. später p. 519, Anm. 43.

[17] Vgl. u.a. ebenfalls im *Epitaph. Bion.* 92[a–f] die Beurteilung des inte-
ressanten Sonderfalls von 6 Plusversen im Cod. Salmanticensis (Non.)
durch K. Latte (*Gnomon* 23 [1951], p. 253, Anm. 1) und V. Mumprecht
(*op. cit.*, pp. 105 f.); anders z.B. Bühler, *Die Europa des Moschos* (Wiesbaden, 1960), p. 14.

[18] *Bucoliques Grecs*, texte établi et traduit, Tome II (Paris, 1927), z.St.

Variante durchaus ein gewisser Sinn entlocken, und zwar nicht
etwa "ich neide dem Frosch durchaus nicht, dass die Nymphen ihm
zuhören" (so V. Mumprecht, *op. cit.*, p. 112), sondern vielmehr
"das Los des Frosches, mag er auch den Bion überleben, ist
deshalb nicht beneidenswert, weil er ein so unbegabter Sänger
ist" (vgl. auch Theoc. *Id.* 7. 41). Die Variante – oder Konjektur –
τῷ verdankt ihr Dasein wahrscheinlich einem Textverständnis,
das in der Entfaltung des Gedankens der Nennung des Frosches
eine der Nennung der Pflanzen vergleichbare Funktion zuweist.[19]
Es braucht wohl kaum ausgeführt zu werden, dass und warum
dies schwerlich der Intention des griechischen Dichters entspricht.

(b) Mit dem Hinweis auf die Möglichkeit einer Divergenz des
Textverständnisses am Schluss des ausgeschriebenen Passus des
Epitaphios Bionos ist der Punkt unserer Darlegungen erreicht, an
dem es von Nutzen sein kann, einen Blick auf Eobans Übersetzung der Stelle zu werfen, die übrigens dort für neun Verse des
griechischen Originals zwölf lateinische benötigt.[20] Sie lautet,
Theoc. *Id.* 19 (in Wahrheit: Ps. Mosch. 3), *vers. Lat.* 139 ff.:

> *Heu mihi quod malvae virides et adhuc redolentes,*
> *Atque apium viride, et quod totum floret anethum*
> *Saepe reviviscunt, et in annum deinde reverso*
> *Sole renascuntur. nos magni, nosque potentes,*
> *Cum semel occidimus, quam primum fata subimus,*
> *Condimur in terram, atque intra cava busta reclusi*
> *Perpetuo durum dormimus tempore somnum.*
> *Et tua clare Bion nunc molliter ossa quiescunt,*
> *Perpetuoque tacens, terra sepeliris in alta.*
> *Batrachon at Nymphis placuit superesse poetam,*
> *Et semper cantare aliquid, quod scilicet illi*
> *Haudquaquam invideo, nam pessima carmina cantat.*

[19] Auf dem Wege zu einer solchen Auffassung ist, trotz ihrer richtigen
Verteidigung der Textform ταῖς, vielleicht auch V. Mumprecht (*op. cit.*, p.
110), wenn sie den unempfindlich weiterquakenden Frosch ausdrücklich
neben die "trotz dem schmerzlichen Ereignis weiterblühenden Pflanzen"
glaubt stellen zu sollen, also Pflanzen und Frösche parallelisiert.

[20] Ich muss die Übersetzung nach der (postumen) Ausgabe von 1545
zitieren (*Francoforti ex officina Petri Brubachii*), die einer griechischen
Ausgabe Θεοκρίτου Εἰδύλλια κτλ. beigegeben ist, da mir die Erstausgabe
von 1531 leider nicht zur Verfügung steht.

Bemerkenswert ist hier gegen Schluss, wie die Übersetzung den Sinn des griechischen Verses

ταῖς Νύμφαισι δ' ἔδοξεν ἀεὶ τὸν βάτραχον ᾄδειν

durch Hinzufügung von *superesse* genauer zu verdeutlichen bemüht ist:

Batrachon[21] *at Nymphis placuit superesse poetam,*
Et semper cantare aliquid eqs.

Hier ist das Los des Frosches, der überlebt, wirklich mit dem Los Bions verglichen, d.h. es liegt jene Exegese vor, auf die man geführt wird, wenn man die Textfassung τῷ (Call.) – die sich Eoban in der Tat zu eigen macht (*quod scilicet illi haudquaquam invideo*) – für die richtige hält. Dass der griechische Text, nach dem Eoban übersetzt hat, tatsächlich die "Calliergiana" von 1516 oder 1517 – nicht etwa "Aldina" (1495) oder "Juntina" (1516) – ist, zeigt ein Blick auf Bestand und Anordnung der Dichtungen.[22]
(c) Nachdem wir die Übersetzung des entscheidenden Passus im *Epitaph. Bion.* kennengelernt haben, empfiehlt es sich, die *imitatio* im *Dürer-Epicedion* erneut anzuschauen, und zwar über die früher von uns ausgeschriebenen Verse hinaus (p. 284, Vers 102–113):

Intereunt herbae, flores moriuntur adulti,
   Sed redeunt vitam restituente Deo.
Nos rerum dominos, naturae opera optima matris,
   Cum semel occidimus, fata redire negant.
Praeterea floret breve ver mutabilis aevi,
   Quod sumus hoc vitam dicere paene pudet.
Tot vetulae durat cornicis vita per annos,

---

[21] Das lateinische *batrachus* ist vorwiegend für den "Froschfisch" belegt (vgl. Plin. *HN* 32. 145). Wenn Eoban sich unter Verzicht auf *rana* die Beibehaltung von βάτραχος gestattet hat (*batrachon* statt *batrachum* bei Vorziehung an den Versanfang – und diese scheint der humanistische Übersetzer um der Deutlichkeit seiner Interpretation willen gewollt zu haben – schon aus metrischen Gründen notwendig), so konnte ihm das z.B. der latinisierte Titel *Batrachomyomachia* leicht nahelegen, vgl. schon Stat. *Silv. praef.*
[22] Dieser ist z.B. in Gow's Ausgabe der Bibl. Oxon. leicht zu gewinnen, die für die Frühausgaben die Reihenfolge der in ihnen enthaltenen Gedichte leicht überschaubar macht (*Praef.*, pp. XIV f.).

Saecula tot cervos vivere posse ferunt.
Igne suo Phoenix onerantes exuit annos,
  Exuvias reparans corporis inde novi.
Invida cur non hoc homini natura dedisti?
Vivere nempe feris dignior ille fuit.

Die zweite Hälfte des ausgeschriebenen Zusammenhangs zeigt, dass hier nicht wie in der Übersetzung vom chokierenden *superesse* des Frosches die Rede ist: als Repräsentanten des Tierreiches, bei denen zumindest die Möglichkeit besonderer Langlebigkeit besteht, werden Hirsche (*cervi*) sowie Krähen (*cornices*) genannt und dem Menschen gegenübergestellt; den *batrachos* konnte Eoban eben im *Dürer-Epicedion* nicht brauchen. Es liegt nahe zu fragen, ob Eoban jene Tierbeispiele aus eigenem hinzutut oder ob er sie einer literarischen Anregung verdankt. Dass letzteres tatsächlich der Fall ist, erscheint als ziemlich sicher, und zwar lassen sich verschiedene Möglichkeiten der Herleitung denken. In der ersten Elegie auf Mäcenas lauten die Verse 1. 113 ff. wie folgt:

redditur arboribus florens revirentibus aetas:
  ergo non homini quod fuit ante redit?
vivacesque magis cervos decet esse paventis
  si quorum in torva cornua fronte rigent?
vivere cornices multos dicuntur in annos:
  cur nos angusta condicione sumus?

Dass von der ungewöhnlichen Langlebigkeit der *cervi* und *cornices* hier im gleichen motivischen Kontext wie im *Epicedion auf Dürer* die Rede ist (*redditur arboribus florens ... aetas; ergo non homini* eqs.? ∞ *flores ... redeunt; nos rerum dominos* eqs.), könnte für die *Mäcenaselegie* als Vorbildstelle sprechen.[23] Wahrscheinlicher ist aber die Herleitung aus dem *Hesiodion* des Ausonius, 5. ecl. p. 93 Peiper = *Anth.* 647 (*De aetatibus animantium*), weil dort in Übereinstimmung mit Eoban – und Abweichung von der Mäcenaselegie – noch eine Erwähnung des Vogels Phoenix folgt:

[23] Die Annahme, dass Eoban die *Elegie auf Mäcenas* gekannt hat, macht keinerlei Schwierigkeit: seit ihrer Auffindung durch Enoch d'Ascoli, der sie bei einer in den Jahren 1451–1455 unternommenen Reise anscheinend in Dänemark entdeckte und dann nach Italien brachte, konnten sie das Interesse der Humanisten erregen, das vermutlich umso lebhafter war, als die Dichtung Vergil zugeschrieben wurde.

Ter binos deciesque novem super exit in annos
iusta senescentum quos implet vita virorum.
hos novies superat vivendo garrula cornix,
et quater egreditur cornicis saecula cervus.
alipedem cervum ter vincit corvus, et illum
multiplicat novies Phoenix, reparabilis ales.

Da die entsprechenden Verse des originalen Hesiod bei Plutarch
zitiert sind (*De def. or.* 11, p. 415 [III 71–72 Paton-Pohlenz],
vgl. *frg.* 304 Merkelbach-West), ist es nicht ganz ausgeschlossen,
dass Eoban die Stelle aus Plutarchs *Moralia* kannte,[24] aber es
liegt gewiss näher, mit Ausoniuslektüre zu rechnen.[25]
(d) Ist damit – erstmals, wenn ich recht sehe – die Stelle des
Dürer-Epicedion, der unsere besondere Aufmerksamkeit galt, als
ein *textus*, d.h. hier "Gewebe" mit einer durch *Epitaph. Bion.* und
eine weitere Vorbildstelle inspirierten Motivkontamination erkannt, so ist nun noch darauf hinzuweisen, dass C. Krause beim
Epicedion auf Mutian[26] das Vorhandensein gewisser Spuren der
Theokritischen Studien[27] grundsätzlich bereits bemerkt hat, ohne
freilich dem Phänomen weiter nachzugehen.[28] Anders als beim
Dürer-Epicedion wird im *Mutian-Epicedion* Eobans Klage um
den verstorbenen Freund ganz ausdrücklich mit der des sizilschen
(*Trinacrius*) Dichters um den dahingeschiedenen Bion gleichgesetzt (p. 291 der Ausgabe von 1564, Vers 33 f.):

Flere libet quali doctum flevisse Biona
Carmine Trinacrius creditur ante senex.[29]

---

[24] Die ed. princeps der *Moralia* erschien 1509 (Aldus et Demetrius Ducas).

[25] So urteilt auch R. Merkelbach, dem ich für brieflichen Hinweis zu danken habe – aus seiner Sammlung von Parallelstellen ist für unsere Zwecke vor allem noch Plin. *HN* 7. 153 von Interesse –; vgl. *reparabilis* mit *reparans* (*Epiced.*).

[26] *In funere doctissimi viri Mutiani Rufi Epicedion* (pp. 290 ff.); über seine Veröffentlichung vgl. unten, p. 520.

[27] Zur Beurteilung des *Epitaph. Bion.* als "theokritisch," die bei dieser Formulierung vorausgesetzt ist, vgl. oben, p. 512, Anm. 12.

[28] C. Krause, *Helius Eobanus Hessus*, Bd. I (1879; Neudruck 1963), p. 414, Anm. 4.

[29] Gemeint ist Theokrit, der angebliche Verfasser des *Epitaph. Bion.* Abweichend hiervon verlangt in dem anderen Zusammenhang des *Dürer-Epicedion* (p. 283, Vers 89) der *Siculus senex* die Deutung Archimedes.

Es ist also kein Zufall, wenn gerade der auf diese Identifizierung folgende Vers (35) sich als der Eingangsvers des *Epitaph. Bion.* herausstellt:

Tristia lugentes suspiria ducite silvae!

Will man die Übernahmen aus dem Vorbildgedicht richtig würdigen, so erscheint lehrreicher als manche Einzelheit an späterer Stelle – etwa *Epiced. Mut.* p. 292, Vers 57 *Hessicus Orpheus* ∾ *Epitaph. Bion. vers. Lat.* 23 *Doricus Orpheus* [30] (griechisch an entsprechender Stelle: ἀπώλετο Δώριος ᾿Ορφεύς) – eben die Aufforderung an die Natur, in die Klage um den Verstorbenen einzustimmen. Wenn im Folgenden das genau Vergleichbare nebeneinandergestellt wird, so erweist sich dort die Bewahrung des Wortlauts der Vorbildstelle jedenfalls dann als recht weitgehend, wenn man bedenkt, dass es, formal gesehen, hexametrische in elegische Dichtung umzusetzen galt:

Epitaph. Bion. (*vers. Lat.*) 5 *ff.*:

> *Nunc nemora et saltus miseris ululate querelis,*
> *Tristibus o maesti flores spirate corymbis,*
> *Nunc lugubre rosae rubeant, nunc triste papaver.*
> *Nunc hyacinthe sonet tua littera, scilicet ai ai:*
> *Non tamen hoc satis est ai ai, plus ergo loquatur,* [31]
> *Litterulasque velis foliis inscribere plures.*
> *Occidit indigna confectus morte poeta.*

Epiced. Mut. 37 ff.

> *Nunc nemora et saltus miseris ululate querelis,* [32]
> > *Nunc lacrimas habeat quaelibet herba suas.* [33]
> *Tristibus heu maesti flores spirate corymbis,* [34]
> > *Lugubribus iaceant lilia mista rosis.* [35]

---

[30] Lautet der Vers im *Epitaph. Bion. interiit fato crudeli Doricus Orpheus*, so muss das *Epiced. Mut.* beim *Hessicus Orpheus* aus metrischen Gründen den Plural *fatis crudelibus* wählen.

[31] Dieser und der folgende Vers ist die ausführlichere Entsprechung zu den wenigen Worten des Originals πλέον "αἰαῖ" / λάμβανε τοῖς πετάλοισι (Vers 6 f.).

[32] Identisch mit *Epitaph. Bion.* 5.

[33] Umsetzung von *Epitaph. Bion.* 4 (*nunc tristes plantae lacrimarum fundite guttas*).

[34] *Epitaph. Bion.* 6 (dort *o* statt *heu*).

[35] Umsetzung von *Epitaph. Bion.* 7.

Nunc Hyacinthe sonet tua littera, scilicet ai ai,[36]
Non tamen ista satis plena querela fuit.[37]
Ergo notas folio plures inscribe rubenti,[38]
Longius ut possit littera scripta queri.[39]
Occidit indigno sublatus funere Rufus,[40]
Rufus ab Hessiacis notus ad astra iugis.[41]

Man möchte gerne wissen, ob Eoban zum Zeitpunkt seiner Abfassung des *Dürer-Epicedion* (April 1528; Dürers Tod: 6/4/1528) zwar den *Epitaph. Bion.* bereits kannte, sich jedoch seiner Übersetzung noch nicht zugewandt hatte – oder ob *interpretatio* und *imitatio* bei ihm zeitlich mehr oder weniger zusammenfallen. Diese Frage wäre ohne das, was das *Epicedion auf Mutian* lehren kann, höchstens mit einer gewissen Wahrscheinlichkeit im Sinne der zweiten der beiden angedeuteten Möglichkeiten zu lösen: Wenn das Manuskript der von Eoban erst nach seiner Übersiedlung nach Nürnberg (Mai 1526) begonnenen Theokritübersetzung[42] im Jahre 1530 oder kurz davor in den Druck ging – die Auslieferung der Erstausgabe erfolgte zur Ostermesse 1531 –, so bereitet es bei Beachtung der Stellung des *Epitaph. Bion.* innerhalb der vom Übersetzer zugrundegelegten "Calliergiana"[43] wohl kaum Schwierigkeiten anzunehmen, dass Eoban im Frühjahr 1528 gerade an der Latinisierung jenes *Epitaphios* arbeitete, ja sie vielleicht soeben abgeschlossen hatte. Dem angedeuteten Gedankengang wird man zunächst nur eine gewisse Probabilität zubilligen können; diese lässt sich indes durch genaue Beachtung der im *Epicedion auf Mutian* vorliegenden

[36] *Epitaph. Bion.* 8.
[37] Umsetzung von *Epitaph. Bion.* 9.
[38] Dies eine Weiterentwicklung von *Epitaph. Bion.* 10.
[39] Herausgesponnen aus dem *plus ergo loquatur* am Schluss von *Epitaph. Bion.* (*vers. Lat.*) 9.
[40] Vgl. nicht nur den ähnlichen Vers *Epitaph. Bion.* 11, sondern auch *Epiced. Mut.* 9: *postquam est indigno consumptus funere Rufus.*
[41] Identisch mit *Epiced. Mut.* 10, also refrainartige Wiederholung.
[42] Vgl. C. Krause, *Helius Eobanus Hessus*, Bd. II (1879; Neudruck 1963), p. 91; dort ein überzeugender Hinweis darauf, dass Eobans einst in Erfurt begonnene griechische Studien ernstlich erst in Nürnberg mit Hilfe des Camerarius intensiviert wurden.
[43] Vgl. oben p. 513, Anm. 16; die im Verhältnis zu der Anordnung in der "Juntina" beträchtlich frühere Stellung von Mosch. 3 (= *Epitaph. Bion.*) in der "Calliergiana" ist den Angaben der Oxoniensis von Gow (Praef., pp. XIV f.) leicht zu entnehmen.

Verhältnisse zur Sicherheit und Evidenz erheben: Wofern in Fällen, in denen die lateinische Übersetzung des *Epitaph. Bion.* nachweislich relativ frei ist, gewisse Entsprechungen im *Epiced. Mut.* den Eindruck machen, aus eben jener Übersetzung weiterentwickelt,[44] also im Verhältnis zu ihr "hysterogen" zu sein, setzt ein solcher Eindruck mit Notwendigkeit voraus, dass die Übersetzung nicht erst *nach* dem *Epicedion auf Mutian* entstanden sein kann. Gegen eine solche Auffassung wird man allerdings chronologische Bedenken geltend machen, da doch Mutian schon zwei Jahre *vor* Dürer gestorben sei (30/3/1526). Nun, anders als mit dem *Dürer-Epicedion* hat sich Eoban mit dem *Mutian-Epicedion* eben Zeit gelassen, erst nach mancherlei Aufforderungen – u.a. einem Brief Jonas' von 1527[45] – scheint er sich an die Abfassung gemacht zu haben; eine sich aktuell gebende Sonderausgabe hat er deshalb gar nicht erst erscheinen lassen, vielmehr das *Mutian-Epicedion* erstmalig innerhalb der Sammlung *Illustrium ac clarorum aliquot virorum memoriae scripta Epicedia* von 1531 herausgebracht. Die entwickelten Überlegungen sprechen dafür, *Mutian-Epicedion* und *Dürer-Epicedion* relativ nahe aneinander heranzurücken, d.h. beide Trauergedichte sind nicht nur in sachlichem, sondern auch in zeitlichem Zusammenhang mit der 1531 erschienenen Theokritübersetzung zu sehen. Übrigens sind Eobans Theokritstudien, und damit berühren wir zuletzt auch ein biographisches Moment, mit den Namen Mutian und Camerarius – diesen haben wir schon als Adressaten des *Dürer-Epicedion* genannt[46] – deutlich verknüpft: seinem Freunde Mutian verdankte Eoban, der zunächst nur Vergils Nachahmung der griechischen Idyllenpoesie und die der Italiener gekannt hatte, die erste Lektüre einer lateinischen Übersetzung verschiedener Theokritgedichte,[47] und dass ohne Camerarius' Hilfe

44 Vgl. z.B. den lehrreichen Fall p. 518, Anm. 35.
45 Vgl. C. Krause, *op. cit.*, Bd. I, p. 414 Anm. 2 (*Ionas Eobano*, Wittenb. 1527: *Epp. fam.* 291).
46 Vgl. oben p. 508, Anm. 3.
47 Vgl. C. Krause, *op. cit.*, Bd. II, p. 91: "Den eigentlichen Vater der Idyllenpoesie, Theokrit, lernte Eoban erst lange später (um 1520) und zwar nicht sowohl im Original, als in einer nur einzelne Idyllen umfassenden metrischen Übersetzung eines gewissen Martin Phileticus kennen": diese Übersetzung hatte ihm eben Mutian geliehen (vgl. Krause, *op. cit.*, p. 91, Anm. 1 und den Brief Eobans an Johannes Lange, Erfurt, 1520; *Epp. fam.* 217). Phileticus' Übersetzung weckte dann gleichsam den Appetit nach mehr.

Eoban nicht als *Theocritus* (und *Moschus*) *Latinus* hervorge-
treten wäre, lehrt nicht nur Camerarius' eigene Theokritaus-
gabe,[48] sondern auch der zwischen ihm und Eoban geführte
Briefwechsel.[49] Man wird annehmen dürfen, dass die Vergäng-
lichkeitsreflexion des *Epitaph. Bion.* beide besonders beein-
druckt hat, wie sie noch auf Carducci gewirkt hat.[50]

---

[48] *Theocriti graeca poemata cum praef. graeca ad G. Heltum* (1530).

[49] Vgl. ferner Camerarius' im Jahre 1553 veröffentlichte *Narratio*
(*de Hesso*) C 5 a: "*Quem conatum* (sc. *traductionem Theocriti*) *omnibus ego
rebus adiuvare studebam.*"

[50] Bei seinem Gedicht *Pianto antico* hat Carducci nachweislich an den
Passus in Ps. Mosch. 3 (*Epitaph. Bion.*) gedacht, hat er doch in seiner
Ausgabe von 1873 den abgekürzten griechischen Text (ὕστερον αὖ ζώοντι
καὶ εἰς ἔτος ἄλλο φύοντι ... καὶ σὺ μὲν ἐν σιγᾷ πεπυκασμένος ἔσσεαι ἐν γᾷ)
ausdrücklich als Motto dem Gedicht vorangestellt (*Nuove Poesie di
Enotrio Romano* [Imola, 1873], p. XXV).

IV. HISTORICA

THE MEDIEVAL CANON LAW OF CONTRACTS, RENAISSANCE "SPIRIT OF CAPITALISM," AND THE REFORMATION "CONSCIENCE": A VOTE *FOR* MAX WEBER [1]

BENJAMIN NELSON

Do we truly wish to understand the relations of religion, law, economic ethics, moral impulse in the affairs of the Middle Ages, Renaissance, and Reformation?

Are we impatient to improve on the answers we are able to give to questions put to us by Max Weber, Sombart, Troeltsch, Tawney and other more recent scholars?

If our answers to these questions are in the affirmative, then we have little time to lose in making some changes in the ways in which we have been relating to such questions.

I

Quite understandably, a fairly high proportion of the nineteenth century scholars who pioneered in the advance of economic history began as jurists drawn into a close study of the development of business enterprise by their forensic concerns.[2]

[1] Earlier versions of some parts of the present essay were read to the annual meetings of professional societies over a number of years, notably *The American Historical Association, The American Society for the Study of Church History*, and *The American Catholic Historical Society*. The two latter had their meeting in joint session. At a few points I have followed the wording of an already published paper, "The Usurer and the Merchant Prince," which is cited in the bibliography in note 2 below.

[2] It is not possible at this time to detail the original sources and secondary writings used in the present essay. A handy bibliography of the items will be found in my book, *The Idea of Usury: From Tribal Brotherhood to Universal Otherhood* (Princeton, 1949), published now in a somewhat augmented edition under the imprint of the University of Chicago Press (1969). Particular attention is called to the entries which are starred in both the original bibliography and in the added references. A New Postscript will offer assessments of the literature and viewpoints since 1949.

Needed clarification of unfamiliar aspects of the evolution of directive

True to the traditions taught by their venerated teachers, they paid long and loving attention to the commentaries, treatises, and learned opinions (*responsa*) of the Italian civilians, who enjoyed such extraordinary renown in the later Middle Ages and Renaissance as veritable "monarchs of Jurisprudence."

systems of moral and religious regulation (embracing the *rationales* of conscience, casuistry and cure of souls) in the West will be found in the following studies:

Kirk, K. *Conscience and Its Problems. An Introduction to Casuistry* (London, 1927).

Lottin, Dom. Odon. *Principes de morale*. 2 vols. (Louvain, 1947).

*–. *Psychologie et morale aux xiie et xiiie siècles*. 6 vols. (Louvain, 1942–1949).

McNeill, J. T. *A History of the Cure of Souls* (New York, 1951).

Wood, T. *English Casuistical Divinity during the Seventeenth Century* (London, 1952).

Two volumes may serve to introduce the *consilia* literature:

Engelmann, W. *Die Wiedergeburt der Rechtskultur in Italien durch die wissenschaftliche Lehre* (Leipzig, 1938).

Ermini, G. *Guida bibliografica per lo studio del diritto commune pontificio* (Bologna, 1934).

Two newly published anthologies assemble basic papers which have been written in the course of the debates over Weber's thesis. The first-mentioned collection by Eisenstadt represents recent, mainly American, statements by sociologists and historians. The second-mentioned collection represents the older critiques and studies by H. Karl Fischer, F. Rachfahl, E. Troeltsch, and Weber himself:

Eisenstadt, S. N. ed., *The Protestant Ethic and Modernization* (New York, 1968).

Winckelmann, J. ed., *Max Weber: Die protestantische Ethik, II: Kritiken und Antikritiken* (Munich and Hamburg, 1968).

The following constitute the main papers I have written which are relevant to the wider as well as immediate issues involved in this paper:

Nelson, B.

1944   "The Legend of the Divine Surety and the Jewish Moneylender." With Joshua Starr. *Annuaire de l'Institut de philologie et d'histoire orientales et slaves*, Tome VII (1939–1944), pp. 289–338. New York: *Editions de l'Institut:* H. Grégoire.

1947   ' The Usurer and the Merchant Prince: Italian Business Men and the Ecclesiastical Law of Restitution, 1100–1550." *The Journal of Economic History*, Supplement, VII (May, 1947), pp. 104–122.

1949   "Blancardo (The Jew?) of Genoa and the Restitution of Usury in Medieval Italy." *Studi in onore de Gino Luzzatto*, Vol. 1 (Milan, 1949), pp. 96–116.

1963   "Casuistry." *Encyclopaedia Britannica*, Vol. VI, pp. 51–52. Reprinted in 1967.

1964   "In Defense of Max Weber: Reply to Herbert Luethy." *Encounter* 131 (August, 1964), pp. 94–95.

1965   "Self-Images and Systems of Spiritual Direction in the History of

The first change we must make is to cease acting on the basis of defenses formed against the excesses of earlier days.

Single minded concentration on aggregate trend analysis can have the paradoxical effect of closing off our accesses to most critical stretches of individual and social behavior. Cultural *traditions* and struggles over authoritative norms can no more be neglected by historians of the intricate transition from the Middle Ages to the modern era than they can by anthropogists describing the life of a primitive people. Neglect the learned opinion of jurisconsults, the treatises of cases of *conscience*, the decision of courts – all the different sorts of courts, including the "Court of Conscience" – and we lose all chance of understanding how the Church actually defined and punished the manifest usurer against whom such paralyzing sanctions were directed in the Church's basic legislation on this score from the Second Lateran Council to the Council of Vienne. We should continue to regard it as an insoluble riddle, as so many do now, that the men of the Middle Ages while irreconcilably opposed to the giving as well as the asking of naked interest on a loan (*mutuum*) readily approved divisions of profits in partnerships (*societates*) where risks were shared. Gains of partners implied for them entirely praiseworthy outcomes of the legitimate relations of members of a *fraternal community*. As Max Weber and other scholars of an

European Civilization." *The Quest for Self-Control: Classical Philosophies and Scientific Research*. S. Z. Klausner, ed. (New York, 1965), pp. 49–103.

1965 "Probabilists, Anti-Probabilists, and the Quest for Certitude in the 16th and 17th Centuries." *Actes du Xme Congrès internationale d'histoire des sciences (Proceedings of the Xth International Congress for the History of Science)*, Vol. I (Paris, 1965), pp. 102–107.

1965 "Max Weber's *The Sociology of Religion*: A Review Article." *American Sociological Review* 30 (August, 1965), pp. 595–599.

1968 "The Early Modern Revolution in Science and Philosophy: Fictionalism, Probabilism, Fideism, and Catholic 'Prophetism.'" *Boston Studies in the Philosophy of Science, III*. R. S. Cohen and M. Wartofsky, eds. (Dordrecht, Holland, 1968), pp. 1–40.

1968 "Scholastic *Rationales* of Conscience, Early Modern 'Crises of Credibility' and the Scientific-Technocultural Revolutions of the 17th and 20th Centuries." *Journal for the Scientific Study of Religion* 7 (Fall, 1968), pp. 157–177.

1969 "*Conscience* and the Making of Early Modern Cultures: The *Protestant Ethic* beyond Max Weber," *Social Research* 36 (Spring, 1969), pp. 4–21.

earlier generation knew, that is indeed how very many partnerships were actually founded and functioned. Naked interest was usury, which none would take except from an enemy under the law of war.

If we wish to know whether and to what extent the later Middle Ages and Renaissance were permeated with the ethic of "capitalism," we must quickly embark upon a fresh appraisal of an immense number of sources, old and new, juridical, theological, logical, legislative, financial, ascetic.

The following sorts of materials, for example, need to be reassessed: the Church's basic legislation on restitution as well as on usury – the major decrees extend from the Second Lateran Council (1139) to the Council of Vienne (1311–1312); the commentaries on the *Corpus* of Justinian and the *Decretum*, and the papal decretals by canonists and civilians alike; the learned opinions (*consilia et responsa*) of renowned jurisconsults on litigation involving usury and other forms of commercial turpitude; the proceedings against usurers in the courts, lay and ecclesiastical, including those of the *outer forum*, such as the court of the bishop, and that of the *inner forum of conscience*, the confessional; royal decrees, municipal and guild statutes; the wills and testaments of leading enterprisers in different lands of Europe until the year 1600; and not least, the evidences of literature and the fine arts – poem and story, Gothic facade and Renaissance portrait.

Stereotyped and unverified allusions to easily misunderstood passages in subtle theologians will never substitute for close analyses of the monumental remains in the form of learned treatises and opinions (*consilia, responsa*) of the authoritative civilians and canonists of the trecento and quattrocento. Our first bit of proof concerns the matter of profits in partnerships mentioned above. Where, let one ask, will one find a more impressive account of the law and ethical ideas concerning forms of association than in the treatise *De duobus fratribus* of Petrus de Ubaldis? So far as I know, no mention of either his name or his authoritative work will be found in recent writings on religion and the rise of capitalism. Yet without a precise understanding of the juristic and moral roots of loan, partnerships of various sorts, sale, deposit, exchange (*cambium*) and other contracts, no understanding of the medieval schema is possible. Our second proof involves the critical matter of *consilia*. There is not a single study in any language known to me of the consultations on usury and ill-gotten gains in the incredibly rich collections of data. My own essay on "The Usurer and the Merchant-Prince" listed below is the only paper I know which discusses a case of restitution of usury *on the basis* of these materials!

II. MODERN AND CONTEMPORARY STEREOTYPES

The second change we must make is to look behind the inherited sterotypes which have been severely blocking the progress of research in this area.

In the present section we shall be considering the four following interlocking sets of stereotypes:

(1) Popular assumptions relating to the cultural (religious, legal, social, economic) roots of the medieval law of usury.

(2) Alleged casuistic loopholes and "extrinsic titles" contrived by scheming jurists and impatient businessmen who conspired to evade the usury law.

(3) The relevance of the canons to a variety of agents, money-changers, moneylenders, merchants, pawnbrokers, Jews.

(4) The measure of rational spirit in the so-called Renaissance and the extent to which this Renaissance was congenial to unfettered enterprise.

The following remarks shall deal with instances of all these stereotypes.

These older emphases started to grow weaker even before the end of the last century. During recent decades, the horizons of legal history have given way to the newer perspectives of policy-oriented theoretical economists and econometricians.

The "reactive" element in this latest orientation has resulted in the threat of a new excess in the circles of historians intransigently committed to change. Concentration on indices and interpretations of data purely in aggregate-behavior terms leads easily to a new absolutism, one which blacks out the vitalities of men moving about in the worlds they inhabited and the worlds by which they were possessed.

A. On the Religious and Juridical Roots of the Law of Usury

1. For several centuries now, at least since the days of Calvin, it has been popularly assumed that the medieval aversion to usury was the consequence of the failure of the untutored exegetes of the Middle Ages to understand the real import of Scriptural allusions, especially of Luke 6 : 35 – *Mutuum date nihil inde sperantes*. It has also been asserted that the ultimate rationale discovered for the law of usury by the Church was the so-called Aristotelian doctrine of the sterility of metals. Neither of these general assumptions is genuinely helpful.

Both Luke and Aristotle were pressed into service by the medieval theologians and jurists, but the driving forces in the canonist formulation of the law of usury were a compelling set of moral views and judicial tools. To put first things first: the medieval thinkers conceived the problems of usury primarily in *moral* and juridical, rather than in *economic* terms.

Now and then, a stray theologian like the excessively neglected Robert de Curzon (d. 1219), Innocent III's Cardinal-Legate to France just before the Fourth Lateran Council of 1215, might insist on exhibiting the significance of the practice and theory of usury for every aspect of Christian life and thought, including the financing of Church constructions. Or, a canonist like Pope Innocent IV could proclaim the ill-effects of usury on the incentives to labor and the output in agriculture. The overwhelming majority of the medieval thinkers stressed the moral components of the prohibition of usury.

2. Usury was a sin and a crime, they insisted, because the taking of usury was the decisive expression of an egocentric morality which did violence to the Christian emphasis upon the transcendent spiritual values: the superior significance of other-worldliness, the religious vocation, and the quest for eternal salvation. The habit of accumulation associated with the professional practice of usury seemed to cause men to deny the supreme value of alms, to lead them to abjure the imitation of Christ's poverty, and above all to violate the Christian injunction of universal brotherhood.

All mankind constituted a universal brotherhood under the common fatherhood of God. To medieval writers, the loan was the occasion for the practice of Christian charity, rather than an economic transaction. For a Christian to take usury from his neighbor – indeed even for a Jew to take usury from a Christian – was deemed an act of fratricide. In the state of the gospel, to which all men were called, all were brothers, and it was regarded as horrible and damnable to take interest from one's own brother. The medieval view was stubbornly *interpersonal*, and not, as is the modern, ruggedly individualistic or *superpersonal* or *impersonal*, i.e., concerned with the natural rights of individuals, the maximum wealth of nations, the greatest good of the greatest number, etc.

3. The juridical tools which lay to hand were derived almost entirely from Roman law. Roman law's analysis of contratcs rather than the Aristotelian theory of money suggested the matrix for the medieval theory.

Starting from the framework of a formalist theory of contracts, medieval theorists found it impossible to consent to the taking of interest on loans because the contract of loan (*mutuum*) was by nature gratuitous, and only articles of a certain type were properly the subject of a *mutuum*. It made no difference if one pointed out that the articles or commodities transferred in a *mutuum* were capable of yielding an increment to the debtor. From the formalistic view, such increment was accidental. It was not necessarily implied by the undeniable fact that in a *mutuum* legal title or *dominium* was transferred from the lender to the borrower. For the lender to argue that he was entitled to some kind of usury because he incurred risk by putting his money at the disposal of the borrower was in the opinion of the medieval thinkers rank nonsense. The creditor's uncertainty in a loan was a *psychological* fact which in no way, in the universal opinion of medieval writers, detracted from the *juridical reality* that the real risk in a *mutuum* was borne by the borrower and not by the lender.

To Catholic theologians and jurists, therefore, it was patent that the borrower bore the risk in a loan. Was not the borrower obligated to return the equivalent of the principal of the loan even if the money dissolved in his hands or if he lost it in a minute after receiving it? From that point of view the creditor had no need to fear and suffered no risk whatsoever. When real risk was suffered, as in a commercial partnership, where the capital was ventured or in hazard, and where the investment was subject to the contingency of loss, Catholic writers found no difficulty in adjudging profit to the investor. In such an agreement, they assumed, the investor did not transfer possession but retained title and still bore the risks during the period of partnership.

The understanding of the medieval Catholic attitude to usury is further confused by many mistaken assumptions. Only a selected number of these may be isolated here for special consideration.

4. Since the time of W. J. Ashley, at least, it has been custom-- ary to make a sharp distinction between the medieval treatment of "consumptibles" and "fungibles" as if the medieval jurists and theologians permitted the taking of an increment in the loan of what they called "fungibles" and forbade it only in the case of what they called "consumptibles." This position rests upon the notion that consumptibles *are* and fungibles *are not* consumed in the act of exchange and the transaction of a loan has different effects if one type of commodity rather than another is at stake. In the case of consumptibles, medieval writers insisted it is impossible to take a price for the use of a thing and the thing itself inasmuch as the thing is consumed in its use. Customarily the category of consumptibles is said to include such things as apples, grain, wine, and other perishable articles – including money, which in the medieval period is thought of as an object of consumption or at least an object which is consumed in the process of exchange; fungibles are generally described as houses, estates, and other properties which are not destroyed by their use.

In truth, a distinction between such types of articles was made in the medieval period but the current terms, consumptibles and fungibles, do not accurately characterize this medieval distinction, from a technical point of view. Indeed, these phrases are not to be found in our sources at all. They are evidently post-medieval in origin. The author of a recent text on Roman-Dutch law claims to find these terms in the work of Ulrich Zasius, perhaps the greatest German jurist of the Reformation era. Indeed, Zasius' biographer, the learned Roderick Stintzing, credits Zasius with having invented the term *res fungibiles*.

In medieval as well as in Roman law, the opposition between what has been called *consumptibles* and *fungibles* is not an opposition between articles of consumption and other types of goods and properties, but rather a distinction between goods which are quantifiable in terms of weight, number and measure and which therefore permit of return *in genere*, and articles which have in themselves a unique irreplaceable utility and are destroyed by the act of consumption.

This implies that what Ashley and all the textbook authors often have called a *consumptible* may be a *fungible* in the proper sense and what they legitimately called a *fungible* could be a *consumptible* in Ashley's sense. *In point of fact, things properly the subject of loans (mutua) are both consumptible and fungible.* As articles of consumption, they are individually consumed by the process of exchange and do not have any life apart from the use which is made of them (and, therefore, to the pre-Reformation writers, do not entitle the creditor to a double price – a price for the sale, and a price for the use of the thing).

Notwithstanding the perishable character of these articles, they are replaceable and therefore fungibles. The repayment which is made in a *mutuum* is not a restoration *in specie* of the specific thing which changes hands, but a return of the same number, weight, or measure of the things involved. Indeed, to misconstrue the fact that it is precisely *fungibles* which are alone in the province of the *mutuum* is to misconceive the whole medieval theory of loan and usury.

5. It would be unfair to leave the impression that W. J. Ashley deserves to be remembered only for his slips in understanding. Indeed, his chapter on the "Canonist Interpretation of Usury" remains a classic. Yet here we must begin with him because of a construction that has grown since his time.

The Historical School of Political Economy of the late nineteenth century deserves credit for indicating the economic and social grounds for the medieval abhorrence of usury. Ashley and a number of other writers pointed the way toward a more sympathetic appraisal of the Church's usury program. Very few scholars remain who contend that there is nothing behind the medieval usury law but philological absurdity and moral perversity. *If anything, the trend of recent writing on the subject has been going to the other extreme.* Twentieth-century historians and apologists who are disposed to square the medieval economic

theory with modern economic values and analysis, will be found
to adopt two contradictory points of view. Some writers, including many notable moral theologians in authoritative texts
and treatises for seminarians, assert that the jurists and theologians of earlier days are not to be blamed for failing to envisage
contemporary approaches to capital and interest, since they had
no point of reference in the economic setting of the medieval
world. If, in other words, the scholastics failed properly to distinguish between consumers' and producers' loans, it was because
of the rudimentary development of investment opportunities in
their economy. Most frequently, this account of the situation is
justified by references to selected documentary remains of the
early Middle Ages.

The newer writers have begun to insist that the medieval
doctrine on interest and usury far surpasses modern writings
from Cassell to Keynes in the subtlety of its economic analysis.
The clue to the character of medieval economic analysis is now
declared to be a profound awareness of a need to check hoarding,
to stimulate productive investments, to tax people for exerting
the liquidity preference. In this spirit, the extrinsic titles, notably
the title known as *lucrum cessans* are treated as anticipation of
the recent analysis of opportunity costs. Keynes himself, indeed,
agreed at one time that the core of his distinction between savings
and investment was anticipated by the reviled canonists.

The "historical" standpoint, in short, has itself engendered a
number of confusing stereotypes with reference to the medieval
law of usury. To look at matters in this light is to assume a
latterday economic attitude foreign to the jurists and theologians
of the Church. There is ample evidence to prove that the archi-
tects of the anti-usury program were aware of the fact that a
borrower was often in a position to reap considerable profits from
a loan. In their eyes, this had nothing to do with the case. What
mattered alone was that the profit was being solicited or demanded within the framework of a contract which, in their eyes, was
gratuitous in its very nature.

Students of the legal development of different cultures,
notably those which make a claim to sacredness, should have no
difficulty in understanding the authority which a great juridical
and moral tradition can have over the minds of the principal

spokesman of great religious communities. The insistence upon a predominantly jural point of view is felt to be the sole guarantee of the continuity of the community and the survival of the accredited way of life under the acknowledged rule of law. It is for this reason, above all, that religious systems of morality tend almost irresistibly to assume juridical dress and to plod their way to innovation by the devices of casuistry. Casuistry is less the fruit of a libertine distortion of the sacred texts in the interest of private pressure groups, than the inevitable armature of conscience seeking to make itself effective among the complex ambiguities of the here-and-now.

B. Casuistic Loopholes and So-Called "Extrinsic Titles"

Very few medieval writers, after the full reception of the Roman law schemata of contracts in the twelfth century, had any hesitation in allowing reasonable returns in a wide variety of contracts (purchase and sale, lease and hire, partnership, *et al.*). What the ecclesiastical authorities would not allow in particular was *profit* on a *mutuum*, that is, pure usury. It made no difference, indeed, whether the profit was secretly hoped for or openly extorted – both were usury. On this point, the disallowance of naked interest, the medieval doctors never compromised. To claim profit on a *mutuum* was for them to violate all law – divine, natural, ecclesiastical, and even, civil. The seeming exceptions to this prohibition in the Old Testament and the Roman law were identified as temporary concessions to the Hebrew and Roman people, respectively. Still – and this has confused all but a handful of modern commentators – the medieval writers had no difficulty in allowing what, following the civilians, they called *usurae compensatoriae* (compensatory indemnities) and *usurae punitoriae* (punitive default damages). What they rejected was *usurae lucratoriae* (usurious *profits* on a *mutuum*). It was this type of usury – usurious profits on a *mutuum* – which was demanded by the manifest usurer openly and explicitly and by him alone.

Modern writers have also generally misstated the evidence concerning the medieval attitudes to the so-called "exceptions" to the absolute prohibition of usury. Even a glance at any of the commentaries upon the *Decretum* of Gratian and the *Decretals* of

Gregory IX indicates that already in the thirteenth century the ranking jurists summing up ecclesiastical regulations allowed the taking of an increment under special circumstances. A hexameter doggerel in the *Summa aurea* of Cardinal Henricus de Segusio, familiarly known as Hostiensis, lists a dozen situations – elsewhere he adds another to make it thirteen – in which an increment above the capital may be taken. These are, however, to be differentiated from the so-called *extrinsic* titles, which remain so sadly misunderstood despite the continuous referral to them in current writings.

In the main, modern authors enunciate propositions of the following order concerning the so-called exceptions and extrinsic titles: the prohibition against usury was completely evaded by the use of casuistical loopholes. So, for example, it is stated that what was disallowed under the name of usury on a loan could be perfectly well taken under the name of damages, *damna*, in accordance with the legitimate title called *damnum emergens*. Enterprisers were also in a position to claim a return upon their capital in compensation for profit opportunities they lost as a result of the loan and in the course of the loan. Thus we are told that anyone who made a loan in the Middle Ages had only to allege that he had lost an opportunity to make a profit, which brought into operation the title *lucrum cessans*. We are also informed that medieval writers acknowledged the right of a lender to claim an increment in compensation for the risk of his capital. This is known as the title *periculum sortis*.

Concerning these and other alleged exceptions to the universal prohibition of usury in loans the following needs to be said:

a. The so-called exceptions and extrinsic titles were not in the first place devised to circumvent the law against usury, though there is no denying that could be exploited to that end. There is not the slightest evidence that the motives of the jurists and theologians who debated those delicate questions in the twelfth and thirteenth centuries were tainted with the desire to undo Church law.

b. For that matter, it is altogether mistaken to suppose that the various contractual arrangements into which different types of businessmen entered originated as schemes for evading the ecclesiastical restrictions. The sundry types of partnership, the contracts of deposit, the letters and bills of exchange, and so forth, developed and were used quite spontaneously and can be traced in most instances to exceedingly ancient commercial practices. To be sure, any one of these arrangements could be exploited to conceal an illegitimate reception of usury in a loan.

c. Neither the *damnum emergens* nor the *lucrum cessans* nor the notion of *interesse* as distinguished from *usura* was particularly medieval in origin. All of these concepts derived directly from Roman law and there seems little point in undertaking to demonstrate, as is currently being done, that these so-called "tricks for evading the usury law" originate among the medieval Hebrews or Muslims. No sooner had the jurists adopted the outlines of the Roman law theory of contract than they were obliged systematically to think through the contingencies which might permit a lender to ask for an increment above the principal of a loan.

Damna et interesse are not to be thought of exclusively as civil law damages, but also as criminal law forfeitures and punishments. No one had a right to claim *damna* unless there was a clear demonstration that there had been a delay in making payments at maturity; moreover, in ecclesiastical thought, whether juristic or theological, the *damna* had to be proved specifically. In short, there were no *damna* unless there was delay (*mora*) in making payment at maturity, and there never was an average rate for all transactions.

Here we have hit upon a decisive distinction between the medieval jural and the modern economic mode of analysis. Without the notion of an average rate it is impossible to have an organized calculus of expectations which is so necessary for the capitalist order. There are many cases in the *consilia* literature involving disputes over the amount of *damna* claimed. Unlike the mercantilists of the seventeenth century, medieval writers never discuss the relative bearings upon the favorable trade balance and national welfare of *different rates of interest*. The clearest indication of the medieval aversion to the concept of average rate will be found in the extraordinary attack upon the interest provision in the *monti di pieta* by the great commentator on St. Thomas, Thomas de Vio (Cajetan).

d. The punitive character of *damna* may clearly be seen in the penalty clause, the so-called *poena conventionalis*. The *poena conventionalis* was not, in the opinion of canonists and theologians, usury masquerading as a charge for lateness in repayment. It was more like punishment for a crime done than the monetary reparation for a loss incurred. In the language of the noted French sociologist Emile Durkheim, the *poena* was originally repressive rather than *restitutive* in character. The usual penalty in the documents of the twelfth and thirteenth centuries is thus a penalty of double, sometimes quadruple, the capital lent.

The dread character of the payments is pointedly reflected in the gruesome tales of the Middle Ages. Overtones of these will be noted in the *Merchant of Venice*. On first glance there might appear to be a contradiction between the gratuitous character of the loan and the punitive nature of the penalty. But second thought might suggest that the two go hand in hand. May it not be that the forfeiture is especially severe where the transaction was grounded in love and charity? The penalty thus becomes a token of rage resulting from the shock of ingratitude or blighted friendship.

Again, with the *poena* as with *damnum* and *lucrum*, it needs to be remembered that the forfeiture and penalty clauses do not originate among the scheming medieval canonists, but go back to the deepest antiquity.

e. Modern writers have been exceedingly careless in tracing the fortunes of the extrinsic title known as *lucrum cessans*. St. Thomas opposed it, as it happens, arguing that one was not justified in claiming compensation for profit one might not have made. Writers in the late Middle Ages and Renaissance show somewhat greater indulgence to the title *lucrum cessans*. Not all, but a number of noted thinkers, agree that a lender might well lay claim to an increment above the capital, if the extension of a loan had been the cause of a failure to realize a profit opportunity. But here also the medieval and Renaissance jurists maintained strict reins upon enterprise. It is simply not to be imagined that anyone was free to claim whatever the traffic would bear from a borrower.

A number of conditions had to be fulfilled before one could rightfully assert the title *lucrum cessans*. In the *first place*, there had to be *mora* or delay in repayments. *Secondly*, the lender had to be able to demonstrate that he was a merchant who was habitually engaged in the practice of trade and had a continuous, even a current, disposition to invest. *Thirdly*, the lender would have to prove that the opportunities for gain in legitimate enterprise were numerous, that market conditions promised a substantial likelihood of profit. *Fourthly*, the merchant had also to prove that the capital which had been lent was not surplus money held in reserve, but working capital, which otherwise might readily have gone into investment channels. *Fifthly*, anyone alleging the title might be called upon to demonstrate the specific opportunities which he had lost.

Cases involving all of these restraints will be found in the consultations of the authoritative jurists of the Renaissance cities, and it is no surprise to discover that some of these cases involve firms and families of the greatest reknown, such as the Strozzi of Florence and others. Saint Bernardino of Siena and St. Antoninus of Florence, who are consistently cited as symbols of the conquest of market mentality in Italy, reject the right of nobles and artificers to allege the title *lucrum cessans* in contracts of deposit, when the capital is safe and not undergoing genuine risk. Indeed, members of the elder branch of the Medici firm were called upon to make restitutions of usury because they had participated in questionable arrangements of this sort, i.e., in so-called "deposits at discretion."

There is great need at the moment for a systematic review of the cases bearing upon individual contracts. Again and again, one encounters opinions of outstanding jurists which disallow the receipt of interest in the contract of deposit, where the convention clearly masks a *mutuum*. The test was the status of the capital in the course of the transaction, whether it was or was not treated as venture capital, that is, committed to risk. Also, innumerable cases rule out the receipt of assured profits in a contract of partnership. Such an agreement is always described as a so-called *societas leonina*, that is, one in which the dormant partner claims the lion's share of the spoils without himself undergoing any risk.

Had these limitations not existed, the Fuggers of Augsberg should not have had such great difficulty in persuading University faculties of the legitimacy of the so-called triple contract, over which polemics raged throughout the sixteenth and seventeenth centuries. The intricate efforts to establish a basis for an assured gain to be offered by the Fuggers to the creditors failed of approval in the last analysis. Notwithstanding the support of this ingenious arrangement on the part of latitudinarian Jesuits in the sixteenth century, the bulk of the writers rejected the claim to assured gain.

Other cases exhibit the working of the doctrine on bills of exchange or the notion of *cambium*. Again, here, the jurists were most cautious in ferreting out exchange arrangements which simply disguised *mutuum* contracts.

C. *The Bearing of the Usury Laws on Enterprisers*

One of the most popular and persuasive in this long series of stereotypes relates to the bearing of ecclesiastical regulations on enterprisers – whether they were usurers, bankers, money-changers, or moneylenders, Christian, Jew, or whatever. Many of the most eminent writers – R. H. Tawney is an outstanding instance – suppose that the ecclesiastical law of usury was aimed against the ruthless extortioners of the peasants in the country-side and not against the financiers who did business with the kings and popes. This again is a latterday economic point of view foreign to the concepts of the medieval jurists.

The target of the Church's enforcement program was the manifest usurer who publicly and notoriously rendered himself accessible to all comers and so, like the prostitute in the brothel, furnished the direct occasion for scandal and despair to his Christian neighbors. Anyone who manifestly committed the crime of usury by sitting at his table in the public square or elsewhere with or without official license of the commune or prince, whether he were Jew or Christian, cleric or layman, merchant-prince or pawnbroker, was, in the eyes of the Church, a manifest usurer, subject to the sanctions laid down by the basic Decretals from time of the Second Lateran Council of 1139 to the drastic regulations of the Council of Vienne of 1311–12.

Manifest usurers, exclusively, were made subject to a host of paralyzing sanctions which incapacitated them at every turn in their life in civil and religious society. Thus, those failing to complete restitution and satisfaction incurred excommunication and infamy. In addition, they forfeited a host of basic rights: the right to act as witness, the right to hold public office, the right to assign property by testament, the right to participate in the sacraments, the right to receive consecrated burial.

A man might be active in commerce – it mattered little whether the traffic was over land or over sea, local or "international" – he might invest in partnerships and maritime loans; he might buy and sell, let and hire property; he might simultaneously violate municipal regulations and Christian ethic by demanding more than the "just price"; indeed, he might even engage in occasional, intermittent, secret or "mental" usury; but unless he were in fact judged a manifest usurer, he did not incur the aforementioned major sanctions promulgated by the general councils. To be sure, anyone benefiting from illicit traffic of one sort or another was under an obligation to return the spoils. But this obligation was enforced by the dread sanctions of the external forum only in the case of manifest usurers.

Current presuppositions as to the omnipresence of economic motivations have led recent writers to underestimate the role of non-economic factors in the Church's campaign against usury and the degree to which the Church interpreted the practice of open usury as a provocative challenge to its pretensions to police Christian society.

In the Church's scheme of things, the Church had a paramount interest in the elimination of scandal from the community of Christians and the punishment of open insubordination to the authority of the hierarchy.

It was the flamboyance of the manifest usurer, the notoriety of his violation of ecclesiastical prohibition against taking profits on loans, which brought down the wrath of the Church. Legitimate traders and financiers were clearly distinguished from pawn-brokers in not practicing direct usury, at least not manifestly or notoriously.

As I have elsewhere written in summary of the theory and practice of restitution of usury and ill-gotten gains between 1100 and 1600: from the peculiar vantage point of the historian of the theory and practice of restitution, the Renaissance is that period in European history which witnesses the accomplishment of a major revolution in the patterns of European society: the establishment of the merchant-prince as cynosure. With the

advent of the Renaissance, the great merchant is no longer
confused with the pawnbroker-usurer. The latter was to remain a
scapegoat and an object of contempt for a long time to come.

By the second quarter of the fourteenth century, public
sentiment as well as ecclesiastical law in the key economic areas
of the later medieval and Renaissance worlds had made a clear
distinction between two figures, originally indistinct. At one pole
cowered the degraded usurer-pawnbroker, whether he were a
Christian or a Jew. At the other pole there proudly stood the
merchant-prince – city father, arbiter of elegance, patron of the
arts, devout philanthropist. In the celebrated fable of the Bard
of Avon, it will be remembered, Shylock and Antonio are locked
in mortal combat.

D. Law, Moral Sentiment, and the "Spirit of Capitalism" in Renaissance Italy

Here, as in many other areas already noted which relate to the
economic ethic of the late Middle Ages and the Renaissance, the
debate has shed much more heat than light. Just now, one senses
the onset of a new phase. Ripples of excitement are attaching
themselves to the more remote corners of this inquiry. Despite
this fact, one cannot say that much new ground has been broken.
The scientific study of the ruling *social ethic* in respect to economic
affairs in Italy from roughly the year 1300 to 1600 has hardly
begun. Here again I must emphasize the difference between an
"externalistic 'aggregate-behavior view' of *economic* units" and an
"holistic" view of sociocultural process, the understanding of the
conduct of men in the light of all the flows of influence which
impinge on them – including the cultures of conscience – and
the workings of their consciences and the consciences of others.
The extent of new forays into this terrain is slight by comparison
with the mass of current research on the ways of enterprises and
enterprisers in that era. Thus, there has been little advance made
to date in regard to the controversies between Max Weber and
his principal critics – the controversies between Weber and Sombart, Weber and Keller, Weber and Brentano. There is no great
loss – and some good is done – if we raise the questions in the
form in which they were left at Weber's death in 1920.

Is it true, as Sombart alleged, that a perfect parallel and

prototype of Benjamin Franklin can be found in the *Della famiglia* of Leon Battista Alberti? Is Keller correct when he suggests that the casuistic innovations of the fifteenth century, notably the views on the "industry" of merchants found in the writings of St. Bernardino of Siena and Antoninus of Florence, are capitalist in character? Are we justified in agreeing with Brentano that the disenchanted ethic of Machiavelli is stimulus enough for the growth of capitalist enterprise?

So far as I know, there has been no substantial review of these problems in the literature since Weber's death. Indeed, some exceedingly important contributions have gone unnoticed because they did not happen to have been a part of the debate. One could cite, in this connection, a very important chapter by G. Biagi on the *Libro di buon costumi* of the fourteenth century Florentine, Paolo di Pace da Certaldo. In Biagi's account, done in 1908, Paolo becomes a fourteenth-century predecessor of the author of *Poor Richard's Almanac*. Another work which has suffered neglect for unaccountable reasons, Giovanni Marcotti's study of Giovanni Rucellai, offers a striking analysis of that noted merchant's commonplace book, the *Zibaldone*. No one has yet attempted to relate Rucellai's other writings, especially his account of his pilgrimage to Rome in 1450, to this problem. I allow myself to add, in passing, that few exercises in comparative history could be more instructive than a comparison of Rucellai's pilgrimage report with that of the great German merchant-philanthropist, Jakob Heller of Frankfurt, who became a follower of Luther.

Studies of attitudes to economic affairs as these are found in medieval French literature are legion, but where shall one look for a solid account of such attitudes in the Italian *novelle* from the thirteenth through the sixteenth centuries? As for the Italians, we are only now beginning to have monographs of consequence from this standpoint on any of the major Italian writers, including Boccaccio, Giovanni Fiorentino, Bandello, and others.

The study of social ethics and economic spirit in the Renaissance is in its infancy. Alfred von Martin's efforts deserve praise, but his ambitious booklet on the *Sociology of the Renaissance* offers an excessively fleeting look at the issues. Speaking more

closely within the context of the present paper, we should have
to say that none of Weber's critics in this field – neither Amintore
Fanfani nor H. M. Robertson nor others – has yet met Weber on
his own ground. Recent essays by Paul Kristeller and Charles
Trinkaus on the moral philosophies and attitudes of the Italian
humanists offer some hope for more substantial progress in the
future. The *consilia* or consultations which report the opinions of
the authoritative jurists on the issues under dispute or in litigation
remain largely untapped treasures for every aspect of the
history of European culture and civilization. It is only necessary
to examine any of these volumes of consultations at random to
discover how slow the jurists were to accept the notions of utter
freedom of enterprise. Firms and families of the greatest eminence
including that of Jacques Scaglia de Tifi, the "bizarre Florentine"
at the Court of the Counts of Burgundy in the late thirteenth century, who has become celebrated through the study of Armando
Sapori, the family and firm of the Strozzi, and even the Fuggers
appear here in the position of defendants, charged with the
illegalities and improprieties which call for amendment and
restitution.

A great part of the confusion – it hardly needs saying – results
from the failure of the participants in the debate to define with
any degree of precision the meaning of the terms "capitalism"
and the "spirit of capitalism"! In some interpretations, capitalism is equated with any evidence of economic exchange or use of
money or pursuit of gain. Every instance of an effort to accumul-
ate wealth, whether through military conquest, through political
expropriation or through downright theft and swindle is deemed
capitalistic. Under such a view, the system of capitalism and its
accompanying spirit must by necessity be as old as history itself.
Notwithstanding Weber's warnings on this score, many writers
proceed as if he had never written and continue to make these
faulty equations. The successive works of Henri Pirenne are the
most striking illustrations of this situation, and it is no wonder
that he sees the capitalist enterpriser and spirit in the eleventh-
century Saint Godric of Finchale, who crowned a life of beach-
combing and fitful accumulation by a conversion to the religious
life.

Max Weber stands out above all others as the scholar-historian-sociologist who recognized and stressed the differences between *casuistic concessions to circumstances* – economic, social, intellectual – and the *establishment of a new "conscience."* Although Weber never explicitly set forth the history and logic of these notions, it is evident that he had profoundly covered a great deal of the ground in the course of his own research and writing.

To date, Weber has been followed by only a small number of historians and sociologists. Chief among these have been Ernst Troeltsch and R. H. Tawney – in the second and third decades of the present century – and a small band of sociologists inspired by Talcott Parsons – in the more recent period. Only a handful of historians across the world have shared a sympathy for Weber's approach.

Weber insisted on the need to see that the breakthrough came with the provision of new, positive, religiously-related premia for methodical and conscientious activity of a gainful nature in this world.

A "crucial experiment" both for Weber's views and my own may be found in the test of the widespread claim that the dominant *ethos* of the late Middle Ages and Renaissance was "capitalist." I will close this section on one pivotal aspect of this issue, an issue, I am bound to say, on which I share Weber's point of view. Sombart and many others after him down to our day have contended that St. Bernardino of Siena (1380–1444) – others mention St. Antonino of Florence (1409–1459) in the same connection – decisively modified the traditional teachings on usury. Did this actually happen? My answer must be that these claims have by now the character of clichés. When placed in proper perspective, there is little of strategic significance in the theologians of the early *quattrocento* for which we cannot find parallels or premonitions in the writings of such authoritative canonists of the mid-thirteenth century as, for example, Goffredus de Trano and Cardinal Hostiensis. The much vaunted emphasis by these Renaissance theologians on the *industria* of merchants was neither so unprecedented nor so influential as is universally assumed. In any case, it is not to be imagined that the acknowledgement of the service performed by the enterpriser led Renaissance theologians to justify the taking of naked interest on a loan (*mutuum*).

One does not have to plod one's weary way through the labyrinthine folios of Bernardino and Antonino to get at the contemporary understandings of their teachings – one has only to examine the handy biographies of these notables in the *Lives* by Vespasiano da Bisticci. The very men whom modern writers celebrate for having subtly contrived to undo the Church's hallowed teachings prove in Vespasiano's account to have been exceedingly vigorous in denouncing commercial turpitude and claiming restitution from profiteers and usurers, alike. If either Bernardino or Antonino had dared to deny the traditional teachings on usury, he would have been denounced as a heretic, rather than canonized as a saint.

No one who wanted to preserve his skin – whether he was a theologian or jurist, a civilian or canonist, a shopkeeper or tycoon – openly challenged the essentials of the medieval analysis until the appearance of the Protestant reformers. Those who doubt this would do well to examine closely the *Tractatus de usuris* (1403) by the eminent Florentine jurist Lorenzo Ridolfi (Laurentius de Ridolfis). It is true that Lorenzo justifies the receipt of returns (*interesse*, not *usura*) on investment in municipal loans (the *mons*) – as later others were to legitimize the taking of interest (*interesse*, not *usura*) in the *monti di pietà*: the pawnshops promoted by the Franciscan Observants in the latter half of the fifteenth century. Despite all this, however, the fundamental outlines of the traditional theological and legal critiques of usury persisted wherever Catholic cultures prevailed. The notion, by now an article of faith among many economic historians on the Continent as well as in this country, that the allowance of *interesse* in the medieval sense was tantamount to the abandonment or the demolition of the medieval idea of usury is simply an error and a source of confusion.

III. A LOOK BACK

Enough has now been said to suggest that in my view the relations of religion, law, and the rise of "capitalism" are much more tangled, chromatic, and elusive than is generally taken to be the case. Too often, current estimates of the bearing which theological and legal theories have upon the trading and money-ending classes of pre-Reformation Europe prove to be marred by a neglect and misunderstanding of basic sources. Unlike many of my colleagues who deal with economic and business history, I find it neither possible nor desirable to deny the relevance of religious imperatives and legal norms for the conduct of business in the medieval and early modern eras. Both the course and the pace of Western economic development during the epoch of transition to "modern society" were very significantly affected by religious, ethical and juridical ideas, ideals and institutions.

As I have intimated, I have been convinced by few criticisms of the Weber-Troeltsch-Tawney thesis urged by historians and sociologists over the last sixty-five years. Weber's views seem to me to stand up very well against the contentions of Henri Pirenne, Henri Sée, Lujo Brentano, H. M. Robertson, Kurt Samuelsson, Herbert Luethy and H. Trevor-Roper. Nor can I agree with the modernizing constructions of familiar studies of the economic morals and doctrines of the Jesuits of the sixteenth centuries, including those of Fathers James Broderick and Bernard Dempsey and Professor John Noonan.

If we wish to improve our understanding of the issues posed by Weber, Troeltsch, and Tawney, I must repeat: we would do well to change our ways in a number of particulars. Postures formed as defenses against the excesses of the past need to be abandoned as being less likely to issue in progress than in the ceaseless cycle of misunderstanding. Neglect of any sector of the documentary evidence for whatever reason only insures the reign of stereotypes.

Not Weber, but his less circumspect followers and critics among contemporary historical and sociological publicists, should be blamed for the spread of the unrealistic characterizations of the social situation and religious outlooks of the later medieval and Renaissance Church and enterprisers, which have been called into question in the present essay.

The cure for this is, however, not as simple as many current scholars suppose. New documents will not of themselves heal our wounds. We need most of all a deeper understanding of the ways of men as they went about the making up of their minds in all the worlds they inhabited. We must do all in our power to get a secure grasp of all the matrices of decision in all the spheres of action and thought – the spheres of conscience, the jural casuistries, the ideals of community. Otherwise we shall never have the disinterested assessment of the religious teachings, moral sentiments, and economic life in the evolution of Western civilization so many of us have so long been seeking.

In my own writings over the last two decades – from the *Idea of Usury* (1949) to the present – I have placed stress on the breakthrough in the *rationales* of *conscience*, the centre of the "guidance system" of all the "decision-matrices" affecting the belief and behavior of all individuals and groups. If I am correct, the new doctrines of usury proclaimed by Luther and Calvin, especially their unprecedented treatments of the Deuteronomic commandment, have vastly more importance than Weber was prepared to admit until, perhaps, in his very last course of lectures in 1920. As I have elsewhere argued, the breakthrough in the exegesis of Deuteronomy speeded the advance of the spirit of *Universal Otherhood* – a growing form of brotherhood in which all become brothers by being equally others.

My conviction is that Weber might himself have come to this very conclusion if he had been allowed to carry forward his research in the spirit of the magisterial essay he wrote in the last year of his life as the "Author's Introduction" to the posthumously published *Collected Essays in the Sociology of Religion* made available after his death in a manner which has continued to perplex readers to the present hour.[3]

Graduate Faculty
New School for Social Research
New York, New York

---

[3] I am privileged to offer this essay as a tribute to the work and person of Philip Merlan. His wonderful writings have been of continuing joy to me during all the years in which we have worked at a great remove from one another. We have been separated in point of place and in the focus of our scholarly research, but not, I believe, in spirit.

GENERAL INDEX

Abamon: 227–239
Adequate Theorem: in Petrażycki, 358–370
Amon: 234–235
Anebon: 227, 232–233
Aristotle: *De An.* 404b18 ff., bibliography, p. 146, n. 1; *De An.* 404b18 ff., relationship of Plato to, 146–148; *De An.* 404b18 ff., relationship of Speusippus to, 158–159, 161–162, 169; *De An.* 404b18 ff., relationship of *Timaeus* to, 151–154; *De An.* 404b18 ff., relationship of Xenocrates to, 148–149, 148, n. 7, 160–161, 164–165; *Metaph.* Z, displacement of text in, 75; *Metaph.* Z 7–9, 75–87; *De partibus animalium* 1.1.641a14–b10, 88–94; the character of his ethics, 116–124; system of ethics built on contingent views, 119; ethics contrasted with Plato, 195–196; form in, 77–87; Prime Mover cannot serve as sanction of moral values, 118–119; theory of knowledge contrasted with Plato, 196–197; nature of living beings in, 88; his view of nature discussed, 120–124; relationship of soul to life, 128–129; soul in his biology, 89–94
Aristotle's Will: in Arabic text, 265; in codex Ayasofya, Istanbul, No. 4833, 266–269
Aurelius, Marcus: *Meditations*, C extracts, mss. of, 187; X extracts, mss. of, 184–186; fate of ms. of owned by Reuchlin, 189–192; first printed quotations from, 188–189; ms. of mentioned in library catalogue in ms. Egerton 602, British Museum, 192; materials for text of, 183–184
Aurelius, Marcus: mentioned as philosopher in scholium of Plato's *Republic* 5.473c, 193
authority: nature of, 433–444

Barigazzi, Adelmo: review of his *La formazione spirituale de Menandro*, 465–482
al-Baṣīr, Yūsuf: refutation of metempsychosis by, 281–290
Bayle, Pierre: 356
beauty: and Socrates, 320–323
becoming: 77, 80–83
Berens, Johann Christoph: 308, 312
Brentano, Franz: portrait of Husserl, 341–345

canon law of contracts: 525–548
capitalism: 525–548
Catullus: 510–511
causality: 398–411
Chinese philosophy: structure of, 298
conflict: of reason and desires, 207–209
conscience: and usury, 527–529
consolatio: etymology of, 224
consolation literature: 223–226; bibliography of, 226, n. 9
Crantor of Soloi: writer of consolation literature, 226
Cratylus: as transmitter of Heraclitean thought to Plato, 3, 7, 9
Critias: identity of, 15–16, n. 12
criticism: philosophy as, 412–416
culture: and the history of philosophy, 298–301

daimon: in Socrates, 317–320
Delphic oracle: in Philo, 245–250
Diog. Laert. 10.136: 454, n. 20
Dionysus: and Socrates, 307, 316
displacement of text: in Arist. *Metaph.* Z, 75; in Hippolytus, *Elenchos*, 240–244

doxography: 294–295
Dualists: 285
Dürer, Albrecht: and Eobanus Hessus, 508–521

eidos: in Proclus, 65–74; in Middle Ages, 70–72; the supreme *eidos* as the Absolute, 73
elegy: 509
Epicurea (Ecloga): 447–460
Epicureanism: in the early 17th century, 346–357; of Pierre Gassendi, 346–349; and Uriel Da Costa, 349–354; and Isaac La Peyrère, 354–355
Epicurus: his style of philosophy, 454–460; and Theocritus, 454–460
Epitaphios Bionos: 511–514
ethics: of Plato and Aristotle contrasted, 195–196

First Cause: meaning of in Proclus, 70
form: in Aristotle, 77–87

genius: 485
Goethe, Johann W.: 503–507; and Hamann's Socrates, 325; and Mozart, 485–502; *Die natürliche Tochter*, 503–507
Golden Age motif: used by Posidonius, 256–257; by Lactantius, 257, 259; source of in Lactantius, 258
Gorgias: in Goethe, 503–507

Hamann, J. G.: 306–310, 331–340; influence on Amalie von Galitzin, 330–340
harmony (of life): 337–340
Hellenistic philosophy: the limits of its influence on the poetry of the age, 461–464
Hellenistic poetry: not necessarily directly related to the philosophy of the age, 461–464; how it should be interpreted, 462–464
Hemsterhuis: 335
Heraclitus: influence on Plato, 3, 4, 5, 9
Hesiod: *Erag* 758¹, Proclus on, 504
Hessus, Eobanus: 508; and Albrecht Dürer, 508–521
Hippolytus: *Elenchos*, displacement in text of, 240–244
history of philosophy: types of, 293–305
Holy Spirit: Socrates and, 317
homoiosis: in Plutarch, 46–47; two types in Plotinus, 62–65

homoiotes: in Plato's *Parmenides*, 58–62
Hume, David: 314, 356
humility: 333, 338
humor: and Hamann, 326
Husserl, Edmund: portrait of, 341–345

Iamblichus: 227–239
Ibn-abi-Usaibi' a: as source for text of Ptolemy's *Vita Aristotelis*, 267, 269
infinite: does not have likeness to the finite or $A = B$, but B does not $= A$, 57–58, 63–64

Kant, Immanuel: 308, 312, 333, 401–405
Kierkegaard, S.: 326
knowledge: theory of, 210–215; theory of in Plato and Aristotle contrasted, 196–197
knowledge of God: in Philo, 248–250
knowledge of oneself: in Philo, 245–250
knowledge and philosophy: 302–303

Lactantius: demons discussed in, 260–262; attitude to Epicureans, 252; God as source of truth in, 251–252; on the history of the true belief in God, 251–263; influence of Greek thought in, 253–254, 253, n. 9; influence of hermetic literature on, 258–259, 262–263; attitude to Plato, 252–253; on the beginnings of polytheism, 259–262; possible influence of Posidonius on, 253, n. 9, 254, 256
likeness: two types in Plotinus, 62–65; in Proclus, 65–66
likeness and the analogy of Being: from Plato's *Parmenides* to Proclus, 57–74
Lucretius: 454

memory: 213–214
Menander: and the Peripatos, 461–484; relationship of his works to Aristotle and Theophrastus, 476–482; relationship of his works to Epicurus, 476–478; the roots of his spiritual makeup discussed, 465; to be considered as poet and not as follower of any philosophic school, 483–484
metempsychosis: refutation of in Yūsuf al-Baṣīr, 281–290
methexis: in Plato's *Parmenides*, 58–62
Mozart: and Goethe, 485–502; *Magic Flute*, 485–502

al-Mubaššir: as source for text of Ptolemy's *Vita Aristotelis*, 269

nature of living beings: in Aristotle, 88
Nietzsche, F.: 306–329
nomos: in Pindar, 270–280

Oates, W. J.: discussion of his *Aristotle and the Problem of Value*, 117–124
origin of matter: 229–230

pastoral: 451–454
Perrault, Charles: on Menander, 469
perspective: philosophy as, 416–432
Petrażycki: Adequate Theorem in, 358–370
phenomenology: and Schutz, 384–397; typification and the world as taken for granted, 383–397
Philo: Delphic oracle in, 245–250; direct knowledge of *Timaeus*, 26; knowledge of God in, 248–250; knowledge of self in, 245–250, lambda schema of numbers in, 30; nature of the *Timaeus* commentaries used by him, 25–35; Posidonian ideas in, 29–30, 32–35
philology and the history of philosophy: 296–297
philosophy: as criticism, 412–416; history of and culture, 298–301; and knowledge, 302–303; as perspective, 416–432; and philology, 296–297; presuppositions in history of, 301–302; structure of Chinese, 298; types of history of, 293–305
pietism: 332, 339–340
Pindar: new Arabic fragment of discussed, 270–280; mss. of new Arabic fragment of, 270; *nomos* in, 270–280; *nomos* and *aletheia* joined in new Arabic fragment of, 274–275
Plato: *Cratylus*, 5–10; *Cratylus*, arguments for date of, 10; *Cratylus*, bibliography of studies on, 5, n. 4; *Cratylus*, reason for etymological passages in, 9; *Cratylus*, sources of etymological passages in, 6, 7; relationship to Cratylus, 3–11; theory of knowledge contrasted with Aristotle, 196–197; his first mover in Arist. *Physics* VIII, 171–182; his progress in philosophy, 10; attitude to popular religion of, 24; Socratic stages in, 4; ethics contrasted with Aristotle, 195–196;

theia somata in, 12–24; *Timaeus* 29C–D, 431–432
Plotinus: *homoiosis* in (two types), 62–65; criticizes Aristotle's entelechy, 194–222
Plutarch: the audience to which his works are addressed, 37–38; relationship to Gnosis, 49; attitude to *homoiosis* formula, 46–47; *De Iside et Osiride* 13, 496; as monist, 51–52; reasons for lack of systematic presentation of Platonic problems in, 38; his relationship to the Platonists of his era, 36–56; Pythagorean elements in, 39, 44, 45, 46; his approach to philosophy compared with that of Plotinus, 55–56; attitude toward the three basic principles of the world, 40–47; Syrian's criticism of, 53
polypragmosyne: new meaning of the term in Menander, 464–465
Porphyry: 205, 227–239
Posidonius: Golden Age motif in, 256–257; influence on Lactantius, 253, n. 9, 254, 256; influence on Philo, 29–30, 32–35; influence on Plutarch, 39; influence on Strabo, 254–255, 255, n. 11, 12
Praxilla: frg. 1 = 747PMG, 454, n. 19
presuppositions: in the history of philosophy, 301–302
Proclus: 228–229; on Hesiod's *Erga* 758¹, 504; on the reduction of likeness to the one supreme cause, 65–69
Psellus: 228
Ptolemy: copies Andronicus' version of Aristotle's Will, 265; nature of his *Vita Aristotelis*, 264–269; rediscovery of his *Vita Aristotelis*, 264–269
Pythagoras: influence on Plato, 4; on Plutarch, 39, 44, 45, 46
al-Qifti: as source of text of Ptolemy's *Vita Aristotelis*, 269

Rationalists: 313
Renaissance Italy: law, moral sentiment, and the spirit of capitalism in, 542–546
Romanticism: 334

Šarḥ al-uṣūl al-ḫamsa: 288–290
scepticism: and Epicureanism in the early 17th century, 346–357
Schutz, Alfred: and phenomenology, 384–397
sleep: 200, 204, 205–207

Socrates: and beauty, 320–323; and
Dionysus, 307, 316; and *daimon*,
317–320; and Goethe, 325; and
Holy Spirit, 317; and humor, 326;
in Nietzsche and Hamann, 306–329;
and tragedy, 324–326
Soul: in Aristotle's biology, 89–94; as
entelechy of body, 194, 198, 200,
203, 215–218; as form of body, 200–
201
Souls: transmigration of, 218–220
Spinoza, Baruch de: 355–356
Strabo: Posidonian influence on, 254–
255, 255, n. 11, 12
substance: nature of, 76–87
suffering: problem of, 282–290
systems: in philosophy, 302, 303–
304

theia somata: nature of in Plato, 12–
24
Theocritus: 513–515; and Epicurus,
454–460; *Idylls* of, 448–454; *Idyll*
7.21–23, 451, 451, n. 15
theurgy: and Iamblichus, 231–239
Timaeus Locrus: relationship to Eu-
dorus, 25
traditions: cultural, 527–528
tragedy: and Socrates, 324–326

Tragedy, The Birth of: Socrates discussed in, 307–329 *passim*
translation: of philosophical sources,
295
transmigration: of souls, 218–220
truth: and perspective, 424–432
typification: and phenomenology and
the world as taken for granted, 383–
397, especially 389–394

usury: 530–535

value: existence and, 371–382; location of, 371–376; realization of,
377–382
virtue (neoplatonic): 235–237
Vita Aristotelis: Arabic epitomes of,
264–269

Wagner, R.: 307, 327
Weber, Max: 542–546
Wise men: motif of early non-Greek
inspired wise men used by Posidonius and Strabo, 254–255; by Justin,
256
world: causal structure of, 398–405;
as taken for granted in phenomenology and typification, 383–397,
especially 386–391

INDEX TO PASSAGES ANALYZED
IN CLOSE DETAIL

Aristotle: *De An.* 404b18 ff., 146–170; *De Interpretatione* 3.16b19–25, 95–115; *Metaph. Z.* 7–9, 75–87; *Metaph.* A6, 987a29, 3–4; *De Part. An.* I. I. 641a14–b10, 88–94; *Physics* VIII 259b1–b31, 175–182

Goethe: *Die natürliche Tochter* 1064–1067, 503–507; *Zauberflöte*, Part II, 485–502

Hessus, Helius Eobanus: *Epicedion in funere Alberti Dureri*, 508–521

Hippolytus: *Elenchos* 5. 7. 34, 241–242; 5. 12. 2, 242–243; 5. 26. 36–37, 243; 6. 32. 6, 244

Iamblichus: *De mysteriis (Aegyptiorum Chaldaeorum Assyriorum)*, 227–239

Pindar: Arabic fragment of in Aya Sophya 2890, f. 125, Fatih 5323, f. 74, Köprülü 1608, f. 120^v, 270–280

Plato: *Criti.* 107a–b, 12–24

Plotinus: *Enn.* 4. 7. 8^5, 199–222

Vita Aristotelis: in Arabic ms. codex Ayasofya, Istanbul 4833, f. 10a–18a, 266–269

Yūsuf al-Baṣīr: *Kitāb-al-Muḥtawī*, ch. 24, 281–290